ADULT DEVELOPMENT AND AGING

Second Edition

ADULT DEVELOPMENT AND AGING

K. Warner Schaie
The Pennsylvania State University

Sherry L. Willis
The Pennsylvania State University

Little, Brown and Company
Boston   Toronto

Library of Congress Cataloging-in-Publication Data

Schaie, K. Warner (Klaus Warner), 1928–
   Adult development and aging.

   Bibliography: p.
   Includes index.
   1. Adulthood. 2. Life cycle, Human. 3. Adulthood—
Psychological aspects. 4. Aging—Psychological aspects.
I. Willis, Sherry L., 1947–   . II. Title.
HQ799.95.S33 1986   155.6   85-23790
ISBN 0-316-77290-9

Library of Congress Catalog Card No. 85-23790

ISBN 0-673-39090-X

9 8 7 6 5 4 3

ALP

Printed in the United States of America

Photograph Credits

Cover photo: Andrew Brilliant and Carol Palmer.
Chapter 1: Page 19, Alice Kandell/Photo Researchers, Inc.; *page 15,* Frank Siteman/The Picture Cube.
Chapter 2: Page 43, Peter Vandermark; *page 52,* Ellis Herwig/The Picture Cube; *page 69,* Elizabeth Crews/Stock Boston; *page 72,* Peter Vandermark; *Chapter 3: Page 92,* Peter Vandermark; *page 99,* James Foote/Photo Researchers, Inc.; *page 107,* David Powers/Stock Boston; *page 123,* George Bellerose/Stock Boston. *Chapter 4: Page 135,* Peter Vandermark; *page 141,* Courtesy of Professor Bernice L. Neugarten, Northwestern University, Professor of Education; *page 151,* Frank Siteman/Jeroboam; *page 152,* George Cohen/Stock Boston; *page 154,* Reprinted by permission from *Thematic Apperception Test* by Henry A. Murray; Cambridge, Harvard University Press, 1943; President and Fellows of Harvard College. *Chapter 5: Page 174,* Peter Vandermark; *page 182, Janet Knott/The Boston Globe. Chapter 6: Page 196,* Ginger Chih/Peter Arnold, Inc.; *page 206,* Ted Dully/The Boston Globe; *page 211,* James Holland/Stock Boston. *Chapter 7: Page 221,* David Krasnor/Photo Researchers, Inc.; *page 231,* Keith Gunnar/Photo Researchers, Inc.; *page 236,* Dan Walsh/The Picture Cube; *page 240,* Elizabeth Crews/Stock Boston. *Chapter 8: Page 257,* left, © Joel Gordon 1980, right, © Joel Gordon 1978; *page 269,* Janice Fullman/The Picture Cube; *page 272,* Peter Vandermark. *Chapter 9: Page 280,* R. Weldon/Jeroboam; *page 283,* © Joel Gordon 1980; *page 303,* Suzanne Arms/Jeroboam. *Chapter 10: Page 327,* Peter Vandermark; *page 336,* Peter Vandermark; *page 344,* Jerry Howard/Positive Images; *page 335,* Terry McKoy/The Picture Cube. *Chapter 11: Page 375,* © Carol Palmer 1986; *page 380,* Peter Vilms/Jeroboam; *page 386,* Rose Skytta/ Jeroboam; *page 396,* Stephen L. Feldman/Photo Researchers, Inc. *Chapter 12: Page 409,* Jim Harrison/ Stock Boston; *page 418,* © Joel Gordon 1972; *page 425,* Peter Vandermark. *Chapter 13: Page 451,* Janice Fullman/The Picture Cube; *page 460,* Jerry Howard/Positive Images; *page 461,* Palmer/Brilliant; *page 465,* Bettye Lane/Photo Researchers, Inc.

Preface

The "graying of America" is at hand. Consider these facts. The post-World War II baby boom generation, comprising one out of every three Americans, is now approaching middle age. One of every four Americans is already fifty years of age or older, and the numbers of those eighty-five or older will double by the year 2000. Those 100 or older will triple in number by the end of this century! By the year 2025, 64 million Americans will be sixty-five years of age or older.

Only now are we coming to grips with the implications of the burgeoning population of older people. Our increasing longevity as well as the need for understanding its ramifications has spurred considerable scientific research, especially during the last two decades. On college and university campuses, the demand has grown for courses that concentrate attention on the broad period of adulthood. How an individual's development is influenced by a rapidly changing society, and how careers, marriage, family life, and psychological functioning are affected have become vital questions.

Our objective in doing this textbook is to present, in a clear and readable manner, a comprehensive look at the phenomenon of adult development and aging. We seek to introduce you to current theory and research on the major psychological issues, and we provide background on those social and biological aspects of development that are essential to understanding behavioral age changes.

The book begins with a chapter that sets the stage for our study. In addition to reviewing the demographic changes in our society, we present theoretical models for the study of aging. We also examine the current state of research in the field, and we look at issues in research methodology.

The order of the remaining chapters corresponds generally to the major *stages* of adult life: young adulthood, middle age, and late life. Each "section" consists of several chapters that cover *topics* or *processes* and an integrative chapter devoted to particular issues germane to the life stage being addressed. The section on young adulthood, for example, begins with three topical chapters on families, careers, and personality development, followed by an integrative chapter. The topical chapters were placed in this section because young adulthood is a time when important decisions are made about getting married and having children, choosing a career, and defining personal identity. The topical chapters in the middle adulthood section deal with intimacy and life style, motivation, and responsibility and failure. Intellectual development, learning and memory, biological development and mental disorders follow the integrative chapter on the middle years.

The material we cover in the topical chapters is not limited, however, to the life stage for which they happen to be particularly relevant. The flow of human lives is not that easily segmented! Career choice, for example, may be of paramount importance to young adults, but matters relating to career development permeate much of adulthood. Our chapters on careers, although placed very early in the book, includes material on occupational development in middle age and career reevaluation and change in later life. Our intent then is to present an integrated picture both of the psychological processes that determine adult development and the stages of human experience. We make extensive use of a life-span approach by following psychological processes as they develop from young adulthood to the very end of life.

During the four years since the first edition of this book, research on aging has continued at a furious pace. We have attempted in this second edition to incorporate the new findings and provide more extensive documentation for our discussion. Most of the new material does not replace older findings, instead it supplements or expands the research literature base, now numbering over 2000 references.

In this second edition more attention has been devoted to understanding behavioral aging within the context of biological and societal changes. While maintaining the original structure, which worked well in our own teaching, we have substantially expanded our discussion of the demography of aging and of issues such as the establishment of family relationships in young adulthood, working women and dual careers, and problems of the elderly related to Alzheimer's disease, alcoholism, and sleep disturbances. The sections on theories of aging, personality, and memory have also been markedly expanded in the light of recent research findings.

Although we emphasized the need for longitudinal data in the first edition, we nevertheless had to base much of our data on cross-sectional findings. In this edition we are now able to present data for many topics that come from at least short-term longitudinal follow-up studies. We have tried to present a sound and thorough review of scientific research in this book while avoiding jargon and excessive or unnecessary technical detail. New to this edition is a research article at the end of each chapter. It contains a more extensive presentation of a recent representative research study or a piece of expository writing that is particularly relevant to a major issue covered in that chapter. Several resources have been provided for students who wish to pursue major issues in greater depth. These include suggestions for further readings at the end of each chapter and a listing of major reference volumes and journals dealing with the study of adulthood and aging at the end of the book. A companion volume to the first edition, *Readings in Adult Development and Aging,* remains in print and is available as a convenient adjunct for those who would like to pursue original sources keyed to the topics covered in this book.

Creating and revising a textbook is no mean task; it requires the harmonious efforts of many skilled professionals. We wish to acknowledge our great appreciation of the people at Little, Brown and Company — in particular, our editor Mylan Jaixen, who guided this revision with sympathy and insight. We would like to acknowledge the contribution of reviewers who read all or part of the manuscript and helped to improve both coverage and clarity. We wish to thank: Marvin Berkowitz, Marquette University; Janet Johnson, University of Maryland; Rick Scheidt, Kansas State University; and Linda Smolak, Kenyon College.

Dan Otis helped in smoothing stylistic incongruencies arising from the interweaving of new material with that retained from the first edition. Anna Shuey handled the clerical and technical details associated with revising the original manuscript.

There is much yet to be learned about adult development and aging, but a much clearer picture has begun to emerge as the results of intensive scientific research accumulates. The picture you are about to form as you read these chapters is as comprehensive and accurate as we could make it. This picture, however, often differs from the one that is painted from the many erroneous beliefs or myths many people hold about adult development and aging. Our interpretation of the research literature is much more optimistic than the popular myths would have us believe. In our view, moving from young adulthood to old age is not so much a series of "life crises" as a progression of challenges and opportunities. We hope to convince you that even the last years of life can be a great period of personal creativity and satisfaction. Not the least purpose of this book is to encourage you about the potential richness of your own life in the years to come and to help you understand the lives of those adults you may care for. We hope that you will find this endeavor both informative and interesting.

K. W. S.
S. L. W.

Brief Contents

Contents

ADULT DEVELOPMENT AND AGING

An Introduction

This is a book about the psychology of adult development and aging. One would think it nearly impossible to cram all the scientific theories and research on these topics between the covers of a single volume but, surprisingly, quite the opposite is the case. Time and time again we encounter a question about adult development — a reasonable question, a researchable question, one whose answer would have social as well as scientific value — and we have to admit that, if it has been investigated at all, the studies are few, use uncertain measures of concepts too broadly conceived, or sample poorly from a population too narrow for meaningful generalizations. Popular beliefs abound, sometimes contradicting one another, and we often lack the data to choose among what may be either correct beliefs or nothing but unfounded myths.

A Book Preview

The task before us is to examine the available research evidence and, from this, to formulate the most plausible conclusions about adult development and aging. To organize this task in a sensible fashion, it is necessary to make decisions about how the material is to be presented. In particular, the findings of developmental psychology can be presented in one of two ways: chronologically or topically. A book organized chronologically uses the life span as the organizing principle, covering, in the case of adult development, first young adulthood, then middle age, then old age. The biological, cognitive, and social processes that occur in any period of life are discussed together or in neighboring chapters; in the following section the same processes are discussed again, in reference to the later age period. In contrast, a topical organization follows a process throughout the life span. Each chapter discusses a different topic as it applies to young adults, the middle aged, and the elderly. Instead of chapter titles like "Young Adulthood," we would have chapters on "Biological Development," "Personality Development," "Families," and "Careers." In a chronological organization, "starting a career" would be one of several topics discussed in the section on young adulthood, and "retirement" would be discussed many chapters later, in the section on old age. In a topical organization, initial choice of career, midlife career changes, and retirement would all be found in a single chapter.

There are advantages and disadvantages with each type of organization. A chronological organization is more "lifelike"; a book so organized reads like a biography or a collection of biographies. Each chapter is a mix of biology, intellect, personality, and society, just as a real life is. One of the disadvantages of such an organization is that many of the issues of adult life do not change significantly from one age to another, and thus one section essentially repeats what was said before. Another disadvantage is that the chronological organization "chops ups" the processes, making it difficult to get a full picture. You might read in the section on middle age, for example, that measured IQ tends to be stable during this period. You try to remember what you learned chapters back about intellectual development in young adulthood: Did it decrease during this period? Increase? And what, you wonder, will happen to the curve in old age? Does IQ remain stable throughout life?

The topical approach gives you the full picture of each process across the life span. In addition, many of the theories of greatest use in adult development are limited to one topic: a theory of intellectual development, a theory of personality development, a theory of careers, a theory of the family life cycle. These theories are difficult to present in a book with a chronological organization, because the research from which they grew is fragmented across the different chronological stages. The chief disadvantage of the topical approach is that it fragments the individual. It cuts us up into our personalities, as distinct from our intellects; it excludes our concerns about our families as it discusses our careers. The topical organization is more abstract than the chronological organization; it lacks the smell of real life.

One could say, with only slight exaggeration, that a chronological organization makes a book more interesting, whereas a topical organization makes it more informative. We would like this textbook to be both interesting and informative, so we have combined elements of the two organizing principles. As befits a scientific textbook whose primary purpose is to inform, our fundamental organization will be topical. However, we have arranged the substantive chapters into three sections that correspond roughly to the three major periods of adult life: young adulthood, midlife, and old age. For example, the first section contains three topical chapters — on families, on career development, and on personality development — followed by a chronologically organized chapter on young adulthood. Each topical chapter covers the entire life span, from young adulthood to old age; careers are followed, for example, from first job through retirement and even beyond. Nevertheless, they are the topical chapters most germane to a discussion of the period of young adulthood, which is dominated by concerns about intimacy and marriage, career choice, and personal identity. Thus they form a basis for our discussion of young adults in the fourth chapter in the section.

In the second section, topical chapters on the relationships between men and women through the life span and on motivation prepare us for a discussion of middle age. Middle age is often a period of reevaluation. Many middle-aged adults reevaluate their marriages, and other aspects of the man–woman relationship may also become a concern — a perceived loss of sexual attractiveness, for example. Middle-aged people may fear that decreased "drive" will thwart their need to escape from a career that no longer interests them. Fears and uncertainties of this sort may precipitate a "midlife crisis."

In the final section, on old age, the four topical chapters cover intellectual development, learning and memory, biological changes with age, and mental health. Again, these chapters take their topics from young adulthood through old age. But obviously now we are involved with the concerns of the elderly: Does intelligence begin to decline at age thirteen or eighteen or something ridiculously young, or is it maintained throughout adulthood? Can an old dog learn new tricks? What has happened to my memory? What can I expect in the way of sensory losses in vision and hearing? What exactly is "aging"? What are my chances of becoming senile? What exactly is "senility"? All these matters prepare us for the final chapter, which integrates the major events of the last stage of life, including death.

There has been a veritable explosion of knowledge in gerontology in general and the psychology of aging in particular. The publication rate of research relevant to the psychology of adult development and the aging has grown to more than 1,000 articles and chapters per year (Birren, Cunningham, and Yamamoto, 1983). Obviously, we do not have room to discuss all of the 4,000 new studies that have appeared since the first edition of this text was published. What, then, has been our rationale in deciding what old material to discard, what new material to include, and what new material to ignore?

A major temptation in revising and updating a text in a scholarly manner is to delete references to older studies and replace them with new ones. This temptation must be resisted; for, as the astute student will realize, the most novel and recent studies tread on uncharted territory (unless they are confirmations of earlier work). Until they have been carefully reviewed and critiqued by qualified colleagues, it may be questioned whether they deserve to be incorporated into a textbook. Furthermore, more recent studies may not be as rigorous and precise as the older work in the literature; newer studies are sometimes premature publications of incomplete data instigated by the "publish or perish" anxieties that plague many promising young academics.

Our decisions have been greatly influenced and made much easier by a careful reading of the recently published second edition of the *Handbooks of Aging* (Birren and Schaie, 1985; Binstock and Shanas, 1985; Finch and Schneider, 1985) and by carefully attending to recent relevant chapters in the *Annual Review of Psychology* and the *Annual Review of Gerontology and Geriatrics*. We found that relatively little material could be deleted and much had to be added. Many of the additions are of primary sources from the late 1970s and early 1980s whose relevance and meaning are now clear enough to be considered a firm addition to the current state of the art.

At the end of each chapter we provide a concise summary of the most important information and the interpretive statements we think are particularly noteworthy. We also provide references to recent review chapters and readable books that will be of interest to those who wish to inform themselves about the topics covered in more detail. These references would also be a good place to start in a search for materials for a term paper. Finally, we have provided a box summary of a research article or piece of expository writing that describes an interesting contribution in some detail. If the summaries intrigue you, we certainly suggest that you find the article in the library and read it in its entirety.

A Bit of History

Why, you may ask, is the field of adult development clothed in relative research darkness? The answer is that the field is a rather new one in psychology. We are only in the beginnings of it, and although research is now booming, we have a long way to go to equal the comprehensive understandings that have been attained, say in the psychology of perception or even in the psychology of *child* development.

But this makes no sense either, you say. How can a topic that covers 75 percent of human development go unstudied for so long? Adults do almost everything of importance in a society: work, marry, make war, create art, exercise power, organize religions. Why have developmental psychologists ignored them for so long? Some of this neglect may be explained by the values and theoretical biases of the early pioneers in the developmental sciences. Freud, for example, proposed that "the child is the father of the man" and thought that most of the events of adulthood could best be explained by an understanding of early childhood experiences. Similarly, many developmental researchers have been oriented toward discovering how individual behavior gets acquired in the first place. They moved only slowly into the study of its growth through childhood into adolescence and were even more reluctant to tackle the complexities of behavioral maintenance, change, and decline as adulthood is reached.

Until quite recently most people considered age-related changes during the adult years to be quite rare. It was believed, for example, that one's personality was well set by the age of maturity, that changes were unlikely and maybe even impossible. Family and career decisions were made early in life and then held to throughout life; divorce was rare and so were midlife career changes. Sexual abilities were believed to decline during the adult years, but sex was a taboo topic, so no one knew for sure. Intellectual abilities were also believed to decline, especially toward the end of life, and tests of intelligence were among the first psychological measures used to compare adults of various ages — leading to questionable conclusions, as we shall see. There was interest in intellectual and biological development in old age, but until the present century relatively few people lived long enough to attain this status.

THE RISE OF GERONTOLOGY

The first glimmerings of a developmental psychology for adults came at the far end of the field, in the study of aging (Riegel, 1977). Advances in sanitation, nutrition, and medical knowledge made possible the incredible changes in life expectancy observed not only in this country but throughout the world, providing subjects for study as well as the need to study them. In the United States, a child born in 1900 could not reasonably hope to reach the age of fifty, whereas life expectancy today is well over seventy. Put another way, the percentage of people over sixty-five in the United States population has risen from less than 5 percent in 1900 to approximately 12 percent today and is projected to reach 21.1 percent by the year 2030 (U.S. Bureau of the Census, 1982b). By the time people born during the "baby boom" — in the decade following World War II — reach old age, the number of old people will exceed 50 million, more than double the number today. The median age in this country (half the people are younger, half are older) will be nearly forty, compared to about thirty today.

What is the cause of this population explosion among the elderly? A number of variables affect the composition of our population; the most important are changes in fertility, mortality, and migration. Since most immigrants spend their childhoods in their native country and migrate as young adults, their chief demographic effect is on the average age of the population. Considered in the context of other demographic factors, the influence of immigration is relatively minor but in the face of the large numbers of illegal immigrants entering the country may become of growing importance.

Fertility, the number of babies born in a population, is of much greater importance. Most of us are familiar with one recent period of high fertility rates — the "baby boom" period that occurred in the United States between 1947 and 1967. It is less well known, however, that the fertility rate has fluctuated throughout our history. There were relatively few people born, for example, during the depression years between 1931 and 1940 and, more recently, between 1971 and 1980. The latter period is sometimes called the "baby bust."

Changes in fertility have a profound effect on the age distribution of the population. This can be seen in the population pyramids in Figure 1–1, which show how the age structure of our population will change between 1985 and 2050. The data are from the 1980 United States census. Since everyone who will be age seventy or older in 2050 has already been born, we have an accurate knowledge of how large some parts of the population will be many years in advance; indeed, we may err on the side of conservatism because mortality rates will probably decline. Younger age groups, who have not yet been born, are estimated on the basis of current fertility levels.

Several features in Figure 1–1 are worth noting. In the 1985 pyramid, the "depression" cohort now between the ages of forty-five and fifty-four is quite small. This group has had several advantages. They faced relatively little competition from age peers as they grew up. When they retire between 1990 and 2005, they can rely on the cohort that follows them, the baby boom group, to provide them with an adequate income. They will face less competition for support and services than either the cohort before them or the cohort that follows them.

The baby boom generation faces a different prospect as it turn into a "gerontic boom." When they retire between the years 2015 and 2030, they will have to rely for their income on the relatively small cohorts that follow them. The *dependency ratio* of persons not gainfully employed (children, those retired, and those unemployed) to those persons who are in the work force during this period will be unusually small. That is, the number of persons who pay taxes and contribute into the social security system will be shrinking, while the number of persons receiving pensions and requiring extensive health care will be markedly increasing. Likewise, the number of persons who become newly available to provide professional and personal care services will be small compared to the increase of individuals in need of greater support and care by others. During this period, there will be a great many old people but relatively few *very* old people. Later, this situation will reverse, and there will be many very old and relatively few young old people. The baby-bust cohort, when it retires, will have to compete for services with a much larger group of very old and increasingly fragile baby boomers.

Over the sixty-five years from 1985 to 2050, the population pyramid will become increasingly rectangular, and the median age of the population as a whole will increase from 31.5 to 41.6 years — a full decade. The imbalance between men and women in old age is likely to increase. This is one of the reasons that we will pay close attention to sex differences in adult development throughout this book. When we speak of the very old, we will be speaking of a predominantly female population.

The increase in the older population is also affected by decreasing mortality rates, of course. These rates are already quite low, and further declines are expected before the end of the century (National Center for Health Statistics, 1980). Our progress in preventing premature death has dramatically increased a person's chances of surviving to a very old age. It is currently estimated that by the year 2045, 95 percent of all deaths will occur between the ages of seventy-seven and ninety-three; the average age of death (not including those who die from accidents or violence) will stabilize somewhere around age eighty-five (Fries, 1980, 1985).

Life expectancy figures at birth markedly underestimate life expectancy as figured at later ages. This fact is made clear by Figure 1–2, which charts life

FIGURE 1–1.

Projected population (in millions) by age and sex: United States, 1985–2050.

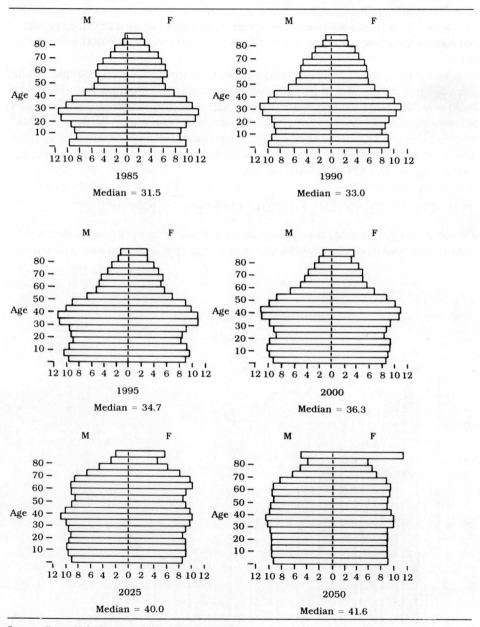

Source: From U.S. Bureau of the Census, 1982b.

expectancy in terms of average number of years remaining at various ages. Note that until early adulthood, on average, it appears that we actually do lose one year for each year we live. As we get older, however, we lose less time for each year we survive. In midlife, for every five years we live, we lose only four years. In the five years from age eighty to eighty-five, we lose only two years! What is happening, of course, is that once we have survived the hazards of late middle age and early old age, reductions in the mortality rate increase the likelihood that we will live even longer.

The rise in the proportion and absolute number of elderly people in the population will force us to make a number of structural changes in society. The elderly will have to be integrated into the social structure so that more of them can actively participate. Many changes of this sort will generate problems of interest to psychologists and other social scientists (Schaie, 1982b; Swenson, 1983). This consideration in recent years has stimulated scientists to increase their investigations of mature and older persons.

THE STUDY OF ADULT DEVELOPMENT AND AGING

Gerontology is the study of the phenomena of the aging process from maturity into old age, as well as the study of the elderly as a special population. (A closely

FIGURE 1–2.

Average years of life remaining at various ages.

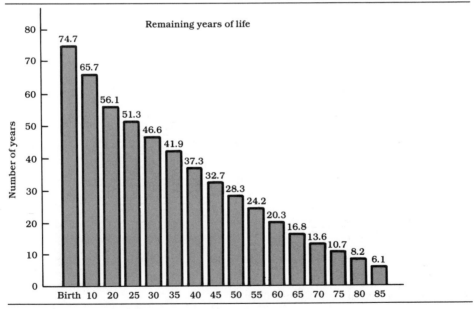

Source: From National Center for Health Statistics, 1983a.

related word is "geriatric," which refers to the medical treatment of the elderly; the root word is the Greek *geras*, meaning "old age.") In the United States, the first important psychological studies in gerontology were published in the 1920s, but barely more than a trickle of research can be noted until the 1950s (Charles, 1970). In a review published in 1961, the author remarked, "More research seems to have been published in the decade of 1950–1959 than had been published in the entire preceding 115 years the subject may be said to have existed" (Birren, 1961, p. 131). Reviewers writing in 1980 had seen the trickle of research grow into a stream, almost a torrent; from 1968 to 1979, they computed, psychological publications in gerontology had increased by 270 percent (see Figure 1–3) (Poon and Welford, 1980), and well over 1,000 new items are now published annually (Birren, Cunningham, and Yamamoto, 1983).

Nevertheless, much more basic and applied research is needed. Currently, one of the impediments to developing knowledge is the reduction in federal support for the training of basic and applied researchers. Paradoxically, the passing of the baby boom has reduced the number of students interested in the topics that will become a major social problem in their later adult lives (Santos and VandenBos, 1982; Storandt, 1983).

FIGURE 1–3.

Number of psychological aging publications per year from 1880 to 1979.

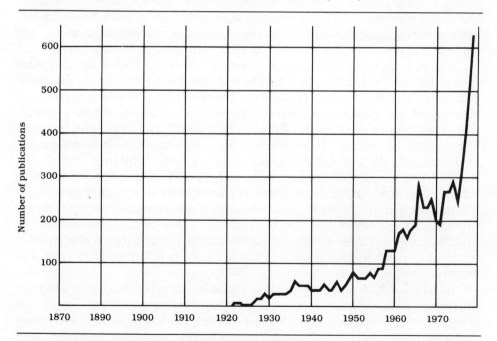

Source: From L. W. Poon and A. T. Welford. Prologue: an historical perspective. In L. W. Poon, ed., *Aging in the 1980s.* Washington, D.C.: American Psychological Association, 1980, p. xiv. Copyright 1980 by the American Psychological Association. Reprinted by permission of the publisher and author.

Besides having an interest in old age, psychologists have begun to investigate the psychological development of adults between the ages of eighteen and sixty-five. One of the reasons for these new concerns, one to which we have already alluded, is the disruptive effect that our fast-paced, technologically advanced society has on the lives of adults. Frequent changes in jobs and spouses, for example, make lives stressful and personal adjustment problematic. The ability of the "old dog" to learn "new tricks" becomes an increasingly important factor in adjustment, so that age changes during the adult years in learning ability, memory, and general intellectual competence become interesting to scientific psychologists.

Recently, too, there has been a surge of interest in what psychologists call "normative life crises" (Datan and Ginsberg, 1975) and what a best-selling author called "passages" (Sheehy, 1976). By whatever name, these are major transitions in adult life, events that provide great opportunities and great risks. These transitions are often called "normative" because they are experienced by most persons in our society. Keep in mind, however, that what is normative in one culture or one generation may not be perceived as such in another. Nevertheless, there are many examples of what would indeed be normative transitions for most of us. Getting married is one, having children is another; starting out in a career is a transition, and so is retiring. Turning forty is a mystical transition, reflecting people's beliefs that it is the midpoint of life as well as the social fact that one is no longer a "young adult" and has entered the life stage we call "middle age." Normative transitions form the basis for several theories of adult development, much as normative events in childhood — toilet training, entering school — are important in the psychology of child development. *death, puberty etc.*

Another source of the present research interest in adult development emerged almost by accident. In the 1920s and 1930s, several groups of psychologists began long-term studies of children. The researchers observed, tested, and interviewed the same children every few years or so to assess their physical, intellectual, and personality development. By the 1940s and 1950s, these subjects had reached adulthood. There seemed no good reason to abandon the investigations simply because the subjects were no longer children. Indeed, the studies seemed to provide a rare opportunity not only to study adult development but also to relate significant events in adult life (such as the breakup of a marriage) to experiences in childhood. Prominent examples of such studies are the Berkeley Growth and Guidance studies (Eichorn et al., 1981). A good deal of the research in adult development owes its existence to the fact that adult subjects about whom much was already known became available for study (Charles, 1970; Poon and Welford, 1980).

But studies that were designed to describe the life experiences and growth of children may not be the most satisfactory source of data on adulthood. The appeal of such studies is that they provide more meaningful data on development than do the studies comparing different age groups that are so common in the literature on adult development and aging. These age-group comparison studies of midlife have yielded little information because behavioral and biological changes occur rather slowly during adulthood; such age differences as are found in these studies are often the result of generational differences between cohorts rather than individual development (see the discussion of cross-sectional and longitudinal methods later in this chapter). Recently, however, a substantial number of longitudinal studies have been instigated as an alternative to age-group comparison studies and studies designed to examine children. These longitudinal studies have been explicitly conceptualized to study individuals from young adulthood to old age (Migdel, Abeles, and Sherrod, 1981; Schaie, 1983c). As a result, we now have a much larger body of data on adult development that actually tracks the development of individuals. Recent studies have been published in such areas as physiological aging (Shock et al., 1984), health and behavior (Palmore et al., 1985; Siegler, 1983), personality (Schmitz-Scherzer and Thomae, 1983; McCrae and Costa, 1984), career development (Bray and Howard, 1983b), and intelligence (Cunningham and Owens, 1983; Schaie, 1983b; Siegler, 1983).

A final reason for the interest in adult development was that certain issues in the scientific study of psychology required extending existing work with children into adulthood. For many years, research on these issues provided the only substantial body of data in adult development and, in addition, clarified the particular methodological problems faced by workers in this area. One of the earliest (and most enduring) of these issues is intellectual development. Early research suggested that the growth of intelligence, as measured by standard IQ tests, was essentially complete by the age of thirteen (Yerkes, 1921). Most adults, including adult psychologists, found this result a bit startling; they demanded more research. The issue spawned a series of studies and the testing of people ranging in age from ten to eighty (e.g., Miles, 1931). The peak age was moved up a bit, to around twenty, but the apparent decline of intellectual ability thereafter gave rise to further controversy that is not entirely resolved even today. We will discuss the issue and the controversies in Chapter 9 on intellectual development; here we merely note the vital historical role research on specific issues such as intellectual growth has played in the psychology of adult development.

THE MYTHS OF AGING

One of the grand purposes of science is to dispel the myths surrounding the phenomena under study. A myth is a belief based on something other than systematic study of the matter. For example, one might assert, "Old people no longer engage in sexual intercourse!" This statement might be based on jokes heard at work, a general notion of old people as physically incapable (expecially of sexual activities), or even anecdotal evidence such as the verbal denials of modest grandparents. (See Table 1-1 for a list of some myths on aging.) Myths are not necessarily incorrect; sometimes scientific investigation turns up evidence of their validity. But they are usually distorted and often dangerous, to the extent that they dictate social policy or personal interactions. For example, myths about old people and mental illness — primarily the assumption that mental confusion in old people means they are becoming "senile" — prevent effective treatment of what in many cases is a reversible condition such as depression or physical illness. Even senile patients can be helped considerably by proper treatment (Santos and VandenBos, 1982).

TABLE 1–1.
Myths about adult development and aging.

In this table are listed some of the common beliefs about adult development and aging, beliefs that have been formed without much scientific evidence pro or con. Some, it turns out, are true; some are partly true; and many are mostly or completely false. By the time you finish this book, you will be in a much better position to evaluate these myths.

Chapter 2

Nuclear families in today's society have little contact with kin.

Extended families were common in earlier eras of American life.

Mothers commonly experience great distress when the last child leaves home.

Aging parents often reverse roles with their adult children, becoming childishly dependent on them.

Remarriages among old people are generally unsuccessful.

Chapter 3

Most people have the same career for a lifetime.

Work is central to an individual's sense of self-worth.

The shock of retirement often results in deteriorating physical and mental health.

Chapter 4

Personality is relatively stable during the adult years.

People become more conservative and inflexible in old age.

Chapter 5

Young, enthusiastic people are more creative than old people.

Chapter 6

Women don't enjoy sex much after menopause.

Old people are not very interested in sex.

Most child molesters and exhibitionists are old men.

Impotence is usually psychological, except in old men, when it is more or less inevitable.

Men are more interested in sex than women.

Rape is the result of the intense sexual needs of some men.

Chapter 7

Old people are harder to motivate than young people.

Old people get rattled more easily.

Achievement motivation is highest in young adulthood.

Old people should keep active to keep their spirits up.

Old people prefer to reduce the number of their activities and friendships.

Chapter 8

Most women experience severe physical symptoms during menopause.

Menopause often results in nervous breakdowns.

Most adult children can't wait to ship their aging parents off to a "home" of some sort.

All men experience a "midlife crisis."

A good leader is one who is able to solve problems effectively.

Chapter 9

Intelligence peaks around the age of twenty or thirty and then declines steadily.

With age comes wisdom.

Those who are most able in their youth, decline the fastest in old age.

Chapter 10

Old dogs can't learn new tricks.

A failing memory is the worst intellectual problem in old age.

In old age, memories of the distant past are clear and vivid, but memories for recent events are fuzzy.

With all their intellectual deficits, old people don't benefit much from education.

Chapter 11

Women live longer than men because they don't work as hard.

Soon people will live to 150 or 200.

There are certain groups of people in South America and Russia who live to extraordinarily old ages.

Elderly patients do not respond well to surgery.

After sixty-five, the majority of people are unhealthy.

It is possible to "worry oneself sick."

Hard work never killed anybody.

Chapter 12

Most old people become senile sooner or later.

Senile old people cannot be helped by psychotherapy.

Women are more susceptible to mental disorders than men.

Unmarried people are more susceptible to mental disorders than married people.

Chapter 13

Most people over sixty-five are financially insecure.

Most people over seventy-five are in nursing homes or other institutions.

Rarely does someone over sixty-five produce a great work of art, science, or scholarship.

Most people who are faced with their imminent death try to deny it.

Negative stereotypes Myths about the aging process result in negative stereotypes — oversimplified and biased views of what old people are like. The "typical" old person is often viewed as uninterested in (and incapable of) sex and as on the road to (if not arrived at) senility. They're conservative, too (rigid, set in their ways), or so the stereotype would have us believe. Old people are tired and cranky, passive, without energy (Green, 1981). They're weak and dependent on others. Children perceive older people as having some positive personality traits but lower physical capacities. If physical capacities are more important to children than positive personality traits, then elderly persons will be viewed less positively than younger adults (Mitchell et al., 1985).

This negative stereotype, most of which is either questionable or highly exaggerated, affects the behavior of not only the elderly, and younger people in interaction with the elderly, but also of young adults and middle-agers. "Growing old" is so negatively valued that many adults will try, often desperately, to preserve at least the look of youth — dyeing their hair, dressing like a teenager, romancing those young enough to be their children. The effect on the behavior of the elderly is even more pronounced and considerably more malignant. Perceived by others as forgetful, uninteresting, and incompetent, many old people begin to accept the same stereotype as an accurate description of themselves. They avoid social interaction because they think they're dull; they refuse to learn a new skill because they believe themselves incapable. Physical symptoms of serious but treatable disease may be ignored because they are viewed as inevitable accompaniments of the aging process (Rodin and Langer, 1980).

Ageism Discrimination against the elderly simply because of their age is *ageism*, a relatively new -ism that is taking its place among social issues such as racism and sexism (Butler, 1975; Butler and Lewis, 1982). Like discrimination on the basis of race or sex, ageism in the job market involves rejection of someone as incapable on grounds other than the direct assessment of capability. The employer decides that an old person (or a black or a female) cannot handle the job and so chooses instead someone else (usually a young, white male) even though, had the applicants been given a valid test of job performance, the older applicant might have scored the highest. Ageism can be found, too, among the medical profession, where, as one reviewer puts it, "Health practitioners in general seem to assign lower priority to service to the elderly than to service to any other age group" (Kalish, 1975, p. 74).

The myths of aging lead to negative stereotypes which, in turn, lead to ageism and the exclusion of old people from many activities in society. It's an insidious process, one that can be halted and reversed only by solid evidence contradicting or qualifying the myths (Swenson, 1983). We plan to present such evidence, to paint as accurate a picture of "growing old" as is presently possible. We consider it important. We hope that you will find it informative — and interesting as well.

Theories of Adult Development

In order to understand and organize the empirical findings in a scientific field it is often helpful to provide some theoretical models. Some fields are dominated by elegant theoretical structures that provide explicit assumptions and postulates that permit formal tests of propositions regarding the body of knowledge that is to

To prejudge that someone can't handle a job because of age is ageism.

be organized. Such an advanced stage has not yet been reached in the study of adult development and aging. Indeed, in many areas of adult development we find little more than a variety of speculative theories; we often cannot choose among them without considerably more research. We shall review the major theoretical contenders in the sections to which they apply, but we need to say a few words about theories in general. How does one go about formulating a developmental theory? What approaches are common, and what seem to be the chief explanatory constructs?

Before we proceed further we need to distinguish between *developmental theories* and *models of development*. A developmental theory organizes the concepts of a broad field of study. By contrast, models of development describe a schematic that informs how a specific developmental process is thought to occur or how such a process is organized. We first discuss the broad theories and then focus on specific developmental models.

A developmental theory is one that describes and explains changes in behavior with age and also differences in such changes between individuals or groups (Baltes and Willis, 1977). In other words, a developmental theory should be able to describe and explain the course of *your* intellectual growth or decline over the adult years; it should also be able to do so for groups to which you belong, such as "Americans," "males" or "females," and "middle class" or "lower class." In addition, a good developmental theory should be able to describe and explain why you and your best friend might change with age in different ways or at different rates, and why males and females or blacks and whites might change differently. A developmental theory, in short, is concerned with *age changes*.

Before we begin our discussion of the theories themselves, we should explain the various concepts of aging that have influenced research on adult development. Different definitions are derived from biology, the social sciences, and psychology. Several biological definitions have been offered. Edmund Cowdry, one of the fathers of biological gerontology, suggested that aging could be viewed as either an endogenous or an exogenous process. In the endogenous view, aging is an involuntary process that operates cumulatively with the passage of time to result in the adverse modification of cells. In the exogenous view, aging would be regarded as a consequence of impairments attributable to infections, accidents, or poisons in the external environment (Cowdry, 1942). These views together comprise a comprehensive and very broad definition of aging. A narrower definition is offered by Handler: "Aging is the deterioration of a mature organism resulting from time-dependent, essentially irreversible changes intrinsic to all members of a species, such that, with the passage of time, they may become increasingly unable to cope with the stresses of the environment, thereby increasing the probability of death" (1960, p. 200).

We will pursue the biological bases of aging in more detail in Chapter 11. Here we will simply point out the basic implication of the biological viewpoint: an aged organism is one that experiences difficulties with self-regulation and hence has trouble adjusting to environmental stress. We should mention that self-regulation, too, has biological, psychological, and social dimensions.

Although a biologist's purpose might be served adequately by a definition based on an organism's probability of survival, such a definition would prove frustrating to psychologists, who are often concerned with outcomes that do not bear directly on the organism's ability to survive. Furthermore, as we shall see, some functions actually increase with age — wisdom is one example — and others show vast individual differences at various life stages. The biological definitions do not reflect these possibilities, being concerned with forces that result in the organism's deterioration. An alternative definition offered to include the psychologist's concerns is more satisfying: "Aging refers to the regular changes that occur in mature genetically representative organisms living under representative environmental conditions" (Birren and Renner, 1977, p. 4). Note the stipulation in this definition that changes to be called "aging" must occur in representative organisms under representative conditions. Many animal experiments used to simulate human aging may be misleading because they examine subjects under isolated conditions in germ-free environments that have little in common with the natural environment. The age changes in behavior displayed by such animals would probably not reflect what one would find in a representative habitat. For example, a comparison of maze-running speed between young and old laboratory rats might be invalidated by the fact that the old animals have become obese because they had effortless access to food and, being confined in cages, did not have the need or opportunity for exercising their muscles as would have been the case in a natural environment. In the same way, human laboratory studies may impose conditions that would alter the behaviors one would see in a field setting. A further concern in human studies is the distinction between aging and disease. Some of the diseases of old age, such as cancer and heart disease, are not inevitably part of the aging process. Their high incidence in old age, however, may result from adverse changes in the immune system that can increase susceptibility to disease, and these adverse changes may be a normal result in aging.

A definition of aging from the social sciences considers the individual's position with regard to a social timetable consisting of age norms about which there is broad consensual agreement in society (Hagestad and Neugarten, 1985; Riley, 1985). In this view, people experience stress when their expected life course sequences and rhythms are upset. Life transitions that are "on schedule" do not seem to elicit psychological dysfunctions (Pearlin, 1982). Unlike the biological view of aging, in which aging should be impervious to historical developments, the social view would suggest that aging is influenced by historical changes in cultural norms. For example, at the turn of the century, a woman who was not married at age thirty would have been considered "off-time," whereas today, when later marriages are more common, such a woman might well be considered "on-time" (Neugarten, Moore, and Lowe, 1968). Other changes in the formation and dissolution of the modern family (see Chapters 2 and 6) may also display social timetables. Some predictable events in the life course, such as widowhood for women, are of course less governed by social timetables, although they too may be affected by historical events such as wars and changes in public health practices.

How do we apply these perspectives to the study of adult development? We are accustomed to thinking of aging in terms of the number of years that have elapsed since a person's birth, and chronological age is in fact used as a major yardstick in aging research, but we should recognize that there are other ways to denote a person's position in the life span (cf. Schaie, 1984a; Schaie and Hertzog, 1985a). Chronological age is an index that has little meaning by itself. What matters is what happened to the individual as time passes (cf. Wohlwill, 1973; Birren and Cunningham, 1985; Schaie and Hertzog, 1985a). The alternative definitions of aging from a biological, sociological, and psychological point of view also lend themselves to the development of nonchronological time frames that for some purposes may be more informative than calendar age. A person's *biological age* is his or her position with regard to remaining life expectancy. The fortunate person whose vital organ systems are in above-average condition would be able to beat the average survival odds expressed in charts such as our Figure 1–2. Such a person would have a biological age lower than his or her chronological age. A person's *social age*, on the other hand, would be determined by judging his or her position in the life course against the average ages at which various positions are reached. These positions are determined by cultural norms. To make such a judgment, one might assess such surface characteristics as manner of dress or speech patterns and more fundamental characteristics such as the life stage of the person's preferred leadership roles. Finally, a person's *psychological age* would indicate how he or she functions in response to environmental demands. Depending on one's level of functioning, one could be psychologically younger or older than one's chronological age on such adaptive behaviors as intelligence, learning ability, memory, and motor skills or on such subjective dimensions as motives, feelings, and attitudes. The biological, social, and psychological age concepts may be quite independent of one another, converging only during extremes such as young childhood and very old age (Birren and Cunningham, 1985).

THEORETICAL APPROACHES

Why do people change with age? As we have seen there are many approaches to this question in psychology, approaches that differ in whether they concentrate on the person or the environment, the individual or the social group, and the behavior or its meaning within a repertoire of behaviors.

Within psychology, several major approaches can be distinguished (see Table 1–2). The behavioral or social-learning approach focuses on environmental determinants of behavior and behavior change, in particular, the environmental outcomes of behavior — rewards and punishments (Ahammer, 1973). This approach also places great importance on the role of modeling or imitating the behavior of persons to whom we have formed emotional attachments. A social-learning theorist might approach the effects of marriage on adult development, for example, by viewing it as an interaction in which each spouse rewards certain behaviors and discourages others. In discussions, each spouse will encourage the other to express the same view of the world and will punish "heretical" beliefs with silence, dispute, and other forms of nastiness. Thus happily married couples should become increasingly similar in attitudes and values over the years, as indeed appears to be the case.

Another traditional approach to human development applies *Freudian* or *psychoanalytic theory*. In general, psychoanalytic theory focuses on emotional conflicts and unconscious mental processes. Emotional conflicts are often triggered by social responsibilities, duties, or realities that do not fit with one's selfish desires (id impulses). Hence psychoanalytic theory is often applied to major

TABLE 1–2.

Theoretical approaches to adult development.

Approach	Author(s) associated with approach	Topical area to which applied
Behavioral, social-learning	Bandura (1969, 1977b) Seligman (1972)	Learning, motivation
Psychoanalysis	Freud (1946) Erikson (1964, 1979)	Personality, motivation
Humanistic approach	Maslow (1970) Kohlberg (1973) Whitbourne (1985)	Motivation, moral development, self-concept
Individual differences	Cattell (1971) Guilford et al. (1976) Schaie (1977/78)	Intellectual development, personality
Information processing	Sternberg (1980)	Learning, memory
Dialectical approach	Riegel (1975)	Personality, life crises

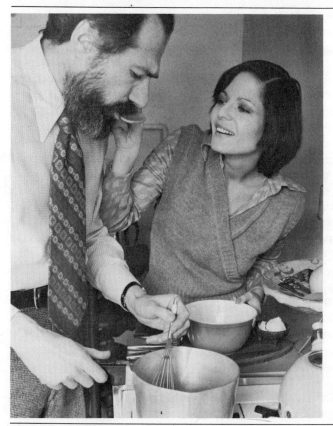

Happily married couples tend to grow more alike in their attitudes and interests because they tend to encourage one another's similarities and discourage the dissimilarities.

transitions in life — parenthood, menopause, death of a spouse. Erik Erikson, who expanded the psychoanalytic theory of development from childhood to the adult years, describes conflicts about intimacy, productivity, and integrity that he feels are major themes of adult life. *can jump stages. w/out paying price.*

The *humanistic approach,* taken by authors such as Maslow, focuses on motivation, especially on the higher (more spiritual) motives that distinguish the human species from lower animals. There is an emphasis on personal growth and "self-actualization," which is defined as the desire to become the best person one can be. Humanistic theorists remind us that the "whole person" (rather than "mechanistic" principles of learning) must be considered when trying to predict what an individual will do next in life. To use a humanist's example, human beings who succeed at a fairly difficult task are not likely to try the same task again (as a simple reward theory of learning might predict). Most humans aspire to somewhat more each time; they set their sights higher and higher, until finally their reach exceeds their grasp. *any testing.*

Other approaches we will find useful in the psychology of adult development include the *individual-differences approach,* which is most commonly represented in the use of psychological tests such as intelligence tests. The *information-processing approach,* which grew from analogies with computer operations, will be prominent in our discussions of memory and perception. Social psychology contributes the *attribution approach,* which in essence states that people attribute events to certain causes; they may be right or they may be wrong, but either way their behavior is likely to be a function of their attributions. People who attribute their sickness to the fact that they live close to a nuclear power plant, for example, are likely to move or at least protest. These various approaches are not incompatible and often complement one another, as when a psychological test is used to assess the basic ways an individual processes information, and these basic "schemes" are also the primary determinants of the attributions one makes.

One of the newest approaches in psychology is called dialectical. The *dialectical approach* is well suited to the study of human development because it focuses on change; it focuses on oppositions and contradictions and their eventual resolution and synthesis. In its best-known dress, a dialectical process involves three stages: thesis, antithesis, and synthesis. For example, in dialectical reasoning, a thought (thesis) suggests a contradiction (antithesis); the paradoxical truth of both the thesis and its antithesis results in a synthesis, a new level of understanding that somehow combines the truth in both thesis and antithesis. This synthesis becomes a new thesis, suggests a new contradiction, and is itself synthesized into a still higher level of understanding. It is a self-perpetuating, never-ending sequence that can lead to remarkable insights (Rychlak, 1968).

In adult development, the dialectical approach views people as active and changing organisms in continuous interaction with an active and changing environment (Riegel, 1975, 1976b). Psychologists who take the dialectical view look for incongruities and conflicts. They may be interested in such concepts as the "midlife crisis," in which some people recognize that their hopes and dreams are incongruent with their present lives. These psychologists would consider the potential for growth as well as the threat of depression, withdrawal, and psychological injury during the midlife crisis. The dialectical approach is also reflected in the psychoanalytic theory of Sigmund Freud. For example, according to Freud, when people say they love their mother, it means (1) they love their mother *and* (2) they hate their mother. How can both be true? Freud was able to show that the tension of these opposites was behind the ambivalent behaviors so often directed toward one's mother (Geiwitz and Moursund, 1979).

MODELS OF DEVELOPMENT

Cutting across the theoretical approaches are certain basic assumptions about the general nature of the developmental changes that occur in adult life. For example, some psychologists prefer to think of adult life as a series of discrete *stages,* whereas others tend to view the same changes as more or less continuous. To illustrate the stage notion in an extreme fashion, we can point to the butterfly, a distinctly different and far more beautiful stage of an organism that once was a caterpillar. In adult psychology, somewhat the same philosophy is applied by theorists who view the middle-aged person as the butterfly who grew from the larva of a young adult.

Psychologists who disdain the stage conception of development claim that much is lost in such broad categorizations. The stage approach can indeed cloud the immense changes that occur within a stage and thus distort our picture of the developmental process; this is in a sense the cost of using the stage approach. What one gains from such an approach is a sharper contrast between periods of development that are different in important theoretical aspects. The change from one stage to another may be so abrupt that to define it as *merely* a change of sizable degree misses the point that a new quality has emerged in the new period. Life after puberty, after menopause, after retirement is qualitatively different from that before. The question thus becomes whether or not the changes are great enough that the benefits of a stage analysis outweigh the costs.

In addition to the distinction between stage and continuous models, there are differences in assumptions about fundamental *trends* in adult development. Trend models are basically of three types: increment, stability, and decrement. Theories of child development, for example, typically use increment models for most variables: intelligence increases with age, and so do social skills and biological capacities. For the description of adult development, decrement models are more common: certain biological capacities decrease and, according to some theorists, so do basic intellectual abilities. Other variables may be considered fairly stable during the adult years; many personality variables fall under the rubric of the stability model (Schaie, 1973, 1977).

Often distinctions are made within a model. The decrement model is often divided into the "irreversible decrement" model (an inexorable decrease, usually biological, is claimed) and the "decrement-with-compensation" model, which suggests that decreasing biological capacities are often moderated by social experience to produce stable or even increasing socialized abilities. Vision often follows a decrement-with-compensation model; biological visual abilities decrease but are compensated for by social interventions such as eyeglasses.

Another useful model attempts to summarize the multiple causes that influence adult development. Figure 1–4 lists three major sets of factors that influence individual development: normative age-graded, normative history-graded, and nonnormative life events. These sets of influences interact to produce developmental change over the life span (Baltes, 1979).

Normative age-graded influences are the biological and environmental factors that are highly correlated with chronological age. These are the variables that have traditionally been studied by developmental psychologists. Some, such as menarche, puberty, and menopause, are biological. Others involve socialization and the acquisition of normative age-correlated roles, such as entering schools, marrying, and retiring.

Normative history-graded influences are events that are widely experienced in a given culture at a particular time. These events may be environmental, as with an economic depression, war, or other political dislocation, or they may be biological, as with environmental pollution, malnutrition, and large-scale epidemics.

FIGURE 1–4.

The interaction of three systems of influences regulating the nature of life span development.

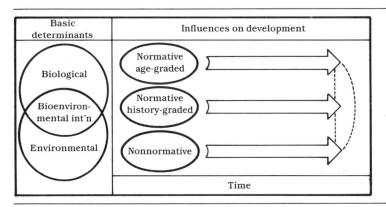

Source: From P. B. Baltes. Life-span development psychology: Some converging observations on history and theory. In P. B. Baltes and O. G. Brim, Jr., eds., Life-span development and behavior (Vol. 2). New York: Academic Press, 1979. Reprinted by permission.

Obviously, biological and environmental events are often mutually influential. In developmental research, these influences are called "cohort effects" if they only affect one generation and "time-of-measurement" or "period" effects if they occur for a limited time but affect the entire population that is exposed to their influence. For example, the great depression in the 1930s was a period effect because it impacted virtually all persons then living in our society. By contrast, we can speak of a Vietnam cohort effect, because it was primarily those persons who were of the right age to be conscripted into military service during that conflict who were maximally affected. Research designs that differentiate these dimensions are discussed later in this chapter.

Nonnormative influences are factors that may be significant within the life of a particular person but are not necessarily experienced by everyone during their lifetime. These may be favorable events such as winning a lottery or succeeding in one's job, or unfavorable events such as unemployment, divorce, or a serious disease (Schaie, 1984a).

The relative significance of these three types of developmental influence may vary in different behavioral change processes and at different points in the life span. For example, age-graded influences may be especially important during childhood and then again in old age, whereas history-graded and nonnormative influences may predominate in early and middle adulthood. This would explain why child development researchers focus on age-graded influences while those who work on adult life have favored an emphasis on history-graded and individualized nonnormative experiences (Baltes and Willis, 1978; Baltes, 1979; Hultsch and Plemons, 1979).

Research Methodology

The psychology of adult development is a branch of scientific psychology and thus shares the methodological concerns of the parent field. One finds in adult developmental psychology much the same kinds of data, generated by the same procedures, as in other fields of psychology. The experiment, the correlational study, the survey will all be as much in evidence here as elsewhere. Psychologists in this field have trouble finding an adequate control group to which to compare their experimental group; they have problems generalizing their results beyond the peculiar individuals they happened to observe; and they worry about statistics distorting their data. They are no different in these regards from other scientific psychologists (Kausler, 1982).

CROSS-SECTIONAL AND LONGITUDINAL STUDIES

In certain respects, however, psychologists who investigate adult development have problems beyond those shared with other researchers. The consideration of one such problem begins with a basic distinction between an *age change* and an *age difference*. An age change is one that occurs in an individual as he or she grows older: at fifty, for example, the individual's reactions might not be quite as quick as they were at twenty-five. An age difference is one that is observed in a comparison of two people (or groups) of different ages: the person in our example at age fifty might be found to have slower reactions than another person of age twenty-five. Often we are interested in age changes (what happens as people grow older), but the only data we have often come from research on age differences (where the performance of different age groups is compared). We must be cautious in assuming that age differences reflect age changes; as we shall see, sometimes they do, sometimes they don't.

The distinction between age changes and differences corresponds to the data generated by two different experimental designs (see Figure 1–5). A *cross-sectional design* compares groups of people varying in age and thus allows us to record age differences. A *longitudinal design* involves the observation of the same individuals at two or more different times; the data are age changes. To illustrate, two researchers might use the different designs to investigate income across the span of life. One, using a cross-sectional design, will compare the average income of representative samples of twenty-five-year-olds, thirty-year-olds, thirty-five-year-olds, and so forth, up to the age of sixty-five. The second researcher will use one sample of people, checking on their income every five years, at twenty-five, then at thirty, then at thirty-five, and so forth. One difference in the designs is thus immediately apparent. The cross-sectional study can be completed in a day, whereas the longitudinal study will take forty years! You will not be surprised to learn, therefore, that cross-sectional studies are much more abundant than longitudinal studies.

FIGURE 1–5.

Cross-sectional studies test different groups of different ages, all at the same time. Longitudinal studies test the same group at different ages, requiring several tests at different times.

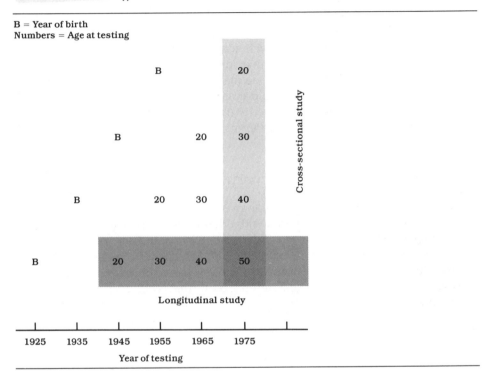

Age and cohort To understand the differences between cross-sectional and longitudinal designs, it is helpful to consider the variables involved. One, of course, is *age*, which is a variable in both designs. A second variable is *cohort*, which is usually defined as the people born in the same year (or period of years). If you were born in 1966 you are in the 1966 cohort; your parents probably belong to cohorts born in the 1940s or so. Cohort is similar to the concept of generation, as in "generation gap"; it is used to distinguish people by time of birth.

Now consider the two designs. The subjects in a longitudinal design all belong to the same cohort, whereas the subjects in a cross-sectional design belong to several cohorts, each representing an age group. As a result, the age differences produced by a cross-sectional study may be due to age *or* they may be due to cohort differences. Imagine a cross-sectional study of liking for Frank Sinatra's music. You would not be surprised to find that older people like him more than younger people, but you would be unwilling to conclude that liking for Frank Sinatra increases as one gets older. Most of the age difference, you might assert, is an effect of cohort, not of age. People who are old today were members of the "younger generation" who adored Sinatra when he was also young. Today's cohorts will grow old and, forty years from now, listen with rapt attention to a gray-haired Madonna!

By comparing results from cross-sectional and longitudinal studies, cohort effects often become apparent. For example, the Bureau of the Census often puts out statistics on the average income of various age groups. Graphs of these statistics invariably look like the one in Figure 1–6: an increase to middle age and then decline until retirement. These statistics are often interpreted as reflecting the normal course of an individual's earnings over the life span, but they are *cross-sectional* data on *age differences,* subject to misinterpretation. A longitudinal study shows that individuals studied over their lifetimes almost always increase their earnings right up to the time of retirement (Ruggles and Ruggles, 1974). The cross-sectional data misled us because each new cohort made more money at each stage of life than preceding cohorts. Thus, though men between fifty-five and fifty-nine typically earn more than they ever have before in their lives, their earnings are less than men between forty-five and forty-nine who started at higher salaries and received greater increases than the older men (U.S. Bureau of the Census, 1981a).

Age and time   Longitudinal studies observe the same cohort at two or more points. The data they produce are age changes, and interpretation is not clouded by possible differences between cohorts. However, longitudinal studies have their own difficulties, not the least of which is the extreme expense, in both time and money, necessary to mount a well-designed investigation. Nor are longitudinal studies free from potential misinterpretation. Here the confound that can affect the external validity (generalizability) of our findings is represented by what is often referred to as "time-of-measurement" effects. Findings of change in longitudinal studies can be attributed either to a true developmental change of the sort we want to discover (a change with age in intellect or memory or personality) *or* to something else, something that happened between the first and second times the subjects were observed that has nothing to do with advancing age (Schaie, 1982a).

Imagine you were running a longitudinal study of attitudes toward the war in Vietnam during the late 1960s and early 1970s. You might well find that your subjects, tested first in 1965, then in 1970, and finally in 1975, had become increasingly intolerant of our nation's involvement in Southeast Asia. What does your finding mean? Does it mean that people become less accepting of war as they grow older? (Is it a true developmental change?) Or, as is considerably more likely in this case, does it mean that social-historical events occurred between testings that resulted in a change in nearly everyone's attitude toward the war?

Practice effects are also time-of-measurement effects. A longitudinal study involving tests (e.g., IQ tests) requires repeated testing with the same measures. What looks like an increase in the skill being assessed may be no more than familiarity with the test items.

FIGURE 1–6.

(a)Median income of white males by age, 1980. (b) If each generation earns ever-increasing income, but also each generation makes more at each stage of the life span, a cross-sectional study can misleadingly make it appear that income drops toward the end of one's career.

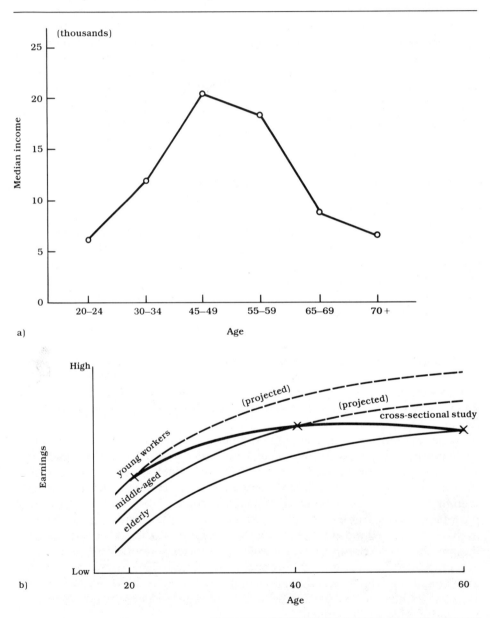

Cross-sectional studies do not have difficulties with time of measurement, since all subjects are observed at a single time. Thus, in summary, cross-sectional studies confound age and cohort or generational effects; longitudinal studies confound age and time-of-measurement effects. The life of a scientist is not an easy one!

There is another type of study that in a sense completes the list of possibilities, at least for simple designs. Called a *time-lag* design, it involves the observation of people of the same age at different times. Suppose you are interested in the sex life of twenty-year-olds and, specifically, in the differences between such activities today and in 1900. Assuming someone had surveyed young people on this issue in 1900, you could survey a new sample of young people today and compare the data. Age is held constant; it is not a variable. The researcher is typically interested in the direct study of cohort effects — differences between generations. The confounded variable is time of measurement. If you found today's twenty-year-olds reporting more sexual activity, perhaps generations truly differ; but perhaps, between time 1 and time 2, society has become more open and honest about reporting such activity.

SAMPLING DIFFICULTIES

One of the chief impediments to sensible conclusions about research in adult development and aging is the difficulty in gathering (and holding on to) appropriate groups of subjects. Subjects are generally presumed to be a *sample* of a larger population; the sample we want is one that is *representative* of the larger group. But there are many ways a sample becomes unrepresentative, making *generalization* of the results uncertain, perhaps invalid.

A representative sample will produce data that can be generalized to a larger population. The people who run opinion polls have an obvious need for representativeness in their samples, for they wish to generalize to very large groups, often the entire population of the United States. In voter surveys, the population is "people eligible to vote" or "people likely to vote." The goal is to predict the actual vote on election day or at least to determine accurately what the vote would have been, had the election been held on the day the survey was taken. Unrepresentative samples can result in very misleading data, showing one candidate ahead when in fact he or she is far behind. In some polls taken early in this century, Republicans were overrepresented because the telephones were used to solicit opinions; in those days, the Republicans were richer and thus had more of the phones.

In adult development, people with more money, more education, and better jobs are usually included in samples more often than less fortunate individuals. These people are easier to find (they belong to clubs and organizations) and easier to persuade to participate (they believe in research and are proud of themselves and their lives). Thus many of the samples providing research findings to be discussed in this book will not be representative of the adult population in general, but only of the middle class. In addition, men are much more frequently studied than women. The debate regarding the factual basis of the so-called mid-life crisis, for example, is concerned almost entirely with the life experience of middle-class males (Levinson, 1978; Bray and Howard, 1983b). There is a rather desperate need for studies of women, minorities, and the working class. In the meantime, we must be cautious in generalizing the research findings beyond the population of which the sample can reasonably be called representative.

People who do longitudinal studies face particular problems in sampling. Not only do they need to find a representative sample, they also have to keep it — to recover it for each subsequent retesting. Between observations, some people die (especially if the subjects are elderly), some people move away (and may not even leave a forwarding address), and some people develop an antipathy toward science (refusing to participate in the next round of tests). Usually the loss makes the sample less representative, for the subjects who die, move away, or become stubborn generally have less education, less income, and less prestigious jobs. In short, if the sample was not biased toward the middle class to begin with, it is likely to be so by the time the longitudinal study is completed (Schaie, 1977; Schaie and Hertzog, 1982).

SEQUENTIAL DESIGNS

Some of the difficulties of interpretation inherent in simple cross-sectional and longitudinal designs can be alleviated with more complex designs called *sequences*, shown in Figure 1–7 (see also Baltes, Reese, and Nesselroade, 1977; Schaie and Hertzog, 1982). A *cross-sectional sequence* consists of two or more cross-sectional studies, covering the same age range, executed at two or more times. For example, we might compare age groups ranging in age from twenty to eighty in 1970 and then repeat the experiment in 1980 with a new sample of subjects in each age group, still from twenty to eighty. A *longitudinal sequence* consists of two or more longitudinal studies, using two or more cohorts. For example, suppose we begin a longitudinal study of age changes between twenty and eighty by observing twenty-year-olds in 1960, with the plan of observing each of these subjects again, every ten years, until they are eighty. This is a simple longitudinal study. In 1970, however, we begin a second longitudinal study of the same age range, choosing a new sample of twenty-year-olds — those of the 1950 cohort; the previous cohort was born in 1940. The two longitudinal studies (running in sequence) define the simplest case of a longitudinal sequence.

Schaie's "most efficient design"   K. Warner Schaie (1965, 1977), who has made extensive studies of research methodology in adult development, has proposed a "most efficient design," which generates data useful for many informative analyses. The most efficient design is a combination of cross-sectional and longitudinal sequences, created in a systematic way. In brief, the researchers begin with a cross-sectional study. Then, after a period of years, they retest these subjects, which provides longitudinal data on several cohorts — a longitudinal

FIGURE 1–7.

Longitudinal and cross-sectional sequences. Longitudinal sequences use two or more cohorts; cross-sectional sequences test the same age groups at two or more times, using independent samples.

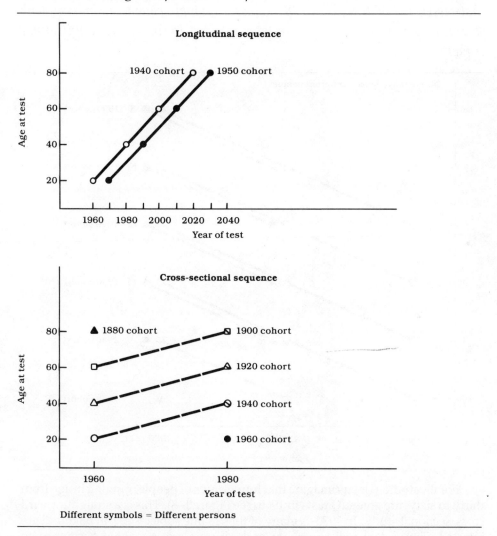

sequence. At the same time, they test a new group of subjects, forming a second cross-sectional study — and, together with the first cross-sectional study, a cross-sectional sequence. This whole process can be repeated over and over (every five or ten years, say) with retesting of old subjects (adding to the longitudinal data) and first-testing of new subjects (adding to the cross-sectional data).

nothing from here on test to end chapt.

FIGURE 1–8.

Schaie's most efficient design. In 1960, four groups are tested (a cross-sectional study). They are retested in 1970 and 1980 (a longitudinal sequence with repeated measures). New groups from the same cohorts are first-tested in 1970 and in 1980 (cross-sectional sequences, independent samples). These new groups are later retested to form new longitudinal sequences.

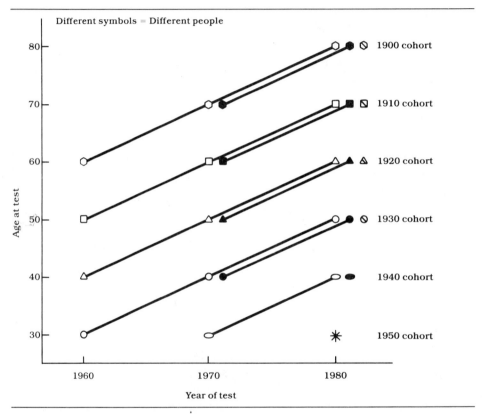

For illustration, let us imagine that four groups of people, ranging in age from thirty to sixty, are given IQ tests in 1960 (see Figure 1–8). This is a straightforward cross-sectional study. In 1970 as many of these same subjects as can be found are retested. These data will show, for each of four cohorts, what happened to average IQ scores as the subjects grew ten years older. At the same time, we recruit new subjects who are in the same age groups as the original subjects and test their IQ for the first time. (We would probably add a new cohort of people who, at the time of the second testing, are thirty years old, to make this second cross-sectional study comparable to the first.) This second cross-sectional study should yield results similar to the first; if it does not, we will have interesting clues to the nature of intellectual development.

Later, in 1980, we can retest the 1960 sample for the third time, adding more data to our longitudinal sequence. We can also retest the subjects who were new in 1970, adding an entirely new longitudinal sequence. And we can recruit more new subjects, forming a third replication of our cross-sectional study. As you can see, we will have generated a wealth of data.

Analyses Data from Schaie's most efficient design or comparable designs can be analyzed in several ways. The way of greatest interest to developmental psychologists is to pit age changes against cohort effects (Schaie and Baltes, 1975). This approach would permit a strong test of the irreversible decrement model. To do this we would need at least two cohorts, and we must observe each cohort for at least two different ages. To simplify our illustration, consider only the changes in IQ scores between the ages of sixty and seventy. These people in our hypothetical study who were sixty in 1960 (the 1900 cohort) and seventy when retested in 1970 would be compared with those people who were sixty in 1970 (the 1910 cohort) and seventy in 1980. Do their IQ scores increase, decrease, or remain stable over the ten-year period? If the irreversible decrement model was valid, we should find similar decline patterns for both cohorts. In a "traditional" longitudinal study we would have data only for a single cohort and would not know, therefore, whether the observed change would hold true beyond the specific cohort that was studied. For example, it is possible that one cohort will show an increase while the other shows a decrease; or one cohort will increase at a slower rate than the other. One cohort may have a higher average IQ than the other at both sixty and seventy, though the increase or decrease may be similar for the two cohorts. Obviously a lot of interesting comparisons can be made from this type of analysis, which is called a *cohort-sequential* analysis (see Figure 1–9).

Another strategy is called *cross-sequential*. First as the cohort-sequential analysis pits cohort effects against age effects, the cross-sequential analysis pits cohort effects against time of measurement. At least two cohorts are compared at two or more times of measurement. This strategy is particularly appropriate for data sets that fit the adult stability model discussed earlier. No age changes are expected, and the primary interest turns to identifying the presence and magnitude of cohort and time-of-measurement effects. The cross-sequential analysis is helpful when the researcher is interested in, say, the effects of some event or sociocultural change that occurs between the two times of measurement and, in addition, suspects that different cohorts might react differently. For example, the effects of the "sexual revolution" of the 1960s might be compared for a cohort whose members were young adults in 1960 and a second cohort whose members were in their early forties in 1960. In addition, if there is reason to suppose that time-of-measurement effects are slight or nonexistent, cross-sequential analysis can be used to estimate age changes, since subjects are obviously older at the second time of measurement.

FIGURE 1–9.

Analyses of cross-sectional and longitudinal sequences can compare two or more cohorts at two or more ages (cohort-sequential), two or more cohorts at two or more times of measurement (cross-sequential), or two or more ages at two or more times of measurement (time-sequential). The data in time-sequential analyses must be from independent samples, but data in the other analyses can be repeated measures or generated from independent samples of the same cohorts.

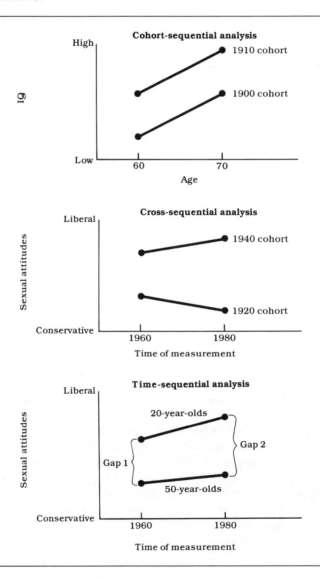

If the cohort-sequential analysis pits cohort against age, and the cross-sequential analysis pits cohort against time of measurement, we have one logical possibility left: the *time-sequential* strategy pits age against time of measurement. People of at least two different ages are compared at two or more times of measurement. For illustration consider a study of changes over time in the generation gap; the attitudes of fifty-year-olds are compared with those of twenty-year-olds, both in 1960 and in 1980. We might find that the difference between age groups narrows between 1960 and 1980, or perhaps both age groups become more liberal in their attitudes but the gap between them remains sizable. The time-sequential method is also appropriate for a test of the decrement-with-compensation model. In the case where a new compensatory method is introduced (say a computerized memory prosthesis or a drug affecting the declining behavior), the time-sequential method would show that age differences over the same age range would be smaller at Time 1 than at Time 2.

Repeated measures versus independent samples In a typical longitudinal study, *repeated measures* are taken of the same subjects at different times. Another possibility is to use the same research design but with *independent samples* at each point on the longitudinal time scale. If we are interested in intellectual development, for example, we might begin a longitudinal study by testing the IQ of thirty-year-olds, with plans to retest these same individuals every ten years; these would then be repeated measures. The alternative would be to draw a new (independent) sample *from the same cohort* every ten years. Thus, in ten years, when our thirty-year-olds are forty, we find a new representative sample of forty-year-olds instead of retesting the old batch. The independent sampling approach works well when a large sample is drawn from a large population frame. If small samples are used it would, of course, be necessary to make sure that successive samples are matched on factors such as gender, income, and education to avoid possible differences due to selection and biases.

What do we gain from the independent-samples procedure? First, we gain a replication of sorts of the repeated-measures study, a second look at the same trends. If, for example, our typical longitudinal study shows decreases in average IQ from age thirty to sixty, the independent-sample study should show the same thing. Of course, we cannot use the independent-sample data to follow a particular individual. We cannot say that Joan Doe, in particular, increased her IQ scores; nor can we say that 87 percent of our subjects decreased and 13 percent increased. But we can say that the averages for the cohort decreased or increased.

In addition, independent samples allow us to estimate the effects in the repeated-measure study of such problems as losing subjects due to their inability or unwillingness to be retested; practice effects can also be examined. The independent samples are new each time and thus reflect what the composition of the single sample of the repeated-measure study would have been if no subjects had been lost between testing. As a new sample, the subjects have not taken our tests before, so practice effects can be estimated by comparing this "no-practice" group with the repeated-measure sample, who practice each time the measures are repeated.

Finally, if the longitudinal study is a longitudinal sequence (that is, if at least two cohorts are studied), then the independent-samples replication will form a cross-sectional sequence, providing valuable information for cross-sectional analyses at each testing period. Suppose we begin our longitudinal study with four cohorts, ranging in age from thirty to sixty, retesting each cohort every ten years. In ten years, in addition to the retestings, we test new, independent samples for each cohort. The retestings are longitudinal but the new testings form a neat, cross-sectional study of the age range forty to seventy. As we mentioned before, to be maximally efficient, one could add a new cohort, a new group of thirty-year-olds, and begin a second longitudinal sequence, to be retested for the second time. Thus the independent samples comprise (1) a replication of the original longitudinal study, (2) a new cross-sectional study, and (3) the start of a new longitudinal sequence. It is not surprising, then, that independent samples are included in Schaie's "most efficient design."

DEVELOPMENTAL RESEARCH

The primary goal of developmental psychologists is to describe and explain age changes. To do this, they try to estimate age changes by observing the age differences in cross-sectional studies, which works reasonably well if cohort differences in the variable under study are slight. Such an assumption is unreasonable when young adults and the elderly are compared. But it makes sense when comparison is made of relatively small age slices; for example, comparing late middle-aged with young old persons, or comparing persons in their twenties with those in their thirties. Or the researchers use longitudinal studies that directly record age changes for a variety of individuals. But longitudinal studies are expensive and obviously time-consuming. In addition, the pure effects of age might be masked by social-historical changes between measurements. Large segments of the original sample may die, move away, or refuse to be retested, changing the sample in significant ways that hinder the researchers' ability to generalize their results to a larger population. And tests that were used on twenty-year-olds in 1920 may be considered obsolete by the time they are retested as eighty-year-olds in 1980. Problems, problems.

But longitudinal studies have the great advantage of measuring directly the changes in characteristics such as an individual's intellect or personality or brain function as he or she grows older. Longitudinal studies produce data that provide at least partial answers to such questions as: Do some people increase in intelligence as they grow older, and some decrease? How much variability is there? What causes the variability? Does the intelligence of people in "intellectual" jobs increase, while it decreases for people in "manual" jobs? Does an increase in blood pressure relate to a decrease in intelligence? As expensive and time-consuming as longitudinal studies are, they provide data that are among the most important for theories in developmental psychology.

It is worth noting that developmental research, which covers the life span, encounters somewhat different difficulties at different stages of life. In a child-development textbook, for example, you will find a discussion of the difference between cross-sectional and longitudinal studies, but the sense of danger will be less. In child studies, cross-sectional and longitudinal studies often produce similar results. One reason is that child studies cover a smaller age range. Two-year-olds might be compared with four-year-olds, for example, and it is not likely that cohort differences will be pronounced in a span of two years. Also, many of the age changes in childhood are based on biological changes; the maturation of the brain and nervous system or the sexual-reproductive system, for example, accounts for fairly uniform changes in intellect and sexual activity among children. Adulthood, on the other hand, covers fifty-five years of the average seventy-five-year life span, and social events rather than biological events are often the primary determinants of change (Flavell, 1970). Thus cross-sectional studies of adults, which confound cohort effects with age effects, are fraught with danger; the time span is longer and the variability of social causes is much greater than the variability of biological causes. Longitudinal studies are much more important therefore in the study of adult development than they are in child development.

Summary

1. The organization of this book is both topical and chronological. The first section covers psychological topics of greatest interest to the chronological period of young adulthood — family, career, and personality development — followed by an integrative chapter on young adulthood itself. Each topical chapter, however, covers the life span from young adulthood to late life. The second section, which ends with a chapter on middle age, includes topical chapters on motivation and the relationship between men and women. The final section, which ends with a chapter on late life, has topical chapters on intellectual development and biological development, learning and memory, and mental health.

2. The scientific study of adult development and aging has surprisingly recent origins. One reason is that, in the past, people simply assumed the adult years to be a time of stability, especially in one's career, family life, and personality. Another reason is that, in the past, there were very few elderly citizens, so aging was less of an issue.

3. The number of elderly people in the population has increased dramatically since the turn of the century, primarily as a result of decreases in premature death. In the decades ahead, the median age of the population of the United States will increase substantially, which will require certain structural changes in society. Gerontology is the study of the aging process from maturity to old age and the study of the elderly as a special population.

4. One of our major goals in this book is to evaluate the myths (untested assumptions) of adult development and aging. Inaccurate myths often lead to

negative stereotypes of aging and ageism, unfair discrimination on the basis of age.

5.   Theories of adult development attempt to explain changes with age and also differences in such changes between individuals or groups. Different disciplines have offered varying definitions of aging. A person's biological age is his or her position with regard to remaining life expectancy. A person's social age is determined by judging his or her position in the life course against the "average" ages at which various positions are reached. A person's psychological age is how he or she functions in response to environmental demands. The *behavioral* or *social-learning* approach focuses on the rewards and punishments people receive from actions in their environment. *Psychoanalytic* (Freudian) theories focus on emotional conflicts and unconscious mental processes. *Humanistic* theories stress distinctively human motives, such as self-actualization; the *individual-differences* approach relies heavily on psychological tests (such as IQ tests); the *information-processing* approach tries to track information from the environment from perception through learning and memory to decision and response; *attribution* theories explore the ways in which social perceptions of the environment affect behavior and behavior change. The *dialectical* approach focuses on contradictions, conflicts, and crises and their resolutions (syntheses). Theories of any type can be classified as *stage theories* or not, or as theories that assume *incremental, stable,* or *decremental* trends in development. Another developmental approach takes into account three major sets of factors that influence individual development: normative age-graded life events, normative history-graded life events, and nonnormative life events.

6.   One of the key distinctions in research methodology for studies of adult development is between *cross-sectional* and *longitudinal* designs. Cross-sectional designs compare several age groups *(cohorts)* at the same time and thus yield data on *age differences.* Longitudinal designs compare the same cohort at different times and thus yield data on *age changes.* Longitudinal studies suffer from subject loss, practice effects, and historical changes that affect behavior, but cross-sectional studies are usually more prone to erroneous interpretations, because they confuse age effects with differences between generations (cohorts). Another major research problem in adult development is that of finding a *representative sample* of subjects; white, middle-class males are vastly overrepresented in the research literature. Longitudinal studies have the further problem of *keeping* the representative sample once it is recruited; lower-class subjects, for example, tend to drop out in disproportionate numbers.

7.   *Sequential* designs are complex combinations of the simple cross-sectional and longitudinal designs. A *cross-sectional sequence* consists of two or more cross-sectional studies run at different times. A *longitudinal sequence* consists of concurrent longitudinal studies of two or more cohorts. Schaie's "most efficient design" includes both cross-sectional and longitudinal sequences formed by retesting the subjects of an earlier cross-sectional study while first-testing new subjects in a new cross-sectional study. Analyses of the resulting data can be *cohort-sequential* (cohort versus age), *cross-sequential* (cohort versus time of measurement), or *time-sequential* (age versus time of measurement). *Repeated measures*, which longitudinal studies provide, can be compared with measures from *independent samples*, which are provided by separate cross-sectional studies at the times of the longitudinal measurements, to estimate the effect of subject loss in the longitudinal study.

SUGGESTED READINGS

Baltes, P. B., and Willis, S. L. (1977). Toward psychological theories of aging and development. In J. E. Birren and K. W. Schaie (Eds.), *Handbook of the psychology of aging* (pp. 128–154). New York: Van Nostrand Reinhold. Discusses basic issues of scientific theory and the discipline of psychology as they apply to the study of adult development. Provides requirements for and an overview of psychological theories of aging and development.

Birren, J. E. and Cunningham, W. R. (1985). Research on the psychology of aging: Principles, concepts and theory. In J. E. Birren and K. W. Schaie (Eds.), *Handbook of the psychology of aging.* (2nd ed.) (pp. 3–34). New York: Van Nostrand Reinhold. A thorough discussion of issues and problems of research on aging. Lists some of the requirements for valid studies and provides suitable cautions against over interpreting limited research findings.

Hagestad, G. O., and Neugarten, B. L. (1985). Age and the life course. In R. Binstock and E. Shanas (Eds.), *Handbook of aging and the social sciences* (2nd ed.) (pp. 35–81). New York: Van Nostrand Reinhold. Provides a social-psychological background for our understanding of adult development, discussing issues such as the social definition of time and aging, group variations in pattern of aging, social age norms, and age-related transitions.

Riegel, K. F. (1977). History of psychological gerontology. In J. E. Birren and K. W. Schaie (Eds.), *Handbook of the psychology of aging* (pp. 70–102). New York: Van Nostrand Reinhold. A scholarly account of the Anglo-American, Continental European, and dialectic approaches to the study of adult psychological development.

The Aging in the Coming Decade

For many years at the beginning of their fields' development, researchers and human service workers focused on the earlier stages of life. The later years were largely ignored, in part because few people survived into old age, but also because health professionals were reluctant to treat the elderly and the elderly were often suspicious of health professionals. Today, older people are still underserved, but we now recognize that relatively few old people need massive support. It is also clear that preventive measures and prompt intervention can ensure in many cases that old age will not be a disastrous period of life. To provide such services, however, one must be familiar with some of the changes that occur as people grow older.

It is well known that elderly people suffer from chronic ailments more often than younger people, but the effects of these ailments are not so well known. Only 20 percent of persons under age seventeen have one or more chronic diseases, but the figure for those over age sixty-five is a whopping 81 percent — a rather grim figure. Most of these ailments are relatively minor, however. The major activities of only 26 percent of the elderly are at all limited, and only 16 percent are not able to carry on the major activities of daily living. To state this more positively, 84 percent of the elderly are capable of caring for themselves completely or almost completely. The problems that do occur are likely to reduce the efficiency of functioning. For example, the elderly may suffer from sensory deficits, tiredness, circulatory problems, and declines in psychological functioning. Contrary to popular stereotypes, only 6 to 8 percent of the population over age sixty-five suffers from an organic mental disorder. The figure climbs to 20 percent among those over age eighty, but that still leaves four out of five very old people in full possession of their mental faculties. In sum, although it is undeniable that some elderly people face serious health problems, most of the elderly are in reasonably good physical and psychological condition.

In attempting to assess how the elderly population will change over the next decade, gerontologists have the advantage that their future clients already exist. Their characteristics can be determined quite readily. One thing we know is that there will be more of them. By 1990, there will be about 30 million people over age sixty-five, about 12 percent of our total population. A disproportionate part of this group will be the old old, who require more services. The new group reaching retirement age will have received better health care when they were young and will also have received more education. The typical older person today has had a grade school education or less; during the next ten years, the average level will rise to include at least some high school. Most people retiring today are blue-collar or semiskilled workers, but this too will change, reflecting the job shift toward high technology and white-collar occupations. In the coming decade, many more women will be retiring from their jobs, so the problems related to retirement will no longer be chiefly a concern of males.

The elderly of the next generation will have more economic resources and much higher expectations about the quality of life. These higher expectations may cause certain problems. The benefits for older generations are financed by younger generations, who may not be able to support the large group of elderly at the level they have come to expect. There may be serious intergenerational conflicts. One possible solution would be to extend mandatory retirement beyond age seventy.

The newly retired of the next decade are also likely to be increasingly militant and involved in the political process. They will demand greater consideration from the professional service sector. Unlike earlier generations, they will not be suspicious of professional service resources, nor will they be reluctant to take advantage of the services they are entitled to because they consider this to be accepting charity or admitting to personal incompetence. They may also have to rely more on professional services than current elderly people do: the trend toward smaller families means that there will be fewer relatives available to care for aged family members. The increases in longevity that we expect will mean that some people will have to spend the period immediately before and after their own retirement caring for their very old and fragile parents.

How will these developments influence the professional care needs of the elderly in the years to come? In considering this question, several influential factors must be kept in mind. First, it is the very old population that will need the most services; the young old will not differ markedly from people at midlife. Second, health care for the chronically ill, who constitute a large portion of the elderly who require services, will be provided in the community rather than in institutions. Third, the energy and sophistication of the elderly in the community are increasing, and they are going to demand greater involvement in their own care.

Much of the effort that is going to be required of professionals over the next decade will involve education. One important area of concern will relate to stereotypes about aging, which can become self-fulfilling prophecies. Health workers often deal exclusively with the disadvantaged and unhealthy elderly; they will have to familiarize themselves with the active, healthy majority of the elderly population. Educators must also inculcate the attitude that the elderly are just as valuable clients as younger people, and they deserve the same high-quality service.

A second area of concern is health education. An increasingly successful job is being done to convince the public that people must control their drinking, smoking, and dietary habits in midlife to ensure that they will be physically fit in old age. This effort should be extended to the area of mental health. The elderly should be taught how to recognize the symptoms of mental health problems and how to seek help when they are discovered; the public must be convinced that mental health problems in later life are as important and worth treating as those at younger ages.

A third area of services concerns the transition to retirement from the world of work. Since retirement in the future is likely to be a complex negotiated process, the health care system will probably have to become more deeply involved in it, making diagnostic appraisals that will influence the decision to retire and helping people cope after retirement.

Finally, efforts must be made to provide more comprehensive arrays of community services, ranging from services for those who can function completely independently through services for those who are completely dependent. Such systems of care and support must be buttressed by diagnostic assessment facilities designed for comprehensive care.

The implementation of programs such as these is a formidable challenge and a responsibility for all segments of our society. By facilitating the transition from middle to old age, however, we can ensure that the lives of older people will involve a minimum of stress and help the elderly preserve as many opportunities and as much freedom as possible. Our success in these ventures is a reflection of the quality of life in our country and a measure of the commitment of professionals to raising that quality for the elderly.

Schaie, K. W. (1982). The aging in the coming decade. In K. W. Schaie and J. Geiwitz (Eds.), *Readings in adult development*. Boston: Little, Brown and Company.

Chapter Two

FAMILIES

Our Primary Relationships

Pick up here again.

The Leslie family spans the adult years, from Linda, a young woman struggling with decisions about career and marriage, to her great-grandmother Lavinia — proud, eighty-seven, and dying of cancer. Linda's father, Larry, feels that the magazine articles about "midlife crisis" may be right on target; he seems to be suffering through one of his own. His father, Leonard, has been recently retired and just as recently widowed; he is considering remarriage, though both Larry, his son, and Lavinia, his mother, are opposed to the idea.

A very brief sketch, yet we already know much about the Leslie family. The concerns of such a family are easily understood, for they are our concerns as well. The great issues in adult life are as powerful as they are universal, providing the fuel for great drama, great novels, and mediocre soap operas. All adults have either firsthand experience with these issues or they have extensive secondhand knowledge that allows them to anticipate their concerns and imagine their behavior at later stages of the life cycle. The decisions of young adulthood, the reevaluations of midlife, the reorganization that occurs in old age — these are familiar to us all. We understand something about the various stages of family life: getting married, having children, experiencing the empty nest, grandparenthood, widowhood. If we learn that Lavinia, at eighty-seven, is becoming forgetful, it comes as no surprise, nor are we surprised to learn that her hair has turned gray — or that Leonard, at sixty-nine, has lost his. Both Lavinia and Leonard worry about becoming a burden to their children and grandchildren. Well, you might say, that's quite understandable.

Linda is in the process of making decisions about career and marriage, but decision about one affects her decision about the other. Larry's concerns about his career at midlife similarly affect his relationship with his wife. Leonard, like Linda, is thinking of marriage, but he worries about his son's disapproval; Linda by contrast is likely to face disapproval only if she *doesn't* marry. In real life any change — in career, in health, in motivation — affects the other aspects of life as well.

Beginning with the first paragraph of this chapter and continuing throughout the book, we describe the trials and tribulations of the Leslie family; Linda, age twenty-two; her father, Larry, age forty-six; Larry's father, Leonard, age sixty-nine; and Leonard's mother, Lavinia, age eighty-seven. As the alliterative names suggest, these are fictionalized accounts of people in various stages of life. What is discussed, however, is not fictional; the concerns and problems, the ideas and motivations of each family member are real, not only to the real-life models for the Leslies, but to many of their peers.

The story of the Leslie family provides illustrations of major themes and, to some extent, anecdotal evidence. One of its major purposes is to show the continuing theme of the interrelation among the generations within the family as the primary context of human development. You encounter the Leslies again in the chronologically organized chapters on young adulthood, middle age, and old age. Their story provides a vehicle for discussing the disparate contents of the topical chapters as they relate to one another in real life. For no person moves through the life course in isolation, and the family throughout remains the context within which change and continuity of lives can best be understood.

Interdependent Relationships

From the beginnings of history, families have been the key to civilization and the representation of primary relationships among people. A family traditionally begins with a man and a woman who decide to satisfy one another's sexual and intimacy needs on a permanent basis. Spouses also provide helpers for one another; in all families, there is a division of labor. In the typical family, children soon add to the size of the family and bring their own desperate needs; they would perish without proper care but most parents need their children as well, to provide love, respect, a sense of immortality, a view of the world through innocent eyes, and the many other things children can offer their mother and father.

A family serves many functions for its members. One useful way to summarize these functions is to view the family as a system of *interdependent relationships*. Each family member has a specific role to play in the system, and other family members depend on him or her to play that role. Young children depend on their parents for the basic necessities of life (food, protection), and sometimes very old parents become similarly dependent on their adult children. Even the youngest and oldest participate to some extent in the division of labor among family members. In addition to these "labor" dependencies, there are also important emotional dependencies between husbands and wives and between parents and children.

When a child becomes an adult, we often think of this change as a shift from

An interdependent smiling contest. *Totally dependent.*

dependence to independence. Young adults, even older adolescents, often speak of their newly gained "independence" and what it will mean for them. What in fact it typically means, of course, is an opportunity to explore possible mutual dependencies with other people in a love relationship, and, eventually, to have children who are dependent on *them* (and on whom *they* depend in ways they could never quite perceive when they were playing the child's role). Thus a better way to conceptualize the changes of young adulthood is to see them as movement from one interdependent system to another. What has happened then is that one family has reproduced itself; a new family has been created.

Consider the interdependencies of family life from the point of view of an individual throughout the life span. One begins life almost totally dependent, relying on instinctive or culturally prescribed nurturant tendencies in parents. Very soon after birth, however, parents begin feeling rewarded by certain of their infant's behaviors; a smile, for example, can make a parent's day. The parents become dependent on the child, in a sense, for the fulfillment of their need to be needed. Thus *inter*dependency begins, even though the most important, the more pressing dependencies are the child's. As the child grows, the balance of the interdependencies shifts, until finally the child becomes an adult, breaks away, and forms a new family. Now the more important, more necessary dependencies become responsibilities, in terms of adults' relationship with their children (and, perhaps, their aging parents). In one's relationship with one's spouse, of course, there is a more nearly equal division of labor and emotional dependencies that must be shared if they are to have any meaning. As one grows older, the balance of interdependencies shifts again; one's children become more self-reliant and one becomes less so. Retirement, which usually means a reduction in income and status, and old age, which may bring some decrease in personal competencies, often result in more dependent conditions for the later years of life.

In 1983 approximately 73 percent of the 83.9 million households in the United States were composed of families. Married couples accounted for 60 percent of the households; families headed by males (without wives present) accounted for 2 percent; and families headed by females (with no husband present) accounted for 11 percent of the households. The remaining 27 percent of the population constituted nonfamily households; that is, they were either living alone or with nonrelatives (U.S. Bureau of the Census, 1984b).

Of course, in many cases the modern family no longer follows the traditional linear pattern from marriage and the birth of children to the "empty nest," retirement, and death. Repetitions of events in the family cycle are common. Following a divorce, a second family is often started; in 1980, 44 percent of all marriages were remarriages for one or both of the partners (National Center for Health Statistics, 1983c). Through remarriage, interdependencies may develop horizontally across families. A child may have a brother or sister from his biological parent's marriage, stepbrothers and sisters from a remarriage, and half-brothers or sisters when the remarried parent and stepparent decide to have another baby — not to mention relatives from the other biological parent's remarriage. It is not unusual for the pattern of relationships to grow even more complicated. Forty percent of all children who experience remarriage following divorce will experience another divorce (Bumpass, 1981). Remarriage following the death of a spouse in old age is also becoming increasingly common (Glick, 1980). Changes are occurring in other aspects of the family cycle as well. For example, some people are abandoning retirement in favor of a new career.

Although one's relationship with one's family (or families) may change throughout life, the basic structure of the family remains more or less the same. If we view the family in terms of the interdependencies among family members, we will have a better perspective on the specific issues that affect families throughout the life span (the topics to be covered in this chapter): choosing a life's partner, for example; having children; living in a nuclear or extended family; and coping with "empty nests" (when the children grow up and leave the home). The concept of interdependence also helps us understand the continuing relationship between adult children and their aging parents; the transmission of values and traditions from generation to generation; and the relationship between grandparents and grandchildren. Finally, we will examine a few of the new forms of the family (single-parent families and homosexual couples, for example) and discuss the possible effects of such alternate lifestyles on adult development.

Choosing a Mate

How does a family begin? One of the first developmental tasks of young adults is to split apart from one nuclear family (parents and offspring) to set up another (Havighurst, 1972). Thus the family reproduces itself. The first step in this process of sociological reproduction is choosing a mate.

The reasons that people give for marrying are often diverse and complex. They include such obvious themes as falling in love, the legitimization of sexual relationships (see Chapter 6 for further discussion of sexual aspects of relationships between men and women), satisfying needs for companionship, communication and sharing, providing security and legal rights for children, and last but not least satisfying social expectations and needs for conformity. Not infrequently the marriage decision may be influenced by the fact that most of one's peers already have married.

Choosing a partner with whom you want to share life's joys and duties (someone with whom you want to establish interdependency) is typically marked by a marriage ceremony. In this chapter we will discuss the most common pattern; a young man (average age twenty-four) and a young woman (average age twenty-two) meet, fall in love, and get married. There is evidence that the degree to which this pattern describes families in this country is decreasing slightly, as more people choose to remain single or marry later in life and as different family arrangements, such as homosexual and communal relationships, become more common. The probability of the marriage decision may also be affected by the experience of one's parents having had a happy or unhappy marriage; those with unhappily married (but not with divorced) parents have less favorable attitudes toward marriage (Long, 1983). Some of these less frequent patterns will be discussed at the end of this chapter and also in Chapter 6. Our immediate concern is with the over 90 percent of young people who unite, in public ceremonies, in heterosexual alliances formed before the elder of the pair reaches the age of thirty-five (Carter and Glick, 1976; Glick, 1977; Rodgers and Thornton, 1984).

WHY MARRY YOUNG?

Many social and economic influences can affect the average age of marriage. People tend to wait a bit longer during economic recessions, and they marry a bit earlier after a period of unavailability of marriage partners (such as might be caused by war). On the whole, however, the range of variation is at most a few years (Rodgers and Thornton, 1984). Young adulthood is unquestionably the period of a person's life when marriage decisions are made. One reason for this is biological. Marriage provides each spouse with a convenient and usually desirable sexual partner at a time when physical health is good, stamina is high, and hormones are raging. Biologically, young adulthood is an optimal time to have children (which is undoubtedly why nature has programmed youthful bodies with high sex drives). Miscarriages, birth defects, and other indications of less efficient biological functioning are more likely to occur with older parents as well as with parents who are in their early teens.

WHO'S THE LUCKY PERSON?

Choosing a mate is a process of considerable interest to many people, as any young person engaged in the process can attest. In the good old days and, indeed, in many societies today, the individuals about to enter marriage had very little to say in the matter; their mates were chosen for them, often when they were quite young. The notion that love is important in a relationship was considered not only ridiculous but also dangerous: young people in love were believed to act impulsively without thinking about the economic, political, and social ramifications of the potential union. Love in marriage is fine, but it should come after marriage, not before (Mace and Mace, 1960).

The nature of love and attachment has been studied by few psychologists. Maslow, writing over thirty years ago (1953), distinguished between D-love (deficiency love), the objective of which is to form an attachment to another person for the primary purpose of satisfying one's own selfish needs, and B-love (love for the being of another person) which represents an unselfish emotional investment that emphasizes sharing and giving of oneself. He also differentiated the intrinsic and extrinsic functions of relationships. Fox (1975) distinguished two kinds of love: *love as fission*, which splits apart, and *love as fusion*, which creates strong bonds. Rougemont (1956) made a distinction between the feeling of *being in love* and the act of *loving*. More recently, Lasswell and Lobsenz (1980) have identified six basic styles of loving: best friends love, game-playing love, logical love, possessive love, romantic love, and unselfish love. (See Chapter 5 for further discussion of love relationships in young adulthood.)

The dominant approach to love in Western culture has typically been romantic rather than scientific. In this romantic view, love is destroyed by fulfillment. That is, reality intrudes on the fantasy of an idyllic relationship and as a result progressively destroys the fantasy. To strengthen the bonds between newlyweds, many societies encourage them to remain isolated from everyday affairs and seek privacy (Cozby and Rosenblatt, 1971). This practice is reflected in our own custom of the honeymoon.

Whether based on romantic love or not, in the United States today the choice of mate is largely left up to the individuals involved, even though this has not always been the case (see Chapter 5, p. 178). Parents usually offer some advice and sometimes make demands, and friends often are willing to criticize potential mates, but unless the choice exceeds certain broadly defined bounds of acceptibility, the two lovers usually have their way. This does not mean, of course, that the process of mate selection is unpredictable, governed only by the irrational choices Cupid makes for love's arrows. On the contrary, the person you will choose (or have chosen) for a life's partner is one of the most predictable choices psychologists have yet uncovered.

Some theories of mate selection view the process in terms of a series of "filters" that screen out unacceptable candidates at various stages of an intimate relationship (Udry, 1971, 1974). For example, as shown by the representative filter theory in Figure 2–1, the pool of all possible dating partners is first screened through a *propinquity* filter. Propinquity means closeness in a geographic sense. What this filter represents is no more than the simple fact that if two possible mates are close to one another, they are more likely to meet, to date, to fall in love, and to marry. If you live in Iowa City, Iowa, there may well be a perfect mate for

FIGURE 2–1.

A filter theory of mate selection. The "filters" represent variables that predict whom one will choose as a marital partner; they do not necessarily reflect conscious decisions.

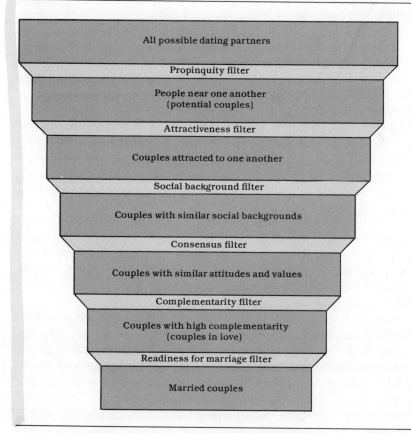

All possible dating partners

Propinquity filter

People near one another
(potential couples)

Attractiveness filter

Couples attracted to one another

Social background filter

Couples with similar social backgrounds

Consensus filter

Couples with similar attitudes and values

Complementarity filter

Couples with high complementarity
(couples in love)

Readiness for marriage filter

Married couples

Source: From J. Richard Udry. Figure 9–1 "The Multi-Stage Mate Selection Filter," in *The social context of marriage*. 2nd ed. New York: Lippincott, 1971. Copyright © 1971, 1966 by J. B. Lippincott Co. Reprinted by permission of J. Richard Udry.

you living in Phoenix, Arizona. Unfortunately, the chances are poor that you will ever meet this person. Not only are you more likely to meet someone who lives in your own city, but also, once you have met, a romance carried out in person usually wins out over a romance carried out long-distance, by letters, phone calls, and occasional visits (Mussen et al., 1979).

Next there is an *attractiveness* filter, which is a screening process you can appreciate from your own experience. Among the people you encounter, some are more attractive as potential mates than others. This is where your own particular notion of "good looks" enters in and also a number of other factors having to do with physical features. What is "too fat" for you, or "too thin"? What is "too short" or "too tall"? One rather subtle physical factor that enters the selective process is age. In the United States, the groom is expected to be slightly older than the bride, and typically is, by two or three years (Carter and Glick, 1976). According to custom, the husband can be up to ten years older or up to three years younger than the wife without much problem. If these limits are exceeded, parents and friends may apply pressure to break up the relationship. This custom is based on the notion that the man is the "breadwinner" of the family and should "establish himself" before taking on a young, dependent bride. As more women develop careers of their own, we can expect more marriages in which the woman is as old as or older than her mate.

The third filter in Figure 2–1 screens potential mates on the basis of *social background*. People tend to marry those who are similar in religion, political affiliation, education, occupation, and social class. Some of these factors (race and religion, for example) have become less important in recent years, but others (education and occupation, for example) have become more important. Marrying someone "of like mind" (someone who is striving for similar goals in life, someone who has the same basic values you have) is still important, and social background factors such as related occupations and similar educational level are still among the clearest indicators of like-mindedness.

As the relationship continues, the potential mates learn much about each other's specific attitudes and values and have less need to depend on the broad social-background indicators of similarity. Joe and June may both be white Lutheran Republicans with college degrees, but they might still disagree violently on issues such as abortions, the value of money, and the proper role of women in today's society. Similarity in certain personality traits is also important in mate selection, in marital satisfaction, and stability of the marriage (Skolnick, 1981). The *consensus* filter is based on such specific attitudes. Then comes a *complementarity* filter to indicate that beyond similarity of attitudes, values, and goals, we want a mate who complements us ("completes" us) — someone who is strong where we are weak. Thus a person who likes to dominate the relationship will search for a submissive mate (Winch, 1974).

Finally there is a *readiness* filter, which is based simply on the fact that people tend to enter first marriages within a very limited age range, usually between eighteen and twenty-five (Carter and Glick, 1976). Thus individuals will often marry whomever they happen to be dating at the "right time" — when they graduate from high school or college, for example. Graduation ceremonies and similar events often convey the message that it's time to settle down — to get a job and to choose a mate. And who is better to fill the role of mate than the person you love at the moment?

An alternative scheme of mate selection was proposed by Adams (1979), whose concepts are based on earlier work by Kerckhoff and Davis (1962). It differs from Udry's filter theory in that it pays more attention to the process of establishing the couple bond rather than emphasizing the elimination of sources of future marital friction. Adams offers the following sequence:

1. Attraction to marriage itself — a conscious, expressed desire to marry.
2. Propinquity.
3. Early attraction, based on such surface behaviors of the partner as gregariousness, poise, similar interest and abilities, physical appearance and attractiveness, and similarity to one's ideal image.
4. Perpetuation of attraction, aided by the reactions of others, including being labeled as a couple; disclosure — opening up to each other; and pair rapport — feeling comfortable in each other's presence.
5. Commitment and intimacy, establishing a bond.
6. Deeper attraction, which may be enhanced by (a) value consensus or co-orientation, providing validation of each other's viewpoints; (b) having feelings of competence reinforced; (c) perceiving other similarities in the partner, such as attractiveness, levels of emotional maturity, emotional expressiveness, self-esteem, race, ethnic group, religion, and matching birth order.
7. Deciding that this is "right for me" or "the best I can get."
8. Marriage.

A problem in determining a developmental sequence of mate selection is that most such sequences assume that marriage is the ultimate goal, the validating end state. Yet relationships may develop over time without ending in legal marriage. In fact, the actual decision to get married may be precipitated not by the stage the relationship has reached, but by such incidental factors as getting a job, pregnancy, parental strictness, or the death of a parent. A domino effect may also be observed. A couple may begin to consider marriage if it seems that most of their friends are getting married. By the same token, a couple who would like to get married may hesitate if most of their friends are still single. Nevertheless, although it may not be safe to conclude that every couple that marries has completed a developmental sequence, most relationships do fall into some variation of this pattern.

Having Children

The typical American family increases in size sometime in the second year of marriage. This pattern is becoming less typical as more and more couples delay parenthood or decide not to have children at all; the number of children per family is also decreasing rapidly (Van Dusen and Sheldon, 1976; Douvan, 1979). A recent Gallup poll (February 1985) showed the smallest proportion of people desiring large families since Gallup began to record such preferences in 1936. The proportion of respondents who said that they wanted to have four or more children declined from 34 percent in 1936 to 11 percent in 1985. When asked to indicate the ideal number of children that a family should have, 56 percent wanted two; 21 percent said three; 8 percent wanted four; 3 percent wanted five or more; 4 percent said one; 2 percent wanted no children, and 6 percent had no opinion. Other recent research also bears on the question of whether parenthood remains a desirable adult role. A recent survey of 213 undergraduate women (Knaub, Eversoll, and Voss, 1983) disclosed that 95 percent of the respondents expected to become parents, but 77 percent also indicated that it was important to first enjoy one's social life and have children later in the marriage, and 73 percent disagreed with the notion that women are happier if they have children early in their marriage. But when all is said and done, by far the most common "script" for American families still involves marriage when quite young and the first baby within a year or two after that.

Why do couples have children? The most direct answer to that question, especially if one considers the many centuries before effective contraceptives were developed, is that couples engage in sexual intercourse, and babies appear on the scene soon thereafter. No doubt Mother Nature has made sex enjoyable, nearly irresistible, so that members of our species will reproduce themselves; having children is certainly "natural" in that sense. But what are the other reasons, beyond the instinctive imperative to perpetuate human life?

Are there other reasons? One could argue that the fact that sex is pleasurable is evidence enough that people would be unlikely to have children otherwise; potential parents must be induced by strong biological rewards to fulfill their potential. Similarly, the search for ways of preventing conception has been one of humanity's longest struggles, recorded among the most primitive tribes throughout history. An example is a recently discovered medical prescription written by an Egyptian physician around 1850 B.C. for a vaginal paste made from crocodile dung: neither the popularity nor the effectiveness of this concoction is recorded (Himes, 1963). Once the act was done, the contraceptive failed, and the child born, a final desperate means of birth control — infanticide — was common throughout history and in almost every known culture (deMause, 1974). This is certainly not the history of a species with a pronounced "natural" desire to have children!

Nevertheless, for most adult humans, parenthood is still the ultimate source of meaning. Gutmann (1975), for example, discussing what he terms the "parental imperative," suggests that parenthood as a vital species activity exercises a controlling role over the entire life span. Just as our relationship with our parents was instrumental in shaping our childhood, so our adulthood gets shaped by the relationship with our children.

Many people express social reasons for having children. In the interdependent system we call a family, children often contribute their part to the family's welfare, doing chores even when quite young. In less technologically advanced societies, children provide a sort of insurance policy for one's old age. The rules of exchange here are something like "I'll care for you when you're young if you care for me when I'm old." Even in advanced societies, social security systems represent an intergenerational transfer of resources, with the aggregate of the younger generation contributing the resources that pay the pensions of the current elders (Schultz, 1985).

The older children also help protect the family. Even in the United States, it is the "older sons" we send out to do battle against enemies. Some cultures have strict norms about "revenge," such that one attacks a parent with the knowledge that the sons, and possibly the daughters too, will come looking for retribution sooner or later.

In broader social groups, children are often seen as the key to a better life in the future. Although the population-gorged nations of the world present apparent evidence to the contrary, many people believe that there is power in numbers and worry when their particular social group reaches zero population growth or when some other group seems to be reproducing more rapidly than their own. Proposals for involuntary birth control in certain instances (e.g., sterilization of unmarried welfare mothers who have had three children) are seen by the social groups with higher birth rates as an attempt to limit their future power, with perhaps some justification. In a country where each adult has one vote, there is power in numbers, especially if the leaders of the group can get the members to vote as a bloc.

Children also can be educated and thus lead us to a better society. Many people believe that the answers to various social problems (for example, racism, sexism, and ageism) lie in the "proper" education of children; humane attitudes can replace bigoted ones with the right kind of instruction. This view probably overestimates the importance of schools in forming social attitudes and ignores the fact that the white male "establishment" figures who are often accused of supporting the institutions of racism and sexism are also in essential control of the schools. But the belief that children can be taught to avoid the mistakes of their parents or their parents' generation is hardy and has some elements of truth.

PERSONAL SATISFACTIONS

In Erik Erikson's scheme of life, the intimacy crisis of young adulthood is followed by the *generativity crisis* (Erikson, 1963). The generativity crisis begins soon after love and marriage (that is, in young adulthood) and continues throughout the middle years of life. Although generativity has also to do with work, production, and creativity, it finds its most direct expression in having children and then guiding them to maturity. In Erikson's words, "the fashionable insistence on dramatizing the dependence of children on adults often blinds us to the dependence of the older generation on the younger one. [The mature adult] needs to be needed, and maturity needs guidance as well as encouragement from what has been produced and must be taken care of" (Erikson, 1963, pp. 266–267).

The perceived value of children was studied in a series of 2,025 interviews of a national sample of married women under 40 and their husbands (Hoffman and Manis, 1979). They were asked to discuss the advantages of having children as compared to having no children at all. The most frequent responses indicated that children provide "something useful to do," that they "bring love and companionship," and that they make you feel like a "better person."

Although many would argue that the "need to be needed" is more culturally than biologically determined (Skolnick, 1978), caring for a dependent individual can be a very rewarding experience. The need for nurturance, as psychologist Henry Murray (Murray et al., 1938) called it, is related to another need that finds deep satisfaction in the parent–child relationship: the need for power. Many parents enjoy exercising authority over their children and making decisions for them, operating as a kind of benevolent dictator.

Many other personal satisfactions of parenthood could be listed. Humans also have a need to love and a need to be loved in return. Children can satisfy these needs and, in addition, provide opportunities for touching, cuddling, and kissing in a world that provides few other outlets for the need for physical contact. Children are also young and active; they are often interesting; they often provide excitement and drama. Finally, children also fulfill certain symbolic needs. Many people see their children as a continuance of themselves, a human form of eternal life.

Most young parents truly enjoy their children, and it is in having and raising children that generativity finds its most direct expression.

THE PAINS OF PARENTHOOD

With all the social and personal reasons for having children, it is perhaps surprising that social pressures in support of parenthood are necessary. Although childless marriages are becoming more acceptable, they are still not considered quite normal. Many people view childless women as selfish, irresponsible, immoral, unfeminine, and unhappy (Skolnick, 1978). Childless couples are subjected to direct pressure from parents and friends and also to subtle hints such as *"When* are you planning to have your first child?"

The social stigma attached to childlessness is an indication that the pleasures of parenthood are balanced by considerable costs, tempting many people to forego the experience. Parents, as they are apt to keep reminding their ungrateful offspring, "sacrifice" great quantities of time, energy, and money to raise their children. Although such sacrifices are to some extent expected, few young couples can anticipate the profound disruption children will make in their lives.

Some couples found that troubles began during pregnancy (Masters and Johnson, 1966; Meyerowitz and Feldman, 1967). Major problems included restrictions on sexual activity and feelings about loss of attractiveness among pregnant women. Newly married couples regard sex as an important aspect of marriage — many men consider it the most important. After the birth of the first child, sex dropped to the least important aspect for women and to second place for their husbands (Reedy, Birren, and Schaie, 1981). Golden-wedding couples' retrospective reports confirmed this trend (Parron and Troll, 1978). However, many husbands showed increasing solicitude toward their pregnant wives and took over more household tasks than at any other time of marriage. In fact, they would have been willing to do more than their wives let them do (Feldman, 1971).

Why does the first birth so often precipitate a crisis? Several explanations have been offered. One view concerns the shift from a dyad of two people to a triad of three. Psychologists studying small groups have shown that triads tend to be unstable, with the weakest member joining one of the two stronger members. In the traditional new family, the baby and mother often become closely knit, leaving the father out (Freilich, 1964). Recent changes in family patterns leading to greater father participation in child rearing, however, largely ameliorate this development (Hoffman, 1983).

Russell (1974) found that new mothers had a number of complaints, however. They worried about their appearance and their poor physical condition. They were often exhausted and felt unable to keep up with the housework. They resented being tied down and were concerned about being competent mothers. Their husbands also lost sleep and had to adjust to new routines and responsibilities. Money was also a problem, and fathers were frequently forced to seek ways of increasing their income. According to LeMasters (1957), many new mothers gave up satisfying jobs, which compounded the financial problem, although this trend is changing with more women remaining in the job market (see Chapter 3). Mothers also felt that they had become less sexually attractive, whereas fathers felt that mothers had suddenly become less sexually responsive. Decreases in sexual opportunities may well be at the heart of both complaints.

Despite these problems and others, Aldous (1978) concludes that most couples "negotiate the transition period with no great sense of crisis" (p. 162). Furthermore, this study and others (e.g., Hobbs and Wimbish, 1977) suggest that earlier investigations may have exaggerated the sense of crisis experienced by parents. But the description of parenthood as a stressful transition still seems warranted. For middle-class women, who before the birth of their first child tend to have an unrealistic and overly romantic notion of motherhood, the transition is particularly difficult. In the average home the birth of the first child doubles the amount of time the wife spends at housework (Peskin, 1982) (see Figure 2–2); it also cuts in half the amount of time she spends in conversation with her husband (Udry, 1974). Contrary to the myth that children improve a marriage, research evidence suggests that children put a significant strain on the relationship between husband and wife. Childless wives are generally happier and more satisfied with their marriages than mothers; mothers are more likely to see their marriages as restrictive and to report marital problems (Veroff and Feld, 1970; Bernard, 1973). Childless husbands also have happier marriages than do fathers.

Several factors have been shown to make the transition to parenthood easier for those who do decide to have children, including a strong marital bond that can weather the intrusion of a third person, adequate finances, and enough preparatory time — at least three years between wedding and baby. Couples that found time to be alone together in the evening and in which the husband got up at night with the baby reported fewer problems (Daniels and Weingarten, 1982).

THE ROLE OF THE FATHER

Studies of traditional families consistently find that from birth on mothers feed and caretake more than fathers even when adjustment is made for the time available for caregiving activities by the mother and father (Parke and Tinsley, 1981). This fact is not due to lesser childrearing competence on the part of the father; fathers have been shown to have the capability to carry out caregiving activities competently even though they generally contribute less time to this type of activity than do mothers (Parke and Sawin, 1976). In addition the father's indirect participation in caregiving may positively influence the mother's behavior (Lewis and Fiering, 1981). Both mothers and fathers engage in play activities with their infants and children, but fathers spend more of their time with their children in play than do mothers. In a study of middle-class families, for example, it was found that fathers spent 40 percent of the time involved with their infants on play, while mothers did so only for 25 percent of the time (Kotelchuck, 1976). Fathers and mothers also differ in the style of play to provide different types of stimulation and learning opportunities. Fathers' play tends to be more physical and arousing, while mothers' play is more verbal, instructional, and employing the use of toys (Power and Parke, 1982).

Timing of parenthood makes an important impact on fathers' participation in childrearing activities. For example, adolescent fathers are out of step with a normative life course; for them child-care activities interfere with the possibility

FIGURE 2–2.
Hours of housework as a function of age of youngest child.

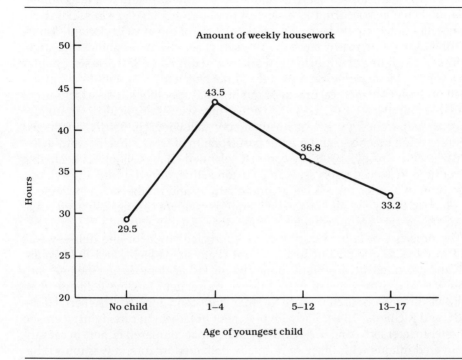

Source: From Peskin, J. (1982). Measuring household production for the GNP. *Family Economics Review, 3,* 16–25.

of making life-stage-appropriate educational and vocational progress (McKluskey, Killarney, and Papini, 1983). There are further differences in father involvement between those who have children early and late in the marriage. Men who have children early have more energy for activities central to the father role such as physical play (Parke and Tinsley, 1981). But these advantages of early fathering are offset by financial and time strains and the competing demands (equally felt by most women) in simultaneously establishing a career and a family. When parenthood is postponed, a career may already have been established, or career development may no longer have as central a role (Feldman, Nash, and Aschenbrenner, 1983). Late-timed fathering permits greater flexibility in balancing these demands. Patterns of collaboration between the spouses may also have been developed prior to the advent of children when these come later in the marriage. In any event, late-timed fathers, in one study, were found to spend three times as much time on the care of preschool children as did early-timed fathers (Daniels and Weingarten, 1982).

One of the most significant changes in the structure of modern American families has been the increased involvement of the father in childrearing activities. Since families are social systems, changes in the quantity and quality of father–child interactions also affect the mother–child relationship (Hoffman, 1983). Changes in fathers' participation were both unplanned and planned. Unplanned changes occurred as a consequence of other changes in social structure that had unanticipated effects on fathers. One of the most important of such structural changes occurring since the 1950s has been the increasing participation of women with young children in the work force (Hoffman, 1984; also see Chapter 3). In addition, greater involvement of the father began to occur right from birth as a result of changes in medical practices and hospital operations. These include the rise in the number of caesarian deliveries, increase in survival of premature babies, the shortened period of hospital stay following childbirth, liberalized hospital visiting practices, and greater participation of fathers in labor and delivery (Parke and Tinsley, 1984). By contrast, planned change involved deliberate interventions in social processes and customs that directly alter the relative distribution of gender-related behaviors in fathers and mothers. An example of such planned change would be the deliberate decision of couples to assign equal or major child-care responsibilities to the father (Russell, 1982).

The presence of fathers during the second stage of labor and delivery was found to increase attachment to the infant (Peterson, Meehl, and Leiderman, 1979), and extended father–infant contact by the father alone during the newborn period was found to result in more intense subsequent feeding behavior than traditional hospital visitation with mother and child together (Keller, Hildebrandt, and Richards, 1981). Early involvement of fathers in caregiving seems to carry over to later fathering behavior. In a study that compared fathers of caesarian-delivered infants with those of normally delivered infants, it was found that the fathers of the caesarian-delivered infants were more likely to share caregiving responsibilities both shortly after delivery (Grossman, Eichler, and Winickoff, 1980) and at six months after birth (Vietze et al., 1980). Similarly, fathers of premature babies have been found to be more active in the feeding and care of infants than fathers of term babies, both in the hospital and later at home (Yogman, 1983).

While the changes in medical practice have been important in changing the fathers' involvement at the beginning of childrens' lives, later involvement has largely been impacted by the increase in the participation of women with young children in the labor force. The husbands' participation in family work was found to increase from an average of 16 percent to 25 percent when their wives were employed (Walker and Woods, 1976). Although this may simply mean that employed mothers are spending less time on housework, there is evidence that fathers' increased participation indeed reflects increased involvement in child-care activities (Hoffman, 1984) and that there has been a value shift in our culture toward greater family involvement by husbands (Pleck, 1983).

A number of pioneering attempts have been made to enhance the role of the father in sharing child-care experiences and responsibilities. These have involved family arrangements that emphasize role sharing between parents (Russell,

1982), or institutional settings such as the Israeli kibbutz which encourage increased father participation (Sagi, 1982). Both these settings seem to facilitate the development of higher verbal ability and career expectations on the parts of children who have had more intensive involvement with their fathers.

In spite of the marked changes described above there is still considerable resistance to the changed sex roles involved for the father. A unique family policy adopted in Sweden some ten years ago, for example, permits paid sick leave for nine months for any parent staying home to take care of a new infant. Yet fewer than 15 percent of new fathers took advantage of this policy during its first five years of existence. Nevertheless, this natural experiment provided opportunities to compare fathers and mothers as primary caregivers (Lamb et al., 1982). The findings of intense home observations are surprising. Regardless of the father's involvement in caregiving, mothers did exhibit greater evidence of smiling, touching, and vocalizing toward their infants, a pattern equally characteristic of traditional families. The researchers conclude that:

> Differences between maternal and paternal behavior are remarkably robust, remaining stable despite variations in the relative involvement of mothers and fathers in childcare. This suggests either that behavioral differences (in childcare) are biologically-based or that they are deeply internalized during years of socialization. We will not be able to evaluate these alternative explanations until we are able to study parents who are themselves reared in a nonsextyped fashion and allocate family responsibilities in a nontraditional fashion. (Frodi et al., 1982, p. 6)

If as a society we wish to encourage fathers to take a greater role in the rearing of their children it will be necessary to provide additional cultural support systems for fathers and their families. Such support systems could include increases in the provision of prenatal and postnatal training classes for fathers to help them acquire caretaking skills and learn about normal development. Fathers should be encouraged to become involved in labor and delivery, and father–infant interaction during the newborn period should be facilitated (Klaus and Kennell, 1982). Paternity leaves are also needed to provide opportunities for fathers to share in the early care of infants. The research we have reviewed in this section, in sum, would suggest that such efforts would benefit not only the children, but also serve to enhance the cohesion and viability of the nuclear family unit under the changed conditions of our contemporary society.

What Ever Happened to the Extended Family?

Many of the problems young couples face with the birth of their first child would be less pressing if there were a grandparent or two around, and maybe an aunt or uncle — if, in other words, the couple lived in an *extended family* instead of a *nuclear family*. The nuclear family consists of a husband, a wife, and their offspring. The extended family consists of the nuclear family *plus* relatives (kin). Everyone has both a nuclear and an extended family; the issue has to do with the role of kin in the lives of individuals. Is kinship less important than it used to be? Is the nuclear family isolated? Were the "good old days" better, when the interdependencies of family life were spread more broadly among the extended family, many of whom lived in the house of the nuclear family?

As research evidence accumulates, it is clear that two pervasive myths, both incorrect in fact, make discussion of the role of kin in family life difficult. The first myth is that extended families "under one roof" were common in early America. The second related myth is that the nuclear family of today is isolated and that kin support and influence have all but disappeared. The first myth, that extended families living together were common in older days (in colonial America, for example) has been rather thoroughly discredited by research using diaries, sermons, novels, and other literary sources of olden days (for example, Seward, 1973; Smith, 1981). The early settlers of the United States brought with them the practice of a two-generation household (that is, the typical nuclear family) — a practice that was normally continued in the new country. Married adults living with married brothers or sisters were rare, and three-generation families were uncommon, if for no other reason than that the average life expectancy was around forty years. Old, dependent parents sometimes moved in with their adult children, but this is as true today as it was then.

The notion of the nuclear family of today as an isolated unit, more or less devoid of support from the extended family, was enunciated by several sociologists in the late 1940s (Linton, 1949; Parsons, 1949). In a general theory on the effects of industrialization, it was proposed that the isolation of the nuclear family came about because of industrial society's need for a mobile labor force — that is, for workers who were willing to leave the family farm. In the industrial society, new institutions take over the support functions of kin: banks lend money in times of need; clinical psychologists, psychiatrists, and clergy offer emotional aid; and day-care centers replace grandmothers.

Although kinship apparently plays a lesser role in industrial society than it did in predominantly agricultural economies, the degree of isolation of the modern family was probably exaggerated by early theorists. The collective participation of family members in education, recreation, economic welfare, religion, and protective activities has diminished, but its importance as a source of mutual affection has probably increased (Cottrell, 1960). Bureaucratic organizations may have assumed greater responsibility in providing services to the elderly, but younger family members have taken on an important role in acting as a mediating link between the elderly person and the bureaucracy (Kreps, 1977; Sussman, 1977; Shanas and Sussman, 1981). It seems that the functions of the family have been redefined, but they do not appear to be diminishing. The typical pattern today is what some researchers have called the *modified extended family* (Litwak, 1960a, 1960b; Sussman and Burchinal, 1962). See further discussion of intergenerational support in Chapter 8.

One index of family functioning is the frequency of contact among family members. Research shows that most Americans remain in fairly close touch with their aging parents, their adult children, their brothers and sisters, and numerous other kin (Shanas et al., 1968; Shanas, 1980; Hagestad, 1984a). In her 1975 survey of noninstitutionalized elderly people, Shanas (1979, 1980) found that 18 percent of the respondents with children actually lived in the same house with one of their children. It does not appear that most older persons would like to live with kin — research shows that they prefer intimacy at a distance (Treas and Bengtson, 1982; Brody et al., 1983). This preference is realized for a fairly larger number — 34 percent of those contacted in the Shanas study lived within ten minutes commuting distance from a child. Surprisingly, respondents who lived alone maintained the same levels of contact with their offspring as those who lived in shared households. Half of the elderly who had children saw at least one of their children during the preceding week. Even when relatives live far apart, modern technology makes it much easier for them to remain in contact than it was formerly.

The exact extent and nature of contact between kin vary considerably by class, race, and other characteristics. Among older people, those who come from working-class backgrounds have more contact with children (and less with other relatives) than their middle-class counterparts do (Riley and Foner, 1968; Shanas et al., 1968). There are several possible explanations for this tendency. First, working-class families simply tend to be larger, so there are more children available to make contact. Second, middle-class children generally live at greater distances from their parents, often because their occupations require that they move to new locations. As you might expect, the relative infrequency of visits is balanced to some extent by the fact that the visits they do make tend to be longer (Harris et al., 1975). These findings are concerned primarily with face-to-face contacts, however; other important forms of communication such as telephoning or writing may also play a significant role (Wilkening, Guerrero, and Ginsberg, 1972; Moss, Moss, and Moles, 1985). There is considerable economic interdependence among kin of all races, with parents providing at least emergency financial support for their adult children — and vice versa (Troll, 1971). In addition to money and valuable property, the extended family often provides valuable services, such as help with moving and, of course, babysitting. Other benefits that family members derive from each other are less tangible. Some of these benefits have occurred throughout history. For example, associating with the elderly exposes the younger generation to behavioral models of aging that provide them with anticipatory socialization for their own old age (Troll, Miller, and Atchley, 1979). But other benefits are reflections of new patterns of intergenerational interaction.

One such development is that, despite disparities in chronological age, family members are entering into "social age" peerships in ways that have no historical precedent. With large numbers of older people returning to school, for instance, it's not unusual for members of two or even three generations of a family to be students at the same time. This is an example of a "renewal activity" initiated by older relatives, but social peerships may also result when younger relatives experience "accelerated activities" such as early widowhood or early retirement (Guemple, 1969; Hagestad, 1981). While relatives belonging to different generations may provide valuable support to each other, the situation is so novel that unambiguous norms and guidelines concerning behavior have yet to develop. In some cases, this can lead to disorganized and confusing intergenerational involvements (Hess and Waring, 1978).

Another development is that the average ages at marriage and at the birth of children declined throughout the last half of this century, although they are once again rising (U.S. Bureau of the Census, 1983b). In the early 1900s, adjacent generations were separated by an average of thirty years, but today the mean length of a generation is only about twenty years (Troll et al., 1979). Coupled with the increase in longevity, this "generational acceleration" (Hagestad, 1981) means that four generations may be formed in the time it used to take to form three generations (Bengtson and DeTorre, 1980).

A consequence of these trends in longevity and the decreasing distance between generations is that relatives are spending more years together, especially female relatives. Formerly, women usually experienced the deaths of their mothers in middle life, whereas today it is more often an event of the immediate preretirement years (Winsborough, 1980). Sex differences in longevity, however, mean that one women in five who gives birth to a son in her early twenties will outlive him (Metropolitan Life, 1977). Even so, their shared lifetime will have been considerably longer than it would have been a few generations ago, and the evidence shows that the degree of emotional interdependence is as great as it ever was.

The Empty Nest

One of the major events in a family is the launching of the youngest child into a family and career of his or her own. The mother is typically between the ages of forty-five and fifty: the father may be a few years older. Together they face a new adjustment — life in the empty nest; they are, in the words of social scientists, a *postparental family.* *under 50 in 1900.*

Like the large numbers of old people in general, the postparental family is largely a phenomenon of the twentieth century. Until 1900 or so, the average parent died about the time the nest was emptying, the cycle of life fulfilled. The number of children in an average family has also decreased considerably, so that the youngest is typically launched when the parents are still relatively young. Thus, when the number of postparental families increased dramatically, scientists began to wonder about the psychological effect of the empty nest. They worried mostly about the mother, especially the homemaker who had defined her own identity in terms of her children. As one postparental mother put it, "My daughters were both nineteen when they married. I didn't want them not to marry, but I missed them so much. I felt alone. I couldn't play golf. I couldn't even play bridge. I don't have a profession, and I couldn't take just any job" (Deutscher, 1968, p. 267).

Although the empty-nest experience is often talked about as if it primarily impacts on women, men may equally be confronted, albeit in somewhat different ways. Because of the man's traditional role as the family's primary economic provider he may have spent little time with his children as they grew up and is now faced with bemoaning many lost opportunities for closer relationships with them (Rubin, 1980).

For most people, however, the emptying of the nest is not a particularly troubling experience. Indeed, many people find that their lives change for the better. Adolescent children are in some respects a burden: they are expensive; they challenge authority; they have learned how to create conflict between parents, if it suits their purposes. When they finally leave, the parents have more time for themselves. "For the first time that I can remember, my evenings are free," said one happy postparental mother (Deutscher, 1968, p. 265). There is finally time for new projects, travel, or simply personal pleasures and finally the money to finance them. In the typical family, the burden of children falls more heavily on the mother; although she is supposed to suffer more from the flight of her young birds, she is also the one who benefits more from their launching. Her housework, which doubled with the first child, is cut in half as the last child leaves.

The parents find themselves in the position of "husband and wife" again; they are no longer primarily "father and mother." Although this confrontation with their marriage can force them to admit they no longer have much in common — leading them to divorce in extreme cases — the normal pattern is a deep satisfaction of a loving relationship that is again allowed to flourish. Most parents also experience a deep contentment from the successful completion of what they see as one of "life's duties": to bear and raise children to the point where the children can manage on their own. Over half of the empty-nest spouses in one study saw their postparental life as preferable; most of the others said life was about the same; only 6 percent considered their lives worse than before the last child left (Deutscher, 1968). Longitudinal research following women through the various stages of family life yields similar results: parenthood becomes more oppressive during the children's adolescence and happier when they leave home (Lowenthal and Chiriboga, 1972). Most women do not fear the empty nest; they look forward to it.

Research findings on marital satisfaction provide a similar picture. As Figure 2–3 shows, satisfaction with marriage by both husbands and wives drops until the postparental period; then a rise begins that carries them eventually to the level of satisfaction seen otherwise only during the period of newlyweds' bliss (Rollins and Feldman, 1970). Further analysis shows this increase in marital satisfaction to be rather directly related to the amount of time the couple spends doing things together (Miller, 1976; Orthner, 1975). Thus the *opportunity* to recreate the interpersonal relationship that led them to be married in the first place (the opportunity to spend time on themselves) can lead to a more satisfying union. For most people, the empty nest turns out to be a rather happy place.

Our discussion should not convey the message that there are no problems associated with this life transition. As Rubin (1980) points out, however, the

FIGURE 2–3.

Marital satisfaction across the life span.

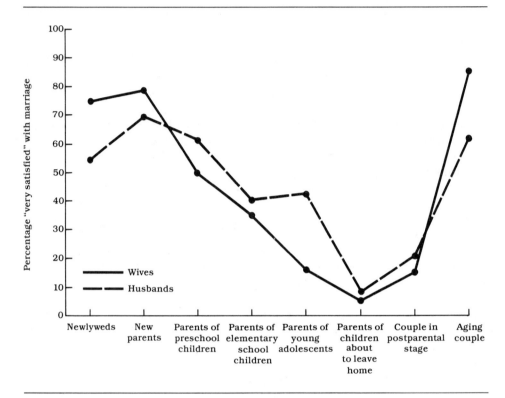

Source: From Rollins, B. C., and Feldman, H. Marital satisfaction over the family life cycle. *Journal of Marriage and the Family*, 1970, 32, 20–28. Copyrighted 1970 by the National Council on Family Relations. Reprinted by permission.

problems are concerned with the contemplation and confrontation of the next stage of life; they likely deal with anxieties of the future, rather than with nostalgia for the past.

Adult Children and Their Parents

One thing to keep in mind while discussing families is that parents are also "children"; they too have parents, and in this age of increased life expectancies, there is a good chance that their aging parents will be alive. Indeed, in some instances one or both of the aging parents may move in with adult children about the time their own offspring have grown up and moved out; the empty nest is filled once more (Brody, 1985).

Aging parents move in with their adult children for different reasons, often for a combination of reasons: chronic illness of one or both of the aging parents (a handicapping illness not severe enough to require hospitalization); the death of one, leaving the other emotionally bereft and incapable of providing for him- or herself; and retirement, after which some elderly parents move closer to their adult children and sometimes move in with them, especially if their resources are limited. About 18 percent of all people over sixty-five who have living children do live with them (Shanas, 1980; see also Atchley and Miller, 1980). But economic, emotional, or health considerations may leave no practical alternative. As Brody (1978) has observed, it is ironic that this new role of parental caretaker has emerged for individuals in the postparental stage. Having experienced the empty nest, often with pleasure, they find that once again they are responsible for relatives. This stage is followed by yet another — the "re-emptied nest" stage that follows the death of aged kin.

The burden of caring for aged relatives has traditionally fallen to women, but providing care is often a problem when women work outside the home. In 1981, almost 60 percent of the women between forty-five and fifty-four and 40 percent of those aged fifty-five to sixty-four held jobs (U.S. Department of Labor, 1982), and it is the women in this age group who are likely to have to care for elderly parents. Their involvement in the labor force inevitably restricts their capacity to provide satisfactory care. Also see Chapter 8.

Whether or not the aging parents are living with their adult children, certain conflicts are bound to arise between the two generations. Psychologists in the past have focused on the "generation gap" of parents and young children; of course a similar gap exists between elderly parents and their adult children. Like all parent–child pairings, the two members have had different life experiences and thus different views in life — different habits, different values. There may be social-class differences if the children have moved up on the social scale. But the major differences in a rapidly changing, technologically advanced society such as ours are generational.

Generational differences ("cohort" differences) exist simply because growing up in one era is different from growing up in another. People who were young adults in 1920 or 1930 are likely to have quite different views on such issues as sexual morality, work, and patriotism than their children, who were young adults in 1940 or 1950. The elder group tried to choose a career in the midst of the great economic upheaval we call The Depression (Elder, 1974; Elder, Liker, and Jaworski, 1984). There were no television sets, contraceptive devices were crude and ineffective, and the threat of venereal disease without penicillin effectively inhibited promiscuity. The World War (later to be numbered WW I) was just over, a grand adventure, with the United States standing as the saviour of Europe. The younger group knew and used automobiles and airplanes as part of daily life. Machines were often a threat to their jobs, as human labor was replaced by automation. Unions grew strong, accepted as part of the American scene by the younger generation, although quite foreign to the individualistic mind of the elder (Klineberg, 1984).

DO ROLES REVERSE?

As parents age, the balance of family interdependencies may shift to give the adult children more and more responsibility for their elderly parents. In a sense, roles reverse, with the offspring assuming the nurturant, parental functions and the aging parents on the receiving end for a change. The adult children may provide financial support, the most typical case, or nursing care. They may also advise their parents on how best to utilize existing governmental programs (to which they are major contributors through taxes). Nevertheless, both economic and affectual exchanges are likely to involve a great deal of reciprocity (Litwak, 1981).

Some "role reversal" is bound to occur. Indeed, if the adult children were not to make available to their own parents some of their knowledge, their competencies, and their financial achievements, they would be looked on with disfavor by the community. Nevertheless, the notion of role reversal in old age is considerably exaggerated. Especially since the advent of government programs such as Medicare and food stamps and the increasing prevalence of private pension plans, the ability of most elderly parents to care for themselves is adequate. Many people see their income as sufficient (Schultz, 1985). They fear debilitating illnesses more, and in fact it is more often the severely handicapping diseases that make them dependent on their adult children (see also Chapter 13).

This dependence may cause conflict and strain between generations. The decreasing age distance between generations and increasing life expectancy mean that many parents and children are growing old together. Children have traditionally been the chief source of support for the aged, but children who are themselves approaching retirement and suffering financial and perhaps physical constraints may be angered when they must care for elderly kin (Blenkner, 1969; Treas, 1977; Brody, 1978; Shanas, 1980). Furthermore, the middle-aged person may face conflicts between responsibilities to aged kin and obligations to children and husband or wife. Brody (1981) has spoken of this as a "middle generation squeeze" resulting from having to meet the needs of both a younger and an older generation (see also Hill et al., 1970; Silverstone and Hyman, 1976; and Schwartz, 1979). Many families today have only one middle generation, but the number with two is growing steadily due to increasing life expectancies and decreasing intervals between generations (Neugarten and Moore, 1968; Neugarten, 1979). Although the two middle generations in some families may share in providing care to the senior generation, many middle-aged kin may eventually have to cope with dependency relations involving two generations of aged parents, aging in-laws, and even aging relations from former marriages or the later remarriage of an aging parent (Schwartz, 1979).

REMARRIAGE IN OLD AGE

Old persons who have lost a spouse through divorce or death are particularly likely to be dependent on their adult children for emotional support, and the children often worry about their aging parents living alone. For these reasons and several others, many older people remarry, preferring the conjugal state to living alone, with children, or in an institution. These marriages are not typically looked on with favor by the couple's children, in spite of the potential benefits; often there is direct and open opposition. Aging parents are accused of acting childishly or impulsively. They are not showing the proper respect for their dear, departed spouse. And, they are thought to be too old for such romantic nonsense (certainly too old for S-E-X!).

Remarriage late in life may disrupt the interdependencies of the family, threatening both the financial and emotional relationships between parents and adult children. In particular, the children may fear that their inheritance will be lost or complicated, although they will rarely state this fear explicitly. Emotionally, their aging parent will now be related by marriage to at least one additional person and usually to another complete family, with the spouse's children and grandchildren now entitled to make demands on their parent's time and energy. Married older persons also tend to live further away from their children (Treas and Bengtson, 1982). With all these reasons, it is no wonder that many of the prospective brides and grooms in late-life marriages feel pressure to call it off. In one study, over 25 percent of those who did get married confessed they almost didn't (McKain, 1972), which suggests that there is an even more sizable number who succumb to pressure and never make it to the altar at all.

In spite of the lack of support these elderly couples receive, their marriages tend to be notably successful. Of the 100 late-life marriages in one survey, only 6 were considered unsuccessful (McKain, 1972). Most of the couples had known each other for several years. Often they were previously related by marriage (for example, a woman would marry the widowed husband of her late sister) and there were a few storybook romances, where childhood sweethearts had drifted apart, only to find each other again in the twilight of their lives. The old brides and grooms also had a reasoned view of what to expect from marriage. They didn't expect radical changes in their lives or their personalities — who has such dreams at seventy? Instead they expected (and got) the satisfactions of companionship — someone to discuss things with, someone to do things with — and they felt they were useful to their new spouses. "The need to be needed does not fade in the later years" (McKain, 1972, p. 65).

Grandparenting

As parents age, their children age too, and eventually become parents in their own right. The elders become grandparents. We have created an image of grandparents as "benign, gray-haired angels with enormous compassion and capacity for use and abuse" (Bischof, 1976, p. 292). In fact, however, most people become grandparents in their late forties or early fifties, and at least in the early years of grandparenthood, they are thoroughly involved with their own careers, with little time for their grandchildren. By the time they retire, the eldest grandchild is in his or her late teens, thoroughly involved in teenaged activities, with little time for grandparents.

Although many new grandparents may consider themselves much too young for the role, most welcome it and derive great satisfaction from interactions with their grandchildren (Robertson, 1977). Dissatisfactions, when they occur, are primarily conflicts between the grandparents and parents over childrearing methods. Especially when the grandmother plays a primary role in raising the child, as often happens in families in which the mother continues to work after childbirth, the children may experience contradictory demands from the two older generations. Also, the father may withdraw from this battleground between mother and grandmother, increasing the adverse effect on children (Hurlock, 1975).

More often, however, the middle generation acts as a mediator in exchanges between grandparents and grandchildren (Wood and Robertson, 1978; Robertson, 1975, 1977). One study of young adults aged eighteen to twenty-six found that nearly two-thirds said that their parents influenced the involvement they maintained with grandparents (Robertson, 1976). Hill et al. goes so far as to characterize the middle generation as "the lineage bridge across the generations" (1970, p. 62). On the other hand, some youngsters report that they feel closer to their grandparents than to their parents (Troll, 1980).

Several styles of grandparenting have been identified (Neugarten and Weinstein, 1964). The most common style, characteristic of about one-third of grandparents, was called *formal*. These grandparents saw their role in rather traditional terms: they occasionally indulged the child, occasionally helped the parents with chores such as babysitting, and expressed a constant interest in their grandchild; but they took a "hands-off" position in regard to child training, leaving that responsibility to the parents. A second common type of grandparent was the *fun-seeker*, whose relationship to grandchildren was characterized by informal playfulness. The *distant* grandparent was a shadowy figure who emerged on holidays, birthdays, and other special occasions with ritual gifts for the grandchild. Two other types of grandparents were less common. A few women were *surrogate parents*, usually because the mother worked. And a few grandparents, almost always men, played the role of *reservoir of family wisdom*; as you might expect, the families in which this role was possible were old-fashioned and patriarchal, with an authoritarian grandfather who sought to control both his adult children and his grandchildren.

Age was one chief determinant of grandparenting style. If the grandparents were over sixty-five, the formal style was most common. For younger grandparents (fifty to sixty-five), the fun-seeking style was more frequently reported. There are several possible interpretations of these data. One is that people become more formal in their style as they grow older; that is, they approximate more and more the traditional image of grandparents. Another interpretation is that older generations had a more traditional view, whereas more recent generations value less formal, fun-seeking interactions with grandchildren. Still another possibility has to do with the age of the grandchildren. Perhaps grandparents are more playful with young children but more formal with older grandchildren. The meager research evidence available tends to support this last interpretation (Kahana and Kahana, 1970; Kalish, 1975), but probably all three are at least partially correct.

In her study of role conceptions among 125 grandmothers, Robertson (1977) offers an alternative typology of grandparenting. Robertson distinguishes a social and a personal dimension of grandmothering. The social dimension emphasizes societal needs and the influence of the larger society. The personal dimension focuses on the attitudes and expectations concerned with personal factors and individual needs. On the basis of these distinctions, four types of grandmothers can be described. On one extreme is the *appointed* type who has high expectations in both the personal and the social aspects of the grandmother role. It is these grandmothers who are most involved with their grandchildren. They tend to be as concerned with indulging and enjoying their grandchildren as they are with doing what is morally right for them. On the other extreme is the *remote* type of grandmother, who is detached from her grandchildren and has low social and personal expectations of the grandparent role. *Symbolic* grandmothers emphasize the normative or moral aspects of the grandparent role, whereas the *individualized* grandmother emphasizes the personal aspects. Robertson found that 37 percent of her respondents preferred the grandparent role to parenthood. These women see grandmothering to be easier, affording pleasure and gratification without requiring them to assume major responsibility for the care and socialization of the child.

Robertson (1976) also examined grandchildren's perceptions of grandparents. She found that the vast majority of her working-class respondents (aged eighteen to twenty-six) expressed very favorable attitudes. Their primary expectation was that grandparents should provide emotional gratification and nurturance. Two-thirds of the young adults questioned felt that adult grandchildren had a responsibility to help their grandparents when necessary and without pay.

Other research has evaluated the meanings of grandparents to children. Kahana and Kahana (1970) noted that children's perceptions changed with age. Four- and five-year-olds liked their grandparents primarily because they were indulgent, whereas eight- and nine-year-olds placed more value on fun-seeking and active grandparents. Eleven- and twelve-year-olds were relatively detached from their grandparents. Kahana and Kahana concluded that children have less preference for doting grandparents as they grow older.

And what effect does involvement with grandchildren have on grandparents? Old people active in the grandparent role are likely to see part of themselves in their grandchildren; they have a sense of "biological renewal" and take vicarious pride in their grandchildren's accomplishments (Neugarten and Weinstein, 1964). As a result, they know more about, and are more interested in, things that concern young people; their perspective on life is far wider than that of the old person without frequent interactions with grandchildren. Active grandparents are likely to take more interest in community and national affairs, even in issues that do not concern them directly. For example, they are more likely to vote for school bonds, for the sake of their grandchildren's education.

Interactions between grandchildren and grandparents are in many cases surprisingly frequent. Nearly half of all grandparents are in almost daily face-to-face contact with their grandchildren, and three-quarters see their grandchildren at least twice a month (Harris et al., 1975). In a sample of elderly widows, Lopata (1973) found that feelings of intimacy toward grandchildren were determined largely by frequency of contact, but more recent research suggests that feelings of closeness prevail even where interaction with grandchildren is low (Wood and Robertson, 1978).

Despite the prevalence of positive attitudes toward grandchildren, more than 20 percent of the elderly who live in the community and 60 percent of those who are institutionalized say that the grandparent role is of little significance (Kahana and Coe, 1969). Community residents view grandparenthood as a means for remaining socially engaged, as we have seen. Institutionalized respondents are largely disengaged from society and hence have little need or opportunity to play social roles. Based on data from studies of modernization in developing countries it has been also argued that the importance of the grandparent role may be waning (Nahemow, 1984). It is argued that the grandparent role may be more important when it comes at the end of life; when the new grandparent is still vigorous and active, other societally valued roles may take precedence.

Transmitting Values and Traditions

The relationship of grandparents to grandchildren (that is, of the first to the third generation) is an interesting one in terms of the transmission of societal values and traditions. Parents have the major responsibility for socializing their children, and thus inevitable conflicts arise between parent and child over the degree of conformity to the parents' standards the child is willing to accept. Grandparents can force themselves into this fracas by constantly criticizing the childrearing techniques of the parents or the behavior of the grandchildren, but they can also stand aloof from the battle. As more or less "objective bystanders," they are often in a position to influence their grandchildren in ways the parents might find difficult. Feeling no need to rebel against the grandparents, the child often finds it easier to communicate with them, to discuss with them the meaning and importance of the manners and values the parents are trying so hard to instill.

GENERATION GAPS

Grandparents and grandchildren tend to form unspoken agreements about areas they can discuss without violent and unproductive arguments. Both avoid the sensitive areas — creating what are called "demilitarized zones" by one researcher (Hagestad, 1978) — thus increasing their influence in other nonsensitive

Grandparents and grandchildren typically provide love and support for one another.

areas. Sensitive areas include a number of issues in which the younger generation has a vested interest because they view changes as a "contribution" of their age group and, thus, in part, an aspect of their personal identities (Troll, 1980). The sexual revolution is a prime example: young people tend to believe that their sexual attitudes are far more sensible than those of previous generations. Their grandparents, who probably believed the same when they were young, are often willing to let their grandchildren's opinion stand, letting fly not much more than an occasional snipe.

By contrast, parents do not have the privilege of avoiding sensitive issues in the upbringing of their children. They are responsible for their children's welfare, and most parents therefore feel they *must* intrude if they perceive their children developing in disadvantageous directions. Thus parents are most subject to the conflicts spawned by the generation gap.

Research suggests that the generation gap is highly exaggerated (Alpert and Richardson, 1980). In most families, there is considerable overlap between the values of parents, children, and the children's friends — the "peers" who are supposedly influencing the children in ways different from the parents' ways. Typically these three groups have social, economic, religious, educational, and geographic commonalities — social-background factors that promote similar attitudes and values. For example, the peers of a white, Catholic, lower-middle-class, "ethnic," blue-collar adolescent who lives in one of our larger cities are likely to share more values with the adolescent's parents than with upper- or upper-middle-class WASP young people of the same age (Conger, 1977b). In many respects, therefore, peers may actually reinforce parental values.

Parents, in return, often support the values of their child's peer group. For example, many parents place great emphasis on popularity and social success and thereby strengthen the child's desire to conform to peer expectations (Mussen et al., 1979). Also, many parents are quite confused by our rapidly changing society and believe their advice and guidance are not very valuable or useful (Douvan, 1979). They foster conformity in their children by relying on peer-group democracy (one child, one vote) to make decisions: "Well," they ask, "are the other kids in your class allowed to do that?"

Relationships between successive generations may be burdened by family stresses over which neither generation has any control. In an interesting analysis of the impact of the Great Depression on intergenerational relationships, Elder, Liker, and Cross (1984) found that under economic pressures fathers tend to become more arbitrary and explosive figures who trigger similar behavior in their children. The long-term effect for the children was seen to be irritability leading to erratic work histories and career breaks. However, this pattern was unique to fathers who had been characterized as "hostile" prior to the onset of the economic pressures, but not by those fathers who were characterized as affectively close to their children. Another finding in the same study indicated also that the disruption and increasingly aimless character of men's lives in hard times that affected the next generation was often counterbalanced by the increasingly stronger role and authority of women. Evidence on the impact of sociocultural change on intergenerational relationships is provided also by studies of developing countries in the throes of industrialization. For example, a study of families in Taiwan conducted in 1973 and 1980 showed dramatic changes in the interactions of parents and adult children as a consequence of societal changes with respect to the acceptability of women working outside the home prior to marriage, a choice virtually unavailable to the earlier cohort, but taken by 83 percent of the later cohort (Thornton, Chang, and Sun, 1984).

Parental influence is likely to be stronger in moral and social values, whereas peer influence is stronger in peripheral matters such as taste in music and entertainment, fashions, and patterns of interactions with the same or opposite sex (Conger, 1977b). Studies of the parents of radical college students in the 1960s, for example, showed that parents and students were in essential agreement on the causes the students were championing. But the parents were upset by the students' long hair, irregular hours, and slovenly clothes (Troll, 1980).

SOCIALIZATION AND BILATERAL NEGOTIATIONS

Socialization in general is one of the major functions of a family. In its broadest definition, socialization is the attempt of a social system to ensure continuity through time.

> One of the classic dilemmas of human society has been the maintenance of a functioning social order despite successive invasions of neophytes: a younger generation lacking the skills and values to perform the intricate social roles of adulthood. The problem of generations, from this perspective, is to successfully transmit information that enables the young to function effectively in the increasingly complex social positions they encounter in adult life. (Bengtson and Black, 1973, p. 208)

It is family life which provides the major portion of the solution to this problem, generation by generation.

More specifically, "socialization refers to the process by which the individual acquires those behaviors, beliefs, standards, and motives that are valued by his or her family and the cultural group to which they belong" (Mussen et al., 1979, p. 328). In many instances, socialization techniques are intentional and direct, involving rewards for desired behavior and punishment for unacceptable actions. Usually, however, transmission of values and traditions proceeds by more subtle processes (Bengtson, 1975). In particular, observational learning occurs as the parents go about their day-to-day activities under the surveillance of their dependent children (Bandura, 1977a). The parents (and grandparents and other relatives to a lesser extent) serve as models for effective and appropriate behaviors. These behaviors may be as simple as choosing the right fork at a fancy dinner or as complex as acting out the social role of a male or a female in our society. Observational or imitative learning is sometimes called *identification*, especially when it refers to actions derived from a young child's need to be like his or her parents and to share in their competencies during the childhood period of extreme dependence.

In the young child, devoid of skills and lacking a well-developed sense of personal identity, the socializing function of the family may proceed without conscious intent to instruct or to learn. Later, especially in adolescence and beyond, socialization takes on a more deliberate flavor and becomes, as some theorists view it, a kind of *bilateral negotiation* (Bengtson and Black, 1973). The older generation champions the values it has tested and found useful, whereas the younger generation seeks an easier way, a new approach, a higher purpose. It is important to recognize that socialization is a two-way (bilateral) process, with the older generation changing along with the younger. Indeed, in a technological society such as the United States, the young often learn of innovations before their elders (Mead, 1970); they may have to explain to their parents or grandparents how a new mass transit system operates, what a new government program provides, or why they haven't lost the respect of their peers because of premarital sexual relations.

Family life socializes individuals in part because it is an example of the same kind of social contract that binds the broader society. Like the broader society, families consist of members who are dependent on one another for valuable commodities and services. At times family members with divergent interests must rely on traditions or "judges" to settle disputes; they must either accept the decision or challenge the unwritten contract under which their family exists. In their interactions with other family members, they experience greed and altruism; anger and affection; cooperation and competition; dominance and submission. It is in the family setting that children first encounter democracy and authoritarianism. This is where children learn to appreciate (or depreciate) art, develop attitudes toward religions and labor unions, learn how to "have friends over." In general, the family provides the processes and mechanisms that enable the child to relate to the broader society — even if that relationship is criminal, rather than supportive or accommodating.

Observational learning plays a major role in the transmission of skills and values from one generation to the next.

The bilateral negotiations that constitute socialization in the family do not cease, of course, when the children grow up and move out. Aging parents continue to play a major role in "training" their adult children to become parents in their own right. Similarly, adult children and aging parents must constantly renegotiate their reciprocal exchanges, as the parents grow old and normally lose some of their independence (Blenkner, 1969). The adult children may have to become more supportive and perhaps even assume caretaking functions, where-as some aging parents must accept the aid and comfort of their children. In many families, the difficulty middle-aged people have with their rebellious children "pulling up roots" is equaled only by the stubbornness of their aging parents trying to maintain their "independence" in the face of a few but obvious needs.

Nevertheless, it is clear that positive social ties are important to the well-being of older people. In one study, elderly medical patients were asked to rate the person they trusted and confided in most. The scale used included statements such as "I can count on this person to stand by me" and "We really enjoy spending time together." The researchers found that the strength of emotional bonds was an important predictor of the patients' perceptions of their own health and life satisfaction (Snow and Crapo, 1982). Another study asked members of three generations within families about the degree of trust, fairness, understanding, respect, and affection characterizing relations among family members. Although all three generations reported high levels of solidarity, older parents reported somewhat stronger emotional ties than did their middle-aged offspring (Bengtson, 1971). This may be true in part because members of different generations have different needs and interests. Younger family members may wish to establish and maintain their independence from their parents, whereas older people may have a stronger stake in family lineage and values (Bengtson and Kuypers, 1971). The elderly may also value the family more because of the positive attitudes toward the family that prevailed in earlier decades when they were growing up.

That family solidarity exists is well documented, but its causes and consequences are not well understood. In a paper that emphasized the dynamic nature of family emotional life, Bengtson (1981) called attention to familial aging processes that shape perceptions and generate understanding. He identified four problems that may serve as an impetus to family change. First, role transitions such as retirement or widowhood alter family members' expectations of one another. Second, aging may alter the balance of autonomy and independence of family members, as we have discussed with regard to parent–child role reversals in later years. Third, there is a problem of maintaining a just and equitable balance of giving and receiving between generations when aging alters the needs and resources of each. Fourth, there are issues related to the continuity of families and their traditions. Developments in each of these areas have the potential to strengthen or weaken family solidarity.

Family Forms

"The family is a dying institution," or so we're told in publications ranging from the grocery-store tabloid to the most prestigious of scientific journals. "The family is in crisis," or so we've heard from people ranging from the president of the PTA to the president of the United States. The ostensible reasons? The sexual revolution. The women's liberation movement. The skyrocketing divorce rate (the permissive divorce laws). The selfishness of young people today (the permissive child-training techniques taught by Dr. Spock). Abortions. Homosexuals. Communists. The list seems endless. Perhaps it is of some comfort to know that the same dire predictions about the demise of the family have been recorded in every century since we've begun our recordings.

The future of the family is a discussion beyond our mandate in a textbook on adult development and aging. What does concern us is the fact that family forms are changing and that many adults now live in households quite different from the nuclear family of American mythology. Here's one statistic: only 16 percent of America's families are nuclear in the traditional sense of having a breadwinning father, a homemaking mother, and resident children (Howard, 1978). Put another way, about 30 percent of all "households" in the United States (which include single and individual unrelated roommates as well as families) are occupied by a married couple with children (Masnick and Bane, 1980). Many of these wives (about 46 percent) work, making the family unconventional at least in that sense. A sizable proportion of these families are "reconstituted": at least one spouse has been married previously. There may be children from the previous marriage as well, which complicates the web of family interdependencies in ways social scientists are just now beginning to understand.

The postparental family (the mother and the father after the nest has emptied) is another traditional family form, one we have discussed in this chapter. Married couples with no resident children, which includes postparental families and childless couples, constitute 34 percent of present households; by 1990 they will drop to about 27 percent (Masnick and Bane, 1980). But married couples in general, with or without children, who presently account for 65 percent of households, will drop to less than 55 percent by 1990!

SINGLE-ADULT HOUSEHOLDS

The rapidly shrinking share of households accounted for by married couples is a result of the rapidly increasing share contributed by single adults. Single-adult households in the United States are quite a mixed group, including everything from young adults who have just begun to search for mates to widows. About 5 percent of adult males are classified as "never married" with 6 percent "previously married" but now living alone. Together, "single-male-headed households," presently 11 percent, will jump to 16 percent by 1990 (Masnick and Bane, 1980). More people are remaining single, more people are divorcing, and more people are remaining single after divorce.

About 5 percent of adult females were classified as "never married," and 19 percent were "previously married but now living alone." Widows, who will be discussed in more detail in Chapter 6, constitute 11 percent of the latter, and divorced or separated women account for the remaining 8 percent. Together, "single-female-headed households," presently 24 percent, will jump to 29 percent by 1990. Most of this increase will be due to increases in the never-married and divorced categories.

With so many single-adult households, questions are raised about social isolation. Fortunately, increases in life expectancy mean that most single adults will have living parents, at least into their fifties and in many cases longer. Older single adults (usually widows) generally have living children. Brothers, sisters, and other blood relatives also imbed the single individuals in a kinship system that supports them to some degree. Very few people are totally isolated. When kin fail, close friends and roommates sometimes function as "substitute family."

Families headed by unwed females increased by 470 percent between 1960 and 1975, and the number of such families is expected to double again by 1990 (Masnick and Bane, 1980). Most of these "unmarried females with children" are teenagers — or *were* teenagers, to be more exact, when the families were formed. About 11 million teenaged girls get pregnant every year; that's about one of every ten (Guttmacher Institute, 1976). About 60 percent of these pregnancies result in the birth of a baby, and the remaining 40 percent are terminated by abortion or miscarriage (one-third of all abortions in the United States are obtained by teenagers). Most of the babies born are kept, rather than given up for adoption. These new families begin in crisis, headed by teenaged unwed mothers who lack the skills and the experience either to hold a good job or to provide a "normal" environment for the infant.

These young women, together with divorced mothers of dependent children, form a group sociologists call "female-headed families." About one in four of all families headed by someone under the age of twenty-five is a single-parent family, and over 95 percent of these are headed by a female (Bronfenbrenner, 1975). Single-parent families are usually poor, although the single parent works in about 70 percent of the cases. Of increasing concern is the fact that an increasing proportion of single-parent families exist below the poverty level. When considering all families with female heads-of-household who had children under eighteen, the 1970 Census reported 27 percent of such families to be below the poverty line. By the 1980 Census this proportion had increased to an alarming 39 percent (U.S. Bureau of the Census, 1983b).

> When one realizes that in single-parent families, the mother is likely to be working, the number of children in the family is likely to be large, and the family is likely to be faced with all the other burdens of poverty, including inadequate housing and deteriorating neighborhoods, the strain in the family becomes particularly evident. (Mussen et al., 1979, p. 389)

HOMOSEXUAL RELATIONSHIPS

Until quite recently, homosexual behavior was severely condemned in our society; it was considered morally wrong and psychiatrically unhealthy, and it was against the law. In the past decade or two, however, there has been an accelerating acceptance of homosexuality. In 1973, for instance, the American Psychiatric Association removed homosexuality from its list of psychiatric disorders.

One result of the decreasing suppression is increasing openness. People with a predominantly or exclusively homosexual orientation have been admitting publicly that they are gay — "coming out of the closet." Gay liberation movements demand respect for this alternative sexual preference and equal treatment for gays under the law. Books, magazine and newspaper articles, plays, and movies about the homosexual experience proliferate. All this publicity might lead one to suppose that the incidence of homosexual behavior is increasing, but research indicates that it is not (Hunt, 1974). About 2 percent of American adult males are exclusively homosexual, and another 3 percent are bisexual. The figures for adult females are about half those for men. These percentages have not changed since Kinsey's studies in the 1940s (Kinsey, Pomeroy, and Martin, 1948; Kinsey et al., 1953) or since earlier surveys around 1900.

Despite the openness of homosexuality today, stereotypes of homosexuals in the media remain essentially negative. Few films, for example, approach sexual preference as a routine personal characteristic. A surprisingly large number of motion pictures portray gay characters as clearly (and needlessly) psychopathic or criminal or incorporate into their plots incidents in which gay people are brutalized or killed (Russo, 1981).

Confronted with a world that is often less than accepting, homosexuals are just as needful of the interdependencies of family life as heterosexuals. Increasingly, as societal sanctions lessen, pairs of homosexuals who are committed to one another are forming families, with "marriage" ceremonies that are acknowledged by their friends, if not always by their church or community. It is not unusual for some families to include children from a previous heterosexual union. Research on such committed couples shows little difference in emotional adjustment or activity patterns from similar heterosexual couples (Bell and Weinberg, 1978). Female homosexuals (lesbians) are more likely than males to form long-term monogamous relationships. Like heterosexual women, lesbians tend to consider sexual aggressiveness and promiscuity offensive or immoral. They prefer partners of similar social background, unlike male homosexuals, who often seek out strangers of other social classes and races for sexual encounters (Diamond and Karlen, 1980). There is very little lesbian prostitution, but male homosexual prostitutes are common.

Male homosexuals are more likely to form a family along the lines of heterosexual male roommates (Diamond and Karlen, 1980). That is, the relationship may continue for many years, and it may be emotionally very supportive; a division of labor similar to that in ordinary marriages typically evolves. But sex is sought outside the relationship. Males in this sort of relationship are about average in measures of psychological adjustment (Bell and Weinberg, 1978).

The pressures of family life are magnified for homosexuals. In addition to the scorn, derision, and sometimes overt violence perpetrated on the homosexual couple by members of the surrounding community, introspective doubts and fears threaten the relationship. Kinship ties to parents, siblings, and even children are threatened by the revulsion with which society views homosexuality; introducing one's gay lover to one's parents has recently been the theme of many comic dramas, but in real life it is more often a tragedy. Homosexuals have great difficulty in retaining custody of their children and find it virtually impossible to adopt children. Outside the law of state and church, homosexuals may find that they cannot visit their partner in a hospital or nursing home (Kelly, 1977). If the partners should die, they often are excluded from the funeral and may not be able to show their sorrow openly; they cannot file a malpractice suit as "a surviving spouse," and problems of inheritance abound.

In the face of problems such as these, gay men and lesbians have been obliged to make a special effort to be self-reliant. Many cities have gay and lesbian self-help groups, most of which depend heavily on volunteers. One such organization is Senior Action in a Gay Environment (SAGE). Founded in New York City in 1977, SAGE provides social services to elderly lesbians and gay men. A number of services are offered. "Friendly visitors" visit older lesbians and gay men on a regular basis. Those who receive visitors may be homebound or need help with activities such as shopping or trips to the doctor. Another service, "telephone reassurance," involves regular phone calls to the elderly. SAGE also organizes monthly social events such as tours, dances, dinners, and discussion groups for the large number of older lesbians and gay men who are self-sufficient but have few opportunities for socializing. Gay and lesbian people who are elderly today grew up during a period when society was even less sympathetic to them than it is now. Many lack the support of a traditional family. SAGE and similar groups offer understanding for the special problems of the elderly gay and lesbian population and help provide a measure of social cohesion to what might otherwise be a population of isolated individuals (Gwenwald, 1984).

IN SUM

As the plight of single-parent and homosexual families indicates, there is indeed a crisis in many families in today's world. The kinds of needs that are satisfied in the more traditional family are not being satisfied as well in some of the new family forms, which is unfortunate in light of the fact that the traditional forms are becoming less and less frequent. We see less and less, for example, of the old-fashioned nuclear family with a mother who prefers not to be employed; some of the problems that arise in dual-career families are discussed in Chapter 3. Divorce, discussed in Chapter 6, and death, discussed in Chapter 13, "dismember" a family — disrupt the nuclear family, and in some cases injure it seriously. Families without children are becoming more common.

It seems that the family as an institution is not dying; it is simply changing. The "new" family forms are not new in the sense that they have never before been observed. In some cultures around the world, female-headed families are the rule, not the exception. Divorce rates rise and fall from time to time, from culture to culture. Homosexual pairings are found in many cultures as well. The incidence of one family form or another is probably a function of economic forces (such as those created in the industrial revolution and those we are now experiencing in the computer-based technological revolution). These economic forces are not easily modified, and economic trends are not easily altered. We may wish for a return to traditional family forms, but realistically we must predict a retreat from them.

What effects do these changes in family forms have on adult development? To answer this question, we have to understand many things. We need to know more about the *advantages* of the new forms. For example, the family of today is more mobile than before, which is probably a factor in increased income and a higher standard of living. The *variety* of family forms today means that people have several options when deciding on how best to satisfy their family-related needs. There is more *freedom*, which can be dangerous but which also presents opportunities for growth and achievement unlikely or impossible in more rigidly structured societies. It is possible, for example, that some spouses are achieving degrees of intimacy unknown to couples who lived in times when marriage was based primarily on duty and responsibility.

We also need to know more about who or what is filling the needs that once were filled by families. Relatives, friends, and lovers may take up the slack for a missing spouse. Government organizations and private businesses provide many of the services families once provided for themselves: protection and defense, for example; insurance; day-care centers; and advice on everything from choosing a career to educating children about sex. Did families in the past do it better?

We want to say yes. But this response is more of a dream than empirical fact, hopelessly bound up with our sense of a difficult present and our nostalgia for what we think of as a happier past (Demos, 1970). Perhaps the family of today is in crisis. But was there ever an era when the family was *not* in crisis? The 1950s, for example, are sometimes held up to us as a peaceful era, one in which the family functioned effectively. Research shows this view to be seriously overdrawn, if not patently false (Skolnick, 1978). The revolts of the 1960s, by blacks, by young people, and by women were the products of unresolved tensions in the "peaceful" 1950s. For these groups at least, the 1950s were not the answer; they were the problem.

> Earlier periods of American history do not reveal any other golden ages of the family either. . . . Rather than witnessing a decline in the family over the past decade and a half, we are recovering from a long amnesia during which important family issues were ignored. We are finally taking up the unfinished business of working out the relations of men and women, parents and children, home and work, family and society in a modernized, industrial, bureaucratic society. (Skolnick, 1978, pp. 35–36)

Summary

1.   A family can be viewed as a system of *interdependent relationships* in which each member depends on others for some needs and fills some needs for the others. An example is the division of labor in a family, in which commonly even the youngest and oldest family members participate. With today's high rates of divorce and remarriage, the events of the family cycle and relations between family members are more complicated than ever before.

2.   A family typically begins with a marriage of young people. The interdependencies on which marriages are based are sexual, emotional, and familial (the desire to provide a context for having children). The emotional interdependency of young couples involves a constant conflict between the need to be independent and the need for emotional intimacy with another person, a conflict Erikson calls the *intimacy crisis* of young adulthood. The nature of love is understood primarily in romantic rather than scientific terms in Western culture.

Choosing a mate is a process that can be viewed as filtering out unacceptable possibilities on the basis of propinquity (geographical nearness), attractiveness, social background, attitude similarity (consensus) and complementarity, and temporal readiness for marriage. Another scheme suggests that people pass through a certain sequence of stages in selecting a spouse.

3. The birth of the first child is often a crisis for the new family, severely altering the interaction of the spouses and the work duties of the mother. Mothers worry about loss of attractiveness and are often exhausted, whereas fathers must often seek additional income. Having children is part of what Erikson calls the *generativity crisis*, which has to do with creativity and production in careers too, but finds direct expression in the creation of new life. There is little evidence of a natural desire for children, but most people derive great satisfaction from their children once they are born. Children make parents feel needed and provide a link to the future — a possibility of a better life, a kind of eternal life.

4. Although traditionally mothers take greater responsibility for the care of children than do fathers, there have been marked changes in the father's involvement in child care since the 1950s. Greater involvement of fathers has been caused by the increased participation of women with young children in the work force and as a result of changes in medical practice and hospital operations which facilitate father participation in the care of the newborn. To a lesser degree changes have occurred also due to conscious efforts in changing sex roles with respect to child-care participation.

5. It is often said that the nuclear family (parents and children) is isolated from kin (the extended family) in today's world. This myth is based on the belief that extended families were common in earlier eras of American life (not true) and on the belief that nuclear families of today have little contact with kin (also not true). Family relationships remain strong, although they may take a different form than they did in earlier years.

6. As children grow up and leave home, the parents remain behind in an *empty nest* or a *postparental family*. Parents in general, and mothers in particular, are supposed to be distressed by this event, but research shows the opposite: satisfaction with completing a life's task (raising children) and renewed intimacy with one's spouse.

7. The empty nest is sometimes filled by an aging parent who moves in because of economic, emotional, or health considerations. It is not true, however, that most adult children and their aging parents reverse roles, with the aging parents becoming dependent on the children. An older person in our society may become more dependent in limited respects, but typically relationships between adult children and aging parents simply become more mature: one adult interacting with another, with bonds of affection and duty. When parents do become dependent, their adult children may find themselves in a "middle generation squeeze," having responsibilities to both a younger and an older generation. Remarriages of old people who have lost a spouse are often discouraged by their adult children, however, in spite of the great satisfactions the elderly bride and groom seem to derive from such unions.

8. Grandparents tend to be formal (traditional, ritualistic), fun-seeking, or distant (with little contact). The ages of grandparents and their grandchildren are crucial determinants of grandparenting style, with older grandparents holding more traditional views and having older grandchildren, with whom the period of similar definitions of "fun" has long since passed. Some grandmothers emphasize either the social or the personal dimension of the grandparent role; others devote equal attention to both. Some grandparents are quite detached from their grandchildren.

9. The transmission of values and traditions from one generation to another — *socialization* — is accomplished in many ways: two of these are by direct teaching and by example (modeling). Parents, much more than grandparents, have the responsibility of guidance, which often results in "generation-gap" conflicts. Children tend to accept their parents' influence in important moral and social values; peers may have more influence in superficial values involving tastes in dress and music (which define identity in a generation). As children grow older, a type of *bilateral negotiation* develops, as each generation champions the values and behaviors it has found important and useful; the parents sometimes learn from their children as much as the children learn from their more experienced parents. Although all three generations report high levels of family solidarity, grandparents feel the strongest emotional ties to family members.

10. The nuclear family, especially the old-fashioned version with a nonworking wife, is becoming less and less common. New family forms include nuclear families with two careers, increasing numbers of postparental families (as life expectancy increases), and vastly increasing numbers of single-parent families and individuals living alone or with roommates. We discussed the problems of teenaged, unwed mothers and homosexual couples, and the future of the family. Viewed through the scope of science and research, the past is not as good and the future not as bad as we tend to believe.

SUGGESTED READINGS

Aizenberg, R., and Treas, J. (1985). The family in late life: Psychosocial and demographic considerations. In J. E. Birren and K. W. Schaie (Eds.), *Handbook of the psychology of aging* (2nd ed.) (pp. 169–189). New York: Van Nostrand Reinhold. Families are defined and an authoritative account is presented on kin networks; intergenerational transfers and relationships of families and their elders are discussed.

Hobbs, D. F., Jr., and Wimbish, J. M. (1977). Transition to parenthood by black couples. *Journal of Marriage and the Family, 39,* 677–689. Reviews research on attitude changes by black couples as parenthood is attained. Somewhat counters the position taken in this chapter that parenthood is often a traumatic experience, at least for blacks.

Lasswell, M., and Lobsenz, N. M. (1980). *Styles of loving.* Garden City, NY: Doubleday. A very readable account of the diverse ways in which men–women relationships are established, as well as the processes and problems that contribute to the successful or problematic maintenance of relationships both within and without marriage.

Seward R. R. (1973). The colonial family in America: Toward a socio-historical restoration of its structure. *Journal of Marriage and the Family, 35,* 58–70. Discusses the history of the family in early American society, including an evaluation of the truths and myths about the prevalence of the extended family in America.

Marital Attitudes Across Time

Attitudes are influenced by a great many factors. As we have seen, it is often difficult to distinguish between those caused by cohort differences and those caused by aging *per se,* particularly when one has to rely on data from cross-sectional studies. Longitudinal research is more reliable, but it is also more difficult to conduct. Perhaps the best approach is to use multiple research strategies.

Carole K. Holahan recently undertook two related studies of changes over the last forty years in attitudes concerning marital satisfaction and egalitarianism in marriage (1984). The first was a longitudinal analysis of changes in the attitudes of a sample of people from the Terman Study of the Gifted. This sample, originally assessed in 1940 at the age of about thirty, was assessed again in 1981 at the age of about seventy. In the second study, the responses of a group of people who were thirty years old in 1981 were collected for comparison with the responses of the older group.

All subjects were asked to fill out a three-part questionnaire. The first part asked about the subject's marital status. In the second part, a group of nine questions was used to assess views about the ideal marriage. Since the studies were intended to clarify both longitudinal and cohort differences, the questions had to be chosen from a test administered to the Terman sample in the 1940s. This permitted comparisons between the attitudes of the 1940 Terman group, the attitudes of the same group forty-one years later, and the group that was about thirty years old in 1981. The nine items consisted of such statements as "The husband should be some years older than the wife" and "The father should take an active interest in the discipline and training of the children." The respondents marked their answers on a five-point scale ranging from 1 (decidedly not desirable) to 5 (very essential).

The third part of the questionnaire covered marital satisfaction. Seven items were used to construct a scale of marital satisfaction. Respondents were asked to rate on a scale of 1 (untrue) to (4 completely true) such statements as "When my spouse and I are alone together we are almost continuously gay and delighted with each other" and "My spouse never does or says anything that either irritates or bores me in the slightest." Subjects were also asked to rate their marital happiness and assess how often they regretted their marriage.

Of the 1940 Terman group, forty-eight men and fifty-four women filled out the questionnaire sent to them in 1981. Of the comparable group of subjects who were about thirty years old in 1981, eighty-seven women and seventy-four men filled out the questionnaire.

The results tended to contradict some popular expectations and to confirm others. It is widely believed, for example, that people become more conservative with age. This would lead one to expect the Terman subjects at seventy to have more traditional views than they did at thirty. The study found, however, that the subjects had developed more egalitarian views as they aged. This was especially true for the Terman women concerning role relationships in marriage: there were declines in the numbers who thought that husbands should be older than wives and that husbands should wear the pants in the family. The older women also believed more strongly that the same standard of sexual morality should apply to both sexes. Both sexes also expressed greater acceptance of the view that the wife should work or have independent income. This longitudinal trend toward egalitarianism, however, was considerably less dramatic than the trend evident in the cohort differences. The women who were thirty in 1981 had much more egalitarian views than the women who were seventy in 1981.

Another manifestation of the trend toward egalitariansim was the finding that the men who were thirty in 1981 were much more involved in family life than the Terman subjects were when they were thirty. The younger group was more likely to express love in words, to participate in the disciplining of children, and to advocate that husbands and wives take vacations together. But despite these areas of accord, marital satisfaction was found to be lower in the younger cohort for both men and women. It appears that increased egalitarianism involves more strain than the more traditional pattern, in which less negotiation is necessary for smooth functioning.

The trend toward egalitarianism notwithstanding, there is evidence that sex differences in some areas are quite stable. This was especially true with regard to the wife's being fully informed about the family finances. In both the longitudinal and cohort comparisons, women were much more likely than men to believe they should be fully informed. Women were also more likely to favor a single standard of sexual morality for both sexes and to favor having a separate budget of their own.

Several results indicated that developmental changes in role behavior in adulthood may occur. Although the Terman men became more egalitarian as they aged with regard to the husband's wearing the pants in the family, there was no difference between the men who were thirty in 1940 and the men who were thirty in 1981. This was one of the few areas where the longitudinal differences were greater than the cohort differences. This suggests that men adhere more strongly to traditional sex roles related to dominance in young adulthood than in later years of marriage.

In general, cohort differences for men were greater than longitudinal differences. For women, on the other hand, the longitudinal changes that occurred often matched cohort differences. The Terman women were more responsive to recent social changes in gender roles on items directly concerned with independence and equality for women than were the Terman men. This suggests that perhaps the attitudes of a dominant group change less than those of a nondominant group when a sociocultural change is occurring.

In summary, the study indicated that the marital attitudes for the Terman subjects changed considerably between the ages of thirty and seventy in accord with the societal trend toward greater gender roles equality. Although the study could not distinguish developmental and cohort effects, it did suggest certain hypotheses concerning the probable causes of longitudinal differences. In two instances, longitudinal effects for men occurred in the absence of cohort effects, which favors life cycle explanation for men on those attitudes. In general, however, longitudinal changes were consistent with sociocultural developments. A plausible hypothesis would suggest that sociocultural change reinforces developmental changes in aging.

Holahan, C. K., (1984). Marital attitudes over 40 years: A longitudinal and cohort analysis. *Journal of Gerontology, 39*, 49–57.

Chapter Three

CAREERS

Earning a Living

Grace Clements earns her living as a felter in a luggage factory (Terkel, 1974). She presides over an eight-foot-square tank full of ground wood, ground glass, fiberglass, various chemicals, and water; the temperature at her work station reaches 150°F in summer. Once every forty seconds, a copper screen emerges with a new piece of felt luggage; dry, it will weigh only three pounds, but now, wet, it's more like fifteen. Grace covers it with a rubber sheeting for two or three seconds to draw out the excess moisture — a "couple of seconds to rest in," she says, comparing her present job favorably to her old job at the punch press, where she punched out hard-sided luggage without such respite. Then, balancing the wet bag on her shoulder, she reaches for a hose and sprays the copper screen to keep it from plugging. She turns around, walks to the hot press behind her, takes off the hot, dried piece placed there forty seconds ago, puts on the new, wet felt, pushes the button to activate the press, inspects the just-completed piece, counts it, stacks it. When she gets a stack of ten, she pushes it along and begins a new stack. She turns back to her tank where the copper screen is rising once more — the Creature from the Green Lagoon. Forty seconds per piece. No talking allowed; she might make a reject. She is not allowed to go to the bathroom until her break; she has two ten-minute breaks, plus twenty minutes for lunch. Her arms are scarred with burns from the hot press. She has trouble hearing the phone at home because the noise at the factory is deafening.

Grace Clements is in her mid-forties. She has worked in factories for the past twenty-five years. She dreams of retiring with her husband to a place near the lake where she can raise flowers in a little garden.

Grace Clements has a tough job — a factory job, a working-class job. She doesn't like her job: it's boring and it's demeaning. Why does she do it? "Ya gotta eat!" Survival is her answer, as it is with most workers. But why does she choose to earn a living in this manner and not some other? What was her first job? How did she choose it? What were her plans? Why did she change jobs from time to time? Did the fact that she's a woman affect her career as worker? She looks forward to retirement, to a return to a little piece of the garden of Eden, but how will it really be for her? Will she miss her job? Will she miss being active? Will she miss the weekly paycheck?

These are the questions we explore in this chapter — not only for Grace Clements, of course, but for people in general. By way of warning, we should note that most of the research has ignored Grace Clements and others like her — working-class people. Instead, researchers have focused on upper-middle-class subjects — physicians, lawyers, businessmen (sic) — and therefore have formulated a sort of theory of the upper crust. Future research on career development may rectify this imbalance, but for now we must be suspicious about the extent to which these theoretical notions can be applied to other groups, not only the working class, but also women (including homemakers) and minority groups.

Working

For most people, including Grace Clements, the primary purpose of work is to earn a living. Some are lucky enough to earn their living in activities they would pursue whether or not they were paid for them; many successful artists fall into this category. And money is rarely the sole reward in a job: there are opportunities for friendships, for the exercise of motivations for power and achievement, for solving interesting problems and creating valuable goods and services. Some workers (homemakers, for example) do not receive money for their efforts (relying on spouses to provide their living in a marital barter system). Others have no need for money, and work for them is like a hobby, activity pursued for its own sake. Nevertheless, for most people, a job is first and foremost a way of earning money, which the worker can exchange for the necessities of life and perhaps a few luxuries too.

A career is a lifelong pattern of work. The word "career" derives from the French word for racetrack or racecourse; it aptly implies the course of jobs, occupations, and vocations through which we race in a lifetime. There was a time when career and job were more or less synonymous, when a young adult chose an occupation (carpenter, teacher, salesperson) and stayed with it for a lifetime. Today, however, people are likely to have several quite different occupations and certainly many different jobs during their lives. Indeed, many young adults deliberately plan for a series of jobs. Realizing that the first job they choose is not likely to be their last, they think in terms of "what this job might lead to" or the valuable experience they will gain that might support their application for a different job.

People's jobs are a major element in their sense of who they are, in their sense of personal identity. Many people introduce themselves with their occupations: "I'm Mary Watts. I'm a real estate broker." One's job affects one's life in so many ways. A college commencement address by William Lowe Bryan says it well:

It is your good fortune to have a wide choice of occupations among which to choose. It is no light matter to make the choice. It is to elect your physical and social environment. It is to choose where you will work — in a scholar's cloister, on a farm, or in the cliffs of a city street. It is to choose what you will attend to, what you will try for, whom you will follow. In a word, it is to elect for life, for better or worse, some one part of the whole social heritage. These influences will not touch you lightly. They will compass you with subtle compulsions. They will fashion your clothes, and your looks, and your carriage, the cunning of your hands, the texture of your speech, and the temper of your will. (Bischof, 1976, p. 213)

Work is a lifelong endeavor, an important consideration even for those who don't happen to have jobs at the time. Children, for example, begin institutional preparation for the world of work around the age of six or so. In our culture, they begin formal schooling; in other cultures, they may begin an apprentice relationship with an older worker. From age six onward (in some instances, even sooner) they are asked, "What do you want to be when you grow up?" The appropriate answers are job titles. If a child should happen to say, "I want to be a cheerful and happy person," adults would reply, "How cute! But what do you want to do?" As schooling continues and some degree of personal choice is allowed in a student's course of study, the student's electives are often part of the occupational choice process. Should it be typing, preparing oneself for a clerical career, or mathematics, in preparation for working with computers?

Choosing an Occupation

In many respects choosing an occupation is similar to choosing a spouse. There are family pressures to take this job and not that one. Social background factors to some extent determine one's choice and one's satisfaction with the choice once made. Similarity of interests between job applicant and satisfied members of a profession predict happiness on the job as similarity of attitudes and values plays a role in predicting marital success. When people are ready to choose a job, they select from among those available at the time, just as the "readiness factor" influences their choice of mate. Beyond computer dating services, we don't see many professional matchmakers these days; but professional intermediaries who match people with jobs (vocational counselors, employment agents) are becoming more common. Job selection is also a reciprocal process, like mate selection: as the individual checks out the employer, the employer checks out the potential employee. One or the other might terminate an unsatisfactory relationship in a kind of industrial "divorce": the employer might fire the employee, or the employee might quit. As you will see, vocational development like marriage, is a process that continues throughout the life span. It begins before adolescence and does not end when one takes a first job.

FAMILY INFLUENCES

Like many other areas of development, choice of a career is strongly influenced by the family. Of major concern in the study of development are the *processes* by which the family influences its members' vocational aspirations, expectations, and the occupational status they eventually attain (Schulenberg, Vondracek, and Crouter, 1984).

The family influences vocational development in two major ways. First, the family can provide *opportunities* for the developing individual. These may be as simple as a set of encyclopedias or trips to the library or as complex and demanding as paying the tuition to private schools or using one's business and social connections to see that a child is accepted at an Ivy League university. Second, the family influences vocational development through *socialization* and parent–child relations. A young man who has a close relationship with his father is likely to be affected by the father's hopes for his future, and most children learn values that resemble those of their parents. The pressures exerted by families may be either direct or indirect. One set of parents may insist that their child enter a premedical program at college. Another may try to direct a child's interest in a certain direction in the hope that he or she will choose a career of which the parents approve.

The family's influence on career choices is reflected by the finding that family socioeconomic status (SES) is correlated with children's occupational status aspirations and expectations and their eventual occupational attainment. Even among those who attend college there is a tendency for students from higher SES backgrounds to have greater educational opportunity. One study found that students from low SES backgrounds tended to go to colleges with lower admission standards than students from higher SES backgrounds, even when the students were of equal ability (Karabel and Astin, 1975).

The correlation between SES and vocational expectations is considerably stronger for men than for women. Research shows that a father's occupational status is directly related to the son's educational attainment, which is in turn an important influence on the son's occupational attainment (Blau and Duncan, 1967). A physician, for example, may have both the money and the inclination to send a son to a prestigious school. A degree from such a school will assure that the son has a good chance of getting a high-prestige job.

The exact nature and causes of this link between a father's occupational status and a son's attainment in education and occupation are not clear, but several factors seem to be influential. It appears that men tend to hold values for themselves and their children that are consistent with the demands of their jobs. Working-class men, whose jobs require compliance with authority, tend to value obedience and conformity in their children, whereas middle-class men, whose jobs depend more on self-direction, tend to value initiative and independence in their children (Kohn, 1977; Kohn and Schooler, 1983). Thus fathers may teach their sons values that are appropriate for occupations resembling their own, which would tend to increase the sons' chances of entering such occupations. Mortimer (1974, 1976) and Mortimer and Kumka (1982) did in fact find a strong tendency for college males to choose jobs similar to their fathers' in terms of prestige, income, extent of work autonomy, intrinsic occupational rewards, and job complexity. Male senior college students from business families were more concerned with extrinsic values such as high income and advancement, whereas sons from professional families were more concerned about the intrinsic people-oriented aspects of their occupations. The extent of "occupational transmission" from father to son was greatest when sons reported a close relationship with the father, and when the father had high occupational status.

Further support for the view that families influence career-related values comes from a ten-year longitudinal followup of Mortimer's study (Mortimer and Kumka, 1982). Mortimer found that parents' occupational successes and parental support had intensified the respective values of the two groups of sons (business vs. professional), even following college.

Evidence regarding the influence of socioeconomic background on females' vocational choices is less clear-cut. Several studies suggest that high SES and nontraditional career choices are highly correlated. Among high school females, a high SES background was found to be a significant factor in discriminating those planning careers in science and those planning to be housewives or office workers (Burlin, 1976).

Of the variables related to socialization, it appears that female career orientations, expectations, and achievements are affected by both whether or not the mother works during the daughters' childhood and adolescence, and the relationship between the father and daughter. Having a mother who works outside the home increases the chances that the daughter will work outside the home. Indeed, the mother's employment status is the single most consistent predictor of the daughter's aspirations in a nontraditional career (Huston-Stein and Higgins-Trenk, 1978; Auster and Auster, 1981). Furthermore, the father's attitude toward working women is important. Several studies have found that, among college women, career aspirations are related to the father's attitude toward housewife and career roles (Oliver, 1975; Ridgeway, 1978). The father's attitude may influence the daughter's choice of a career by encouraging nontraditional socialization practices and by exposing the daughter to career options, including the father's own. The father can also provide a countermodel of predominant cultural attitudes, thereby reassuring the daughter that choosing to have a career is not incompatible with male approval (Weitz, 1977). This type of father is more likely to be supportive of his wife's working and thus the daughter can observe the satisfactions as well as stresses of a dual-earner family.

VOCATIONAL INTERESTS AND PERSONALITY

One approach to conceptualizing personality as it relates to vocational interests distinguishes six personality types: investigative, social, realistic, artistic, conventional, and enterprising (Holland, 1966, 1985). Theoretical descriptions of the six types are given in Table 3–1. Briefly, the investigative person likes to work with ideas (and is therefore likely to choose a scientific occupation); the social person likes to work with people (and might therefore be found in human services or religious work); the realistic person likes to work with objects (and is therefore likely to be found in mechanical occupations); the artistic person likes to work with emotions (and might therefore be found in the arts or other creative occupations). Conventional persons are conformists; they are practical, conservative, neat, correct, but lack spontaneity, originality, and flexibility. Occupations in finance (bank teller) or business (accountant or office manager) suit this pattern of interests. Finally, enterprising persons are adventurous and persuasive; they like to dominate. The enterprising individual enjoys work in business — in sales and supervisory positions, in particular.

The relationship of personality type to career choice is generally moderate but significant. In other words, personality doesn't explain *all* aspects of career choice, but it has an influence. One study showed the *average* scores of college-graduate workers in the medical field to be highest on the investigative scale, as the theory predicts (Walsh, Horton, and Gaffey, 1977). Similarly, careers in the ministry appear to draw people who score, on the average, highest on the social scale. Both males and females in car sales (an "enterprising" occupation) average highest on the enterprising scale (Benninger and Walsh, 1980). But these averages include some individuals whose personalities do not fit the characteristics of the job: a minister with strong intellectual interests, a salesperson with artistic interests. These "misfits" usually adapt in one of three ways: (1) they quit their jobs and try to find one more to their liking; (2) their interests change to become more in line with their jobs; or (3) they reconstruct their work to satisfy their interests. In the latter case, our intellectual minister might shy away from social duties, preferring to dig through books for religious insights. Or the artistic salesperson might begin work on a novel about life on the used-car lot!

Most of these personality characteristics can be predicted from family background (Grandy and Stahmann, 1974; Holland, 1985). Enterprising individuals, for example, typically grow up in an urban rather than rural area. Their parents, who are usually relatively well-to-do, value popularity and material rewards. Conventional persons tend to have fathers who place a low value on curiosity and independence. Their mothers, on the average, base their childrearing techniques on the principle that suppression of naughty behavior (sex, aggression) is of paramount importance.

Where a family lives also has predictive value. The offspring of a family that lives in Seattle, Washington, the home of Boeing, are more likely than average to choose a career in the aircraft industry; children growing up in a coal mining region are more likely to consider mining occupations. Ethnic and religious values also play a role. Jewish culture, for example, values education highly and influences disproportionate numbers of Jewish children to seek academic careers. Many people who grew up in a Catholic family have at least considered the possibility of taking vows to become a priest or a nun.

Personality types such as those described by Holland tend to remain stable

TABLE 3–1.

The six basic personality types and their relationship to vocational preferences, as defined by the theory of J. L. Holland.

Investigative

The model type is task-oriented, intraceptive, asocial; prefers to think through rather than act out problems; needs to understand; enjoys ambiguous work tasks; has unconventional values and attitudes; is anal as opposed to oral. Vocational preferences include aeronautical design engineer, anthropologist, astronomer, biologist, botanist, chemist, editor of a scientific journal, geologist, independent research scientist, meteorologist, physicist, scientific research worker, writer of scientific or technical articles, zoologist.

Social

The model type is sociable, responsible, feminine, humanistic, religious; needs attention; has verbal and interpersonal skills; avoids intellectual problem solving, physical activity, and highly ordered activities; prefers to solve problems through feelings and interpersonal manipulations of others; is orally dependent. Vocational preferences include assistant city school superintendent, clinical psychologist, director of welfare agency, foreign missionary, high school teacher, juvenile delinquency expert, marriage counselor, personal counselor, physical education teacher, playground director, psychiatric case worker, social science teacher, speech therapist, vocational counselor.

Realistic

The model type is masculine, physically strong, unsociable, aggressive; has good motor coordination and skill; lacks verbal and interpersonal skills; prefers concrete to abstract problems; conceives of himself as being aggressive and masculine and as having conventional political and economic values. Persons who choose or prefer the following occupations resemble this type: airplane mechanic, construction inspector, electrician, filling station attendant, fish and wildlife specialist, locomotive engineer, master plumber, photoengraver, power shovel operator, power station operator, radio operator, surveyor, tree surgeon, tool designer.

Artistic

The model type is asocial; avoids problems that are highly structured or require gross physical skills; resembles the investigative type in being intraceptive and asocial; but differs from that type in that he has a need for individualistic expression, has less ego strength, is more feminine, and suffers more frequently from emotional disturbances; prefers dealing with environmental problems through self-expression in artistic media. Vocational preferences include art dealer, author, cartoonist, commercial artist, composer, concert singer, dramatic coach, free-lance writer, musical arranger, musician, playwright, poet, stage director, symphony conductor.

Conventional

The model type prefers structured verbal and numerical activities and subordinate roles; is conforming (extraceptive); avoids ambiguous situations and problems involving interpersonal relationships and physical skills; is effective at well-structured tasks; identifies with power; values material possessions and status. Vocational preferences include bank examiner, bank teller, bookkeeper, budget reviewer, cost estimator, court stenographer, financial analyst, IBM equipment operator, inventory controller, payroll clerk, quality control expert, statistician, tax expert, traffic manager.

Enterprising

The model type has verbal skills for selling, dominating, leading; conceives of himself as a strong, masculine leader; avoids well-defined language or work situations requiring long periods of intellectual effort; is extraceptive; differs from the conventional type in that he prefers ambiguous social tasks and has a greater concern with power, status, and leadership; is orally aggressive. Vocational preferences include business executive, buyer, hotel manager, industrial relations consultant, manufacturer's representative, master of ceremonies, political campaign manager, real-estate salesperson, restaurant worker, speculator, sports promoter, stock and bond salesperson, television producer, traveling salesperson.

Source: J. L. Holland. *The psychology of vocational choice*. Waltham, MA: Blaisdell, 1966, p. 16. Reprinted by permission of the author. See Holland, *Making vocational choices: a theory of vocational personalities and work environments*, Prentice-Hall, 1985.

over time, as do vocational interests. Longitudinal data collected over a twenty-year period indicate that vocational interests remain about the same from late adolescence onward (Strong, 1955; Johannson and Campbell, 1971).

The relationship between Holland's vocational interest typology and a three-dimensional model of personality has been examined (Costa, McCrae, and Holland, 1984). Personality traits in the Costa model are divided into three broad domains: Neuroticism (N), Extraversion (E), and Openness to Experience (O). Neuroticism includes such traits as anxiety, hostility, depression, and vulnerability. Extraversion includes traits such as warmth, assertiveness, gregariousness, and positive emotions, and Openness to Experience covers areas such as aesthetics, feelings, actions, ideas, and values (see also Chapter 4, p. 162). The Holland types and the NEO model tend to support each other. For example, the personality dimension Openness to Experience includes the same people as the Holland type categories investigative and artistic, as you would expect. The social and enterprising types fell into the NEO category of Extraversion. These relationships were found for both men and women. Furthermore, the NEO categories tend to confirm the occupational preferences suggested in the Holland types. Openness to Experience was related to occupational preferences for professions such as author, journalist, research scientist, and anthropologist. Extraversion was related to occupational preferences such as advertising executive, sales manager, marriage counselor, and manufacturer's representative. Thus comparisons with the NEO model tend to confirm the accuracy of the Holland types.

On all six Holland types, significant sex differences have been found (Costa, McCrae, and Holland, 1984). Women fall more often into the artistic, social, and conventional categories. This tendency was found in all age groups. The preference for work in these areas is in accord with the roles and values traditionally associated with women in the United States.

Career theories based on personality type are not without limitations, of course. Such perspectives are overly static and simplistic, and they do not take into account the context in which decisions are made. Career decisions are not made by personalities acting in a social vacuum. Rather, there is a dynamic interaction between the person and the sociocultural environment. It is also important that interactions between the work-related and nonwork-related

The world of work has been changing dramatically for women. Today there are more job opportunities open to women, and they comprise about half of the work force.

aspects of a person's development be taken into account insofar as they affect career aspirations and achievement. For example, career choices may be moderated by the individual's marital and family commitments. Personality types can take us only so far in understanding vocational decisions; we need to understand the interactive contributions of the environment as well.

ASSESSING VOCATIONAL INTERESTS

Most of us have taken a "vocational interest test" at one time or another, perhaps in high school or as a part of an employment counseling service in college. Among the most common tests in current use is the Strong–Campbell Interest Inventory (SCII). The SCII is designed to measure career likes and dislikes. Most of its items are answered "like," "dislike," or "indifferent," in response to various occupations (e.g., dentist), school subjects (e.g., physics), activities (e.g., repairing a clock), amusements (e.g., skiing), and types of people (e.g., very old people). An individual's pattern of responses can be interpreted on several levels. At the highest level are the six vocational-personality types discussed previously: investigative, social, realistic, artistic, conventional, and enterprising. Most people do not appear to be "pure" types and may earn a high score on two or three scales.

Slightly less abstract are twenty-three "basic interest" scales, which represent general occupational interests such as agriculture, public speaking, and science.

Finally, at the most analytical level, the SCII gives scores for 162 specific occupations, such as psychologist, photographer, architect, forester, and physical education teacher. The scores on these scales indicate the similarity between the person taking the test and satisfied men and women in the various professions, whose answers to the same items were used to construct the scales. To illustrate, almost all men who are satisfied with their careers as engineers respond "dislike" to the item that asks them to consider the idea of acting on stage. So males who say they dislike acting are given one point for being similar to engineers, and those who say they like acting have one point subtracted from their engineer score. Considered together, the answers give a good picture of the individual's general similarity — in *interests* only, not in ability — to people already in a profession (D. P. Campbell and Hansen, 1981).

Vocational interest inventories are useful predictors of vocational choice and satisfaction. For example, in any given occupation there are five times as many men who have high interest scores for that occupation as there are men with high scores for any other occupation. In terms of job satisfaction, if we compare interest scores of satisfied professionals with those dissatisfied in the same profession, the average score for happy workers will be about double that for unhappy workers (Perry, 1955). *Counter - sets curriculum*

Vocational interest tests do not predict the occupational choices of women as well as those of men (Sundberg, 1977). This is probably due to the fact that, historically, women have been less able than men to choose careers that suit their tastes and talents. They have faced discriminative practices that have reduced or prevented their participation in some occupations, or they have subjugated their interests to those of their husbands and families.

Establishing a Career

Once an occupation is chosen (sometimes with great care and sometimes without much deliberate thought on the matter), the individual next faces the problems of what psychologists call "early professional socialization." Workers must learn exactly what it is that they are supposed to do. They must learn how to get along with coworkers, even with those who are unfriendly and competitive; how to respond to authority, including when to conform and when to complain; how to defend themselves, to protect their own interests. They have to learn who can do what for them — that is, they must decipher the true power and service relationships, which do not always correspond to official titles.

THE DREAM

In Daniel Levinson's theory of adult development (Levinson, 1978), the "novice phase" of early adulthood — up to roughly the age of thirty — is characterized by

Disciple of Ericson

four major tasks. One is getting married and starting a family. The other three have to do with the individual's career: choosing an occupation, forming a Dream, and finding a mentor. The Dream is an individual's general expectation of what he or she will become, or would like to become. When we say something like "Never did I dream I'd be a company president at 29!" or "This job is a dream come true!", we are using "dream" in Levinson's sense. The Dream is more structured than pure fantasy, less articulated than a plan; it is "a vague sense of self-in-adult-world." As a vision of the kind of life a person wants to lead as an adult, the Dream, of course, includes images of a certain kind of family life and community environment, but for most people occupational concerns are central.

One of life's chief tasks, according to Levinson, is to define the Dream in greater and more realistic detail — in effect, to try to live up to it. First choices of occupation and career are obviously important. An individual may be forced, for various reasons, to enter the world of work on a track other than that which would most likely lead to Dream fulfillment. Approximately half of all young people aspire to professional status, but only 20 percent of the work force are in professional jobs (U.S. Bureau of the Census, 1983b). Members of minority groups and women may face discrimination. In 1983, only 6 percent of all individuals in managerial or professional occupations were black (U.S. Bureau of the Census, 1984a). An individual may be pressured by family or economic need to enter a career other than the one in his or her Dream. For whatever reason the conflict between reality and the Dream develops, it is likely to be a source of stress and depression for the young worker; it also contains the seeds of emotional and vocational "crisis" at later stages of the individual's career.

Even for people who embark on the career of their Dreams, the first experiences with their jobs can be shocking. The Dream, especially when newly formed, contains many fantastic elements, so the real world never quite measures up. There is inevitably some degree of "reality shock" (Van Maanen and Schein, 1977), as new assistant professors discover how much time is wasted in committee meetings, as new carpenters discover that supervisors play favorites, as new factory workers discover how little the union can do for them, even when safety is the matter in dispute. Encountering reality is part of articulating the Dream, of course, and, for most people, adaptation follows reality shock; the fantasy aspects of the Dream may not disappear completely, but the realistic elements come to play a greater role.

A number of the propositions in Levinson's theory of adult development have also been addressed by data from a longitudinal study of managers conducted by American Telephone and Telegraph (AT&T) beginning in 1956. The goal of the study, which was called the Management Progress Study (MPS), was to investigate various facets of the lives and careers of managers and to examine factors related to ability and personality that could be used to predict career success and life satisfaction (Bray, Campbell, and Grant, 1974; see also Howard and Bray, 1980; Howard and Wilson, 1982; and Howard, 1984). A total of 422 young lower-level managers participated in the initial phase of the study. All were white males, and all were part of the pool from which future middle- and upper-level managers would be drawn. There were two classes of men: college graduates hired into the first level of management and men without a college degree who had joined the company as craftsmen but had been promoted into management.

The research began in 1956, when the men participated in tests and exercises for three days at an assessment center. The men were rated on multiple dimensions thought to be important among managers. There were annual interviews during the first seven years of the study. In year eight and year twenty of the study, the three-day battery of tests was administered again.

Data from the AT&T study support and extend Levinson's concept of the Dream and a period of reality shock (Howard and Bray, 1980). During the first seven years, "expectation inventories" were administered annually. These inventories were designed to gather information on the hopes and dreams of the subjects concerning various aspects of their careers, including when they expected to advance, salary increases anticipated, and additional work responsibilities they would assume.

The findings showed that although the young managers began with very high expectations, they rapidly became more realistic. The major drop in expectations had occurred by year five of the study, when the college men were on average twenty-nine years old and the noncollege men were on average thirty-four. The desire to advance had decreased. Desires for further promotions also dropped fairly early. Aside from adjusting to the reality of the career plateau, many men had sound reasons for not wanting further promotions. Promotions often meant being transferred to a new location, which families objected to, especially when they had teenage children who would have had to leave their school and friends. Another consideration was that working at a higher level of management would entail more work and more responsibilities and less time for family-related activities. (Work-related motivation is further discussed in Chapter 7.)

This is not to say that most managers were dissatisfied with their jobs or with their lives in general. They generally found much satisfaction in the challenge of their jobs and in doing their jobs well. Their inner work standards — the extent to which they met their own personal standards of achievement — did not decline.

Limitations in the broader applicability of both the Levinson theory and the AT&T research should be noted. Both focused primarily on the careers of white-collar professional workers who had linear career paths; some of them, at least, could hope to advance up the hierarchical ladder to positions of greater responsibility and higher pay. Many workers, however, do not have such orderly career paths. Service workers, blue-collar workers, and unskilled laborers generally have few opportunities for vertical advancement. Another shortcoming of the Levinson and the AT&T studies is that they dealt almost exclusively with white males. The career patterns of women and members of minorities may differ considerably from those of white males at every stage, including the initial stage of reality shocks, when it is helpful to find a sympathetic individual with more experience to serve as a guide through the novelties of the new career.

THE MENTOR

The worker usually does not face the trials of reality shock alone. Typically, guidance is provided through the early years (the early professional socialization) by another person. This guide has been called the *mentor* (Levinson, 1978). The mentor is usually an older person, at least in terms of experience; he or she may be one's supervisor or boss, a teacher, a senior colleague, or even a friend, neighbor, or relative.

The functions of the mentor are many, and all are quite important to the career development of the young worker. The mentor is partly a teacher, training a protégé. Mentors may also serve as sponsors, using their influence to facilitate the young worker's advancement. Mentors provide counsel on both the technical and the often-unwritten social aspects of the job — "Don't invite both McAfee and Messick to the same party." The mentor is also a model, from whom the young worker can learn through observation.

Success in a career often depends on the quality of the mentor relationship. This fact raises some interesting questions, on both the individual and social levels. An individual usually has some choice in the mentor. Graduate students, for example, typically choose the faculty member with whom they want to work; plumbers may choose the master plumber to whom they want to apprentice themselves. One of the many questions in the choice is whether to choose a powerful mentor who may rarely be available for advice or a less senior mentor who can do more counseling. The senior vice president of a large bank would certainly be in a good position to help an aspiring manager up the corporate ladder, but such a person is unlikely to be available often for the daily consultations on routine matters that mentors are most helpful in providing. On the other hand, the vice president could provide introductions to key business contacts and clients. Often, the individual must choose between an influential mentor and one who is commonly available for discussions.

One of the many social issues raised by the need for mentors concerns working women. Women, on the average, probably have a greater need for a good mentor than men, since they may have been excluded from childhood training experiences society provides for boys — newspaper routes, for example, or even competitive sports, where young males are taught how to compete fairly, how to play on a "team," the importance of a "game plan," and other "virtues" that many scholars have characterized as the basis of the American free-enterprise system (see Harragan, 1977). In spite of what may be greater need, however, women often have considerably greater difficulty finding a good mentor although this may vary across disciplines (Busch, 1985). For one thing, female mentors have been scarce, since the world of work has been dominated by men. Although the absolute number of women in the work force has increased dramatically, there are still relatively fewer women in upper-level management positions who can serve as mentors. For example, 12 percent of men in the work force are in executive, administrative, or managerial roles compared with 7 percent of the female work force (U.S. Bureau of the Census, 1983b). Available research suggests that women with female mentors are significantly more productive than women with male mentors (Goldstein, 1979). Although male mentors are not necessarily less effective for women than female mentors, there are frequently sexual overtones to the relationship between an older man and a younger woman. As a result, there may be conflict and confusion in the relationship — a disruption of rapport — even if there is no overt behavior that one or the other party finds offensive.

Career Development

Young adults spin their Dreams from their values. If they think money is important, they will dream of a high salary. If they think recognition is important, they might picture themselves winning a Nobel prize. An environmentally oriented young attorney might envision a "landmark case" victory over a major industrial polluter. Values are the stuff Dreams are made of, and when workers express dissatisfaction with their jobs, it is often because important values are not being fulfilled.

There continue to be significant generational differences in vocational values. Young people in the 1960s and 1970s were said to be less interested in material success, and they viewed American industry as exploitative and overly concerned with profit at the expense of human needs and the quality of the environment. Compared with older workers, young people of more recent generations are said to place more value on individual expression; they did not want to become a small cog in a large, impersonal machine.

Although young people today seem to be more "career minded" than those of the late 1960s and early 1970s, they still are considerably less willing than youth in the 1950s to put up with arbitrary, authoritarian, or impersonal treatment by employers (Yankelovich, 1974, 1981; Jones, 1980). They view some American business practices with cynicism (Howard and Wilson, 1982). A recent trend in the mid-1980s has been a decline in applications to professinal schools, such as medicine, law, dentistry, and veterinary science, suggesting a transition in career orientations. In contrast, applications to computer science and engineering programs have increased. These young people have not lost, however, their desire for work that is personally rewarding, and they want friendly coworkers.

A second longitudinal study at AT&T begun in 1977 confirms the prevalence of value-related changes among more recent cohorts (Howard and Wilson, 1982). The project was designed to parallel the original MPS study of 1956. By the 1970s, the managers at AT&T were a more diverse group, and the sample of subjects consisted of about half women and one-third minorities. The 1970s cohort is of particular interest since it represents a portion of the baby boomers — a generation expected to have significant impact due to its being a much larger cohort than preceding or succeeding generations.

The study noted some similarities between the 1956 and 1977 cohorts, but also a number of striking differences. In terms of intellectual ability, the two groups were similar, although the more recent cohort was better educated. There were few differences in need for achievement — both groups preferred to work toward goals such as accomplishing something of great significance or doing a difficult job well. Inner work standards — the extent to which the subjects wanted to do a good job and met personal standards of achievement — were about the same for the two cohorts.

But in terms of motivation for upward mobility as measured by high job status and salary, the two cohorts differed significantly. The 1977 cohort did not expect the major rewards and satisfactions in life to be associated with work. Their expectations regarding the future were lower too. In the 1956 cohort, 60 percent of the managers expected in the first five work years to advance to a challenging job that offered significant job-related opportunities. In the 1977 group, only 45 percent expected this. There were no gender-related differences in motivation, but minorities scored significantly higher in both motivation and expectations. The primary motivation for minorities was the financial reward, not the power or challenge associated with advancement.

Another area of difference between the two cohorts involved leadership — activities such as directing others, assuming responsibility for subordinates, and motivating others to follow one's directions. In 1956, 49 percent of the earlier cohort rated high in this area; only 22 percent of the 1977 cohort rated high.

This does not mean that managers today prefer to be followers. Of the 1956 participants, 68 percent rated high on the dimension "need for superior's approval." Only 37 percent of the later group scored high in this area. As one participant put it, "People with authority often earn it with time rather than ability. My ambition is never to have a company, government, or person capture my soul and spirit because of financial shackles" (Howard and Wilson, 1982, p. 37).

If new managers do not want to be leaders or followers, what do they want? A clue comes from the finding that they scored higher than the earlier cohort on matters pertaining to emotional support. On scales measuring such tasks and qualities as assisting others less fortunate, treating others with kindness and sympathy, and being generous to others, the 1977 group outscored the 1956 group by 74 percent to 49 percent. The new managers were more likely to expect to give emotional support as well as to receive it.

Findings such as these have been confirmed by other studies (Jones, 1980; Yankelovich, 1981). What are their implications for the future of corporate management, business, and society at large? Although the new values are at variance in some respects with traditional business expectations, many people approve of the turning away from materialism, power-seeking, upward-striving, and competition and the movement toward individual freedom, leisure, and cooperation. With forces pulling in both directions, our culture may be at a turning point. It is clear that the objectives of entrepreneurial enterprises and current personal value systems of more recent cohorts may be out of phase. Unless efforts are made to bring them into accord, we may lose effectiveness in many of our systems of social organization (Howard and Wilson, 1982).

Noncollege youth suffer similar frustrations. In the 1950s and 1960s, blue-collar youth were much more traditional than college youth in their career orienta-

Young people of the late 1960s and early 1970s, such as this Vista volunteer, had a great desire for work that contributed to the health and welfare of others.

tions. They were satisfied with a steady job with decent wages. More recently, however, they have begun to express a desire for self-fulfillment and individual expression in their work (Yankelovich, 1974, 1981). Unfortunately, blue-collar young people are even less likely than their college-educated peers to obtain a job with opportunities for such personal satisfactions.

Just as the divorce rate indicates rising expectations and dashed hopes in modern marriages, studies of career changes show some turmoil among workers. Sometime in midcareer, many people begin a preliminary analysis of their Dream — how it has changed, how close they have come to fulfilling it, and whether or not they seem to be headed toward eventual fulfillment (Sheehy, 1976; Neapolitan, 1981). It is a time of reevaluation. Earlier career choices are reconsidered. Is the job meeting my expectations? Have my values and my interests changed to such an extent that the job is no longer in line with them? With increasing life experiences most individuals become more mature. Their personal sense of who they are — their personal identity — has stabilized, and there has been a deepening, if not a change, of interests.

SETTLING DOWN

The midcareer period for many involves a time for settling down with one's job choice (Levinson, 1978). The choice has been made, and it has been reevaluated; now it is time to "get serious." Levinson identified two major tasks in this period of life: to establish one's niche in society and to strive for advancement. The first task, to establish a niche, involves attempts to create stability, not only in one's work but in one's life in general. In one's work, it means focusing on one's career (forgetting attractive alternative careers, at least for a while) and trying to become as good at one's chosen profession as one can possibly be. The second task, striving for advancement, involves trying to move up "the ladder" to a more responsible and prestigious position. A worker may seek to reach a supervisory position; an executive may seek to become head of his or her department; a college teacher wants to be a full professor. To some extent these two major tasks conflict, for advancement often entails risk and change. For example, an aspiring young executive may be asked to move to another city, where a vice presidency is open; he does not want to disrupt the stability he has achieved in his home and community, but a refusal to move may end his chances for significant promotion.

During this period, the process of settling down takes on for some a special flavor, which Levinson (1978) calls "Becoming One's Own Man" (BOOM). The men in Levinson's study began to speak of their needs to become "senior members" at work, to have independence and authority. The mentor is often cast off, and the individual takes full responsibility for his own life.

Climbing the ladder of success, however, is not as easy as the Dream depicts. Most professions are pyramidal, with very little room at the "top." In business, for example, there is only one position in top management for every fifteen or twenty middle managers; in the factory, there is only one supervisory position for even thirty to forty line workers.

MIDCAREER REALISM

Levinson (1978) has proposed that the early forties, from about forty to forty-five, is the period of the *midlife transition* (Levinson, 1978). The first half of life has ended (or so it seems), and before one can begin the second half, a thorough examination of the life-so-far may be required. Careful and mature evaluation of one's life most often, but not invariably, results in what Levinson (1978) calls *de-illusionment* (rather than "disillusionment," which presupposes a cynical reaction to the loss of cherished beliefs). Since people's dreams about themselves are to some extent unrealistic, appraisals are likely to be negative and emotionally depressing. People are forced to realize that certain long-held assumptions and beliefs about themselves and their world are simply not true. They must face the fact that they are not going to become the president of the company or win a Nobel prize. Even if, objectively considered, their careers have been successful, some at midcareer tend to see themselves as failures, because their Dreams required more (also see discussion of midlife transitions in Chapter 8).

The de-illusionment and fears mentioned by Levinson may be most characteristic of people involved in the professions and from upper-class environments in which upward mobility is expected and highly valued. As we have seen, the MPS study begun in 1956 (Bray and Howard, 1980) revealed that many workers in their mid-thirties or older did not consider further advancement critical to their job or life satisfaction. That is, career success and life satisfaction were not related. Given many workers' realism regarding promotions, what else can we say about work at midcareer?

First, although the desire for advancement may decline in midlife, workers still seek job challenges and find satisfaction in accomplishing tasks. They maintain their high inner work standards (Bray and Howard, 1980). Another development is that they seek greater autonomy, freedom to be independent in their work (Boffey, 1985).

Second, the relative importance of work in most men's lives tends to decrease as a function of age and relative career success. For the least successful — those who advance little or not at all from their entry-level position — family, recreation, community service, and other nonwork roles assume greater importance. The process of "disengagement" from work began as soon as the early thirties. Although most still want job challenges and maintain inner work standards, they are less motivated to put in additional time and effort at work. Those who reached average levels of advancement, experience disengagement at a later period. For men who achieved above average success in work, there was actually an increase in the importance they attach to their job. These findings are reflected in Figure 3–1. The vertical scale represents ratings of the importance that interviewed men gave to their occupation relative to other areas such as marriage and family and religion. The horizontal axis are the years in which ratings were made in the AT&T study. At year 20 of the study, the men were in their mid-forties, on the average. Note that at the beginning of the study, the men did not differ in their ratings of the importance of work. As you can see, for those who achieved higher positions (levels 4 through 6 of the management hierarchy) the importance of occupational

FIGURE 3–1.

AT&T Study. Changes in ratings of the relative importance of work for men attaining various management levels. Ratings on a 7-point scale of the importance of work were made from interviews conducted in years shown on horizontal axis.

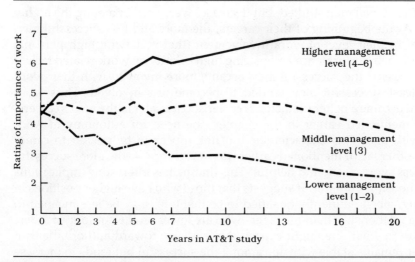

Source: From A. Howard and D. W. Bray. Career motivation in mid-life managers. Paper presented at the Annual Meeting of the American Psychological Association, Montreal, Canada. Reprinted by permission.

life tended to increase with time whereas those who remained at lower management levels gradually came to consider their work less important relative to other aspects of their lives (Howard and Bray, 1980).

A final finding of the study was that lower-level managers, especially those at the first, or bottom, level of the corporate hierarchy tended to become more nurturant and caring as time went on. Those at the very highest levels became progressively more remote and detached and showed less inclination to be sympathetic and helpful (Howard, 1984).

CAREER SUCCESS AT MIDLIFE

We have seen that men who do not rise in the corporation as quickly as they expect often cease to consider upward mobility to be of paramount importance. But what of the men who are successful in the corporation? Are they different in terms of ability and personality characteristics from those who don't advance as far? Again, the MPS study begun at AT&T in 1956 provides some information (Bray and Howard, 1983a,b; Howard, 1984).

The researchers defined as successful those men who had reached level 4 or above of the corporate hierarchy by year 20 of the study; there were six levels of management. Having conducted assessments of the men throughout the twenty-year period, they had a body of data that would describe not only which characteristics were correlated with success, but at what point these characteristics appeared and whether they changed as the managers advanced. Some of the characteristics associated with success were present at the beginning of the career, but others were the result of changes that came with success. Bray and Howard found that the most significant early predictors of career success included intellectual ability, interpersonal skills, and motivation for advancement. For example, motivation for achievement — the desire to get ahead — tended to decrease with age for all men studied, but decreases were smaller among the highly successful. At the beginning of their careers, the more and less successful men were similar in their level of work involvement (that is, having high personal standards for their performance and placing high priority on work-related tasks), but as time passed the successful men became more involved with their work while the least successful men tended to become less involved. Thus work involvement became a better predictor of career success later in the men's careers.

As we mentioned earlier in the chapter, the need for autonomy in work increases with age. This characteristic did not appear to be related to career success. Another factor mentioned earlier was nurturance — the more successful tend to be less sympathetic and helpful. This finding has interesting implications regarding choosing a mentor. It suggests that those who have higher positions in the company, albeit eminently qualified to be mentors, may be less inclined to enter such a relationship than managers who are lower on the corporate ladder.

Contrary to what one might expect, the tendency toward authoritarianism decreases or remains stable with age among the successful but tends to increase with age among the less successful. A related characteristic, behavioral flexibility (the ability to change one's own behavioral style to accomplish goals), becomes progressively more important at higher levels of career success. Dominance, the desire to be a leader and direct undertakings in which one is involved, is a good predictor of success at all stages of the career (Howard, 1984).

As you can see, success in the corporation seems to require certain characteristics and to breed certain others. It appears that the skills and capabilities one exercises on the job also influence how one thinks and reacts outside the work environment, as we will explain in the next section.

"SPILLOVER" EFFECTS OF WORK ON INDIVIDUAL AND FAMILY DEVELOPMENT

Work by Kohn and Schooler (Kohn and Schooler, 1983; Schooler, 1984) indicates that the nature of the work one does influences both intellectual and nonintellectual aspects of one's development. Kohn and Schooler studied the complexity of the work environment along three dimensions: routinization, closeness of supervision, and substantive complexity of work. Substantively complex work is work that requires the employee to deal with ideas and people. Such work involves the use of initiative, thought, and independent judgment. Work on an assembly line, for example, is generally simple and repetitive; the worker may spend the entire workday doing the same task over and over again. At higher levels, work often involves making independent decisions on a variety of complex matters. A doctor, lawyer, or manager in a corporation must deal with complicated problems of all kinds on a daily basis.

A ten-year longitudinal study of the relationship between work complexity and intellectual flexibility showed that the two factors were related (Kohn and Schooler, 1983). Men who had jobs that required independent decision-making and that involved working with a complex set of environmental circumstances tended to become more intellectually flexible. This finding was maintained when prior levels of intellectual flexibility were controlled for. The work one does affects how one thinks. Consider the case of a physician who operates a general practice in a small city. Every day, she will meet a variety of patients, each of whom will have a medical complaint of some sort. In every instance, the doctor must determine the nature of the complaint and the best approach for dealing with it. She will see patients of all social backgrounds and all ages. Some will have life-threatening illnesses. The doctor must use her training, insight, and personal skills to attempt to chart a course for the patient to regain his or her health.

The doctor must also try to keep up with new medical developments, visit patients in the hospital, deliver bad news and good news, and decide when more tests are necessary or the services of a specialist are required. She may even make house calls. In cases of child abuse or sexual abuse, she may have to deal with social workers or other government agents. The result of having to deal with such an enormous range of problems is that the doctor must remain intellectually vigorous, open-minded, and flexible enough to deal with various situations that arise. Insofar as a job imposes diverse and complicated demands on an employee, the implication is that she is more likely to remain intellectually flexible. Research indicates that men and women react to complex environments in the same way (Miller et al., 1979).

By contrast, a person who works in a relatively static environment and does the same task over and over again is likely to progress in the opposite direction. An assembly-line worker must deal with the monotony of repeating the same task over and over again. There is little room for any kind of independent thought or judgment — indeed, the worker who tries to act on his or her own is likely to cause problems and get in trouble. He or she is likely to be reinforced for following orders, doing the job, and not rocking the boat. In such circumstances, there is little support for an intellectual orientation, and such an environment will tend to encourage conformist values and behaviors.

There is some evidence that people generalize from their work to other aspects of their lives, not only in their psychological functioning but in their leisure activities. Those who have jobs that require intellectual flexibility are likely to prefer more intellectual pursuits outside work (for example, reading, attending plays). This finding applies equally to men and women (Miller and Kohn, 1983).

This spillover from work to nonwork areas of life has been confirmed by a study conducted by Crouter (1984a), who investigated blue-collar workers at a factory where participatory management strategies were used. At this factory, workers were divided into teams which managed the manufacturing process — they decided who was to do what and when. Crouter found that these employees carried over some of their work-related characteristics to their interactions at home. They were more willing to use a democratic approach to resolving conflicts at home. They had better listening and communication skills, and they were more willing to tolerate give-and-take in exchanges with their families. There was also some negative spillover. Workers were often fatigued, especially supervisors who constantly worried about what was happening at work and received many phone calls at home about work problems. Crouter (1984b) has also found spillover from family to work. Women with young children are most likely to report high levels of spillover, in contrast to mothers of older children and to fathers regardless of their position in the family life cycle.

CAREER CHANGES AND STRESSES

Career changes in midlife are becoming increasingly common. There are many reasons for such changes. Technological innovation, for example, results in career shifts, as workers move from jobs rendered obsolete by automation or new techniques or into more attractive jobs created by the new technology. Look at the "help wanted" section of a newspaper and ask yourself how many of the listings would have been there twenty-five years ago, or fifty years ago. New jobs are being created at an increasingly rapid rate; many former jobs are being drastically transformed due to technological change. In fact, the days of a single career in life are virtually gone (Sarason, 1977).

A recent advertisement by IBM illustrates the types of job changes one might experience in one's work life with today's rapidly changing technology (*The New*

York Times, May 17, 1985, p. 15). In 1964 Wayne Hazelwood joined IBM as a typewriter assembler. He was well qualified and good at his job, but IBM made changes in the way they manufactured typewriters. The job Wayne had been performing was no longer necessary. So, in 1975, Wayne was selected to take an intensive training program in typewriter inspection. Wayne became a Selectric typewriter quality inspector. He did well, but in time new developments in typewriter technology required the learning of new skills. In 1980 Wayne took a training course in manufacturing instruction and began using his sixteen years of experience in IBM's production line. In 1985 Wayne is in his fourth career at IBM as a member of the electronic card assembly technical staff. Retraining and learning new job skills have become critical aspects of how companies and employees adapt to a changing world.

People are spending longer periods than ever before in the labor market. In 1900, when the average worker spent only twenty-one years in the labor force, career changes were much less common. By 1980, the average working life had grown to thirty-seven years. A person could begin a new career as late as age forty-five and still put in the twenty years required to earn a retirement pension. The longer period of work also increases the chances that a person's job will change significantly enough that he or she may be motivated to try something new. We can expect it to become increasingly difficult to find people who have kept the same job throughout their lifetimes.

In discussing some megatrends forecasted to occur in our society in the next two decades, Naisbitt (1984) suggests that we are rapidly moving from an industrial to an information society and this is affecting the types of jobs available and the types of job-related skills required. More jobs are concerned with providing and using information (for example, teachers, clerks, lawyers, technicians) than with directly producing goods. Almost all professions deal primarily with use of information. Two factors affecting an information society are the rate at which the volume of information is increasing and the rapidity with which information can be accessed. For example, the volume of scientific and technical information is now doubling every five years. Due to technological advances, there can be almost instantaneous transmission of information; the sender and receiver of information are brought much closer together. In such an information society, the knowledge and skills one uses in his or her profession (physician, engineer, and so on) changes at a very rapid rate. The term "half-life" of scientific information has been coined to describe the time it takes for 50 percent of one's professional knowledge to become invalid or obsolete (Dubin, 1972). For computer scientists, the half-life is only two or three years; among engineers, it is five or six years (Cross, 1981).

An increasing number of professional organizations will grant continuing certification only when the individual proves that he or she has kept up with current developments in the field. In California, certified public accountants are required to complete 80 hours of continuing education every two years to retain their certification. Physicians specializing in family practice must prove their competence by being recertified every six years. They must take a written exam to show that they are familiar with contemporary practices in all the basic areas of family practice, including internal medicine, surgery, obstetrics, pediatrics, psychiatry, neurology, and community medicine (Cross, 1981).

People's responses to rapid change impacting their lives vary. For those who don't keep up with changes in their professions, there is the threat of obsolescence. Knowledge obsolescence has been defined as when the individual uses theories, concepts, or techniques that are less effective in solving problems than others currently available in the field of specialization (Dubin, 1972). Knowledge obsolescence does not reflect an age-related *loss* of ability; rather, it reflects individuals not continuing to learn and update themselves as new knowledge and techniques become available. Levels of obsolescence are higher in fields that change rapidly. It is estimated that by the mid-1980s 75 percent of all occupations will involve use of knowledge of computers in some way (Naisbitt, 1984); thus some level of computer literacy is required of most workers today. As previously illustrated by the discussion of Wayne Hazelwood, both industry and employee must bear responsibility for the necessary retraining and updating required in a rapidly changing work world.

Naisbitt (1984) and others (Zuboff, 1982; Turkle, 1984) have suggested other types of concerns regarding rapid technological change as it relates to the workplace. Greater concern with personalization and a sense of control may result from what is perceived as an increasingly impersonal high technology. For example, the computer terminal has become some employees' primary focus of interaction; employees report feeling isolated in an impersonal work situation. In a Volvo plant in Sweden a computer system was installed to monitor assembly operations. A feedback device was programmed to flash a red light signaling a quality control problem. The workers protested against the device, insisting that the supervisory function be returned to a foreperson. They preferred to answer to a human being with whom they could negotiate, argue, and explain rather than to a computer whose only means of "communication" was unidirectional. There may also be a growing concern with values and ethics as a result of being confronted with high-tech choices never before experienced. For example, the arbitrariness of the meaning of death with high-tech medicine has resulted in some medical schools employing professors of philosophy and theology on their faculties to gain a broader perspective of life–death decision-making.

Americans dislike "boring" jobs; they believe work should be stimulating, provocative, and challenging (Lowther, 1977; Howard and Wilson, 1982). We may switch careers late in life simply because a job that was challenging at first has lost its allure. Most tasks are interesting the first time, but they may be less interesting the third time, or the tenth time. Once one has mastered a job, one may want to look elsewhere for challenges (Kohn and Schooler, 1983). From the standpoint of the company, the effectiveness of an employee may decrease, in spite of obvious competence, because motivation decreases (Cherniss, 1980; Paine, 1982).

A work-related problem of increasing concern is that known as "burnout." The topic began to gain attention in the mid-1970s, with a book by Freudenberger (1974). As a clinician, Freudenberger reported a number of case studies of burn-

Most of the research on the midlife transition has ignored the blue-collar worker, whose dialectical crises may be quite different from those of white-collar professionals.

out, particularly in the human service professions; his focus was on the psychodynamics of the problem. He defined burnout as a state of physical and emotional depletion resulting from conditions of work (Freudenberger and Richelson, 1980). Burnout is a process that occurs when workers perceive a discrepancy between their work input and the output they had expected from work. For example, a mental health counselor may perceive herself to be a caring, committed professional willing to spend long hours and become personally invested in the progress of her clients; however, over time she may become "burned out" with her profession due to excessive client loads, lack of progress by her clients, and insensitivity of the bureaucracy. There are wide individual differences in the symptoms associated with burnout; these include feelings of helplessness and hopelessness, physical and psychological depletion, sense of unending stress, development of a negative self-concept, and the perception of little or no "payoff" in terms of job outcomes and achievements.

Current research suggests that burnout should be conceptualized and studied as a multidimensional problem involving personal characteristics of the individual, situational factors contributing to burnout, and the organizational and cultural contexts within which burnout occurs (Edelwich and Brodsky, 1980; Pines and Aronson, 1981; Paine, 1982; Farber, 1983). A number of personal characteristics associated with an individual's being particularly vulnerable to burnout have been identified; these include being too idealistic, setting unrealistic goals for self and clients, over identifying with others, high need for self-affirmation, and high work orientation. A number of characteristics of the work environment associated with burnout have also been identified. These work environments often involve excessive workloads, not only in terms of number of hours of work expected, but also in terms of the complexity of the work and frequent changes in work demands, sometimes associated with rapid advances in technology. The worker's role may be ambiguous, lacking clarity in terms of the worker's rights, responsibilities, status, and the goals the worker is to strive toward in the job; as a result, the worker may experience a sense of loss of control and autonomy on the job. There may also be insufficient resources to accomplish the job and administrative indifference or interference. These stressful and unpleasant work environments may be partially a result of changes occurring at the societal level. For example, the increased specialization of many jobs results in a fragmentation of work. The worker is involved with only one small segment of producing the total product, or in providing services to the client; there may result a loss of sense of accomplishment and a loss of autonomy. Likewise, the increase in bureaucracy and the number of layers of organizational administration may lead to a reduction in communication among the various layers of administration and a sense of depersonalization.

Women and Careers

Although a number of the studies we have been citing were based on research with male subjects, women experience many of the same developmental tasks. However, the world of work has been changing dramatically for women. For one thing, women represent a much larger proportion of the work force today than they did formerly. In 1953, only one woman in three worked outside the home. In 1985, women became the single largest group in the U.S. labor force, surpassing the number of white males, traditionally the largest work force group. Women now comprise approximately 45 percent of the total work force (U.S. Bureau of the Census, 1984a). While in 1940 the majority of women in the work force were single, today the majority of women are married and many have children. Women have not achieved equality in the workplace, however. There is a substantial difference between the sexes in the kinds of jobs they take and the pay they receive for them.

As you can see in Figure 3–2, women are disproportionately represented in certain kinds of occupations. Although women are represented in all occupational groups, they remain concentrated in clerical and service jobs. Almost two-thirds work in either technical/clerical or service-related occupations. Occupational segregation results in domination of certain sectors of the labor force by men and others by women, out of proportion to their overall participation in the work force. Many women hold "pink-collar" jobs, which are low-paying white-collar jobs held predominately by women. In 1980, one-fourth of all women in the labor force were in just five job categories — secretary, household worker, bookkeeper/billing clerk, elementary/secondary school teacher, and waitress. Only 15 percent of women work in blue-collar jobs, primarily in the lower-paying operative jobs (as assemblers, inspectors, or machinery operators, for example), rather than the more lucrative craft jobs.

Employers have traditionally assumed that the typical female employee is not interested in a career, that she will soon marry and begin to have children, which

FIGURE 3–2.

Occupational distribution of employed men and women in each job category, 1980. Data include persons sixteen years of age and older.

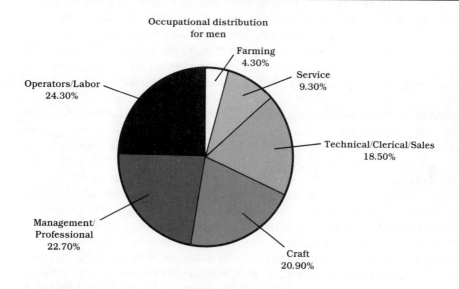

Occupational distribution
for men

Farming
4.30%

Service
9.30%

Operators/Labor
24.30%

Technical/Clerical/Sales
18.50%

Management/
Professional
22.70%

Craft
20.90%

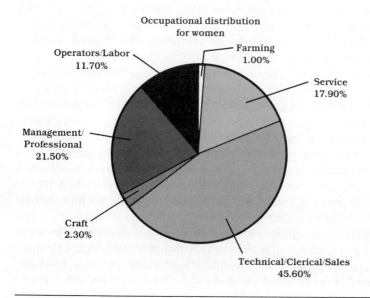

Occupational distribution
for women

Operators/Labor
11.70%

Farming
1.00%

Service
17.90%

Management/
Professional
21.50%

Craft
2.30%

Technical/Clerical/Sales
45.60%

Source: From U.S. Bureau of the Census, 1983b.

will force her to leave the work force and care for them. This may be one of the reasons that many traditionally "female" jobs have no career track and provide few opportunities for promotion. Service work is a good example; few service workers ever make it to even the lowest rung of the management ladder (Fox and Hesse-Biber, 1984). But the assumption that women will leave work to raise a family is inaccurate. Most female workers are not looking for Mr. Right; they are already married. Many have childrearing responsibilities in addition to their jobs (U.S. Bureau of the Census, 1984a). In 1984, over 50 percent of all women with children under age six were in the labor force; among those with children between six and seventeen, the figure was over 65 percent (U.S. Bureau of the Census, 1984a).

Attitudes about working while being a parent have changed considerably. In 1943, 20 percent of a group of female undergraduates said they wanted to work full time with a minimum interruption for childbearing; in 1980, the percentage in a similar group had risen to 53 percent (Mirra Komarovsky, *The New York Times* Op. Ed. Page, January 23, 1981; cf. Catalyst Fact Sheet, October 1983).

Why do women work? A recent poll by Roper Organization (cf. Catalyst Fact Sheet, October 1983) asked "Are you working primarily to support yourself, to support your family, to bring in extra money, or for something interesting to do?" Economic necessity was found to be the primary motive for women working. Forty-three percent reported working primarily to supplement the family income. Twenty-seven percent worked to support themselves, 19 percent to support their families, and 14 percent for something interesting to do. Women who work full-time year-round contribute 40 percent of total family income.

Despite the fact that most women work primarily because they or their families need the income, women continue to receive low pay in comparison to men. Although there are far more women in the workplace, their relative earnings have changed little over the last thirty years. In 1955, women earned 63.9 percent of what men earned; in 1980, the figure was only 60.2 percent. The Rand Corporation, a research group, predicted in a recent study that women's wages would be 74 percent of those for men by the year 2000 (Serrin, 1984). Level of education does not seem to reduce the inequity in earnings, although there is greater comparability in pay within the professions than in the sales and service sectors. In 1983, women with four or more years of college earned only 63 percent of what men with the same level of education earned (Catalyst Fact Sheet, October 1983). Even within the same job category, there are gender differences in pay. In 1983, female elementary school teachers earned 87 percent as much as male teachers; female lawyers 88 percent as much as their male counterparts (Serrin, 1984).

Women have been moving into fields more traditionally dominated by men. Psychologists who have studied such women report that they often are strongly influenced by others. Support and encouragement from parents, teachers, friends, and boyfriends/husbands are generally quite important factors, more so than for men in comparable occupations (Auster and Auster, 1981). A woman's mother appears to be the most influential model. Typically, the mother, like her daughter, is a high achiever. She also tends to reward independent actions and achievement strivings in her daughter, from birth on. And she usually has a loving husband who is proud of her accomplishments; the daughter realizes that competition and achievement do not mean that she will be less attractive to men. The daughter sees that relationships between two self-actualizing people can be very satisfying indeed.

As a result of these and other factors, a number of fields that were formerly almost exclusively male now include sizable numbers of females. In 1950, only 15 percent of all professionals were women, by 1983 the figure had risen to 40 percent (U.S. Bureau of the Census, 1984a). Between 1950 and 1983, the number of female lawyers and judges rose from 4 percent to 15 percent, and half of all lawyers graduating in 1983 were women. Nevertheless, the majority of women still hold low-paying, traditionally "female" jobs (U.S. Bureau of the Census, 1984a).

Even those women who do manage to get high-status jobs with good pay may face more problems than men in comparable positions. In 1982, nearly half of the women over age 52 who held senior management positions had begun their careers in clerical positions. Among younger female managers, only 23 percent started in clerical positions, the majority having started in entry-level management positions. In many cases then, the two groups will have taken different career paths. As a result, the older women may be of limited value as role models for the younger women (Catalyst Fact Sheet, October 1983).

Awareness among employers of the implications of the growing number of women in management, the professions, and the work force in general seems to be increasing, but employers are slow to implement changes in the workplace. When Fortune 1300 corporations were asked if they were concerned about two-career family problems because they could affect recruiting, employee morale, productivity, and the corporate profits, 76 percent said they were (Catalyst Fact Sheet, October 1983). However, only 37 percent of the companies surveyed had instituted policies such as flexible work hours. Forty percent thought that certain positions in their firm could not be attained by women who combined parenting with a career; only 27 percent felt the same was true for men. Only 40 percent of the employed women in the United States have some form of paid maternity leave (American Psychological Association Monitor, August 1983), and less than 1 percent of American employers provided any child-care assistance for employees in 1981 (Catalyst Fact Sheet, October 1983).

DUAL-EARNER MARRIAGES

Massed entry of women into the workplace has resulted in a new phenomenon in American society called the "dual-earner marriage," which is defined as a marriage in which the husband works full time and the wife works twenty or more hours per week (Pleck and Staines, 1982). In some dual-earner marriages, both couples have full-time careers. Most research on dual-career couples has focused on couples in academia or the professions. In one such study of highly educated British couples, three patterns emerged (Rapoport and Rapoport, 1971, 1980). These patterns are probably characteristic of dual-earner couples as well. In all patterns, the men worked continuously. The "conventional" pattern involved a woman who worked until she married or had children and then dropped her career to concentrate on being a homemaker. Throughout most of the century, this was the most common pattern. The "interrupted" pattern was one in which the wife interrupted her career while her children were young but intended to return eventually. This is the most common pattern today. In the "continuous" pattern, the wife pursued her career with little or no disruption for childrearing. About a third of women in the study, all of whom had college degrees, followed the continuous pattern, although only one of twenty experienced no interruption at all of her career (Rapoport and Rapoport, 1971, 1980). Evidence suggests that the continuous pattern is becoming increasingly prevalent (Favia and Genovese, 1983).

STRAINS AND GAINS

Dual-earner couples typically experience certain strains and satisfactions that are less common in the conventional family. One large-scale study of dual-earner marriages found that a third experienced moderate to severe conflicts in trying to meet both work and family responsibilities (Pleck and Staines, 1982). Conflicts were more severe when there were greater job demands (such as longer work hours) and when there were scheduling conflicts between home and family responsibilities. Men with working and with nonworking wives reported similar levels of work–family conflict. The burden apparently falls mostly on the women, who reported moderate to severe conflicts between work and family.

In the British study (Rapoport and Rapoport, 1980), four major sources of strain and conflict were identified. The first is work overload. Housework, child care, social arrangements, and the other duties the nonworking wife usually handles still require handling by someone. A growing body of evidence suggests that, especially in two-earner families, domestic tasks are being shared more equally (Maret and Finlay, 1984). Child care is especially likely to be shared (Bird, Bird, and Scruggs, 1984). Even though working wives have fewer domestic responsibilities than nonworking wives, the major responsibility for such duties often falls to the wife.

What determines the extent to which household and childbearing responsibilities are shared by a couple? Several studies suggest that the wife's relative share of the family income is influential (Maret and Finlay, 1984; Bird, Bird, and Scruggs, 1984). Women who earn more are more likely to share domestic responsibilities. They may not necessarily share them with their husbands, however; some studies suggest that husbands assume some responsibilities but that others are delegated to hired household help paid for with the additional income. There is some evidence that husbands who have egalitarian views on sharing household tasks are more likely to assume these tasks themselves (Bird, Bird, and Scruggs, 1984).

The second and third strains on the dual-career marriage have to do with *society's reaction* to mothers who work, and with the couple's own reactions to the same thing. Societal sanctions today may even be on the side of the working wife, but many people still look with disapproval at a woman who pursues a full-time career while her children are young. Indeed, she herself may have *role conflict* between her roles of mother and career woman (Huston-Stein and Higgins-Trenk, 1978). Her husband, in addition, may have his views on the matter, which may or may not coincide with her own.

A fourth major strain felt by dual-career couples has been called *social network dilemmas.* In a couple's social network are their relatives, friends, business associates, and other people with whom they commonly come in contact. A dual-career couple, because of its work overload, has less time for these people in general, which is one of the problems. In addition, the wife's professional acquaintances must often be entertained, like the husband's. Entertaining one's friends, relatives, and business associates can be very time-consuming, and there isn't that much time to be consumed in many dual-earner families.

If these are some of the costs of the dual-earner marriage, what are the gains? As we mentioned, the extra income is one source of satisfaction. The standard of living of dual-earner families is almost without exception higher than that of comparable conventional families (Rapoport and Rapoport, 1971, 1980). Dual-earner families are better equipped financially to deal with emergencies; they can provide a better education for their children, and they are in better shape for eventual retirement. However, for college-educated dual-earner couples, the most important benefit is self-actualization of the wife. Talented individuals (who happen to be women) are creating things, providing services, achieving recognition — in short, they are fully functioning people. Their husbands, with few exceptions, take great pride in their wives' accomplishments, and they see other benefits for themselves as well. Their wives, they perceive, are more vital, more interesting, with more self-esteem and greater competence as a helpmate in life.

CAREER DIFFICULTIES

The problems and benefits of the two-earner family may be exaggerated in the two-career family. For one thing, having two careers in one family is likely to affect the careers themselves. Obviously women who interrupt their careers while their children are young will have some difficulty when they return to their former jobs. They will have to reestablish themselves, perhaps relearn certain skills, and they will find themselves competing for junior positions with others much younger than they (McDowell, 1982; Favia and Genovese, 1983).

Career decisions are generally much more difficult with two careers to consider. One spouse may be offered a good job or a significant promotion in another city, but the move might mean the loss of job or a demotion for the marriage partner. Typically the husband's career is given a somewhat higher priority, and the wife's career is the one that suffers in a conflict (Favia and Genovese, 1983). One reason for this is the traditional attitude toward the male's career as the one that supports the family; the female's is seen as supplemental. Another derives from the tendency of women to marry men who are older than they, which usually means that the husband's career will be more developed (higher income, more status) than the wife's; a decision in favor of the husband's career, therefore, will frequently maximize family income and lifestyle but may handicap the woman's own career development.

Women with Ph.D. degrees typically progress less rapidly in academic careers than men with comparable qualifications (Stoll, 1974; Helmreich et al., 1980). Discrimination may often be a factor in this state of affairs, but another important factor is the geographic constraints placed on a woman's career in a two-career family. Almost all married women in academia have husbands who are also pursuing professional careers, whereas fewer married men in academia have professional wives (Favia and Genovese, 1983). As a result, women with Ph.D. degrees are concentrated in the large urban areas, where there are more colleges and universities in which to work. When they move to a new job, more often than in the case of men it involves no change in geographic location and no change in status (Marwell, Rosenfeld, and Spilerman, 1979). Many professionals move to new jobs in new locations because they have received better offers; moving is part of career advancement. Women, constrained by the two-career family, make such moves less often. If the wife's career is made subordinate to the husband's, there are further constraints on moves that might advance her career.

One response to the geographic constraints of a dual-career marriage is to separate — to live apart (Greenberg, 1980; Time, 1982). More and more professional couples are doing this. The strains of separation, of course, are in many cases equal to or greater than the strains of geographical constraint. Another solution for dual-career couples in the same line of work is to share a job. Two people with Ph.D. degrees might share one full-time position in an academic department. In similar fashion, many dual-career families work together as a team, sharing their professional responsibilities as they do their personal responsibilities. One thinks of prominent examples: Marie Curie and her husband, Pierre, who together won a Nobel Prize for the study of radioactive materials; Irene Joliot-Curie, Marie's daughter, who shared a later Nobel Prize in chemistry with her husband, Frederic; Will and Ariel Durant, who together wrote one of the most popular histories of the world; Franklin and Eleanor Roosevelt, perhaps the most effective political team of our century. In psychology, the American Psychological Association has awarded its most prestigious award, for distinguished scientific contributions, to a husband–wife team: D. Jameson and L. M. Hurvick.

Ethnic Minorities and Careers

Ethnic minorities appear to suffer many of the career disadvantages documented for women in the previous section. In 1983, blacks comprised 9 percent of the U.S. work force; hispanics comprised 5 percent. Examination of the occupational distribution for blacks, compared with that for men and women (shown in Figure 3–2), indicates that blacks are particularly underrepresented in the managerial/

professional sector. Only 14 percent of blacks in the work force were in managerial or professional jobs in 1980 (U.S. Bureau of the Census, 1983b). There has been some progress, however, since only 9 percent of all blacks in the labor force in 1970 were in managerial/professional roles. Almost three-quarters of all blacks in the labor force in 1980 were in three job sectors: technical/clerical/sales (25 percent), service (23 percent), and operators/labor (26 percent). Relatively few blacks are in crafts (9 percent).

The Older Worker and Retirement

The concept of retirement is fairly new in human history. Until quite recently very few workers lived to old age, so the concept had little meaning or usefulness. In the late nineteenth century, Chancellor Otto von Bismarck of Germany established a state pension for people over sixty-five, the first institutional support for retirement. In the United States, the Social Security Act of 1935 established the age of sixty-five as the "time to retire." Before Social Security, most men over sixty-five continued to work — 68 percent of them, for example, in 1890 (U.S. Bureau of the Census, 1976b). Even after Social Security, working after the age of sixty-five was common.

Today we are again seeing significant changes in the concept of retirement. On the one hand, we see increasing pressures and increasing support for early retirement — before the age of sixty-five. On the other hand, government and business policies of "mandatory" retirement at sixty-five have come under fire; in fact, since the passage of the Age Discrimination in Employment Act in 1978, for most workers, "mandatory" retirement has been limited to age seventy under federal law and prohibited altogether in some states (e.g., California and Maine).

In conjunction with changes in attitudes about retirement, shifts in characteristics of the American population have raised several new issues. The proportion of people over sixty-five is increasing. Currently, six workers support one retiree, but by the end of this century, this ratio will have dropped to four workers per retiree; by 2030, the ratio will be three to one. Social Security and other pension systems will become a significant burden on younger workers, and intergenerational conflict may become severe.

Most experts expected the number of workers remaining in the labor force past age sixty-five to increase when the mandatory retirement age was raised to seventy. As you can see in Table 3–2, however, more men retired before age seventy in 1983 than in 1970. Labor force participation by women over sixty dropped during the same period, even though it increased sharply among younger women (Atchley, 1984). Thus it appears that we can expect the burden on the younger generation to continue. People tend to retire as soon as they have enough money to do so. Current discussions about the solvency of the Social Security system portend what may well be a major economic crisis by the year 2000.

TABLE 3–2.

Labor force participation rates, by age and sex: United States, 1970 and 1983.

Age	Male		Female	
	1970	1983	1970	1983
40–44	94.6%	95.0%	52.1%	68.3%
45–49	93.5	93.5	53.0	65.3
50–54	91.4	88.7	52.0	58.3
55–59	86.8	81.0	47.4	48.0
60–64	73.0	56.8	36.1	33.6
65–69	39.0	25.5	17.2	13.9
70+	18.2	12.3	8.1	4.5

Sources: U.S. Department of Labor, 1983; U.S. Bureau of the Census, 1973.

THE OLDER WORKER

In terms of occupations, older workers are heavily employed as managers and administrators, professional and technical workers, service workers and farmers; they have low representation in crafts, sales, clerical, and operatives. Older workers are more highly represented among the self-employed, which permits part-time work and considerable flexibility in scheduling.

Older workers are often victims of stereotyping; they may suffer discrimination based solely on their age even when their competence and qualifications are comparable to those of younger workers (Doering, Rhodes and Schuster, 1983). In analyses of the literature on the performance of older workers, Waldman and Avolio (1984) distinguished between objective measures of job performance and supervisory ratings of performance. Objective measures of job performance (i.e., productivity) showed no decreases or relatively minor decreases in performance with age. However, supervisors rated older workers somewhat lower than younger workers. Further analysis indicated that supervisory ratings were particularly likely to be lower for older workers in nonprofessional jobs.

Stereotypes are often inaccurate. In a review of over 150 studies related to aging and work, Doering, Rhodes, and Schuster (1983) came to the following conclusions:

1. The attitudes and work behavior of older workers (age fifty-five and older) are generally consistent with effective organizational functioning.
2. Job satisfaction is higher among older workers than in other age groups.
3. Older workers are more loyal and less likely to leave their current employer.
4. Healthy older workers have lower rates of absenteeism compared to the young. Unhealthy older workers, however, may have higher rates of absenteeism.

5. Older workers are less likely to be injured on the job. Those who are injured, however, take longer to recover and are more likely to be disabled than younger workers.
6. Older workers do continue to learn and can profit from retraining opportunities.

Several recent studies indicate little or no age-related declines in job performance for older workers in a number of job categories (Rhodes, 1983; Stagner, 1985). Age-related declines in job performance were most likely to occur in jobs which were physically demanding or that were highly speeded. However, due to years of experience older workers are sometimes able to compensate for declines in speed of response and remain as productive as younger workers. Salthouse (1984) examined younger and older experienced typists and found that although the older experienced typists were somewhat slower in speed of response, they were able to process at each glance larger chunks of the information to be typed and thus were able to compensate for any behavioral slowing. The significance of experience, rather than age, was also shown in research examining the performance of older workers in a garment factory. Giniger, Dispenzieri, and Eisenberg (1983) examined the performance of older sewing machine operators on a job involving speed and the performance of quality control examiners on a job involving primarily skill. For the machine operators neither age nor experience was significantly related to performance; there also were no age differences in absenteeism, accident rate, or job turnover. In the case of the examiners, age was not significantly related to performance, but level of experience was directly related to performance.

Despite findings such as these that indicate that older workers function well in their jobs, mature workers, although relatively unlikely to lose their jobs, may have trouble finding work if they are unemployed. Note that the U.S. Department of Labor defines a "mature" worker as any employee age forty or over. One study found that older workers tend to be laid off first in plant closings, mass layoffs, and company reorganizations, even when experience, technical competence, and education were held constant (Parnes and King, 1977; Morrison, 1983). The Age Discrimination in Employment Act of 1978 notwithstanding, unemployed mature workers still face age discrimination. Between 1979 and 1983, the number of age discrimination complaints increased over 300 percent. Even this high figure probably underrepresents the actual frequency of age discrimination; many workers are unaware of the protections offered by the law or are reluctant to become involved in legal tangles. Parnes and King (1977) found that unemployed middle-aged workers eventually did find new jobs, but they were at lower salaries and occupational levels. The longer the period of unemployment, the greater the drop in occupational level and earnings.

There is no question, however, that aging does affect the ability of some people to do some jobs (Doering, Rhodes, and Schuster, 1983). How can an employer ensure that the people he or she hires can manage all their responsibilities without discriminating against the aged? In one study, an Industrial Health

Counseling Service used a system developed by Kaye (1973) to diagnose workers' capacities in seven functional areas: general physique, upper extremities, lower extremities, hearing, eyesight, intelligence, and personality. Job demands were also rated, using the same criteria. Then individuals were matched to jobs according to their functional profiles. As a result of this procedure, many persons over forty years of age were placed in jobs (Quirk and Skinner, 1973).

THE DECISION TO RETIRE

The meaning of retirement has gradually changed over the last few decades (Atchley, 1984). In the 1950s, retirement was considered justified only if a person was physically unable to work (Ash, 1966). Today, retirement has come to embody the notion that, by virtue of their long-term contribution to the growth and prosperity of society, people earn the right to a share of the nation's prosperity in their later years without having to hold a job.

The meaning of retirement, however, becomes more complicated if subjective as well as objective measures of retirement are considered. Atchley (1984) proposed a three part definition of retirement that incorporates receiving retirement benefits, decreased time in paid work, and labeling one's self as retired. Jackson and Gibson (1985) argue that the subjective meaning of retirement for the black elderly is particularly complicated by the fact that many blacks may be receiving no retirement benefits and that decreases in time spent in work may not be that clear-cut, in view of their discontinuous worklife patterns and need to work in old age. Over one-quarter of a national sample of black elderly defined themselves as "not retired," although not working or working less than twenty hours per week (see Box for further discussion of the meaning of retirement for black elderly).

What factors predict the decision to retire? For all men, the two major factors predicting retirement have been health status and adequacy of income in retirement (George, Fillenbaum, and Palmore, 1984). Eligibility for Social Security benefits has been found to be a significant predictor of the decision to retire. These same two predictors have also been identified in studies involving unmarried women. But most women in the work force today are married. Recent studies are beginning to suggest that for married women, the timing of retirement is often a collaborative decision by the couple and that the characteristics of the spouse influence the woman's decision to retire (Gratton and Haug, 1983). A couple will often time their retirements to coincide. Since the woman has traditionally been somewhat younger, she often retires at an earlier age than the husband, often with lower retirement benefits. Thus, for current cohorts of older workers, the adequacy of the husband's pension plan is likely to be a more important determinant of retirement decisions than the woman's retirement benefits (O'Rand and Henretta, 1982). As the worklives and incomes of men and women become more comparable, the factors influencing the couple's retirement decision may also change.

In many cases, retirement is not entirely voluntary. There appear to be two general but quite distinct classes of early retirees (Beck, 1982). The first group is characterized as in poor health, having low income, and possibly unemployed. The second group are in good health, have above average incomes, and, more important, have private pension plans. As you might expect, the second group tend to be in high-status jobs and it is their access to private pension plans that is the strongest predictor of when they retire. However, the first group has been of greater concern to those studying retirement patterns. In the past, the proportion of people retiring for health reasons is estimated to have been as high as 50 percent (Maddox, 1968). The proportion of workers retiring for health reasons is likely to decrease in the future because of improving health care. Today, 9.4 percent of all men between the ages of forty-five and sixty-four are physically unable to work, and another 10.5 percent have physical limitations in the amount or kind of work they can do (Atchley, 1984). Among those under forty-five, only 1.4 percent are physically unable to work. The health limitations of older workers are due in part to premature aging, but job-related injuries are also a problem. You will recall that older workers, although less likely to be injured than the young, are more likely to be disabled when they are injured. Overall, it is difficult to assess the significance of health problems as they relate to retirement. It is likely that people sometimes cite health as the reason for retirement because they see it as more socially acceptable than the simple desire to retire.

Employers may also exert pressure on employees to retire. Such pressure may be applied in several different ways. Sometimes an employer will simply state outright that it's time for a worker to leave. Unattractive job transfers or job reclassifications that significantly change the working conditions may also be used. As yet, there is no way to estimate what proportion of older workers experience such pressures. Relatively few complaints about age discrimination concern retirement. Straightforwardly asking retirees if they retired against their will probably yields underestimates of the number who would like to have continued working, because people do not enjoy describing major career decisions as being out of their control. Even so, various studies have found that between 37 and 50 percent are willing to decide to retire early rather than take an unsatisfactory job or undergo a humiliating job search (Atchley, 1984).

Recently, there have been a number of instances in which workers were offered incentives to retire as early as age fifty-five (Durbin, Gross, and Borgatta, 1984). The older worker may be offered a financial bonus if he or she decides to retire early; or the worker may be allowed to retire early without a reduction in benefits. These workers are typically in very good health. So what factors determine who accepts incentives to retire early and who remains on the job? One study of faculty at a major university found that dissatisfaction with the work setting was associated with electing early retirement. In addition, expectations of adequate income in retirement were related to accepting early retirement options. As might be expected, the amount of time spent considering the retirement option was also positively related to early retirement.

As we mentioned earlier, most workers retire as soon as it is financially feasible (Bixby, 1976; Atchley, 1984). In fact, among more recent retirees, the desire to retire is a more important factor than poor health. Together, poor health and the desire to retire create a situation in which most people retire shortly after the minimum age (Atchley, 1982b). The minimum age of retirement has a much more direct effect on the retired proportion of the population than do mandatory retirement policies. This is illustrated by the fact that the "typical" age of retirement under Social Security quickly went from sixty-five to sixty-three as soon as benefits became available to men at age sixty-two rather than sixty-five — even though early retirement means a reduction in benefits (Atchley, 1984). Early retirement may also be promoted by employer policies that allow employees to generate entitlement of early retirement. Under such plans, supplemental pension payments are provided to keep pensions at an adequate level until the retired person becomes eligible to collect Social Security. Employers may encourage early retirement to make room for the promotion of younger workers, to deal with technological change, or in reaction to plant closings and production cutbacks.

In the next few decades, we are likely to see a variety of highly ingenious retirement plans designed to meet the needs of employers and employees alike (McCluskey and Borgatta, 1981). There may be gradual phase-out plans, in which workers gradually reduce the number of hours they work beginning at age sixty or sixty-five. Workers might be able to devise their own schedules. We may see more job sharing, with two elderly workers sharing one job. Another possibility that a few industries have tried already involves "lateral" promotions in which workers are shifted to positions in the company that can benefit from their experience. The elderly manager might move gradually from an executive to a consulting role in the company.

REACTIONS TO RETIREMENT

One of the many myths of old age is that work is central to an individual's self-concept and that retirement is a sign of declining self-worth. In fact, the average American worker shows very little involvement with his or her work. Most workers are quite happy to quit working; the shock they experience is primarily a severe drop in income and fringe benefits such as company health insurance. Programs that replace the "satisfactions of employment" with "activities that have the form and appearance of productive work" are almost always unsuccessful — unless of course the "workers" are paid (Maddox, 1968). When asked of their "major satisfactions" from work, most people reply "money" (Shanas, 1972; Atchley, 1984).

Although most of us are accustomed to thinking of retirement as an event — one abruptly stops going to work at about the time of one's sixty-fifth birthday — studies suggest that it is actually a *process* involving several phases. These phases are not a sequence of events that everyone goes through, nor are they necessarily associated with any particular chronological age or period of time. Rather, they involve a series of adjustments to the circumstances resulting from retirement. Atchley (1982b, 1934) identified five stages. The *honeymoon period* begins immediately after retirement. It is a euphoric period during which the person tries to do all the things he or she never had time to do before. The honeymoon is based in part on preretirement fantasies concerning what retirement should be like. It may involve extensive traveling. A honeymoon period is more common among those who retire voluntarily and have plenty of money.

Following the active honeymoon period there may be a period of *rest and relaxation*, during which the retired person decides to take it easy. Atchley found that activity levels dropped after retirement but rose to preretirement levels again three years after retirement. There may also be a period of *disenchantment* if retirement expectations do not work out as planned or if plans are disrupted by the illness or death of a spouse. In some cases, this period may involve serious depression. Although the proportion of persons who experience disenchantment is not known, it is thought to be relatively small.

The next phase is called *reorientation*. During this phase, the person takes stock of the retirement situation and explores new avenues of involvement. The goal of this period is to develop a realistic set of choices for providing structure and routine to retirement. The final phase is the development of a stable and satisfying routine in retirement.

Overall, it appears that the majority of people are satisfied with retirement. In a study of differences in the adjustment of white-collar and blue-collar workers, Heidbreder (1972) found that problems were concentrated among those who had low income, poor health, and little education. Adjustment was found to be greatly enhanced by sufficient income, the ability to give up one's job gracefully, and good health.

Atchley (1975a) suggests that adjustment to retirement depends largely on one's hierarchy of personal goals. If one's job is not in a high position in one's hierarchy of priorities, no serious change in personal goals will be occasioned by retirement. If a job is high on one's list of priorities, one may very well attempt to find another job. If a substitute job cannot be found, one's hierarchy of personal goals must be reorganized. This reorganization may be easy if one is involved in a variety of activities, but if one has had few activities other than a job, one must seek alternative roles. If alternative roles are not available, the individual may withdraw from active involvement in life.

Although most retirees do not assess their self-worth in terms of their jobs, a few do. Most are high-salaried executives and professionals with high-status jobs that are intrinsically interesting and involving. When these workers approach the age of sixty-five, they are often reluctant to retire (Streib and Schneider, 1971) and, in fact, are less likely to do so. This is true even though these people typically have less economic need to keep working and have the education and the money to enjoy their leisure. It is a bit paradoxical that wealthy candidates for a "leisure class" are instead the "unexpected candidates for a 'working' class characterized by conspicuous occupational involvement."

Another myth about retirement is that the worker, deprived of the activity

Retirement, for most workers, is more a blessing than a shock.

that gives meaning to life, is likely to go into a physiological decline (Ekerdt, Bosse, and LoCastro, 1983). This syndrome is sometimes called *retirement shock*. The research evidence clearly shows that, except for occasional individuals who were strongly attached to their work, workers do not find retirement debilitating at all (Gratton and Haug, 1983). Longitudinal studies find health declines associated with aging but not with retirement per se (Streib and Schneider, 1971; Ekerdt et al., 1983). Nor is there evidence indicating that retirement negatively influences mental health (Nadelson, 1969). Men who had jobs that required working under stress were more likely to report self-perceptions of improved health after retirement (Ekerdt et al., 1983). Think of Grace Clements at her felting task; her job is a risk to health, and retirement is something to which she looks forward. Of course, many people do die soon after retirement (which may have given rise to the myth), but the cause of death is not retirement shock; people over sixty-five, working or not, have a higher death rate than younger adults. In more than a few cases, the cause of death is an illness that began during the work years and forced an early retirement.

Most people's attitudes about retirement are based on their expectations about retirement living (Atchley, 1975a; Glamser, 1976). In particular, individuals who feel that their pensions plus savings are inadequate to support them and their families in the style to which they have grown accustomed are likely to be anxious about retirement. In addition to financial considerations, people worry that they will not see their friends as often and, more generally, that they will have too much free time with nothing to do (McGee, Hall, and Lutes-Dunckley, 1979). Fortunately, the actual experience of retirement is usually more satisfying than one expects (Streib and Schneider, 1971).

In terms of income, it is true that retired people must make do with less. Postretirement incomes are about half of what they were before leaving work, so perceptions of economic deprivation may temporarily increase (Atchley, 1984). Even with this drop in income, however, the typical household of retired persons does not feel financially strapped (McConnel and Deljavan, 1983). Some may move to less expensive housing, but this is generally in the same geographical area. The great majority do not relocate. The groups that do are the widowed, disabled, well educated, and those living in households other than their own.

Most retired persons consider their levels of activity and social adjustment satisfactory as well. Morale remains quite constant during the retirement transition (George and Maddox, 1977; Palmore et al., in press). Retirement does not seem to produce significant changes in life satisfaction or scores on measures of self-esteem either (Streib and Schneider, 1971; Atchley, 1982b). In terms of activity, most people continue to do in retirement the same kinds of things they did when they were working. About a fifth decrease their amount of non-job-related activity; about a third increase it to fill the gap left by retirement. These are relative measures, however, and must be interpreted with caution. A person who was uninvolved before retirement might increase his or her level of activity and still face large amounts of unfilled time.

THE FUTURE OF RETIREMENT

As an expectation on the part of individuals and an institution in our society, retirement is well established. Commitment to a job as an end in itself is declining, so we can expect people to look forward to retirement. Given the growing number of older adults and the resulting strain on Social Security and other retiree benefit systems, however, we can perhaps anticipate a reversal of the trend toward lower minimum retirement age (Atchley, 1984). Note that Public Law 98-21 increased the eligibility age for full Social Security benefits from age 65 to age 67, beginning in the year 2000. Social Security benefits are unlikely to rise above their current levels. During the next two decades, income is likely to remain the major problem associated with retirement.

Summary

1. A career is a lifelong pattern of work. In many respects, choosing a career is similar to choosing a spouse. In both areas, family pressures and social background are influential. One approach to vocational interests as they relate to personality, the Holland types, distinguishes six personality types: investigative, social, realistic, artistic, conventional, and enterprising. Each type is associated with certain types of professions. The family has a powerful influence on its members' career aspirations. Sometimes influence is expressed directly, as when a child is pressured to pursue a particular career; more often it is indirect, a reflection of family socialization practices, values, and interests. The Strong–Campbell Interest Inventory is a frequently used measure of career likes and dislikes.

2. One of the most important tasks in adult life is establishing a Dream of what one would like to become. Most young workers begin with high expectations, but according to the AT&T study, they lower their sights once they have come into contact with the realities of the workplace. Some workers are helped to rise in their profession by a mentor, a more experienced person working in the same field.

3. There is a good deal of evidence that younger workers today have different values than those of previous generations. A followup study to the 1956 MPS study at AT&T found some significant differences. The later study, begun in 1977, found that young managers had less motivation for upward mobility than their counterparts of 1956. They were also less inclined to be leaders — or followers. They did not expect the major rewards and satisfactions in life to be associated with work.

4. Midcareer is a period of reassessment, of establishing a niche in society, and striving for advancement. The midlife transition typically begins in the early forties. This phase often involves reevaluation of one's unrealistic expectations. Although most men continue to seek job challenges, the relative importance of work in men's lives tends to decrease, especially among the less successful. Success in a corporation seems to require certain characteristics and to breed certain others. Dealing with a complex, demanding environment tends to keep people intellectually flexible. Those who work in static, repetitive environments often learn conformist values. Practices at work often carry over to the life of the employee outside work. Career changes are quite common today. Those who don't keep up with their field risk technological obsolescence.

5. The number of women in the work force has increased dramatically over the last several decades. Many work in low-paying, low-prestige occupations. The majority have childrearing responsibilities as well. The number of women in the professions is increasing. Although employers are beginning to recognize the implications of the large number of women in the work force, few have made changes to accommodate them.

6. The status of retirement in the United States is changing. The mandatory retirement age has been raised to seventy, and the number of people retiring before sixty-five is increasing. Older workers are often the victims of stereotypes, but research shows that they are better employees than younger workers in some respects. Older workers may have trouble finding jobs if they are unemployed. In many cases, retirement is not entirely voluntary. Poor health and employment problems contribute to early retirement. Most workers retire as soon as it is financially feasible. Atchley suggests that retirement is actually a process involving five stages: a honeymoon period, rest and relaxation, disenchantment, reorientation, and the development of a stable and satisfying routine. It appears that the majority of people are satisfied with retirement. There is no evidence of physical decline associated with retirement age per se. Retired people do have to manage with less money, but most do not feel financially strapped. Most retirees consider their levels of activity and social adjustment satisfactory.

SUGGESTED READINGS

Aldous, J. (Ed.). (1982) *Two paychecks: Life in dual-earner families.* Covers a variety of issues related to families in which both husband and wife are employed.

Doering, M., Rhodes, S. R., and Schuster, M. (1983). *The aging worker: Research and recommendations.* Beverly Hills, CA: Sage. Extensive literature review on various issues related to the older workers, including work attitudes, job performance capabilities, and policy implications.

Kohn, M. L. and Schooler, C. (1983). *Work and personality: An inquiry into the impact of social stratification.* Norwood, NJ: Ablex. Reports from a series of studies examining the causal relationships among personality factors, the work environment, and intellectual functioning.

Naisbitt, J. (1984). *Megatrends.* New York: Warner Books. A forecaster's speculation regarding ten megatrends predicted to occur in America in the coming decades; a number of these trends involve the world of work.

Palmore, E. (Ed.) (1986). *Retirement: Causes and consequences.* New York: Springer. Summary of longitudinal research findings on antecedents and outcomes of retirement.

Stagner, R. (1985). Aging in industry. In J. E. Birren and K. W. Schaie (Eds.), *The handbook of the psychology of aging* (2nd ed.). New York: Van Nostrand Reinhold. Review of the literature on the issues related to the older worker.

Work and Retirement Among Blacks

Virtually no research has focused exclusively on the work and retirement of older blacks. A few work and retirement studies include some black–white comparisons (e.g., Parnes and Nestel, 1981), but little research or writing has been devoted to an investigation of factors related specifically to work and retirement experiences *within* the black population. The primary purpose of this article is to provide preliminary data on the work and retirement experiences among the black elderly from a recently conducted national sample survey of the black American population.

The National Survey of Black Americans involved a probability sampling of the total noninstitutionalized black population in the continental U.S. The survey involved face-to-face interviews with 2,107 respondents by black interviewers 1979–80. The data to be reported involved a subset of 544 black Americans, fifty-five years and older.

One of the first considerations in undertaking this analysis was to define retirement. Three groups of black elderly (over age fifty-five) were described. Group 1 consisted of those aged fifty-five or older who were working twenty hours or more per week. Group 2 consisted of those who worked less than 20 hours a week or not at all and who, when asked why they were not working, replied that they were retired. Members of Group 3 consisted of those who worked less than 20 hours per week or not at all, but, when asked why they were not working, gave reasons other than retirement; they did not perceive themselves to be retired. We will call these groups the working, the retired, and the nonworking nonretired, respectively.

About 26 percent of the subjects were found to be working, 46 percent reported themselves retired, and 28 percent were nonworking but did not report themselves to be retired (nonworking, nonretired). The working group, as might be expected, was found to have higher incomes. The working elderly were found to be younger than the retired elderly — 79 percent of the retired were sixty-seven years old or older. Interestingly, however, a third of the nonworking nonretired were also sixty-seven or older, which suggests that blacks' decisions to describe themselves as retired are not based solely on chronological age. The nonworking nonretired were generally in the lowest income and education categories.

The study found that the black elderly as a whole were highly dependent on public funds such as Social Security as their largest single source of income. They were likely to be working to supplement their incomes — even those who suffered from infirmities. Contrary to expectations, most were found to be financially independent, receiving no financial assistance from relatives, friends, or children.

In terms of subjective appraisals of their financial situation, those working were found to be most likely to describe themselves as being better off than they were three years earlier. However, of the three groups, the retired were the most likely to report having no worries about paying their bills.

On a number of other measures, the retired were found to be better off than either of the other two groups. They were found to have higher levels of life satisfaction, happiness, and personal control. Their psychological adjustment was better. They were also more likely to report that they had gotten what they wanted out of life. The authors interpret these findings to support the notion that life in retirement, by providing a regular income and relief from the vagaries associated with a disadvantaged position in the labor force, may be happier and more secure for elderly blacks than life in the work force. It appears that leaving the labor force is related to psychological well-being, for blacks as for others.

The study also developed a profile of the retired black elderly. Many retired relatively early because of poor health. In fact, blacks have been found to be more likely than whites to retire early for reasons of poor health. The most common activity pattern was working in the house or garden. Contrary to popular belief, only a small minority (10 percent) of the group was found to participate in church and church-related activities. Forty percent of the women and 20 percent of the men belonged to clubs and organizations, but the men were somewhat more likely to do volunteer work. About half of the retirees said their financial circumstances were about the same as before retirement; about 30 percent said they were in far worse financial circumstances. When asked what they liked best about retirement, about a third said "freedom." Men were more likely than women to see boredom as a major problem, whereas women saw having no money as a problem. Although only 12 percent reported missing anything about their previous jobs per se, 60 percent of the men and 46 percent of the women said, however, that they missed people at work. Among those who did have problems with retirement, about half said the problem was not being ready to retire. The vast majority reported no problem finding things to do or making adequate financial arrangements.

The authors suggest that it may be particularly important to consider prior work histories and life experiences in studying the retirement experiences of blacks. A work pattern of poor jobs with few benefits and little stability has implications for the types of resources and benefits available to blacks in retirement. The lack of benefits and available resources may force some of the black elderly to work long past the average age of other demographic groups. The authors suggest that though retirement status has been judged to be inferior to working status by others, retirement with Social Security benefits may provide blacks a stability of income and financial security not known during their years spent in an unstable and unsupportive labor market.

In discussing social policy implications of their findings, the authors note that the black elderly are highly dependent upon Social Security and public funds because they are often the sole source of support in retirement. Thus, blacks may be particularly affected by decisions that influence the basic payment structures of Social Security or that raise the age of eligibility under Social Security.

Jackson, J. S. and Gibson, R. C. (1985). Work and retirement among the Black elderly. In Z. Blau (Ed.), *Work, leisure retirement and social policy*, Greenwich, CT:JAI Press

Chapter Four

PERSONALITY DEVELOPMENT

Continuity and Change

By the time Susan came in for counseling, she was already known to the counselor (McKinney, 1965). He had heard about her from her landlady, who noted her inability to get along with other students, her problems with her courses, and her lack of personal cleanliness. Susan's academic adviser (Susan was a graduate student in classical languages; her goal was to teach Latin in high school) convinced her to see the counselor; before her first session, the adviser sent the counselor a note: "I feel she is becoming less and less promising as a useful member of society; hence, I raise some questions as to the desirability of her continuing with graduate work. I would like some advice from you."

Susan was one of ten children in a desperately poor family that lived in the backwoods of Arkansas. She lived in a house with no electricity, no running water, no glass windows, a house that "couldn't have cost more than $20." Her mother died of tuberculosis when Susan was four. Six or eight years later her father died, and the family was split up among relatives. In the small high school in Arkansas she attended, the Latin teacher had special prestige, leading her to make the same occupational choice. Though she was not particularly intelligent, she worked very hard at school and never, never gave up. The fact that she made it to graduate school at a major university is a minor miracle, an astounding achievement on Susan's part.

Susan's academic achievements, however, cost her dearly in other areas of adjustment. "Ever since . . . high school I have been . . . paying my own way. I realize that in this world nobody's going to do anything for you; you have to do it all yourself. I have taught in a rural school, I have worked as a waitress, and I have even worked in people's kitchens. It is because of my work and ability that I am here, and I don't intend to have my plans disrupted."

Susan had no interest in counseling, other than in gaining a letter evaluating her positively as a degree candidate. Her attitude toward teachers, advisers, and her fellow students was one of hostility and defiance. Given a poor grade, she would fly into a rage, accusing her teacher of prejudice and incompetence. As one person said of her, she had "a personality style based on a *once-accurate* perception of a blasted, withered, starved life, where no quarter is given and none expected." Susan's view of life, however, was neither accurate nor adaptive in a new environment, and she couldn't adjust. Indeed, in response to criticism of her appearance, she reacted by cultivating a dirty, slovenly look; in response to poor grades, she reacted by drinking and carousing: "After all the insults I have received about being a stupe, I decided to be known as a drunken and immoral bitch rather than a constitutional inferior."

A remarkable and in many respects an extremely admirable woman, Susan was nevertheless failing the major tasks of young adulthood. Although fiercely independent, she was confused about her personal identity, especially since her view of herself was not mirrored in the responses of others; she was doing a lot of role playing. Her career plans were based more on a need to win approval and prestige than on any deeply felt desire to teach Latin, or even to teach. Her few teaching jobs ended in disaster, usually when she and the principal got into a fight. When she finally, incredibly, after having been dropped by several departments for poor grades, earned a Ph.D. in Community Development, she never used it to get a job of any kind.

Her greatest failure was in establishing intimacy. She had practically no friends, and her relationships with men were distant and exploitative. She told her counselor she had never been close to anyone, not even her brothers and sisters. She said she would never marry. She said she needed affection, all right, but "I want to be a person with no ties." If she did marry, she would choose a husband who would give her status — not somebody in business, maybe someone at a university. Her dates were merely opportunities to play the role of "a drunken and immoral bitch."

Susan built up strong defenses against the rejection and hostility she experienced as a child, defenses that were serving her poorly as a young adult. She was suspicious and untrusting, which denied her the intimacy she wanted and needed. She projected her own hostilities onto other people, and then she often behaved so as to elicit the hostility she had assumed. She not only had made a very bad adjustment to the world, but she was so heavily defended against rejection and hurt that it was almost impossible for a sympathetic soul to get through to her, to help her. (Paranoid clients, for this reason, are generally among the most difficult for psychotherapists.)

Susan eventually married (an accountant) and became a housewife. She fought constantly with her husband and his relatives, so it is doubtful she achieved much intimacy in her marriage. If there is a ray of hope for Susan, it is in her child, a son. She loves him, but more importantly, she does not fear and distrust him; he and only he has been able to enter her shell. Perhaps as he grows older, he can crack the shell and let this remarkable woman realize some of her immense potential.

In this chapter, our topic is personality development. Susan's story is a good one to illustrate the interplay between characteristics of the person (personality) and the environment that together determine behavior. On the surface, Susan's life is not particularly unusual: she went to school, got a degree, got married, and had a child. Her personality makes her story interesting, providing a subplot of continuous conflict with others, and with herself as well. Her personality allowed her to achieve the heights she did, and her personality made the achievement valueless. How are we to understand such personality characteristics?

The primary issue in the study of adult personality development is *change versus continuity*. This paradox is central to much of the study of adult development (see Chapter 1). We tend to think of personality in general, and adult personalities in particular, as stable and enduring, one of the few unchanging features in a changing world. "Good old Bert Moore," we say, "we can always count on his being cheerful, witty, honest, and kind. He was that way when he was in grade school, and he's still the same today." On the other hand, we like to think at least of the *potential for change* in one's personality. We all hope, for example, that Susan's son will be able to transform Susan, open her up to love and trust and quench some of the fires that drive her so relentlessly toward unsatisfying goals. In fact, when we think about it, we all know cases of radical personality change: someone who in youth was hard and persistent but in later life is peaceful and philanthropic; someone who in youth was weak and vacillating but in later life is self-assured and assertive; someone altered by a great event — an alcoholic who dries out after a serious automobile accident, a moral degenerate who finds in religion the basis for a new life.

Early experiences set a powerful course for further development, and personality characteristics once established are strongly reinforced by most of us remaining in a relatively constant environment. Nevertheless, there are many early experiences (good or bad) that may not have long-lasting effects because they are related primarily to the need of a particular life stage; for example, the survival of the young infant through that period when the infant is totally dependent on caregivers (Kagan, 1980). This discontinuity makes it possible for the individual to be responsive to meaningful events that occur later on in life and as we will see can lead to substantial change within individuals. Such individual changes will rarely lead to total reversals of early personality patterns. Rather they will involve a relatively limited positive or negative adjustment in response to the event that causes the change. This is why *average* patterns of personality development show remarkable continuity in spite of the many individual personality changes that occur throughout life.

Approaches to Personality

In addition to the issue of change versus continuity in adult personality, we will be faced in this chapter with the problem of defining personality. Personality theorists have struggled with definitions since the beginnings of psychology, often resorting to metaphorical statements that describe "personality" as "an entity of the sort you are referring to when you use the first person prononoun, 'I' " (Adams, 1954) or "what a person really *is*" (Allport, 1937). Most theorists prefer a definition that sounds a little more scientifically respectable; the classic, from Gordon Allport in 1937, suggests that personality is *the dynamic organization within the individual of those biosocial systems that determine his or her unique adjustment to the world.* The "biosocial systems" include such things as personality traits, habits, motives, and values that are partly biologically based (inherited, for example) and partly the result of learning and experience (social). These biosocial systems are interrelated (organized). In active (dynamic) interaction with the environment, they determine an individual's unique adaptation to life.

Theories of personality differ primarily in their choice and definition of the "biosocial systems" they view as most effective in explaining human behavior. The *psychoanalytic approach* begun by Sigmund Freud, for example, divides the human personality into id, ego, and superego, which represent impulsive, realistic, and moralistic tendencies in the individual. The *individual-differences approach* emerged from early attempts to develop psychological tests for measuring human characteristics; personality traits or, more globally, personality types are the units usually employed. A *learning approach* to personality implies we will hear about habits controlled by stimuli and reinforcements. The *humanistic approach* is noted for its resistance to attempts to reduce explanations of human behavior to those which have worked for lower animals; it is marked by discussions of higher human motives such as self-actualization. The *cognitive approach* emphasizes the fact that the way people *perceive* their world is the most direct determinant of their behavior. The "biosocial systems" in the cognitive approach are social perceptions, beliefs, attributions (ideas about what causes what), and the like.

All these approaches have been used to describe the course of personality development in the adult years. Every theory has its advantages and disadvantages, of course, and each seems to have a place in the overall attempt to understand what happens to the personality as it ages. Each approach seems to be particularly well suited to some aspect of adult development, and in regard to that aspect we generally find a body of research influenced by that approach. The psychoanalytic approach, for example, focuses on ego development through the life span; we will discuss theory and research in this area in the following section. This will be followed by an example of the cognitive approach. The individual-differences approach focuses on age differences in personality test scores; research on personality assessment will be covered in the latter part of the chapter.

The other approaches to personality development will be discussed in Chapter 7 on motivation, since most of the topics influenced by these approaches fall into areas traditionally considered motivational.

Ego Development

Sigmund Freud formulated his psychoanalytic theory of personality over many years, beginning in 1900 with the publication of *The Interpretation of Dreams.* Over the next forty years or so, Freud and his associates, including Carl Jung, revised and extended the psychoanalytic theory until Freud's death in 1939. Since Freud's death, further modifications and extensions have been accomplished by a number of important theorists, including Erik Erikson, Anna Freud (Sigmund's daughter), David Rappaport, and many others. The resulting theory is an extremely complex approach to personality and therapy, which we cannot describe here in detail (see Geiwitz and Moursund, 1979). Three aspects of psychoanalytic theory have proved to be most influential in the study of adult development:

1. The notion of *unconscious mental processes.* This led to the development of *projective tests* containing ambiguous stimuli. It is assumed by the authors of such tests that these stimuli can be described in ways that reveal (without our awareness) our deepest desires and values (Schaie and Stone, 1982).
2. The notion of *defense mechanisms,* cognitive tricks we play on ourselves to reduce anxiety and personal embarrassment.
3. Above all, the notion of *ego development,* which is based on the idea that we are constantly defining our personal identities as we live our everyday lives.

The definition of personality in terms of three parts — *id, ego,* and *superego* — came rather late in Freud's theory. In the early formulations, conflict, which presumably caused mental disorders, was viewed in terms of unconscious ideas in opposition to conscious intentions. As Freud encountered a greater variety of mental disorders, it was clear that some of them involved conflict between unconscious ideas and equally unconscious intentions. To improve his theory's ability to represent conflict, therefore, Freud introduced the constructs of id, ego, and superego, and portrayed conflict as a discrepancy between the aims of two of these parts.

The id is the power system of the personality, providing energy (sexual and aggressive) for the actions of the individual. It is said to operate on the *pleasure principle,* which holds that what is immediately pleasurable is good and that unpleasant events should be avoided — regardless of the later consequences. The id does not tolerate delay of gratification.

The ego is the strategist of the personality. It operates on the *reality principle,* which focuses on the distinction between what can be accomplished and what cannot. The ego moves to satisfy the desires of the id in a realistic manner, by assessing the situation and planning actions in a logical sequence to achieve a certain purpose. The ego is Machiavellian; it has no moral principles. Unless arrest and imprisonment made theft impractical, the ego would steal to satisfy the id. It would steal, that is, except for pressure from the superego.

The superego is the moralist of the personality, that part of us which fills us with pride when we do "good" (ego-ideal) and with shame when we do "bad" (conscience). Freud believed that the superego develops from interactions with parents, as the parents interpret for the child the moral principles of the society.

Needless to say, the desires, plans, and demands of the id, ego, and superego are often in conflict. Imagine a sex-starved hedonist, a humorless computer scientist, and a frock-coated Puritan minister chained together and turned loose in the world, and you have a reasonable approximation of what Freud was trying to say about personality (Geiwitz and Moursund, 1979). The id, ego, and superego cannot break their chains and go their separate ways. They have no alternative but to adjust to one another. The result, in the psychoanalytic representation of life, is the adult human personality.

DEFENSE MECHANISMS

As the individual matures, the ego takes on greater power and responsibility. To control the impulsive id and the moralistic superego, the cunning ego often relies on cognitive tricks called *defense mechanisms* (A. Freud, 1946). Defined slightly differently, defense mechanisms are adaptive techniques designed to provide psychological stability in the midst of conflicting needs and stresses that are part of human existence; they are characteristic ways of dealing with anxiety, aggressive impulses, and frustrations (Butler and Lewis, 1982.)

One of the most common defense mechanisms used by middle-aged and elderly people is *denial*, a form of *repression* — driving an idea out of consciousness. For example, denial of aging itself is a way some people use to handle the anxieties and uncertainties of increasing age (Butler and Lewis, 1982). Almost a third of the people in one study, all of whom were seventy or older, considered themselves "middle-aged" rather than "old" or "elderly" (Bultena and Powers, 1978). Denial of one's own imminent death is also common, as is denial of the death of a loved one, as we shall see in Chapter 13. Also often denied are some of the sensory and energy losses that often accompany growing old. Another form of repression involves a *selective memory*, which recalls the pleasant moments of one's past but banishes the unpleasant. As Nietzsche once said of distasteful actions in his past, "My memory says that I did it, my pride says that I could not have done it, and in the end, my memory yields." The man who formulated the concept of repression, Sigmund Freud, made frequent errors in dates and facts when trying to recall his experiences with cocaine in young adulthood (Geiwitz and Moursund, 1979).

Another common defense mechanism is *regression*, which is defined by a return to less mature behaviors. Some people react to growing old by acting "babyish," that is, by assuming a very passive and dependent role. In one study, about 10 percent of a sample between the ages of seventy and seventy-nine were classified as "succorance seekers," which means they wanted others to take care of all their physical and emotional needs (Neugarten, Moore, and Lowe, 1968). Often these seekers move in with an adult child who is then expected to play the role of parent.

Other defensive behavior patterns common enough to warrant a name are often used by adults, although perhaps no more often than by children. In *projection*, an anxiety-arousing impulse is denied in oneself and "projected" instead into another person. A man anxious about his own sexuality may complain that "everyone" has been making sexual advances to him; another, harboring unconscious aggressive impulses, may assert that adult children, physicians, and politicians dislike him and are out to do him harm. In *displacement*, the true object of a sexual or aggressive impulse is repressed and a new, less threatening object is substituted. Angry at her "deteriorating" body, an aging woman may complain that the world is going to ruin. In *reaction formation*, an objectionable idea is replaced by its opposite. Unconscious hate may be covered over by conscious love, or desperate sexual desires under the surface may result in a prim life and antipornography tirades; as one investigator described a man who used reaction formation as a characteristic defense, "he was positively allergic to pleasure" (Vaillant, 1977, p. 146).

Isolation involves separating an idea from its emotional significance. Issues that might provoke too much anxiety if discussed in personal terms, for example, might be handled if the discussion is "abstract" and "objective." In other words, one who is anxious about sexual desires for people other than one's spouse may start a discussion on the nature of marital fidelity. This form of isolation, called *intellectualization*, is in some situations a valued ability in our culture: scientists and judges, for example, are expected to consider the evidence of a matter without letting emotions "distort" their judgment. A good sense of humor is another form of isolation. A man in World War II found himself in a farmhouse surrounded by German soldiers; he turned to his buddy and commented, "Isn't this just like a Grade-B western!" (Vaillant, 1977, p. 117). Isolation is more frequently used by people as they grow older, whereas other defenses, notably reaction formation, are observed less often (Vaillant, 1977).

Sublimation is the ingenious defense in which one satisfies base impulses while acting in a way highly valued by society. For example, an artist may be driven at some deep psychoanalytic level by the desire to smear feces. But instead the artist smears paints in pleasant patterns and earns, not scorn, but universal acclaim.* Similarly, a musician with conflict about putting things in his or her mouth (part of an old desire to suckle at the mother's breast) may relieve it by playing the oboe. Novelists may have the best of all possible worlds; they can write about the most direct and vulgar expression of the basest motives and be praised for their efforts — psychoanalytically at least, an incredible feat. Successful human development in the adult years is the successful sublimation of potentially evil instincts into socially acceptable behaviors that benefit, rather than

---

*We hope a footnote will suffice to note that the motives represented in any occupation are many, and that not all artists are driven, even unconsciously, to smear feces or otherwise express vulgar desires.

Creative activities like finger painting allow children to make a mess in a socially acceptable way and introduce them to the defense mechanism we call sublimation.

harm, other people. Freud curiously thought that women were less capable of the society-bulding aspect of sublimation because he viewed women as having weaker superegos. It is interesting to note that this was Freud's attempt to explain the more limited participation of women in the world of work and professional accomplishment.

ACTIVITY AND CAUTIOUSNESS

Apart from the defense mechanisms, described by psychoanalytic theory, that people of all ages are presumed to use, there are similar processes that have been described by researchers working with elderly persons. Old people use certain defenses against anxiety and uncertainty that are particularly appropriate to their life circumstances. Notable among these are activity and cautiousness.

Activity is a common enough defense at younger ages as well. Following some unexpected tragedy, such as the loss of a spouse or a job, the victim might be heard saying something like, "Well, I'll just bury myself in my work." In the later years of life, after the age of sixty or sixty-five, such tragedies as the loss of spouse or job become frequent, although the anxiety does not necessarily decrease. Activity — "working off the blues" (Butler and Lewis, 1982) — is still one of the most common and effective defenses. We have already mentioned, for example, that some of the most successful retirements are engineered by people who base their whole program on activity: building things, getting involved in church activities, and so on. Activity is a form of meditation; it keeps your mind too busy to think about your problems. As noted in Chapter 3, however, such activities have to be meaningful; activities that merely have the appearance of productivity simply do not suffice (see also the discussion of disengagement versus activity theory in Chapter 7, p. 235).

Cautiousness is another way some elderly people defend themselves against the anxieties of old age. As people grow older, they tend to become more careful, trading off speed of response in order to increase accuracy (Botwinick, 1978; Salthouse, 1979, 1982). They often appear to be motivated by the desire to avoid mistakes more than to succeed at a task. For example, some older people, more often than younger subjects, will make no response at all to a question on an intelligence test (Zelinski, Schaie, and Gribbin, 1977). Such *omission errors* earn no credit, of course, but they are generally regarded differently than *commission errors*, that is, actual responses that are incorrect. In similar fashion, older people are more likely to use the "no opinion" response to questions about their attitudes in national opinion surveys (Gergen and Back, 1966; but see Glenn, 1969, for some qualifications). When faced with situations in which there is a chance of considerable gain but also some chance of loss (for example, when someone has an opportunity to change jobs to a company that could be very successful but could also fail), many more older people than younger people are unwilling to take any chances at all (Botwinick, 1978).

Interestingly enough, the tendency of older people to select less risky (and consequently less demanding) situations seems to hold only when the payoff is relatively limited (Okun and DiVesta, 1976). When the expected reward for selecting a more demanding situation becomes substantial, older persons are as likely as younger ones to prefer the riskier situation (Okun and Elias, 1977).

Many people over the age of forty or fifty perceive some decline in their ability to compete with younger adults in tasks that require quick response. In compensation (in defense), they may reorder their priorities; they may begin to value accuracy, quality, and other "timeless" characteristics more. An aging psychologist may strive to put out one or two "superior theoretical papers" and wonder about the young psychologists who put out a dozen research papers a year that are only slight variations of one another. An aging quarterback values his knowledge highly, his ability to stand in one place as 280-pound linemen struggle to reach him, his cautious approach, his ability to withhold a response until the defensive pattern becomes clear and he knows when and where a receiver will break into the open. He may not be able to move around as quickly as a younger quarterback or to throw a football as far, but are these abilities the important ones? Not in his mind.

Cautiousness is very often a virtue, for many aging quarterbacks and for many aging psychologists. Sometimes, however, it results in inferior performance, in terms of both slowness and poor quality. In various sorts of ability tests, for example, older people earn lower scores on the average than younger people. Some of these age differences may represent a decline in the ability being tested, but typically some of the difference is due to the increased cautiousness of older people. They are unwilling to venture a guess on a questionnaire item, or they slow down on a manual task, perhaps believing that to do two things out of two successfully is better than to do four things out of six — even though the test is scored for the number of tasks completed, not for the percentage of tasks tried and accomplished successfully (Birkhill and Schaie, 1975). As a result, many studies comparing the abilities of younger to older subjects show much more decline than actually exists.

The cautiousness of older people may well exaggerate the apparent decline in such abilities as intelligence, learning and memory, and perception. Perhaps one of the clearest examples of the effect of cautiousness on an interpretation of psychological research is in sensory psychology. Consider the typical hearing test: the examiner presents tones at varying degrees of loudness and asks when the individual hears them. Subjects who are very cautious will not say they have heard the tone until it is quite loud. A number of research studies have confirmed the hypothesis that traditional hearing tests considerably overestimate the degree of hearing loss in older people, confusing actual loss with cautiousness of report (Rees and Botwinick, 1971).

STAGES OF EGO DEVELOPMENT

In the view of psychoanalytic theorists, personality development over the life span is largely a matter of ego development. In less theoretical terms, the processes and abilities we use to cope with reality emerge and are strengthened; they become more complex, more integrated. Our defense mechanisms become more mature, utilizing such gross adaptations as denial and projection less, utilizing more refined adaptations such as intellectualization and sublimation (Vaillant, 1977). The ego adjusts to the peculiar demands of the id, the superego, and the environment.

To describe ego development, theorists have often used the notion of developmental stages. As in all stage theories the life span (or some part of it) is broken into time periods, each characterized by a set of developmental issues. These issues are different, in degree if not in kind, from those in other periods.

Erik Erikson's (1963) extension of the psychoanalytic stage approach into the adult years marked a rather sharp departure from previous theories of ego development, which tended to see the personality as relatively fixed by the age of five or six. Although Erikson's most famous concept, the *identity crisis,* is placed in adolescence, the turmoil of deciding "who you are" continues in adulthood, and identity crises may recur throughout life, even in old age. The identity crisis, in some respects, is the central issue of ego development, as the ego tries to define its powers and limitations in regard to the strength and nature of the individual's desires (id) and, simultaneously, in regard to the restrictions imposed by the rights and powers of other people and society as a whole (Gould, 1975, 1978).

The *intimacy crisis* was discussed in some detail in Chapter 2, since it is the primary psychosocial issue in the young adult's thoughts and feelings about marriage and family. The primary issue of middle age, according to Erikson, is *generativity versus stagnation.* Broadly conceived, generativity includes the education of one's children; productivity and creativity in one's work; and a continuing revitalization of one's spirit that allows for fresh and active participation in all facets of life. Specifically, the midlife career problems described in Chapter 3 are manifestations of the generativity crisis. Marital difficulties of middle age are other manifestations, and so too are the fevered attempts of many middle-aged men and women to "improve themselves" through sometimes outlandish therapies, mystical religions, and even "physical meditation" (which some people call "jogging"). Successful resolution of the generativity crisis involves the human virtues of caring, giving, and teaching, in the home, on the job, in life in general.

The final years of life, in Erikson's view of ego development, mark the time of the *integrity crisis*, when individuals look back over their lives and decide either that they were well-ordered and meaningful (integrated) or unproductive and meaningless — in which case, instead of integrity, there is despair. The people who despair approach the end of life with the feeling that death will be one more frustration in a series of failures. In contrast, the people with integrity accept their lives (including their deaths) as important, with occasional setbacks, of course, but on the whole satisfying. In a sense, ego integrity is the end result of the lifelong search for ego identity, a recognition that one has coped reasonably successfully with the demands both of the id and of society (Erikson, 1979, 1982).

Of course, the processes of ego development do not manifest themselves in the same way for everyone. People have different needs, values, and goals and ego must attempt to organize and harmonize them in its own unique fashion. For some people, the process will be relatively easy; for others, it will be extremely difficult or impossible. As a result, people reach different levels of ultimate development. A formal model that discusses the mechanisms that may be involved in this individuation of adult ego development has recently been presented by Pascual-Leone (1983).

According to Loevinger (1966), people at different stages of development face fundamentally different tasks and approach them in different ways. Men and women who are in the lower stages are subject to strong, primitive impulses, and they tend to express their needs immediately. Since their ego functions are underdeveloped, they do not resolve conflicts efficiently or schedule their activities effectively. In the long run, they are unable to satisfy many of their needs without feeling guilty or treading on other people's toes and arousing their hostility.

Those who have achieved higher levels of ego development, on the other hand, have more sensitive and sophisticated ways of integrating their needs and values. The lives of such people are more complex than the lives of those at lower levels, however. They may be troubled by moral concerns or abstract problems that would be meaningless or nonexistent for people at low ego levels. As a result, a high level of ego development does not necessarily lead to greater satisfaction or happiness (McCrae and Costa, 1983).

Another aspect of ego functioning has been described by Block (1981), who contends that two dimensions can be perceived. The first, ego resiliency, is the person's ability to meet new demands. Those who have high ego resiliency are resourceful and flexible and able to adapt themselves to novel circumstances. Those who have low ego resiliency tend to be hypersensitive, moody, and uncomfortable with themselves and their environment. The second dimension, ego control, is concerned with the ability to master one's impulses. People who are overcontrolled tend to be strongly conformist, narrow in interest, and poor in the ability to interact with other persons. Undercontrolled persons tend to be spontaneous, inclined toward immediate gratification of impulses, and willing to attempt new relationships and ways of doing things. The importance of developing and maintaining flexible personality styles has recently been further supported by showing that persons with flexible attitudes and behaviors in midlife showed greater maintenance of intellectual abilities into old age (Schaie, 1984b).

JUNG ON ADULT DEVELOPMENT

Carl Jung was certainly one of the most original thinkers in the history of psychology. He was allied for a brief period with Freud and his analytic theory of personality bears many resemblances to that of Freud, but his theory also represents an early form of humanistic psychology. One facet of Jung's theory is concern with adult development; most personality theories stress development during childhood.

One of the key ingredients of Jung's theory is the concept of balance. Each part of an individual's personality must be in balance with the other parts; each must be given expression in one way or another, or it will find its own expression — in neurotic symptoms, for example, or in terrifying dreams. In particular, Jung distinguished two major orientations of the ego: toward the external world, an orientation he called *extraversion;* and toward inner, subjective experiences, which he called *introversion.* Jung considered both orientations necessary for psychological health. There must be balance between the two, he claimed, because individuals need, at times, to deal with the social world and, at other times, to reflect on their values and to observe their reactions to the happenings in their lives. Unfortunately, people often display one orientation almost exclusively, which is the basis for our categorizing people as socially active, gregarious, party-loving extraverts or introspective, bookwormish introverts.

A general age trend exists in regard to introversion–extraversion, according to Jung (1960). Young people are much more extraverted than older people. Indeed, young adults are forced to focus largely on their relationship with the outside world, for they are choosing mates, choosing careers, having children, and otherwise carving their niches in society. Sooner or later, however, their need for balance will cause them to become introverted. As they reach middle age and beyond, the pressures of making crucial decisions about the external world lessen somewhat. The death of parents leads to a lessened need for career success because it is no longer necessary to display a "dutiful child" role. All these events, according to Jung, lead most persons to turn their energies to exploring their internal worlds.

Another and related age trend involves the masculine and feminine parts of our personalities. In Jung's theory, young adults tend to express only one sexual aspect, often taking considerable pains to inhibit the other. The particular behaviors to be expressed are usually defined by sex-role stereotypes, which may differ from culture to culture or from generation to generation. In our culture, the male role is active and aggressive and the female role is passive and nurturant. As people age, however, the suppressed part of their personalities will come out, according to Jung; we should expect men as they grow older to express more behaviors that earlier in life would be considered feminine, and likewise expect women to show more traits that in their youth would have led to their being rather masculine. This does not mean that there is a reversal of sex roles. What this trend accomplishes is to provide a greater sense of balance (androgeny) that permits both men and women as they age to express personality styles that fit their individual needs and circumstances rather than being governed by the societally imposed sex-role stereotypes.

THE KANSAS CITY STUDIES

A large-scale series of investigations known collectively as the **Kansas City Studies of Adult Life** provides some evidence bearing on age differences in introversion–extraversion and masculinity–femininity (Neugarten, 1977b). Although the differences may not exist for the reasons Jung suggested, older people showed an increasingly passive and fatalistic orientation toward the external world, together with an increasing preoccupation with self and a growing introversion. The forty-year-olds believed they could influence their environment with bold action, but the average sixty-year-olds were more likely to see the world as controlling them. At sixty, conformity and accommodation were the primary means of coping with the environment — a defensive posture psychologists sometimes call "passive mastery." Introspection became more frequent, in the specific forms of contemplation, reflection, and self-evaluation.

Similarly, Jung's hypothesis that men become more feminine and women more masculine receives support from the Kansas City Studies (Neugarten and Gutmann, 1968). Subjects ranging in age from forty to seventy were asked to tell a story about a picture that depicted a young man and woman and an old man and woman, the four apparently in conversation (see Figure 4–1). Subjects over fifty-five were much more likely than younger subjects to describe the old man as passive rather than authoritative and the old woman as assertive rather than submissive or under the control of husband and children. From this and other studies, one reviewer concluded that "older men seemed more receptive than younger men of their affiliative, nurturant, and sensual promptings; older women, more receptive than younger women of aggressive and egocentric impulses" (Neugarten, 1973, p. 320).

Sharp-eyed readers will note a slight contradiction in the findings just reported: How can women become more introverted, adopting a style of passive mastery, at the same time they are presumably becoming more assertive and aggressive? Current research evidence does not permit us to resolve this contradiction entirely. Some investigators believe that the bulk of the evidence supports the notion that both men and women become more introverted with age but that sex differences decrease or disappear; thus men, in youth more extraverted than women, increase in introversion at a faster rate than women

FIGURE 4–1.

Adult family scene, used as a projective test in the Kansas City Studies.

(Neugarten, 1973). Other psychologists hold that women actually become more extraverted with age, as men become more introverted, leading to the "unisex of later life" (Gutmann, 1975). In this latter view, the different parenthood roles of the two sexes determine the early differences in introversion–extraversion.

In a more recent cross-sectional study, using the Bem Sex Role Inventory (Bem, 1978), sex-role attributions of 426 women and 378 men were studied at eight stages in the family life cycle from adolescence through grandparenthood (Feldman, Biringen, and Nash, 1981). Characteristics studied included leadership, autonomy, acquiescence, nonassertiveness, compassion, tenderness, social inhibitions, and self-ascribed masculinity and femininity. Most of the life stage differences found were associated with the particular life stage of the family rather than with chronological age. Both femininity and masculinity varied only within gender, and at that quite modestly. Women showed greater tenderness than men at all life stages, except during the married-childless grandparenthood stages. Men were more autonomous and less acquiescent then women during the stage of expecting a child and during young parenthood, but not at other stages. Other changes occur in complex ways and reveal both diverging and parallel developmental differences occurring for men and women with role shifts related to the stage of family life that they are in. In a related study conducted in Australia involving a sample of dating, cohabiting, and married couples and divorced partners (Cunningham and Antill, 1984), it was found, however, that masculinity and femininity scores were more related to the individual's involvement in work or education than to the stage of family development. In this study employed women were found to have lower femininity scores, and their male partners lower masculinity scores, than did nonemployed women and their partners. Women who were engaged in graduate education had lower femininity scores than those who were not. The latter study, however, did not extend beyond the period of working life and therefore does not challenge previous findings on the convergence of sex-role related behaviors in old age.

As primary breadwinners, men must suppress emotional sensitivity and dependency needs to succeed as economic providers. Later in life, the demands of parenthood subside, and men can afford to express tenderness. Women, on the other hand, are traditionally the primary caregivers, so they must suppress their aggressiveness to avoid breaking up the family or damaging a child's developing personality. When they grow older and have adult children, they reap a number of rewards: receiving a good deal of affection and having a certain amount of power over their kin. Freed from their earlier restrictions, they find outlets that give them more recognition — that is, they become more aggressive (Brown, 1982). Women generally adjust better to the role losses of old age because they are socialized to expect less consistency in their roles (Cool, 1981; Elwell and Maltbie-Crannell, 1981).

These different age changes for men and women have been noted in many cultures around the world (Gutmann, 1977). Finding them in several cultures with economies ranging from agricultural to highly technological adds weight to the conclusion that a basic developmental process is involved and not simply one dictated by specific events in a particular society (Fry, 1985).

The multivariate approach to the study of personality in old age pioneered in the Kansas City and related studies has also contributed to our understanding of adaptation in old age. For example, Neugarten, Havighurst, and Tobin (1968) described four major personality types that had different adaptive patterns as they aged. Those individuals who displayed an *integrated* pattern that was characterized by flexible and adaptive attitudes and by behaviors that were conducive to continued involvement with, or consciously programmed disengagement from, their social environment showed high life satisfaction. But high life satisfaction was also shown by the *armoured* type, those individuals whose personality organization reflected a need for tight control over their impulse life and who either held on to their earlier life roles or who defended themselves against threats from the losses posed by their aging by constricting their social contacts and closing themselves off from experience. By contrast, low life satisfaction was expressed by the *passive-dependent* type, who were either leaning on other persons for emotional support or who were characterized by an apathetic response to their environment, the "rocking chair" people. Low life satisfaction was also shown by those individuals who fit into an *unintegrated* personality type who showed a disorganized pattern of aging. Even though these persons were able to maintain themselves in the community, they were characterized by declines in psychological and physiological functioning and by low levels of activity and interaction. Similar findings showing the importance of personality styles to adaptive behavior and satisfaction in later life have been reported by Lowenthal, Thurnher, and Chiriboga (1975) and by Schmitz-Scherzer and Thomae (1983).

A COGNITIVE LIFE SPAN APPROACH

In contrast to stage models derived from psychoanalytic theory, *cognitive approaches* to the study of personality assess development in terms of the individual's own conception of how his or her life should proceed. An interesting example of such an approach is Whitbourne's (1985) formulation of an individual "life span construct" that relies on distinguishing how a person's own life course differs from age norms and expectations that exist for society as a whole.

The life span construct has two basic structural components, the *scenario* and the *life story*. The scenario consists of a person's expectations about the future. As soon as a sense of identity develops in adolescence, one begins to acquire some notion of what one wants to do with one's life and to imagine what one will be doing at various points in the years to come. Our suppositions about how our lives will progress are strongly influenced by culturally determined age norms: society expects us to reach certain transition points at specific periods of our lives. Throughout our lives we continually compare our actual performance to the scenario we had imagined for ourselves, using it as a basis for self-evaluation and adjusting it as circumstances dictate.

Consider, for example, the case of a high school senior who has decided that she wants to be a scientist. Her scenario might well include events and circumstances such as these: She expects to graduate with the class and then go to a four-year college, where she will major in biology. She expects that she will have many women friends and perhaps a boyfriend. After college, she knows that she will have to go to graduate school, but she isn't sure whether a doctorate will be necessary. Subsequently, she imagines herself doing research in a laboratory of some sort. She expects to marry at some point and vaguely assumes that she will eventually have children, but these are matters about which she is unsure at present. She expects to remain in contact with her friends and make new friends among her colleagues at work. In the distant future, she has an image of herself addressing a large audience at a convention of some sort and being loudly applauded when her speech is finished. In short, she expects herself to ultimately be successful.

She will use this scenario as a guide for planning and a means of assessing her progress toward her goals. Every time she passes an important transition in her life — graduating from school, getting her first job, publishing her first paper, getting married — she will compare her actual performance to the way she imagined life would be at that point; her progress will influence how she feels about herself. If she gets a doctorate by the time she is twenty-six, she may feel very proud of herself. If she is not married by age thirty-five, she may begin to fear that she will miss out on having children. As a result, she may begin to denigrate herself in some ways. Inevitably, the scenario she originally imagined for herself will change; she might marry and have children immediately after college and put off continuing her education for a few years.

As the person moves into the scenario she has imagined, she begins to build a life story. This is the second component of the life span construct. The life story is the narrative of personal history into which one organizes the events of one's past life to give them personal meaning and a sense of continuity. It is called a "story" because the person alters it as it is retold, distorting the actual events into a pattern that she finds acceptable. If the woman in our example didn't graduate from college until she was twenty-eight, she might tell herself that she graduated "in her twenties, like most people who go to college"; this permits her to think of herself as "on time" according to the development schedule she has set for herself. She might make other distortions as well, simplifying the circumstances surrounding complex decisions or exaggerating the importance of events of which she feels proud. Together with the scenario, the life story encompasses the individual's sense of the future and the past; it is the central principle around which people organize and assess their progress through their own lives.

CHANGE AND CONTINUITY OF THE SELF-CONCEPT

The self-concept is one of the basic elements of the personality, so we can perhaps expect tendencies toward stability or change in self-conceptions to be representative of the personality as a whole. Studies of various aspects of the self-concept indicate that, in most respects, it is quite stable over long periods. Some changes do occur, however (see Ryff, 1984; Chapter 5, this volume, p. 171).

One study investigated the stability of self-concepts among several hundred people undergoing one of four major adult transitions: leaving home after finishing high school, having one's first child, having one's youngest child leave home, and retiring from work. In all four age groups, the structure and interrelationships among different dimensions of the self-concept remained stable over a five-year period. The level of self-assessment did change for some of the dimensions but not for others. What remained stable over time included the concept of personal security, amiability, and assertion. Changes were noted in other dimensions, however, including social poise, self-control, and hostility (Pierce and Chiriboga, 1979). Other studies yield similar results. One showed substantial stability over the fourteen years of early adulthood (Mortimer, Finch, and Kumka, 1982). Another, which involved subjects ranging from age nine to age eighty-nine, found no significant age differences in self-conceptions (Monge, 1975).

Body image — how one feels about one's physical self — is closely related to self-concept. Most of us would expect there to be significant shifts in a person's body image as the person ages. Although there has not been much research in this area, and such studies as have been conducted are cross-sectional rather than longitudinal, the findings suggest that aging does not have a negative influence on body image (Plutchik, Weiner, and Conte, 1971; Berscheid, Walster, and Bohrnstedt, 1973). The popular view that older people consider themselves un-attractive does not appear to be accurate.

Sex-role identification is another significant realm of the self-concept. In this area, there do seem to be some changes as people age, but they are relatively modest. Fitzgerald (1978) investigated sex-role-related self-concepts using a measure that assessed variations along two major dimensions, nurturance and dominance. His findings were that college males described themselves as more aggressive than older males considered themselves. The older males, however, scored higher in areas such as cooperation and nurturance. Younger women scored higher than younger men on scales related to cooperativeness, docility, and dependence, but older males had dominance scores only slightly higher than those of older women. Other studies also suggest that traditional sex differences in self-concepts are less evident in older men and women compared with younger individuals (Ryff and Baltes, 1976; Hyde and Phyllis, 1979).

The assumption that the self-concept should become more positive with age is compatible with formulations of adult development such as Erikson's (1982) contention that the positive resolution of the final psychosocial crisis results in ego integrity, implying a sense of positive self. But others, such as Buehler (1968) and Rosow (1974), who emphasize the restriction of socialization and role loss in old age would argue that there ought to be negative changes in self-concept. The empirical literature, depending on what self-concept dimensions are studied provides some evidence in either direction (see also Breytspaak, 1984). The resolution of this apparent paradox, as already mentioned in our discussion of age changes in role identification, may be that it is not age per se but rather one's stage of life or the particular environmental demands of a job or education that significantly influence one's self-concept (Bengtson, 1973; Feldman, Biringen, and Nash, 1981; Cunningham and Antill, 1984).

Individual-Differences Approach to Personality

When Charles Darwin formulated his theory of evolution based on "the survival of the fittest," differences among the individual members of a species (which are more fit than others?) became an important area of study. Francis Galton, an English biologist, became interested in human evolution and even proposed a program of eugenics for improving the survival abilities of the English people: he proposed that the more intelligent members of the human species should parent most of the children, thereby increasing the average level of intelligence in the population. To identify the more intelligent individuals, of course, Galton needed some means of assessing intelligence, and thus he pioneered the development of intelligence tests. In a sense, he simultaneously pioneered the individual-differences approach in psychology, which, since Galton's time, has always relied heavily on psychological tests.

SELF-REPORT INVENTORIES

The first significant personality test was called the *Personal Data Sheet*, which was developed to screen recruits for the United States armed services during World War I (Woodworth, 1920). The Personal Data Sheet was simple in theory and in practice. The author, psychologist Robert Woodworth, first made a list of symptoms generally considered to indicate emotional maladjustment. From the list, Woodworth constructed 116 questions (such as "Do you usually feel well and strong?") that could be answered yes or no. The total number of questions answered in the direction Woodworth thought of as maladjusted constituted the "psychoneuroticism" score; if the soldier scored high enough, he was seen by a psychiatrist.

The Personal Data Sheet is a type of personality test called a *self-report inventory*, so called because the individual is asked to report on his or her own feelings and activities. The most famous of the self-report inventories is the *Minnesota Multiphasic Personality Inventory* (MMPI). The MMPI consists of 566 items of the form, "I am frightened to read of prowlers in my neighborhood," to which the individual responds true, false, or "cannot say." From the pattern of responses, the individual receives scores on the scales originally designed to discriminate between normal and psychiatric populations. One scale, for example, is the mania scale, on which a high score presumably indicates manic tendencies (tendencies to become extremely excited).

In addition to its uses for psychiatric diagnosis and clinical counseling, the MMPI is also used extensively for personality research with normal subjects. Researchers may want to know, for example, if old people are more depressed or more paranoid than young people. The investigators would not look for the extreme scores that indicate severe depression or debilitating paranoia, but only for differences between the averages for young and old subjects.

One question we can ask of studies using the MMPI is whether or not they show an increase with age in introversion, as Jung predicted and as the Kansas City Studies showed. The answer is usually yes. Consider, for example, data on 50,000 patients at the Mayo Clinic in Rochester, Minnesota (Swenson, Pearson, and Osborne, 1973), shown in Figure 4–2. (Psychiatric and acutely ill, nonambulatory patients were excluded from this tabulation.) Both males and females show a general increase with age on the MMPI introversion scale, although women are somewhat more introverted than men throughout the life span. These are *age differences* from a cross-sectional study, and we cannot be sure that they reflect true age *changes*. But the data do support the hypothesis of an increase in introversion. Similar results were obtained for men in other investigations as well (Brozek, 1955; Calden and Hokanson, 1959).

What of Jung's other hypothesis, that men become more feminine and women become more masculine? The Mayo Clinic data support only the female portion of this hypothesis. Older women have more masculine interests than younger women, but older men also show an increase in masculinity (see also Feldman, Biringen, and Nash, 1981).

Other MMPI scales also show similar patterns for men and women. Depression shows essentially no change over the life span, in spite of many theories asserting that depression becomes more common in later life. Psychopathy (unemotional disregard for laws and social norms), paranoia, psychoasthenia (excessive worry, lack of confidence, compulsive behavior), schizophrenic tendencies, and mania all decrease systematically over the life span. Depression, therefore, which does not decrease, is *relatively* higher in older people; this fact may account for its apparent increase (Gynther and Shimkunas, 1966). In the Mayo Clinic patients, two scales increase to middle age and then decrease: hypochondriasis (excessive concern with physical health) and hysteria (physical symptoms caused by excessive anxiety, such as "writer's cramp"). These two scales thus represent evidence of sorts for a midlife crisis in neurotic concern for what's happening to one's body (see also Aaronson, 1958; Brozek, 1955; Hardyck, 1964).

Other cross-sectional investigations of MMPI trends with age corroborate the Mayo Clinic data, for the most part (see Chown, 1968; Schaie and Marquette, 1972; Savage et al., 1977; Shanan and Jacobowitz, 1982). In particular, young adults tend to score higher than older people on the scales measuring psychopathy, schizophrenic tendencies, and mania. These scores paint a picture of the average youth as someone with an energetic (manic) approach to life and attitudes that run to the unusual, if not the bizarre (schizophrenic) and untraditional, if not immoral (psychopathic). Around middle age, there is a transition from concern with impulse control to concern with physical and mental health (Aaronson, 1960). Older adults are more introspective and introverted than young people, and possibly more susceptible to depression.

Age differences in average MMPI scores are rarely sizable and some studies show no statistically significant differences at all (Canter et al., 1962). The MMPI has also been criticized because many of the scales are scored for the same items, building in correlation between scales, and because scores are affected by the tendency to deny socially undesirable items (Schaie and Marquette, 1972). Because of cohort differences in socially desirable attitudes (Schaie and Parham, 1976), it may therefore follow that the MMPI does not discriminate equally well between the young and old (Davis, Mozdzierz, and Macchitelli, 1973; Schaie and Stone, 1982). The apparent decrease with age for some MMPI scales, shown in Figure 4–2, could simply reflect a greater desire by the older cohorts to appear socially respectable.

Another self-report inventory commonly used to investigate age changes in personality is the *Sixteen Personality Factor Questionnaire* (16 PF) constructed by psychologist Raymond B. Cattell. The 16 PF was designed for normal adults and provides scores on sixteen general personality traits (or factors) that are usually described by two ends of a personality dimension. Examples are reserved–outgoing, humble–assertive, and shy–venturesome. Even more general dimensions (called second-order factors) can also be assessed, notably extraversion and anxiety.

There have not been many longitudinal studies of personality development. In one of the few, a brief test that estimates thirteen of the sixteen characteristics in the 16 PF was given to people aged twenty-one to eighty-four (Schaie and Parham, 1976). The test was administered twice, once in 1963 and again in 1970. The results were quite revealing. Only a single trait was seen to be changing systematically with age — "excitability," which increased as the subjects grew

FIGURE 4–2.

Cross-sectional data on representative MMPI scales. Note that increasing masculinity is shown directly for females and indirectly, through decreasing femininity, for males. For six scales not shown, hysteria followed the pattern for hypochondriasis; the others (schizophrenia, mania, psychasthenia, and paranoia) showed general decline, like psychopathy.

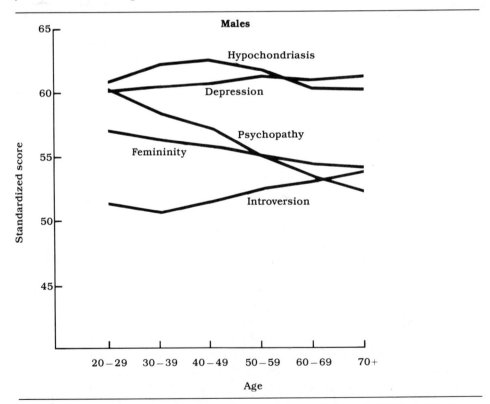

Source: Data from Table 1 in Swenson, M. W., Pearson, J. S., and Osborne, D. (1973). *An MMPI source book*. Minneapolis: University of Minnesota Press.

older. Many of the other traits showed age differences that on statistical analysis were actually found to be cohort differences. For example, people born in earlier years (which of course makes them older) were "more reserved, less outgoing" than people born in later years. This age difference makes one think of introversion and our hypothesis that introversion increases with age, and indeed this trait is one in the composite of traits that make up the second-order introversion factor. But this age difference turned out to be attributable, not to true age change, but to differences in generations. People born in later years (the younger subjects) were less reserved than older subjects, but they did not become more reserved as they got older. Apparently people born in different generations were taught different things about the proper amount of reserve to show in social situations; once learned, this lesson is carried by the members of each generation throughout life.

This study did not include examination of certain 16 PF traits that could not adequately be assessed with the brief test used. Thus it provides no estimate of cohort differences versus age changes on emotional stability (ego strength) and the dimension that runs from "sober and serious" at one pole to "enthusiastic and happy-go-lucky" at the other. Both of these have been found to differ across ages in cross-sectional studies (Sealy and Cattell, 1965; Fozard and Nuttall, 1971), with older subjects more stable and more serious. The latter trait is a major component of introversion as well and one of the prime contributions to the finding of increasing introversion with age (Chown, 1968).

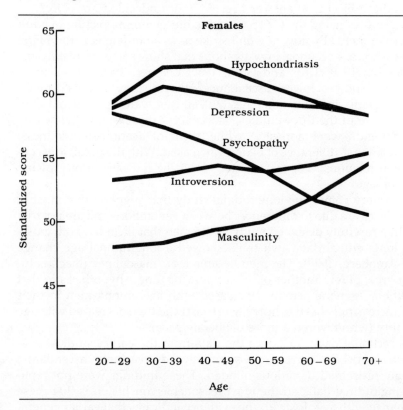

Another longitudinal study, however, used the complete 16 PF. Testing 331 men and women who were fifty-four to seventy years old at the time of first measurement (between 1968 and 1970), the researchers found practically no age changes over an eight-year interval (Siegler, George, and Okun, 1979). In addition, the correlations between testings were very high. Similar findings occur for data coming from the Boston Normative Aging Study of veterans. A comparison of data for 139 persons who took the 16 PF in 1965–1967 and again in 1975 showed that there was no significant change for fourteen of the scales. For the two scales where change was observed, Intelligence and Social Independence, movement was in a positive direction (Costa and McCrae, 1978; McCrae and Costa, 1984). These studies indicate high stability of personality characteristics. There was no change in average scores as people grew older, and the ranking of people also did not change much. The sizable differences between generations suggest that early childhood experiences are crucial in the formation of personality; the absence of age changes and the high correlations in the adult years suggest that, once formed, personality does not change a lot.

A self-report inventory somewhat similar to the 16 PF is the *Guilford–Zimmerman Temperament Survey* (GZTS). The GZTS provides scores on ten personality dimensions or traits, such as friendliness, emotional stability, and thoughtfulness (Guilford, Zimmerman, and Guilford, 1976). Each trait score is based on the individual's response to thirty items such as "You are often in low spirits," which the subject is to answer "Yes," "?" (if undecided), or "No."

What have studies using the GZTS to add to our emerging picture of adult personality development? By now, it won't strike us as an unfamiliar story. First we have three early cross-sectional investigations that show some interesting age differences (Bendig, 1960; Titus and Goss, 1969; Wagner, 1960). In all three studies, older men showed lower "ascendance"; that is, they described themselves as more submissive and more hesitant and as wanting to avoid conspicuousness. In two of the three studies, "sociability" decreased with age (the men had fewer friends, were more shy), while "restraint" (serious-mindedness) and "personal relations" (tolerance of people) increased. With the possible exception of "personal relations," all these factors could be indications of growing introversion with age.

Next in our story comes the longitudinal study that suggests that most of these age differences are due to differences between generations and are not true age changes. In a carefully designed study of 915 men that included both cross-sectional and longitudinal data, two traits showed a longitudinal age change (Douglas and Arenberg, 1978). The men became less "masculine" (macho attitudes) as they grew older, another bit of support for Jung's hypothesis to that effect. In addition, "general activity" increased with age among men in their twenties (they increasingly liked to hurry, work fast) and then decreased with age for men over fifty (who favored a more deliberate pace).

The cross-sectional data, including the data from the earlier studies, suggested that men also became increasingly submissive (decreasingly "ascendant") and increasingly restrained or serious-minded. These findings were not replicated in the longitudinal data, so the most reasonable conclusion is that these traits do *not* change with age. Instead, the evidence indicates that earlier genera-

Is this young man likely to become more reserved as he grows older (an age change), or do earlier generations have different standards of social behavior (a cohort difference)?

tions (men born in times more distantly removed from the present) were taught to be more restrained and more submissive.

Thoughtfulness and tolerance declined in the longitudinal data but not in the cross-sectional analysis. The conclusion one draws from this pattern is that between 1958 and 1968, when the first test was given, and 1968 and 1974, when the second test was given, society in general changed its attitude toward these traits. People of all ages became less reflective and introspective and less tolerant, more critical of people and social institutions. Considering the events that transpired between testings — the war in Vietnam and at least the early stages of the Watergate crimes — an increase in cynicism is hardly surprising. These findings are consistent with a study using an MMPI-type scale of "social responsibility" (personal integrity plus a sense of obligation to society) which also showed a general decline in recent years (Schaie and Parham, 1974).

In another analysis of essentially the same sample of men, correlations over periods of six and twelve years were computed from the longitudinal data (Costa, McCrae, and Arenberg, 1980). These correlations were surprisingly high: around .73 for the average scale over twelve years and between .80 and 1.00 when corrected for the unreliability of the test. Together with the absence of age changes in mean scores, the high degree to which rankings are maintained indicates an exceptional amount of stability in the personality characteristics measured by the

Several studies show that men feel emotions more deeply and express them more openly as they grow older.

GZTS (see also McCrae and Costa, 1982). Combining what we know of results from the MMPI, the 16 PF, and the GZTS, a fairly consistent picture emerges of personality development in the adult years. It is a picture, first and foremost, of stability and continuity, and not one of frequent and extensive change. Psychologists have long considered personality to be an *enduring* organization of traits, and the test results support this view, for most people.

A second major conclusion from the test studies is that many of the age differences we once thought of as personality development are in fact differences between members of different generations. A number of cross-sectional studies, for example, show that older people are more reserved (16 PF) or restrained (GZTS) than younger people. Here is a personality trait we would almost expect to change with age. Don't older people become more serious-minded? Aren't younger people more happy-go-lucky, becoming more reserved with age? Apparently not. The evidence from two major longitudinal studies, one with the 16 PF and one with the GZTS, shows that reserve/restraint differs between generations but does not increase with age within a given generation.

Three personality dimensions give evidence of change with age. One is masculinity, for which the evidence applies only to men. As men age, they become less comfortable with "masculine" activities such as hunting; and they report that now that they're older, they feel emotions more deeply and express them more openly — admitting fear, for example, and crying when sad.

The other personality traits that show age changes are two that we would expect to be positively related: excitability (16 PF) and general activity (GZTS). But one, excitability, goes up with age, whereas the other, general activity, goes down. Another contradiction in the research literature? Perhaps. Another possibility, however, is that both findings are valid, that the "activation" described by general activity is different from the "activation" described by the excitability factor. General activity refers to "pace"; a high score indicates someone who is energetic, rapid-working, active, and sometimes impulsive (Guilford, Zimmerman, and Guilford, 1976). This quality seems to decrease with age. Excitability, on the other hand, refers to a quality of instability in arousal level, an inability to keep one's emotions on an even keel, as reflected in a tendency to become perplexed and befuddled by relatively trivial incidents. This quality seems to increase with age. In fact, these two self-reported personality traits may be related to two characteristics of the human nervous system, which also appear to change in different ways with age. To put it rather glibly, older people seem to be harder to "turn on" than younger people, but also harder to "turn off" (Marsh and Thompson, 1977). The older nervous system is less active generally, but it is also less stable.

PROJECTIVE TESTS

A projective test is one in which the stimuli, which are comparable to questions in other tests, are deliberately made vague and ambiguous. For example, the best-known projective test, the Rorschach Inkblot Test, uses inkblots that were originally created by dropping ink on papers and folding them in half. The individual is shown each blot in turn and asked what it makes him or her think of. In another popular projective test, the Thematic Apperception Test (TAT), pictures rather than inkblots are used as stimuli. The theory behind projective tests is that persons must "project" their own personalities onto the ambiguous stimulus in order to construct a coherent response. Thus, in describing the inkblot, individuals are supposedly telling us about their basic needs and values. (There is considerable doubt, however, that this assumption is correct and that the Rorschach, the TAT, and other projective tests actually measure what they purport to measure; see Anastasi, 1976.)

Susan, the suspicious and hostile young woman whose story began the chapter, told TAT stories of talented individuals who fail because of circumstances beyond their control. She described a world full of cheating, jealousy, and aggression. To the picture in Figure 4–3, she responded, "This is an artist's conception of the outer and inner life of a young woman. Outwardly, she is young and attractive and has the vehemence and independence of a man; but she is looked on by others, and in turn views herself, as unattractive, inadequate, and aged" (McKinney, 1965, p. 226). Several stories told of her need for intimacy; characters saw "romance and beauty in spite of the drudgery and sordidness around . . ." (McKinney, 1965, p. 227).

FIGURE 4–3.

Susan described this picture as an artist's representation of the inner and outer life of a young woman (presumably herself).

In studies of adult personality development using the Rorschach, one of the more common findings is that older people are more likely than younger people to make responses considered indicative of introversion (e.g., Ames, 1965). Similar results have been obtained with the TAT. Asked to tell brief stories that might account for the scenes depicted in the TAT pictures, older subjects tend to describe introspective, shy, conforming characters to whom things happen beyond their control, while younger subjects relate stories of active, outgoing, assertive people who *make* things happen (Neugarten and associates, 1964). It is primarily these results that led one reviewer to conclude that studies of personality change "add up to the generalization that introversion increases with age in the second half of life" (Neugarten, 1977b, p. 636).

The reversal in sex-role behaviors that we have discussed previously is also found in TAT-type studies (Neugarten and Gutmann, 1958). Presented with the picture in Figure 4–3, older subjects (aged fifty-five to seventy) tended to see the older woman in the picture as dominant over the older man, whereas middle-aged subjects (aged forty to fifty-four) described more traditional sex roles, with the older man dominant. In addition, older men seemed more receptive than younger men to their "feminine qualities," such as their emotionality and their need to care for someone (nurturance). Older women "projected" more aggressive and selfish attitudes than younger women, presumably showing a change toward "masculine qualities."

Projective tests must be interpreted with care for subjects of all ages, but it is worth mentioning that older subjects present unique problems. Many older people may give unusual responses because they don't see the stimuli clearly or because they can't hear the examiner's questions (Caldwell, 1954; Eisdorfer, 1960). Also, consider a picture of an old person interacting with a young person presented for story-telling to an old and a young subject. People are likely to identify with the character in the picture closer to their own age, and to form the story around that character. In essence, they are telling stories about two *different* pictures, one with the older person as hero, the other with the young person as the center of attention. Comparing their stories may tell us something about their age, but little about their personality.

Some researchers have proposed that it would be better to use TAT-like forms specifically designed for use with older persons. Examples of such tests are the Senior Apperception Technique (SAT) developed by Bellak (1975) and the Gerontological Apperception Test (GAT) by Wolk and Wolk (1971). Use of these special techniques is quite problematic, because these authors portray the elderly figures on the test cards as being physically decrepit, in socially submissive situations, and wearing old-fashioned clothes. Older persons responding to these cards may either have great difficulty identifying with the elderly figures, if they are still in good health and live an active life in the community, or may give responses that the professional interviewer might interpret as evidence of pathology, but that are no more than accurate descriptions of the characteristics built into the stimulus material. Consequently, these special materials have not been found any more useful for work with the elderly than standard TAT cards (Schaie and Stone, 1982).

Change and Continuity in the Adult Personality

What is the nature of personality change with age? Is one's personality relatively stable throughout life, or does it change significantly? Are there general trends reflecting universal or nearly universal changes in personality that occur as one grows older?

These are important questions, and we cannot answer them adequately yet. The research evidence does suggest, however, that very few general trends exist. Few personality traits systematically increase or decrease with age. Perhaps "excitability" increases or "general activity level" decreases. Perhaps people become more introverted as they grow older. Perhaps men become a little less macho and women a little more so. Beyond these few personality characteristics, there is precious little evidence for general change.

People tend to *perceive* that they have changed more than they have in fact. In an intriguing study, personality test scores of people first tested in 1944, when they were about twenty years of age, were compared with their scores in 1969, when they averaged forty-five (Woodruff, 1983; Woodruff and Birren, 1972). The test measured personal and social adjustment. There were no significant differences over the twenty-five year period, supporting the conclusion that personality changes in very few general ways. At the time of the second testing, however, the participants were asked to take the test again; this time they were to answer each question as they thought they probably had answered it back in 1944. These "remembered" scores were quite a bit lower than the real scores. People imagined themselves as less well adjusted twenty-five years previously than they actually were. They perceived that they had improved considerably over the years, even though the true test scores showed no evidence of change at all.

THE POTENTIAL FOR CHANGE

To say that there are few general trends in personality development in the adult years does not mean that personality change is impossible or even infrequent. In fact, personality changes are quite common, even in the twilight years. The absence of general trends simply indicates that change, when it does occur, is in different directions for different people, and that age by itself is not the major factor.

Life experiences have an influence on one's personality. Losing one's job after thirty years can be disillusioning; the individual may become anxious and depressed, less confident. In another case, a satisfying marriage may provide a solid base in life, turning an anxious personality into a vital, optimistic, and self-assured personality. The death of a loved one, an increase in responsibility for others, a religious conversion, drug addiction, medical problems, psychotherapy — all these can change an individual's personality in significant ways. It is characteristic of such life experiences, however, that they are not experienced by everyone or at the same age or life stage. Psychologists sometimes call them "nonnormative events" (see Baltes, Cornelius, and Nesselroade, 1979; Schaie, 1984a). The death of one's child, for example, is not "normal" in the sense that it does not happen regularly to everyone at the same time; in contrast, a normal or normative event like retirement usually occurs around the same time in the life of every worker. Normative events, to the extent that they have a general influence on personality, should result in clear age changes on personality measures. Nonnormative events also result in change, but for the individuals experiencing them and not for others the same age.

Just as normative and nonnormative events may influence the personality as a whole, they may also have an effect on specific aspects of the personality. The self-concept is one such aspect. Many researchers have noted that the stability or variability of the self-concept may be a function not purely of intrapsychic forces or "distant" circumstances such as childhood experiences but of environmental events occurring in one's current life (Seligman, 1975; Moss and Sussman, 1980;

Costa and McCrae, 1982; Mortimer, Finch, and Kumka, 1982; Schmitz-Scherzer and Thomae, 1983). Glenn (1980), for example, notes that as the social environment becomes more stable in adulthood, some attitudes and values become more stable. This is not to say that "distant" life experiences are uninfluential. It has been shown that life experiences throughout the decade after college have significant effects on feelings of competence at the ten-year point. Specifically, employment insecurity has a negative effect on feelings of competence, whereas income, work autonomy, and close relationships with one's father have a positive effect (Mortimer and Lorence, 1979; Mortimer, Finch, and Kumka, 1982).

This relationship between environmental events and self-concept is a reciprocal one. Just as events may influence self-concept, self-concept may influence the kind of life stresses one experiences. For example, those whose self-concepts reflect neurotic tendencies tend to have more marital troubles, lower job satisfaction, and other problems (Costa and McCrae, 1980a,b). Certain personality variables from the 16 PF (such as conscientiousness, tendermindedness, and practicality) are better predictors of well-being than are social status variables (George, 1978). Furthermore, Thurnher (in press), in an eight-year longitudinal study of developmental turning points and self-concept, found that people rated high in self-control were likely to perceive turning points positively, whereas those who tended to be anxious and depressed perceived turning points negatively.

Thus it appears that people who have better-adjusted self-concepts may achieve objectively and subjectively better life situations, which in turn enhance their self-concepts. It also appears that certain types of self-concepts are predisposed toward well-being, independent of life events (Mortimer, Finch, and Kumka, 1982). Earlier self-concepts may influence later objective and subjective events, and these events contribute to the further stability or variability in self-concept.

As we have seen, the correlations of self-report inventories administered at two or more times as the individuals grow older are generally high (McCrae and Costa, 1984). This is another indication of the basic stability of the adult personality, but the high correlations by no means preclude the potential for change. For one thing, descriptions of oneself by oneself tend to be more stable and consistent than other measures of personality — descriptions by others, for example (Kelly, 1955) — and actual behavior patterns (Mischel, 1968). Even so, correlations that run as high as .70 still leave 50 percent of the variability of test scores unexplained. Some of this variability is unexplained because of imperfections in the test itself, but a good deal must be attributed to true shifts in the ranking of people on the personality characteristic in question. In personal terms, some people who were among the highest in, say, dominance at age twenty-five may fall to the middle ranks by age forty or fifty; others who were low may move up.

The *average* score for a given trait is likely to remain the same, which means that the people whose scores on the trait increase are balanced by people whose scores decrease. As they grow older, people experience a variety of nonnormative events, changing them in different ways. There is very little *general* change, but there is quite a bit of *individual* change.

The Nature of the Adult Personality

Even though research on personality change in the adult years is beset with difficulties of measurement, experimental design, and interpretation, a glimpse of the nature of the adult personality seems to come through. First one is impressed with the number of age differences in personality that turn out to be due primarily to differences between generations. Indeed, one could conclude that the most important fact about an individual's personality is the year of birth. Someone born in 1900 grew up in different circumstances from someone born in 1950. Methods of child training were different; interactions between children and parents, between brothers and sisters, and between friends were different; values and attitudes were different, and education was different; historical events were different. In short, life was profoundly different for people growing up in the early 1900s, compared to people growing up in the 1950s and 1960s, and these differences made for sizable differences in certain personality characteristics.

Second, the adult personality, once formed, appears to be remarkably stable. This is perhaps as it should be, for the changing world is difficult enough without our close friends radically altering their identities from one meeting to the next. There are a number of reasons to expect a significant degree of stability, of course. For one, the adult personality is a highly complex *organization*. Traits, habits, ways of thinking, ways of interacting, ways of coping all are patterned in a completely unique fashion for each individual. Like any organized system, the adult personality *resists* change, for change in one part requires change or realignment in the other, interrelated parts. Reflect on the case of Susan, for example, with which we opened this chapter. Her personality, "based on a once-accurate perception of a blasted, withered, starved life," was not well suited to her new environment. But instead of changing her personality, she fortified it, erecting new defenses against new threats, new "blasts." Her defiant persistence, which had served her so well in her youth, was too deeply ingrained to change easily. Her aggressive attitudes caused her to see others as hostile, at once both justifying and releasing her own hostility.

Once formed, the adult personality is unlikely to change radically, even in such pressing circumstances as retirement and impending death. In fact, personality is one of the prime determinants of how someone will react to such pressures. We have discussed different reactions to retirement, for example. People with well-integrated personalities had little difficulty "mellowing out" in what they perceived to be the final stage of a successful life cycle. People with poorly integrated personalities encountered the same event with despair and hostility, turning "sour" in the last years of their lives.

Although they run counter to popular preconceptions about older people, findings from several studies spanning several decades of life and using different measurement instruments indicate that self-esteem of middle-aged or older individuals equals or surpasses that of younger subjects (Hess and Bradshaw, 1970;

Nehrke, Hulicka, and Morganti, 1980; Atchley, 1982). This may simply be a result of cohort differences: older respondents may have had higher levels of self-esteem throughout their lives than younger cohorts do now. A more plausible explanation is that the results reflect changes resulting from maturation. Despite the losses and difficulties that often accompany old age, it appears that people can maintain or even increase their level of self-esteem as they age. A third possible explanation suggests that people with higher self-esteem have greater longevity. Although there are no longitudinal studies relating self-esteem levels to rates of subject attrition, Antonovsky (1981) found that self-esteem is a protective factor, increasing a person's resistance to stress and contributing to physical health. In a related study, it has been found that the reactions of elderly women faced with poor health and decreasing social activity depend largley on their personalities (Maas and Kuypers, 1974). Those who reacted to their misfortune with bitterness, compared to old women in general, were rated as undependable, stingy, irritable, critical, aloof, moody, cold, unsympathetic, cheerless, devious, and generally negative. They were self-indulgent and self-pitying, with tendencies toward depression. They disliked having demands placed on them, and they withdrew in the face of threats. Those who reacted more positively to their situation were rated as straightforward, not defensive, and independent. Personally, they were charming, interesting, not moralistic, and socially perceptive; not surprisingly, they were well liked by others. Other studies have found personalities to be a major and lifelong determinant of well-being (Costa and McCrae, 1985).

Another source of stability in adult personality is the tendency to choose environments that suit the individual's personality and to avoid those that might demand change. As people with acrophobia avoid tall buildings and Ferris wheels, people in general avoid situations in which their personality puts them at a disadvantage; shy people avoid public speaking, for example. Kind, gentle people who like a slow pace choose to live in small towns, thereby creating a match between personality and social environment that promotes stability in both. As we have seen, people tend to choose mates with similar interests and values and careers that fit with their personal identities.

Different patterns of stability or change in personality may depend on the type of personality organization established early in life (Block, 1971, 1981; Shanan and Jacobowitz, 1982). One study, for example, identified two types of personality organization in women: traditionalism and independence (Livson, 1976). She found that the "independents" showed far more discontinuity than the "traditionalists" from adolescence to middle age. Another study found differences in continuity of lifestyles between two groups of small-town elderly people, those characterized as positive and as active (Keith, 1979).

Although adults' personalities are generally stable, certain critical events may disrupt patterns for whole groups as well as individuals. The Great Depression had an important influence on the generation then in its adolescence, for example. The exact nature of this influence, however, depended on the individual's earlier socialization (Elder, 1979). In a major German longitudinal study of personality, people's stability seemed to depend on a complex interaction among age, sex, social condition, health, and a variety of psychological predispositions (Thomae, 1980; Schmitz-Scherzer and Thomae, 1983).

The potential for change in personality is then a fact of life. The human animal is characterized by its ability to adapt, to adjust to changing conditions. The human animal is a learning animal. Thus, when the environment presents "learning dilemmas" (Dollard and Miller, 1950) in the form of situations that require readjustment, people do change, sometimes radically. Even in Susan we can see the potential for change, through interaction with her child.

More and more investigators are concluding that "the search for 'invariant' and 'unidirectional' developmental functions in adulthood is not a useful approach" (Baltes and Schaie, 1976, p. 721). Instead we are probably better off examining the sources of stability *and* change in the continuous interaction of individual and environment (Riegel, 1976a; Bandura, 1977b).

Summary

1. Personality is dynamic organization within individuals of those biosocial systems (traits, habits, values) that determine their unique adjustment to the world. Various theories of personality have been proposed, including the psychoanalytic theory of Sigmund Freud and individual-differences theories, which stress personality traits assessed by psychological tests.

2. Psychoanalytic theory divides the personality into *id, ego,* and *superego,* which represent impulsive, reality-oriented, and moralistic tendencies in the individual. The ego uses *defense mechanisms* such as denial, regression, projection, intellectualization, and sublimation to defend itself against the anxiety and guilt caused by unacceptable or unrealistic id or superego demands. Elderly people also use activity and cautiousness as defense mechanisms.

3. Erik Erikson extended the psychoanalytic theory of ego development into the adult years, describing three stages in which *intimacy, generativity,* and *integrity* are major concerns. Loevinger claimed that people at different stages face fundamentally different tasks and approach them in different ways. Carl Jung, who was briefly allied with Freud, also theorized about the adult years. Two of Jung's chief hypotheses were that people become more *introverted* with age and that men and women become similar — men becoming more feminine, women becoming more masculine. The Kansas City Studies of Adult Life found support for both hypotheses.

4. The *cognitive life span* approach to the personality has two basic components, the *scenario* and the *life story.* The scenario consists of one's expectations about the future. One continually compares one's actual experiences with the scenario one had imagined. The life story is the narrative of personal history into which one organizes the events of one's past life to give them personal meaning and a sense of continuity. This approach differs from psychoanalytic approaches in that personality development is assessed in terms of the individual's own conception of how his or her life should proceed.

5. The self-concept tends to remain stable over long periods of adult life. Perceptions of body image are not significantly influenced by aging either. Studies indicate that traditional sex differences among men and women diminish with age; it may be one's stage in the family life cycle rather than aging per se that actually influences traditional sex-role identification. Events in the life environment may also influence self-concept, which will in turn influence what kind of experiences one has.

6. The individual-differences approach to personality development compares test scores at different ages to determine stability or change. Stability is indicated by no difference in average trait scores, which suggests no general trend with age, and by high correlations between scores at different ages, which suggests little shifting in the ranking of individuals. Correlations can be computed only if the same individuals are involved at different ages, that is, if the study is longitudinal.

7. On the *self-report inventory* known as the MMPI, cross-sectional studies show older people as more introverted, but both older men and older women are more masculine than younger adults. Younger people appear as more energetic, with attitudes that are more unusual and more amoral. One of the few longitudinal studies of 16 PF scores found only "excitability" increasing as subjects grew older.

8. The GZTS, in cross-sectional studies, showed a number of age differences which, in longitudinal studies, turned out to be probably cohort or generational differences and not true age changes. Only "masculinity," which decreased for men, and "general activity," which decreased for men over fifty, appeared to be changing systematically with age. Correlations over a twelve-year period were very high, another indication of stability in the adult personality.

9. *Projective tests* such as the Rorschach inkblot test and the TAT ask subjects to "project" their needs and values into a story about an ambiguous stimulus (inkblot, picture). Cross-sectional studies show older people more introspective and introverted, with older men more passive (feminine) and women more assertive (masculine).

10. In sum, the psychoanalytic and individual-differences approaches, both of which rely heavily on psychological tests for empirical results, paint a picture of the adult personality, once formed, as remarkably stable. Since personality is a highly organized system of traits, habits, and values, we should perhaps expect a fairly high degree of stability. Even levels of self-esteem appear to persist into later adult life. There is a pronounced tendency of individuals to place themselves in environments, including marriages and careers, that promote the stability of their personalities. Nevertheless, the human animal is characterized by exceptional adaptability, and the potential for change is significant, especially if unexpected changes in the environment ("nonnormative events") demand it. This adaptability to changing circumstances is amply demonstrated by the widely diverging "average personalities" formed by cohorts growing up in different social eras.

SUGGESTED READINGS

Bengtson, V. L., Reedy, M. N., and Gordon, C. E. (1985). Aging and self-conceptions: Personality process and social contexts. In J. E. Birren and K. Warner Schaie (Eds.), *Handbook of the psychology of aging* (2nd ed.) (pp. 544–593). New York: Van Nostrand Reinhold. Review of the research literature covering theories, methodological issues, and a social-psychological view of self-concept development.

Fry, C. L. (1985). Culture, behavior, and aging in the comparative perspective. In J. E. Birren and K. W. Schaie (Eds.), *Handbook of the psychology of aging* (2nd ed.) (pp. 216–244). New York: Van Nostrand Reinhold. Provides a cross-cultural perspective of aging in industrial and nonindustrial societies, including discussions of gender and ethnicity as they affect aging.

McCrae, R. R. and Costa, P. T., Jr. (1984). *Emerging lives, enduring dispositions: Personality in adulthood.* Boston: Little, Brown. An account of a major longitudinal study of personality that provides strong support for the proposition that personality remains quite stable across the life course.

Schaie, K. W., and Parham, I. A. (1976). Stability of adult personality traits: Fact or fable? *Journal of Personality and Social Psychology, 34,* 146–158. Reports results of another longitudinal study of adult personality traits and develops a model that accounts for the origin of the different patterns of age change and generational differences observed in the study.

The Self-Concept and the Stability of Personality: Cross-Sectional Comparisons of Self-Reports and Ratings

Does personality change with age? The popular view is that it does — we expect older people to be more reflective, less active, less receptive to change, and generally more conservative than younger people. The theoretical views of Jung, Erikson, and others also suggest that people's personalities change as they age. Many studies have been conducted on this matter, but their findings tend to contradict the popular assumption, indicating that personality in fact remains stable. One might expect this to lay the matter to rest. However, the issue and the studies that attempt to resolve it are not as straightforward as they at first appear.

The problem is that studies of personality rely heavily on self-reported information — the aging people themselves provide the responses used to determine whether their personalities have changed. It has been argued that these self-responses reflect not the status of the actual personality but the status of the self-concept. The two may be related, but they are not identical. The personality is a set of consistent dispositions and styles — emotional, interpersonal, and experiential — that characterize an individual. The self-concept, by contrast, is what a person thinks he or she is like. "The self-concept is not the 'real self' but, rather the picture of the self" (Rosenberg, 1979, p. 7). It has been argued that at some point during maturation, probably early adulthood, the self-concept may become crystallized, or fixed. In other words, once a young person develops a certain image of him- or herself, he or she may tend to maintain it throughout life — even though the person's actual personality may change dramatically. Thus, a gruff, irritable elderly man may continue to think of himself as the kindly, gentle person he was as a young man. If this were found to be the case — if self-reports reflect self-concept rather than personality — the effect would be to invalidate the many studies that indicate that personality tends to remain stable throughout adulthood.

The issue, then, is whether the self-concept remains stable as the personality changes. How can such a question be addressed? In a 1982 study, McCrae and Costa took this approach: they reasoned that, to disentangle self-concept and personality, nonself-report methods of personality assessment would have to be used. The best alternative, they decided, was one in which the personality of the subject was rated by an outside observer. Such an observer would have to be intimately acquainted with the subject, however. This led to the choice of the subjects' spouses as the other raters. Presumably husbands and wives would recognize personality changes in their spouses as such; their assessments would not reflect the subject's self-concept.

Data from the study came from the Neuroticism–Extraversion–Openness (NEO) Inventory (discussed in Chapter 3). As you will recall, the NEO Inventory is used to assess a variety of characteristics in the three broad domains given in the title. Both self-report and spouse rating data were available on 139 men and 142 women ranging in age from twenty-one to eighty-nine. Stated simply, the assumption was that if self-concept remains constant while personality changes with age, the correlation on the NEO between self-reported scores and spouse rating should be greater among younger couples than older ones.

The findings? Correlations tended to remain quite constant. The self-report showed great stability across the life span. Comparison of these self-reports with spouse ratings indicated that self-concept and personality tend to run parallel courses of stability over the years twenty-five to ninety. This suggests that self-concept probably corresponds quite closely to the actual personality. Both, it appears, remain stable across the life span.

McCrae, R. R., and Costa, P. T., Jr. (1982). The self-concept and the stability of personality: Cross-sectional comparisons of self-reports and ratings. *Journal of Personality and Social Psychology, 43*, 1282–1292.

Chapter Five

YOUNG ADULTHOOD

Independence Versus Intimacy

Linda Leslie is twenty-two years old. She is, in her words, "about to become an adult."

"What is an adult?" we asked.

"Adults earn their own money," Linda replied. "Adults make their own mistakes. Adults are on their own."

"Aren't you a little old to be entering adulthood? Don't you think eighteen is the dividing line?"

"Maybe it is for some people. Maybe it's even younger for some people. Me, I've been going to college, still spending my parents' money. Now I've got my degree, and I'm on my own. I'm about to become an adult."

"What do you plan to do with your life?"

"What questions! 'What is an adult?' 'What do you plan to do with your life?' What's next? 'What is the purpose of life?' "

"Let's see. . . . No. It's 'What is truth?' "

"All right! That I can answer! Life's plans? Well, it may please you to learn that I've decided to become a psychologist — a clinical psychologist, in private practice. I've been accepted at the University of Minnesota, in the clinical psychology program. I'll be working as a research assistant next year, to pay for my graduate work."

"How did you happen to choose psychology as a profession?"

"I wish I could give you a logical answer. I was a mathematics major in college, believe it or not. I was pretty good, too, usually second or third in class on tests and things. I liked math a lot — its clarity, the structure of it. In my senior year, though, we were working on a lot of physics-type problems. That was maybe a little less interesting. But the main thing, I guess, is that I just got interested in people. I feel I should make a contribution in life, and I would like to help people with their problems. Psychology seemed a good choice."

Linda's mother, Laura, asked a question. "How about a family, dear? Are you and Steve going to get married? I would like to see some grandchildren before I die." Laura chuckled, as if her death were an incredible thought.

"Steve is my boyfriend," Linda explained. "Actually, we've been living together for about six months. What do you call someone you're living with? Someone suggested 'mingle' — halfway between single and married. Steve is my mingle."

"You didn't have to tell them that, dear," said Linda's mother.

"Mrs. Leslie has a good question. Are you and Steve planning marriage?" we asked.

"How about if I tackle 'What is truth?' instead?! I don't know. What's going to happen? He's going on to graduate school in mathematics at M.I.T.; I'll be in Minnesota. Will we drift apart? I suppose so. Why is it I have to choose between a career and a family?"

"In my day, there was no choice," said Leonard Leslie, Linda's grandfather. "A girl grew up, got married, had children — and in that order, too."

"Times are changing, Gramps."

"Yes, I know. And if you want my opinion, it's all to the better. In my day there were some terribly bright women, terribly talented. All gone to waste."

Linda's mother frowned. "Raising a family isn't a waste," she said. Her comment evoked no response, except for a scowl from her husband, Linda's father.

"Do you have a good sense of who you are?" we asked. "Who is Linda Leslie? What are her values?"

"I'm clearer now than I was, that's for sure. Linda Leslie is . . . well, I don't know . . . a basically optimistic person. She likes people. She's not very selfish. She wants to help. She's intelligent and capable, capable really of doing just about anything she wants to. She'll make an *outstanding* psychologist! [She laughs.] She doesn't have false modesty; she's quite self-confident. She's a loving person, who someday will team up with an equally loving and sensitive man to make one helluva pair. They'll have maybe a couple of kids, and they'll share the responsibilities of raising them. Equally. Except for pregnancy and birth, of course."

"That's my granddaughter, all right," exclaimed Leonard. "Damn good woman, that's what she's going to be. A damn good woman."

"Shut up, Grandpa!" said Linda's mother. "Don't swear!"

The Period of Young Adulthood

It is not easy to define when a child becomes an adult. No single answer would fit all people. In some cultures, young people barely into their teens assume the full responsibilities and privileges of adulthood, whereas in other cultures men and women stay with their parents until well into their thirties, struggling to get a start on their own. In our society, the age of eighteen confers some legal status (the right to vote, for example) and many young people, finished with high school, begin their careers. They become adults by Linda Leslie's definition: they earn their own money. Others postpone final career decisions for more schooling in colleges or in the armed services.

The transition to adulthood, then, is marked by a number of developments. The young person may get a job, get married, become a parent, or join the military. Schooling may end, or the person may continue to college. In many cases, the young person moves to a new place of residence. These events may occur simultaneously or sequentially. Their timing and the pattern in which they occur varies for individuals and for different cohorts.

The timing and pattern in which these normative events occur are determined in part by societal expectations and historical events. It is expected that the young person will make certain transitions at specific periods of his or her life and also that the transitions will occur in a certain order. When the usual order and timing of transitions are disrupted, it may pose problems for the individual and for society. For example, we generally expect people to be economically independent before they marry and have children. If the economy and job market are poor, however, a person may have to begin marriage and parenting "off time," later than social norms would suggest. Acquiring additional schooling can have a similar effect.

Social expectations concerning what constitutes "normative" transition events to adulthood have changed historically. As the length of compulsory schooling has increased, for example, the age at which one is expected to enter the labor force has changed. Almost one-half of young adults in the United States now seek some form of post-secondary education, and thus further delay entry into full-time jobs. Historically, young women only briefly entered the job market, prior to marriage. Increasingly, women are staying in the workplace after marriage and during the childbearing years.

The transitions of young adulthood, then, vary with the individual, cohort, economic conditions, and a variety of other social factors. The relationship of cohort and social class membership to the timing and sequencing of the transitions to adulthood has been examined in an interesting study by Featherman, Hogan, and Sorenson (1984). In this study, two cohorts of young men — one born between 1929 and 1933, the other born between 1934 and 1939 — were studied longitudinally between the ages of fourteen and twenty-nine. For each month during this fifteen-year period, changes in the lives of the subjects were noted, resulting in an unusually detailed chronology of transitional changes.

Figure 5–1 presents the total number of months from ages fourteen to twenty-nine spent in each state: in school, working, and married. The bar graph is shown by cohort, race, and social class (father's occupation). Note that the earlier cohort (1929–1933) was involved in the Korean War and spent six months more time in the military than did the younger cohort. Partly as a function of greater military service, the earlier cohort spent fewer months at work and married than did the later cohort during this fifteen-year period. That is, their transition to work and marriage was delayed by military service.

The major racial differences found involved schooling and employment. Compared to whites, blacks spent fewer months in school and more months at

FIGURE 5–1.

Average person-months spent in school, at work, and married from ages fourteen to twenty-nine by birth cohort (1929–1933, 1934–1939), race (black, white), and father's occupation (blue-collar, white-collar).

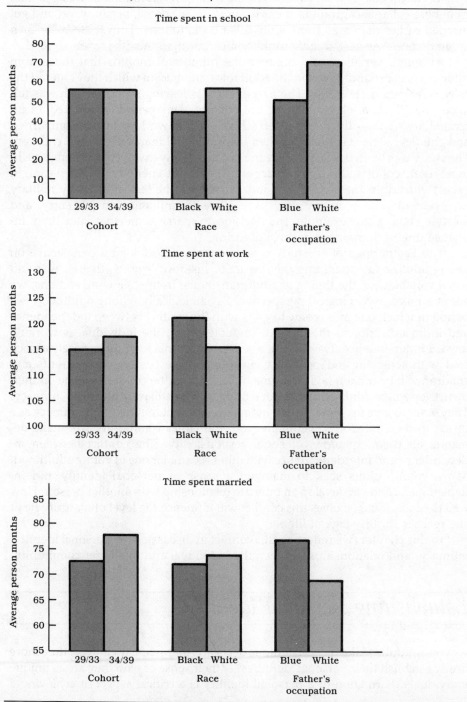

Source: Adapted from D. Featherman, D. Hogan, and A. Sorenson. Entry into adulthood: Profiles of young men in the 1950s. In P. B. Baltes and O. G. Brim, Jr., eds., *Life-span development and behavior* (Vol. 6). New York: Academic Press, 1984. Reprinted by permission.

work in full-time jobs. In general, blacks began working, married, and became parents at earlier ages than whites. The major social class difference was that men from blue-collar backgrounds spent fewer years in school, began work, and got married earlier than men from white collar backgrounds. Thus, blue-collar men entered states associated with adulthood earlier than the other men studied.

Although variations did occur in the number of months that those from different backgrounds spent in the adult roles, the *order* in which they entered the roles remained quite stable. The first event was leaving school, which was followed by taking a job or entering the military. This period constituted an intermediary stage — the man had left school and was working but was unmarried and childless. The stage ended when the individual married and had children. The study was limited, of course, by the fact that it only involved male subjects. In more recent cohorts, due to voluntary enlistment and a period of peace, we might expect entry into the work force and marriage to be less affected by military involvement. The economy may have a greater influence on job entry; and lifestyle choices (for example, the decision to marry somewhat later) may influence timing of marriage and childbearing.

The Featherman et al. study was essentially a sociological perspective on young adulthood, examining the impact of historical events (that is, war and social variables) on the timing of adult transitions. In the following sections, we adopt a more psychological perspective. Psychologically, young adulthood is a period in which one must come to grips with the conflict between independence and intimacy. Prior to this period, in adolescence, the individual is working toward independence. Developing a sense of personal identity is closely associated with achieving independence. Eventually, the ties between parents and children will be broken (at least some of them), and the children will be on their own; they will be adults. But they soon find that they still want and need intimacy. They want to give up some of their independence, but they also fear intimacy as a threat to their freedom. Eventually, too, the larger community will make demands on them, in terms of social responsibility. The conflict between independence and interdependence with others is a major one in young adulthood. Many young adults seek to maintain a sense of personal identity and independence, and yet develop an intimate relationship with another person. How well the individual resolves this conflict will influence the level of maturity he or she reaches in this stage of life.

In this chapter, we reflect on this conflict in discussions of personal identity, intimacy, and relationships between the individual and the larger community.

Establishing Personal Identity

As young adults make the momentous decisions that shape their lives, they more firmly establish their personal identities — their sense of who they are as unique individuals. Formation of a personal identity is a critical aspect of achieving a sense of independence — of differentiating oneself from parents and others. The choices of a career and a mate constitute a large part of personal identity. Children, too, become a significant part of one's identity, in some cases almost an extension of oneself. Several different perspectives have been offered on the nature of identity and how it changes in young adulthood and throughout life.

IDENTITY AND THE SELF-CONCEPT

The term "identity" is most closely associated with Erikson (1963, 1968), who introduced the concept of the "identity crisis" to describe the fifth stage of the eight stages of development throughout the life span. An identity crisis may occur during adolescence in response to the rapid physical and emotional changes that occur during this period in combination with increasing social expectations for adult behavior. The adolescent must integrate into an earlier identity as a child such important characteristics as a new physical appearance, new abilities, new feelings, and new roles (Whitbourne and Weinstock, 1979). If the adolescent manages to integrate these characteristics into a consistent whole by questioning and exploring alternative possibilities for adult life, then he or she achieves a new level of ego identity. If the adolescent is overwhelmed by the changes occurring and the range of possibilities available, identity diffusion occurs. Expanding on Erikson's work, Marcia (1967) has suggested that the adolescent may forego an identity crisis in either of two ways. The young person may preclude the crisis by *foreclosure*, by accepting unquestioningly parental beliefs and attitudes. For example, the child goes into law because the parents want to have a "lawyer in the family." Alternatively, the young person may remain in a state of indecision, making few commitments and indicating little concern with forming an identity.

The identity crisis is most often associated with adolescence, since that is considered the period when identity issues predominate, but Erikson believes that identity continues to be an issue throughout adulthood. New concerns such as intimacy and generativity arise that affect and are affected by identity. Whitbourne and Weinstock (1979) have suggested that it may be more useful to think of the search for identity as a lifelong *process* than as a discrete stage or phase. In other words, they do not think of adult identity as a unitary construct or static phenomenon. A person's level of identity integration will vary by social role (for example, spouse, employee) and also in response to life events. One may have a clear-cut identity as a manager at work but have difficulty with one's identity as a spouse (especially as a result of recent sociocultural changes in sex-role expectations regarding spousal roles; see Chapters 3 and 4). Furthermore, there may be changes in a person's identity as he or she moves through the adult life course. For example, as children leave home, both fathers and mother may redefine their parental and spousal roles.

Erikson's stages and related concepts such as identity and intimacy have been difficult to quantify and study empirically. Thus, although there has been much theorizing, there have been few substantive studies, especially longitudinal studies (see Whitbourne and Weinstock, 1979).

Whitbourne and Waterman (1979) conducted a ten-year longitudinal follow-up study of college students initially assessed in terms of Erikson's stages in 1966. They found significant *longitudinal* changes on a measure of psychosocial development between 1966 and 1976 for men and women (Figure 5-2). In addition to an overall psychosocial development score, the scale scores were derived for six Eriksonian stages. Advances in scale scores occurred for the two stages that would be expected to change during this age range, that is, identity and intimacy. As a second part of the study, a current cohort of college students was tested in 1976 for comparison with the 1966 cohort that was initially tested ten years earlier. In the *cross-sectional* analysis, comparing the 1976 scores for the two cohorts, a significant age/cohort effect was found. That is, in 1976, the 1966 cohort's (alumni) overall scores on psychosocial development were significantly higher than those of the 1976 college sample, again suggesting age-related change (Figure 5–2). The identity and intimacy scale scores of the 1966 cohort were higher than the 1976 cohort's scores; however, these differences were not statistically significant. Finally, in a *time-lag* comparison the scores of the earlier cohort when it was in college in 1966 were compared with the 1976 college sample. The 1976

FIGURE 5–2.

Mean overall Inventory of Psychosocial Development scores used in the longitudinal, cross-sectional, and time-lag comparisons.

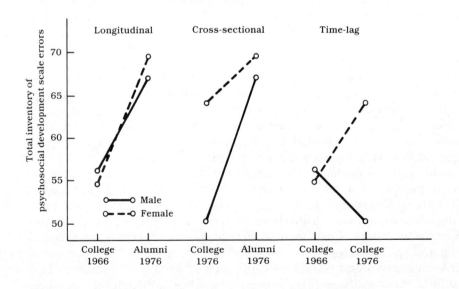

Source: S. K. Whitbourne and A. S. Waterman. Psychosocial development during the adult years: Age and cohort comparisons, *Developmental Psychology*, 1979, *15*, 373–378. Copyright 1979 by the American Psychological Association. Reprinted by permission of the publisher and author.

women scored significantly above the 1976 men and the 1966 women, whereas the 1976 men scored significantly below the 1966 men and women. There was little difference between males and females for the 1966 cohort; however, there were large sex differences for the 1976 cohort. There are several possible explanations for this finding. There may be sampling differences between the 1966 and 1976 cohorts for women. Different college selection criteria for women may have been in use in 1966 and 1976 — a larger and more diverse group of women were attending college in 1976 than in 1966. On the other hand, it may be that the societal changes in sex-role expectations that occurred between 1966 and 1976 had a positive influence on the psychosocial development of women but had a negative influence for men. In addition, these hypothesized societal changes from 1966 to 1976 appear to have affected the gender differences for the 1976 cohort much more than for the 1966 cohort. While there are large gender differences for the 1976 cohort, gender differences for the 1966 cohort are small and remain fairly constant across the ten-year period. In summary, the longitudinal data in this study provide empirical support for age-related changes in the level of psychosocial development, as defined by Erikson. In addition, one interpretation of the time-lag analyses is that the psychosocial development of women and men may be influenced differentially by historical trends.

THE MULTIDIMENSIONAL VIEW OF THE SELF-CONCEPT

Another approach to the study of the self-concept involves conceptualizing it in terms of a number of personality traits rather than examining identity as the focus of one stage of psychosocial development. Mortimer, Finch, and Kumka (1982) used self-ratings on a number of personality characteristics to identify four factors associated with self-concept: competence, well-being, sociability, and unconventionality. Competence reflected one's appraisal of oneself as active or passive, strong or weak, competent or incompetent, and successful or unsuccessful. Well-being involved perceiving oneself as happy or unhappy, relaxed or tense, and confident or anxious. The sociability dimension reflected whether one saw oneself as social or solitary, interested in others rather than interested in oneself, open or closed, and warm or cold. Unconventionality involved perceiving oneself as impulsive or deliberate, unconventional or conventional, and a dreamer or practical.

The subjects in the Mortimer et al. study were male students who graduated from the University of Michigan in 1966 or 1967. The subjects were administered the self-concept scales when they entered as freshmen in 1962 and 1963, and they were reassessed as seniors. Seventy-four percent were followed up again in 1976, when most were in their early thirties. This sample was exceptional in terms of the level of professional status attained — by the time they were reassessed in 1976, half had obtained a professional degree in a subject such as law, divinity, or dentistry. This cohort is of particular interest since it consists of baby boomers, who are now approaching midlife. The baby boomers have been receiving a good deal of attention lately because they are a large group compared to the cohorts that preceded and followed them and thus have had a significant impact on societal structure.

In comparing the self-concept scores of the subjects when they were freshmen, seniors, and in their thirties, four main questions were asked. First, does the self concept, as a construct, remain constant over time? That is, does the self concept involve the same dimensions (competence, well-being, and so on) over time, and do the relationships among the dimensions remain stable? The researchers found that the self-concept does indeed have the same "meaning" over time; the same dimensions of the self-concept were relevant at all assessment points.

Second, does a person's rank ordering in the group tend to remain stable over time? The researchers found that it did — for example, a person who had a high rank in 1966 on a dimension was likely to have a high rank in 1976 as well.

Third, are there quantitative changes in an individual's self-concept scores across time? That is, compared to his earlier level on a given dimension, does a subject's score tend to change or remain the same? The results showed that changes do occur. As a rule, the subjects' feelings of well-being and competence declined between their freshmen and senior years and then increased after graduation. Why? It has been suggested that the declines are a result of the stresses of late adolescence and college. Once the individual begins to successfully adapt to adult roles, his sense of well-being and competence increases. Earlier research produced the same finding (Brim, 1977).

It was also found that unconventionality and sociability decline after graduation. It has been suggested that sociability declines because men who have graduated find themselves under pressure in their careers and from their families and have less time for friendship and sociability.

The fourth question concerned the relationship between life events and changes in self-concept over the period from 1966 to 1976. Life events were assessed objectively and subjectively. For example, work-related events were judged objectively by level of income and work autonomy. Self-evaluations of career progress and marital satisfaction were also obtained in 1976. First, competence levels as assessed during the senior year were found to be predictive of attainment in work in 1976. That is, self-competence as a senior was positively related to higher levels of income and work autonomy in 1976. Self-competence as a senior was also positively related to the individual's self-evaluation of his career progress, marital satisfaction, and general life satisfaction in 1976. Second, it was found that life events occurring between 1966 and 1976 were predictive of the level of self-competence in 1976. Specifically, it was found that high work achievements (assessed in terms of income and work autonomy) were positively related to self-evaluations of competence in 1976. The implication of these findings is that there is a reciprocal relation between self-concept and life events during the transition to young adulthood; life experiences appear to be partially determined by earlier levels of self-competence. But these life experiences also significantly contribute to the level of self-competence at later periods of development.

Establishing Intimacy

"I need somebody to love," Linda Leslie explained. "It's very important for me to share my life. When I accomplish something, I want someone to celebrate with; when I have a problem, I'd like some advice from someone who's interested in what happens to me; when I think of something profound or funny, I want to share it. I need to give. I have a lot of talents. I'm a nice person, sensitive, skilled at anticipating the desires of other people. I want somebody to use those talents on."

Like Linda, most young adults desire an intimate relationship and the opportunity to share experiences with another. However, the young adult's need for an intimate relationship may present certain problems. Typically, young adults have just attained independence from their parents, and they are struggling to understand who they are as unique human beings. Their identity crises help them to distinguish the "me" from the "not me." The need for intimacy runs counter to these identity and independence needs. The need for intimacy calls for opening up the "me" to another person, giving up some of the hard-won independence, and redefining identity, at least to some extent, in terms of the values and interests of a pair of people rather than those of an individual.

To a large extent, maturity in young adulthood is a function of an individual's ability to balance the two opposing needs for independence and intimacy. Without a degree of independence, the person loses self-respect and personal initiative and may eventually define his or her identity *solely* in terms of the intimate relationship (marriage); intimacy itself is threatened, for the spouse may discover that the person is not very interesting and shows no promise of self-improvement. Without intimacy, on the other hand, there is loneliness and despair.

ELEMENTS OF INTIMACY

According to Erikson, the stage of intimacy versus isolation marks the transition into adulthood. To achieve intimacy, the individual must establish a close, mutually satisfying relationship with another person, whether it be a sexual partner, spouse, or friend. In Erikson's view, intimacy need not involve physical or sexual intimacy. It exists in any relationship involving an emotional commitment between two adults, whether they be family members, friends, or lovers. The intimacy involves a union of two identities but allows each person the freedom to remain an individual. Isolation occurs when the individual's defenses are too rigid to permit a union with another person. Out of the successful resolution of the intimacy versus isolation problem evolves the motivation for generativity that characterizes the next stage, which is concerned with producing and caring for a new generation and helping to improve society.

But do people really perceive themselves as experiencing such changes in personality during young and middle adulthood, and are young adults more concerned with intimacy than adults at other ages? These questions were examined in a cross-sectional study by Ryff and Migdal (1984) in which young and middle-aged women were questioned about (1) the major concerns that occur between young and middle adulthood and (2) the nature of the changes that occur between young and middle adulthood. The young women were asked about their current concerns and about what concerns they expected to be most important in middle age. The middle-aged women were asked to recall what had been their major concerns when they were younger and also to explain the changes that had occurred in middle age.

The younger subjects did in fact regard intimacy as being more important in their current lives than it would be when they were older, and the older subjects thought it had been more important when they were younger. The middle-aged women also thought they had become more concerned with generativity as they aged. The younger women, however, did not confirm the theory on this point. They thought of themselves as currently being more concerned with issues related to generativity than they would be when they were middle-aged.

Erikson's stage theory focuses on the psychosocial changes that occur within the individual during an age period. Some evidence, however, indicates that the concerns of cohorts may vary across historical time. Veroff, Douvan, and Kulka (1981) reported the findings of two national studies on subjective well-being,

One of the major tasks of young adulthood is to establish an intimate relationship without losing one's independent identity.

conducted in 1957 and 1976. They found that the 1976 subjects tended to be more introspective and also significantly more concerned with intimacy than the 1957 group.

Rogers (1972) took another approach to the study of intimate relationships. Rather than regarding an emphasis on intimacy simply as a stage in development, he analyzed the elements common to intimate relationships at all ages. He found that such relationships had four factors in common. First, he found that there was a mutual commitment — not a commitment to love and honor one another forever, but a commitment to work to keep the relationship growing for both partners. Second, there was communication occurring at a meaningful level. Third, expectations that were not based on the actual desires of the individuals in the relationship were broken down. The goals and needs of the relationship were defined in terms of the partners' needs and desires, for example, not in terms of societal or parental expectations. Fourth, the identities of both partners were developed. Ideally, as the partners grow individually, the relationship itself is enhanced. Each partner encourages and supports the growth of the other.

ROMANTIC LOVE

Intimacy is characteristic of relationships between friends, siblings, colleagues, and others, but the form of intimate relationship of most concern to many young adults is what is sometimes called a romantic love relationship. What is special or unique about this form of intimate relationship? This question has been addressed by poets as well as psychologists; the latter have attempted to define precisely what is meant by "romantic love."

Z. Rubin (1973) was one of the first social scientists to rigorously study the similarities and differences among various types of close relationships. He sought to differentiate liking and love as attitudes that predispose a person to think, feel, and behave in certain ways toward another person. By so doing, he focused on the cognitive or belief aspects of liking or loving. He developed two scales, one to assess how much a person was liked and another to assess how much a person was loved. He found that there was only a modest relationship between how much one liked and how much one loved another person, which suggests that liking and loving are two distinct attitudes. It was found that women distinguish more sharply between liking and loving than men do.

A number of researchers (Berscheid and Walster, 1974; Rubin, 1974; Davis, 1985; Sternberg & Grajek, 1984) have suggested that there are two dimensions in a romantic love relationship that set it apart from other intimate relationships. The first dimension involves passionate emotionality, whereas the second dimension involves caring.

Passion At least three aspects of the passion dimension have been discussed in the literature (Davis, 1985): (1) emotionality, (2) sexual desire, and (3) fascination/exclusivity. "Falling in love" is usually characterized by a number of emotional responses, including a pounding heart, flushed face, and knotted stomach. But is there actually an emotional state that is unique to romantic love? Or is the basic emotional state and the attendant physiological arousal the same for many types of emotional experiences — is it only the individual's *interpretation* of the situation that differs? In other words, is romantic love more in the heart or more in the head (as Rubin's research would suggest)?

Berscheid and Walster (1974) contend that the emotional aspects of love occur as a result of two conditions. First, the individual must be intensely aroused physiologically, and second, the situational cues must dictate to the individual that romantic love is the appropriate label for the feelings. Romantic love may involve much stronger forces than other types of intimate relationships because it involves physiological arousal. Since high levels of physiological arousal cannot be sustained indefinitely, the authors suggest, the emotional aspects tend to be unstable and fickle. Why, then, do people remain "in love," even when not emotionally aroused? Berscheid and Walster (1978) suggest that in addition to emotional aspects there is companionate love, the affection one feels for someone with whom one's life is deeply intertwined. If the relationship is built on a sufficient number of shared endeavors and positive experiences, an enduring companionate form of love will remain between periods of passionate love.

The second aspect of passionate love involves sexual desire — the desire to be near the loved one, to touch, to kiss, to have intercourse. Of course, sexual behavior often occurs outside the context of love relationships. Sexual behavior always involves the physiological arousal that is also characteristic of passion. Whether sexual behavior can be regarded as an *expression* of romantic love depends on how many other aspects occur, such as psychological intimacy, exclusivity, and extreme caring.

The third aspect of the passion dimension concerns fascination and exclusivity. Fascination generally occurs for a relatively short period, during which lovers are so preoccupied with each other that they tend to devote their attention to each other, even when they should be involved in other activities. The element of exclusivity concerns the fact that lovers have a special relationship that precludes having the same relationship with a third party. Typically, the couple is sexually monogamous and gives priority to each other's concerns in other ways as well.

Extreme caring The second dimension that distinguishes romantic love from other types of intimate relationships is extreme caring. The two lovers give the utmost for each other, even perhaps to the point of extreme self-sacrifice. A well-known example of this type of caring occurs in O. Henry's short story "The Gift of the Magi," in which a man pawns his treasured pocket watch to buy his beloved a set of combs for her beautiful hair, only to find that she has cut and sold her hair to buy him a gold chain for his watch.

Figure 5–3 depicts the dimensions characteristic of intimate relationships and those unique to romantic love (adapted from Davis, 1985). Many types of intimate relationships, such as friendships and relationships with relatives, involve such characteristics as willingness to share, openness and lack of defensiveness, enjoy-

FIGURE 5–3.

Model of the relationship between intimacy and romantic love. Romantic love involves aspects of intimacy plus passion and caring.

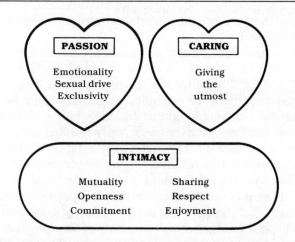

Source: Adapted from Davis, K. E. Near and dear: Friendship and love compared. *Psychology Today,* 1985, *19,* 22–30. Reprinted with permission. Copyright © 1985 (APA).

ment of each other's company, and respect for each other as individuals. Romantic love involves all these characteristics plus the two other dimensions we have discussed — passion and caring the utmost. At any given time one of these dimensions may be more evident than the other, but over time, various aspects of both dimensions will come into play in sustaining the relationship (Sternberg and Grajek, 1984). It is the aggregation of all these aspects that sets romantic love relationships apart from other kinds of intimate relationships.

LOVE THROUGH THE AGES

To most Americans today, love relationships seem to develop in a "natural" progression. One develops a liking for someone, which turns to love, which is followed in turn by sexual involvement and, in many cases, marriage. We tend to assume that this has always been the natural sequence for relations between men and women. In fact, however, our current conceptions concerning the relationship between love, sex, and marriage developed rather recently. It is true that marriage and sex have always been linked, but the relation of love to marriage and sexual expression has varied widely throughout history. The notion that love should be a primary basis for marriage developed in the eighteenth century; it is only in the present century that it has grown to be the predominant view (Hendrick and Hendrick, 1983).

Development of the modern perspective on love and marriage has paralleled a number of other social developments, especially those that pertain to the role of women in society. In ancient Greece and Rome, women were uneducated and were considered legally and morally inferior to men. A major role of marriage was to provide a social context for producing children; it was also a way for a male to increase his estate. In most societies, marriages were arranged by the parents of the couple to be married.

In 1000–1300 A.D., a new, romantic approach to relationships evolved. This new approach, which has come to be called "courtly love," involved emotional exaltation, adoration, and an intensely devoted pursuit of the beloved. The pursuit was highly ritualized; for example, songs were composed, poetry was written, and tournaments were fought in the lady's honor. The goal was to win the lady's attention and favor, but marriage rarely resulted. In many cases, both the lady and her suitor were already involved in arranged marriages.

Although it was stylized and impractical, the development of courtly love did support the notion that a woman could be intensely loved by a man. It also fostered a range of forms of behavioral expression between men and women. The notion of love marriages developed during the Reformation and Renaissance, although the traditional arranged marriage remained the norm for a long time. At first, love was considered only one possible basis for marriage, and not the most important one. Other considerations, such as status, family alliances, and economic security, were important, and they remained important today in many cases.

Hendrick and Hendrick (from whose 1983 account much of our information on the history of romantic love is derived) suggest that the growth of the concept of love in marriage is related to increasing societal recognition of the value of the individual as a unique and important entity in his or her own right, regardless of status, social class, and other such considerations. A sociocultural perspective, then, would suggest that societal recognition of the intrinsic worth of the individual was a necessary precursor to the concept of love marriages, and to the subsequent development of the concept of equity in marriage relationships as well.

INTIMACY AS A DYNAMIC PROCESS

Like identity, intimacy can be conceptualized as a developmental *process*, rather than the focus of a certain stage. As the partners in a relationship grow and change, so does the relationship itself. Two questions are often asked by young adults about the nature of romantic involvements. The first is, "Is what I feel really love?" The second is, "Will our love last?" or, in some cases, "Why did our love die?" We have already addressed the first question in our discussion of the various dimensions of intimate relationships and romantic love. It is in considering the second question that it is useful to consider intimacy as an ongoing process rather than a fixed state (Whitbourne and Weinstock, 1979).

Over the course of an intimate relationship, a couple's patterns of involvement may change because the two individuals continue to develop and because the modes of communication and conflict resolution change. Huston, McHale, and Crouter (1984) examined changes in the feelings and behavior patterns of newlyweds over the first year of marriage. All the couples were married for the first time. They were from working-class backgrounds and were in their early twenties. They were interviewed separately and together and filled out a number of questionnaires many times over the first year of marriage.

Changes in subjective feelings over the first year of marriage followed a consistent pattern. Husbands and wives were both less satisfied with their patterns of interaction, less in love, and less pleased with married life in general at the end of the first year. The authors caution, however, that this does not mean that the couples were unhappy, disillusioned, and dissatisfied. After a year of marriage they were less euphoric than they were shortly after marriage, but their responses were still on the positive side.

Another dimension of married life studied by the researchers was changes in behavior and activities over the first year. The total number of activities the couple engaged in together did not change significantly, but the types of activity did change. The major change was that the proportion of instrumental tasks (such as house chores and shopping) increased while the number of leisure activities decreased by 20 percent over the year. Since instrumental tasks are less pleasurable than leisure activities, it may be that some of the decline in satisfaction that occur during the first year resulted from associating the spouse more with doing unpleasant tasks. The amount of time that husbands and wives spent talking together also decreased, from an average of about one hour and twenty minutes per day two months before marriage to one hour a day a year later. Sex-role patterns of behavior were quite traditional and did not change over the year. Wives did 65 percent of all household tasks, and this did not change throughout the year. The amount of cross-sex-role behavior also remained constant throughout the year.

The most striking change the authors found was in socioemotional behavior. The greatest change was a reduction in the rate at which partners did and said things that brought each other pleasure — for example, complimenting each other, saying "I love you," or doing something to make the other person laugh. The number of pleasurable activities reported declined by about 40 percent overall. Spouses spent less time talking about the quality of their relationship, making efforts to change their behavior, and explaining their desires and concerns to each other. On the positive side, the number of negative or displeasing events remained quite small across the whole period of the study.

The authors caution that although there were significant changes in feelings and behavior, the differences were a matter of degree; there was not a change to dissatisfaction. The affective tone of the marital interaction remained positive. (Of course, some newlyweds do become disillusioned and separate during the first year.)

How were changes in feelings and changes in behaviors related? The most striking relationships between feelings and behavior were found in the realm of socioemotional behavior (rather than the realms of companionship and sex-role behaviors). The relationship between positive feelings about the marriage and positive socioemotional behaviors, such as compliments and displays of affection, was strongest early in the year. On the other hand, the relationship between negative feelings about marriage and negative socioemotional behaviors, such as criticism, anger, and unresponsiveness, became more pronounced at the end of the first year. Indeed, at the end of the year, feelings about marital satisfaction were much more highly related to negative than to positive socioemotional behaviors. Furthermore, negative socioemotional behavior early in the year was predictive of negative socioemotional behavior later in the year. The researchers concluded that couples who experienced negative socioemotional behavior early in their relationship may be particularly at risk because of the predictive nature of the early negative behavior.

Are these same patterns found among couples who live together before marriage? The researchers hypothesized that cohabiting couples would have experienced declines earlier in their relationship, but couples who had been living together for an average of ten months before marriage reported the same pattern of decline in romantic feelings and positive interactions as the other couples. Two explanations have been offered for this finding. First, it may be that the cohabiting couples simply did not live together for a long enough period to influence the onset of declines. Second, the act of marriage is so imbued with romance in our culture and so significant an event that, regardless of how well the couple knows each other, they may make an extra effort to be on good terms before marriage.

Community Involvement

Linda Leslie has been working on the campaign of Toni Buchanan, a local attorney running for the school board. "I had no idea what it would be like!" said Linda. "I thought it would be like my campaign for student body president in high school. But it's been incredible: the dirty tricks (on both sides), the ridiculous coverage by the media. To listen to the newspapers, Toni wants to spend your money until the bank repossesses your family home; and Bill Boyd, her opponent, wants to close the schools altogether. It makes you wonder how the system works at all."

"Why did you get into the campaign?" we asked.

"Well, I got to know Toni when we were both working on the Westside Benefit Show, after the tornado hit. She's really a concerned lady; she's really interested in the education of our kids and what's happening to the schools. She got me interested, too. I started reading about some of the guys on the school board. The only reason they're on the board is to keep their taxes down. And to keep *Catcher in the Rye* out of the high school library. I got to thinking about my kids — if I ever have any — and I asked myself, 'Do I want to send my kids to a school run by these types?' Well, the answer to that is clear, and the next step is to do something about it."

In addition to the balancing of identity and intimacy in their personal lives, young adults face the task of determining their relationship with the larger community. No longer does their world consist simply of family and friends in the home, school, and church; the city, the state, the nation, and the world enter their sphere of interest and influence. Many factors play a role in the young adult's increasing involvement with a broader community: the right to vote, the right to hold office, and other legal rights granted on attainment of adult status; a career, which introduces governments into one's life in many ways (regulates one's business, demands one's taxes, and so on); marriage and a family, which introduce responsibilities that cannot be fulfilled without community support.

Community involvement for many individuals entails defining social or political ideologies one can identify with and becoming active in community organizations. For many people, their church or synagogue is the primary vehicle of social participation. For others, political parties, unions, or special interest groups provide opportunities for community involvement. Some people do little more than contribute to charity now and then. One of the major factors in the degree of community involvement is the "orderliness" of one's career (Wilensky, 1968). Young people who settle down in one location and who embark on a career that promises to move them job by job up the ladder to some higher goal are much more likely than those with less orderly careers to join and participate in community organizations, to get involved in local issues, and to give generously to charities. Perhaps they have the most to gain if the community is healthy and functioning effectively, and the most to lose if the social contract is poorly written and executed.

One aspect of aligning oneself with the larger community involves affiliation with a particular political ideology. In the United States, most political activity is organized around either a liberal or a conservative political ideology. Is there a relationship between an adult's political ideology and personality characteristics evident in adolescence? Do people perceive themselves as becoming more liberal or conservative as they age? In an attempt to answer these and other questions, Mussen and Haan (1981) examined longitudinal data from the Berkeley and Oakland growth studies. Subjects' political ideologies were determined by self-ratings taken in 1968–1970 when most subjects were in middle adulthood. Personality data were available from adolescence and young adulthood. The data showed that differences in the personalities and social orientations of conservatives and liberals were already clearly evident during adolescence and these personality characteristics remained stable over long periods of time. At multiple assessment points in the longitudinal study from early adolescence to middle age, liberals were rated as being more philosophically concerned and more rebellious than conservatives, as valuing independence more, and priding themselves more on objectivity. Conservatives were consistently rated higher than liberals on submissiveness and seeking reassurance. Mussen and Haan caution, however, that personality characteristics account for only part of the variation found in an

The interests of individuals do not always coincide with those of state and nation.

individuals' political ideologies and behavior. An individual's political views may also be strongly related to social and economic trends and to historical events.

The subjects were also asked to compare their present (middle age) ideological self-ratings with their perceived orientations at age twenty-one and with their parents', childrens', and spouses' current views. Both liberals and conservatives perceived themselves to have become more self-consistent in their political orientations over time. Liberals rated themselves as more liberal than they had been when they were younger and more liberal than their parents and spouses, but not more liberal than their children. The conservatives regarded themselves as more conservative than they had been at twenty-one and more conservative than their children and spouses, but more liberal than their parents.

In addition to becoming involved in the community via social organizations, such as churches and political parties, young adults must increasingly grapple with issues of social responsibility at the individual level. The level of responsibility an individual feels toward others in the community who are in distress (for example, being a Good Samaritan) has been the focus of research, precipitated in part by a much publicized incident occurring some twenty years ago (Shotland, 1985). In 1964, Kitty Genovese was brutally murdered as her cries in the night were unanswered by thirty-eight of her neighbors. The attack began at 3 A.M., when the neighbors heard sounds of the struggle and went to their windows. Some were ineffective helpers, turning on their lights, opening their windows, and shouting. No one went down to rescue her. One person finally called the police, after deliberating for some time on what action to take. A series of studies by Darley and Latane and others indicated that a person is less likely to help someone in trouble when other bystanders are present. This "bystander effect" has been shown to occur in all types of emergencies, medical and criminal. The effect occurs because witnesses diffuse responsibility (for example, someone else will call the police); membership in a group of bystanders lowers each person's likelihood of intervening. Moreover, the research indicates that if people are going to intervene, most do it in the first few seconds after they notice the emergency. Bystanders also behave very differently if they assume a quarreling man and woman know each other or are strangers. They are more reluctant to intrude if they assume it is a "lovers' quarrel" rather than a woman being attacked by a stranger.

What types of people are willing to intervene directly when a crime is in progress? Huston and Geis (Shotland, 1985) found active interveners to be very self-assured and certain that they could handle the situation by themselves. They were likely to have specialized training in first aid, lifesaving, or police work. These people were more likely to have been victimized themselves and to have witnessed more crime in the prior ten years than people in general. Similarly, spontaneous vigilantism, in which bystanders not only apprehend a criminal but mete out punishment themselves, tends to occur under special circumstances. Spontaneous vigilantism happens only in response to certain types of crimes. First, the crimes generate strong identification with the victim (for example, being mugged or robbed in one's own neighborhood). Second, the crimes are particularly threatening to the local community's standards.

Citizens' willingness to break the law is also influenced by their perception of the actions of others (Loftus, 1985). A recent IRS survey found that 20 percent of those surveyed admitted to cheating on their taxes recently, but claimed that they only cheated a little bit (about $100) (Loftus, 1985). Although only 20 percent admitted cheating, the individuals surveyed estimated that 40 percent of all taxpayers cheat. Many reasoned that since a lot of rich people pay no taxes at all, if someone with less income underpays a little, it's no big deal. Thus an individual's willingness to aid neighbors in distress as well as citizens' rationalization of income tax cheating appear to be influenced by perception of the response or nonresponse of others involved. In the case of Good Samaritanism, one's willingness to aid the victim is influenced by whether other bystanders are present. In the case of tax cheating, citizens often rationalize their behavior based on assumptions of what others are doing.

Summary

1.   The transition to adulthood is marked by a number of changes — in legal and marital status, place of residence, and occupation. The timing and pattern of these changes are determined in part by social institutions and historical events. People who seek additional education, for example, may postpone marriage and childbearing until they are older. Social class and racial differences exist in the ages at which people enter into states (for example, marriage) associated with young adulthood, but the *order* of occurrence of these events remains quite stable.

2.   Erikson introduced the concept of the "identity crisis" to describe the period, which most often occurs during adolescence, when the maturing individual must integrate new abilities, feelings, roles, and a new physical appearance into an earlier identity as a child. Others suggest that the search for identity is a lifelong process, not a discrete stage or phase.

3.   The self-concept can be conceptualized in terms of a number of personality traits, not just in terms of identity during one stage of psychosocial development. A study by Mortimer et al. based on this view of the self-concept indicated that it tends to involve the same dimensions over time but that changes do occur in the quantitative level of different dimensions.

4.   For Erikson, the stage of intimacy versus isolation marks the transition into adulthood. Isolation occurs when a person's defenses are too rigid to permit a union with another person. Research comparing younger and older women indicated that the younger group was in fact more concerned with intimacy than the older group.

5.   A number of researchers have distinguished two dimensions of romantic love relationships that set them apart from other intimate relationships: (1) passionate emotionality and (2) extreme caring. At least three aspects of the passion dimension have been described, including emotions, sexual desire, and exclusivity. The caring dimension of romantic love may be so strong that the couple would endure extreme self-sacrifices for each other. Romantic love may seem the normal basis for marriage today, but this view didn't evolve until the eighteenth century.

6.   Intimacy, like identity, can be regarded as a developmental process. A study of newly married couples indicated that their feelings and patterns of behavior changed, often for the worse, over the first year of marriage. Nevertheless, the couples tended to regard their mates and their marriage as more positive than negative after the first year. The same pattern was found among couples who lived together before marriage.

7.   Young adults also face the task of determining their relationship with the larger community. This relationship can take a number of forms. Research shows that individuals' political ideologies in middle age are associated with personality traits evident in adolescence.

SUGGESTED READINGS

Featherman, D. L., Hogan, D. P., and Sorenson, A. (1984). Entry into adulthood: Profiles of young men in the 1950s. In P. B. Baltes and O. G. Brim (Eds.), *Lifespan development and behavior*, Vol. 6., pp. 159–202. New York: Academic Press.

Kelley, H. H., Berscheid, E., Christensen, A., Harvey, J., Huston, T., Levinger, G., McClintock, E., Peplau, L. A., and Petersen, D. (Eds.). (1983). *Close relationships*. New York: Freeman.

Shotland, R. L. (1985). When bystanders just stand by. *Psychology Today, 19,* 50–55.

Sternberg, R. and Grajek, S. (1984). The nature of love. *Journal of Personality and Social Psychology, 47,* 312–329

Whitbourne, S., and Weinstock, C. (1979). *Adult development: The differentiation of experience.* New York: Holt, Rinehart & Winston.

The Development of Investment and Commitment Scales for Predicting Continuity of Personal Relationships

Much of the research on personal relationships in young adulthood has focused on the factors which are important in the early stages of the formation of a relationship. The filter theory presented in your text is an example of a model examining the factors which are important in relationship formation. However, there is growing awareness that the development of personal relationships is a *process*, and that different factors may be important at different phases in the relationship. In studying personal relationships, one may need to consider multiple factors or dimensions (e.g., love, commitment, passion); different factors may be particularly salient at different phases of the relationship. Lund hypothesized that while love, involving positive feelings toward the other, may be particularly important in the early stage of a relationship, factors such as commitment and investment may become increasingly important in maintaining and continuing a relationship. This study involves two stages. In the first stage measurement scales were developed to assess the factors of love, rewards, commitment, and investment, as these apply to personal relationships. The second stage of the study involved a longitudinal study of college seniors' personal relationships to examine the relative importance of these four factors in predicting the continuity of the relationships after college graduation.

SUBJECTS

The subjects were 129 college seniors (M =50; F = 79), who were involved in heterosexual relationships that had lasted, on average, two years. The mean age of the subjects was 21 years. The subjects were at different stages in their relationships: 19% — casual dating; 16% — seriously involved; 43% — exclusively involved; 12% — engaged; and 10% — married.

PROCEDURE AND MEASURES

Subjects completed a questionnaire twice, once during the winter of their senior year and the second time during the summer following their senior year. Previous research on college student relationships had shown that the end of the academic year is the most likely time of breakup. The stress of career decisions and geographical moves following college graduation would seem to make the summer after the senior year a likely time for the breakup of relationships, and thus a critical period for studying factors related to the continuity of relationships.

At each assessment period, subjects completed four measurement scales, assessing the factors of love, rewards, commitment, and investment. The love scale was a shortened version of Z. Rubin's Love scale, examining positive feelings regarding one's partner. Example items were: "One of my primary concerns is my partner's welfare," "I feel I can confide in my partner about virtually everything." The rewards scale focused on how rewarding the subject found the relationship to be, the similarity of attitudes and interests of the partners, and the partner's ability to fulfill needs of the other. The investment scale assessed how large an investment they had made in various aspects of the relationship (e.g., time spent together, gifts, etc). The commitment scale examined a subject's expectations regarding the continuity of the relationship and how difficult the subject felt it would be to terminate the relationship.

FINDINGS AND DISCUSSION

The authors were able to develop four scales, which differentiated between the factors of love, rewards, commitment, and investment in personal relationships; the scales were positively related to each other, but each scale was found to measure a factor distinct from the other three factors. This scale differentiation permitted the authors to examine each factor as a predictor of relationship continuity.

What factors were the best predictors of the continuance of the relationship following college graduation? Participants winter scores on the commitment and investment scales were found to best predict the fate of their relationships in the summer. Although love usually accompanied commitment, commitment and investment alone told more about the likelihood of a relationship lasting over time.

Changes in love and commitment from winter to summer were studied. There was a small but statistically significant increase in commitment; love showed no change over time. It was found that those scoring higher on investment during the winter were most likely to report increases in commitment in the summer; those with low initial investment scores did not show increases in commitment.

Findings from studies, such as this one, suggest that research on commitment and investment, as well as love, are needed to examine the progress of a relationship. Personal investment in a relationship strengthens commitment to the relationship, which makes continuing it more likely. The author suggests that commitment and investment may be construed as "barriers" which develop over time in a relationship and which make leaving a relationship more difficult. Happy relationships hold together not only because of the positive pull of factors such as love and rewards, but also because of the growing strength of "barriers" such as commitment and investment, which decrease the likelihood of relationship dissolution.

Lund, M. (1985). The development of investment and commitment scales for predicting continuity of personal relationships. *Journal of Social and Personal Relationships, 2,* 3–24.

Chapter Six

MEN AND WOMEN

Together and Apart

In Wallace Stegner's Pulitzer Prize winning novel, *Angle of Repose,* Susan Burling, shocked by the unexpected engagement of her two closest friends, Augusta Drake and Thomas Hudson, considers a similar union with a quiet Westerner named Oliver Ward. The year is 1873.

> She was quickly reassured that he was not impossible, at least for any society short of Augusta's. He was most admiring of her talent and respectful of her friends, he was as big and restful as she had found him in the library in Brooklyn Heights, he had a way of speaking lightly of things without persuading her that he felt them lightly. He was not talkative, but once wound up he charmed them all with his stories of life in California. Her parents sat up late to hear him, though when her New York friends visited they went early to bed. He could play chess — that promised cozy evenings. Her father said he had never seen a man pick a basket of apples faster. And when he took hold of the oars of a rowboat, the rowboat nearly jumped out of the water.

> Augusta, Susan's best friend, had been as shocked by Susan's inclinations as Susan had been by Augusta's engagement. Augusta:

> "I never expected to see you fall in love like a shopgirl with the first handsome stranger."
> "You're forgetting yourself!"
> "Sue, I think you're forgetting *yourself.* What does this young man do?"
> "He's an engineer."
> "In California."
> "Yes."
> "And he wants to take you out there."
> "As soon as he finds the right place, with some permanence in it."
> "And you'll go."
> "When he sends for me, yes."
> Augusta resumed her pacing, throwing her hands outward in little distracted gestures. She straightened a picture on the wall without stopping. She bent her head to gnaw on a knuckle. "What about your art? What about everything we've worked for?"

"My art isn't that important. I'll never be anything but a commercial illustrator."

"You know that's utterly wrongheaded!"

"I know I want to marry him and go where his career takes him. . . . I can go on drawing. He wants me to."

"In some mining camp."

"I don't know where."

But this exchange came later, after Oliver's visit. Oliver's visit had been a puzzle to Susan — for example, where to take him on excursion.

Long Pond and Black Pond, liked by New York visitors, were not enough for a man who had seen the Yosemite and ridden the length of the San Joaquin Valley through square miles of wildflowers. So she and Bessie and John took him to Big Pond, eight miles back in the woods, a wild romantic place where a waterfall poured into a marble pool and then fell through diminishing pools to the lake.

It was incorrigibly Hudson River school — brown light, ragged elms, romantic water. There they sat on the grass confronting nature. . . . Susan sketched a little while he stood admiring by. They did not spoon, though Bessie strategically led her husband away so the two could be alone. Having no acceptable way of expressing their feelings directly, they probably vented them in nature . . ., she struck speechless by a view, he with his hat in his hand before the purity of her sensibility.

Late in the afternoon they were back at their picnic spot at the top of the fall. She had always responded strongly to storms, rain in the face, wild winds, wild water, exciting crossings of the Hudson through floating ice. On this day she lay down and hung her face over the cliff to see down the waterfall. At about the same time, and for similar reasons, John Muir was hanging over the brink of Yosemite Falls dizzying himself with the thunder of hundreds of tons of foam and green glass going by him. Muir had a good deal farther to look down, but Susan Burling had something her fellow romantic did not. She had Oliver Ward hanging onto her ankles to make sure she didn't spill over.

Anxious? Not on your life. In these days when a girl goes to bed with anybody who will pat her in a friendly way on the rump, few will be able to imagine how Oliver Ward felt, holding those little ankles. He would not have let go if fire had swept the hilltop, if warrior ants had swarmed over him from head to foot, if Indians had sneaked from the bushes and hacked him loose from his hands. As for Susan Burling, upside down and with her world whirling, that strong grip on her ankles was more than physical contact made sweet by the fact that it came between the bars of an iron cage of propriety, touch asserting itself against a thousand conventions. It was the very hand of the protective male. When she came up out of her dizzying tete-a-tete with the waterfall she was in love. (Stegner, 1971, pp. 51–55)*

The relationship between men and women is an exceedingly complex topic, and various aspects of the relationship have been dealt with in different chapters of this text. We discussed the couple within the context of the family in Chapter 2 and considered issues related to dual-earner marriages in the context of our discussion of work in Chapter 3. Since finding a mate is a normative task of young

*Excerpts from *Angle of Repose* by Wallace Stegner. Copyright © 1971 by Wallace Stegner. Reprinted by permission of Doubleday and Company, Inc. and A. M. Heath.

adulthood, we further explored the processes of intimacy and romantic love in Chapter 5. In this chapter we discuss issues of sexuality and then turn our attention to aspects of male–female lifestyles which occur outside the married couple relationship. We consider issues related to divorce and widowhood and to alternative lifestyles, including singlehood, cohabitation, and communal living. As a result of demographic changes in our society, increasing proportions of individuals can expect to spend some part of adulthood in a state outside the traditional married couple relationship. Consider that over 40 percent of marriages end in divorce and 70 percent of elderly women experience widowhood. It is becoming increasingly important, then, to consider male and female relationships and lifestyles outside the marriage bond.

Sexual Relationships

How should we describe sexual relationships between men and women across the life span? Two volumes by Alfred Kinsey and coworkers, *Sexuality in the Human Male* (1948) and *Sexuality in the Human Female* (1953), contain some of the most extensive data ever published on sexual behavior, and much of what is reported about sexual behavior is based on these reports. However, Kinsey's research is limited in at least two respects (Starr and Weiner, 1982). First, older adults were underrepresented in Kinsey's sample so that the research does not provide a truly life-span perspective of sexual behavior. Second, although Kinsey the biologist gave us mountains of descriptive information about sexual behavior, he did not examine many important psychological questions, for example, regarding the meaning and importance of sex. Of course, sex is a total human experience, not just a biological function, and it is important that we treat it as such in our discussion (See also Chapter 7, p. 222). In this chapter, we begin with a description of patterns of sexual behavior across the life span, consider age-related changes in biological functioning as they influence sexual behavior, and then turn to examination of individuals' attitudes regarding the meaning and importance of sex. It is these latter issues which may be most instructive in considering sexuality in later adulthood.

SEXUAL INTERCOURSE

Different methods have been used to study the frequency of sexual intercourse at various points in the life span. Beginning in adolescence, premarital intercourse is usually discussed in terms of the percentage of boys and girls who are sexually active. After marriage, sexual intercourse is typically recorded in terms of frequency per week. For subjects over the age of sixty, the method of study shifts again from frequency per week back to the proportion of older adults who report themselves to be sexually active.

Among unmarried college females, the percentage who were sexually experienced increased from 32 percent to 58 percent between 1968 and 1978; among college males, the percentages increased from 40 percent to 62 percent over the same period (Barrett, 1980). A more recent study showed that this trend is continuing. Between 1965 and 1980, the percentage of college males who were sexually active rose from 65 percent to 77 percent; for females, the figure rose from 29 percent to 64 percent (Robinson and Jedlicka, 1982). These figures show that premarital intercourse is much more common than it was a few decades ago, especially among girls and young women.

After marriage, the frequency of sexual intercourse in an average week reported by young married couples, spouses aged eighteen to twenty-four, is a little over three (Hunt, 1974). The frequency of marital coitus gradually decreases with age to about once a week for husbands and wives between forty-five and sixty. Previous surveys show the same pattern of regular decline with age, although the frequency of sexual intercourse at all ages is greater today than it was in the past (see Figure 6–1).

In all these comparisons, we must allow for the possibility that some of the differences may reflect changes in the willingness to report what to many people are very private activities. An increase in reports of premarital sex among girls and young women may be partly a decrease in modesty, for example, rather than a significant change in behavior. Similarly, married couples interviewed more recently are more likely to report accurately (or even exaggerate!) than people interviewed in the 1940s, and older cohorts in cross-sectional studies are likely to have different standards of confession than the younger cohorts. Nevertheless, it is doubtful that an increased willingness to admit sexual activity can account for all the increases in reported behavior. Most likely the incidence of sexual intercourse has increased, although changing attitudes about discussing such activities may make the increase appear somewhat greater than it is in fact.

For subjects over the age of sixty, scientific attention shifts from frequency per week back to percentages. According to the Kinsey reports (Kinsey, Pomeroy, and Martin, 1948; Kinsey et al., 1953), which reflected the sexual attitudes and activities of the 1940s, 95 percent of the men at age sixty were sexually active, with 70 percent at age seventy. Not quite 70 percent of the married women aged sixty were active and 50 percent of those aged sixty-five. The lower percentages of sexually active women may be partly due to their having spouses older than themselves and possibly in poor health. In a more recent study of 800 older adults, Starr and Weiner (1982) found that 92 percent of men sixty to sixty-nine years old were sexually active, compared with 88 percent of the married women.

Over the age of seventy-five, sexual behavior does decrease significantly. However, studies differ in the proportion of elderly over seventy-five who are sexually active. Some studies report only 25 to 30 percent of married people remain active (McCary, 1978; Tsitouras, Martin, and Harman, 1982). In contrast, Starr and Weiner reported almost 90 percent of their seventy- to seventy-nine-year-old subjects to be sexually active. There have been very few reliable studies of the sexual relations of very old men and women, but some individuals in their

FIGURE 6–1.

Sexual intercourse among married couples (male and female estimates combined). Comparing the 1970s to the 1940s, the bad news is that frequency still declines with age. The good news is that frequency for all age groups is up; it's better to be forty and average today than it was to be thirty and average in the 1940s.

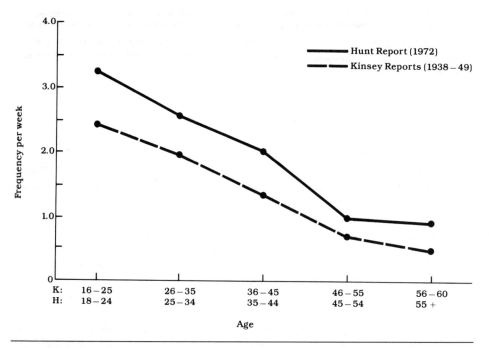

Source: Hunt, 1974; Kinsey et al., 1948; Kinsey et al., 1953. From P. H. Mussen, J. J. Conger, J. Kagan, and J. Geiwitz. *Psychological development: a life-span approach.* New York: Harper & Row, 1979.

eighties and nineties are still active. In an exceptionally healthy sample of elderly, Starr and Weiner found that only 15 percent of the eighty- to ninety-year-old people in their study reported themselves to be totally sexually inactive. Even centenarians (over 100) have reported interests not infrequently fulfilled (Leaf, 1973a). In sum, the data show that, barring loss of opportunity through death, severe illness, or some other catastrophe, many old people maintain a moderate program of sexual activity throughout their lives. Frequency of sexual intercourse in old age is highly correlated with frequency of sexual activity in the first two years of marriage and general level of sexual activity between the ages of twenty and thirty-nine (Martin, 1981). In sex as in other areas of functioning, the adage "use it or lose it" may be a fairly accurate summation of what to expect as one ages.

BIOLOGICAL CONSIDERATIONS IN SEXUAL INTERCOURSE

A number of biological factors affect sexual intercourse between men and women. The sex hormones (estrogen and progesterone in females; androgens, including testosterone, in males) have a notable influence on sexual interest and behavior at many points in the life span. In adolescence, these hormones regulate puberty which, among its other characteristics, involves a dramatic increase in the sex drive. In a mature woman, the female hormones regulate the menstrual cycle and may have effects on sexual desire through that cycle. Sometime around the age of fifty, a sizable decline of estrogen in women accompanies the cessation of menses in the event known as menopause, which has variable effects on sexual intercourse.

In many subhuman animals, hormones control a rigid, clear-cut relationship between reproductive fertility in the female and sexual responsiveness in both male and female (Ford and Beach, 1951). In humans, this relationship is much weaker and rather easily overcome by nonbiological influences. Menopause is a good example. With fertility at an end, most women experience a number of physical symptoms, notably a significant reduction in vaginal lubrication, which are largely a function of significantly decreased estrogen levels. In lower animals, a decrease in estrogen brings a decrease in sexual drive, but, in humans, menopause has no direct effect on sexual capability or interest. In spite of vaginal dryness, many women report an increased sex drive; their fear of pregnancy is gone, and they enjoy the "pure" tenderness and sensuality of the physical communication with their partners (Neugarten et al., 1968; Butler and Lewis, 1982). Almost 80 percent of the women in the Starr and Weiner (1982) study reported that menopause did not affect their sexual activity or that it improved. (See Chapter 8 for psychological effects popularly associated with menopause.)

A prominent finding by Kinsey was the age-related differences for men and women in biological factors related to intercourse. As men grow older, biological factors do affect their ability to make love (Masters and Johnson, 1970; Comfort, 1980). By middle age, the average man takes two or three times longer than a young adult to have an erection after stimulation, ejaculates semen with half the force of youth, and after age fifty has a longer refractory period, requiring as much as twenty-four hours before he can have another erection. In contrast, there is little change in a woman's sexual response capability through much of adulthood, with some decline in the late sixties. On the other hand, men in the fifty- to seventy-five-year-old age group can remain erect longer before coming to orgasm than those in the twenty- to forty-year-old age group; this has been noted as a positive factor by middle-aged and older adults, since intercourse can be less hurried and there is greater opportunity for mutual satisfaction of both partners.

Impotence — the inability to have or maintain an erection — becomes a major problem for men over the age of fifty. Although reports of impotence vary more widely than other sexual confessions, perhaps for obvious "macho" reasons, it appears that about 35 percent of men between sixty and seventy are impotent (Rossman, 1980). Technically, this means that they fail to induce or sustain penile erection in at least 25 percent of their coital attempts (Masters and Johnson, 1970).

The causes of impotence are uncertain. Some researchers claim that nearly all cases (95 percent) have psychological rather than physical causes (Kaplan, 1974), but careful biological assessment in one study turned up 35 percent with hormonal imbalances (Spark, White, and Connolly, 1980). One of the reasons researchers have attributed impotence to psychological causes is that sexual activity is not highly correlated with the levels of testosterone, the primary male sex hormone (Tsitouras, Martin, and Harman, 1982). But research with animals suggests that erection and ejaculation require complex patterns of nervous system activity; age changes in the efficiency of the relevant mechanisms in the central nervous system may cause impotence long before the necessary hormones decrease (Elias and Elias, 1977).

Nevertheless, the *fear* of losing potency remains either the cause or a major contributing factor in most cases of impotency. Sex, self-esteem, and self-image are closely related. Often one or two episodes of impotency are brought on by physical exhaustion, intemperate consumption of alcohol, physical illness (for example, diabetes), or prescription drugs (for example, sedatives). The individual begins to fear that he will never be able to perform adequately again (therapists call this "performance anxiety") because he thinks impotence is what normally happens to old men. The fear acts as a self-fulfilling prophecy, causing that which is feared. Often performance anxiety combines with other psychological factors, such as anxiety about sex due to, say, a strict religious upbringing. Fortunately, impotence can be successfully treated by a combination of psychotherapy and physical therapy in about 70 percent of the cases (Masters and Johnson, 1970).

For whatever reason, the physical inability of the male is by far the most common hindrance to sexual intercourse among middle-aged and elderly couples (Pfeiffer, Verwoerdt, and Davis, 1972; Butler and Lewis, 1982). Illness in one or the other spouse is another hindrance not uncommon in the later years of a couple's relationship. But many older people continue to have sex even after the onset of chronic physical conditions. Most men remain potent after a prostatectomy. Impotence is more common among those who have diabetes, but it can be reduced if the disease is properly controlled. Sexual potency may be lower after the onset of heart disease, but this is often a psychological or pharmacological problem. Psychologically, one's confidence in one's physical abilities may be lower. In addition, medications for cardiovascular problems can decrease potency as well as increasing the likelihood of depression. Contrary to popular myths, sudden deaths due to heart attacks during intercourse are very uncommon (Butler and Lewis, 1982).

SEXUAL ATTITUDES

Obviously sexual attitudes play a major role in sexual behavior throughout the life span. The increased sexual activity of unmarried adolescents and young adults can be traced to changes in cultural and personal attitudes about premarital intercourse (Robinson and Jedlick, 1982). Similarly, new attitudes toward marital coitus have been influential in the increased frequency with which intercourse has been reported in the past few decades. A negative effect of attitudes can be seen in women whose sexuality suffers after menopause, women who are often the victims of myths: "I was afraid we couldn't have sexual relations after the menopause," said one woman (Neugarten et al., 1968, p. 196), "and my husband thought so too." We can also see the negative effect of performance anxiety in older men.

Many sexual attitudes are age-related. In the minds of many Americans, sex and old age don't seem to go together (Starr and Weiner, 1982). Behavior that is considered appropriate in a young man or woman may invite ridicule or scorn in an old man or woman. Witness the "dirty old man" character that appears frequently in television sketches, comic novels, and everyday gossip: he is a man interested in sex, "dirty" only because he is old. Many people think of child molesters and exhibitionists as old men. Old men, in fact, are the least likely of any age group to engage in such deviant behaviors. Similar disapproval applies to older women with sexual interests. One rationale for such disapproval is a belief that age brings dignity, a dignity that is somehow offended by sex (Diamond and Karlen, 1980). Children, even adult children, often cannot accept the fact of their parents' sexuality. In one study, over half the college students surveyed thought their parents had sexual relations monthly or less often; a quarter of them believed their parents had essentially given up sex completely (Pocs et al., 1977). The myth of the old person uninterested in sex is accepted by some old people, too, who thereby deny themselves pleasurable release from sexual tensions and the tender feelings of being loved, of being needed, and of being intimate.

Another rationale for the assumed incongruity between sex and old age is an overemphasis in our society on the physical aspects of sexuality. There is perhaps the mystique that sex is most pleasurable between individuals with attractive, youthful bodies and that to be satisfying an orgasm must always be achieved. One young medical student questioned how exciting sex could be between two people with flabby bodies, wrinkled skin, and old faces? However, many older adults do report finding sex satisfying and pleasurable; 75 percent of the elderly in one study reported that sex now was the same or better than when they were younger (Starr and Weiner, 1982). In their interviews with 800 elderly, Starr and Weiner (1982) found that in discussing their sexual activities, the older adults emphasized the quality of the experience, rather than just its frequency. They talked about the pleasure of being unhurried and of not feeling they had to perform or reach a specific goal. Some reported sex was better because of greater understanding, increased self-awareness, loss of worries such as pregnancy, and a greater appreciation and meaning of the sexual experience. Others emphasized the importance of being flexible in one's attitudes and sexual behaviors, and the potential for achieving sexual gratification in a variety of ways, rather than focusing only on intercourse and orgasm. One seventy-two-year-old woman explained "your sex is so much more relaxed, I know my body better and we know each other better — sex is unhurried and the best in our lives" (p. 11). A sixty-nine-year-old man summed it up: "Sex is one of the pleasures of life. It is also one way in which men and women overcome loneliness and frustration. There's the added pleasure

Contrary to myth, many elderly people continue to express their needs for tenderness, caring, and sexual intimacy.

as we grow older, we can still enjoy sex and thus are still to be counted as total men and women" (p. 37).

Another age-related sexual attitude has to do with the relative ages of the partners. In general, in our society it is expected that the male be slightly older than the female. By late middle age or early old age, however, a man can date and even marry someone "young enough to be his daughter." Although a few tongues will wag, the reaction is nowhere near the uproar that follows an old woman dating a young man. Perhaps progress toward general equality between the sexes may someday equalize these reactions as well.

SEX DIFFERENCES IN SEXUALITY

Sexuality is expressed differently in males and females, of course; anatomy differs, physiology differs, and reproductive roles differ. The two sexes were designed to be complementary, not identical. Questions of sex differences in sexuality, therefore, arise in areas where we might reasonably expect similarities, where differences in attitudes and behaviors are a source of conflict rather than cohesion. Are there differences in sexual interest, for example, so that one or the other party desires more sexual activity than the other? Should different moral standards be applied to men and women, as represented by the concept of the double standard?

Females generally show less interest in sex and exhibit less sexual activity than males, although differences in attitudes and behaviors are rapidly disappearing (Barrett, 1980; Broderick, 1982). Married women are more likely today than previously to view sexual intercourse as a form of recreation and, therefore, to enjoy it, to experiment with new forms, and to demand consideration of their sexual needs and desires. Wives and unmarried women more commonly initiate sexual activity than they did in the past.

From data such as these, one could easily draw the conclusion that the differences in sexual attitudes and behavior that were prevalent in the past were due not to any fundamental difference in need and desire but to cultural traditions and childrearing techniques that *assumed* that females are less interested in sex. Given a more nearly equal opportunity to express sexual desire, women are today showing that these assumptions of disinterest were largely in error (Broderick, 1982; Starr and Weiner, 1982). This view, though perhaps held by a majority of psychologists who know the research evidence on sex differences in sexuality, is not without its opponents. Opponents cite studies of subhuman animals, in which the pattern of an active, aggressive male and a passive female is commonly observed (Eibl-Eibesfeldt, 1972; Harlow, 1975). They cite studies of tests designed to measure libido (sexual drive), which suggest an innate (not learned) disposition that men have in considerably greater quantities than women (Eysenck, 1976). All these arguments, however, are open to alternative interpretations that picture the human sex drive, relatively free of the powerful hormonal influences found in subhuman species, as influenced primarily by what society cares to teach us on the "nature" of men and women.

If the man's "more intense" sex drive is no good reason for conflict in a relationship, perhaps there is still a source of conflict in the "relative" sex drive at different ages. Gail Sheehy, in *Passages* (1976), claims that men and women are quite similar in their sexual interests as adolescents and in the "unisex of old age," but that they are quite divergent in between. The divergence and convergence form what Sheehy graphically terms "the sexual diamond." The divergence, in which the seeds of conflict reside, is greatest in the late thirties and early forties, when women supposedly experience a surge of sexual desire and capacity, while men perceive a loss in physical vigor and react to their wives' newly kindled desires with anxiety and impotence. Although there is very little evidence for a sexual diamond of relative desire (and much evidence to the contrary), there is indeed evidence that many women are able to free themselves from cultural inhibitions and from the demands of childrearing by their late thirties, at a time when their biological capacity for sexual response is still high (and in some respects higher than in youth), allowing a "late bloom" of sexual desire (Starr and Weiner, 1982). The evidence also suggests, however, that most husbands welcome the bloom and seek to nourish it, rather than fear it.

Extramarital sex The generally permissive attitude of the "new morality" toward premarital and marital sexual practices does not extend to extramarital sex. Articles and movies about mate swapping notwithstanding, both men and women, young and old, still view sexual fidelity as essential to the marriage contract; infidelity is considered a serious moral offense (Hunt, 1974). The frequency of extramarital affairs has not changed much in recent decades, except among younger women (Broderick, 1982). Kinsey and his colleagues (1949, 1953) reported that, among young adults, 24 percent of the men and 8 percent of the women had had at least one extramarital liaison. Research, reporting on extramarital behavior twenty to thirty years later, found that while the proportion of men had not changed much, the proportion of women is much closer to that reported by males (Broderick, 1982).

Among the reasons given for entering into an extramarital relationship, by far the most important is resentment and dissatisfaction with the marriage itself. Next in importance seems to be premarital sexual patterns (the more sexual partners one had before marriage, the more likely one is to be extramaritally active). Men are most likely to be involved in extramarital relations during the first five years of marriage, while for women it is more common after fifteen to twenty years of marriage (Broderick, 1982).

Rape   The study of rape is confounded by the fact that legal definitions of rape vary from state to state. Definitions typically involve three separate elements: sexual intercourse occurs, there is force or threat of force, and the victim does not consent to the act (Frieze, 1983). Of particular concern recently has been the issue of acquaintance rape — a rape in which the victim and rapist are previously known to each other and have been interacting in a socially appropriate manner prior to the incident (Shotland and Goodstein, 1983). How common is acquaintance rape? It is estimated that at least one-third of rapes and rape attempts occur among acquaintances (National Crime Survey, 1981). Ten to 20 percent of college women surveyed reported forceful attempts at sexual intercourse (Kanin, 1971; Koss and Oros, 1980).

Study of acquaintance rape has been fraught with the difficulties of determining whether an incident should be labeled rape and under what conditions such a rape occurs. Individuals have been found less likely to perceive acquaintance rape as "real" rape, compared to rape by a stranger. Part of the ambiguity is related to societal assumptions and norms governing sexual activity among acquaintances, particularly dating couples. For example, there is some evidence that in our society it is commonly accepted for a woman to conceal her genuine interest in sexual contact, and that she may be expected to resist a man's advances at least in the beginning stages of a sexual encounter even though she may later be responsive and consent to sexual relations. Moreover, there is the expectation that it is the male's responsibility to initiate and to take the dominant role in sexual activity (Burt and Albin, 1981). It may be reasoned, then, that some use of force by the male is socially accepted, given the initial, expected resistance by the female.

In a recent study Shotland and Goodstein (1983) presented male and female college students with variations in a detailed description of a date in which the male used low or moderate force to obtain sex, after the female began to protest either early, in the middle, or late during foreplay. Her protest consisted of just pleading or pleading plus a physical struggle. Subjects were more likely to blame the woman and perceive her as desiring sex when the man used low force and the woman did not protest until late in foreplay. The incident was more likely to be viewed as rape when the man used more force and when the women struggled and protested early in foreplay. It was also found that students were less likely to blame the victim, if they were more egalitarian in their attitudes toward women. Persons with low scores on attitudes toward women, typically males, were more likely to blame women in rape incidences. To summarize, the study suggests that subjects' decisions about whether a rape has occurred involve assessments of both the degree of violence/force used by the male and the degree of desire or lack of desire (for example, verbal and physical protests) offered by the woman. The incidence was most likely to be considered a rape when greater force and stronger protests occurred.

An even more thorny issue is that of marital rape. Indeed, laws in at least twenty-nine states specifically prohibit a man from being prosecuted for raping his wife (Frieze, 1983). Current studies suggest that marital rape is most likely to occur in marriages that are violent in other ways as well. One study found that over one-third of battered women also reported being raped by their husbands (Frieze, 1983). This study also found that marital rape was rare in nonviolent marriages.

In contrast to acquaintance rape, rape by a stranger is generally considered a crime of violence and power, rather than an act of passion (Diamond and Karlen, 1980). The purpose of the rapist is not to relieve sexual tension but to hurt and to dominate. The psychology of rape describes an angry man, frustrated by incompetence, who feels inferior in a world in which he is supposed to be superior; rape is his attempt to reestablish his power (Russell, 1975). Viewed as a political act, rape represents the violation of a woman's rights in an unequal society and, as such, has justly been a *cause célèbre* among feminists (Brownmiller, 1975).

The sexual arena is a microcosm of the larger society, as the politics of rape demonstrates. There is no doubt that societal beliefs and attitudes about the proper role of women in relation to men influence sexual behavior and satisfaction, no less than other male–female interactions. Many of the sex differences we have discussed in this and other chapters (3, 4, 5) are due to the active role men are expected to play. As the politics change, as women achieve more nearly equal opportunity in business, science, the professions, and other areas of social life, we can expect the "male superior" attitude in sexual relations to decline as well.

Marital Instability

"The fundamental loneliness goes when two can share a dream together." So go the lyrics of a once popular song, expressing well the intimacy most couples hope to achieve in their marriages. But increasingly often these days intimacy does not grow with the years; instead it withers. Eventually the couple takes a close look at an empty relationship and calls it quits. Divorce.

What happened? What went wrong?

In this section we will look at some of the factors that can impede or disrupt marriage. We will consider the growing incidence of divorce and the "ripple" effects to adjacent generations in the family.

DIVORCE: INCIDENCE AND ATTITUDES

The divorce rate in the United States has been climbing rapidly; "sky-rocketing" is the term aptly used by some journalists. As Figure 6–2 shows, the number of divorces increased rapidly for a brief period following World War II (around 1945) and then fell back to a slower but steady increase (National Center for Health Statistics, 1984). In the 1960s, however, the divorce rate began accelerating. In 1974, for the first time, more marriages were ended through divorce than through the death of a spouse (Glick, 1980). The Census Bureau estimates that four of every ten marriages contracted by women born between 1945 and 1949 will eventually end in divorce (U.S. Bureau of the Census, 1976a). If the divorce rate continues its spectacular rise, men and women marrying today will have about a 50:50 chance of a lifelong union (Doherty and Jacobson, 1982).

FIGURE 6–2.

Divorce rates per 1,000 married women 15 years of age and older (1925–1981).

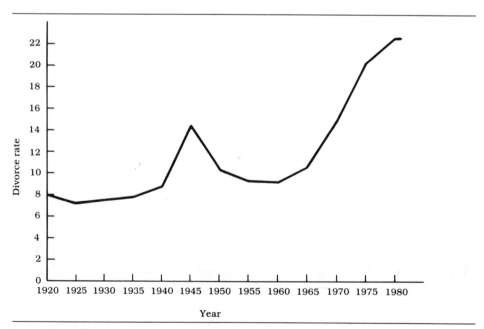

Source: From the National Center for Health Statistics, 1984.

As divorce rates soar, attitudes about divorce are changing, too, each partly a cause and partly an effect of the other. For centuries, divorce was permitted only in the most extreme cases of flagrant adultery or cruelty (and divorced people were not allowed to remarry). One of the major reasons for low divorce rates in the past was the unequal status of men and women. The wife was considered "property" of the husband. Uneducated and almost totally dependent on their husbands for financial support, most women could not survive by themselves. Thus a man's divorcing his wife was viewed as roughly akin to deserting his children; "incompatibility" has never been considered a justification for casting off one's children, and the same reasoning protected the wife.

In nineteenth-century Europe, the wife's status improved somewhat. Marriage had been considered solely an economic arrangement — a good wife, like a good horse, was a good worker — but now a new element was added: emotional intimacy (Burgess, Locke, and Thomes, 1963; Doherty and Jacobson, 1982). A husband was expected to *love* his wife, to be affectionate and friendly, to be a good companion. Although slowly at first, attitudes about divorce began to change, adding "the withholding of affection" to adultery and cruelty as reasons one might seek a divorce.

More recently, largely since 1960, a new attitude toward marriage has further reduced inhibitions about divorce. Many people today have the notion that marriage should be a positive experience, that they have a right to a happy marriage (Doherty and Jacobson, 1982). Divorce is considered acceptable on no greater grounds than that the marriage is dull. Such an attitude argues incompatibility is reason enough for divorce, and we find this attitude represented in the no-fault divorce laws of many states today.

DISRUPTION OF THE MARITAL RELATIONSHIP

If we were to arrange couples on a scale of marital satisfaction, those who divorce would certainly fall at the low end of our scale. But it is not always the least happy people who get divorced. Many very unhappy people remain married for the sake of the children or for religious and economic reasons, and some couples who divorce were quite satisfied with their marriages. One spouse may have found someone else he or she loves more, or two careers may split the couple geographically. Government policies such as easing divorce laws or increasing public assistance to divorced parents with dependent children can affect the divorce rate without changing the average level of marital satisfaction (Moles, 1979).

Data show that the likelihood of divorce is greatest in groups with certain characteristics. Those who marry young are more likely to get divorced. Among women, the highest rates are found among those who marry for the first time before age eighteen (Spanier and Glick, 1981). There is also a correlation between divorce rates and educational level. People who have less than a high school education have high divorce rates, whereas those who have college degrees tend to have higher levels of marital stability.

The income of the husband is consistently related to marital stability; men with higher incomes are less likely to divorce (Norton and Glick, 1979). Exactly the opposite finding is true of women; women with higher incomes are more likely than wives with lower incomes to divorce (Cherlin, 1979; Kelly, 1982). Higher incomes for women are also associated with higher levels of education. Thus women who have graduate training are much more likely to get divorced than those who have just an undergraduate degree (Spanier and Glick, 1981). Money can reduce one prominent source of stress in a marriage — financial worries — and thus promotes stability. In fact, recent longitudinal research suggests that *instability* of the husband's employment and income may be a critical factor in the increased incidence of divorce in low income families (Kelly, 1982). An independent income for the wife, however, makes it possible for her to survive on her own and thus lessens the financial obstacles to her divorce.

As the effect of women's income shows, much of the problem of divorce comes down to the balance between intimacy and independence. Divorce is the disruption of intimacy, a splitting apart of two interdependent people into two independent agents. The attractions of intimacy are pitted against the attractions of independence, which include sexual enjoyments with other people, unencumbered self-actualization, and the opportunity to make important decisions all by oneself (Levinger, 1979; Kelly, 1982). As intimacy breaks down from the pressures on the relationship, independence becomes more attractive.

The deterioration of a marriage is rarely a sudden development. In many cases, divorce is the culmination of a long process of emotional separation and growing independence. The final months of a marriage are usually remembered as unhappy (Thompson and Spanier, 1983). Recent research evidence confirms that a mutually shared decision to divorce is uncommon. One partner typically wants to terminate the relationship more than the other. When a divorce or separation is suggested, it is usually the wife who raises the issue first (Kelly, 1982). This is probably because women tend to become dissatisfied with a marriage that is not working sooner than men do. It also usually falls to the mother to inform children of the impending divorce. Mothers maintain closer ties with and receive more support from children before, during, and after divorce (Hagestad, Smyer, and Stierman, 1984).

THE PERSONAL EFFECTS OF DIVORCE

The breakup of the intimate relationship between a man and a woman is a very stressful event. Most people perceive divorce as a kind of failure. Even an unhappy marriage has some benefits, and the idea of living alone elicits considerable anxiety for many people. One woman said, "When the idea occurred to me that I could live without Dave and be happier, my immediate next feeling was just gut fear. It's really hard to explain. It was just terror" (Weiss, 1979, p. 203). These feelings of anxiety appear in men and women whether the marriage has been happy or not, whether the divorce has been sought or not.

The spouse's respective role in terminating the marriage has been found to be significantly related to certain behaviors, feelings, and overall adjustment in the immediate postseparation period (Kelly, 1982). Since many separations are not mutually decided, the separation is an extremely stressful experience, particularly for the rejected spouse. Feelings of humiliation and powerlessness are common. Many rejected spouses appear to have been completely unprepared for their partner's decision to divorce. While they may have felt as ungratified by the marriage as their partner, they themselves were not actively contemplating divorce and were shocked by the decision. Marital discord of even extreme intensity did not equally prepare each spouse for divorce. For the men and women who did not participate in the spouse's decision to divorce, the period of greatest divorce-related stress occurred more often immediately after learning there was to be a divorce. In contrast, for spouses who decided to divorce, the period of greatest stress was prior to the separation during those months and years of agonizing over whether to divorce. Spouses who initiated the divorce often did so with sadness, guilt, and anger, but a clear differentiating feature was their sense of control and the absence of feelings of humiliation and rejection. They had often rehearsed and mentally prepared for their separation status.

Most divorces occur in the early years of marriage when people are relatively young, which raises the possibility that the patterns associated with divorce may be different among middle-aged and older people. A study of divorce at midlife, however, concluded that there are some similarities. Again, it was the women who first became dissatisfied and considered the possibility of divorce. Perhaps as a result, women found that the time prior to the decision to divorce was the most stressful, whereas men reported more trauma after the decision had been made (Hagestad, Smyer, and Stierman, 1984).

Another study (Chiriboga, 1982) showed that adults over the age of fifty reported greater psychological stress after a separation than did younger people. The older group reported greater disruption of their social lives, experiencing difficulty going alone to such places as restaurants and the theater. Their personal lives were disrupted more as well; they felt that their lives were more disorganized and out of control. In general, they were more unhappy and less optimistic about the future. These findings may be a result of the deeper entrenchment of middle-aged and older adults in a certain social order and of the difficulties in adjusting to unmarried life. They may also perceive themselves as having fewer options for the future than younger groups do. One study found that men especially had trouble anticipating what life would be like a year in the future after their lifestyles had changed (Chiriboga, 1982).

The stress of divorce is apparently too much for some people, who succumb to serious mental or physical disorders (Bloom, Asher, and White, 1978; Kelly, 1982). Physical illness of almost every variety is more common among divorced and separated people than among the married or never-married. Presumably this is due to stress, which can affect the body's resistance to disease. Similarly, stress can affect mental health; divorced people are disproportionately represented in psychiatric facilities, and their alcoholism and suicide rates are higher. In some cases, of course, the physical or mental problem may have existed before the divorce — in fact, may have precipitated the divorce — but there is no question that divorce itself is a traumatic event in the lives of most people who experience it.

However, most divorced people experience improvements in well-being by three years after the final separation (Spanier and Furstenberg, 1983). There is some evidence that those who have the strongest sense of well-being are the most likely to remarry within three or four years after separation. The converse is also true: a happy remarriage contributes to a sense of well-being. Remarriage is three times as likely for men as for women, in part because age norms suggest that wives should be younger than husbands. Thus most men over age forty remarry, but a third of all divorced women never remarry (Spanier and Furstenberg, 1982).

In an interesting study comparing the reactions of widows and divorcées to the loss of a spouse, Lopata (1980a) found that life is often more difficult for the divorcées (see box at end of chapter). The divorcées perceived themselves as having lost more status and respect than the widows. They also felt that they were more likely to be taken advantage of, that remarriages would be unhappy, and that they were more of a "fifth wheel." Unlike widows, most divorcées had negative memories of their husbands. Thus this study highlights the particular negative effects of divorce for women, which goes beyond loss of spouse per se.

CHILDREN, DIVORCE, AND THE "RIPPLE EFFECT"

The place of the child in the American family has changed historically in the twentieth century. On the one hand, a greater proportion of couples now have children than in the past. The proportion of childless couples has decreased from about 20 percent in the early 1900s to only 10 percent in the 1970s due largely to improved fertility treatments and a lower incidence of maternal deaths (Doherty and Jacobson, 1982). There may now be a reverse trend in that more couples are opting for a child-free lifestyle, but it is still premature to determine this trend. While more couples are having children, it is also the case that more children are being reared in single-parent families due to increasing divorce rates. The number of children whose parents have divorced is at an all time high (Spanier and Glick, 1981).

Children in a marriage have two contradictory effects on the relationship between the man and the woman (Hoffman and Manis, 1978; Lerner and Spanier, 1978; Zeits and Prince, 1982). On the one hand, children disrupt intimacy. They come between the husband and the wife and force them into roles of father and mother. They require time and energy, previously reserved for the husband–wife relationship. They may cause arguments about childrearing methods and general goals and plans. As a result, American couples with children in the home tend to be significantly less happy with their marriages than childless couples (Levinger, 1979). As one researcher said, "Almost as soon as a couple has kids, their happy bubble bursts. For both men and women, reports of happiness and satisfaction drop . . ., not to rise again until their children are grown and about to leave the nest" (Campbell, 1975, p. 39).

If the disruption of intimacy by the advent of children is an effect that moves the couple closer to divorce, the second effect is opposite, promoting marital stability. Children in a sense create the family, the system of interdependent members we described in Chapter 2. For many people, the opportunity to raise children is one of the prime reasons for getting married in the first place. If divorce is contemplated, pressures are brought to bear by relatives, friends, the community, and the spouses themselves to keep the family together. Divorce becomes less appealing for many people because they will be forced to live apart from the children, whom they love. Thus children are a force for keeping the marriage intact, just as they are simultaneously a force driving the husband and wife apart. There is some evidence that women with children, especially three or more, are less likely to get divorced (Spanier and Glick, 1981). It is not clear, however, whether having children decreased the likelihood of divorce or whether divorce simply interrupts childbearing. Also, the parents in families consisting of many children are likely to be older, and older families have lower divorce rates.

When a divorce occurs, it has a "ripple effect." That is, divorce not only affects the couple, but also the two adjacent generations, the couple's children and also the grandparents (Hagestad, 1984b). The children are likely to lose close contact with one parent and, often, with their grandparents and other kin on one side of the family. This is most often the father's side, since mothers generally win custody. Thus paternal grandparents, in particular, may face the loss of active grandparent roles. On the other hand, bonds with the grandparents of the side that wins custody of the children are often strengthened (Hagestad, 1984b).

Alternative Lifestyles

Changes in attitudes toward men–women relationships, the increasing entry of women into full-time employment and professional roles, and the growing number of divorces have contributed to many men and women seeking alternative types of lifestyles. These new forms range from singlehood, in which there is no intimate commitment to one other person, to communes, in which modified commitments are made to several people, rather than to a single person. It is important to note that the lifestyles considered in this section do not involve a "couple relationship" or family unit. Alternative lifestyles involving a couple relationship, such as a gay couple, or involving a family unit (for example, single-parent household) were discussed in Chapter 2.

SINGLEHOOD

Singlehood has traditionally been thought of as a stage of young adulthood prior to the young person's entering into a marital relationship. A small segment of the population has remained in singlehood throughout adulthood, choosing not to marry. However, due to societal change, singlehood is becoming a state that an individual may enter and exit from multiple times over the adult life course. For example, given that 40 to 50 percent of all marriages today are ending in divorce, a significant proportion of the adult population returns, at least temporarily, to singlehood following the dissolution of marriage. Moreover, many elderly are single, due to the death of a spouse. The average widow can expect to spend ten to twelve years in singlehood. Clearly, the experience of singlehood is qualitatively different depending on one's life stage and one's experiences prior to the state of singlehood. In an earlier section of this chapter, we have dealt with some of the feelings and experiences those recently divorced may encounter as they reenter singlehood. Later in this chapter we will discuss issues related to widowhood. Issues related to singlehood from the perspective of a never-married young adult have been considered in Chapters 2 and 5. Finally, the box article for this chapter contrasts singlehood experienced as a widow versus a divorcée.

COHABITATION

For many young people, and for a surprising number of middle-aged and older adults as well, cohabitation — an unmarried adult sharing the same living quarters with an unrelated adult of the opposite sex — is a nice compromise between the loneliness of singlehood and commitments of a legal marriage. For most

Today it is not uncommon for an unmarried adult to adopt a child.

doesnt have to be sexual.

cohabitors, living together is a kind of "intense dating," a way for people who are not yet ready for marriage to have a close sexual relationship (Bower and Christopherson, 1977). The number of cohabiting couples grew significantly during the 1960s and 1970s, and there is evidence that this trend is continuing (Spanier, 1983). Between 1975 and 1980, the number doubled, and today about 4 percent of all couples living together are unmarried. Although we often stereotype cohabitors as young couples who have not been previously married, cohabitors are a diverse group. Approximately 45 percent of all men and women in a cohabiting relationship have been previously married. As expected, 72 percent of all cohabiting households have no children present, but 28 percent have at least one child. Cohabitors do tend to be young adults. Almost 40 percent are in the twenty-five to thirty-four-year-old age group (Spanier, 1983).

Several factors are probably involved in the continuing increase in cohabitation. First, acceptance of cohabitation in society has grown. Second, it is becoming more acceptable to delay having children until after age thirty, so women feel less pressure to marry young. Men are waiting longer to marry too. It may be that cohabitation is regarded today as an extension of courtship. Most people involved in cohabitation expect to marry in the future. Their future spouses will in some cases be the people they have been living with, but not always; only rarely is cohabitation viewed as a "trial marriage." Although living together, many cohabitors keep certain parts of their lives separate. In their study of traditional marriages and heterosexual cohabitations, Schwartz and Blumstein (1983) noted a sharp distinction between the two groups with regard to financial matters. Whereas husbands and wives tended to pool their incomes, such that the money's ownership got lost, cohabitors often kept separate bank accounts. Thus the relative contributions of each partner were much more evident. Cohabitation helps the participants clarify their ideas about marriage and the kind of person with whom they would like to share their lives. Most participants say that they also learn a lot about themselves in these intimate encounters; it helps them mature, they say, and they gain a better sense of personal identity (Macklin, 1972; Broderick, 1982). Nevertheless, if they marry, cohabitors may encounter many of the early marital adjustments experienced by noncohabiting couples (see Chapter 5).

NEW FORMS

Many new forms of the intimate commitment we call marriage have been suggested and tried. *Open marriage,* for example, allows both spouses openly to seek friends and interests outside the marriage (O'Neill and O'Neill, 1972). Compared to what we suppose would have to be called the traditional or closed marriage, the open marriage overcomes some of the restrictions at the expense of potentially disruptive jealousies; a little more individuality is traded for a little less intimacy.

Some scholars have proposed that, given today's divorce rate, we have already entered an era in which the most common form of marriage is *serial marriage* (Toffler, 1970). In serial marriage, each individual marries more than one other — in a series, of course, not all at the same time. Some people have begun to anticipate at least the possibility of divorce by specifying the economic arrangements in the case of separation or by considering their union to be a short-term contract — say, five years, with an option for renewal.

Group marriage is one of the least conventional forms of marriage today, involving typically three or four people. Women who express an interest in group marriage hope that a "new situation" will ease the sense of isolation they feel at home with their children, freeing them from dependence on their husbands; they also hope that group marriage will release them to utilize their talents — allowing them to take a full-time job, for example (Ramey, 1972). Men considering group marriage are impressed by the economic advantages, with multiple incomes and reduced expenses "per capita." The disadvantages of group marriage include the fact that it is a situation with no cultural support or guidelines, requiring a tremendous investment of time, effort, and emotional energy (Constantine and Constantine, 1972). Beset with jealousies, sexual and otherwise, most group marriages dissolve in a year or two.

Group marriage is a specific form of *communal living*. Other types of communes range from the structured and reasonably successful kibbutzim (collective settlements) in Israel to various loosely structured and usually unstable communes in the United States. A study in the mid-1970s estimated that there were about 3,000 communes in the United States, up from about 500 in the late 1960s (Stinnet and Walters, 1977). The more successful communes tend to have structured patterns of authority, often dictated by religious or political beliefs shared by the participants.

There is much evidence that members of communes are not seeking to establish a radical new form of family living but instead are trying to reestablish an old form: the extended family. They find that day-to-day living is easier and loneliness is less frequent when one shares responsibilities with other people who have similar needs and interests. An interesting recent development is communes for elderly people whose need for intimacy and a division of labor among friends is no less than that of the younger adults we commonly associate with communal living. Stop

Widowhood

Most old men are still married, but most old women are widowed and alone. Between the ages of sixty-five and seventy-four, about 40 percent of the women are widowed, compared with 9 percent of the men. Among those seventy-five and older, 70 percent of the women are widowed, compared with 24 percent of the men (Uhlenberg and Myers, 1981). The reasons for this disparity between the sexes in the last years of life are clear: women generally marry older men and, in addition, have a longer life expectancy than men. As a result, the average woman in the United States can expect to live between ten and twelve years as a widow. Her chances of remarrying are slim and they have been getting slimmer throughout this century. In 1900, it is estimated that there were 2.2 widows for every widower; today the ratio of older unmarried women to unmarried men is about 5 to 1 (Lopata, 1980a), and by the year 2000 it will be 6.5 to 1 (Hagestad, 1984b). Fortunately, perhaps, many older widows do not consider getting married. Seventy-five percent of a sample of older urban widows said they did not wish to marry, citing as reasons loss of independence, not wanting to care for another sick spouse, and fear of fortune hunters (Lopata, 1980a). In any case, eligible males over sixty-five, if they do marry, often marry women under sixty-five. Given the greater opportunity to find a mate, widowed men over sixty-five are eight times as likely as old widows to remarry.

Elderly women whose husbands have died experience a host of economic, social, and psychological difficulties. Income tends to be low, about a third of what it was before the husband died; a third of all widows live on incomes below the poverty line (Lopata, 1980a). Many widows, particularly those who live in cities, receive little financial or service help from children or relatives. Over half of the urban widows in one study said they did not have help in making decisions or in house repairs. Eighty-seven percent said they received no help with their cars, which increased the chances that they would have to sell their car and thereby restrict their mobility and social interaction, as well as their ability to get necessary medical services (Lopata, 1980b). The problem is complicated by the fact that most elderly widows live alone, usually in older homes which are considerably more expensive than new homes to operate and maintain. This trend toward living alone has been growing in recent decades. Two-and-one-half times as many widows lived alone in 1970 as in 1940, and three-quarters of all women over sixty-five years old are heads of their own households. Women report that they prefer to live alone because they want to remain independent and manage their own homes and work. They also wish to avoid the disadvantages of living with their children.

Other effects of widowhood can be equally severe. Losing a spouse can cause loneliness of at least two types: social loneliness and emotional loneliness (Weiss, 1973; Lopata, 1980a). The death of a spouse immediately removes the source of most of an individual's social interactions (Fiske, 1980). In addition, many of a person's relationships with other people and with social organizations are organized in terms of a husband–wife unit. Friends, especially those in couple-to-couple contexts, may find interactions with an unattached individual difficult. The widow (or widower) may find that going out to a movie theater, a restaurant, or even church is less pleasant and satisfying by oneself. Some people, embarrassed by signs of grief, may avoid the widow and may even justify their avoidance by assuming the individual wants or needs to be alone. Emotionally, the surviving spouse is deprived of his or her most intimate relationship and of the person to whom he or she was most important. At the same time, they cease to be loved by a person and they lose the person they loved most; the sense of loss is often and quite understandably very severe. On a less profound level, the widow or widower misses the companionship of his or her spouse and the spouse's partnership in the division of labor (Peterson, 1980).

Unlike many cultures, the United States does not have a well-defined social role for widows to play and even looks with some disapproval on those men and women who continue grieving too long. Since widowhood is more likely in old age, social support for widowhood is somewhat greater then. As a result, young widows often experience a more difficult adjustment than older women in the same circumstances (Blau, 1961). Not only are the young widows more likely to lack friends and relatives in the same circumstances, but they may feel the unfairness of the situation more strongly. The older widow's role is clear and more acceptable, and she is also more likely to have friends in a similar position.

The psychological effects of widowhood may be extremely painful. Two stages of grief are often experienced. During the stage of acute grief (mourning), the widow or widower attempts to adjust to the loss of the most significant person in her or his life. This stage usually takes somewhat less than a year. The health of the widow or widower suffers. Some researchers claim that the death rate rises sharply (Maddison and Viola, 1968; Parkes, Benjamin, and Fitzgerald, 1969), but this conclusion is controversial (Clayton, 1971; Kalish, 1976). Loneliness, anxiety, and depression are commonplace. In the first month of bereavement, crying and sleep disturbances are frequent. A sizable percentage of widows and widowers — about one in five — report terrible feelings of guilt, believing that they should have been able to do something to prolong the life of their spouse (Clayton, Halikes, and Maurice, 1971).

During the second stage, the bereaved person gradually reconstructs an identity as a partnerless person. If the individual's health is good and finances are adequate, chances of leading a happy and satisfying life are fairly good (Cumming, 1969; Glick, Weiss, and Parkes, 1974). Some widows, however, find it quite difficult to "move on" with their lives. They understand, at least vaguely, that society allows them a brief period of extreme mourning and that then they are expected to pull themselves together. These widows find that they cannot, and this alarms them more. Still grieving for their departed spouses, frightened, with a profound sense of hopelessness, they may withdraw from life and become true social isolates (Lopata, 1975). Over time, this withdrawn lifestyle can result in a relatively rapid decline in intellectual competence (Gribbin, Schaie, and Parham, 1980). Lack of community sympathy for the widows' plight combined with their lack of social skills tends to produce passive, helpless old women. These widows have difficulty with adaptive activities, such as joining a club or a church, moving to a new neighborhood, finding a job, or turning a stranger into a friend.

One of the changes which may result from widowhood is a change in self-perception. The older, more traditional and particularly less educated women reported no change in themselves as a result of becoming a widow. However, many more educated and socially adept widows report greater feelings of competence and independence. This does not mean that they look back at their

Many elderly men and women maintain a strong self-identity even after losing a spouse.

marriages negatively, but that they experienced a positive change in themselves after the acute grief period was over.

A woman's reaction to widowhood depends not only on her personal resources but also on the nature of her relationship with her husband before his death. This, in turn, has been shown to be related to the couple's socioeconomic status. Well-educated, middle-class couples tend to be more communicative with each other, sharing their lives and spending their leisure time together much more than working-class couples do (Lopata, 1980a). As a result, middle-class couples may be quite mutually dependent, and widows from such couples may experience severe disruption of their lives when their husbands die (Lopata, 1975). The activities of working-class couples, on the other hand, tend to be much more segregated along gender lines. Men's contacts are with coworkers and with other men at sports and other leisure events. Women's contacts are with other female family members and with women at female-oriented church and volunteer activities. As widows, working-class women grieve over their husbands' deaths, but their identities and lifestyles may undergo less change. Thus middle-class women may encounter more disruption of their social worlds following the deaths of their husbands than do working-class women, whose social lives were more independent and segregated to begin with.

Variations are also found in how widows speak about and remember their deceased husbands (Lopata, 1981). Some widows tend to idealize or even "sanctify" their former husbands, remembering them as being far more perfect than they actually were. In a group of women who tended to sanctify their husbands, one in four strongly agreed with such statements as "my husband had no irritating habits," and half thought that their husbands had been unusually good men. Sanctification of this sort may have some useful functions for the survivor. The process of grieving involves preserving the memory of the deceased in the memories of survivors. At the same time, mental health demands that the process of grieving be completed. Sanctification may permit both — the husband is remembered in such favorable terms that he becomes distant, unreal, and otherworldly, and distancing the husband in this way helps the widow end her grieving (Lopata, 1981).

Although there are far more widows than widowers in the United States, widowers face some special problems (Lopata, 1980a). Mental illness and death are more common in surviving spouses of both sexes when compared with all elderly, but the risk appears to be greater among widowers. Since men are relatively likely to depend on their wives as their major social support and as their means of keeping in contact with others, they are more likely to suffer from isolation when their spouses die. Women, on the other hand, often have social support systems of family members and female friends. The more severe problems of widowers may be related to the need to have a confidant to maintain psychological health. Extreme social isolation has been identified as a factor that precipitates psychiatric illnesses (Lowenthal and Berkman, 1967), and marriage and social relationships are important in maintaining the well-being of older adults (George, 1978). On a more practical level, older widowers may face additional problems because they often lack experience in dealing with routine household chores.

Relationships: Change and Continuity

The nature of the intimate relationship between man and woman is constantly changing, constantly aligning itself to the changing society in which it is embedded. Medical discoveries such as effective contraceptives and cures for venereal diseases have changed the nature of sexual interactions. Technological advancements have created occupations in which strength and speed count less and intellect more; women compete successfully with men for these jobs. Thus women are becoming liberated, and this fact is bound to affect the man–woman relationship. In some respects, the changes will be of negative or at least dubious value: witness, in this chapter, the rising divorce rate and the conflicts of the dual-career marriage. In other respects, the changes cannot help but improve life: consider, for example, the plight of the isolated widow, passive, dependent, helpless primarily because she was taught to be passive and dependent and because she was not taught how to cope on her own (Lopata, 1975). The liberated widow will do better; she will have more resources.

The traditional stereotype of a relationship between a man and a woman in American society assumes that men are assertive, logical, and competent, whereas women are warm and nurturant (Broverman et al., 1972). This stereotype fit society when the man was the "bread-winner" and the woman raised the children at home. Today, however, the majority of married women work; they need to become more assertive, more logical, more skilled. Men, dealing with women who are their equals in the world of work and faced with greater responsibilities if they wish to have children, need to become more nurturant, more sensitive to their feelings and the feelings of others. There is already considerable evidence that today's society rewards men and women who are "androgynous," that is, who are both warm and sensitive *and* assertive and competent (Geiwitz, 1980). A change to relationships between more complete individuals is hardly to be feared; it is a change to be welcomed.

Nevertheless, throughout the uncertainty, conflict, excitement, and wonder that change can bring to a relationship, "the fundamental things apply, as time goes by." The fundamental things about a relationship between a man and a woman are intimacy and sharing, and no social change is likely to affect the priority of these qualities. An intimate relationship was, is, and ever shall be a vulnerable position, an opening up of oneself to another person, a sharing not only of life's tasks but also of life's conflicts and fears.

Summary

1. According to national surveys, three-quarters of all college males and two-thirds of all college females are sexually active. Young married couples make love about three times a week; middle-aged couples, about once a week. Barring chronic illness, most elderly couples remain sexually active well into their seventies. There is marked decline of sexual activity after the age of seventy-five, but individuals as old as 100 or more are still capable of expressing love in a physical way.

2. The most common reason for an inactive sex life among elderly couples is male impotence, which has a variety of physical and psychological causes; physical and psychological therapies are generally effective.

3. Changes in sexual attitudes are correlated with changes in premarital and marital sexual activity. Negative attitudes toward sex among the elderly result in jokes about and unfair stereotyping of the "dirty old man" and the postmenopausal woman.

4. Women in our culture, on the average, are less interested in sex and engage in less sexual activity than men. A good portion of these sex differences in sexuality is apparently due to cultural norms against the expression of sexuality among women; as attitudes become more liberal, sex differences are decreasing. Extramarital sex is still considered immoral by old and young alike, although sex differences are disappearing there too. Rape, by a stranger, a crime more of violence than of passion, is usually an attempt by a frustrated, hostile man to reestablish power and dominance.

5.   Divorce rates have been skyrocketing, to the extent that a marriage today has about a 50:50 chance of remaining intact 'til death do them part. Attitudes about marriage — from "wives as property" through "marriage involves love" to "marriage should be a positive experience" — have changed along with the divorce rate and may be partly causal. The economic liberation of women, however, is also a cause. Divorce is often the result of a long process of marital deterioration. It appears to cause more psychological stress among older couples.

6.   Children have contradictory effects on a marriage, drawing the couple closer together and at the same time disrupting the couple's intimacy. When divorces do occur, they have a "ripple effect" on grandparents and children. The number of children of divorced parents is today at an all-time high. Divorce is a traumatic event in the lives of people who experience it. A few years after a divorce, however, many people experience improvements in well-being.

7.   Alternative lifestyles include singlehood, cohabitation, and new forms of marriage defined by adjectives such as open, serial, and group. Communal living can take a variety of forms.

8.   Seventy percent of the women over age seventy-five are widowed, compared with 24 percent of the men. Relatively few widows remarry. Many widows experience financial hardships. The emotional loss that occurs when a spouse dies also has serious effects. Two stages of grief are often experienced. Some women have trouble recovering from their grief. The ease or difficulty of one's recovery is related to one's social status and prior relationship with one's spouse. Some widows tend to sanctify the memory of their husbands. Widowers, although fewer in number than widows, face certain special problems.

SUGGESTED READINGS

Doherty, W. J., and Jacobson, N. S. (1982). Marriage and the family. In B. B. Wolman (Ed.), *Handbook of developmental psychology*, pp. 667–680. Englewood Cliffs, NJ: Prentice-Hall. This chapter examines issues such as trends in marriage and the family, the influence of marriage and parenthood on adult personality development, and the relationship of marital status to physical health and mental health.

Kelly, J. B. (1982). Divorce: The adult perspective. In B. B. Wolman (Ed.), *Handbook of developmental psychology*, pp. 734–750. Englewood Cliffs, NJ: Prentice-Hall. This chapter examines issues such as factors associated with marital instability, the decision to divorce, the separation period, and postdivorce adjustment.

Lopata, H. Z. (1980). The widowed family member. In *Transitions of aging*, pp. 93–118. New York: Academic Press. This chapter examines the social, familial, and economic aspects of widowhood.

Schwartz, P., and Blumstein, P. (1983). *American couples: Money, work and sex*. New York: William Morrow. Detailed interviews with married couples, heterosexual cohabiting couples, and homosexual couples.

Starr, B. D., and Weiner, M. B. (1982). *The Starr–Weiner report on sex and sexuality in the mature years*. New York: McGraw-Hill. Detailed report of survey of 800 older adults on sexual attitudes and behavior.

Divorcées and Widows:
Similarities and Differences

In the United States we place a high value on a woman's being married. It is an important source of status for women, who still have fewer opportunities than men to obtain status on their own and who until recently were expected to obtain prestige vicariously through the achievements of their husbands and children. A 1980 paper by Kitson and coworkers addressed several questions pertaining to the loss of the married status for women. Does the shift from being married to being divorced or widowed lead women to hold attitudes that restrict or otherwise influence their relationships with others? Do widows and divorcées report similar attitudes, or does one group feel more restricted in its relationships than the other? Do they tend to idealize their departed or deceased husbands?

The loss of a husband through death or divorce has a broad range of social consequences for the wife. She may see herself differently as well as be perceived differently by others. One of the functions of grief is to help the former wife construct an image of herself as a partnerless person. In the context of this study, several hypotheses suggest themselves. First, divorced and widowed women may respond similarly because both have a devalued status — no longer married. Second, widows and divorcées may offer different reports of the restrictions in their relationships because they lost their husbands in different ways. Among widows, the departure of the husband was not desired; as a result, they may be treated considerately by others and they may not perceive their relationships with others as suffering. Divorce, on the other hand, is desired by at least one of the partners, so the divorcée may be perceived as not deserving sympathy and support from others, and she may feel that her relationships with others are restricted. A third hypothesis is that the status of the widow is more clearly defined culturally. There are norms for mourning a death, but not for mourning a divorce. The transition to unmarried status, then, may be easier for the widow, but because she is expected to conform to norms she may feel more restricted in her relationships than the divorcée. Finally, as newly unmarried women adapt, they may restructure reality in creating memories of their former spouses. Widows may tend to idealize them, whereas we might expect divorced women to "vilify" them. A divorced woman who did not want a divorce would be less likely to view her husband negatively. Thus we would expect the two groups to differ greatly in their memories of their spouses, but that the "unwilling" divorcées would differ from the widows less than the "willing" divorcées.

Three sets of data were used to test the hypotheses. The first set was from a longitudinal study of adjustment to divorce among a group of black and white men and women from metropolitan Cleveland, Ohio. The sample was drawn from county court records. The other two data sets involved probability samples of widows in the Chicago area. The average age of the divorcées was 30.7 years. The average age for the two widow samples was 66 and 51 years, respectively. The sample differences in age of divorcées and widows are representative of population differences in these two groups. In order to adjust the effects of age on the findings, a statistical adjustment was made in the analyses of attitude scores.

The widows and divorcées were asked to respond to two attitude scales. One scale focused on their sense of restriction in relationships with others. The second scale focused on attitudes toward their former spouses. One item on the restriction scale, for example, was "women lose status when they become widows (divorced)." Scores on these items ranged from 1 (agree strongly) to 4 (disagree strongly). On the attitudes toward former spouse scale, subjects were instructed to indicate which word from each pair of adjectives (for example, kind–cruel; warm–cold) more closely described their former spouses.

The data did not support the first hypothesis, that the widows and divorcées would respond similarly on items pertaining to restrictions in relationships because both have experienced a loss of status. The divorcées reported feeling much more restricted and isolated from others than do the widows. The divorcées were more likely to report that their friends were jealous about them when the friends' spouses were around. The divorced were also more likely to feel that those who remarry may be very unhappy in their new marriages. Divorcées more often reported seeing themselves as a "fifth wheel." The widows were less likely to report being taken advantage of than the divorcées. Finally, the divorcées were more likely than the widows to report that women lose status and respect as a result of their change in marital status. In general, the data supported the hypothesis that widows have less restricted attitudes about social relationships than divorcées.

The evidence also indicated that widows had more favorable memories of their spouses than the divorcées did. As expected, divorcées who wanted the divorce had more negative images of their ex-husbands, whereas divorcées who did not want the divorce had more positive attitudes toward their spouses and so more closely resembled the widows. For both the divorced and the widowed, ambivalence about the departed spouse can create long-term adjustment difficulties. The widow may be aided somewhat in her adjustment to the loss of her spouse by the pleasant memories she has of him. The divorcée tends to have less pleasant memories.

Overall, the analysis suggests that the divorcée would seek and receive less support from others. The status of widow involves more firmly established expectations for behavior as well as clearer expectations regarding the behavior from others, which may aid the widow in her adjustment. There are less clear expectations regarding the expected behavior of divorcées or how others are to react to her; these ambiguities may make her adjustment more difficult. Data on the physical and mental health status of the widowed and divorced do indicate that there was generally more physical and mental health disturbances among the divorced than among the widowed. In sum, the study shows that many divorcées have unpleasant memories of their spouses, restricted relationships with others, and a sense that a remarriage would not be happy. For them, the past, present, and future may appear bleak.

Kitson, G., Lopata, H., Holmes, W., and Meyering, S. (1980). Divorcées and widows: Similarities and differences. *Journal of Orthopsychiatry, 50,* 291–301.

Chapter Seven

MOTIVATION

The Whys and the Wherefores

No formal def.
Have models of it.

A politician removes a spot from his suit (need to avoid unpleasant stimuli) because he does not wish to make a bad impression (need to avoid shame), and thus diminish his chances of winning the approval and friendship of Mr. *X* (need for affiliation) from whom he hopes to obtain some slanderous facts (need to explore and inquire) relating to the private life of his political rival, Mr. *Y*, information which he plans to publish (need to communicate information) in order to damage the reputation of Mr. *Y* (need for aggression) and thus ensure his own election to office (need for achievement) (adapted from Murray et al., 1938, p. 87).

This brief episode in the life of an unscrupulous politician depicts the efforts of psychologist Henry Murray to understand the motivation of a simple behavior: picking a spot from a suit. How complex the motivations of even the simplest behaviors! The motivation*s* — plural. Some needs seem more basic, involving biological drives, while other needs seem to have been acquired through learning and acculturation.

An episode like Murray's can be created rather easily, with almost any action as the point of beginning, by asking "Why?" over and over. Why did he remove the spot? To make a good impression on Mr. *X*. Why does he want to make a good impression on Mr. *X*? Because he wants Mr. *X* to like him. Why? So he can obtain slanderous facts. And so on, and so on. "Why?" is the fundamental question of motivational psychology. Put somewhat more precisely, motivational theorists attempt to account for *choices:* why this and not that?

One of the problems in studying motivation is that the term itself has no commonly accepted definition (Elias and Elias, 1977). There is no one all encompassing theory of motivation. Rather, we have numerous specific models that focus on a specific type of motivation. These include theories of achievement motivation, moral reasoning, and physiological arousal. Some theorists emphasize a "push" conception to motivation while others emphasize a "pull" conception. In the push view, motivation is concerned with the needs and drives from

Use compare contrast? (2 sources)
1. General Source,

within the person which "push" behavior. These drives are the result of biological or psychological needs that create a state of arousal. The state of arousal results in activity to satisfy the needs. For example, depriving a person of food results in a biological need that produces a hunger drive. The hunger drive creates a state of arousal and a push toward behavior to satisfy the hunger. Spence (1958) is the author of one of the best-known drive conceptions of motivation, and it is in the context of this conception that most of the research on primary biological needs such as hunger and thirst has been conducted. Much research on primary biological needs has been conducted with animals, since it would be unethical to deprive humans of such basic needs.

The pull conception of motivations focuses on the goals, incentives, and valences that "pull" behavior. Behavior is "pulled" toward achieving or maintaining certain goals or outcomes. Motivation is a function of how attractive or desirable a certain goal is for an individual and the likelihood (probability) of attaining that goal. Much of the motivation research in work settings has involved this conception of motivation. For example, how much one is willing to strive to become assistant manager is a function of how desirable this job position is (the "pull") and one's perception of the probability of achieving this position.

Many of the goals that "pull" behavior are learned or acquired through socialization; they are not primary biological drives. In many cases, however, it is not clear the extent to which human drives are biologically based or a product of socialization. In animals, for example, sexual activity is considered a biological drive. Much human sexual activity is a result of both hormonal activity and the specific forms of human sexuality that have been learned through socialization. Motives that are acquired through socialization and that are therefore uniquely human are considered to be complex or higher-order motives. Examples include the need for achievement, moral and religious incentives, and the need for self-actualization.

It should be noted that in the study of human motivation, we deal primarily with people's *perceptions*. We cannot directly observe higher-order goals, drives, and motives. Rather, we infer people's goals, needs, and motives from their behavior and what they tell us about their needs and desires in questionnaires and self-report inventories. Accordingly, some investigators see themselves as studying "motivated behavior" rather than motivation per se (Whalen and Simon, 1984). A researcher, then, might study eating behavior rather than the hunger drive and mating behavior rather than the sex drive.

The study of the drives, needs, and goals that motivate people is a complex field in itself. The issue of development across the adult years poses an even more complex question: How do motives change as adults develop and age? Several areas of change have been suggested (Wigdor, 1980). First, there may be changes in the intensity or strength of certain drives, such as hunger. These changes in intensity may be related to physiological and metabolic changes. Second, the temporal nature of certain goals may change. The aged may be more concerned with short-term or present-oriented goals than with long-term or future-oriented goals. An older person would probably be more interested in current changes in the neighborhood than in long-term plans for the development of a downtown area that might take twenty years. Third, there may be qualitative changes in the nature of motives. The elderly might be more motivated to read meaningful or personally relevant materials than highly novel or speculative materials.

As we noted earlier, there is no one global theory or approach to the study of motivation. Rather, we will be considering in this chapter a variety of domain-specific models of motivation (arousal, achievement, and so on). In our discussions, we progress from a more biological approach to motivation to an increasingly cognitive approach to the study of motivation. The chapter is organized to consider first the more basic needs or drives and then to move to more complex and higher-order motives and goals. Our discussion will begin with physiological drives (hunger, thirst, arousal) and how they change as people age (see also Chapter 11). We then consider the influence of cognitive factors on motivation and how one's feeling of control over one's life can affect one's behavior. Next, we describe the factors that influence achievement motivation during adulthood, and two perspectives on the value of remaining active during old age. Finally, we discuss moral and religious values and the process of self-actualization.

Physiological Drives

The concept of arousal is central to the study of physiological drives. According to the push approach, biological or psychological needs result in drives, which produce a heightened state of arousal. Arousal results in activity (for example, eating) designed to satisfy the biological need. Thus arousal is central to the process of meeting physiological needs. It rarely occurs by itself, but it can be considered by itself, as we do later in this chapter. Here we examine the role of arousal in several physiological drives.

HUNGER AND THIRST

There is growing acknowledgment that eating behavior in humans involves an interaction between physiological needs and external situational factors (Rodin, 1981). Exactly how internal (physiological) and external factors interact in regulating eating is still being debated, but recent research on obesity has yielded some clues. Rodin (1981) suggests that external cues such as the sight or thought of food may trigger an internal, physiological state of arousal. Physiological arousal plays an important role in the regulation of eating. There are large individual differences in basal levels of arousal and rates of arousal activation, and these differences may be the basis for individual differences in responsiveness to external cues (for example, sight of food). Those who experience hyperarousal in response to external stimuli may be especially prone to overeating.

Lunch programs for senior citizens provide nourishing meals and a chance to socialize.

Overarousal to external cues may also be associated with metabolic changes such as secretion of insulin (Rodin, 1981). People who are overaroused by external cues have been found to oversecrete insulin when they are shown appetizing food. Oversecretion of insulin is associated with feeling hungry. Oversecretion also speeds the conversion of sugar into fat and can thus enhance fat storage. Hence persons who become overaroused by external cues may oversecrete insulin, resulting in feelings of hunger; they may then consume more calories in order to balance this metabolic output.

There are several age-related physiological changes that affect hunger and thirst drives in the elderly. We briefly note three of these changes. First, recent research suggests that there are small but measurable declines in a number of the senses as people age. Small declines in the ability to detect sweet and salty tastes (Moore, Nielsen, and Mistretta, 1982) and to identify or label odors (Schiffman and Pasternak, 1979) have been found (see also Chapter 11). Our feeling hungry and our enjoyment of a meal involve the senses of smell, taste, and touch. Decrements in the senses can then reduce the appeal of eating. Second, there is evidence that the functioning of the central nervous system slows with aging and that the basal metabolism rate drops as a result (Wigdor, 1980). A decrease in the basal metabolic rate often results in a reduction in physical activity. As one becomes less physically active, one's need for food also decreases. Third, there are age-related changes in the hypothalamus which reduce the reliability of homeostatic control in the aged. That is, the hypothalamus may become less sensitive in reading blood levels and less efficient in making adjustments in blood glucose levels. Thus there may need to be changes in the eating patterns of the elderly to compensate for this inefficiency. For example, some older adults may need to eat smaller quantities but more frequently to maintain appropriate blood glucose levels.

Eating and drinking are not completely controlled by physiological needs or drives, of course. Eating and drinking habits are learned across a lifetime (Wigdor, 1980). In our culture, eating is often a social affair. It is a time to converse with others, to celebrate a happy event, or to console ourselves in stressful or unhappy situations. In old age, the motivation to eat may be more a function of lifelong eating habits and the immediate social situation than of the need to satisfy basic drives. The social incentives to eat may be reduced if, for example, one's spouse has died. There is less motivation to prepare a meal for only one person, and eating alone can be depressing. Some elderly people suffer from malnutrition even when they have money for food because they lack the social incentive to prepare meals or to eat alone.

SEXUAL ACTIVITY

Sexual activity, which is defined as a physiological drive in animals, is determined in humans largely by learning, previously developed habits, and situational circumstances. There may be age-related changes in arousal — older animals and humans may need more stimulation to achieve sexual arousal. Moreover, sexual activity in old age is increasingly determined by social circumstances. Many older adults, particularly women, have lost their sexual partners, and thus have less opportunity for remaining sexually active. See Chapter 6 for further discussion of biological and social aspects of human sexuality.

UNDERAROUSAL VERSUS OVERAROUSAL IN THE ELDERLY

For the past fifteen years, there has been a continuing debate over whether there are changes in physiological arousal with age and how these changes relate to behavior (Elias and Elias, 1977; Marsh and Thompson, 1977). Some contend that the poorer performance of the elderly in learning tasks is a function of underarousal; others argue that the problem is overarousal.

The major research supporting the overarousal hypothesis was conducted by Eisdorfer and his colleagues (Eisdorfer, 1968; Eisdorfer, Nowlin, and Wilkie, 1970). These researchers noted that older persons do less well in learning experiments. They make more errors of omission than commission (that is, they fail to make a response more often than they make a wrong response), and they make an especially large number of errors when the pace of the task is speeded up. This leads to the hypothesis that errors of omission were a result of increased situational anxiety, or overarousal. The hypothesis was supported by research that showed that omission errors decreased and the elderly's performance improved when the pace of the task was slowed. To examine the hypothesis further, a measure of arousal that was independent of learning performance was needed.

Eisdorfer assessed arousal by measuring levels of free fatty acid (FFA) in the blood, since FFA level reflects a metabolic response to stress.

The research showed that in a learning experiment, older adults did have higher levels of FFA than younger adults. Furthermore, after the study the FFA levels of the older adults returned to normal much more slowly than those of younger adults. These findings suggest that older people are overaroused and that they remained in an overaroused state longer than do young adults. A final experiment was undertaken to determine whether lowering arousal levels experimentally (that is, reducing FFA levels) would improve performance in learning tasks. In this experiment, subjects were given the drug propranolol, which blocks autonomic nervous system arousal but has little influence on central nervous system functioning. The learning performance of the experimental group was compared with that of a group who received a placebo. The results showed that the experimental group had lower FFA levels and also fewer total errors during the learning experiment. Unfortunately, the most direct measure of over-arousal, a decrease in the number of omission errors compared with commission errors, did not show a significant drop. Nevertheless, this research has been interpreted as evidence that decrements in the learning performance of the elderly may be associated with overarousal and not solely with cognitive factors. It should also be noted that the Eisdorfer research has never been fully replicated (Woodruff, 1985).

The studies indicating that underarousal is the problem have used different physiological measures of arousal and different behavioral measures than the studies indicating overarousal is the problem (Woodruff, 1985). As we have seen, overarousal studies have typically used biochemical measures such as FFA level and cognitively stressful behavioral measures such as learning tasks. The underarousal approach has assessed arousal with bioelectric measures such as galvanic skin response and heart rate (Marsh and Thompson, 1977). Behavioral measures focus on conditioning and vigilance tasks. These types of tasks tend to be repetitive and boring, so the elderly may not have been motivated to perform at their best.

Why the conflict in these overarousal versus underarousal findings? Part of the problem, of course, is the use of different measures. Another aspect, however, is related to the growing consensus that autonomic arousal is not a unitary concept. Various forms of arousal may differ functionally and anatomically (Lacey, 1967). This creates problems in the useful study of physiological arousal as it relates to age changes in meaningful behavior.

Arousal has been studied with regard to the central nervous system, as well as in relation to the autonomic nervous system, as we have described above. Research on age-related changes in arousal within the central nervous system supports the underarousal hypothesis. The electroencephalogram (EEG) is often used in this research (Woodruff, 1985). Various EEG frequency bandwidths have been associated with stages of arousal ranging from deep sleep to alert problem-solving. Very slow EEG frequencies called delta waves are associated with deep sleep, whereas theta waves are associated with light sleep and the transition to wakefulness. Alpha frequencies occur during alert wakefulness, and the faster beta frequencies are associated with thinking and problem-solving. Studies have found that there is a tendency for EEG frequencies to slow with age. Figure 7–1 shows age differences in EEG for delta (sleep) and alpha (wakefulness) stages. Note for both the delta and alpha stages the smaller amplitudes of waves and the slower frequencies in the older subjects. The question is whether this slowing of

FIGURE 7–1.

Age differences in EEG. In both cases note the smaller amplitudes of waves and the slower frequencies of the older subject. Also the older subject shows shorter duration bursts of such rhythmic activity. Recordings were made during alert wakefulness for alpha rhythms and during sleep for delta rhythms.

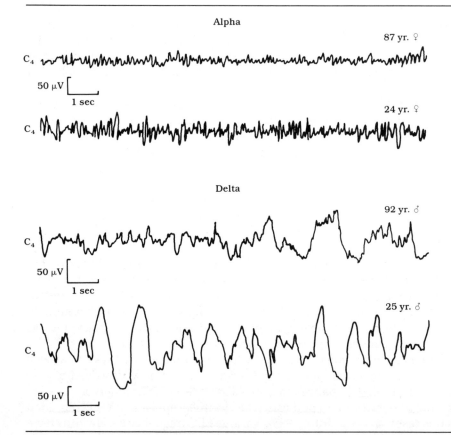

Source: Data from P. Prinz reported by G. R. Marsh and L. W. Thompson. Psychophysiology of aging. In J. E. Birren and K. W. Schaie, eds., *Handbook of psychology of aging*. New York: Van Nostrand Reinhold, 1977, p. 236. Reprinted by permission of P. Prinz.

EEG frequencies, especially alpha frequencies, is related to age changes in behavior and thinking. Reliable relationships have been found between the slowing of alpha frequencies and cognitive impairment among institutionalized groups of elderly (Woodruff, 1985). Such a relationship, however, has not been found among elderly people dwelling in the community. Thus the nature of the relationship between EEG frequency and behavioral competency in community-dwelling elderly remains unclear.

ANXIETY

In the preceding section, the case for age-related changes in physiological arousal was presented. However, individuals, including psychologists, rarely discuss arousal per se. We do not describe ourselves as being simply aroused, but rather provide a cognitive label for the arousal — anxiety, elation, fear, and so on. Anxiety has been defined as an aroused state characterized by vague fears. Like many emotions, anxiety can be said to be partly biological (involving an aroused state) and partly cognitive (a label that is given to the aroused state). Personality psychologists have focused on self-reports of anxiety or on behaviors said to manifest anxiety, rather than on physiological indexes of arousal. Age-related changes in anxiety, studied as a personality dimension, have been examined longitudinally as part of the Normative Aging Study (McCrae and Costa, 1984; see also Chapter 4). In this study, longitudinal changes are examined in three dimensions of personality: neuroticism, extraversion, and openness. Anxiety is considered a component of the neuroticism dimension, the other components being depression, hostility, and vulnerability. Although one might expect anxiety to increase with age because of the increasing stresses and losses people face as they grow old, the data indicate that this does not occur. Anxiety tends to remain quite stable with age. This has been demonstrated with longitudinal studies involving both self-reports (Costa and McCrae, 1978; Douglas and Arenberg, 1978) and with ratings by professionals (McCrae and Costa, 1982). Similar conclusions are made when anxiety is conceptualized as a personality trait and assessed through personality inventories and questionnaires; when projective techniques are used (Rosen and Neugarten, 1960); and when interviews are used (Cameron, 1975).

Cognition and Motivation

In many cases, what we think about a situation — our cognitions, as psychologists call them — determines how we respond to the situation. If we believe that our behavior will affect the outcome, that we have control over the outcome, then we will respond differently than if we believe the outcome is due to chance or luck. In this section we discuss the relationship between an individual's perception of control and behavior in various situations. We also consider how negative stereotypes about aging or loss of physical ability may result in an older adult's perception of a loss of control, leading to learned helplessness.

CONTROL

There is great variation in the degree to which we can control events around us. We make judgments about the probability of being able to control these events (Mineka and Hendersen, 1985). These judgments influence our behavior; they help determine where we will direct our efforts, how long we will persist, and how effectively we will work. For example, how long and hard we study for an exam depends in part on whether we believe that the grade we receive will be largely determined by our efforts. There are a number of domains in our lives in which the degree of actual personal control can be assessed.

How does one make an accurate judgment about the controllability of an outcome? Weisz (1983) suggests that in order to make accurate judgments about one's control over an outcome, one must be able to assess two factors:

1. *Contingency* — the degree to which the outcome is contingent on the behavior of a person like myself. Is the outcome controllable by means of my behavior?
2. *Competence* — the degree to which one is capable of producing the behaviors on which the desired outcome is contingent.

Many factors may limit contingency. Events influenced by chance are non-contingent. Events such as the occurrence or nonoccurrence of a thunderstorm or the outcome of a roll of the dice are uncontrollable because they are not contingent on our behavior. Nonchance conditions, such as those involving human attitudes, may also affect the contingency of an outcome. For instance, the outcome of a job interview may be highly noncontingent for certain individuals because of the racial bias or sexism of the interviewer. The second factor in determining controllability is personal competence, that is, my capacity to produce the behavior on which the desired outcome is contingent. The fact that school grades are administered fairly (that is, contingent on actual school performance) may or may not mean that I have a high level of control over my grades. The degree to which I can exert control will depend on my capacity to produce the kinds of performance (for example, correct answers on a test) on which good grades depend.

A composite judgment regarding both contingency and competence is required in assessing the controllability of an outcome. Weisz and Stipek (1982) suggest that the factors of contingency and competence have not been clearly distinguished in previous research on control. Rotter (1966) in his research on *internal* versus *external* locus of control has emphasized the contingency factor. A person has an internal locus of control when he or she assumes that the relationship between action and outcome is under his or her internal control. A person has an external locus of control when he or she assumes that the relationship between action and outcome depends on external causes beyond the person's control. On the other hand, Bandura (1981) has emphasized the competence component in control, referring to it in terms of self-efficacy.

Some research indicates that normal adults slightly overestimate their control over events (Lewinsohn et al., 1980). Even for an outcome totally determined by chance, adults tend to perceive that they have some control over the situation. What affects this illusion of control? Personal involvement, being able to make a choice, and experiencing a sequence of outcomes in which there is success on the first few trials produce an illusion of control. For example, being able to pick one's number in a purely random lottery has been shown to increase one's perception of control (Langer, 1975). It may be that people perceive contingencies when none exist in order to avoid feelings (anxiety, depression) that things are not under control; also, perceiving events to be contingent on one's behavior may enhance self-esteem (Langer, 1977).

Another well-documented finding is that normal adults assume more personal responsibility for favorable outcomes than for unfavorable ones. Greenwald (1980) has labeled this tendency *beneffectance* and suggests that there are advantages to beneffectance in that it enhances our persistence in a task and enhances our sense of well-being. Illusory control and beneffectance may be psychologically adaptive for normal adults. This is suggested by recent research that indicates that very accurate assessments of personal control are most characteristic of depressed people (Abramson and Alloy, 1980). A depressed person's judgments were found to be particularly accurate in situations in which actual control was quite limited; in these situations normal adults often showed an illusion of control beyond that which actually existed. In a laboratory task in which the contingency between the students' behavior and outcome was manipulated, depressed students' judgments of contingency were found to be very accurate. However, nondepressed students were much less accurate and showed a tendency toward beneffectance (Alloy and Abramson, 1979).

The causal relationships between accuracy of contingency judgments and depression need further study (Weisz, 1983; see also Chapter 12). It may be that a depressed mood causes people to view their impact on events accurately, making them "sadder but wiser." Or perhaps a very clear view of one's actual control over events makes some people depressed. A recent experiment was designed to assess whether changing the mood of normally nondepressed or depressed students would alter their perceptions of contingency. Naturally nondepressed students who were made temporarily depressed made accurate contingency judgments on a laboratory task. Naturally depressed students who were made temporarily elated overestimated the contingency of outcomes on their behavior, suggesting that mood may influence the accuracy of adults' contingency judgments (Alloy, Abramson, and Viscusi, 1981).

There has been little research on the accuracy of contingency reasoning among the elderly. However, there is little doubt that for some older adults there is a substantial loss of actual contingency for a number of important outcomes. This is particularly evident for elderly in institutions. A large number of everyday life outcomes (for example, choice of meals and timing of dining, bedtime, mobility) are no longer contingent on the elderly's behavior. Their behavior does not determine when they eat or what they eat, or when the lights are turned out at night. In the following section we discuss some intervention studies that have attempted to modify institutionalized older adults' perceptions of contingencies.

The second factor in accurate judgments of controllability involves perceived competency. There is evidence that normal adults may exaggerate notions of their own competency. In one experiment college students predicted the outcomes of a number of coin tosses; a second group merely observed students predicting the outcomes. Afterward, all were asked "How good do you think you are (she is, for group observing) at predicting outcomes like these?" This sort of competence question is somewhat silly, since coin tosses are chance events and everyone should be equally competent. However, students who actually participated in making predictions judged themselves to be more competent than did students who merely observed (Langer and Rodin, 1976).

Depressed adults do not seem as susceptible to this illusion of competency in chance situations. Depressed and nondepressed students were studied in a game involving betting on dice throws (Golin et al., 1977). Half the students threw the dice themselves; half observed the experimenter throw the dice. Before the dice were thrown the students rated their confidence that they would win. It was predicted that nondepressed students would operate under the illusion of control and therefore rate themselves as more competent, when they were actually throwing the dice (personal involvement in a chance situation). In contrast, it was predicted that depressed students perceive themselves to be less competent and therefore would rate themselves as more confident when the experimenter threw the dice. These predictions were supported.

The elderly may be particularly likely to underestimate their competence in many important life events (see also Chapter 12). Langer (1982) reviewed a number of relevant studies and concluded that a person's perception of in- competence can be influenced by (1) being assigned a label that denotes inferiority (for example, being labeled "old" in our society suggests less competence), (2) being denied an opportunity to engage in a task that one formerly engaged in but that is now engaged in by another (for example, retirement), and (3) simply allowing someone else to help you (adult children's insistence on helping their elderly parents may not always be beneficial). Comparisons across generations may also negatively affect the elderly's perceptions of their competence. The elderly may interpret comparisons with their adult children or grandchildren as reflecting age-related decline, when part of the discrepancy in performance may be due to cohort differences (for example, educational level, life experiences).

LEARNED HELPLESSNESS

The concept of learned helplessness was first developed in experiments with dogs (Seligman, 1975). These dogs were put in a standard laboratory situation in which they were supposed to learn to escape from electric shocks, in the following way. A dog is placed in a shuttlebox, which has two compartments separated by a short barrier the dog can easily leap over. The lights dim and then, ten seconds later, a slight but unpleasant shock is delivered through the grid floor of the compartment the dog is in. The dog typically leaps the barrier to the other side, which is not electrified. Eventually it leaps when the lights first dim, avoiding (or escaping) the shock altogether. A simple avoidance-learning task.

Some dogs, however, could not learn this simple task. Twenty-four hours before the shuttlebox test, they had been placed in hammock-like harnesses and subjected to several shocks. These shocks, unlike those they experienced later in the shuttlebox, could not be avoided, escaped from, or controlled in any way. In short, the dogs experienced true helplessness. Later, in the shuttlebox where they could in fact control their destiny, they still acted as if they could not. They did not leap the short barrier to safety; they simply sat and whined. It is as if they had become fatalists, accepting shocks as a way of life. They had learned helplessness.

Learned helplessness, depression, and deteriorating performance have been associated with a person's perception of loss of control (Alloy et al., 1984). It has recently been suggested that there are two types of helplessness — personal and universal. In both forms the individual believes the outcome is not contingent on his or her behavior. However, in *personal helplessness*, the person perceives that some other people would be able to meet the desired goal or avoid the undesirable event, but that he himself (or she herself) cannot. This perception can lead to depression, difficulties in initiating responses, persistence problems, and loss of self-esteem. In *universal helplessness*, the person perceives that no person could avoid the undesirable event. People experiencing universal helplessness may be depressed and have some personal deficits, but they do not suffer loss of self-esteem as do those experiencing personal helplessness.

Weisz and Stipek (1982) have suggested that contingency of outcome and one's perception of competence are related to personal and universal helplessness. People who believe their failures result from noncontingency will experience universal helplessness, whereas people who perceive failures as resulting from their own incompetence will experience personal helplessness.

The concept of learned helplessness has become popular with psychologists in personality and social psychology. Generalizing to real-life situations, psychologists described the social environments of culturally deprived individuals (Garber and Seligman, 1980). Archie, for example, age fifteen, is waiting for his chance to quit school. School has been an unending series of shocks and failures for him: questions with no answers because he doesn't know some of the words in the questions, interactions without joy because the other kids think he's stupid. Nothing he does seems to have any effect on these "shocks." Archie is ready to enter the shuttlebox of life, and he has learned how to be helpless. He is likely to endure passively any shocks he encounters outside school, just as he does in school. His chances of success are not good.

Psychologists interested in adult development and aging also saw potential applications in their fields (Langer, 1982). Fatalistic adults who can't seem to cope with the simplest problems and the even greater number of old people who face life without passion, accepting whatever comes their way: have these individuals learned to be helpless? Have they, like the dogs, experienced shocks beyond their control so frequently and consistently that they've given up trying?

One way to test this notion is to provide "therapy." If people are suffering from learned helplessness, then they should be helped by experiences in which good events occur because of something they do. In one such program, the elderly patients in a nursing home were encouraged to make decisions for themselves, were given decisions to make, and (most notably) were given responsibility for something outside themselves — a plant (Langer and Rodin, 1976). Almost all these patients showed improvement in mental alertness. They were rated as more active and happier, both by nurses and by themselves. In contrast, old people not involved in this "individual responsibility" program showed little if any improvement.

In another study, the event to be controlled was a visit from a friendly college student (Schulz, 1976). The visits for some of the residents of this retirement home were random (that is, unpredictable, uncontrollable) although equal in frequency and duration to the visits the other residents had. The other residents (the experimental group) could specify when and for how long the visitor would come. Although the visits were equally enjoyable in both conditions, the elderly residents with a sense of control were happier and were rated by staff as having a greater "zest for life" than the residents whose visits were determined by external forces.

Both of these studies were followed by additional studies of the same subjects, to see if the interventions had had any long-term effects. The nursing-home patients in the first study (the ones who had been given a plant to care for) were still psychologically and physically healthier than the comparison group after eighteen months (Rodin and Langer, 1977). In the other study, involving visits from college students, the responsibility group did not fare so well (Schulz and Hanusa, 1978). These subjects (residents of a retirement home) were less healthy and less happy than the control group twenty-four months after the initial assessment, and also after thirty and forty-two months. They were more, not less, likely to die.

Why was the momentary feeling of controllability long-lasting in one case and transient in the other? One possible answer lies in the attributions subjects make, that is, the way they perceive the manipulations of the experimental psychologists (Abramson, Seligman, and Teasdale, 1978; Weisz, 1983). In both studies, the subjects in the responsibility groups were able to exert some control over their lives — caring for a plant, requesting visits from students. As a result, their spirits were raised; they were no longer helpless. Then the experiment came to an end, and the psychologists left. In one case, the manipulation had involved pep talks about personal responsibility combined with situations (including plant care) in which that responsibility could be exercised. When the researchers left, the situations (including the plant) remained. In psychologists' jargon, the attribution of personal control was stable, and thus the beneficial effects continued. In the other study, the experiment's end meant no more visits. The subjects probably thought, "Well, I *had* control, but now it's gone." The attribution was unstable. Indeed, to perceive oneself as helpless, then briefly as in control, and then as helpless once again may be a particularly depressing sequence of events.

Elderly people who are given responsibility for something other than themselves, such as a pet, generally are more mentally alert, active, and content.

A taste of responsibility may whet the appetite, producing frustration with the normal (less controllable) environment of the retirement home.

It should be mentioned that the experimenters anticipated that subjects might be upset when the study was over (Schulz and Hanusa, 1980). The subjects were warned that the visits would eventually cease (the students, after all, had to return home for summer vacation). The visits were not stopped abruptly, but gradually. And the students were encouraged to continue friendships that had developed, as many did. The poorer status of the responsibility subjects at the time of the followup assessment was slight, not even reaching statistical significance. Nevertheless, it would probably have been wise to substitute another "responsibility manipulation" for the visits when the experiment was completed — perhaps something like the pep talks and plants of the other study. Perhaps then the feelings of personal control would have endured.

Humans seem able to develop the feeling of personal helplessness through many routes (Schultz, 1980). Direct experience with unavoidable unpleasant experiences, like those in the original dog experiments on learned helplessness, is one route; a series of failures is another. But experience is not necessary; one can develop the illusion of incompetence simply by being labeled "assistant" in a miniature social system where "assistant" is the position of least status (Langer and Benevento, 1978). Moving into an institution where the labels "elderly" and "patient" define one's status relative to "staff," who do most things for the elderly patients, is an even more powerful change in one's life. It is no wonder that many adults in their later years show the slackened motivation and depression that accompany the feeling that one is no longer in control, that one is helpless, that all now is hopeless.

On the other hand, for most older adults, feelings of helplessness can be alleviated and a sense of control can be reinstituted with equally simple manipulations: pep talks, something or someone to care for. The many therapies available to increase one's sense of "self-efficacy" (the power to have an effect) have special meaning to people whose feelings of helplessness are their major problem in life (Bandura, 1981). We return once again to many of these issues in Chapter 12, in our discussion of mental health and aging.

Achievement Motivation

Closely related to learned helplessness and control as motivational concepts important in the study of adult development is *achievement motivation*. As commonly conceptualized, achievement motivation involves behaviors in which individuals know that their performance will be evaluated (by themselves or by others) in terms of some *standard of excellence* (Atkinson and Birch, 1978; Raynor and Entin, 1982). This evaluation may result in a judgment of *success* or *failure.*

Many people, including many psychologists, believe that achievement motivation decreases in the second half of life. As one investigator puts it:

> career drives are likely to . . . dominate the years of young adulthood, perhaps even to the point of resulting in minimal contact with family. If by forty or forty-five, the career-oriented individual has achieved economic security and success, the need to "get ahead" (the achievement need) may be much less in evidence, and the former career-oriented individual may turn more frequently to family or to community activities as sources of gratification. "Affiliation" or "service" needs then may be more important. (Kuhlen, 1968, p. 116)

In support of this notion are studies showing that men tell stories with fewer achievement themes after middle age; themes of power gradually replace them (Veroff et al., 1960).

However, evidence on the maintenance of achievement motivation and other needs comes from a cross-sectional study comparing elderly college graduates in their seventies and eighties with graduate students, matched by field of study, who were in their early twenties (Schaie and Strother, 1968). Males and females were equally represented in both age groups. Of particular interest was the finding that need for achievement remained as important in the need hierarchy for the older group as for the graduate students. Other needs that were equivalent for the old and the young were the needs for autonomy (independence), the giving and receiving of affection, new experience, self-examination, and, interestingly enough, aggression. Some age differences were found, however. The older group was higher than the young adults in needs for deference (conformity), order, and endurance (persistence). They were lower in the needs for heterosexual expression, attention, and dominance.

Study of developmental changes in achievement motivation are limited due to lack of longitudinal data and the fact that various measures of achievement motivation have been employed in different studies. Achievement strivings may take multiple forms in adulthood. Research from the AT&T study discussed in Chapter 3 (Bray and Howard, 1983b) provides some data on longitudinal changes across adulthood in two types of achievement strivings: Need for Advancement and Inner Work Standards. Need for Advancement is defined as motivation to advance along the career ladder faster and further than one's peers. This type of achievement striving was assessed with interview ratings, personality and motivation questionnaires, and projective tests. Inner Work Standards are defined as motivation to perform to the best of one's ability on the job one currently holds and having one's own high standards of work performance, even though a lesser level would satisfy one's superiors. The focus of Inner Work Standards is on motivation to perform well regardless of one's place in the hierarchy. This form of achievement motivation is assessed with interview ratings, projective tests, and, most importantly, with performance on simulated work exercises.

The study found that people who were motivated by Need for Advancement were oriented toward upward mobility and financial rewards. They had a desire to lead and were self-confident and outgoing. Those who were motivated primarily by Inner Work Standards and less by Need for Advancement were less outgoing and had a strong sense of responsibility and a strong desire to be accepted and do the proper thing. They were likely to be persistent.

How did these two types of motivation change over the years? Were they related to job success as measured by the level of management the person eventually reached? You may recall from Chapter 3 that these motives were assessed three times, at year 0, year 8, and year 20. Figure 7–2 shows the ratings for each motive at the three assessment points, charted according to the management levels (1–6) reached at year 20.

The top graph shows that, on average, managers declined in Need for Advancement over time, regardless of the level of management they reached. Bray and Howard (1983b) suggest that this decline may reflect the realization that in a pyramid organizational structure, they had reached a plateau and would not advance further. The bottom graph, on Inner Work Standards, shows a different pattern. Although the *average* rating for this motive remained steady over the twenty years for the total group, those at the higher management levels had increasing work standards, whereas those at the lower levels had lowered their standards. In other words, levels of Inner Work Standards seemed to have been progressively shaped by career success; it appears that career success is a good motivator of Inner Work Standards. Nevertheless, it is interesting to note that

FIGURE 7–2.

AT&T study of managers. Average assessment ratings of two motives (Need for Advancement and Inner Work Standards) over time (year 0–20) by management level achieved (N = 266).

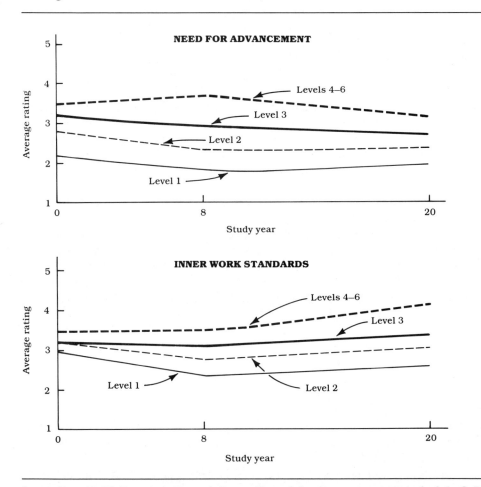

Source: From D. W. Bray, & A. Howard. Personality and the assessment center method. In C. D. Spielberger & S. N. Butcher (Eds.), *Advances in personality assessment Vol. 3.* Hillsdale, NJ: Lawrence Erlbaum Associates, 1983. Copyright © 1983 by Lawrence Erlbaum Associates, Inc. Reprinted by permission.

Inner Work Standards remained relatively constant from year 8 to year 20 even for the majority of managers who did not reach the higher levels. This suggests that adults in midlife continue to be motivated to perform competently and to meet their own inner standards even in the absence of external reinforcements such as vertical career advancement.

This study involved only males when it was begun in 1956, but a second study begun in the late 1970s did include women. The 1977 study found no gender differences in Need for Advancement, whereas women were rated somewhat higher in terms of Inner Work Standards (Howard and Bray, 1980). In terms of desire to lead others, however, women had lower ratings than men; the desire to lead is considered a necessary quality for a manager in today's business world. Again, cohort differences since 1977 among women entering the business world may have altered this finding.

Disengagement Versus Activity

The role losses suffered by the elderly and the possible morale problems that result from role loss were first recognized in the 1940s, in the early days of social gerontology (Cottrell, 1942). To avoid these problems and grow old gracefully, it was assumed that one must keep active, continually finding new interests to replace work and new friends to replace those who have moved or died (Havighurst and Albrecht, 1953). This perspective came to be known as the *activity theory* of aging, even though there was no explicit theory about the relationship between social activity and adjustment in old age until 1972 (Lemon, Bengtson, and Peterson, 1972). In the 1960s, however, an alternative arose which suggested that old age is a time to slow down and enjoy life, that activities should be curtailed and one's number of friends should be reduced to a manageable number. This view, known as *disengagement theory* (Cumming and Henry, 1961), aroused considerable debate and excited renewed interest in more explicit consideration of activity theory.

DISENGAGEMENT

Almost all old people experience some disengagement — some reduction in activities and in encounters with other people — whether they desire it or not. In the original statement of disengagement theory, these reductions were seen as *natural* and, in some sense, *ideal* (Cumming and Henry, 1961). According to disengagement theory, people are at least accepting of the reduction in activities; in most cases they *want* the reduction, and work to achieve it. Social withdrawal "is accompanied by, or preceded by, increased preoccupation with the self and decreased emotional investment in persons and objects in the environment; . . . in this sense, disengagement is a natural rather than an imposed process" (Havighurst, Neugarten, and Tobin, 1968, p. 161).

The research on which disengagement theory was initially based was a cross-sectional study of a small number of elderly residents in Kansas City. Cumming and Henry (1961; Hendricks and Hendricks, 1977) derived several basic tenets regarding disengagement theory from this study. First, in an ideal sense the process of disengagement should be a mutual endeavor between the person and society. The disengagement process, they said, could be initiated by the older person or by society. The aging person could withdraw rather markedly from

An active life is more satisfying than an inactive one, and school volunteer work is one of many opportunities for involvement.

some groups of people (for example, former business associates) while remaining close to others (for example, family). But in some cases, the timing and needs of society and the individual will differ. Society, for example, may force a person to retire before he or she is ready because it needs to open up jobs for younger people and maintain the equilibrium of the social system. In the process, it may define older people as no longer useful or dependable. By the same token, a person may be ready to retire well before he or she reaches the age of sixty, but society dictates that we should work until at least that age. Second, Cumming and Henry argued that the process of disengagement is inevitable and universal, although there may be cultural and individual variations in the timing. Much criticism of the theory has focused on the assumed universality of the disengagement process and the lack of attention to individual differences. More recently, Cumming has emphasized differential disengagement as an avenue for maximizing adjustment.

Disengagement theory had the happy result of stimulating a great deal of research on the relationship between activity and life satisfaction in old age. Unhappily for the theory, however, most of the research supported the rival activity theory. Indeed, one could say that disengagement theory, as originally presented, has been rather thoroughly discredited (Hochschild, 1973). Most studies showed a rather sizable correlation between social *engagement* and satisfaction. Most old people regret the reduction in their activity levels, increasingly so with age (Havighurst, Neugarten, and Tobin, 1968). Nevertheless, the research generated by the theory (much of it designed to refute the theory) has added immensely to our understanding of the process of aging.

Some theorists have suggested that the satisfactions of disengagement come only very late in life, after the age of seventy or so. To test this hypothesis, correlations between activity level and life satisfaction were computed separately for people under seventy and over seventy; no significant difference was found

(Havighurst, Neugarten, and Tobin, 1968). Older old people disliked the reduction in activity as much as the "youngsters" under seventy.

Disengagement can be a consequence of several factors. One of the most prominent of these is role loss as the individual's position in society changes. A woman was an office manager; now she is retired. She was in charge of dependent children; they are now out on their own. She was chairperson of the city airport commission; now she is consulted only infrequently. She was a wife; now she is a widow (Tobin and Neugarten, 1961).

A second factor is more psychological: "With an increasing awareness that his future is limited and that death is not only inevitable but no longer far distant, the older person may be more likely to attend to himself and to whatever is extremely important to him, simultaneously pushing away what is not extremely important" (Kalish, 1975, p. 64).

A third factor in disengagement is biological. Most old people experience some biological loss: some loss in sensory capacity (seeing, hearing), a memory not quite as sharp as it once was, or a reduced energy level. Mild to severe health problems become more probable. Forty-five percent of elderly sixty-five years and older report a limitation of activity due to chronic disease, such as high blood pressure, arthritis, diabetes, heart disease, or kidney disease (National Center for Health Statistics, 1984). In addition, there are increasing chances of eye cataracts, broken bones, and other maladies. These conditions may require some curtailment of social activities.

Observations and studies such as these enable us to come to some conclusions on whether disengagement is voluntary and desired by the elderly. If people reduce their activities because they are forced to, because of ill health or mandatory retirement, they are not likely to be pleased with their disengagement. If, however, social disengagement occurs because one wants to focus on a few of the most satisfying aspects of one's life — one's *closest* friends, one's *favorite* activities — then it can be extremely satisfying and, for this sort of person at least, an optimal pattern of successful aging.

ACTIVITY THEORY, ROLE SUPPORT, AND LIFE SATISFACTION

Although the assumptions of activity theory have been widely accepted as true for many years in social gerontology, the theory was not formally articulated until after disengagement theory had been described. Activity theory is concerned with the relationship between social activity and life satisfaction in old age. Activity is seen as providing roles for an individual, which are necessary in maintaining a healthy self-concept. As a person ages, he or she is often deprived of many of the major roles that have sustained him or her throughout adulthood — when employment ends, children leave home, or a spouse dies, for example. There is a need for optional roles to take their place.

Lemon, Bengtson, and Peterson (1972) were among the first to articulate activity theory. The central assumption in this early articulation was that "the greater activity, the greater one's life satisfaction" (p. 515). They described three types of activities. The most intimate was *informal activity*, socializing with friends, neighbors, and relatives. Less intimate but still social was *formal activity*, participating in voluntary groups that have established agendas — attending meetings, for example. The third type was *solitary activity*, which is activity pursued independently, such as maintaining one's household and pursuing leisure activities on one's own. Several hypotheses were derived, including the following: (1) informal activity is more highly associated with life satisfaction than is formal activity, and (2) formal activity is more highly associated with life satisfaction than is solitary activity. The intimate activities were hypothesized to be most reinforcing and thus to contribute to life satisfaction because they provided opportunities to reaffirm one's important roles and one's perceptions of self with significant others in one's life.

The early research of Lemon, Bengtson, and Peterson provided only partial support for their hypotheses. A replication of the study, however, provided more substantial support. Longino and Kart (1982) found that informal activity was in fact the form of activity most highly associated with life satisfaction, so it appears that intimate activity does provide strong role support and self-affirmation. Formal activity, on the other hand, was related to lower life satisfaction. A third finding of the study was that solitary activity had no influence on life satisfaction.

The important implication of this study is that not all activities are equally helpful in adjusting to losses in old age. The advice commonly given to "become more active, do something, get involved" is insufficient in itself. Sheer frequency of activity is not as important as the quality of the activity. Choice of activities must be based on the needs and personality of the person involved. For most people, however, intimate activity appears to be particularly useful in providing role support.

The importance of individual differences is indicated in another study of personality, activity level, and life satisfaction conducted by Neugarten, Havighurst, and Tobin (1968). These researchers found that people with well-adjusted, "integrated" personalities are generally quite satisfied with life, regardless of activity level. Some of them are very active; some are more selective and focus on fewer activities of higher value; some are withdrawing, disengaging by choice. At the opposite extreme of personality type, people with "unintegrated" personalities are generally dissatisfied, regardless of activity level.

In between these two extremes is where level of activity has its most pronounced effect on morale. People with what have been described as "armored" personalities — ambitious and striving, but with an apparent need to keep impulses and emotions in control — use high levels of activity as a defense against the idea of growing old. Low levels of activity are very disturbing to these people. Similarly, passive, dependent persons need interactions; they need people to talk to, people to help them make decisions. Without activity, they fall into apathy and depression.

Both the disengagement theory and the activity theory of successful aging were phrased in general terms, disregarding individual differences in personality. No single course of aging works best for everyone, just as no one lifestyle is right for all young adults.

Moral and Religious Values

As we move up the ladder of human motivations from the most clearly biological to the most clearly intellectual and social, we increasingly encounter moral and religious values. These values develop from one's own experience, from the teachings of organized religions, or, as is probably most common, from a combination of the two influences. A surprisingly little-studied feature of adult life, moral and religious values have wide-ranging effects on behavior. But as the number of studies of adult development has increased, the information on moral development also has begun to increase, since it is impossible to ignore the strong ethical emphases most adults place on changes in their lives.

MORAL VALUES

Lawrence Kohlberg (1973, 1981; Levine, Kohlberg, and Hewer, 1985) has developed a theory of moral reasoning which focuses on the individual's conception of justice. For Kohlberg moral reasoning involves judging the rightness/wrongness of an action in terms of its impact on the legal rights and well-being of the various people involved. To assess moral reasoning, Kohlberg analyzes people's responses to moral problems, presented in story form. In a classic story, a person must decide if it is morally "right" for a man to steal in order to obtain lifesaving medicine needed by his critically ill wife; stealing is, of course, breaking the law. In such moral problems, universal principles of conscience (for example, saving a life) are juxtaposed with societal/legal regulations (breaking the law). In Kohlberg's theory of moral reasoning, children pass through several stages. In stage 1, the young child judges the rightness or wrongness of behavior solely by whether or not it is rewarded or punished. The parent is the primary authority figure, who rewards or punishes the child's behavior. In stage 2, children judge the rightness or wrongness of behavior, not only by whether it is rewarded or punished but also by whether it satisfies a personal need. Older children begin to internalize these moral standards in stage 3, developing notions of what a "good girl" or a "good boy" is, regardless of whether or not the behaviors are punished or rewarded. Stage 4 usually begins in adolescence, when children recognize the need for obedience to rules, even if the rules are less than optimal; the world is viewed as a giant baseball game, where one may complain mightily about an umpire's decision but still recognize that without umpires the game would be chaos. Many people never progress beyond this law-and-order morality, even in adulthood.

Kohlberg describes additional stages of moral development, all of which supposedly occur in the adult years (Levine et al., 1985). The *social-contract, legalistic orientation* (stage 5) has been described as the official morality of the United States government. What is right is that which the majority of citizens agree on and set into law. Any citizen who disputes any part of this legal code can bring it up for further discussion: the social contract can be revised; laws can be changed. This sort of reasoning has been shown to increase dramatically in young adulthood (Kohlberg and Kramer, 1969; Tapp and Levine, 1972).

In Kohlberg's stage 6, which he claims very few people ever reach, morality is based on *universal ethical principles*. Legitimate legal authorities are rejected as the source of moral authority. Some universal principle of justice is chosen as the arbiter of right and wrong. An example of a universal ethical principle is the Golden Rule: Do unto others as you would have them do unto you. Such principles are philosophical abstractions; they do not involve the particular people or the particular events in question. Only impersonal values, objectively defined, are important. Very few adults ever reach this stage of moral development and reason this way about moral issues. Most recently, Kohlberg has acknowledged that stage 6 has not yet been empirically validated (Levine et al., 1985). Furthermore, stage 6 is not viewed as being logically derived from the preceding five stages. Its development is not based solely on logic or cognitive reasoning ability. This final stage reflects societal values and norms regarding what is considered to be the "highest" level of moral thought.

There has been a good deal of debate about whether level of moral reasoning changes with age. Some cross-sectional research (Bielby and Papalia, 1975) suggests that people over age fifty have lower stage levels of moral judgment than those in the thirty to fifty age range. Kohlberg (1973), on the other hand, has suggested that old age may be associated with new forms and levels of ethical and moral thinking, for some elderly at least.

In a democracy, all citizens are parties to the "social contract" under which the government operates, and therefore all citizens have a right to be heard.

Another form of advancement would involve not progression to a higher stage but greater *consistency* in the application of a moral perspective across different tasks and contexts. Research by Pratt, Golding, and Hunter (1983) found no differences in average stage of moral reasoning for young, middle-aged, and older adults when level of education was controlled. There was evidence, however, that the elderly were more consistent in applying their level of moral reasoning across various tasks. Old age may then be characterized by an increasing coherence in level of moral reasoning.

Why do some people rise to higher levels of moral reasoning than others? From limited evidence, Kohlberg has tentatively suggested two kinds of personal experience that he feels lead to principled morality (Kohlberg, 1973). The first is a moratorium experience in young adulthood. "Moratorium" is used in the sense of *delay* in making major life decisions, such as choosing an occupation, a delay most people engineer by attending college. Taking a year off after high school, traveling around the country before settling down in a "real job," is another way. The moratorium affords the young adult a year or so to explore values and to learn about personal identity before having to face the obligations of adult life. It's a chance to think about the various possibilities before making final commitments.

The second kind of personal experience important to principled morality is called "explicit cognitive-moral stimulation." The individual needs not only the time (the moratorium) to consider moral principles but also the stimulus to do so. A college "moral discussion program" is apparently effective for many students, leading 40 percent to higher levels (Kohlberg, 1973). For others, similar discussions may arise in the course of church activities or political activism. For some, the seeds of moral development planted in the moratorium do not grow until later in life, when the individual encounters "sustained responsibility for the welfare of others and the experience of irreversible moral choice" — the kind of experience one has when supervising others on the job or when making important family decisions.

There have been a number of criticisms of Kohlberg's theory. In his own research Kohlberg (1973) has had difficulty demonstrating that the higher stages (4 and 5) always occur in an invariant sequence; he has found instances in which there appeared to be regression to a lower stage after an individual reached one of the higher stages. The universality of Kohlberg's stages has also been questioned (Reid, 1980). The higher stages have not been demonstrated cross-culturally. Recently, Kohlberg has emphasized that higher stages (for example, stage 6) are indeed value-laden and may reflect the norms and values of particular cultures, most notably Western cultures.

There has also arisen the question of whether the same stages of moral reasoning occur for men and women (Gilligan, 1982). Kohlberg originally developed his theory of moral development on an all-male sample, and much of his research has indicated a gender difference, with many women at stage 3 and many men at stage 4 or 5. Gilligan (1982) argues that women's moral development follows a different course than men's and that Kohlberg's stages and scoring procedures reflect a male orientation toward morality. Kohlberg's theory, she says, is based on a model which assumes that individual achievement in a competitive society is the primary motive for human action. For example, in stage 5 of Kohlberg's theory, relationships and what is "right" is determined in terms of social contracts and legal negotiations. Gilligan suggests that such a conception neglects to consider morality based on responsibility and caring. An alternative form of morality, for example, might place more value on ensuring that human relationships are maintained and seeing that the needs of the vulnerable are met through caring. Gilligan believes this dimension of care and responsibility is a major part of women's moral development. Many women, according to Gilligan, view morality in terms of protecting the integrity of relationships and minimizing the hurt, whereas men see morality as a system of rules for adjudicating rights. In response to these arguments, Kohlberg has recently redefined stage 5 to include the aspect of caring emphasized by Gilligan. At the same time, Gilligan has offered only limited empirical support for her contention that men and women follow different paths of moral development (see Walker, 1984).

As noted previously, Kohlberg's theory has been primarily concerned with moral reasoning in childhood and young adulthood. What types of moral problems do older adults experience? In a recent study a sample of older adults were asked to describe a moral problem they had recently faced (Rybash, Roodin, and Hoyer, 1983). The most commonly reported moral problem involved the relationship between the older adults and members of their families. The elderly reported being concerned about whether advice should be "given to" or "taken from" a family member of another generation. The advice usually dealt with matters of marital or sexual propriety. For example, should one push one's morals on an adult daughter? A second type of family relationship problem involved decisions about caregiving and living arrangements — whether to live with an adult child, whether or not to place a spouse in a nursing home. The second most frequent category of moral problems did deal with moral dilemmas involving legal/societal expectations, but these represented less than a fourth of the total number of problems described. Thus, in the majority of problems reported, there was no conflict with a legal authority, as in many of Kohlberg's stories, in which one had to decide whether or not it was "right" to break a legal or societal contract. Rather, the older adult was faced with much more pragmatic problems, involving primarily family relationships and their rights and responsibilities in relation to these family members.

Currently, there are no longitudinal studies which have examined period effects or cohort differences in moral decision-making. However, national public opinion survey data do suggest that there have been shifts in opinions regarding social issues, such as abortion (Cutler, Lentz, Muha, and Riter, 1980). In 1973 the U.S. Supreme Court ruled that a woman may go to a doctor to end her pregnancy at any time during the first three months. Cutler et al. (1980) examined cohort changes in attitudes about the availability of legal abortion from 1965 to 1977, based on public opinion survey data. The same six questions were asked in 1965 and in 1972 to 1977: "Please tell me whether or not you think it should be possible for a pregnant woman to obtain a legal abortion (1) If there is a strong chance of serious defect in the baby? (2) If she is married and does not want any more children? (3) If the woman's own health is seriously endangered by the pregnancy? (4) If the family has a low income and cannot afford any more children? (5) If she became pregnant as a result of rape? and (6) If she is not married and does not want to marry the man?" Figure 7–3 shows the changes in attitudes about the availability of legalized abortion from 1965 to 1977 for four birth cohorts. The

FIGURE 7–3.
Cohort changes in attitudes about the availability of legalized abortions.

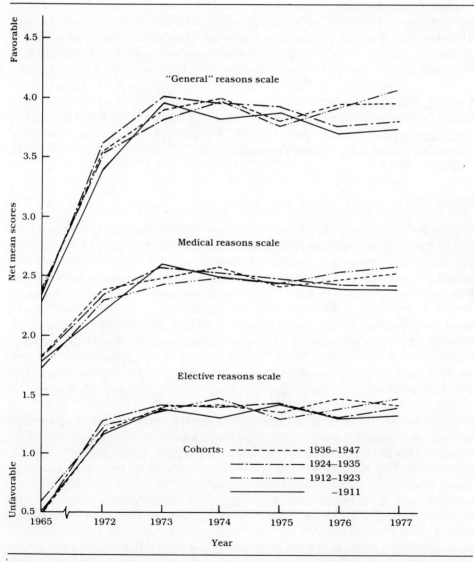

Source: From S. Cutler, S. Lentz, M. Muha, and R. Riter. Aging and conservatism: Cohort changes in attitudes about legalized abortion. *Journal of Gerontology*, 1980, 35, 115–123. Reprinted by permission.

General Reasons Score shows the summed responses to all six questions (maximum score = 6). The Medical Reasons Scale Score shows the summed responses to questions 1, 3, and 5 (maximum score = 3). The Elective Reasons Score shows the summed responses to questions 2, 4, and 6 (maximum score = 3). Note that the major increase in favorable attitudes occurred between 1965 and 1972. Attitudes continued to shift in the direction of being more favorable through 1974, but at a much diminished rate. From 1974 to 1977 the general picture is one of a plateau having been reached around 1974 and no great shift in public opinion from 1974 to 1977. This shift in attitudes appears to reflect a period effect with all four cohorts studied showing similar patterns of change across time. The attitudes of the older cohorts became more favorable from 1965 to 1973 just as did the younger cohorts. Thus there is no evidence from these data that older cohorts were more rigid or conservative; rather their attitudes shifted in the same liberal direction as those of the younger cohorts. Note also that there is greater support for abortion for Medical Reasons than for Elective Reasons; these trends have also remained constant over the time period studied. Attitudes toward abortion appear to have remained relatively stable from 1977 through 1983 with only a slight increase in the proportion favoring abortion. In 1983, 50 percent of the population surveyed supported abortion on demand, as stated in the 1973 ruling (Gallup Poll: Public Opinion, 1983).

RELIGIOUS VALUES

Religious motivation, as we have mentioned, has received little attention from researchers in adult development. This is especially surprising when we consider that church and synagogue are where most social activities outside the family take place. Some people join a church for *extrinsic* reasons that have little to do with religion per se (Hunt and King, 1971). They like the social aspects of the church — the gatherings of friends; perhaps the church affords them status, perhaps it's good for business to be seen there. *Intrinsically* motivated people, in contrast, are drawn to the church because of its teachings; they are more likely to apply these teachings to their everyday life. About 40 percent of all adults report that they attend church or synagogue in a typical week, according to a 1984 Gallup poll. This figure has remained very stable over the past twelve years, declining from an all-time high of 49 percent in 1958.

Much of the literature on religiosity published more than a decade ago tended to focus on a single measure — participation in formal organized religion, which was generally assessed in terms of attendance at church services (Ohrbach, 1961; Bahr, 1970). This is especially true of studies of religiosity in relation to aging. There is growing awareness, however, that religiosity is a multidimensional construct and, more importantly, that the various dimensions are not necessarily highly related. Studies that only examined one aspect of religiosity, then, may have yielded distorted results. When church attendance is used as the primary measure of religiosity, for example, it is often concluded that religious participation declines in later adulthood (Moberg, 1968). This is not necessarily true, however, as we shall see. Unfortunately, almost all research on this matter has been cross-sectional, so we cannot reliably distinguish age from cohort effects.

A number of dimensions of religiosity have been examined. It has been found that one dimension of religiosity is not necessarily highly related to other dimensions of religiosity (Glock and Stark, 1965; Heisel and Faulkner, 1982). Ainlay and Smith (1984) examined three dimensions of religiosity. The first concerned public participation in organized religious activities — attending meetings for young people or adults, attending church services, or serving as a Sunday school teacher. The second dimension was attitudinal and was concerned with whether or not a person considered it important to participate in church activities or serve the home church. The third dimension concerned nonorganizational religious activities such as private Bible study, prayer, and listening to religious programs on radio and television (see box for further description of the study).

A number of studies have found that participation in organized religious activities decreases in old age (Ohrbach, 1961; Blazer and Palmore, 1976; Ainlay and Smith, 1984). The same studies, however, often found that participation in personal nonorganized aspects of religion remains constant or even increases with age (Blazer and Palmore, 1976; Ainlay and Smith, 1984). Mindel and Vaughan (1978) found that 62 percent of their sample reported participating in personal nonorganized religious activities very often. Thus one's perception of oneself as a religious person can encompass more than participating in religious organizations; it also includes private religious behavior. Among aged people, there may be shifts in the form of religiosity. Mindel and Vaughan (1978) conclude, "These data again seem to be saying that we must separate religiosity as a community activity from religiosity as a personal subjective experience. Our data indicate that the elderly in this sample might have disengaged from religion in the community activity sense but they have continued to maintain or perhaps transformed the way in which they experience religion" (p. 107).

Religious activity is one realm in which one can consider the issue of disengagement (Mindel and Vaughan, 1978). There is some evidence that the elderly are *objectively* more disengaged from organizational religion (as measured by church attendance), but that *subjectively* they remain engaged (as evidenced by their level of participation in personal nonorganized religious activities). A finding that further confirms this interpretation is that people's desire to participate in this life of the church remained constant across later life (Ainlay and Hunter, 1984).

It is useful to consider not only the elderly's continued participation in organized religion, but also the church's response to the aged in the congregation. Taylor and Chatters (1984) studied the types of support the church provides for elderly blacks. The most prevalent type of support, reported by 32 percent of the sample, was help during sickness — visiting, moral support, but excluding financial or nursing care. Financial assistance and provision of goods and services (for example, meals) was provided to 24 percent of the elderly. However, the researchers also found that the more frequent church attenders and widows were more likely to receive support. Steinitz (1981) found that receiving assistance from church members and clergy was perceived as a reward for one's past participation in church activities.

Does religion provide spiritual satisfaction and solace throughout life? Are the members of organized religions better adjusted than nonmembers? There are no clear answers to these questions, for there are many different religions attracting a wide variety of people. But "despite the objection of many researchers [Palmore, 1970], the weight of the evidence is in favor of a correlation between religion and a more abundant sense of life satisfaction" (Hendricks and Hendricks, 1977). It is important to note, however, that in the absence of longitudinal data and lagged analyses, one cannot determine the direction of the relationship (that is, whether religion improves life satisfaction or whether people who have high levels of life satisfaction are more attracted to religion). One study, however, may shed some light on this matter. Blazer and Palmore (1976) found that religious attitudes and activities were positively and significantly correlated with happiness, personal adjustment, and feelings of usefulness. Because correlations in older age groups were stronger, it was concluded that religion tends to become increasingly important in the adjustment of older people as they age, despite declines in certain religious activities, such as church attendance.

Self-Actualization

We've come a long way, from hunger to moral and religious values. Is it all motivation? How are all the needs and drives and goals and values that motivate humans related? Is it possible to organize the vast variety of human motivations into one coherent framework? One psychologist who tried was Abraham Maslow (1970).

In Maslow's view, human needs arrange themselves in a hierarchy, as depicted in Figure 7-4. The defining characteristic of the hierarchy is that lower needs must be satisfied before higher needs; in Maslow's term, the lower needs are *prepotent*. The lowest and most compelling of the needs are *physiological*, needs that lead to behaviors necessary for the survival of either the individual (as hunger leads to eating) or the species (as the sex drive leads to childbearing). If unsatisfied, these needs can dominate a person's thoughts and actions; a starving person has no interest in philosophy.

Next in the hierarchy are the *safety* needs. These include the need for security, stability, law and order, and the freedom from fear. If we are reasonably safe, we may begin to express the need for *belongingness and love*. We desire friends, lovers, children. If we do not get them, we become lonely, just as we become hungry without food, frightened if safety needs go unsatisfied.

If love and belongingness needs are satisfied, needs for *esteem* emerge. We need to respect ourselves, and we need the respect of others.

FIGURE 7–4.
Maslow's hierarchy of needs.

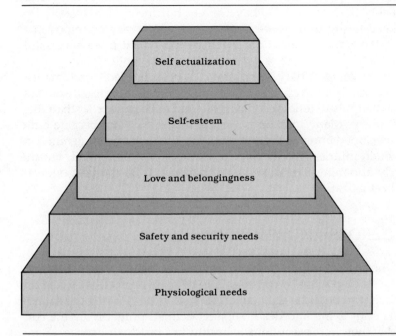

Source: From Geiwitz, J. (1980). Psychology: *Looking at ourselves* (2nd ed.). Boston: Little, Brown.

At the top of Maslow's hierarchy is the need for *self-actualization*. Self-actualization is defined as the desire to become everything one is capable of becoming. It is illustrated by humans struggling to become the best they can be at whatever they do — to reach for perfection.

LIMITED CAPACITY, UNLIMITED DREAMS

It may come as a surprise to learn that Maslow first based his concept of self-actualization on studies of brain-injured soldiers (Goldstein, 1939). The behavioral effects of these brain injuries were many. Some could be traced directly to the injury; the soldier might be blind or partially paralyzed, or have difficulty interpreting or producing speech. Other effects were secondary symptoms that reflected attempts to adjust to a new life with reduced sensory or cognitive abilities. For example, brain-injured patients are typically neat and orderly; they are the favorites of the nursing staff. This symptom can be observed in a wide variety of patients with injuries in widely varying parts of the brain. All of them have lost some of their ability to cope with novel situations and thus, *defensively*, they try to organize their lives to avoid surprises.

Other secondary symptoms could be classified as *compensatory*, attempts to regain a previous level of competence in another way. Therapists often note that patients who have lost a function completely (for example, the totally blind) adjust more quickly than those who have severe but incomplete losses. The partially blind keep trying to improve their vision, which may be impossible, while the totally blind develop their other senses and adjust more successfully.

But a third class of secondary symptoms has been labeled *growth* or *self-actualization* behaviors. There were clear attempts by the brain-injured soldiers, for example, not to simply defend or compensate, but to become *better* than they were before the injury. Many took up a musical instrument and became quite skilled. Others developed unusual cognitive abilities such as computing numbers mentally. With brain injuries, the avenues of expression were limited, but the desire was clearly apparent. The desire was to grow, to be the best one can possibly be: self-actualization.

MASLOW'S HEROES AND THEIR VALUES

Maslow studied normal, healthy people to understand self-actualization more clearly. In fact, he studied what he considered to be *above*-normal, *super*-healthy people, in an attempt to describe self-actualization at its best. His study sample included subjects both living and dead, subjects defined primarily by the consensus opinion that they were exceptionally healthy in a psychiatric sense. Living subjects were interviewed. Subjects who were dead (including historical figures such as Lincoln and Einstein) were examined through biographies and other writings. From these observations, Maslow constructed a list of characteristics of the average self-actualizing person, shown in Table 7–1. It's an interesting list, with few surprises; it depicts what most of us would consider an "ideal" person.

An individual who has had a taste of self-actualization and of the "peak experiences" one can experience in this pursuit may become "addicted." If you experience in a profound way what "justice" means, for example, it can take over your life completely, as you devote yourself to the pursuit of "perfect justice." An artist may begin pursuit of perfect beauty; a philosopher may start tracking truth. Once experienced, the highest needs may become prepotent over the lower needs, according to Maslow. The need for food becomes a need for skill in preparing and appreciating food: the individual becomes a gourmet. The need for sex becomes a need for a sensual, loving experience, part of a contract between two self-actualizing persons.

Goals in general become indistinguishable from what we consider the great virtues in life. According to Maslow, we strive for truth, honesty, beauty, justice, order, and playfulness. Playfulness? Yes! We strive for joy, not pleasure; for satisfaction, not gratification. And the happy, altruistic attitude of play is a basic attitude of the self-actualizing individual.

TABLE 7–1. *Characteristics of self-actualizing types.*

Characteristic	Comment
Self-actualizing people	Self-actualizing people detect absurdities and dishonesties quickly, even their own; they do not live in a dream world.
1. perceive reality accurately,	They are unorthodox, especially in their thoughts. They do not act rebelliously simply because they disagree with the opinions of others. They do not act for effect unless the principle involved is highly valued. They have ideals, in other words, but they also understand reality.
2. even in regard to themselves, and	
3. are not afraid of it.	
4. They are spontaneous and natural.	
5. They focus on problems, not on themselves.	They are not focused on their own personal problems to the exclusion of the problems of society; they think in terms of contributions they can make.
6. They like privacy and detachment;	They are relatively independent of both the physical and the social environment; they enjoy but do not *need* friends.
7. they can be called autonomous.	
8. They have a continued freshness of appreciation.	Life does not become old and stale for them.
9. They have peak experiences.	They have out-of-the-ordinary (mystical) experiences.
10. They have a feeling of relationship with all people and	They are realistic reformers, attempting to improve the lot of all people, and their personal friendships and love-relationships are also more intense.
11. more profound interpersonal relations.	
12. They have a democratic character structure and	They are not prejudiced and they have a strong sense of ethics.
13. discriminate between means and ends.	This follows from the other characteristics, does it not?
14. They are creative.	
15. They have a philosophical sense of humor.	They laugh at absurdities, not at other people's failings.
16. They resist enculturation.	Each is his or her own person.

Source: From James Geiwitz, *Psychology: Looking at ourselves,* 2nd ed. Copyright © 1980 by James Geiwitz. Copyright © 1976 by Little, Brown and Company. Reprinted by permission. The characteristics adapted for use in this table were described by Abraham Maslow, *Motivation and personality,* 2nd ed. (Harper & Row, 1970).

Summary

1. Motivation theories attempt to account for behavior by asking why it occurs. The "push" view suggests that people are motivated by internal biological needs or drives. The "pull" view focuses on the external goals and incentives that instigate behavior. The biological drives that play an important role in the push view are influenced by a variety of physiological and social factors, some of which change with age. Drives result in arousal, which in turn results in activities to satisfy the drives.

2. Anxiety, an aroused state characterized by vague fears, tends to remain quite stable with age.

3. The intimate relationship between cognitions and motivations is also illustrated by the concept of *locus of control*. Locus of control is seen to be either external (other people, impersonal fate) or internal ("I am responsible for the rewards and punishments that come my way"). Older people are more likely than young adults to attribute their failures to internal causes and their successes to external causes.

4. The concept of *learned helplessness* developed originally from animal experiments in which the "locus of control" of unpleasant events (like shocks) was clearly external. Eventually the animals "learned" to be "helpless"; that is, they gave up trying to control their environment through personal actions. In humans, a lengthy learning phase seems to be unnecessary; simply placing humans in a "helpless" environment in which they *perceive* the locus of control to be "external" is sufficient. Therapy for institutionalized old people who suffer from helplessness is effective to the extent that it produces *stable attributions* of internal control; patients in nursing homes who are given more responsibility for themselves and for something outside themselves (a plant, a pet) show great improvement in attitude and behavior.

5. A stable attribution of internal control (a view that one is capable of handling whatever comes one's way) is also a key feature of modern theories of *achievement motivation*. In the AT&T study, Need for Advancement was found to decline over time. The Inner Work Standards of very successful managers tended to increase, whereas those of less successful managers remained stable or decreased. Career success and life satisfaction were not found to be related, however.

6. According to the *disengagement theory*, elderly people welcome a reduction in activities and interpersonal relationships. The *activity theory* holds the opposite, that one must replace lost activities and friends in order to keep one's spirits up. Research more often supports the activity theory, although some people apparently do disengage themselves voluntarily. Whether disengagement is voluntary or not, however, most elderly people experience some reduction in activities, for reasons social (retirement), psychological (the more imminent prospect of death), and biological (disabling illnesses). How they respond to such reductions often depends on their personalities; activity is most important for people who use it as a defense mechanism and for passive sorts who need the stimulation of other people. Studies show that certain kinds of activities, particularly intimate activities, improve life satisfaction more than others.

7. Kohlberg's theory of moral development suggests that people pass through a number of stages as they age. Relatively few people research the higher stages. Studies on whether people's stages of moral development change as they move into old age yield mixed results, but there is little evidence that the elderly commonly operate on a higher moral plane. They may, however, be more consistent in applying their moral reasoning across various tasks. Gilligan suggests that the moral development of women may emphasize different values than the moral development of men.

8. Much of the older literature on religiosity assessed it in terms of a single dimension, church attendance. There is growing evidence, however, that religiosity is a multidimensional contruct and that the various dimensions are not necessarily highly related. It appears that participation in organized religious activities often decreases in old age, but participation in personal, nonorganized aspects of religion remains constant or even increases with age. There is a correlation between religiosity and level of life satisfaction.

9. Maslow's hierarchical theory of motivation describes physiological needs as most basic, followed by safety, belongingness/love, and esteem needs. At the top of Maslow's hierarchy are growth or *self-actualization* needs.

SUGGESTED READINGS

Bandura, A. (1981). Self-referent thought: A developmental analysis of self-efficacy. In J. H. Flavell and L. Ross (Eds.), *Social cognitive development: Frontiers and possible futures*. New York: Cambridge University Press. An essay on the development of an individual's perception of self-competence.

Garber, J., and Seligman, M. E. P. (1980). *Human helplessness: Theory and applications*. New York: Academic Press. Revised discussion of the theory of learned helplessness.

Gilligan, C. (1982). *In a different voice: Psychological theory and women's development*. Cambridge, MA: Harvard University Press. A theory of women's moral development.

Rodin, J., and Langer, E. (1980). Aging labels: The decline of control and fall of self-esteem. *Journal of Social Issues, 36*, 12–29. Article discusses the role of perceived loss of control as it relates to aging.

Rodin, J. (1981). Current status of the internal-external hypothesis for obesity. *American Psychologist, 36*, 361–372. Explores the interaction of internal and external factors related to obesity.

Aging and Religious Participation

Previous studies of the relationship between aging and religious participation have tended to use a single measure of religious participation (i.e., church attendance), and have frequently ignored private forms of religious participation (e.g., prayer, Bible reading). When church attendance has been used as the single measure of religious participation, it has often been reported that religious practices declined in old age. In their study, Mindel and Vaughn (1978) argued that religious participation is multidimensional, and needs to be assessed by a variety of dimensions and indicators. Both public, organizational and private, nonorganizational forms of religious participation need to be examined in studying religiosity in old age. For example, while there may be a decline in church attendance with age, nonorganizational, private forms of religious participation (e.g., private devotion, listening to religious radio programs) may continue or even increase with age. Moreover, church attendance alone does not adequately assess the subjective desire of older people to participate in the life of the church. In another study, Ainley and Hunter (1984) found that even though organizational participation declined among older church members, their desire to participate remained constant and their private religious participation increased. Minlay and Vaughan also found greater private religious participation among the elderly.

If a multidimensional approach is to be taken to studying religious participation, it is important to show that the same dimensions of participation are meaningful at different ages. That is, do people of different ages attach the same meanings to the dimensions of organizational and private religious participation? It is important to determine that a dimension such as private religious participation can be defined and measured in the same way at various ages. If a dimension takes on different meanings at different ages, then it becomes impossible to examine age-related changes in a dimension. For example, it is necessary to show that private religious participation can be defined similarly at age 50 and age 70, before examining whether private participation increases or decreases with age. The purpose of this study was to determine whether three dimensions of religious participation had the same meaning at ages 50, 60 and 70. The three dimensions were: organizational participation, nonorganizational participation, and attitudes toward participation.

SAMPLE AND PROCEDURE

The data for the study was a 1975 survey of five Mennonite and Brethren in Christ denominations. Two percent of all members of the five denominations were sampled, and the authors consider this sample to be representative of beliefs and behaviors for members of these denominations. In this study, only members aged 50 and above were considered; this included 947 adults. Subjects were grouped into three age categories: 50–59, 60–69, 70+ years. Three dimensions of religious participation were studied. The first dimension, public participation, was assessed by worship service attendance, Sunday School attendance, religious meetings attendance, and Sunday School teaching. The second dimension, attitudes toward participation, was assessed by reported interest in Sunday School, interest in serving the congregation, and the perceived importance of church participation. The final dimension, private participation, was assessed by Bible reading, private prayer, private devotion, and religious radio listening.

FINDINGS

The study found that people of different ages do attach the same meanings to public participation, private participation, and attitudes toward participation. It appears that fifty-year-olds and seventy-year-olds are referring to the same things when they discuss a dimension of their religious participation. This provides support for examining age-related changes in religious participation, since the dimensions have similar meanings at different ages.

Second, the research casts further doubt on the assumption that church attendance is an adequate sole measure of religious behavior. The authors suggest that religious participation is multidimensional and hence private as well as public aspects of participation need to be considered.

Third, the findings provide new evidence that private religious involvement is important for the elderly. There is some disengagement from organizational involvement, but this is more than offset by increases in private forms of religious involvement. This suggests that a general religious disengagement among the elderly does not occur.

Ainlay, S. C., and Smith, D. R. (1984). Aging and religious participation. *Journal of Gerontology, 39*, 357–363.

Chapter Eight

THE MIDDLE YEARS

Responsibility and Failure

Larry Leslie is forty-six years old. He feels he is experiencing a midlife crisis, but he sees light at the end of the tunnel. Soon, he thinks, his life will be in order again.

"It's hard not to get a little depressed at my age. Maybe this sounds funny to you, but I've always thought of myself as a young man. When things were tough, I could always say, 'Well, things will get better; I'm still a young man.' In the last couple of years or so, I feel like I've passed some kind of boundary. Suddenly I feel old. My daughter's all grown up; got herself a college degree. My wife's going through her change of life. [Laughs.] Can you imagine a young man with a menopausal missus? A whole bunch of little signs and indications that you aren't the young man you think you are. Finally you have to give it up; you're old."

"You're not so old," we replied.

"See! That's one of the little signs, right there. It used to be that I'd say to one of the guys on my crew, well, I'm a little stiff this morning, I must be getting old. And he'd laugh, like it was a big joke. Now I say it and they don't laugh anymore. They give me sympathy! They try to cheer me up! Man, oh man, is that depressing!"

"OK, so you're forty-six. What's wrong with being forty-six?"

"Now that's a good question! I wish I knew the answer. I don't think there is anything wrong with being forty-six; I mean, I really don't. Some of my best friends are forty-six! But then you look at what I've done recently, and you'd have to say I do think there's something wrong with being forty-six. I'm trying to avoid it, I guess. I'm afraid of it, I guess. I don't know. I really don't."

"What have you done recently that makes you think you're afraid of being forty-six?"

"Well, I quit my job with Evans Construction and started my own outfit. That's gotta rank as one of the dumbest things I ever did. I'm working twice as hard and making half as much, and I have to handle all the headaches too. The regulations, the inspections, supplies, inflation, finding good men. And women. Gotta hire women now too."

"How about your marriage?"

"I've got a good marriage, I guess. I love Laura all right, although she's driving me crazy with this menopause thing. Throws the cover off in the middle of the night, saying she's burning up. Hot flashes, you know."

"What are you afraid of at age forty-six?"

"Being over the hill, used up, no good to anyone anymore."

"Do you think Laura feels the same about herself?"

"Sure. Of course. There's a lot of emphasis in our society on youth and beauty — especially for women. How does a woman over forty cope with this 'youth' stuff?"

"Do you ever talk to her about it?"

"No. We don't talk about much anymore."

The Period of Middle Age

The period of middle age is no more easily defined than "young adulthood" or "old age." If you ask a large sample of people what they consider middle age, they are likely to say that it begins around the age of forty and continues to the age of fifty or fifty-five (Cameron, 1969; Neugarten, Moore, and Lowe, 1968). Although reasonable, this definition leaves the period from thirty-five to forty undefined — neither young adulthood nor middle age — and similarly leaves people between fifty-five and sixty-five without a proper label. These gaps in our social definitions mark transition periods in which people vary considerably in their attitudes and behaviors concerning when middle age begins and ends. Some people are well into middle age by the age of thirty-five, whereas others seem young even after forty. Some people seem very old at fifty, whereas others at sixty-five display the manners, attitudes, and sometimes even the physical appearance of people a decade or two younger. Acknowledging the wide variety of adaptations to age that exist in our culture, especially in the transition periods, we focus in this chapter on middle age as an era that begins between thirty-five and forty and ends between sixty and sixty-five. However, as we elaborate in our discussion of midlife crises versus transitions, there are limitations in using chronological age as definers of developmental periods.

The difficulty in defining and discussing middle age is partly due to the fact that middle age is a twentieth-century development in the human life cycle (Borland, 1978; Lawrence, 1981). Middle age as a period in the life cycle has resulted largely from two major biological and social changes. First, the average life span has increased dramatically during this century, such that it is now normative for an individual to live past the period known as middle age. In 1900, in contrast, the life expectancy was fifty, so that many people died before or during what we call middle age. The longer life expectancy today influences when one begins to become aware of one's aging and mortality; the growing awareness of one's own mortality, typically occurring in midlife, is believed by some to precipitate what has become known as the "midlife crisis" (Jaques, 1965). Second, the empty-nest phase, occurring after the children leave home, is a relatively new stage in the family life cycle; this phase is sometimes called the postparental period. In 1900, women were, on average, fifty-five years old when the last child married (Glick, 1977). Thus, given the lower life expectancy in 1900, the average woman could expect to be a widow before the last child left home (Deutscher, 1968). With increased life expectancy, smaller family sizes, and closer spacing of children, the average couple can now expect to live almost twenty years alone after the last child has left home. Thus the characteristics of the period known as middle age have evolved and changed historically. We may expect that the characteristics of this period will continue to change as a result of future biological advances and social changes.

What are the major developmental tasks of this period known as middle age? In terms of Erik Erikson's theory, people at midlife face the dilemma of *generativity versus stagnation* (Erikson, 1963). Generativity is a very broad concept in Erikson's theory, encompassing parenthood (both having and educating children) as well as most of what we consider as "productivity" and "creativity." One generates products (works hard, effectively) and ideas (is creative). One aspires to be the best one can possibly be, as parent, as worker, and also as spouse, citizen, and tennis partner or vegetable farmer. One works to develop one's virtues and to eliminate or improve one's faults. As Larry Leslie put it, "This sounds stupid, I know, but I always had the goal to become perfect. Perfect! I knew it was impossible, but I always thought that that's what I should try for."

If the individual fails to "generate," if there is no personal growth, then there exists instead a negative quality that Erikson calls stagnation. Of course, some stagnation is unavoidable. Successful resolution of the dilemma of middle age, according to Erikson, shades toward optimism over pessimism and prefers problem-solving to complaining. Erikson (1964) claims that *caring* is the human virtue we associate with generativity. Mature adults are those who care for their children whom they have created, for the work that they have produced, and for the welfare of others in the society in which they live.

Robert Havighurst has listed some of the specific developmental tasks faced by middle-aged people in our culture (Havighurst, 1972). These seven tasks are listed in Table 8–1. In this chapter, we discuss some of the issues that have

TABLE 8–1.

Havighurst's developmental tasks of middle age.

1. To accept and adjust to the physiological changes of middle age.
2. Reaching and maintaining satisfactory performance in one's occupational career.
3. Adjusting to aging parents.
4. Assisting teenage children to become responsible and happy adults.
5. Relating to one's spouse as a person.
6. Achieving adult social and civic responsibility.
7. Developing adult leisure-time activities.

Two of the tasks in the middle years are to develop satisfying relationships with one's spouse and with one's aging parents.

developed from research on middle age — issues that relate rather directly to Havighurst's tasks. For example, we discuss reactions to menopause and other physiological changes in middle age and consider psychological adjustments associated with biological change in midlife. (A discussion of some of the biological aspects of these changes can be found in Chapter 11, on biological aging.) In the past decade, there has been much discussion in the popular literature regarding the "midlife crisis" (Levinson, 1978; Sheehy, 1976). Is a midlife crisis a normative experience in middle age or do most individuals perceive themselves to be going through transitions rather than crises? We consider issues related to this debate in this chapter.

Middle-aged people are in a unique position in their families: they are both parents and children. Not only must they aid their by now adolescent children to become reasonably competent adults, they must also help their own aging parents adjust to lives that may be changing as rapidly as the lives of the teenagers. The children are gaining in responsibility and face the prospect of financial independence. The aging parents are adapting to retirement and to possible physical, social, and financial changes (for example, health problems, loss of spouse, reduced income). In the center of these storms of youth and age are the middle-agers, with their own problems.

Middle-agers are often in positions of maximum responsibility in their families, work, community, and the nation. They are typically at the zenith of their careers, earning capacity, and power. Many middle-agers are in leadership positions in the country's service, economic, and political institutions. In the final section of the chapter, we consider some issues of leadership and responsibility.

Menopauses: Biological and Psychological

Menopause is the time in the life of an adult female when her monthly menstrual period ceases. At the same time her ovaries stop producing a monthly ovum or egg, so she is no longer capable of bearing children. Menopause, the cessation of menses, is part of a longer phase in the aging process known as the climacteric, which is the period when women are making the transition from the reproductive to the nonreproductive stage of life. In most women, menopause occurs between the ages of forty-one and fifty-nine years, with a mode of fifty-one years. It is not clear whether age at menopause has changed historically, as has the age at menarche (onset of menstruation), which has gotten lower with successive generations. It appears that age of menarche and age of menopause are unrelated (Treloar, 1982).

Usually there is a period preceding the final cessation of the menses in which menstruation becomes irregular and a number of other physical symptoms appear; usually this period lasts around two years. The physical symptoms, in addition to menstruation that is increasingly irregular in timing and amount of blood flow, include "hot flashes" and dryness of the vagina. Hot flashes are sudden experiences of heat; they may produce sweating, even skin redness, and they are frequently followed by chills. Typically they last for a minute or so and occur four or five times a day in women who experience them at all. Dryness of the vagina is usually experienced as pain or discomfort during sexual intercourse. Like hot flashes, vaginal dryness appears to be the result of plummeting levels of the female hormone, estrogen. If the symptoms are unusually severe, a physician may prescribe "estrogen replacement therapy," which generally alleviates the symptoms. The therapy may have harmful side effects (it has been associated with increased risk of uterine cancer) and for this reason is controversial (Friederich, 1982; Olesen, 1982). Menopause is followed by some atrophy of the vagina, uterus, and breasts, but such shrinkage is minor for ten or twenty years after menopause and may not even be related to the cessation of the menses. Degeneration of the ovaries leads to decreased estrogen production, which is associated with hot flashes. Other glands, however, can continue to produce both estrogen and progesterone, so postmenopausal women may still have "female" hormones in the bloodstream. The variability of estrogen levels may explain why there are wide individual differences in women's symptoms during menopause.

A number of other symptoms are associated with menopause, although at least some of them have psychological rather than physical origins (Timiras, 1972). Dizzy spells, headaches, and heart palpitations, for example, could result from hormonal imbalance, or they could be psychosomatic; perhaps there is an element of both. Similarly, psychological complaints of anxiety, irritability, impatience, and depression are probably compounded from physical change and psychological reaction. If hot flashes keep the woman awake during the night, for example, she may be tired and irritable the next day.

Evidence is accumulating that most textbook descriptions of the frequency and severity of symptoms during menopause are highly exaggerated (Voda, Dinnerstein, and O'Donnell, 1982). Various studies have shown that 25 to 35 percent of menopausal women exhibit no symptoms at all, except for the cessation of the menses (Crawford and Hooper, 1973; Berger and Norsigian, 1976). Most of those who do exhibit symptoms report no more than mild, occasional hot flashes. The Berkeley longitudinal studies of women during middle age found that 80 percent of the subjects considered themselves to be in good to excellent health. In addition to assessing themselves, the women's health was rated by physicians, whose overall ratings showed no mean change between the ages of thirty-four and fifty (Bayer, Whissell-Buechy, and Honzik, 1982). Likewise, in a study of women who regularly visited a clinic in Hawaii, only one in four menopausal women reported hot flashes or other symptoms (Goodman, Stewart, and Gilbert, 1977; Goodman, 1982). The symptoms reported by menopausal women were just barely more numerous and frequent than the symptoms reported by women of similar age who were still menstruating. The researchers concluded that some of the symptoms might in fact be associated with the aging process, rather than attributable to menopause per se.

THE PSYCHOLOGY OF MENOPAUSE

In spite of evidence refuting them, the myths of menopause remain strong. Many women who are facing or undergoing this natural phenomenon are frightened. One common myth is that couples cannot have sexual relations after the menopause (Neugarten et al., 1968). There is no evidence, however, that women's physical capacity for sex declines after menopause. Men's orgasmic capacity gradually decreases during the adult years, but women's capacity does not decrease, at least until the age of sixty (Starr and Weiner, 1981; Butler and Lewis, 1982). Mental problems are also a common concern. One woman said, "I knew two women who had nervous breakdowns and I worried about losing my mind." Many women dislike the whole idea of menopause because they take it as a sign of old age, that they are no longer attractive, that they are dried up and useless (Stimpson, 1982). Some psychoanalysts have suggested that the loss of childbearing capacity is especially traumatic — it is the "closing of the gates" (Deutsch, 1945) — but very few women mention the inability to have more children (at age fifty) as a chief concern in menopause. They are much more concerned about aging in general.

The actual experience of menopause is, for a vast majority of women, much less negative and, in some respects, much more positive than popular belief would have it (Severne, 1982). Simply not menstruating is counted as a benefit, and not worrying about pregnancy can revitalize a stagnant sex life. Many women report increased vigor after menopause: "I'm just never tired now," said one woman (Neugarten et al., 1968). Most women (and most men too) have at least a few distorted ideas about menopause, and it is these ideas that produce much fear and apprehension. The scarcity of rigorous research on menopause and its effects is a major source of uncertainty and anxiety. A group of older women, asked what was the worst thing about menopause, responded most frequently, "Not knowing what to expect" (Neugarten et al., 1968).

But current menopausal research is beset with methodological problems (Goodman, 1982). First, menopause is a complex biosocial, biopsychological phenomenon, but most research deals only with one or two aspects. For example, research that deals with the physical aspects of menopause without taking into account the woman's socialization experiences, fears, and unfounded beliefs about menopause may inappropriately attribute symptoms solely to physiological variables.

Second, cohort differences probably affect the menopausal experience. Cohorts of women differ, for example, in age at menarche and in the number and spacing of pregnancies, and these factors could affect menopause. Suggestive evidence concerning cohort differences in women's health status was noted in the Berkeley longitudinal studies of middle-aged women (Bayer, Whissell-Buechy, and Honzik, 1982). There are also cohort differences in medical intervention procedures pertaining to childbirth, estrogen replacement, and other matters, and these too may have long-term effects on health during menopause.

Third, there are often sampling problems (Goodman, 1982). The case-history approach often used in menopausal research is biased in that only those women who seek professional help for menopausal complaints are represented. The experience of the many women who have few or no menopausal problems are not reflected in case histories. Finally, without cohort-sequential longitudinal research it is difficult to disentangle the effects of aging from those of cohort differences in reaction to menopause (Goodman, 1982). For example, a common complaint of menopause is insomnia, but increasing sleep disturbance occurs with age as well. A menopausal woman's complaints of insomnia, then, may be a function of increasing age rather than menopause per se.

The evidence we do have suggests that women's behavior is strongly influenced by their culture and by their immediate physical and social environments as well as by physiological factors (Voda, Dinnerstein, and O'Donnell, 1982). For example, it was long believed that the physiological and psychological stresses associated with menopause caused an increase in depression; this depression occurring in women of menopausal age was called "involutional melancholia." However, there is no evidence that the onset of depression in women is correlated with menopause or that depression occurring in the menopausal age group is different from depression occurring at other stages of life (Weissman, 1979). The incidence of depression increases gradually with age in both men and women. The incidence in women is higher throughout the life cycle, probably because women's social roles render them more vulnerable (Butler and Lewis, 1982).

Further evidence pertaining to the role of social factors in women's experience of menopause is presented by Severne (1982). She studied the effects of menopause on Belgian women of higher and lower socioeconomic status and on housewives and working women in each SES group. Those who had a higher SES and held jobs had fewer menopausal complaints and higher life satisfaction during the menopausal period. Figure 8–1 shows the percentage of women reporting high positive evaluations of themselves during three phases of the menopausal period. Self-evaluation ratings reflected women's opinions of their attractiveness and well-being and their satisfaction with family and social life. More than half the high SES women with jobs showed excellent self-rating throughout the period. Lower SES workers and higher SES housewives showed a drop in self-ratings during the menopausal period but a return to higher levels in the postmenopause. Below all other groups were lower SES housewives showing a consistently lower self-rating across the menopausal period. Thus women who have more economic and educational opportunities, who live in a more stimulating environment, and have more options in life may be less prone to some of the psychological difficulties associated with menopause. Findings from the Berkeley longitudinal studies also indicate that women of above-average psychological health at age fifty had social and economic advantages; half were employed part- or full-time outside the home (Livson, 1981).

Cross-cultural research on menopause also reflects the importance of social and environmental factors in determining symptoms of and reactions to menopause. Women of the Rajput caste in India, for example, have fewer menopausal complaints than women in the United States (Flint, 1982). This may be a result of cultural differences. Rajput women live in purdah (that is, they are veiled and secluded) prior to menopause. They are not allowed to be in the company of men other than their husbands. Once they reach menopause, however, cultural taboos against flowing blood and childbirth no longer apply to them, so they are released from the restrictions of purdah and can talk with men. Since their status increases after menopause, it is not an event that they view with foreboding.

THE MALE MENOPAUSE

Well, certainly "the male menopause" is a misnomer! Males do not menstruate and therefore do not cease menstruating. But psychologists and laypeople are intrigued by the parallels between the female menopause and some aspects of the male "midlife crisis," and thus the title, "the male menopause," occurs frequently in magazines and even in college textbooks (as it does here, in ours).

What are the male parallels to female menopause? The biological parallels are weak, almost nonexistent. In men, no single, abrupt event marks the end of the reproductive capacity (Masters, John-Johnson, and Kolodny, 1982). Men lose their reproductive capacity very slowly over the years; sperm production at age sixty, for example, is still about 75 percent of what it was at twenty-five. Hormone levels also decrease gradually. Certain dysfunctions of the hormone production system can result in rapid decreases in sperm counts and behavioral impotence,

FIGURE 8–1.

Percentage of women in each subgroup who showed a very positive self-evaluation (scoring 78–98 points).

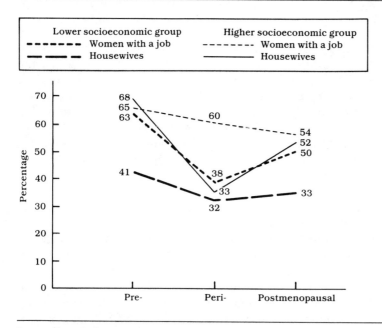

Source: From L. Severne. "Psychosocial Aspects of the Menopause." In A. M. Voda, M. Dinnerstein, and S. R. O'Donnell, eds., *Changing Perspectives on Menopause.* Austin, TX: University of Texas Press, 1982, p. 245. See also A. A. Haspels and H. Musaph, eds., *Psychosomatics in Peri-Menopause.* Lancaster, England: MTP Press, 1979. Reprinted by permission.

and these dysfunctions are more common in middle age than in young adulthood (Spark, White, and Connolly, 1980). These male patients may also suffer some of the symptoms of female menopause: hot flashes, chills, irritability. But in males such dysfunctions are clearly abnormal; they are malfunctions of the biological system that occur rarely on a statistical basis.

Closer parallels to female menopause can be found in the realm of psychological reactions to aging (Brim, 1977). Many women react to menopause as a sign of aging, and men react similarly to similar signs in themselves. Simple, chronological age is one such sign. Many people, both men and women, may react with anxiety and depression to the event of their fortieth birthday, or fiftieth. Hair loss, weight gain, or slowing of reaction time, noticed on the tennis courts or in the church softball league, can send men as well as women into spasms of fear and uncertainty. There is a perception of growing old. There is a feeling of middle age.

What men and women *fear* in middle age is the loss of the admirable qualities of youth and the unavoidable addition of what are perceived to be the unadmirable qualities of age. What they must do, for a successful midlife transition, is balance the young and the old in their lives.

MIDLIFE: A TRANSITION OR A CRISIS?

For the past twenty years there has been intermittent debate in the social sciences regarding how to describe and explain the developmental changes occurring during midlife. Much of the debate has centered around two models for conceptualizing the nature of development in middle age (Perun and Bielby, 1979).

Crisis model One model, which we will call the crisis model, is concerned principally with changes occurring *within* the individual. This model conceptualizes development as involving passage through a series of stages; each stage is characterized by a particular type of crisis which the individual experiences and must resolve in order to advance successfully to the next stage. All individuals are said to experience the same set of stages. It is also important to note that within this conception of development, crises are seen as normative developmental events, experienced by all individuals at specific stages of development. Each stage and its accompanying crisis is typically defined as occurring within a particular chronological age range. A major contributor to this developmental model is Erikson, whose stage theory has been discussed in various chapters of this text. However, interestingly, the Eriksonian stage model does not give special emphasis to middle age and does not single out the crisis of generativity versus despair occurring in midlife for special attention.

As interest in the adult years has grown over the past two decades, there has been increasing attention given to middle age and possible crises associated with it. The term midlife crisis became popular because of an article by Elliot Jaques (1965) on the career crises of artists. In an intensive review of their lives, Jaques found some kind of dramatic change around the age of thirty-five in almost every case. He found that in many instances the period of crisis was precipitated by the individual's recognition of their own mortality. They became concerned about time left to live, rather than time since birth. Some artists (Gauguin, is a prominent example) began their creative work at this time. Others quit, and many died. The people who were artists before and after this crisis usually demonstrated some significant change in their work. Often the change was one of intensity, as impulsive brilliance gave way to a mellowed and more deliberate form of the art.

Adult models of development, such as those by Levinson (1978), Gould (1978), and Sheehy (1976) all emphasize crises occurring in midlife. One of the better known of these adult models had an impact even before it was published. While still working on his book, *The Seasons of a Man's Life*, Daniel Levinson discussed his ideas with Gail Sheehy, who went on to write the best-selling *Passages*. Levinson's research was based on ten to twenty hours of interviews with forty men in the age range from thirty-five to forty-five. Four occupational groups were studied — executives, workers, biologists, and novelists. Based on retrospective biographical sketches given by these men, Levinson conceptualized the life course as divided into four eras: childhood and adolescence, early adulthood, middle adulthood, and late adulthood. Bordering the beginning and end of each era are times of instability and developmental crisis. The period of instability occurring during entry into middle adulthood is given particular emphasis within Levinson's model. He suggests that there are three tasks associated with this crisis period: the man must review his life as a young adult and reappraise what he has done; he must move toward entering middle age; and, finally, he must deal with four sets of polarities which are sources of conflict. These four polarities are young versus old, destruction versus creation, masculine versus feminine, and attachment versus separation. A man may feel young in many ways, yet he may also become increasingly aware of growing old (young/old). He may become more aware of his own mortality and that of others and may have a strong desire to become more creative or generative in his remaining years (destruction/creation). Likewise, every man at midlife must come more fully to terms with the coexistence of masculine and feminine parts of the self (see also Chapter 4). Finally, a man must reconcile his need for attachment with his equally important need for separateness.

Levinson sees these periods of instability as closely tied to specific chronological ages; this period in midlife is said to occur between age forty and forty-five, and Levinson argues that it cannot begin before age thirty-eight or after forty-three. Moreover, these periods of instability are considered to be nearly universal; Levinson suggests that 80 percent of all men experience such a period of crisis in midlife. The period is frequently traumatic and painful:

> For the great majority of men . . . this period evokes tumultuous struggles within the self and with the external world. Their Mid-Life Transition is a time of moderate or severe crisis. Every aspect of their lives comes into question. . . . A profound reappraisal of this kind cannot be a cool, intellectual process. It must involve emotional turmoil, despair, the sense of not knowing where to turn or of being stagnant and unable to move at all. . . . Every genuine reappraisal must be agonizing, because it challenges the illusions and vested interests on which the existing structure is based. (Levinson, 1978, p. 199)

Before considering an alternative model of midlife development, it is important to note several limitations of research conducted within the crisis model, since this model has received such widespread attention within the media and popular literature. First, there has been concern regarding the samples used in these studies. In several instances clinical populations have been used; also, white, middle-class males are overrepresented in the samples. Moreover, as Rossi (1980) has pointed out, the research of Levinson, Gould, and Sheehy are based on the same birth cohort, raising questions regarding generalizability to other generations. To the extent that the problems of midlife are related to specific societal and historical trends and events, we may expect that midlife may be experienced qualitatively differently by various generations. A second concern is that midlife crisis research has been based almost totally on interview data. There has been little attempt to quantify this interview data and subject it to statistical analyses, nor have these researchers cross-validated their findings by use of standardized instruments (McCrae and Costa, 1984). Finally, the major studies cited to support the crisis model are cross-sectional. It is not possible therefore to compare functioning in early or later adulthood with functioning in midlife, and determine whether midlife is indeed marked by a period of greater instability.

Transition model   An alternative conceptualization of development during middle age rejects the notion that crises are normative developmental events. Rather, progression across the life course is seen as being predictable and orderly, for the most part. The individual constructs a timetable for when major life events would be expected to occur. The expected timing of events is based largely on societal age norms. That is, there exists a socially defined timetable for the age at which men and women are expected to marry, raise children, retire, and so on. Much of one's life is construed and evaluated in terms of this social timetable. A proponent of this model is Neugarten (1968), who has studied the impact of midlife events, such as menopause and the empty nest, on nonclinical samples of middle-aged women; these events have been interpreted within the crisis model as being closely associated with onset of the midlife crisis. However, Neugarten found most women did not perceive these events to be exceptionally traumatic; moreover, she did not find these events to co-occur in time with changes in self-perception or in personality characteristics, as a crisis model might predict (see also Chapters 2 and 4). Lowenthal and Chiriboga (1972) found that, if anything, parents were somewhat happier in the empty nest.

One of the few longitudinal studies of women in adulthood examined a group of women who scored above average on an index of psychological health at age fifty (Livson, 1976, 1981). Two patterns of development between the ages of forty and fifty years were discovered. The Traditional group conformed to customary gender-related role expectations in our culture. They were gregarious, nurturant, and placed a high value on closeness with others. The psychological health of this group remained relatively stable from age forty to age fifty. The Nontraditional group *improved* in psychological health over the same period. These women were more ambitious, intellectual, autonomous, and unconventional in their thinking. They were doers, and their interests were intellectual or skill-oriented rather than social. These Nontraditional women had experienced some difficulty earlier in the life span in finding their "niche;" however, once found, these women's psychological well-being improved significantly over the middle-age period. The experiences of the latter group point up the view of middle age as a time of *opportunity*.

Other researchers have also questioned some of the implicit assumptions of the crisis model, including the expectation that a midlife crisis is nearly universal, occurs within a limited age range, and results in significant changes in one's self-perception or one's lifestyle. Epidemiologists find little support for the midlife being a time of excessive stress, when compared with other age periods (Kramer, Taube, and Rednick, 1973). Divorce is most common in the twenties; admissions to psychiatric hospitals show no peak at age forty; suicide is most prevalent in young and old age, rather than at midlife. Longitudinal studies of personality characteristics, such as neuroticism, which from a crisis perspective, might be expected to increase in midlife, have found that such characteristics are remarkably stable over much of the life course (McCrae and Costa, 1983). A study by Farrell and Rosenberg (1981) of 500 men at midlife suggests that for the minority of men in their sample who appeared to have a crisis, the difficulties they were experiencing appeared to have their roots in conflicts and problems originating earlier in the life course.

One of the most dramatic occurrences generally assumed to accompany a midlife crisis is an abrupt and drastic career change. But how common are such midlife career changes in actuality? To find out, Gottfredson (1977) examined civilian employment data from the U.S. Bureau of the Census, classifying job categories into the Holland occupational categories discussed in Chapter 3. He found that job stability (staying in the same job or job category) over a five-year period increased among workers over the age of thirty. Over 80 percent of the workers between the ages of forty-one and fifty-five remained in the same job category during the five-year period studied. Of those who did take new jobs, 60 percent changed to another job within the same occupational category, and only 10 to 14 percent moved to a job in a different category. For men, the most common shift across occupational categories was from realistic "technical" work to "enterprising" work involving management or supervision, an expected career progression.

For current cohorts of middle-aged women, the most common career transition is from not working to entering or reentering the job market. Many women begin working during the empty-nest stage or because they had divorced. Many women see these transitions as a period of excitement and challenge. The woman once again has the opportunity to refocus her energies on her own development and self-actualization.

The Bray and Howard study (1980) of AT&T managers examined predictors of life satisfaction in midlife. At the inception of this study (described in Chapter 3), numerous personality and work-related variables were assessed, and the same variables were assessed twenty years later. At the twenty-year point, an attempt was made to study the participants as middle-aged individuals, not just as managers, to determine early predictors of life satisfaction in middle age. Several values identified in the first assessment were found to predict life satisfaction twenty years later at midlife. These included self-confidence (the belief that one can cope with most situations and that people will treat one well) and emotional stability (having a steady temperament). Those who had high levels of life satisfaction also tended to be less cynical and less selfish early in development, which suggests that they had positive attitudes toward others as well as themselves.

Why do some studies conclude that midlife crises are common while others conclude that they are uncommon? A number of disparities exist between the two camps in methods of research. First, research within the crisis model has drawn more heavily, although not exclusively, from clinical populations, who have sought help because of concerns and problems. Research within the transition model has used nonclinical populations. A limitation of both camps has been the overrepresentativeness of white, middle-class samples. Second, researchers in the two camps have also tended to employ different types of measures. As mentioned previously, the crisis model has been based primarily on interview data. Interviews may be geared to tap "inner turmoil" and may therefore tend to elicit complaints and general "bellyaching." In one major interview study (Vaillant, 1977), many men claimed to be in crisis, but other evidence (for example, radical changes in their careers or marriages) was uncommon. On the other hand, the transition position has supplemented interview data with projective techniques and self-reports or self-ratings of life satisfaction and happiness. Those concerned with personality variables (McCrae and Costa, 1984) have also employed personality questionnaires. As a result of using different instruments and asking different types of questions of the data, the outcome measures of the two groups have been different. The crisis group has relied heavily on case-study descriptions. Readers are left to draw their own conclusions from these case studies regarding whether a crisis has occurred or to accept the author's summary statements. In contrast, the transition researchers have sometimes offered global self-ratings of life satisfaction or happiness in support of their position. The research base of both groups has suffered from a lack of longitudinal studies.

In summary, both models suggest that middle age, as the name implies, is a midpoint, a time to consider and reevaluate the past with its accomplishments as well as failures. Midlife also poses the opportunity, challenge, or threat (depending on one's viewpoint) to look to the future and to consider what still might be. Most individuals, whether or not they perceive themselves to have experienced a crisis, do make whatever adjustments may be necessary and look forward to some of the satisfactions of the second half of life.

Being a Child and a Parent

Larry Leslie is at the same time a child and a parent. He spoke of the particular problems. "There are some very fine lines between help and control. You have to be very careful. Linda's pretty much grown up — on her own, you might say. But she still needs many things from us. Love, for example; the need for love never stops. Heck, I still need it from my dad, and he needs it from his mother. She's eighty-seven! You have to be ready to help on things. Linda might need money. I'll do what I can. She'd probably want a loan, with papers to sign; maybe she'd even insist on some interest. Got to be independent, you know.

"Then there's my father and my grandmother. I still get a lot from them, but the situation is reversing. I'm giving more to them now, and it will probably increase. I lose one child and gain two. That's life, I guess."

"Your father Leonard is retired, isn't he?" we asked.

"Yes, he is."

"Does he have financial worries?"

"Well, of course he worries a little. Who doesn't these days? But realistically he's pretty well off. If he keeps his senses. He's been coming up with some harebrained schemes lately. First he was going to sell the house — our family house, where all of us grew up! He thought a condominium would be good enough. Then he decided to travel around the world. He wanted to go on one of those fancy cruise ships. I mean, everybody would like to travel around the world, but he's got to be a little careful. He's got to protect his investment."

"It's hard to ask this question without sounding insulting. But do you ever think of it as *your* investment? Do you ever worry that he might squander your inheritance?"

"That is insulting, isn't it? I wonder if it's true. You try to think in terms of the welfare of your parents, but I suppose inheritance enters your thinking now and then. He'll decide maybe to give some money to some group — there's this social action group he's joined, for example.

"It's his money. He earned it. Sometimes I wonder if I'm thinking he should save it for me, instead of giving it to them. I don't consciously think about inheritance, though. I don't make plans for it."

"Linda thinks this social awareness in Leonard is a good thing, doesn't she?"

"Oh, sure. She's on his side in this dispute. They're the high-minded, altruistic pair, and I'm supposed to be the hard-headed businessman. Profit is my motive. Well, I don't mind. I'm glad Linda is trying to help people; I'm glad that's her motive. I'm just sorry that the real world isn't like that. It doesn't allow for much altruism. What's that old poem? 'The rain falls on the just and unjust fella, but mostly on the just, because the unjust's got the just's umbrella.' That's what life is really like!"

"One last question: We heard that Leonard is planning to remarry. How do you feel about that?"

"You are really going to paint me out a louse, aren't you? Well, I'm against it. For one thing, Mom died less than a year ago. For another, Lorna is only fifty years old! My father, at age sixty-nine, is going to marry a woman who's only a month or two older than my wife! If you don't think that's silly, at least think of how complicated the family relationships are going to get. I mean, am I supposed to call her 'Mom'? Forget it! I'm against it."

"How does your wife feel about it?"

"She thinks it's a mistake. Linda's also for it. My grandmother is against it. Who needs family squabbles? I've got enough problems with my work!"

THE SANDWICHED GENERATION

Larry Leslie is a member of the generation of middle-aged people who are "sandwiched" between their adolescent or young-adult children and their aging parents (Davis, 1981). Their own problems with career and marriage may seem overwhelming, but they must also be involved in the problems of their children, who are about to begin adult life, and their parents, who are facing the end. Their resources — emotional and financial — may be strained by the simultaneous needs of three or four generations; conflict and guilt are sometimes the result (Morgan, 1981).

Middle-aged people form the "sandwiched" generation, with responsibilities toward both their aging parents and their growing children.

Brody (1981) has spoken of this as a "middle-generation squeeze." Most families today have only one middle generation, but the number with two is growing steadily due to increasing life expectancies and decreasing intervals between generations. In the Leslie family, both Larry and Leonard would be considered middle generations. Although the two middle generations in some families may share in providing care to the senior generation, many middle-aged kin may eventually cope with dependency relationships involving two generations of aged parents, aging in-laws, and even aging relations from former marriages, or the later remarriage of an aging parent (Schwartz, 1979).

Middle-aged people are also sometimes put into the position of evaluating prospective spouses, not only for their young-adult children, but also for their widowed parents. Larry Leslie is a case in point; both Linda, his daughter, and Leonard, his father, are thinking about marriage. His approval or disapproval will probably make a difference, for approved marriages have a significantly higher chance of success, even those of an elderly parent (McKain, 1972).

AGING PARENTS

There is the myth that the adult individual's relationship to his or her parents is extremely difficult, with the aging parents becoming more and more dependent — in effect, reversing previous role relationships. In this myth, the adult children can hardly wait to ship the old folks off to a "home" of some sort. Such a picture is accurate for only a minority of families. In fact, Brody (1985) thinks that caring for aging parents has become a normative part of middle adulthood. A relatively small proportion of the elderly are in institutions, but it is estimated that for every disabled person in a nursing home, two or more equally disabled elderly live with or are cared for by their families. Even when an aged parent would be better off in an institution, children sometimes do not seek the aid their parents need out of a sense of love, obligation, and perhaps guilt.

Care of aged parents has only recently become a widespread concern, in part because of demographic changes such as increases in life expectancy. As parents live longer, they are more likely to become dependent on their middle-aged children for care and to need care for an extended period. In 1980, for example, 40 percent of all people in their late fifties had a surviving parent. Ten percent of those over sixty-five had a child over age sixty-five. Moreover, with today's declining birthrate, we can expect the ratio of potential adult child caregivers to elderly parents to decline significantly.

One researcher has coined the term "filial maturity" to describe the psychologically healthy relationship most adult children develop with their aging parents (Blenkner, 1965). Instead of a role reversal, it is more a state of mutual respect. The adult child becomes "dependable," in a sort of mature identification with the parents as they were at the same age. The aging parents are directly involved,

> first in a modeling capacity, and secondly in a rewarding capacity. In other words, the significance of the parent–child relationship does not end with launching but continues throughout life. The parent who continues to mature throughout his life — to accept his own development as meaningful and satisfying — is helping his children to mature in turn. (Troll, 1971, p. 277)

Who provides care for the elderly? If the older person is married, care is most often provided by the spouse (Cantor, 1983). In this situation, the caregiver is an older person too. You will recall, however, that the majority of older women are widowed or alone, so they must be cared for by someone else. The task generally falls to adult children, especially adult daughters. Cantor (1983) has documented what she calls the "hierarchical compensatory" support system. By this she means that support for the elderly is activated in order from the closest and most intimate to more distant relationships. This hierarchy progresses from spouse, to adult child, to distant relative and/or neighbors, and finally to assistance from formal agencies. Morris, Sherwood, and Mor (1984) found that 96 percent of older persons interviewed identified at least one person as an "informal" source of assistance; 86 percent identified two or more such persons. Very few relied solely (3 percent) or primarily (5 percent) on formal sources of assistance, such as social agencies.

Since over half of all middle-aged women work, caring for aged parents can be something of a strain, especially since women in this age bracket must also care for their own families. Brody (1981) has called women in this position "women in the middle." Working women, however, manage to spend almost as much time helping their parents as nonworking women do, even though they must give up their free time and opportunities for socialization and recreation to do so. Daughters and sons in their sixties spend more time caring for their parents than do children in their fifties; the parents of the older children are, of course, older themselves, and so are likely to need more care.

Most aged parents do not live with their children, but when they do they often move in after the youngest generation has moved out. Brody (1985) has referred to this stage as the "refilling of the empty nest." (See also Chapter 13.)

The type of strain reported most often by adult child caregivers is emotional (Cantor, 1983). The chief worry is about the health of the dependent parent, but there are also concerns about finding sufficient help for their parents. The financial concerns related to caregiving are less troublesome. Strain is related to attitudes about caregiving. Those who believe that family members have a responsibility to other family members felt more strain than those who did not have such feelings.

Have attitudes toward filial responsibility and family care of the aged changed as demographics have changed? In most respects, the evidence indicates that they have not. In a study of three generations of women in families, Brody (1985) found high levels of continuity in attitudes toward filial responsibility. There was a strong belief that families should care for their aged members, even when the middle-aged child was in the work force. Most people felt that care should be provided by both men and women and that the burden should not fall exclusively to the daughters. All generations, including the eldest, agreed that it was better for a working woman to pay someone to care for an elderly parent rather than leave her job to provide care herself. In fact, there appears to be a discrepancy between the expectancies of older people with regard to assistance from their children and what adult children feel they should provide to their older parents. Brody (1985) found that the majority of the oldest generation, but only a minority of the other generations, felt that professional services could replace some family-provided services, that older generations would rather pay professionals for assistance than ask family members. Perhaps this reflects older adults' valuing of independence and their desire not to be a burden on their children.

Leadership

People between the ages of forty and sixty — middle-aged people — run the world. Many of the leaders of government and business are middle aged. In fact, a leader who is not middle aged is marked as unusual: the "brilliant" thirty-five-year-old president of a major company, or the "still vital" seventy-year-old union boss. Thus, for all the problems they face, middle-agers are in power. It's their turn. It's time for their generation, for better or for worse, to run the show.

Why do some people become leaders and others not? What is the nature of leadership? Certainly these are among the most complex questions in all of psychology. Almost everyone is the leader of something, at some level of the society; if nothing else, mothers and fathers are leaders of their families. There are leaders in children's groups; high schools elect presidents of the student body; there are leaders in groups of old people. To sort out the common characteristics of leaders in the wide variety of circumstances they are found in is an exceptionally difficult task.

TWO KINDS OF LEADERS

Much of the research on leadership in organizational settings has focused on contingency models of leadership, which suggest that successful leadership is contingent on a variety of factors. Certain kinds of leaders do best in certain kinds of situations; effective leadership is that which provides the most appropriate match between the leaders and the circumstances.

One of the best-known contingency models of leadership is Fiedler's model (1967; 1978), which suggests that the behavior, attitudes, and performance of the group is a joint function of two factors: a factor called *situational favorableness,* and a factor defined as *leadership style* (Mitchell, 1979; Schneider, 1985). Situational favorableness is the degree to which a situation gives a leader potential power and influence over group behavior. This factor is determined by such considerations as the group's respect for and acceptance of its leader, the degree to which the group is structured, and the extent to which the role of leader is invested with power. Two types of leadership style are recognized. *Task-motivated* leaders are more effective in situations of high or low favorableness. These are the leaders who keep the group to its appointed duty and who try to elicit the best ideas on the

One of the functions of play is to provide relatively risk-free practice in adult activities, as in this play school.

topic at hand. The task leader is the chief problem-solver. *Interpersonally motivated* leaders, on the other hand, are more effective in situations of moderate favorableness. The leader of this type tries to keep group spirits up and morale high, to keep interactions smooth. The interpersonal leader is generally more sensitive to the personal goals and values of the group members and, in a well-functioning group, creates a social environment in which the task leader can work more effectively. In terms of behavior in the group, the task leader is usually asking for or giving suggestions, opinions, and information; he or she is at the center of the questions and answers. The interpersonal leader takes charge when disagreements surface; when fear, anger, and other tensions develop; and when group members become antagonistic, trying to assert themselves and deflate others. To prevent these negative reactions from splitting the group, the interpersonal leader increases the positive reactions in the group by offering rewards and praise for good ideas, by pointing out areas of agreement to balance the disagreements, and by joking or laughing to release tensions that are building. Thus leadership is most effective when the leader is appropriate to the nature of the task or group.

What types of people are more likely to become leaders? How are leaders chosen? People from upper social classes, with more education, with a more "facilitating" social background are more often found in positions of leadership than people from lower classes, with less education, or with no influential family friends. A number of factors have been identified in choosing a leader. First, of course, is knowledge: a person is more likely to be chosen as a leader if he or she is an expert in the area of the group's major responsibility. Second, if no one in the group is an expert, several studies indicate that the people who talk the most during the group's discussion are likely to be chosen as leaders (Zander, 1979). It even appears that quantity of talk is regarded more favorably than quality of talk. Apparently talking a good deal is regarded as a sign that a person is willing to work on a group's behalf and so would be a suitable leader.

Whatever one's initial level of skills, however, "time must be served by moving up the hierarchy" (Bray and Howard, 1979, p. 30). Thus positions of significant leadership are typically reached in middle age. There is some evidence to suggest that the years intervening between first employment and eventual leadership are best used to learn the intangible aspects of leadership — the social-emotional skills, how to deal with people rather than with problems. A mentor relationship with an older employee is particularly valuable in learning the "political" requirements of the job. (See Chapter 3 on careers for a more complete discussion of mentors.)

Summary

1. The period of life called "middle age" begins around the age of thirty-five or forty and ends around the age of sixty or sixty-five. It is a period that, in Erikson's terms, involves the issue of *generativity* — creativity and productivity in family life (children) and in career. *Stagnation* is the opposite, the basis for *midlife crisis*.

2. One of the primary developmental tasks of middle-aged women in our culture is to deal effectively with the launching of their children and the biological . end to childbearing capacity known as *menopause*. Although many woman experience "hot flashes" and some dryness of the vagina during menopause, the frequency and intensity of symptoms have been greatly exaggerated. Women commonly fear menopause for a variety of reasons, but they find that the actual experience is much less unpleasant than they had imagined, and it sometimes has unexpected benefits. Research on menopause is beset with methodological problems. It appears that social and cultural factors have a strong influence on how women react to menopause.

3. There is some controversy over the prevalence of midlife crises (as distinguished from simple midlife transitions). Different measures and different types of studies yield different estimates of the frequency of crises. The nature of the midlife crisis, if it occurs, is probably influenced by the social context. One study of women who were exceptionally healthy psychologically at age fifty found that midlife can be a period of stability and even improvement in psychological adjustment.

4. Middle-aged people are in the "sandwiched" generation, with responsibilities for their adolescent or young-adult children *and* their aging parents. These three generations, contrary to myth, are usually in close touch with one another in our society — giving aid and exerting influence. "Filial maturity" is a term used to describe the characteristic of middle-agers who have accepted their familial responsibilities with competence and good humor. Caring for aging parents has become a normative part of middle age. Contrary to common belief, relatively few elderly are in institutions; most are cared for by family members. The task most often falls to the daughters, who may experience considerable strain if they also have jobs and responsibilities to their own families. Studies indicate that attitudes toward filial responsibility remain constant across generations.

5. Middle age is a time of leadership. Middle-agers fill most of the positions of power in government, business, labor, and education. The contingency model of leadership suggests that successful leadership is contingent on two main factors: situational favorableness — the degree to which a situation gives a leader potential power and influence over group behavior — and leadership style. There are two basic leadership styles. Task-motivated leaders keep their groups working on their appointed task and function as problem-solvers. Interpersonally motivated leaders focus more on keeping group spirits and morale high and smoothing out group interactions. Leadership is most effective when the leader is appropriate to the nature of the task or group.

6. Much remains to be learned about leadership. Social background factors may influence the likelihood that a person will attain a leadership position. Expertise and a willingness to talk a good deal in a group situation are factors that influence whether a person is chosen as a group leader. There is some evidence that learning to deal with people rather than problems is the most important task of the period that precedes a leadership position.

SUGGESTED READINGS

Brody, E. M. (1985). Parent care as a normative family stress. *Gerontologist, 25,* 19–29. Parent care as a normative experience for the individual and families is discussed. Some of the complex factors that interact to determine filial behavior are explored.

Eichorn, D. H., Clausen, J. A., Haan, N., Honzik, M. P., and Mussen, P. H. (1981). *Present and past in middle life.* New York: Academic Press. Report on selected aspects of two longitudinal studies, the Oakland Growth Study and the Guidance Study.

Hill, R. E., Miller, E. L., and Lowther, M. A. (Eds.) (1981). *Adult career transitions: Current research perspectives.* Ann Arbor, MI: University of Michigan. Collection of readings on career transitions occurring in midlife or later.

Troll, L. E., and Bengtson, V. (1982). Intergenerational leadership throughout the life span. In B. B. Wolman (Ed.), *Handbook of developmental psychology,* (pp. 890–910). Englewood Cliffs, NJ: Prentice-Hall. A discussion of changes in leadership roles within families over the life course.

Voda, A. M., Dinnerstein, M., and O'Donnell, S. R. (Eds.) (1982). *Changing perspective on menopause.* Austin, TX: University of Texas Press. This edited volume provides an interdisciplinary perspective on issues related to menopause.

Women's Changing Roles and Helps to Elderly Parents: Attitudes of Three Generations of Women

The changing roles of women in the United States have had far-reaching consequences for many aspects of society, including family life, the birth rate, and child-care practices. Another realm that has traditionally been the responsibility of women is care for elderly family members, and several trends suggest that attitudes in this area may have changed. The first trend is demographic: the number of old and very old people is growing, so there are more elderly people who need care than ever before. A second trend is that as average life expectancy increases, there are more three or four generation families. Ninety percent of the old people with children are grandparents, and 46 percent are great-grandparents. Care of the elderly then becomes a multi-generational responsibility. The third trend has been the entry of middle-aged women into the work force. In 1980, 60 percent of the women between the ages of 45 and 54 worked. Hence, the ease with which care can be provided by female family members has decreased, even as the need for care has increased. The question arises regarding whether the changing lifestyles of women have resulted in significant shifts in gender-appropriate roles toward caring for the elderly. While women have been the traditional caregivers, has there been a shift toward more egalitarian views so that both men and women share responsibility for the aged? In the context of these trends, Brody, Johnsen, Fulcomer, and Lang (1983) undertook a study of women in three generational families to see if changes in women's work roles has resulted in generational differences in attitudes toward responsibility for the care of aged parents.

SAMPLE AND PROCEDURE

Personal interviews were conducted with 403 women who were members of three generational families. The sample consisted of 131 grandmothers (hereafter referred to as G1), 165 middle-generation daughters (G2), and 107 young-adult granddaughters (G3). Included was a subgroup of 75 triads of blood relatives — grandmother, mother, and granddaughter from the same family. The subsample permitted examination of intra-family influences.

The subjects responded to an attitude questionnaire on gender roles and responsibility for care of aged parents. Subjects rated each item on a five-point scale from "strongly agree" to strongly disagree." Three of the attitude dimensions studied were: egalitarian gender roles, receptivity to formal supports (that is, willing to accept services provided by professionals, rather than family members) and stereotypical beliefs. The egalitarian dimension involved items, such as "If a women has a paying job, her husband should share household tasks." A formal supports item was "I would rather pay a professional to do things for me than ask assistance from my family." A stereotypical belief item was: "Sons in a family should be given more encouragement than daughters to go to college."

FINDINGS

One of the most surprising findings was that a vast majority of each generation favored egalitarian sharing of roles. For the statement, "If a women has a paying job, her husband should share in the household tasks, such as washing dishes and doing the laundry," 96 percent of G3 agreed, compared with 88 percent of G2 and 92 percent of G1. These findings suggest that the older generation of women may have been influenced by the women's movement and by increases in women's employment.

Another unexpected finding was that the oldest generation was consistently more receptive to having services supplied by professionals (formal support systems) than were the younger two generations. For example, with the statement, "Professional services can usually take the place of family care," 55 percent of G1 expressed agreement, compared with 22 percent of G2 and 16 percent of G3.

As expected, there were significant generational differences in stereotypic beliefs with the G1s being most stereotypical. For the oldest cohort, 45 percent agreed that sons should be given more encouragement than daughters to attend college. Only 12 percent of G2s agreed and 8 percent of G3s. All three generations agreed that elderly parents should be able to depend on their adult children for various kinds of help. Indeed, despite the increase in the number of women working, the sense of filial responsibility remained strong. On the statement "Older people should be able to depend upon their grown children to help them do things they need to do," 75 percent of G1 expressed agreement. The figure rose to 80 percent for G2 and 83 percent for G3. Thus, the middle-aged and young-adult women seem equally concerned with filial responsibilities. There was no evidence for a cohort effect with successively younger generations seeking a smaller role in filial care. The development of new attitudes favoring women working has apparently not resulted in a decrease in attitudes favoring responsibility toward older family members. If women act on these attitudes, however, they may be subjected to stress from role overload and the conflicts involved in attempting to balance work, child care, and other family responsibilities, with care for aging parents. Possibly adding further pressure is the widespread acceptance of the "myth" of family abandonment of the elderly. Three-quarters of each generation agreed with the statement: "Nowadays, adult children do not take as much care of their elderly parents as they did in past generations."

Some limitations of the study should be noted. The sample was small, principally urban, and exclusively female. Thus, findings cannot be generalized to the population as a whole. Second, it has been demonstrated repeatedly that attitudes and behavior are not identical — one doesn't always do what one believes one should do — so the results must be interpreted with caution. Nevertheless, the study does cast light on an issue that is of critical importance for many families and for society as a whole. Additional research is needed to determine whether the attitudes expressed in the study reflect actual practices and, if they do, how these practices affect caregivers and elderly alike.

Brody, E., Johnsen, P. T., Eulcomer, M. C., and Lang, A. M. (1983). Women's changing roles and help to elderly parents: Attitudes of three generations of women. *Journal of Gerontology, 38*, 597–607.

Chapter Nine

INTELLECTUAL DEVELOPMENT

The Display of Competence

What is intelligence?

No one leaps to answers.

Whom do you consider intelligent?

Einstein. Scientists in general. Philosophers.

Consider this account by Ralph Waldo Emerson, an American philosopher, which is derived from an incident described in his journal:

> The problem posed is to get the calf into the barn, ordinarily not a monumental task, but this time the calf has chosen to be obstinate. It will not go. Emerson pushes from behind. The calf will not budge. Emerson enlists his son Edward in the battle. Emerson pushes from behind while Edward pulls the calf's ears. Success evades them. A servant girl passes by, watches with amusement, offers her help. She thrusts a finger into the animal's mouth; "the calf, seduced by this maternal imitation, at once followed her into the barn." Emerson recorded his appreciation of the servant girl's intelligence: "I like people who can do things." (Fuller, 1970)

Mental ability has long been esteemed in Western culture, for people believe it underlies such important behaviors as learning, problem-solving, and adjustment. Thus intelligence quite understandably was one of the concerns of the earliest psychologists, and the attempts to define it, measure it, even increase it have had a long and often stormy history. Indeed, the storms of controversy rage no less strongly today, as perhaps we should expect when dealing with an ability so highly valued.

Some of the controversy has to do with the role of intelligence in the everyday activities of men and women. One wants to know, for example, if intelligent people are better in school than less intelligent people. Are they more successful in life? Can they repair a clock more efficiently? Can they move a calf? And what other factors besides intelligence are involved in competence? Is competence in the elderly the same as competence in young adults? These questions, which will

278

help us distinguish intelligence from other abilities, are the focus of the first section of this chapter.

In the following sections, we discuss theories and research in intellectual development as it proceeds in the adult years. The questions we seek to answer are relatively simple, such as "Does intelligence decline with age?" The answers, however, are more complex; they vary with age, the specific intellectual function, and even the year in which the individual was born. This last influence, which comprises a host of "generational" factors, is analyzed in some detail. And finally we look at the last few years of life, when illness and social isolation frequently have an adverse effect on intellectual performance. We encounter here a recurring problem in gerontology, that is, how to disentangle the effects of disease from those of aging per se.

Intelligence

The word "intelligence" comes from the Latin words meaning "to choose between," and "the ability to make wise choices" is not a bad definition, although a bit imprecise. "The capacity for learning" is another common definition, one that fits with the original intent and common present use of intelligence tests — to predict scholastic performance. "The ability to manipulate symbols" is a definition that stresses the intellectual (symbolic) aspect of intelligence. *ceiling on intellect is set at birth*

INTELLIGENCE AND COMPETENCE

However we define intelligence, we must be careful to distinguish it from the "intelligent behaviors" it presumably affects. Intelligence is a theoretical construct, inferred from but not the same as competent behavior. On the one hand, we estimate individuals' intelligence by observing them in a number of situations in which they can behave competently or not; we watch them to see if they solve problems effectively and if they learn quickly from success and failure. The more such situations we can observe, the more confident we are in our estimate of a person's intelligence. The so-called IQ tests do much the same thing, presenting the individual with a number of short tasks that can be responded to with or without competence.

On the other hand, intelligence is not identical with competent behavior. Competence is a product of many factors, of which intelligence is only one. Consider, for example, performance on a history test. Here certainly is behavior in which intelligence can be assumed to play a role; indeed, one's test performance could be considered an application of intelligence to a particular situation. But much more than intelligence is involved. One's test score depends also on such factors as motivation (how diligently one studies), prior education (number of previous history courses), and many others.

Does the ability to learn decline with age?

The relationship between intelligence and competence is more clearly defined in theory than in practice. Many of the complaints about IQ tests, for example, concern themselves with this relationship. Some people say that IQ tests are biased against minority groups, whose competence on tests devised by the white Anglo-Saxon majority estimates not native mental ability but the degree of cultural isolation and deprivation. Others say that intelligence is assessed in unusual situations that have little to do with competence in the "real world." Outside the classroom problem-solving often has more to do with motivating a sales force than matching digits with symbols, more with enlisting the aid of a powerful ally than remembering the dates of famous wars (McClelland, 1973). A conservative view of these controversies suggests that caution is in order in interpreting IQ scores for subjects other than the young, white, middle-class students for whom the tests were created and in situations involving competencies other than the educational and vocational ones the tests were designed to predict (see also Schaie and Stone, 1982).

We should be cautious, therefore, also in interpreting research on the intellectual development of adults, especially in the later years of life. We are concerned with tracing the stability of adults' intelligence as it affects their ability to analyze environmental features that define their problems; to form effective plans that enable them to adapt to or to alter environments in ways that alleviate or solve their problems; and to learn from their successes and failures (Connolly and Bruner, 1973). There are a number of reasons to suspect that the competence of adults is not always highly related to their intelligence as estimated by traditional tests. One is that the tasks adults face are different from those of immature students. Children are typically engaged in the *acquisition* of knowledge, whereas adults spend more time in its *application* (Schaie, 1977/78). Adults need to be concerned with the consequences of their acts; life is not for them an intellectual exercise. In order to be successful, adults must be able to organize and integrate information, not simply parrot back the English equivalent of a Spanish verb. They have to sort out the important from the unimportant, the meaningful from the trivial (Labouvie-Vief, 1982; Labouvie-Vief and Blanchard-Fields, 1982).

Another problem with IQ tests and the study of adult intelligence is that these tests may measure different things in adults than in young people. For instance, consider items that require the test taker to do something as *quickly* as possible; the score might be the number of seconds it takes to arrange a series of pictures or the number of digits correctly paired with designated symbols in a given amount of time. Among young people, variations in speed of response on such items may well reflect differences in intellectual abilities, such as memory. Among old people, variations in speed of response are more likely to reflect other factors, such as cautiousness and the physical efficiency of the nervous system (Reinert, 1970). In other words, "speeded" test items may be a good way to estimate intellectual abilities in young people but a poor way in old people, who vary in response speed for more reasons than do young people. Similarly, since young people in our society are more accustomed to tests than older folk, differences in scores found when comparing young and old may be due in part to "test-taking abilities" that have little to do with intelligence (Schaie, 1978). An example of a test-taking ability is the knowledge that one should proceed as rapidly as possible, that it's better to go ahead and answer the questions one knows for sure than to sit and puzzle over those where one isn't certain of the correct answer. In speeded tests, with a limited time per item, this knowledge (which comes from experience) can mean several extra points on the final score.

Perhaps the biggest difference between young and old test takers is motivation. Young people are more interested in knowledge per se; they are curious, and any new bit of information may attract their fancy, no matter how irrelevant to their lives it may be (Schaie, 1977/78). Older people, especially those in the later years of life, are more likely to restrict their interest to knowledge that is useful, meaningful in their own lives. They may not work on a test item if it seems irrelevant: "If Airplane *A* takes off from Point *A* at 7:00 a.m. and Airplane *B* takes off from Point *B* at 8:00 a.m., . . . when and where would they collide?" Young people are interested in the "probable time of collision"; old people would just as soon fly off in a different direction and avoid the crash altogether.

In an early demonstration of the effects of meaningfulness on IQ test scores, two psychologists (Demming and Pressey, 1957) created an "IQ test" with problems designed to be meaningful to the older adult. Their test had no hypothetical pilots flying toward each other on a collision course; instead the characters in their test faced difficulties with the use of the yellow pages of a telephone directory, with legal terms in common contracts, and with the need for help from other people (how to get someone to help with housework or income tax). Older people did better on this "revised IQ test" than younger people, in contrast to the typical result, where young people do better on "their" tests than the older subjects.

ADULT STAGES OF INTELLECTUAL DEVELOPMENT

We are trying to understand the nature of intelligence in adults. We want to know how it is similar to the intelligence of young persons and how it changes. If we are going to construct IQ tests that are fair to older people, we must know more about *wisdom;* we want to know in what sense people become smarter as they grow older.

The famous Swiss psychologist Jean Piaget has described the ways in which children become smarter as they grow older (Flavell, 1963). Infants are said to be at a relatively primitive, sensory-motor stage of intellectual development, learning simple but basic ways of perceiving and reacting to the world. With the onset of speech, children enter a stage in which they grow primarily in the "conceptual-symbolic rather than purely sensory-motor arena" (Flavell, 1963, p. 121). This stage, called preoperational, is succeeded around the age of six by the stage of concrete operations. Operations, in Piaget's theory, are mental routines that transform information in some way — for example, adding two numbers to get a third, or categorizing, as in placing all red objects together. The stage of formal operations is entered around the age of twelve or so and is defined by the ability to use mental operations in abstract material. For example, an adolescent can solve a problem like "If a suitcase can eat four rocks in one day, how many can it eat in two days?" Younger children cannot imagine a suitcase that eats rocks, so they will refuse to solve the problem; they cannot disregard the content of the problems (its concrete aspects) and reason in a purely hypothetical way (using the form, or formal aspects, of the problem).

Intellectual development is not complete at the age of twelve, when the average child enters the stage of formal operations, but Piaget does not discuss later development in much detail. One can assume that there are advances in the use of formal operations, as people progress from "rock-eating suitcases" to elegant mathematical theories of the physical universe, but there are said to be no new Piagetian stages in adulthood (Flavell, 1970). Some psychologists who focus on adult development find this child-centered approach restrictive and wish to expand it, to delineate those changes in the quality of intellectual function they observe in adult subjects. As Erik Erikson and Daniel Levinson expanded the psychoanalytic stages of ego development to the adult years, these psychologists wish to do the same for Piaget's stages of intellectual development.

K. Warner Schaie (1977/78) has used research on adult intellectual development to formulate three or four adult stages* (see Figure 9–1). He begins with the observation that Piaget's childhood stages describe increasing efficiency in the *acquisition* of new information. It is doubtful that adults progress beyond the powerful methods of science (formal operations) in their quest for knowledge. Therefore, if one is to posit adult stages, they should not be further stages of acquisition; they should reflect different *uses* of intellect. For example, in young

---

*Other attempts to extend Piagetian theory into adulthood, too complex to present here, have been offered by Riegel (1975, 1977) and by Commons, Richards, and Kuhn (1982).

adulthood, people typically switch their focus from the acquisition to the application of knowledge, as they use what they know to pursue careers and families. This is called the *achieving* stage. It represents most prominently the application of intelligence in situations that have profound consequences for achieving long-term goals (such as those involving decisions about career and marriage). These situations are not the hypothetical ones posed on IQ tests or encountered in classroom studies, nor are they the problems of childhood whose solutions are closely monitored by parents and society; they are problems the *adult* must solve for him- or herself, and the solutions must be integrated into a life plan that extends far into the future. The kind of intelligence exhibited in such situations is similar to that manifested in scholastic tasks, except that it requires more careful attention to the possible consequences of the problem-solving process. Attending to the context of problem-solving as well as to the problem to be solved may be thought of as being a quality-control process like that used in industry when the consequences of a mistake are severe.

Young adults who have mastered the cognitive skills required for monitoring their own behavior and, as a consequence, have attained a certain degree of personal independence will next move into a stage that requires the application of cognitive skills in situations involving social responsibility. Typically the *responsible* stage occurs when a family is established and attention must be paid to the needs of spouse and offspring. Similar extensions of adult cognitive skills are

FIGURE 9-1.
Schaie's stages of adult cognitive development.

He likes this!
TesT?

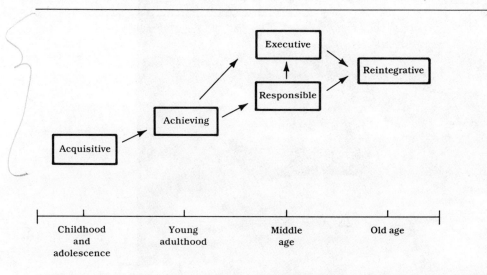

Source: From: Schaie, K. W. (1977/78). Toward a stage theory of adult cognitive development. *Journal of Aging and Human Development, 8,* 129–138. Copyright 1977 by Baywood Publishing Co., Inc. Reprinted by permission.

required as one's career develops and responsibilities for others are acquired on the job and in the community (Neugarten, 1969).

Many individuals' responsibilities become exceedingly complex. These individuals become presidents of business firms, deans of academic institutions, officials of churches, or take one of a number of other positions that are characterized by a need to understand how an *organization* works. Executives of organizations need to know the structure and the dynamic forces — who answers to whom, and for what purpose. They must monitor organizational activities not only on a temporal dimension (past, present, and future) but also up and down the hierarchy that defines the organization. They need to know not only the future plans of the organization but also whether or not policy decisions are being adequately translated into action at lower levels of responsibility. For example, the president of a major bank may decide that "a personal touch" will bring in more customers; he or she then needs to know if the bank tellers and loan officers are following instructions to call each customer by name. Attainment of the *executive* stage, of course, depends on exposure to opportunities that allow the development and practice of the relevant skills.

In the later years of life, beyond the age of sixty or sixty-five, the need to acquire knowledge declines even more; the necessity of monitoring decisions in terms of future consequences also decreases, because the future appears short

---

An executive must monitor the past, present, and future and also the activities up and down the hierarchy that define the organization.

and inconsequential; and executive monitoring is less important because frequently one has retired from the position that required such an application of intelligence. What, then, is the nature of competence in an elderly adult? As Schaie (1977/78) puts it, there is a transition from the childhood question ("What should I know?") through the adult question ("How should I use what I know?") to the question of later life ("Why should I know?"). This stage, *reintegration*, corresponds in its position in the life course to Erikson's stage of personality development, *ego integrity*. The information that elderly people acquire and the knowledge they apply is, to a greater extent than earlier in life, a function of their interests, attitudes, and values. It requires, in fact, the reintegration of all of these. The elderly are less likely to "waste time" on tasks that are meaningless to them. They are unlikely to expend much effort to solve a problem unless that problem is one they face frequently in their lives. They tend to be uninterested in abstract questions (for example, "Which is better, capitalism or communism?") unless the questions relate to their desire to make sense of their lives as a whole (for example, "What is the purpose of life?" or "What comes after death?").

Research on adult competencies requires new approaches to the assessment of intelligence. We need to know more, for example, about the situations in adult life in which intelligence is expressed. In one study, the investigators simply interviewed older individuals they encountered in parks, senior citizen centers, and the like (Scheidt and Schaie, 1978). The subjects were asked to indicate situations in which they had to use their intelligence. "Look for a new place to live" was one common response; "figure out how to pay a debt" was another. Over 300 such situations were collected. On the basis of the situations' attributes, four major dimensions were identified: social–nonsocial, active–passive, common–uncommon, and supportive–depriving. Examples of specific situations that contain each of the sixteen possible combinations of attributes are given in Table 9–1. The dimensions identified in the Scheidt and Schaie study were used to study age differences in perceived competence in a group of 234 persons ranging in age from the thirties to the eighties (Schaie, Gonda, and Quayhagen, 1981; Willis and Schaie, 1985b). The study revealed that older people described themselves as being more competent in situations of common occurrence and those that involved social interactions. Perceived competence declined for situations that involved an active response or had depriving consequences. As a corollary, we may infer that older people feel less competent in nonsocial and uncommon situations and more competent in those that have supportive attributes.

Assessment of Intellectual Functions

As we stated in the section on personality assessment, psychological tests were first developed to identify intelligent people. Francis Galton (a half-cousin of Charles Darwin) believed that human intelligence is mostly inherited and, as a result, he urged his country (England) to begin a program of selective breeding. By allowing the most intelligent people to have the most babies, the English race

TABLE 9-1.

Attributes and illustrative content of sixteen classes of situations

Situational attributes	Social	Nonsocial
High activity		
Common–supportive	Arguing with person about important point.	Gardening in yard, planting seeds, weeding.
	Being visited by son or daughter and their children.	Doing weekly shopping in crowded supermarket.
Common–depriving	Pressured by salesperson to buy merchandise.	Climbing several steps to building entrance.
	Quarreling with relative.	Cleaning apartment or household.
Uncommon–supportive	Having sexual intercourse.	Preparing large meal for friends.
	Traveling around city looking for new residence.	Exercising for a few moments each day.
Uncommon–depriving	Waiting at end of long line for tickets to entertainment.	Moving into new and unfamiliar residence.
	Returning faulty or defective merchandise to store.	Driving auto during rush-hour traffic.
Low activity		
Common–supportive	Seeking aid/advice from friend or family member.	Browsing through family photo album.
	Offering money to son or daughter who needs it.	Making plans for future.
Common–depriving	Hearing from friend that he/she is considering suicide.	Eating meal alone in own home.
	Hearing that close friend has recently died.	Worrying about ability to pay a debt.
Uncommon–supportive	Entering darkened nightclub to take dinner.	Recording day's events in diary.
	Attending art exhibit.	Wading in waist-high water in ocean.
Uncommon–depriving	Opening door to stranger selling product or soliciting opinion.	Slipping on slick part of floor and falling.
	While talkinig with someone, you feel you have unintentionally hurt their feelings.	Discovering you locked keys in car while shopping.

Source: From Scheidt, R. J., and Schaie, K. W. (1978). A taxonomy of situations for the elderly population: Generating situational criteria. *Journal of Gerontology, 33,* 848–857. Reproduced by permission.

would get smarter and smarter, claimed Galton; it would evolve to even greater heights in Darwin's phylogenetic tree.

A TEST OF INTELLIGENCE

But how could the most intelligent people be identified? A test of intelligence must be created. Galton took on the job and in 1883 published the first intelligence test (Galton, 1883). Influenced by British philosophers who considered intelligence to be based on the ability to process sensory information, Galton devised a series of tasks designed to measure how well a person could see and hear and smell and taste and feel. For example, in one task the person was asked to lift two weights and say which was the heavier.

Galton's "mental test" (as he called it) was a dismal failure, showing only trivial correlations with measures of intellectual competence in the real world, such as scholastic performance (Wissler, 1901). Almost twenty years later, a French psychologist by the name of Alfred Binet tried again to construct a test of intelligence. Binet was not out to better the French genetic stock. He had been given a very practical problem to solve by the French Ministry of Public Instruction: they needed a test to distinguish students of low ability (mentally retarded) from those of adequate ability but low motivation.

Binet held a more traditional view of intelligence than Galton, believing that playing chess was a better indicator of it than smelling vinegar. He set out to assess "reasoning, judgment, and imagination" by a series of "cognitive" rather than "sensory" tasks. Instead of lifting weights, for example, the child was asked to tell the difference between the words "yesterday" and "tomorrow." Since Binet's miniature tasks were quite similar to those the children faced in school, scores on his test were highly correlated with scholastic performance. First published in 1905 (in collaboration with Theodore Simon), Binet's tests were quickly translated into other languages, including English. In the United States, Binet's test was translated and revised by Stanford psychologist Lewis Terman in 1916 and is still in common use today as the Stanford–Binet Intelligence Scale.

Terman's first revision introduced the concept of *intelligence quotient*, or IQ. Binet had arranged the tasks (or items) of his test into age scales, each consisting of four to eight items, which children of a certain age should be able to pass. A six-year-old child who passed all the items for seven-year-olds (but no more) would have been said to have a "mental age" of seven, even though his or her real or chronological age was six. Terman simply divided the mental age by the chronological age to get the child's IQ. In our example, the child with a mental age of seven and a chronological age of six has an IQ of $7/6 = 1.17$, multiplied by 100 to clear the decimal, or 117. An *average* IQ by these standards is obviously 100, and 117 indicates a somewhat brighter than average youngster. Since 1960, Terman's method of computing IQ has been changed to more sophisticated statistical techniques, so IQ, properly speaking, is a bit of a misnomer. But even with the new statistics, 100 is set as the average for an age group; higher numbers indicate greater intelligence, and lower numbers lower intelligence than that of the average person of one's age. The term IQ lingers on, perhaps as a tribute to Binet, Terman, and the other psychologists who worked so hard to develop psychology's most successful test.

This short history of intelligence testing is relevant for our discussion of adult intelligence for at least two reasons. The first is to show that the testing movement in psychology had its beginnings in very practical circumstances — the need to predict potential scholastic success. The intelligence test (Binet's) on which all later tests are at least partially based was designed to forecast the school performance of young children (and not, in contrast, the life's performance of old people). Second is a reminder that IQ tests are age graded, that is, the average score for each age level is given the score of 100. A question such as "Who has the higher IQ, an average ten-year-old or an average seventy-year-old?" is meaningless. They both have IQs of 100, the average for any age group.

THE NATURE OF INTELLIGENCE

In the beginning, Binet found himself "in the position of the hunter going into the woods to find an animal no one has ever seen. Everyone is sure the beast exists, for he has been raiding the poultry coops, but no one can describe him" (Cronbach, 1970, p. 200). There was a great deal of debate about how many "animals" were involved. Is intelligence a single, general ability, or are there several different intellectual abilities? Binet favored the idea of a "general ability" (sometimes called the "g" factor), but others who came later into the hunt favored the notion of several factors in intelligence.

Some intelligence tests have several subtests defined by different content. The Wechsler Adult Intelligence Scale (WAIS), the test most frequently used by clinical psychologists for the individual assessment of adult intelligence, has eleven subtests (see Table 9–2). Six of these subtests are called "verbal" because they rely heavily on language. Examples are the vocabulary subtest, in which the subject is asked the meanings of various words, and the comprehension subtest, which is designed to measure practical judgment and common sense with items such as proverbs the subject is asked to explain. Five of the subtests are called "performance" tests because the subject can solve the problems without recourse to language. In the block design subtest, for example, the subject tries to reproduce a visual design with colored blocks. Performance tests were first used in World War I to test illiterate draftees (Garrett, 1957) and have also been useful in testing subjects whose native tongue is not English. As we shall see, old people generally do not do as well on the performance subtests.

The fact that we can construct slightly different subtests on an intelligence test is of course no guarantee that these subtests are measuring different intellectual abilities; they may simply be different ways of measuring the one ability, "general intelligence." Further exploration may take the form of *factor analysis*, a statistical procedure that identifies the basic dimensions or factors in a set of data. For example, if we knew nothing but the distances between each pair of a dozen

TABLE 9–2.

The subtests of the Wechsler Adult Intelligence Scale.

we peaked
) ATE !

Peaks
AS

Don't have to know this.

Verbal Scale

1. *Information:* 29 questions covering a wide variety of information that adults have presumably had an opportunity to acquire in our culture. An effort was made to avoid specialized or academic knowledge.

2. *Comprehension:* 14 items, in each of which the examinee explains what should be done under certain circumstances, why certain practices are followed, the meaning of proverbs, etc. Designed to measure practical judgment and common sense.

3. *Arithmetic:* 14 problems similar to those encountered in elementary school arithmetic. Each problem is orally presented and is to be solved without the use of paper and pencil.

4. *Similarities:* 13 items requiring the subject to say in what way two things are alike.

5. *Digit Span:* Orally presented lists of 3 to 9 digits to be orally reproduced. In the second part, the examinee must reproduce lists of 2 to 8 digits backwards.

6. *Vocabulary:* 40 words of increasing difficulty presented both orally and visually. The examinee is asked what each word means.

Performance Scale

7. *Digit Symbol:* A version of the familiar code-substitution test which has often been included in nonlanguage intelligence scales. The key contains 9 symbols paired with the 9 digits. With this key before him, the examinee has 1½ minutes to fill in as many symbols as he can under the numbers on the answer sheet.

8. *Picture Completion:* 21 cards, each containing a picture from which some part is missing. Examinee must tell what is missing from each picture.

9. *Block Design:* A set of cards containing designs in red and white and a set of identical 1-inch blocks whose sides are painted red, white, and red-and-white. The examinee is shown one design at a time, which he must reproduce by choosing and assembling the proper blocks.

10. *Picture Arrangement:* Each item consists of a set of cards containing pictures to be rearranged in the proper sequence so as to tell a story.

11. *Object Assembly:* In each of the four parts of this subtest, cutouts are to be assembled to make a flat picture of a familiar object.

Source: Reprinted with permission of Macmillan Publishing Company, from *Psychological testing*. 4th ed., by Anne Anastasi. Copyright © 1976 by Macmillan Publishing Company.

American cities, factor analysis would provide us with two dimensions — north/south and east/west, we could call them — that will enable us to describe the location of any of our cities. In a similar fashion, we can use degrees of relatedness (correlations) between each pair of a set of intellectual tasks (like the subtests of WAIS), and factor analysis will tell us if intelligence is one-dimensional or a many-splendored thing.

The answer is both. In a factor analysis of the WAIS subtests, for example, the major dimension was general intelligence, a mammoth factor that accounted for about half the job of description (Cohen, 1957). Three other, much weaker factors were also identified and labeled "verbal comprehension," "perceptual organization," and "memory." The labels are unimportant for our purposes. What the analysis means is that the "country" of the WAIS can be described fairly well with a single dimension, just as one can locate rather precisely most of the cities in Chile with the single dimension of north/south. Three other factors appear to be important for some purposes. An individual high in perceptual/organizational abilities, for example, might do better on certain subjects such as block design than we would expect from his or her general intelligence alone.

One finding of interest to us in this study was the fact that the memory factor, a relatively weak factor among young subjects, became a major factor among older subjects, over the age of sixty. This probably means that specific memory abilities vary more among older people and affect scores on more of the subtests. Vocabulary scores, for example, are for young people largely a function of how much they've learned, but in older adults, more a function of how much they can recall.

If one's goal is to map the "country" of intelligence and not simply that of the WAIS, a wide variety of intellectual tasks should be administered to a large number of people. Factor analysis of a wide variety of intellectual tasks has regularly turned up between six and a dozen major factors, the most prominent of which are listed in Table 9–3 (Thurstone and Thurstone, 1941). The "purest" tests of these factors are sometimes administered as tests of the "primary mental abilities." The most recent adult version of these tests is called the Schaie–Thurstone Adult Mental Abilities Test (STAMAT) (Schaie, 1985).

But what is the nature of the relationship between such elementary "building blocks" of intelligence and the tasks people face in real life? To find out, Willis and Schaie (1985a) administered tests on seven primary abilities to a group of eighty-seven older persons. The group's performance was also assessed on real-life tasks such as interpreting medicine bottle labels, reading street maps, filling out forms, and comprehending newspaper and yellow page advertisements (Educational Testing Service, 1977). The researchers found a substantial correlation between abilities and performance on tasks; correlations varied, however, depending on the task. Furthermore, it was found that composite performance on the real-life tasks could be predicted by several abilities, particularly reasoning, but also by verbal knowledge to a lesser extent.

Another study examined the relationship of the primary abilities to the situational dimensions involved in competent behavior described earlier in this chapter (see p. 285) (Willis and Schaie, 1985b). It was found that competence in social situations was predicted by spatial ability, competence in active situations was predicted by both spatial ability and inductive reasoning, and competence in passive situations was predicted by verbal ability. This also suggests a strong relationship between "building blocks" of intelligence and abilities on real-life tasks.

We have come, then, from the view of intelligence as primarily a single trait to the view of intelligence as really several distinct abilities. One group of psycholo-

TABLE 9–3.

The most common intellectual factors discovered in studies using factor analysis.

V. **Verbal comprehension:** The principal factor in such tests as reading comprehension, verbal analogies, disarranged sentences, verbal reasoning, and proverb matching. It is most adequately measured by vocabulary tests.

W. **Word fluency:** Found in such tests as anagrams, rhyming, or naming words in a given category (e.g., boys' names, words beginning with the letter T).

N. **Number:** Most closely identified with speed and accuracy of simple arithmetic computation.

S. **Space (or spatial orientation):** May represent two distinct factors, one covering perception of fixed spatial or geometric relations, the other manipulatory visualizations, in which changed positions or transformations must be visualized.

M. **Associative memory:** Found principally in tests demanding rote memory for paired associates. There is some evidence to suggest that this factor may reflect the extent to which memory crutches are utilized. The evidence is against the presence of a broader factor through all memory tests. Other restricted memory factors, such as memory for temporal sequences and for spatial position, have been suggested by some investigations.

P. **Perceptual speed:** Quick and accurate grasping of visual details, similarities, and differences.

I. **Induction (or general reasoning):** Early researchers proposed an inductive and a
(or R). deductive factor. The latter was best measured by tests of syllogistic reasoning and the former by tests requiring the subject to find a rule, as in a number series completion test. Evidence for the deductive factor, however, was much weaker than for the inductive. Moreover, other investigators suggested a general reasoning factor, best measured by arithmetic reasoning tests.

Source: Reprinted with permission of Macmillan Publishing Company, from *Psychological testing*, 4th ed., by Anne Anastasi. Copyright © 1976 by Macmillan Publishing Company.

gists has gone even farther, combining logical and statistical analyses to come up with 120 factors in intelligence (Guilford, 1967; Guilford and Hoepfner, 1971). Obviously the issue of how many beasts are raiding the poultry coops is not yet decided. Part of the issue is how detailed a description you want: one farmer might be content with "fox" as a description of the predator(s), whereas another says, "Yes, but one has a limp, another has patches of grey, and there's a third, too, with a funny wheeze." First farmer: "They're all foxes to me." In a similar fashion, we can identify several distinct factors in intelligence, but they tend to be related and can therefore be identified as members of the same "family." However, the distinctions are vital for the study of intellectual development in adults, as we shall see.

An attempt has been made to develop a comprehensive model of intelligence that explains the basic components of intelligence, the processes by which they are established and maintained, and their relationship to everyday competence. This theory, developed by Sternberg (1984), contains three subtheories: a componential subtheory that relates intelligence to the individual's inner world, a contextual subtheory that relates intelligence to the external world, and a third subtheory that relates intelligence to both the internal and external facets.

The componential theory specifies the mechanisms responsible for the learning, planning, execution, and evaluation of intellectual behavior, including the manner in which new information is acquired and selectively compared to old information.

The second subtheory follows from Sternberg's suggestion that the normal course of intelligent functioning in the everyday world involves adaptation to the environment. If an environment fails to fit a person's values, skills, or concerns, the person may attempt to alter the environment to meet his or her needs or to find a new environment that meets them better. Thus contextual theory considers intelligent behavior in terms of the selection of real-world environments relevant to a person's life and how the person shapes and adapts to these environments.

The third subtheory, which relates the inner and outer world to each other, states that intelligent behaviors involve adaptation to novelty, automatization of information processing activities (that is, performing information processing without conscious awareness of it), or both. A person who automatizes processing efficiently can allocate resources to coping with novel situations; conversely, efficient adaptation to novelty will allow automatization to occur earlier in one's experience of new tasks and situations. The notion of allocation of intellectual resources is particularly relevant to the study of intellectual aging. As we shall see, recent data and thinking suggest that the response of older persons to tests is far more selective than that of youngsters, and such allocation is often directed to optimize functions that meet the individual's needs and goals (Baltes, Dittmann-Kohli, and Dixon, 1985).

RELEVANCE OF TEST INSTRUMENTS TO STAGES OF INTELLECTUAL DEVELOPMENT

The simple tasks found in the traditional IQ tests are well suited to measure progress in the performance of many basic skills through the stages of knowledge acquisition described by Piaget (Humphreys and Parsons, 1979). But they are decidedly less adequate for the assessment of adult competence. Even a test that was constructed explicitly for adults, the well-known Wechsler Adult Intelligence Scale (WAIS), described earlier in this chapter, is deficient in several respects. The test was first of all designed with the intent of measuring cognitive dysfunctions in clinically suspect individuals, and second, it was normed on young adult samples, those who in our conceptual scheme would be classified as being in the achieving stage. What we need, therefore, is to construct *adult* tests of intelligence relevant to competence at different points in the life span, just as the traditional test is relevant to the competencies of children in school settings. In the achieving stage, for example, we should expect an increase in the ability to solve *relevant* problems, an ability that should remain high throughout the adult years. In the executive stage, when integration of information from several sources becomes more important, we should expect gains in tasks involving pattern recognition, inductive thinking, and complex problem-solving — fundamental strategies of information processing that might be assessed in ways suggested by cognitive psychologists (for example, Pellegrino and Glaser, 1979; Sternberg, 1982). In the reintegrative stage, we can expect relevancy to become even more important and, thus, a sharp decrease in scores on tests that assess simple information-processing capabilities: When we say to an old man or woman, "Repeat these nine digits backward," he or she may respond, "What on earth for?"

Research on "age-fair" IQ tests has just begun. The development of such tests will require the time and energy of many psychologists over many years; it is a task no less demanding than the original development of IQ tests for school-children.

Intelligence and Age

What happens to intelligence with age? This is the key question in this chapter, although our previous discussions should alert you to the fact that the answers are many, complex, and controversial. Some say intelligence enters a process of irreversible decline in the adult years, because the brain becomes less and less efficient, just as the heart and lungs and other physical organs do. Some say intelligence is relatively stable through the adult years, with the brain providing more than enough capacity for anything we would want to contemplate until serious disease sets in late in life. Some say intelligence declines in some respects (in mental quickness, for example) and increases in others (in knowledge about life, for example).

EARLY CROSS-SECTIONAL STUDIES

If we were to administer a typical IQ test like the WAIS to various groups representative of people their age, we would find that each group has an average IQ of 100. By definition, the average IQ for any age group is 100. This automatic adjustment disguises the fact that a twenty-year-old must earn a higher raw (unadjusted) score to be assigned an IQ of 100 than a fifty-year-old. On one test, a raw score of 80 placed a fifty-year-old slightly above average for his age group — 101 — but a twenty-year-old with the same score would be decidedly below average, with an IQ of 87 (Garrett, 1957). If we compared raw scores across age groups, we would find that the average score was highest in the young adult groups and systematically declined with age. Figure 9–2 depicts an early study of this sort.

The interpretation of these early cross-sectional studies was straightforward and unsuspecting: an individual's intellectual abilities gradually but inexorably decline over the adult years. David Wechsler, creator of the WAIS, believed that the "decline of mental ability with age is part of the general senescent process of the organism as a whole" (Wechsler, 1972, p. 30). In other words, Wechsler believed that mental ability deteriorated in ways similar to the decline of lung capacity, reproductive function, and other physical abilities.

It was soon apparent, however, even from cross-sectional studies, that intellectual decline was not as pronounced in some tasks as in others. Researchers noted that certain subtests on tests such as the WAIS showed less decline than others (Siegler, 1983). Wechsler (1972) began calling these the "hold" subtests, in contrast to the "don't hold" subtests that showed a greater decline. In general, the subtests that "hold" (older adults do about as well as younger) are the verbal subtests, whereas the performance subtests "don't hold" (see Figure 9–3).

New results call for new interpretations. Why should some tasks show practically no decline, whereas others show the older subjects doing much more poorly than the younger subjects? One might point out that the subtests in which

FIGURE 9–2.

This early cross-sectional study would lead us to believe that intelligence test scores decline with age; but read on.

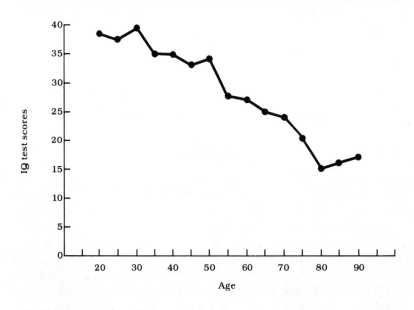

FIGURE 9–3.

Comparative age differences of verbal and performance subtests on the WAIS with age.

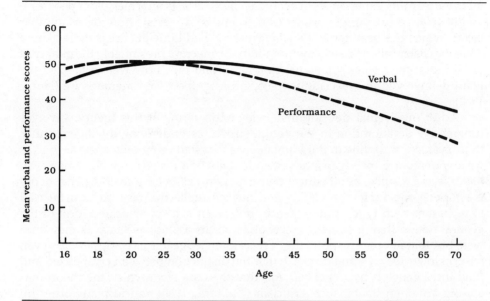

Source: Adapted from Wechsler, D. (1958). *The measurement and appraisal of adult intelligence,* 4th ed. Baltimore, MD: Williams & Wilkins, Co., p. 28. Copyright © 1958 Dr. David Wechsler.

older people do poorly are all "speeded" tests; the scores reflect the time it takes for the subject to solve the problem or it reflects the number of responses in a given time interval. Perhaps older people are just slower, but not dumber. This hypothesis has been partially discredited by research in which the subjects were given *unlimited* time to solve problems and only the number correct was counted (Botwinick, 1978). Older people still do less well on "don't hold" tasks, relative to younger subjects. But, of course, this type of research changes the "problem" considerably, from "How long does it take you to solve it? to "Can you solve it at all?" It is perhaps instructive to see that the slower average speed of solution among older subjects is contributed largely by those who fail to solve the problem at all.

CRYSTALLIZED AND FLUID INTELLIGENCE

One of the most prominent theories of "hold" and "don't hold" tests was formulated by Raymond Cattell and elaborated by John Horn. In factor analyses of cross-sectional studies of several intellectual tasks (not from the WAIS), Cattell and Horn repeatedly discovered that the tests on which older adults do well compared to younger adults show up as a factor they call *crystallized intelligence*. As represented by tests of general information and vocabulary, crystallized intelligence is said to reflect the mental abilities that depend on experience with the world — on education in the broad sense, including both formal schooling and informal learning experiences in everyday life. The tests on which older people do poorly relative to younger adults (the "don't hold" tests) show up as another factor, which has been termed *fluid intelligence*. Fluid intelligence is more akin to what Wechsler called "native mental ability," reflecting presumably the quality of one's brain: how quickly a signal can get in and out, how well organized the neurons involved in associations, pattern recognition, and memory are (Horn, 1982).

Adult intellectual development, viewed in terms of this theory, involves progressive deterioration in the neural structures underlying intelligence and, thus, systematic decline in fluid intelligence. Crystallized intelligence, as long as we do not require speedy responses, should not be affected as much; it may even increase as a result of adult educational experiences. (See Figure 9–4.) The theory is a popular one, for it more clearly specifies the intellectual tasks that can be used to represent each type of intelligence. Indeed, it is a sophisticated form of the general notion that in some respects older adults are not as sharp as they once were but that in other respects they are as knowledgeable as ever, perhaps even wiser. However, we should realize that the distinction between crystallized and fluid intelligence is hypothetical, and that the data from which the theory has sprung are open to statistical criticism (Guilford, 1980) and to many other interpretations (Labouvie-Vief and Chandler, 1978). We consider some of these alternative interpretations later in this chapter.

LONGITUDINAL STUDIES

Widespread use of intelligence tests among college freshmen began in the United States about 1920. By 1950, therefore, it was possible to find a sizable group of fifty-year-olds who had taken an IQ test some thirty years previously. Several psychologists, seeing their chance to run a relatively inexpensive longitudinal study, seized the opportunity by retesting these middle-aged subjects. No one expected results different from those found in cross-sectional studies, which showed a marked decrease in IQ scores after the age of twenty-five or thirty. Thus it came as a bit of a shock to find that not only did the longitudinal studies show no decline in IQ, they showed an increase! The average person got smarter and smarter with age, at least up to age fifty (Owens, 1966). Later followups showed that these subjects maintained their intellectual abilities into their sixties (Cunningham and Owens, 1983).

Most of the first longitudinal studies tested highly educated people (college graduates) whose professional careers required continuing use of academic skills — mathematics, extensive reading, and formal reasoning. Later studies of people at all levels of intelligence and education, in all walks of life, showed the

FIGURE 9–4.

Performances of various age groups on tests used to define fluid, crystallized, and general intelligence.

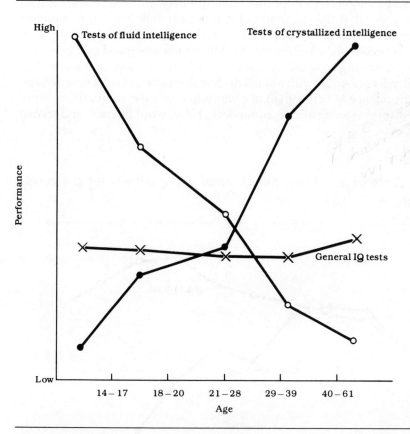

Source: From Horn, J. L. Organization of data on life-span development of human abilities. In L. R. Goulet and P. B. Baltes (Eds.), *Life-span developmental psychology: Research and theory.* New York: Academic Press, 1970, p. 463.

increase in IQ scores to be characteristic only of the highly educated population. But the absence of decline was replicated again and again.

In one large-scale study, features of both cross-sectional and longitudinal designs were combined (Schaie, 1979b, 1983b; Schaie and Hertzog, 1985b). First, in 1956, people ranging in age from twenty-two to seventy were tested — a cross-sectional study. Then, in 1963, as many of these same people as could be found and convinced to participate were retested. This process was repeated a third time in 1970, and a fourth time in 1977. Thus the researchers had four cross-sectional studies in addition to longitudinal data covering a period of twenty-one years.

The cross-sectional studies showed the typical pattern of intellectual decline in the adult years; the longitudinal data told a quite different story. Consider, for example, "verbal meaning," one of the "primary mental abilities" assessed by the investigators — the ability to understand ideas expressed in words. Figure 9–5 is the most dramatic way to represent the difference between cross-sectional data and an estimate of what the longitudinal data would look like if the youngest group of subjects were followed for the rest of their lives (Schaie and Strother, 1968). The cross-sectional data show a peak at thirty-five, followed by a relatively sharp decline. In striking contrast, the longitudinal data suggest increases in this ability until fifty-five or sixty, with a small decline thereafter; even at seventy, the estimated performance is better than at twenty-five. Similar comparisons were made with tests of reasoning ability, numerical ability, word fluency, and spatial visualization.

FIGURE 9–5.

Comparable cross-sectional and longitudinal age gradients for the verbal meaning test.

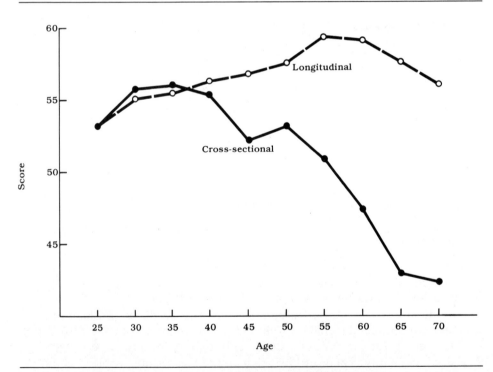

Source: From Schaie, K. W., and Strother, C. R. (1968). A cross-sequential study of age changes in cognitive behavior. *Psychological Bulletin, 70,* 671–680. Copyright 1968 by the American Psychological Association. Reprinted by permission of the publisher and author.

The data just described came from a single longitudinal study over the period from 1956 to 1963. More recently, longitudinal data for five mental abilities have been reported from the expanded investigation covering 1956 to 1977, a period of twenty-one years (Schaie, 1983). Representative findings, shown in Figure 9–6, suggest little if any decline in these abilities until the age of sixty; in several instances, increases are apparent during the adult years. Even after sixty, decline is slight until age seventy-four or eighty-one. *STOP HERE.*

COHORT DIFFERENCES

What accounts for the difference between the cross-sectional and longitudinal results, with the latter not only showing no decline over most of the adult years but also, in some cases, clear increases in intellectual abilities? Why do the longitudinal studies give us such a different picture from the earlier, cross-sectional investigations?

The answer is "cohort" differences — differences among generations. The reason longitudinal studies give different results from cross-sectional studies is that cross-sectional studies compare people of different ages *and* of different cohorts. The differences that have been attributed to age should, for the most part, be relegated to the differences in year of birth. Cross-sectional studies make it appear that intelligence declines steeply over the years, but much of this is an illusion. Longitudinal studies suggest instead that each generation is smarter than the one before.

Why is one cohort more advantaged in intelligence than another? Why is it that people born more recently earn higher averages in IQ tests than their parents or grandparents? Various answers suggest themselves. Over the last several generations in this country, education has improved and the average person gets more of it; among the members of the oldest cohorts, the majority may not have achieved a high school diploma and very few have had college experience. Nutrition has improved in the last seventy or eighty years, and so has medical care; the physical condition of the brains of the more recent cohorts may therefore be superior. The use of tests like those for IQ has burgeoned, and thus later generations may be better than earlier generations at performing well on such instruments.

Cohort differences in intelligence, moreover, are not uniform across different abilities. Figure 9–7 shows the change in cohort level in T-score units (.10 of a standard deviation) for ten cohorts born from 1889 to 1952. As can be seen there was substantial gain for successive cohorts until the one born in 1938 for Space and Reasoning; and until 1952 for Verbal Meaning. Number peaked in 1924 and then went down below the level of the oldest cohort. Word Fluency by contrast actually declined for successive cohorts, but has been gaining since 1938. These differential data suggest that older cohorts are at a particular disadvantage on the fluid abilities.

FIGURE 9–6.

The effect of age on five mental abilities in longitudinal studies. The mental abilities are described in more detail in Table 9–3.

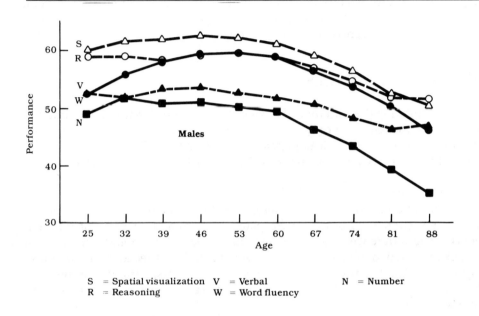

S = Spatial visualization V = Verbal   N = Number
R = Reasoning   W = Word fluency

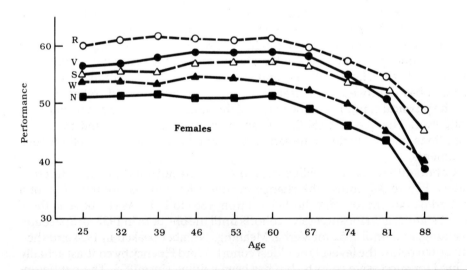

Source: From Schaie, K. W. The Seattle Longitudinal Study: A twenty-one year exploration of psychometric intelligence in adulthood. In K. W. Schaie (Ed.), *Longitudinal studies of adult psychological development*. New York: Guilford Press, 1983. Reprinted by permission.

FIGURE 9–7.

Cumulative cohort changes from oldest to youngest cohort for five mental abilities.

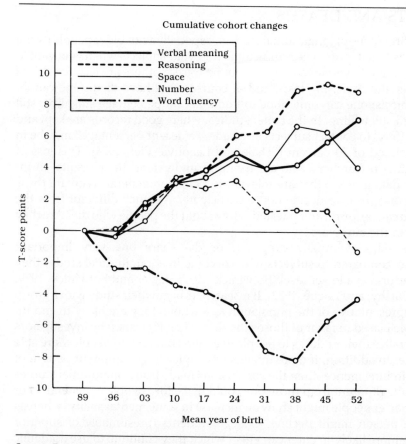

Cumulative cohort changes

Source: From Schaie, K. W. (1983). The Seattle Longitudinal Study: A twenty-one year exploration of psychometric intelligence in adulthood. In K. W. Schaie (Ed.), *Longitudinal studies of adult psychological development*. New York: Guilford Press. Reprinted by permission.

There is some evidence that the differences between generations have begun to run in favor of the earlier-born cohorts. Average test scores on the Scholastic Aptitude Test have been declining since 1962; before that, averages were stable or increasing (Advisory Panel, 1977). The decline has been blamed on many factors, but chief among them are poorer educational standards in our schools and "the passive pleasure, the thief of time" — television. For whatever reason, the youth of today are doing somewhat less well on IQ tests than their elders did at the same age, and this fact will eventually show itself on cross-sectional studies of intelligence. It will then appear that people get smarter as they grow older, a conclusion that will be no more justified than the one based on present cross-sectional studies, that people experience a significant decline in intelligence in the adult years.

DROPOUTS AND DEATHS

One of the difficulties of longitudinal studies, especially with older people over a long period, is that it is often very difficult to find your subjects when you want to retest them. Some have moved and cannot be traced; others are sick, or sick of psychologists and their silly tests; and of course some have died. One cannot retest all subjects; one can only hope to find a decent percentage still alive, still available, and still willing. In the better studies, where good records are kept and systematic efforts to contact subjects are made, "a decent percentage" may be in the neighborhood of 50 percent (Schaie and Labouvie-Vief, 1974). This loss of subjects haunts researchers who are trying to understand their results, to interpret their data in ways that are relevant to people in general. Who are these people who disappear or decide not to participate? Are they different from the subjects who can be found and retested? How about the people who die? Are they different from the survivors?

Subjects who eventually drop out or die share one very important characteristic: compared to subjects who continue in a longitudinal study, they generally perform at a lower level (Botwinick, 1977; Siegler and Botwinick, 1979; Siegler, McCarthy, and Logue, 1982). If researchers begin their study with a group of people representative of the population as a whole, they are likely to end up with a sample biased in favor of those who do well on IQ tests. The investigators cannot generalize their findings to people in general but only to people more able than average. In addition, if more intelligent people show a different pattern of age change in intelligence, then the conclusions made from longitudinal studies would be quite different from those one could make for "people in general." For example, smarter people might show an increase in some mental ability, whereas the average person might decline. College students (presumably of superior intellect) are more likely to enter careers in which they continue to use academic skills, such as abstract reasoning. They might thus maintain or increase their level of functioning on tests of this ability.

One way to determine the effects of dropouts is to compare the people you manage to retest with a more representative sample of the original population. In the large-scale longitudinal investigation we have been discussing, at each time of retesting a new sample of subjects was also tested (Schaie, Labouvie, and Barrett, 1973; Gribbin and Schaie, 1979). Data from these new samples can be viewed as an estimate of what the retested longitudinal group would have done, had they not lost several members due to geographical mobility, uncooperative attitudes, and the other reasons for dropping out. For example, one cohort had an average age of twenty-five in 1956; in 1963, their average age was thirty-two; in 1970, their average age was thirty-nine. These people were compared with a new sample of thirty-two-year-olds in 1963 and a new sample of thirty-nine-year-olds in 1970.

Cross-sectional studies compare people of different generations, who differ in many ways beyond those wrought by aging.

The results from the new samples lead to a not unexpected conclusion: the average scores on tests of intellectual abilities begin a decline somewhat earlier than shown in the longitudinal studies. Figure 9–8 shows comparative results for "verbal meaning" or vocabulary scores. In the longitudinal data, average scores increase until age sixty and then decrease *slightly*, such that even at age eighty-one the average score exceeds that at age twenty-five. In the "independent-sample" data, average scores decrease rather consistently throughout the adult years, although they do not decline to a "meaningfully lower level" until the age of seventy-four.

There are, of course, several ways to interpret these data. One is to say that the longitudinal studies are of little value since they end up with such a special sample, so unrepresentative of people in general (Horn and Donaldson, 1976). Another is to say that the longitudinal data are quite valuable, to show the developmental trends in intelligence among "special" people — the more gifted and more stable, the people who form the foundation of American society (Schaie, 1979a). Still a third point of view might suggest that the decline among people in general, however slight, is particularly misleading because the people added to the special people in the longitudinal samples are precisely those for whom the tests make least sense. Poor, moving from place to place to survive, they have little interest in arranging pictures in a logical sequence or in divining the meaning of the word "fulsome" (Bloom, 1981).

FIGURE 9–8.

Comparison of longitudinal data with independent samples, to assess the influence of subject dropouts.

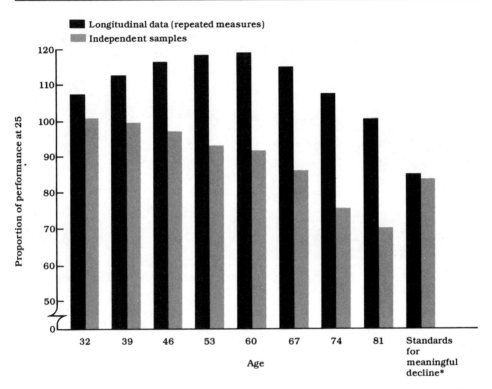

■ Longitudinal data (repeated measures)
▨ Independent samples

*These bars represent a decline to the 25th percentile of 25-year-olds. See section on "Magnitude of Change" for explanation.

Source: Adapted from Schaie, K. W., and Parr, J. (1981). Intelligence. In A. W. Chickering and Associates. *The modern American college*. San Francisco: Jossey-Bass.

MAGNITUDE OF CHANGE

As scientists we often get hung up in our concern to demonstrate the mere presence or absence of change. What we frequently ignore is the question of whether or not a difference "makes a difference," that is, is substantial enough to be important in the practical, everyday lives of the people we're discussing. One way to estimate the meaningfulness of change is to look for changes that drop an age group to the lower 25 percent of twenty-five-year-olds. In other words, suppose that 25 percent of these young people score 84 or less on an IQ test; 50 percent score 100 or less; 75 percent score 116 or less. The average score would be approximately 100. If a group of sixty-year-olds also averaged 100, essentially they would be at the same level as the twenty-five-year-olds; their average would fall at the 50 percent level of the younger group. However, if decline were such that the oldsters averaged eighty-four, their average would fall to the 25 percent level of the younger group. This magnitude of decline is what we will call "of social importance."

Table 9–4 gives the data relevant to this analysis. Note that in the longitudinal data, the average scores are often above 100, indicating *higher* averages than the twenty-five-year-old reference group, and often there are increases through middle age. There is some decline in old age for all measures, but it reaches our standard of importance in only three of seven cases. In two of those three cases, only at age eighty-one does the decline become sizable; in the third, the 25th percentile of youth is reached by age sixty-seven. In two cases, the eighty-one-year-olds are still performing at a higher level than the twenty-five-year-olds! Certainly the idea that people steadily lose their intellectual abilities after the age of twenty-five, dropping into near incompetence by the age of sixty or so, deserves to be called a myth.

The data from the independent samples paint a similar picture, although important decreases are apparent earlier than in the longitudinal data. Here we see averages reaching the 25 percent level as early as age fifty-three for two measures; two more reach that point at age sixty-seven, and two more at seventy-four; one never declines that much.

FREQUENCY OF DECLINE

In addition to knowing the age at which the average person declines, it is also important to know what proportion of people are likely to decline at a given age. Such knowledge is useful in at least two ways. First, it alerts us to the fact that there may be more stability than change in intellectual aging and that some persons may still grow even at an advanced age. Second, just as longevity tables permit life insurance companies to forecast the odds of someone dying, a knowledge of the proportion of those declining at a given age would permit us to determine the probability that intellectual changes will have important consequences. For example, such knowledge would permit us to determine the odds that an elderly president will show mental decline before completing his term in office. In a recent study, frequency distributions were prepared for several hundred subjects to determine how many had declined significantly over the seven-year age ranges from sixty to sixty-seven, sixty-seven to seventy-four, and seventy-four to eighty-one years (Schaie, 1984b). Although data were available for persons under age sixty, they were not examined because very few people of this age show a reliable decline. The researchers tested the five primary mental abilities: verbal meaning, reasoning ability, word fluency, numerical ability, and spatial visualization. The proportions of persons who declined, remained stable,

TABLE 9–4

Age changes compared to standards of meaningful decline.

Ability		32	39	46	53	60	67	74	81	Standards of meaningful decline[c]
Verbal meaning	R[a]	107	112	116	119	120	117	110	103	84
	I[b]	102	102	100	95	95	89	80	74	83
Spatial orientation	R	113	114	117	118	117	110	97	77	71
	I	98	90	89	82	81	68	58	55	71
Inductive reasoning	R	94	97	97	95	96	91	82	74	80
	I	97	90	84	76	72	64	58	53	79
Number	R	110	114	115	116	120	116	103	89	71
	I	116	119	121	115	115	106	98	85	74
Word fluency	R	100	96	95	89	86	74	63	52	83
	I	96	89	85	77	74	60	50	46	82
Intellectual ability	R	107	108	110	109	109	103	93	81	84
	I	103	99	97	90	88	79	70	63	84
Educational aptitude	R	107	112	116	117	118	115	108	101	85
	I	101	100	97	92	91	84	76	70	83

Note: Average score of twenty-five-year-olds is assigned the value of 100, and others are expressed as a percentage of that value. Thus scores above 100 represent increases from age twenty-five, and scores below 100 represent decreases.

[a]R = repeated measurement longitudinal panel.

[b]I = independent sample.

[c]These figures represent a decline to the 25th percentile of twenty-five-year-olds. See text for explanation.

Source: From K. W. Schaie and I. A. Parham. Cohort-sequential analyses of adult intellectual development, NAPS No. 03170, and K. W. Schaie. Age changes in intelligence. In R. L. Sprott, ed., *Age, learning ability, and intelligence.* New York: Van Nostrand Reinhold, 1980, p. 67. © by Litton Educational Publishing, Inc. Adapted by permission.

or significantly gained over the seven-year period are shown in Figure 9–9. Note that, although ability varied greatly in the various areas tested, on average no more than 25 percent of those studied had declined by age sixty-seven. By age seventy-four the decline had risen to about a third, and by eighty-one to more than 40 percent. What is more impressive, however, is the larger proportion of persons who remained stable and the presence of at least a few persons whose performance increased reliably on some ability even at an advanced age.

TERMINAL DROP

We know that people who are no longer living at the time of a longitudinal retesting, if we compare their first test scores to those of survivors, generally scored lower. There are many possible explanations for this fact. The subjects who

FIGURE 9–9.
Proportion of persons who decline, remain stable, or improve over a seven-year period.

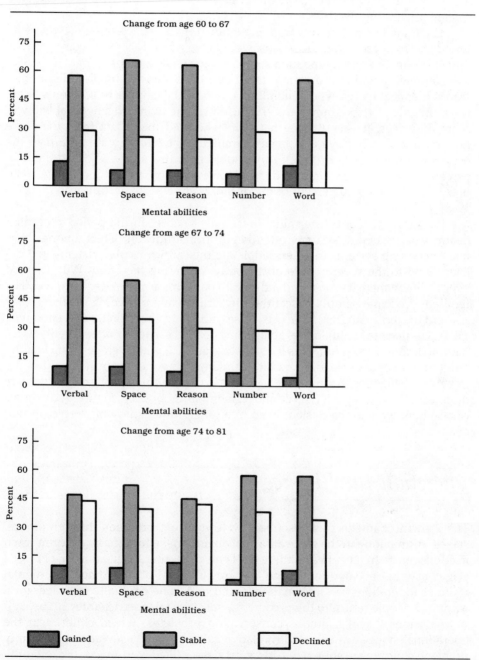

Source: Data are from the Seattle Longitudinal Study (see Schaie, 1979b, 1983c).

die before retesting may have been poor, unable to afford adequate medical care or nutrition, or they may have been ill (sometimes without knowing it) at the time of the first testing; all these and similar factors would predict lower than average scores. But there is another issue involved: Does a dramatic drop in intelligence foretell impending death?

The issue of *terminal drop* was first studied by R. W. Kleemeier (1962), who tested elderly men on four occasions over twelve years. Kleemeier compared the rate of decline for those who died soon after the testing to that for subjects who were still living and found a more rapid decline for those who died. In another study, identical twins, who generally are remarkably similar in IQ scores, were tested in old age (Jarvik and Bank, 1983). When one twin had a noticeably lower score, however, it was always that twin who died first. Data from the Duke Longitudinal Study have also been examined for evidence with regard to the occurrence of terminal drop. Of those subjects in this study who had died, 76 percent showed decline prior to death. However, most of this decline was relatively gradual; only 20 percent of the decliners showed an abrupt drop (Siegler, 1983).

If you think about it, terminal drop makes sense. In the period preceding death, various bodily systems often begin to malfunction. Chief among these malfunctioning systems in older people are the cardiovascular systems that deliver blood to the several parts of the body, including the brain. With its food supply diminished, it is no wonder the brain performs at a less adequate level. The terminal drop may simply reflect the physical decline preceding death.

But the terminal drop, if it exists, raises other questions (Baltes and Labouvie, 1973). The decline of intellectual abilities in later life, especially after seventy: Is it a natural decline with aging, or is it a statistical artifact, with averages from healthy and dying people misleading us into thinking everyone (even the healthy) declines in intelligence? As one review put it, "in the healthy older person, cognitive decline may be a myth" (Jarvik and Cohen, 1973, p. 228). Figure 9–10 shows clearly how we may be misled, even in a longitudinal study of people of high ability.

Piagetian Intelligence

The growth of intellect as described by Jean Piaget proceeds through several stages, culminating in the stage of formal operations, which many children reach in adolescence. In recent years there has been increasing speculation that Piaget's stages may be repeated in old age — in reverse! The ability to perform mental routines (operations) on information is said to decline gradually with age, until many old people return to the preoperational stage (also see Chapter 10, p. 350).

Consider Piaget's famous conservation problems, which children in the operational stages can solve with relative ease. In the conservation of quantity problem, children are shown two identical glasses filled with an identical quantity

FIGURE 9–10.

A hypothetical example showing how terminal drops can lead us to think there is a general decline in intelligence in late life. In the example, subjects maintain their ability until a few years before their deaths. If we happen to test our subjects while one or more are in the middle of a terminal drop, the average scores will be lower than previous years; healthy subjects, however, show no decline.

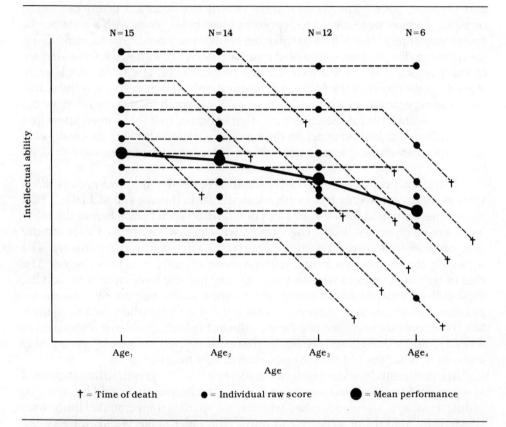

† = Time of death ● = Individual raw score ⬤ = Mean performance

Source: From Baltes, P. B., and Labouvie, G. V., (1973). Adult development of intellectual performance: Description, explanation and modification. In C. Eisdorfer and M. P. Lawton (Eds.), *The
psychology of adult development and aging*. Washington, D.C.: American Psychological Association, p.
174. Copyright 1973 by the American Psychological Association. Reprinted by permission of the
publisher and author.

of liquid. Before the child's eyes, the contents of one glass are poured into a third glass, which is taller and thinner than the others. Young children, under the age of seven or so, respond to the superficial features of their perceptual experience and are likely to say that the taller, thinner glass has *more* liquid, because the liquid rises to a higher level. They cannot mentally adjust the two dimensions (adults would say, "the increase in height is compensated for by the decrease in width"); they cannot perform the proper mental operation.

A number of rather startling studies have shown that old people also do poorly on these simple conservation problems (Papalia and Bielby, 1974). It is as if the basic cognitive abilities that are gained in youth are lost in old age. On the other hand, there is evidence that the mental abilities are not lost, but instead are for some reason not used. To illustrate, consider a study of women aged sixty-five to seventy-five who were tested on a "conservation of surface" task (Hornblum and Overton, 1976). The women were shown two identical green cardboard rectangles which were meant to represent grass fields, each with a little plastic cow in the center of the field; two small red barns were placed close together along the top edge. The women were asked if each of the two cows had the same amount of grass to eat. After they answered, the two barns on one of the fields were moved to other parts of the field, and the question was repeated. Then the whole task was repeated with six and ten barns. "Conservation" was defined as answers, on at least two of the three trials, that indicated that the women knew that moving the barns had no effect on the exposed surface. Although this may seem to you a supremely simple task, only twenty-six of the sixty women were successful.

Then, however, the women who failed were divided into two groups. Each woman was given twenty trials with a task similar to the one she had failed. Half the women were told if they were right or wrong on each trial, whereas the other half were given no feedback. The women with feedback improved very rapidly and, on later tests of conservation of surface, performed nearly perfectly. The women in the comparison group, without feedback, improved only slightly. The ease of training these old women suggests they had the basic *capacity* for solving these conservation problems but for some reason performed poorly. Among the possible reasons are lack of familiarity with the testing situation, lack of motivation (who cares about plastic cows and cardboard fields?), problems with vision or memory, and a misguided desire to please the experimenters by giving silly answers to what the old women perceive as silly questions.

In a similar study, older adults were presented with a green surface supposed to represent a meadow and a number of miniature houses that could be arranged in different ways. They were asked whether the spatial arrangement of the houses affected the amount of grass left to mow. The older subjects did not give the correct solution, which is that the spatial arrangement of the houses is insignificant. Instead, they noted that mowing would be harder and take more time if the houses were arranged such that there were many small spaces between the houses rather than a single large, open space. Time, energy, and the spatial arrangement of the surface were thus seen to be important variables, and these practical concerns influenced how the task was solved. Within these pragmatic parameters, however, the older subjects' thinking was perfectly coherent and logical (Newman-Hornblum, Attig, and Kramer, 1980).

Elderly subjects sometimes complain that they have difficulty with problem-solving tasks that require following experimenter-imposed rules that seem to the subjects to be oversimplified and unsatisfactory given the nature of the problem. When pressed by the experimenter to utilize the rules given, one elderly subject commented, "I know what you want me to do, but it just isn't true," revealing his consternation at being asked to simplify a task he knew to be far more complex than was represented by the experimenter's instructions (Sabatini and Labouvie-Vief, 1979).

It appears that the reasoning of older adults is more socially oriented than that of younger people — they regard decisions as occurring in a complex social context and take that context into account in attempting to make the best decisions. A study by Fengler (1976) illustrates the payoffs of such an approach. In his research on 150 members of the 1973–1974 Vermont legislature, he found that younger members produced twice as many bills as older legislators, but that the bills of the older members were twice as likely to be passed. Thus, in terms of quantity alone, the younger legislators were superior, but the older ones were superior in terms of effectiveness. The younger members took more risks and tended to take a trial-and-error approach, whereas the older members worked more cautiously and deliberately.

These older legislators presumably had to marshal a number of different resources to ensure that their bills passed. It has been suggested that the ability to integrate information from ambiguous or conflicting sources may actually increase throughout adulthood. Kuhn, Pennington, and Leadbeater (1983), in a study of the reasoning strategies of jurors age twenty-one to seventy-three, assessed reasoning in terms of the ability to evaluate various accounts of a crime. Jurors varied widely in their ability to base their inferences on more comprehensive data, to coordinate information, and to avoid basing their conclusions on isolated instances. Although this study did not report any correlations with age, Lougee and Packard (1981) have reported that older adults are commonly judged to be more competent evaluators of such social information.

Despite evidence that the elderly have superior effectiveness in some situations, the research also suggests that performance on certain intellectual functions, as measured by Piaget's tests, does decrease in old age. This has been variously attributed to inevitable neurological deterioration (Hooper, Fitzgerald, and Papaiia, 1971), social isolation (Looft, 1972), and superficial performance factors (Hornblum and Overton, 1976). These studies, however, are all cross-sectional; it seems likely, given the high correlation of Piagetian tasks with general tests of intelligence (Humphreys and Parsons, 1979), that much of this so-called cognitive regression will turn out to be generational differences, not age change. Those age changes which remain after controlling for the generational effects may still be attributable to factors other than inevitable neurological deterioration with age. The ease of training old people in these tasks suggests that the neurological structures necessary for the appropriate behavior still exist.

It may also be that a Piagetian conception of intelligence, however helpful it may be in understanding the development of thinking in children and adolescents, is simply inappropriate when applied to adults. Older people may have different concerns than younger people, and as a result they may use their intelligence differently. If this is the case, then it would be improper to use the early Piagetian tasks in assessing adult intelligence.

Certain researchers do in fact believe that adult thinking differs qualitatively in significant respects from that of younger people. Piaget himself thought that adolescents may tend to a belief in the "omnipotence of reflection." "With the advent of formal intelligence," he stated, "thinking takes wings and it is not surprising that at first this unexpected power is both used and abused. . . . [It is as if the adolescent believes] the world should submit itself to idealistic schemes rather than to systems of reality" (1967, pp. 63–64). That is, adolescents tend to place excessive faith in the "egocentric" systems of pure abstraction they have formulated themselves. They are unwilling to submit their abstract constructs to the tests of the "real world," preferring an internally consistent but inaccurate intellectual perspective on the world to one that is frustratingly vague or incomplete but more closely corresponds to reality.

To put it another way, the adolescent wants to be sure. The adult, on the other hand, is more comfortable dealing with a world that is often ambiguous. Perry, in his study of college students' adjustment to the complexity of university life, found that youth search for a single perspective on truth and are profoundly confused and troubled by the fact that no *one* correct view is apparent, whether in academic matters or in personal decisions. The role of authority, in their minds, is to offer "correct" interpretations; as a result, they become highly dependent on authority because it removes ambiguity. Their failure to realize that the thinker must ultimately accept responsibility for his or her own thought — with no guarantees of certainty — creates a kind of obsession with finding safe techniques to unveil truth (Perry, 1968). The mature adult, on the other hand, perceives tasks as inherently open-ended and ambiguous. A number of authors have noted that the ability to work creatively with ambiguity is a hallmark of mature thinking (Basseches, 1980; Labouvie-Vief and Blanchard-Fields, 1982; Arlin, 1983).

Health, Lifestyle, and "Natural" Development

One of the thorniest problems in the study of old age is the separation of the "natural" aging process from the effects of disease. On the one hand, we would like to know, to use an example from our current concern, what happens to the intellect in a body that lives its full life free from disease and then expires, like the one-hoss shay, at its appointed time. On the other hand, such a desire is unrealistic, since part of the "natural" aging process seems to involve an increasing susceptibility to disease, so that a completely healthy ninety-year-old is just as unusual as a ten-year-old invalid. Nevertheless, disease is a hit-and-miss affair, affecting some old people primarily in their physical functions (as in arthritis) and others primarily in their mental functions (as in the ailments we commonly group as "senility"). Recognizing then that disease becomes more and more likely as one grows older, we want to know the specific effects of specific diseases on the intellectual functioning of older people.

Some diseases affect intellectual behavior directly, by damaging the brain. Others affect intelligence indirectly, by making it more difficult to perform in an intelligent manner. The distractions of pain and economic worries that accompany illness in the later years, for example, often lead to poorer performance on tests of intellectual capacity.

Perhaps the most important diseases affecting intelligence in old age are those classified as cardiovascular — having to do with the heart and blood vessels. When the blood flow to the brain is affected (cerebrovascular diseases), mental abilities usually decline to some degree, although the decline may be temporary. A stroke (a blocking of blood vessels in the brain) may result in permanent impairment, depending on the areas of the brain affected, but even mild cardiovascular disease has been shown to be related to deficits in memory (Klonoff and Kennedy, 1966) and lower scores on the Wechsler Adult Intelligence Scale (Wang, Obrist, and Busse, 1970). Apparently, the lowered blood flow has its effects by decreasing the oxygen supply to brain cells, resulting in temporary "malnutrition" or permanent "starvation" and death of the affected tissue.

Other types of disease may also cause problems in intellectual behavior. Among institutionalized patients who have various types of brain disorders, for example, there is generally a positive correlation between degree of brain impairment and intellectual malfunctioning (Wang and Busse, 1975; Obrist, 1978). Such a relationship may not occur among elderly persons who are living in the community in relatively good health, however, which suggests that changes normally thought to be age-related may actually be a function of disease. Studies that show intellectual declines among the elderly may do so because the elderly population generally includes a considerably higher percentage of people with health problems. When studies systematically exclude patients with even minimal dementia or other physiological problems, it may be found that cerebral oxygen consumption levels among older adults resemble those of younger adults.

Several studies suggest that intellectual declines among the elderly are associated with disease. There is evidence that a relationship exists between intellectual decline and high blood pressure, for example, but the relationship was consistent only when the blood pressure was elevated above a certain critical level (Eisdorfer and Wilkie, 1973). In other words, intellectual deficits are found only when blood pressure is pathologically high.

In several longitudinal studies, it has been possible to retroactively examine performance changes related to dying and death (Riegel and Riegel, 1972; Eisdorfer and Wilkie, 1973). Once subjects had died, the researchers were able to relate performance changes to the onset of the illness that proved to be terminal. This research convincingly shows that intellectual declines related to chronological age were a statistical artifact. Throughout most of their adult lives, people maintained a more or less stable level of performance, with dramatic changes occurring primarily in the five years immediately preceding death. These data support the claim made by some that there may be a brief and precipitous decline as death approaches (Fries and Crapo, 1981).

If declines among the elderly are primarily a function of diseases, it becomes increasingly important to define precisely what we mean by "disease." This is frequently more complicated than one might expect. Some authors, for example, consider senile dementia (Alzheimer's disease) to be merely the extreme end of the spectrum of *normal* aging changes (Terry, 1978). Others contend that the two involve qualitatively different sorts of changes; there is some research support for this view (Valenstein, 1981).

Even when it is possible to discover physiological changes in the brain, it may not be clear how they affect intellectual functioning. It may be tempting, for example, to speculate that minor atrophy of the cortex plays a profound role in intellectual deficits. It appears, however, that even moderate atrophy may be compatible with normal intellectual functioning (Roberts and Caird, 1976; Kaszniak et al., 1979). Another instance of how confusing it can be to relate brain pathology to patterns of intellectual performance is the finding that performance patterns among the elderly may parallel those of young adults with various degrees of brain damage. Such patterns are often found among elderly subjects who have excellent health and levels of social adaptation (Price, Fein, and Feinberg, 1980).

Further data on this matter come from Schaie's longitudinal study, in which the subjects were members of a medical insurance plan; thus fairly complete medical records were available. Only minor relationships were discovered between poor health and mental ability scores, and then only when the most severe illnesses were considered; and only verbal meaning and word fluency were affected. Cardiovascular disease was related to generally lowered mental function. But this finding was due primarily to the fact that cardiovascular disease was more common among older people and people in the lower social classes. When people of the same age and class were compared, those with cardiovascular diseases scored significantly lower only on two measures: number and a composite measure of intellectual ability (Hertzog, Schaie, and Gribbin, 1978). This suggests that one must be cautious in interpreting studies that simply compare people with and without cardiovascular disease. It may not be the presence of disease that is crucial; other factors such as age or social class may be more important.

The participants in the Schaie longitudinal study also provide evidence that changes in one's style of life affect what happens to their IQ scores (Gribbin, Schaie, and Parham, 1980). On the basis of intensive interviews, four types of participants were identified. What we might call the "average Americans" — average social status, intact family, average involvement with their environment — do quite well intellectually as they age, maintaining most of their abilities over the fourteen years of testing. The "advantaged Americans" — high social status, with lives that require or allow them to keep learning new things — do even better, often increasing their test scores over the years. The "spectators" —

average social status, intact family, passive participation in social activities, declining interest in new learning situations — generally show a decline in abilities. Finally, the "isolated older woman" — poor, unhappy, likely to be divorced or widowed, isolated either by choice or circumstances — shows the greatest decline of all. In short, those who live by their wits, die with their wits.

Equally interesting is the finding that favorable lifestyles seem to enhance the development of flexible attitudes (see Chapter 4). Such attitudes at midlife appear to be highly predictive of the maintenance of intellectual functioning into advanced old age. But do flexible attitudes maintain intellectual functioning, or do high levels of intellectual functioning encourage flexible attitudes? The evidence indicates that flexible attitudes affect intelligence. Correlational information on the relationship between intelligence and flexibility has been gathered from longitudinal studies over twenty-one years. The data clearly show that correlations between midlife flexibility and intelligence in old age are much greater than those between intelligence at midlife and flexibility in old age (Schaie, 1983c, 1984b). Similar evidence indicates that lack of environmental stimulation leads to cognitive loss. For example, we know that the greatest risk of cognitive decline occurs among widowed women who have not pursued a career and whose environmental stimulation has been reduced by the death of their spouse (Gribbin, Schaie, and Parham, 1980; Schaie, 1984b).

EDUCATION AND INTELLECT

If we were to summarize the research we have discussed so far, we might say that few intellectual abilities show substantial decline in adulthood until the age of sixty-five or so. Evidence for decline after that age is open to several interpretations: biological, environmental, and various combinations. Suppose one takes the view that much of the decline not due to specific diseases is a result of a restricted social environment (after retirement) and a culture that provides few incentives for further acquisition of knowledge or even the maintenance of knowledge. Then one must perforce accept the hypothesis that, by providing incentives and instruction in later life, we can stabilize declining trends and perhaps even reverse them. We should be able to teach old dogs new tricks. See Chapter 10.

The research evidence suggests that older adults can indeed continue to learn and are an "untapped resource," if we care to put it in such materialistic terms. They are capable of learning and performing at very high levels (Baltes and Labouvie, 1973). Not only can they learn a new job — an important practical skill — but, if given proper incentives, they can markedly improve their performance on tests of "fluid intelligence" — highly abstract skills that often include, in scoring, a measure of response speed (Plemons, Willis, and Baltes, 1978; Willis, Blieszner, and Baltes, 1981).

The evidence of the effectiveness of training efforts has been reviewed by a variety of authors (Labouvie-Vief, 1977; Denney, 1981; Willis and Schaie, 1981, Baltes and Willis, 1982; Willis, 1985; see also Chapter 10 on memory training). In general, it indicates overwhelmingly that significant gains in performance can be brought about, often with very minor interventions. A number of different treatments have been tried. Some studies have assessed the effects of physical exercise (Barry et al., 1966; Powell, 1974) and approaches designed to highlight certain dimensions of tasks (Denney, 1974a; Sanders et al., 1975; Sanders and Sanders, 1978). Others have focused on providing training in the component strategies involved in completing tasks (Labouvie-Vief and Gonda, 1976; Schultz and Hoyer, 1976; Plemons, Willis and Baltes, 1978) or on "performance factors" that may not be directly related to a particular task but do influence cognitive performance. The older person's reluctance to guess would be such a performance factor (Birkhill and Schaie, 1975).

An objection sometimes raised to such research is that training may not actually modify intellectual functioning per se; rather, it may simply provide more "extraneous" support for improved performance by increasing motivation, social reinforcement, or other influential factors. In other words, there may be different kinds of training effects — those that are ability-specific (that actually improve intellectual functioning) and those that are ability-extraneous (that improve performance in ways not related to intellectual functioning). This matter was the object of a study involving eight training sessions and two delayed posttests, one after twenty-five days and the other after twenty-three weeks (Plemons, Willis, and Baltes, 1978). The study demonstrated that training actually does improve skills and not just motivation and other extraneous factors. The researchers found that the results of training fell into a hierarchical transfer pattern. Training was most helpful in improving performance on tasks directly related to the training task. Poorer performance was found on tasks related less directly to the task used in training. Similar effects have since been established in further studies using different target abilities (Blieszner, Willis, and Baltes, 1981; Willis, Blieszner, and Baltes, 1981; Baltes and Willis, 1982). These studies support the contention that the cognitive behavior of the elderly can be modified.

A second objection to research concerning the trainability of the elderly has to do with the failure to use young control groups. The argument is that if deficits among the elderly result from a lack of environmental stimulation, one should not find similarly large training effects among "nondeprived" younger controls. But to function as an adequate control group, younger subjects would have to resemble the older ones in all respects other than ability, and as we have pointed out they do not. Today's elderly have had substantially different life histories than today's young people, and differences discovered between the two groups could easily be a result of these differences (Baltes and Willis, 1982).

A major defect in most of the cognitive training studies mentioned above is that they did not determine whether the elderly trainees had experienced declines before training began. Did the studies actually remediate declines, or did they simply teach the elderly new skills? In a recent study, Schaie and Willis (in press) gave five hours of individual training to 229 older persons ranging in age from sixty-four to ninety-four. The training was on one of two abilities, spatial orientation or inductive reasoning. All the subjects had been assessed over at least fourteen years before the study; about half had shown declines. When the performance of those who declined was examined, it was found that more than half gained significantly, and about 40 percent returned to their predecline level of performance. About a third of those who had not shown declines improved their performance above the previous level. It seems, then, that cognitive training can indeed remediate losses resulting from disuse, but that we need to know a person's prior level before we can be sure whether the improvement with training represents remediation of a loss or new learning.

Although these facts do not deny biological interpretations of intellectual decline in the last years of life (training can help even a brain-injured patient, for example; no one would say otherwise), the research is most compatible with an interpretation of intellectual decline (as measured by IQ tests) in old age that implicates disease and lack of environmental stimulation as major causal factors.

THE NATURAL HISTORY OF INTELLECT

What happens to one's intellectual powers as one grows older? This is the primary question in this chapter, and we have a tentative answer. It is, in fact, not a bad answer, as answers go in the field of adult development and aging. It is an answer based on at least some research.

The pure numbers (the average IQ scores) were at first thought to indicate a gradual decline after the age of twenty-five. Later studies showed this interpretation to be completely wrong, to be an artifact of increasing abilities with successive generations. We now believe that the pure numbers decline only later in life, largely after the age of sixty-five. For advantaged groups, like college graduates, the numbers decline very late, if at all; we're talking about the eighties and the nineties here (Schaie, 1983b).

The numbers for certain tests, those variously called "speeded" or "fluid" or "performance" or whatever, drop somewhat more rapidly, but the reasons for this remain the most controversial. These may be the basic biological aspects of intellect, as some theories assert (Birren, 1974; Horn, 1978). Or these may be the abilities most subject to variations in training, motivation, and historical circumstances (Baltes and Labouvie, 1973; Labouvie-Vief and Chandler, 1978; Geiwitz, 1979).

The decline (if any) in IQ test scores over the age of sixty-five or seventy is similarly subject to several interpretations. In addition to notions of inevitable biological decrement, we could attribute intellectual decline to social isolation, decreasing motivation to perform irrelevant intellectual tasks, disease (including disease related to impending death and terminal drop), or some combination of such factors. All in all, many psychologists have begun to believe that the search for the curve of "normal" deterioration in intellectual abilities is a fruitless task (Baltes and Schaie, 1976). In this view, there is too much variability in age trends to postulate one of these as normal or basic. Some people decline in intellectual ability; others increase. Some abilities seem to be increasing with each new generation; others seem to be decreasing. An environmental event — the development of television, for example — can change age trends for some people and have little effect on others. Thus the search goes on, but it is a search now for the *determinants* of change or stability and much less for inevitable and irreversible decrements.

If you keep your health and engage your mind with the problems and activities of the world around you, chances are good that you will experience little if any decline in intellectual performance in your lifetime. That's the promise of research in the area of adult intelligence.

Summary

1. Intelligence is usually defined as the ability to learn or to manipulate symbols. Intelligence is an inference from competence demonstrated in several situations, but competence involves more than simply intelligence — motivation, for example. The particular abilities and motivations necessary to do well on IQ tests, which were designed to predict scholastic performance, may bias these tests in favor of young people.

2. Adult stages of intellectual development include the *achieving* stage, which involves planning and periodic assessment of programs designed to achieve major goals in career, family, and life in general. In the *responsibility* stage, abilities are applied to both short- and long-term concerns for family units, coworkers, and community groups. In the *executive* stage, planning and assessment abilities are applied to the organizations for which one is at least partly responsible — one's family, for example. In later life, the *reintegrative* stage requires a reintegration of abilities, interests, and values — getting one's priorities in order, for example.

3. IQ tests were developed in the early 1900s by Alfred Binet. *Factor analyses* of such tests typically show a major factor called "general intelligence" or "g." Slightly different analyses have turned up two major factors called *crystallized* and *fluid* intelligence, about six to twelve factors called *primary mental abilities*, and 120 factors in the most complex model of intelligence. Sternberg's comprehensive model of intelligence consists of three subtheories: a componential subtheory that relates intelligence to the individual's inner world, a contextual subtheory that relates intelligence to the external world, and a subtheory that relates intelligence to both the internal and external facets.

4. Early cross-sectional studies of the relationship between age and intelligence showed decline after the age of twenty or thirty. Some tests, usually of simple information-processing abilities that make up fluid intelligence, showed sharper decline than others; tests of general information, vocabulary, and the like (crystallized intelligence) sometimes even increased.

5. Longitudinal studies, the first of which were published around 1950, showed that the cross-sectional studies had been seriously misinterpreted. Many individuals typically show little or no decline in IQ scores with age, and some brighter individuals, in intellectual professions, may actually increase. The cross-sectional studies had reflected not age changes in intelligence but cohort or generational differences in average IQ scores.

6. Interpretations of longitudinal studies have their own difficulties, not the least of which is the problem of dropouts and deaths, subjects who usually score somewhat lower than average on IQ tests. Nevertheless, a "sizable" intellectual decline that reduces the average of an older group to the level surpassed by 75 percent of the younger group was found for only three of seven measures in a major longitudinal study — two of the three only at age eighty-one. In a comparable study using "independent samples" to avoid the problem of dropouts, two measures show a sizable decline (as defined above) at fifty-three, two at sixty-seven, two at seventy-four, and one not at all. The abilities of the majority of people remain stable throughout adulthood and old age, and some older people even increase their performance.

7. Cross-sectional findings that elderly subjects perform poorly on simple Piagetian tasks, such as conservation, probably reflect generational differences. Training studies suggest that even these differences are not in capability, but in motivation, familiarity with the testing situations, or similar factors. Some researchers have suggested that adult thinking differs qualitatively from that of younger persons.

8. Why do some people decline in IQ scores over the age of sixty-five or seventy? One possible answer is normal biological deterioration (of the brain and nervous system, presumably). However, diseases, especially cardiovascular diseases, are a significant factor for some individuals; life-threatening diseases are known to produce a "terminal drop" in IQ scores. Social isolation induced by retirement, deaths among family and friends, and disabling diseases can also reduce one's IQ score. A number of researchers have shown that appropriate training can often remediate declines. It's possible that healthy individuals who maintain an active intellectual life will show little or no loss of intellectual abilities even into their eighties and beyond.

SUGGESTED READINGS

Horn, J. L. (1982). The theory of fluid and crystallized intelligence in relation to concepts of cognitive psychology and aging in adulthood. In F. J. M. Craik and S. Trehub (Eds.), *Aging and cognitive processes* (pp. 237–278). New York: Plenum. An exposition of the Horn–Cattell theory of fluid and crystallized intelligence and a review of cross-sectional data on age differences in the light of that theory.

Labouvie-Vief, G. (1985). Intelligence and cognition. In J. E. Birren and K. W. Schaie (Eds.), *Handbook of the psychology of aging* (2nd ed.) (pp. 500–530). New York: Van Nostrand Reinhold. Reviews recent theorizing on adult intellectual development that proposes further growth and development of intellectual processes beyond young adulthood.

Schaie, K. W. (1983). The Seattle Longitudinal Study: A twenty-one year exploration of psychometric intelligence in adulthood. In K. W. Schaie (Ed.), *Longitudinal studies of adult psychological development* (pp. 64–135). New York: Guilford. An account of the history and results of one of the major longitudinal studies of intellectual development in adulthood.

Willis, S. L. (1985). Towards an educational psychology of the adult learner. In J. E. Birren and K. W. Schaie (Eds.), *Handbook of the psychology of aging* (2nd ed.) (pp. 818–847). New York: Van Nostrand Reinhold. A review of the evidence on intellectual aging and its implications for the education of the adult learner.

Complexity of Life Style and Maintenance of Intellectual Abilities

Researchers have recognized for some time that a person's intellectual performance may change during adulthood. It has proven difficult, however, to distinguish true developmental changes from changes arising from external sources. Examples of several nondevelopmental causes of change can be given. One concerns the "cohort confound," which occurs when researchers mistake differences between generations born at different times for real developmental changes. Life stages may also be influential; virtually all declines in intellectual performance take place after retirement. Factors such as fatigue, anxiety, and cautiousness may reduce intelligence scores among the elderly as well. Another problem concerns such factors as socioeconomic status, birth order, and availability of reading material. These factors are all correlated with *children's* intellectual performance, and they may influence the ability of adults as well. Research is continuing on these matters, but the relationships between these many variables are complex and will be difficult to untangle. A different approach is to see whether cognitive functioning over time is correlated with lifestyle patterns, that is, with the comprehensive sum of all the variables that comprise a certain type of environment. The results of a study of this sort were published in 1980 by Gribbin, Schaie, and Parham.

The study involved 140 subjects, 60 men and 80 women between the ages of forty and eighty-eight. All group members had been assessed on two instruments, the Primary Mental Abilities test and the Test of Behavioral Rigidity, in 1956, 1963, and 1970; thus, longitudinal data on their intellectual performance were available. To obtain the necessary information on their lifestyles, activities, and interests, a twenty-nine page questionnaire called the Life Complexity Inventory (LCI) was developed and administered to the subjects in 1974. On the basis of the initial analysis of the LCI results, eight clusters of item scores were developed. These clusters represented the following areas: (1) homemaker activities; (2) level of social status; (3) subjective dissatisfaction with life status; (4) disengagement; (5) semiengagement; (6) a noisy environment; (7) degree of family solidarity or dissolution; and (8) maintenance of acculturation. The items defining these clusters are listed in Table I.

A number of statistical manipulations of the data were performed. One form of analysis involved correlating environmental circumstances

TABLE I.

Variables comprising item clusters.

A. *Homemaker role*
younger than spouse;
widowed or not married;
much time spent in homemaking activities;
much time spent in solitary activities;
now and previously, spent much time working with hands;
never in military service;
now and previously, high on unnecessary conversation;
female

B. *Social status*
high level of education;
high present and previous income level.
high present and previous occupational status;
perceived time pressure;
many magazines read;
large number of rooms in home

C. *Dissatisfaction with life status*
high present and retrospective dissatisfaction with life;
high present and retrospective dissatisfaction with job;
fewer friends

D. *Disengagement*
high number of passive activities;
few changes in professional roles;
relatively more advanced age;
many solitary activities retrospectively;
few past and present hours spent reading;
low involvement in people-related activities;
low present and past involvement in work activities

E. *Semiengagement*
retrospective upper-middle-class lifestyle;
present home-related activities high;
high number of friends with diverse interests

F. *Noisy environment*
living now and previously close to freeways, airports, etc.;
living in an environment described as noisy in general and bothered by it;
in particular, present and past environment filled with traffic noise

G. *Family dissolution*
number of changes in residence during the past five years;
number of spouses lost by death;
living in multiple-unit dwelling;
living in neighborhood with large elderly population;
widowed or not married retrospectively

H. *Maintenace of acculturation*
high number of fiction and nonfiction books read;
high number of university and/or adult education courses taken;
high number of weeks spent in educational activities

Source: Complexity of life style and maintenance of intellectual abilities. Gribbin, K., Schaie, K., and Parham, I. (1980). *Journal of Social Issues*. 36, 47–61. Copyright © 1980 by The Society for the Psychological Study of Social Issues. Reprinted by permission.

with cognitive functioning as measured on the Primary Mental Abilities test. This instrument provides separate scores on verbal meaning, space, reasoning, number, and word fluency, as well as summary scores on intellectual ability and educational aptitude (see pp. 290). Two findings were of special significance. In general, Social Status was positively correlated with all test scores in all measurement periods; that is, people from higher status levels tended to have higher test scores. Test scores were negatively correlated with Disengagement; that is, disengaged people tended to have lower scores. As the authors state, "These results permit the inference that societal and environmental factors may indeed influence the individual's intellectual and psychological functioning" (p. 53).

The next procedure was to use the LCI cluster scores to identify different subject types. Usable profiles of four types were devised. Type 1 subjects were of average social status, lived in a relatively noise-free environment, had largely intact families, maintained an average level of acculturation, were quite engaged, but expressed strong dissatisfaction with their life status. Type 2 subjects had intact families, maintained acculturation at slightly above average levels, and lived in relatively noisy, accessible environments. Type 3 subjects were homemakers of average social status, average satisfaction with life status, and intact family situations. They were low in maintaining acculturation, and they lived in noisy but accessible environments. They were above average in disengagement and had the highest mean level of semiengagement. Type 4 subjects were older, widowed homemakers of low social status. They were dissatisfied with their life status, and scored highest on the disengagement items, although they did not show high levels of semiengagement. They lived in noise-free but probably inaccessible environments and had the highest levels of family dissolution.

The final step was to determine whether these different subject types maintained different levels of cognitive ability over time. Statistically significant differences were found for all abilities except number. Type 2, the high-status engaged, scored consistently high on all abilities, whereas Type 4, the disengaged, scored consistently low on all abilities. Type 3, the semiengaged, were generally average on all abilities. Type 3, the semiengaged, were generally average on all abilities, as were Type 1, the average-status engaged.

What do these findings mean? The authors conclude that "individuals of particular life-style types are more or less prone to quite specific change on cognitive variables" (p. 58). But since this is a correlational study, one cannot conclude unequivocally that the differences in lifestyle necessarily caused the observed differences in intellectual functioning over time. One might ask whether instead declines in cognitive ability could cause change in lifestyle? Possibly, but this does not appear to be what happened. The group with the largest decline, Type 4, were all widows, and widowhood is not likely to be produced by a drop in cognitive functioning. (But some factor other than widowhood per se is clearly implicated, since there were widows in other groups as well). What seems clearly implicated is that degree of engagement in life's stimulating activities (which in turn is facilitated by the availability of above-average economic resources) is strongly predictive of maintenance of high levels of mental abilities as one ages. The research suggests further that gerontological researchers need to consider the life-environment context in which the person exists to understand more completely the complexities of cognitive development over the adult life span.

Chapter Ten

LEARNING AND MEMORY

Acquiring and Retaining Information

Linda Leslie spoke of her great-aunt, Lucille, her grandfather Leonard's sister. "Lucille's a wonderful person: kind and generous, always cheerful. She lives in the Lakeview Nursing Home now, but she always comes up to the house for Christmas, Thanksgiving, and birthdays — special occasions. As far as I can tell she's in perfect shape except for her memory. She just cannot remember anything that she's experienced recently — what she's just said, who people are. She remembers all the family, of course, but new people. . . . Like my boyfriend Stephen. Every time she runs into him, and I mean *every time,* she says the same thing: 'And who is this handsome young gentleman?'

"Sometimes it gets on your nerves. She asks you about your life, like 'How's school, dear?' Five minutes later she asks the same question. But she's so nice! It's hard to get irritated with her.

"Sometimes it's sad. When Grandma died, Lucille of course went to the funeral. But she kept forgetting why she was there. She kept asking my father, 'What's going on? Why are we going to church in the afternoon?' and later, 'Why are we at the cemetery? Did someone die?' Each time Dad would gently tell her the truth. And each time Lucille would begin to sob again. Her sorrow was repeated over and over, and each telling came as a shock to her.

"Sometimes she's funny! Last Thanksgiving we had received a long letter from a former neighbor who now lives in Arizona, a woman who had been a good friend of Lucille's too. The letter was maybe seven or eight pages long. When Lucille finished a page, she'd put it at the end of the other pages. So when she got to the end of the letter, she started reading the first page over. She read the entire letter about four times, enjoying it immensely each time! Mom said that she knew where Lucille was in the letter because on one page there was a joke, and each time Lucille came to that spot, she giggled. Regular as clockwork."

Learning, Remembering, and Growing Old

Learning and memory are obviously closely related concepts (Botwinick, 1978). People must learn before they can remember, and learning without memory has a limited utility. Learning is often assessed by memory tasks. "How much have you learned?" is translated into "How much can you remember?" Memory is often assessed by learning tasks (for example, memorizing the Gettysburg Address or a list of words). How can we distinguish between learning and memory?

Learning is typically defined as the *acquisition* of a new skill or information through practice or experience. Remembering is typically defined as the *retrieval* of information that has been *stored* in memory. Thus we could speak of a general learning/memory system that involves all three processes: acquisition, storage, and retrieval. Memory is discussed in terms of *information,* that is, how you put information into "the system," how you store it, and how you retrieve it. This is the approach of modern *information-processing theories,* and it is ours to the extent that it is possible. In this view, learning is part of memory — the acquisition or encoding phase.

And now we have to add the other dimension: age. How do learning abilities change with age? How does memory change with age? Does it fade gradually? Do old people (like Lucille) tend to forget new things, remembering better the events from the more distant past?

There are other questions as well. How does society affect the demands placed on learning and memory? For example, we live in a culture marked by rapid technological change, so that much of what we learn in youth is outdated by the time of our maturity. We must learn new techniques, new facts. In less rapidly changing societies, the "elders of the tribe" are often the teachers, the founts of wisdom. In our society, they must learn new skills like everyone else, as new technology alters basic systems of communication, transportation, finance, and recreation. As values change, societal rewards change, and new learning is required.

At various points in time, different approaches to the study of learning and memory have been dominant. Until the early 1960s the associative view dominated the work on adult learning and memory (Hultsch and Deutsch, 1982). In the 1970s and early 1980s information-processing theories of learning and memory have been emphasized. Now in the mid-1980s there is growing concern with a contextual approach. Thus it will be necessary to briefly review research on learning and memory from each of these approaches. We try to provide an integrated view of learning and memory, but sometimes we strain a bit and the roughness is apparent.

In this chapter we first look at research on age differences in an associative approach to learning and memory. We consider some of the reasons why older people may typically not learn as quickly or as well as young adults. Factors such as the pace of learning, cautiousness, and anxiety are discussed, among others.

Then we turn to information-processing research on memory, considering age differences (or the lack of them) on three phases of memory: encoding, storage, and retrieval. Next, a contextual view of memory is considered. Finally, we turn to adult education — learning and memory in the real world — and review some of the factors that affect formal schooling and its benefits for students in later life.

Associative Learning

The associative approach is based on the assumption that learning and memory involve the association of ideas or events that occur together in time (Hultsch, 1982; Kausler, 1982). In this approach, learning involves the formation of a stimulus–response (S–R) bond. These S–R associations represent the contents of memory. The act of remembering involves the individual giving the correct response (R) when the appropriate stimulus (S) is presented. Forgetting involves a weakening of the S–R bond.

THE PACE OF LEARNING

One variable known to affect old learners more than young ones is the pace of learning — the speed with which the task must be performed. A common laboratory task used in associative learning research is the *paired-associate* task. The task is to learn an association between two items, usually words or letters. Typically, the subject is presented with a single word, such as BASKET (this is called the *stimulus* term) and then after a certain time, with a pair of words: BASKET–THEREFORE (the latter called the *response* term). This pair remains in view for a certain time, and then another pair is presented (ORANGE–UNTIL), and so on through a list of a certain number of paired associates. The task is to give the correct response to each stimulus as it appears alone, before the response appears. One obviously cannot give the correct response the first time through the list, but study of the pairs allows most subjects to get some right on the second trial; learning is typically considered complete when the subject gives correct responses to all stimuli on one or two trials in a row. The task, as you can see, is much like learning a foreign language: "Spanish word"–"English equivalent" or NADA–NOTHING.

The pace of learning paired associates can be manipulated in two ways. The time the stimulus term is presented by itself, which is the time allotted for a response, is called the *anticipation interval*. Older subjects perform particularly badly when this interval is short (one or two seconds) and do much better when they have more time to respond (Arenberg and Robertson-Tchabo, 1977). Younger subjects also improve as the anticipation interval increases, but less than older subjects. The second element of pacing in paired-associate learning is the time the pair of items is presented for study; this period is called the inspection interval or

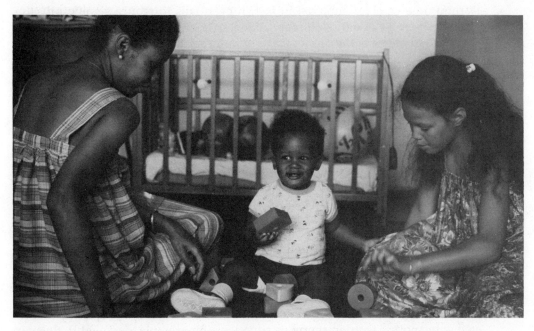

Children of today grow up in cleaner, healthier environments with more "educational" toys than the children of the early 1900s. How does this affect relative performance on learning tasks?

study time. Increasing the study time also improves performance, but old and young subjects benefit about equally (Monge and Hultsch, 1971). If subjects are allowed as much time as they want to study the pairs and to make a response to the stimulus member of the pair — a condition called "self-pacing" — older subjects again benefit more than younger subjects. They rarely increase their study time, however. They spend most of the time on the anticipation (response) interval (Canestrari, 1968).

Cautiousness, Anxiety, and Interference   Adults' ability to perform associative learning tasks may be affected by variables other than pacing. For example, most errors in fast-paced associative learning situations are *errors of omission,* rather than *errors of commission.* That is, the individual makes no response at all to the stimulus member of a paired associate, rather than giving an incorrect response. Errors of omission are said to reflect cautiousness, a reluctance to venture a response unless one is absolutely certain of its accuracy. It has been suggested that the poorer performance of the older adults relative to young adults, as reflected in omission errors, is a function of their being more cautious.

To test the hypothesis that cautiousness is a factor in the learning performance of older subjects, psychologists have usually tried to overcome the cautiousness through requests or demands that some response be made, even if the person knows it is probably wrong. This procedure generally fails to increase the learning rate of older subjects; in fact, it even fails to reduce significantly the number of errors of omission (Taub, 1967).

In another test of the cautiousness hypothesis, however, the data were more supportive (Leech and Witte, 1971). Older subjects were offered a small monetary reward for each correct response. Each *incorrect* response was also rewarded, although at a slightly lower value. Only the absence of a response received an absence of reward. In this situation, the old people significantly reduced their omission errors. This suggests that older people could do better on many tests of learning merely by taking a few more chances, guessing at least when they have some idea of the answer (see also Birkhill and Schaie, 1975).

A second major hypothesis regarding the poorer functioning of the elderly focuses on their being highly anxious about their performance. Support for this hypothesis comes from the research cited in Chapter 7 (Motivation) which indicated that a drug that blocked physiological arousal resulted in significantly fewer errors by old people on an associative learning task, compared to other oldsters given an inactive drug (Eisdorfer, Nowlin, and Wilkie, 1970).

A final hypothesis suggests that in some instances of associative learning, older adults are more susceptible to the effects of interference with prior learning. Older adults' susceptibility to interference has been studied by varying the associative strength of the word pairs learned. When one word is frequently associated with another word in everyday situations (for example, dark–light), the pair is said to have high associative strength. When one word is infrequently associated with another (for example, dark–fast), the pair has low associative strength. If the associative habits of older adults are more established through a greater number of years of experience, it follows that age-related differences should be least for high associative pairs. This appears to be the case. In a comprehensive study, Botwinick and Storandt (1974) presented adults aged twenty-one to eighty years with three lists of paired associates which varied in their associative strength and difficulty. The low-difficulty list consisted of high associative strength word pairs (for example, ocean–water). The moderate-difficulty list consisted of low associative strength word pairs (for example, hair–book). The high-difficulty list consisted of consonant–word pairs (for example, FP–wagon). The researchers found no age-related differences in performance on the easy list, but marked age-related differences in performance on the moderate- and high-difficulty lists. Thus it appears that the associative learning performance of older adults is aided when the task is consistent with previously established verbal habits (high associative strength pairs). The older adults are most handicapped when learning and recall involves forming associations that are contrary or in competition with previously learned verbal associations.

Judging from laboratory studies of associative learning, the rate of learning slows only gradually through the adult years. Only after the age of sixty-five or thereabouts does one's learning become demonstrably poorer than that of young adults. Even then the nature of the age deficit is unclear. Older subjects profit from a slower pace of learning much more than young adults. Moreover, the oldsters may get too anxious or too cautious, or they may suffer from the interference of previously learned associations.

Human Memory

The question of age differences in learning has its counterpart in the psychology of memory, for many old people complain of a failing memory. Donald Hebb, a former president of the American Psychological Association, seventy-five years old at the time commented: "It's very embarrassing when you're lecturing to an introductory class and you have to ask them for the word you want, which may be as simple as 'pavement' or 'bread' " (Cohen, 1980, p. 5). There are even specific myths about the effects of aging on memory. For example, old people are supposed to forget things they've learned recently, but memories from the distant past are supposed to be clear and vivid, sometimes startlingly so.

Learning is part of memory when studied within the information-processing approach — it is the "acquisition phase," as psychologists put it (Craik and Trehub, 1982).

Memory research has been dominated since the 1970s by an approach based on an analogy between human thought and the workings of a computer, an approach called "information processing." Learning, therefore, is viewed as putting information into the information-processing system (Hoyer and Plude, 1980; Poon, 1985). In fact, learning is often called *encoding*. Just as information must be translated into the proper code (or "language") for a computer to process it further, information from the environment must be encoded for the human processing system to store it, use it, and later retrieve it. Studies of memory encoding often overlap with studies of perception, for both involve "initial processing." Now we must turn our focus to the "process" variables that memory psychologists seek to ferret out.

ENCODING, STORAGE, AND RETRIEVAL

Memory psychologists usually distinguish three phases (encoding, storage, retrieval) of the memory process (Erber, 1982; Poon, 1985) (see Figure 10–1). *Encoding*, is the learning or acquisition phase. *Storage* is perhaps the phase most people think of as memory — the laying away of encoded information in "storehouses" for later use. Psychologists in recent years have begun to speak of several different "stores" for information. The *sensory store* is conceptualized as a very brief waystation for essentially unprocessed information from the environment (Hoyer and Plude, 1980). In order for information to be recalled, it must be processed and transferred to the later stores (short-term, long-term). The *short-term* store is presumed to hold relatively small amounts of information for a slightly longer time than the sensory store — commonly on the order of a few seconds. Information in short-term store has been processed in the form of concepts which can be recalled. The phone number you hear from Directory Assistance and try to remember until you can dial the number is largely in short-term store. The sound of the operator's voice, which was first encoded in the sensory store, has been processed to represent a series of numbers now held in short-term store. The *long-term store* is seen as having a very large capacity for storing information, which it can retain over long periods of time. In transferring the phone number from short-term into long-term store, you could organize the information schematically, by remembering that 237 is the local prefix and 3076 are the last four digits of your social security number.

FIGURE 10–1.

The memory system — a very rough approximation of current memory theories. The primary purpose of this chart is to illustrate two basic dimensions: (1) the three phases of memory (encoding, storage, retrieval) and (2) the three storage systems (sensory, short-term, long-term). The additional material is included to give some idea of the differences in encoding, storage, and retrieval for the three stores.

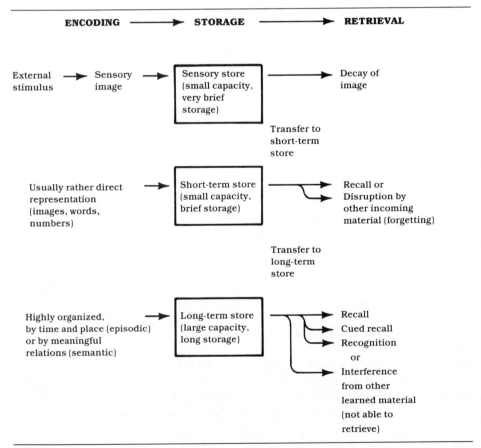

Source: Based on Atkinson J. W., and Shiffrin, R. M. (1968). Human memory: A proposed system and its control processes. In K. W. Spence and J. T. Spence (Eds.), *The psychology of learning and motivation* (Vol. 2). New York: Academic Press.

The final phase of memory is *retrieval,* the finding of the information when it is needed. Forgetting can occur at various stages in the memory process. For example, just after the operator repeated the phone number there may have been a loud noise which distracted you and the information in sensory store decayed before it could be transferred into short-term store. Alternatively, the information may have been transferred into short-term store, but just as you were hanging up the phone, someone told you a date you also needed to remember. Since the capacity of short-term store is small, the phone number was replaced by the date in short-term store, before it could be transferred to long-term store. The major age differences in memory performance are related to short-term and long-term store (Poon, 1985). There do not appear to be significant age differences in sensory store. Thus much of our discussion focuses on short-term and long-term memory.

We review evidence that some of the age difference in memory lies specifically in the retrieval phase. Old people may have the necessary information in storage, but they can't get to it as easily as young people (Craik and Rabinowitz, 1984). One way to show that retrieval difficulties, rather than learning or storage difficulties, are involved is to compare two common methods of retrieval, *recall* and *recognition.* Recall asks simply for the to-be-remembered information: What was the name of your third-grade teacher? What were the words on the thirty-item list we just showed you? Recognition presents possible answers: What was the name of your third-grade teacher, Johnson or McNally? Or, here are sixty words, thirty of which we just showed you; pick out the thirty we just showed you. As you know from comparing your performance on multiple-choice exams to that on essay tests, recognition is generally easier (Burke and Light, 1981). Many times you can recognize an answer that you cannot recall; you can't dredge up "McNally" when asked about your third-grade teacher, but once it's presented, you say, "Well, of course! Mrs. McNally! How could I forget?"

What does it mean, then, that one can recognize material that one cannot recall? It certainly means that the information was learned and stored, because it can be recognized as correct. It means that the individual could not retrieve it when asked for simple recall, though he or she could if presented with multiple choices. It means that the failure of recall was a failure of retrieval, that the search for the desired information in the storehouses of memory failed, even though the information was there, had the searcher gone to the right niches.

Current research suggests that encoding *and* retrieval problems are the cause of the memory difficulties of older adults (Craik and Rabinowitz, 1984). As we point out, however, some of these difficulties occur because older adults do not spontaneously use effective encoding and retrieval strategies. When they are instructed to use these strategies, their performance improves significantly.

Age and encoding As with learning, the typical finding in memory research is one of slight change until the age of sixty-five or so, then more rapid decline (Poon, 1985). This inference of age changes is based largely on cross-sectional studies.

The question is again, what accounts for the age differences we observe?

What is the relative importance of encoding problems, storage problems, and retrieval problems? Does the problem lie in sensory storage, short-term storage, long-term storage, or some combination of all three?

Let us take first the question of age differences in encoding. Encoding, in the information-processing scheme of things, is the learning or acquisition phase, and our earlier discussion of age differences in learning suggests that encoding will be found to be less efficient in older subjects than in younger adults. In particular, a slower pace to learning should make things easier for older subjects, who can then encode the information more efficiently (Craik and Byrd, 1982). Another relevant finding is that if you equate initial learning between young and old groups, memory will be essentially the same (Craik, 1977). An older subject might take twenty repetitions to learn a list of words (where "learned" is defined as two consecutive perfect recitations), whereas a younger subject might take fifteen. But, once the words are learned (by this criterion), memory fades equally in the younger and the older adult. The implication is again that older subjects are less efficient in encoding the material and that, therefore, they require more repetitions or better organized material to build an adequate code.

The work of the short-term store involves the encoding processes discussed below (organization, mediation, depth of processing). It is a temporary store-house for information in which some but not all is prepared for more permanent storage in the long-term store. If the information is bumped out of the short-term store before it is properly encoded, it probably will be gone forever, never to be retrieved from memory. Although this view is certainly oversimplified, it does picture the basic distinction between, and relationship of, the short- and long-term stores.

Organization and encoding   One of the best ways to encode information for later retrieval is to organize it (Kausler, 1982). Here we may think of filing systems as an analogy: if material is filed neatly and systematically in reasonable categories, our chances of finding it when we need it are greatly enhanced. If material is stuffed, without rhyme or reason, into folders as it comes in, we will surely experience difficulty later.

Much research evidence suggests that many older subjects do not spontaneously organize information for later recall (Craik and Rabinowitz, 1984). In one investigation, subjects of various ages were asked to learn lists of words. Each list had several "clusters" of words based on similarity in meaning (ocean and sea, for example) or on relatedness (piano and music); subjects were not told explicitly of the clusterings, however. These natural ways to organize and encode the lists were used frequently by younger subjects but rarely by subjects over seventy (Denney, 1974a). Since the number of words recalled in such a task is highly correlated with the degree to which the subject organizes the list, younger adults did much better than older adults.

If older subjects are instructed in the memory-enhancing advantages of organization, they tend to improve their position relative to the younger subjects (Schmitt, Murphy, and Sanders, 1981). This is especially true of subjects who are both old and of low intelligence on verbal ability (Botwinick, 1978). An example of this type of study is one in which subjects were first given experience in sorting words into categories — experience that trains them in organizing such words (Hultsch, 1971). Later, given a similar list to learn, older subjects did better relative to younger subjects than older subjects who did not have the prior training in sorting (see Figure 10–2).

Mediation and Encoding Another good way to encode information for later retrieval is to use what are commonly called "mnemonic devices," techniques that psychologists typically call "mediation" (Hartley, Harker, and Walsh, 1980).

FIGURE 10–2.

Average number of words learned as a function of age. Prior to learning, half the subjects carried out a sorting task designed to be helpful in organizing word lists; the rest of the subjects performed a task that did not involve sorting.

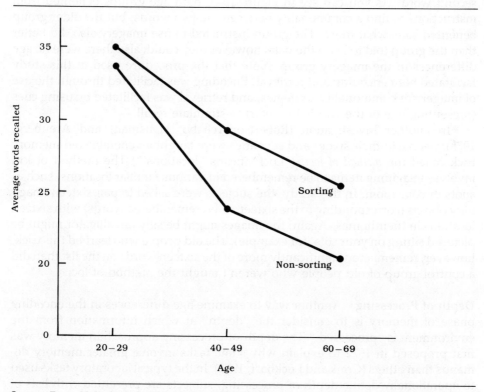

Source: From Hultsch, D. (1971). Adult age differences in free classification and free recall. *Developmental Psychology, 4,* 338–342. Copyright 1971 by the American Psychological Association. Reprinted by permission of the publisher and author.

These techniques use verbal or visual associations to link together pieces of information that might not by themselves have clear relationships. A common verbal mnemonic is the rhyme we use to remember an otherwise forgettable rule of spelling: "i" before "e," except after "c." Visual mnemonics often involve picturing the material to be remembered in some sort of imaginary scene. To remember a shopping list of milk, mushrooms, and cigarettes, for example, one might visualize a cow smoking a cigarette while sitting on a "toadstool." Although bizarre, such images have been shown to improve memory. They are especially useful in the encoding process. Older adults may have trouble forming images, but they can be trained to form them and use them in memory tasks (see the research article in the box at the end of this chapter).

In a study of the effectiveness of various types of encoding instructions (Rabinowitz, Craik, and Ackerman, 1982), younger and older adults were given pairs of unassociated words to learn. Three different groups were instructed (1) to simply learn the pairs as best they could, (2) to think of some property or characteristics common to both words in the pair, or (3) to form a visual image of an interaction of some sort between the two objects named in each word pair. To test retention, one word of a pair was given and the subject was asked to recall the second word. As you can see in Figure 10–3, both age groups benefited from instructions to find a commonality between the two words, but the older group benefited somewhat more. The group instructed to use imagery also did better than the group told to learn the pairs however they could; also there were no age differences in the imagery group. Note that the procedure used in this study facilitated both encoding and retrieval. Encoding was facilitated through the use of imagery or commonality strategies, and retrieval was facilitated by using cues (presenting one of the words in a pair) to stimulate recall.

In another investigation (Robertson-Tchabo, Hausman, and Arenberg, 1976), people in their sixties and seventies were taught a venerable old memory trick called the *method of loci*. ("Loci" means "locations.") The method of loci involves imagining items to be remembered in various familiar locations, such as spots in your room. In this study, the subjects were asked to pair sixteen imaginary objects (corresponding to the sixteen to-be-remembered words) with sixteen locations in their homes. Again, the images might be silly (an alligator might be pictured sitting on your sofa, for example). The old people who learned this trick, however, remembered significantly more of the sixteen words on the list than did a control group of old people who weren't taught the method of loci.

Depth of Processing   Another way to examine age differences in the encoding phase of memory is to consider the "depth" at which information from the environment is "processed." The depth-of-processing approach in memory was first proposed in 1972 to explain why some tasks involve greater memory demands than others (Craik and Lockhart, 1972). In the typical laboratory tasks used to operationally define depth of processing, subjects are presented with lists of words and asked to make certain judgments. They might be asked to decide whether or not the word is in capital letters; this is considered a shallow level of

FIGURE 10-3.

Comparison of young and old subjects' performance on paired-associates learning task under three sets of instructions: (a) learn as best you can; (b) think of some common characteristics; (c) form an image of interaction.

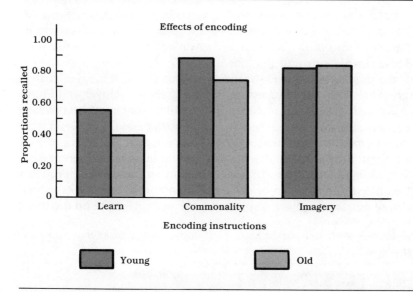

Effects of encoding

Source: Adapted from F. I. M. Craik and M. Byrd. Aging and cognitive deficits: the role of attentional resources. In F. I. M. Craik and S. Trehub, eds., *Aging and cognitive processes*. New York: Plenum Press, 1982, p. 202. © 1982 by Plenum Press. Reprinted by permission of Plenum Publishing Corporation.

processing. A somewhat deeper level is obtained by asking the subjects about the sound of the word: asking them, for example, if the word rhymes with "pain." The deepest level of processing is obtained by asking subjects something that requires them to think about the meaning of the word: Does the word, for example, fit in the sentence: "The girl placed ____ on the table"? In general, the deeper levels of processing involve the word at a *semantic* level; that is, they involve examining the meaning of the word rather than superficial characteristics such as with what letter the word starts. Typically, depth of processing defined in these ways is highly related to later recall of the words; the deeper the level, the more remembered (Craik and Byrd, 1982).

The various depths of processing were illustrated a few paragraphs ago in our description of the Rabinowitz–Craik–Ackerman study (1982). When simply instructed to remember a word or pair of words, the older adults often processed the information at a very superficial level, thinking about their sounds or repeating the word. When they were instructed to identify a common mediator or form an image — tasks that involve deeper, more semantic levels of processing — their performance improved. It appears that visual imagery is associated with deeper levels of processing than words are, so the use of imagery is especially useful for older adults (Craik and Byrd, 1982).

As with their apparent difficulties with organization and mediation, older subjects do not seem to process information as deeply as younger subjects. The data suggest that without direct and detailed instructions, older subjects process words in a list simply by thinking about their sounds, whereas younger subjects process them by thinking about their meaning. It has been shown, however, that age differences can be reduced or eliminated altogether if older adults are instructed in the use of encoding strategies and given additional time to use them (Treat and Reese, 1976; Craik and Rabinowitz, 1984).

Age differences in encoding and the use of organizational strategies (such as mediation and processing) are most evident in *effortful* tasks (Hoyer and Plude, 1980). These are tasks that require constant attention, that may be novel or unfamiliar, or that require a different combination of strategies than that which is typically used (Shiffrin and Schneider, 1977). For example, following a new recipe, driving an unfamiliar car, or driving to a familiar place by a different route would be effortful tasks. *Automatized* tasks, on the other hand, are thoroughly familiar and require little attention or conscious awareness. Such tasks as performing a routine household chore or playing a very familiar tune on the piano

Elderly people are less likely to have difficulty performing familiar tasks than tasks that require concentration and place demands on memory.

from memory could be considered automatized. Effortful tasks require more concentration than automatized tasks and make greater demands on memory. Thus they are an especially appropriate area for the use of encoding strategies that facilitate memory storage. Tasks that have become automatized probably required the use of encoding strategies when they were first learned, but with automatization the need to use these strategies decreases.

In summary, several lines of evidence suggest that part of the age difference typically observed in studies of memory lies in the encoding phase of memory. Older subjects do not spontaneously organize information as quickly or as effectively as younger subjects. They find it harder to form associations, and it takes them longer (Canestrari, 1968; Craik and Byrd, 1982). They tend to use less effective verbal mediators when they mediate at all, instead of visual images. In general, older people do not seem to process information as deeply as young adults. They therefore store less information and obviously can retrieve less.

We still do not know *why* this is true. Motivation seems to play a role; older subjects might not be interested in processing deeply the silly lists presented in experiments, or they might be so anxious that they can't explore meanings in depth (Fozard, 1980). Their information-processing system may be slowing down, making it more difficult for them to make the associations necessary for organization and mediation. Or the average older subject may simply be suffering from less education; perhaps he or she was never taught how to process information effectively, in schools of the early 1900s that emphasized "rote learning." All these possibilities may be correct in part. We return to discuss some of them again, in later sections of this chapter and in some of the chapters to follow.

AGE AND THE STORAGE PHASE OF MEMORY

The second phase of memory, storage, has to do with retention and loss of information. Traditionally, studies of memory storage have been based on questions about *how much* information an individual can store — the *capacity* issue — and questions about *how long* the information can remain in storage before it is lost or displaced — the *forgetting* issue. These studies have usually been guided by a general theory of memory that posits our three storage systems: the sensory store, the short-term store, and the long-term store (Atkinson and Shiffrin, 1968). The sensory and short-term stores are viewed as limited-capacity structures that ordinarily retain information for only brief periods of time; the long-term store is considered to have an almost unlimited capacity, and information is rarely lost from it.

The sensory store New incoming information is initially registered in sensory memory. This memory is sense-specific; that is, the information is stored according to the sensory modality that receives it (Poon, 1985). Visual information is stored for a brief period of ¼ to ½ second after the visual stimulus is viewed. This fleeting memory is called the *icon*, and the visual memory store is called the iconic memory. See Table 10–1 for ways you can demonstrate the presence of the icon to yourself. Facsimiles of auditory stimuli, called *echoes*, are also produced, and the

TABLE 10-1.

Personal demonstrations of sensory memory.

- Close your eyes, then open them for as short an interval of time as possible before you close them again. Note how the sharp, clear image that you picked up stays for a while and then slowly dies away.
- Listen to some sounds, say the tapping of your fingers or a few whistled notes. Notice how the distinctness of the image in your mind fades away.
- Hold your clenched fist out in front of you. Rapidly open your hand, extending two fingers, and then close your fist again. But see the shadowy trace of the fingers remain for a while even after your fingers have again formed a fist.
- Wave a pencil (or your finger) back and forth in front of your eyes while you stare straight ahead. See the shadowy image that trails behind the moving object.

This last demonstration is the most important, for with it you can estimate how long the image lasts. Change the rate at which you wave the object back and forth. Note that if you go too slowly, you lose the continuity of the image between the endpoints of the movement. At what rate does the shadowy image just barely maintain its continuity? You should discover that it takes about 10 cycles every 5 seconds to maintain the continuity of the afterimage. This means that the moving object passes in front of your eyes 20 times in 5 seconds, or four times each second — the visual trace lasts about 0.25 seconds (250 milliseconds).

Source: From Lindsay, P. H., and Norman, D. A. (1977). *Human information processing: An introduction to psychology,* 2nd ed. New York: Academic Press, p. 305. Reproduced by permission.

auditory memory store is called the echoic memory. Many psychologists consider these brief facsimiles to be an initial stage of information processing, holding information in a straightforward way for a short time so that patterns can be recognized for later processing. In the perception of speech, for example, one must remember the first sound of a word long enough to join it to the other sounds and determine the word's meaning.

There is almost no information available on the effects of aging on echoic memory (Crowder, 1980); as a result, we must focus on the iconic memory in discussing the sensory store. Iconic memory is often studied by briefly presenting a stimulus (for example, a letter or letters) to a subject and then presenting a second stimulus that eliminates or "masks" the first one. Iconic memory is assessed as the extent to which the initial stimulus is recalled after the mask. The age differences in iconic memory are small (Walsh, Till, and Williams, 1978; Cerella, Poon, and Fozard, 1982). Since visual systems decline with age (losing, for example, some of their sensitivity at low levels of illumination), we might expect the declines in the sensory store to be larger than they are. It is possible that age differences in sensory storage make some stimuli more difficult for older people to attend to and remember. Speech comprehension is one likely candidate. But the minor deficit's in sensory store that do occur probably don't contribute significantly to the more severe memory problems in long-term store experienced by the elderly. This is because age differences in short-term memory, the next stage of the information-processing system, appear to be small as well (Poon,

1985), and it is in short-term memory that information is prepared for long-term memory.

The short-term store   The short-term store is a temporary memory with a limited capacity. It holds something on the order of three words or so, possibly as many as seven or eight, but certainly less than ten. It holds this information for a brief period of time (on the order of ten or twenty seconds) although longer periods are possible if the material is mentally rehearsed. The purpose of the short-term store is to "work on" the information so that it is in proper form for storing in the more permanent long-term store; for this reason, it is sometimes called "working memory."

Recall that the work of the short-term store involves the encoding processes (organization, mediation, depth of processing) discussed previously. The major importance of the short-term store lies in its preparation (encoding) of information for permanent storage in long-term store; and there are age differences in the facility with which adults use these encoding processes. If information is bumped out of short-term store before it is properly encoded, it probably will be lost forever.

While there are age differences in *encoding* in the short-term store, there do not appear to be age differences in the *capacity* of short-term store (Craik, 1977; Fozard, 1980; Poon, 1985). Capacity refers to the amount of information retained at one time in a given store. Two lines of research converge on the same conclusion. First, studies of *memory span* — the longest string of items (numbers, letters, words) that can be repeated perfectly after a single brief presentation — show few age differences. Memory-span tasks are something like hearing a phone number from Directory Assistance with no pen at hand; you have to recall it perfectly to dial your party. The average memory span for digits is about seven and for words, about five.

A second line of evidence on the lack of age differences in short-term storage comes from what psychologists call the *recency effect* (Poon and Fozard, 1980). Given a list of words to recall, subjects typically do best on the last few words given — the most *recent* items. Older as well as younger subjects show this effect, and the older subjects remember the last few words from the list as well as younger subjects do, albeit somewhat more slowly. Since the recency effect has been attributed to the short-term store (the most recent items are placed in this store, whereas the others must be retrieved from the long-term store), the conclusion again is that old and young people do not differ in the capacity of the short-term store.

Putting information into long-term store may require different memory strategies than holding information in short-term store. If the person wishes simply to hold information temporarily in short-term store, repeating the words or letters is a useful strategy. If the goal is to encode the information for long-term store, however, it is useful to use one of the encoding strategies discussed earlier. In encoding information into long-term store, the problems faced by older adults may be a result of the tendency to use repetition rather than a more appropriate encoding strategy.

The long-term store   The long-term store is, of course, what people generally think of as memory. Whereas the age differences in sensory and short-term memory are minimal, there may be large age differences in long-term memory, particularly when the material to be remembered exceeds the span of short-term store. The use of the encoding processes we have been discussing is crucial if the information is to be remembered and retained in long-term store. Once material has been placed in long-term store, most psychologists regard it as permanent, with loss occurring only in exceptional cases of brain injury or disease. Since the probability of diseases that can affect brain tissue or brain functions is much greater in old people, this sort of loss may be a factor in age differences in memory. Also, some psychologists have begun to ask whether information stored in long-term memory can be changed by the acquisition of more recent information (Loftus and Loftus, 1980). We discuss this issue later in this chapter in the section "Everyday Memories." This effect too would weigh more heavily on older memories, which have had more time to substitute new information. Nevertheless, most of the discussion of age differences in long-term storage center not on capacity or loss but rather on the ease or difficulty people have when trying to locate information in this vast repository of facts and ideas. This is the issue of retrieval, the third phase of memory.

AGE AND RETRIEVAL

We have considered evidence that older adults have more difficulty than young adults encoding information. We now consider evidence that older adults also have more difficulty retrieving the information they have stored. We are, in effect, suggesting that old people have trouble getting the information into their long-term stores and that they also have trouble getting it out. Difficulties in encoding and retrieval account for most of the overall age differences observed in memory experiments (Poon, 1985).

Recall versus recognition   As we mentioned earlier, one way to demonstrate retrieval difficulties is to show that people can *recognize* words that they cannot *recall*. They might not be able to recall BASKET, for example, when asked to dredge up the words from the list just presented, but they can recognize it when asked, "Was BASKET on the list?" A number of studies show that older subjects benefit more than younger subjects when recognition tests are used instead of recall tests (Schonfield and Robertson, 1966; Poon, 1985). Studies show that age differences on recognition tests are small or nonexistent, whereas the age differences found for recall of factual information are significant. Recall and recognition may be affected by different encoding strategies (Smith, 1980; Poon, 1985). The use of efficient encoding strategies may be especially important for recall.

In a twenty-one-year longitudinal study of word recognition and recall (Schaie, 1980), word recognition showed modest gain until age sixty and only moderate decline thereafter (see Figure 10–4). The word recognition test involved a multiple-choice task in which a word having the same meaning as the stimulus word had to be picked from a set of one correct answer and three distractors. In contrast, the word recall test (which required writing all the words beginning with

FIGURE 10–4.

Cumulative age changes by sex from twenty-one-year longitudinal study of word recognition and recall. Word recognition was measured by the Verbal Meaning Test and word recall by the Word Fluency Test (Thurstone and Thurstone, 1949).

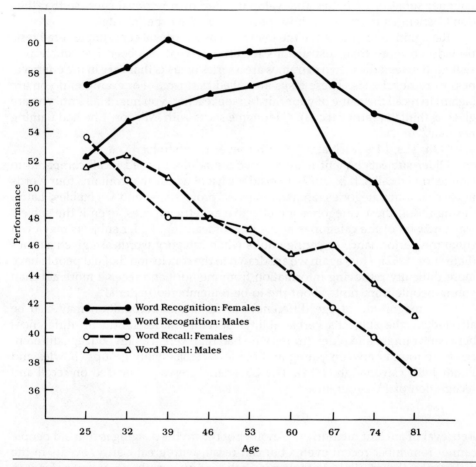

Source: Reprinted by permission of the publisher, from Schaie, K. W. (1980). Cognitive development in aging. In L. K. Obler and M. L. Martin (Eds.), *Language and communication in the elderly*, Lexington, MA: Lexington Books, D. C. Heath and Company. Copyright 1980, by D. C. Heath and Company.

the letter "S" one could think of) showed marked age changes beginning in young adulthood and accelerating in old age (Schaie, 1980). An unexpected sex difference also turned up; the difference between recall and recognition in old age was much greater for women than for men. The sex difference is yet to be explained, but the age changes support the general conclusion of studies comparing recall and recognition: older subjects have a lot of information in memory storage that they cannot get to in difficult retrieval tasks such as recall.

Cross-sectional studies comparing recall and recognition confirm the relative advantage to older subjects in recognition tests, although they generally show slight age differences even in the easier recognition task (Craik, 1977; Botwinick, 1978). One way to interpret these results is to suggest that older subjects benefit more than younger subjects when retrieval cues are improved; recognition tests provide more and/or better cues than recall tests. There is also the assumption that younger subjects are better at developing their own retrieval cues, so that they don't benefit as much from those provided by the experimenter.

Recognition tests provide the item itself as a retrieval cue; simple recall tests provide no more than instructions to retrieve what has been previously presented. Between these two extremes are a series of tasks that vary in the effectiveness of retrieval cues. These tasks are called *cued recall*. For example, if you are (again) to recall the name of your third-grade teacher, you might fail until you are given a "hint" (a retrieval cue): "Her name starts with 'M' " or "She had flaming red hair."

"Oh, yes, Mrs. McNally!" You retrieve successfully.

Older subjects benefit relative to young adults in cued recall compared to simple, free recall (Craik, 1977). Consider a list of words that contains four words in each of four categories: animals, names, professions, and vegetables. Later, during recall, these categories are effective as retrieval cues, even if the subject was unaware of the categories at the time of learning. Older subjects may even equal the performance of young adults when category words are given as cues (Laurence, 1967). Thus again we are drawn to the conclusion that old people have more difficulty retrieving information from memory and receive more aid than young people from hints about the to-be-remembered material.

The magnitude of age differences in recall and recognition may also be affected by the subject's verbal ability. Several studies found no differences between younger and older groups who had high verbal ability, but age differences were found between young and old low-verbal-ability groups (Bowles and Poon, 1982; Cavanaugh, 1984). The Cavanaugh research focused on recall and recognition of TV programs.

Retrieval of ancient memories   Another of the myths of aging is that old people cannot remember recent events but can recall, with great clarity, events in the distant past (Erber, 1981). In the nineteenth century, one theorist went so far as to formulate what has come to be known as Ribot's Law (1882), which states that information is forgotten in a sequence that is the reverse of the order in which it was acquired. In other words, distant events are remembered more clearly than recent events. An old woman, for example, may claim to remember her first day in school "as if it were yesterday," even though the real yesterday seems to have passed from her memory. Is the old woman telling the truth? Is there anything to the myth of ancient memories?

As a general rule, memory for an event is greatest immediately following the event and then declines systematically; recognition memory declines less rapidly than recall. The literature on age differences in remote memory suggests that such differences as occur are minimal. Even though remote memory holds up well in older adults, it is not superior to the recall of recent events (Erber, 1981).

Remote memory is commonly evaluated by testing a subject's recall and recognition of public events that have occurred over several decades. One study, for example, examined recall of events that occurred between the 1920s and the 1970s (Poon et al., 1979). There were no differences in recall of recent events from the 1970s versus remote events (1920s to 1960s). The old remembered the 1970s and 1920s to 1960s events as well as the young.

What is probably happening when people feel that ancient events are clearer in their mind than more recent events is that a particularly sharp memory from the past is being compared with some vaguely encoded events of the last day or two (Erber, 1981). The recent events may be poorly encoded because of distraction, lack of interest, decreasing abilities, or a number of other reasons. The remote events may be in sharper focus also for a number of reasons. Perhaps an uncommon retrieval cue triggers a well-formed memory that is not often retrieved, as when one encounters the name of a person who was a close companion in grade school but who subsequently moved away. People are often surprised at how good their memories are over long periods of time. Or the remote event was of such personal significance that it was thought about (rehearsed) many times after the actual event, leading to an exceptionally strong memory called a "flashbulb" memory (Brown and Kulick, 1977). People who were adults in 1963, for example, often remember with great clarity what they were doing at the moment they heard of John F. Kennedy's assassination.

Young and middle-aged adults probably experience this strange reversal of memory strengths — remote memories are stronger than recent memories — almost as often as old adults. Perhaps old people encode recent events less well than younger adults, and it is possible they rehearse ancient memories more often (reminiscing). But more often the reversal of memory strengths, a natural phenomenon that occurs at all ages, is incorrectly viewed as a sign of aging ("My memory is no good anymore") and for that reason is marked as significant only among older people. The truth is that memory is a notoriously leaky repository in humans of all ages. The myth that old memories are set in mental concrete that has hardened to the extent that it will not accept new inputs — well, that's pure nonsense.

Nevertheless, a few people (like Great-Aunt Lucille) experience atypical difficulties in encoding *new* events. Some, but by no means all, these people are elderly. Probably these difficulties result from temporary or permanent changes in brain function, probably because of changes in brain chemistry (Marsh, 1980). In humans, such changes can be induced in adults of all ages by prescription medications or voluntary use of alcohol, marijuana, and similar drugs; these effects are usually transient. In elderly adults, and sometimes in younger adults, brain disease that results in biochemical imbalance is often reflected in the inability to remember recent events (because they are not encoded and stored), although memory for less recent events is unimpaired (Butler and Lewis, 1982).

Reminiscences strengthen memories of earlier events.

EVERYDAY MEMORIES

In the typical laboratory experiment on memory, subjects are presented with a list of words and later asked to recall or recognize these words. Many researchers have criticized such studies as irrelevant to the kinds of real-life situations in which people use their memories (Hartley, Harker, and Walsh, 1980). The older subjects may have more difficulty than younger subjects in encoding word lists into memory and later retrieving them, but they don't seem to have difficulties remembering the time and place of the experiment; they retrieve with ease information about income, education, number of grandchildren, and other data requested in psychologists' questionnaires; they have no trouble encoding the instructions for the experiment (West, 1986). Elderly subjects may not spontaneously organize word lists for effective recall, but ask a seventy-year-old fan of soap operas to recount the last two weeks of "The Young and the Restless" or "Days of Our Lives" and you are likely to observe a confident, highly organized, and accurate response.

Much remains to be learned about how memory functions in everyday situations. Some memory psychologists distinguish between *episodic* memories, which concern specific events (episodes) that occurred at a specific time and place in the life of the rememberer, and *semantic* memories, which concern general, context-free facts about the world, such as the meanings of words, rules of grammar and arithmetic, personal beliefs, and the like (Tulving, 1972). Many types of everyday memory tasks are episodic in nature (for example, trying to recall a person's name by remembering the situation in which one met the person;

recalling the date on which a given conversation occurred). Present research findings suggest that the elderly do worse than younger subjects on episodic tasks; however, some studies find no age difference in semantic memory tasks (Hartley, Harker, and Walsh, 1980). Kausler has done a series of interesting studies on episodic recall of activities (Kausler and Hakami, 1983). Young and elderly adults were given a series of topics to discuss with the experimenter. Half the participants were forewarned that there would be a recall test (intentional memory) following the discussions; the remaining participants were not forewarned (incidental memory). There was an age difference on the recall task of the topics of discussion; however, there was no age difference on a recognition task of whether or not a particular question was asked during the conversation. Most interestingly, there was no effect for either age group for whether or not the subjects were forewarned about the recall task. Kausler's research suggests that intentionality to remember an activity, like a conversation, is not an important factor in recall. In activities such as conversation, one may not routinely engage in use of the internal memory strategies (for example, organization, depth of processing) which laboratory research has shown to be useful in recall. However, Kausler has also found that many repetitions of an activity are particularly useful in aiding the older adult's recall of the activity.

Episodic memory studies have generally investigated recall of activities which have already occurred. In contrast, prospective memory involves remembering to do something in the future (for example, to turn off the oven when the cake is done, to keep the dental appointment scheduled for tomorrow). Older adults have reported problems with forgetting prospective memory tasks. However, in most studies the older subjects have performed as well or better than the young adults (Poon and Schaffer, 1982). Time monitoring strategies are important in prospective memory tasks. These can include checking one's calendar for the activities of the day, or setting the kitchen timer to remind one when the cake is done. Both young and older adults report using these time monitoring devices.

The contextual approach A recent approach to the study of memory suggests that the processes of memory should be studied in a broader context, taking into account such variables as the subject's prior knowledge of the material to be learned, level of verbal ability, motivation, and other factors. This view, called the contextual approach, maintains that one must examine the interaction between the characteristics of the subject, the type of material used in the task, and memory performance (Hultsch and Dixon, 1984).

This type of research often investigates the processing of information from prose passages, which are certainly more common in everyday experience than word lists. For example, we often obtain general information from written sources such as newspapers and magazines. In one carefully designed experiment, for example, young, middle-aged, and elderly subjects were asked to read short passages of less than 200 words. Later, the subjects were asked to recall the passages, then to give a one-sentence summary, then to complete a partial outline of the passage. No age differences were found in any of these tasks (Meyer and Rice, 1983).

Prose research has yielded two major findings (Hultsch and Dixon, 1984). First, age differences are not nearly as common in text (prose) memory performance as they are in recall of lists. Second, the presence or absence of age differences is a function of the contextual factors that mediate the subject's processing of text materials. Age differences have been found to be smaller when the text material is well organized, when the subject has prior knowledge of the topic, and when the subject has above-average verbal ability (Hultsch and Dixon, 1984).

Several studies indicate that older adults recall the "gist" of a well-organized text passage as well as young adults (Hultsch and Dixon, 1984). If, however, the central meaning of the text is difficult to extract from the prose passage and the subject has lower verbal ability, the elderly may have more difficulty identifying a passage's main idea. The elderly's recall of specific details may be more limited than recall of a central idea (Zelinski, Gilewski, and Thompson, 1980; Meyer and Rice, 1983). This may be because old and young employ qualitatively different processing styles (Labouvie-Vief and Schell, 1982). The old may focus on the main idea, whereas the young are more observant of detail and minor points. Thus what appear to be inefficient processing behaviors on the part of the elderly may actually reflect adaptive changes. As a result of life experiences or lower levels of mental energy, the old may focus on higher levels of meaning devoting less attention to details.

Self-reports of memory   Contextual studies are, of course, another form of laboratory investigation. They may more accurately reflect real-life conditions of remembering than studies of list recall do, but they are still open to the criticism that they give a distorted picture of how people actually use their memories in their daily lives. What can be said about how people use their memories as they go about their daily affairs?

Unfortunately, studies of real-life remembering and forgetting are few and far between. What we do know is based largely on self-reports, which may present a distorted picture of what actually occurs. The studies show that, when questioned about their memory in everyday living, older adults report more memory failures, and they are more likely to be upset when a memory failure occurs (Zarit, Cole, and Guider, 1981; Cavanaugh, Grady, and Perlmutter, 1983). Older adults also reported that they forgot names, routines, and objects more often than young adults did. Memory failures were more common in situations outside the older adults' normal routine and when they were required to recall information they had not recently used. Several studies found that forgetting names was the most commonly reported failure of memory (Zelinski, Gilewski, and Thompson, 1980; Cavanaugh, Grady, and Perlmutter, 1983).

Laboratory studies of memory have focused on the individual's use of internal memory aids (for example, mnemonics, depth of processing). However, in real-life memory tasks, people often use external memory aids (lists, appointment schedules, timers). In terms of the types of information for which they used memory aids and the types of aids used, younger and older adults were quite similar. Older adults used aids more frequently than younger adults did. Both groups used external aids (such as written reminders) more often than internal aids. Thus, although the internal aids most often studied by psychologists are useful and important, they are not the aids used most often by either young or older adults (Poon and Schaffer, 1982; West, 1986). Internal and external memory aids are probably most useful in different types of situations. Internal memory aids may be most useful, for example, in trying to remember a person's name, External memory aids may be particularly useful in prospective memory tasks or when recalling a list of items.

Distortion of long-term memory   It is widely believed by psychologists and laypeople alike that information is permanently stored once it has been placed in long-term memory (Tulving, 1972). The information is not lost even when it cannot be retrieved. Recent research, however, suggests that information in long-term memory can be distorted (Loftus and Loftus, 1980; Loftus, 1983). This series of studies involved complex, real-world events, and the distortions were systematic and predictable. Subjects witnessed a complex event such as a film of a crime or accident; they subsequently received misleading information. Later, they recalled certain events incorrectly — the color of a car, whether a sign was a stop sign or a yield sign, whether there was a barn at a certain location. Several variables were found to influence the likelihood that a memory would be distorted by a postevent suggestion.

First, distortions in memory are more likely when the interval between the event and the presentation of the misinformation is long rather than short. Second, memories of violent events are more likely to be distorted than memories of nonviolent events. Those who see mentally shocking events (for example, crime, accidents) have poorer retention, probably because the encoding of information into long-term storage is disrupted. Third, postevent information is more likely to be accepted if it is presented in an auxiliary clause than if it appears in a main clause of a sentence. That is, misinformation is more likely to be assimilated if it is presented casually and assimilated unintentionally. Fourth, memory distortion is minimized if subjects are warned that the postevent message that they are about to receive might contain misinformation. To be effective, the warning must be given just before the presentation of the misleading information. Once an alteration in memory occurs, it is difficult to induce the witness to retrieve the original memory; attempts to recover the original memory are often unsuccessful (Bekerian and Bowers, 1983). The possibility of distortions of long-term memory is of significance in a number of real-life situations. For example, the credibility of an eyewitness in a court case is based on the assumption of accurate recall of long-term memories. Likewise, national surveys on topics such as voting behavior, health, or crime victimization are based on the assumption that the respondents accurately remember and report events and decisions occurring sometime in the past (Loftus, Fienberg, and Tanur, 1985). Research on the conditions under which memory distortions occur can be useful in judging the accuracy of recall of long-term events in daily life.

Memory complaints, depression, and drug use   The extent of memory problems in healthy older persons has probably been exaggerated by the elderly themselves and by the relatives and professionals who associate with them (Zarit, 1980). This is reflected in the finding that complaints about memory problems, which are quite common, do not correlate with scores on objective tests of memory performance (Kahn, Zarit, and Hilbert, 1975; Perlmutter, 1978; Thompson, 1980).

Significant correlations are found, however, between depression and complaints of poor memory for adults of all ages (Kahn, Zarit, and Hilbert, 1975; Zarit, 1980). Depression has been found to be related to memory complaints both in people with normal brain functioning and in those who have chronic brain syndromes, that is, who have actual pathological disturbances of memory. Memory complaints among the depressed, and perhaps other self-perceptions of cognitive performance, may be influenced by stereotypical age expectations and also by the tendency for depressed persons to underestimate their abilities.

Drug side effects may also affect cognitive functioning in general and memory in particular. Drugs such as tranquilizers, antidepressants, sedatives, and hypnotics are widely prescribed and used in older populations (Butler and Lewis, 1982). Unfortunately, these drugs can reinforce some of the slowing tendencies observed in older people and aggravate any existing sense of aging and depression. In some cases, inappropriate dosages of drugs can result in mental confusion and memory loss. These potential side effects are especially serious in older people because they often have inefficiencies in metabolism. Older people absorb drugs more slowly, distribute them through their bodies differently, and metabolize and excrete them from their systems more slowly than the young. As a result, high levels of medication can build up in their systems over a relatively brief period.

There is also potential for drugs to improve cognitive functioning and memory. Pharmacological research is currently focusing on the use of drugs to improve neurotransmitter and neuroendocrine functioning in the elderly. Unfortunately, the results of research in this area have been disappointing so far (Marsh, 1980; Poon, 1985). Those who investigate the possibilities of pharmacological intervention for the aged face two special problems. First, they must target a specific cognitive process that a drug is supposed to influence. For example, the effect of the drug on long-term memory versus short-term memory must be examined; since most memory problems involve long-term store, this would be the area of most concern. Second, the problems resulting from metabolic variations must be taken into account. Too small a dosage may not help, whereas too large a dosage may have serious side effects. For a particular subject, the dosage would have to fall within a narrow range to be most beneficial. Thus the correct dosage would have to be determined for each individual and careful monitoring would be necessary. See also Chapter 12.

PROBLEM-SOLVING

Many of the learning and memory tasks described in the previous sections were relatively simple problems. Another type of cognitive activity, problem-solving, is more complex and may involve aspects of learning and memory discussed in the preceding sections. Problem-solving requires that a person assess the present state of a situation, define the desired state, and find a way to transform the present state to the desired state (Reese and Rodeheaver, 1985). Thus, to give a simple example, one might recognize that one's phone is not working properly, define a fixed phone as a desirable goal, and figure out how the problem can be solved.

The process of solving a problem has been broken down into four steps (Polya, 1971). The first step is to *understand the problem,* which involves gathering information on the problem and identifying its important features. With our phone example, this might entail understanding that the malfunction may be in the phone itself or may be in the wiring inside or outside the house. The second step is to *devise a plan,* using past experience for guidance. Psychologists are particularly interested in whether the problem-solver identifies relevant strategies to employ in solving the problem. The use of a "relevant strategy" would ensure that one devises an efficient plan that does not involve needless time or expense in having the phone repaired. The plan might be to first determine if the malfunction is in a particular phone, by checking to see if other phones in the house are working properly. If all phones are malfunctioning, then the best "guess" might be that the problem is in the wiring. We might then notify the phone service division, ask if there has been a service disruption in the area or ask that a repair person be sent to examine the wiring.

The third step is to *carry out the plan.* If our plan is a good one, this step should be fairly simple. If troubles arise, then our plan must be revised. The final step is to review *what one has done.* Does the phone work? If one had to approach the same problem again, should one do it differently? Why did the plan work or not work? This series of steps may seem so simple and obvious that one might suppose it has few applications, but it is useful in a variety of contexts. For example, it serves as the basis for the process of managerial problem-solving and decision-making that is taught in business schools (Bobele and Buchanan, 1976).

Unfortunately, most studies of problem-solving have used "laboratory" types of problems rather than problems taken from real life. It is widely assumed that the same steps and variables are used on both types of problems, but there is little documentation for this view. An elderly subject once illustrated this quandary very neatly for one of the authors, asking, "Is this *your* problem or *my* problem that we are going to solve?" Too often, it is the concerns of the psychologist and not the problems of the subject that are addressed through research. Several types of laboratory problems commonly studied are discussed below.

Concept attainment   In concept attainment tasks, items in a set are divided into two subsets in accordance with some characteristics or rule. The subject demonstrates mastery of the rule by distinguishing the items that reflect the rule from those that do not reflect the rule. If the set includes red circles and green circles, the rule might be "Choose the red circle; do not choose the green circle." In more complicated problems, there might be several relevant rules.

A number of studies of this type, in which the performances of younger and older adults were compared, found that the old solved fewer problems than the young (Crovitz, 1966; Offenbach, 1974). One such study (Hartley, 1981) involved a "poisoned foods" task and young, middle-aged, young-old, and old-old adults. The subjects were presented with a "meal" consisting of three courses (appetizer, entree, dessert). They were told whether a diner would live or be ill after eating that meal. Their task was to determine which two courses had been tampered with. For example, Dinner A — oysters, filet, cake — and Dinner B — melon, filet, pie — made the diner ill, while Dinner C — melon, filet, cake — was okay. The problem solution involved identifying the rule: "Illness resulted if the meal had either oysters or pie or both." The elderly groups did less well than the young and the middle-aged groups. Some of the problems encountered were that subjects failed to ignore irrelevant information and the subjects tended to fixate on useless hunches (Hartley, 1981). Although the elderly did not spontaneously employ effective strategies, several training studies have found that the elderly's performance could be improved with brief training procedures (Sanders et al., 1975; Sanders et al., 1976).

Twenty questions   In this type of task, the subject is presented with an array of pictures or words, only one of which is the correct choice. The task is to determine the correct choice by asking less than twenty questions that can be answered with a yes or no. The most efficient strategy is to ask a series of constraint-seeking questions (for example, "Is it an animal?"), each of which eliminates a set of possible answers. Asking questions that refer to only one item is inefficient. Again, the elderly did less well than younger age groups (Denney, 1980), and again their performance improved significantly after training in the use of constraint-seeking questions (Denney, 1979).

Piagetian tasks   Piagetian theory assumes that concrete operational abilities such as classification and conservation develop during middle childhood and that formal operational abilities are achieved in adolescence (Hooper, Hooper, and Colbert, 1984). Do these abilities decline in old age? One hypothesis suggests that operational abilities decline in reverse of the order in which they develop (Papalia and Bielby, 1974; Muhs, Hooper, and Papalia-Finlay, 1980); formal operational thought would decline before conservation. Studies of the elderly's performance on various Piagetian tasks have yielded mixed results. Some show that the elderly do more poorly than younger people (K. H. Rubin, 1973); others find no age differences (Papalia-Finlay et al., 1980). Once again, success is positively correlated with higher levels of education and higher fluid intelligence scores (Reese and Rodeheaver, 1985). Also, training has been shown to improve the elderly's performance (Hornblum and Overton, 1976). Furthermore, there is serious doubt about whether everyone achieves formal operational abilities during adolescence in the first place. One study found that only 30 percent of the adults studied had completed the transition to formal operations (Kuhn et al., 1977). Piaget (1972) suggested that the attainment of formal operations is influenced by one's life experiences, including job and vocational training. A lawyer, for example, may be able to use formal operational thought in presenting a legal argument to a jury but be unable to use this form of thought in solving a physics problem. Moreover, some (Labouvie-Vief, 1982, 1985; Meacham, 1983; Kuhn, Pennington and Leadbeater, 1983) have questioned whether the more advanced stages of formal reasoning are always the most adaptive and useful in real-world problem-solving and daily life.

In summary, these studies suggest that there are age differences in problem-solving. The elderly do less well on a number of types of tasks. Several explanations of this finding have been offered. It may be that problem-solving ability is a function of educational level, fluid intelligence, or both, rather than aging per se. These factors, in turn, may reflect cohort differences. Moreover, brief educational training has been shown to improve all types of problem-solving discussed (Willis, 1985). This suggests that the elderly possess the competence to perform the tasks but do not spontaneously employ the necessary strategies. At present, we do not know why they don't use these strategies or whether, after training, they will transfer the use of these strategies to the problems of real life.

Learning, Memory, and Education

Learning and memory have always been important topics in psychology because of their profound implications for human behavior. Unlike lower animals, who have a vast stock of instinctive behaviors that allow them to adapt to their environments, humans adapt through learning. Life, for us, is an educational process, some of it formal (in schools) but most of it informal (through everyday experience). We hear now and then that education for middle-aged and older adults is senseless. The truth is, however, that adults of all ages can profit from education. Moreover, in a rapidly changing society, adults are in particularly great need of formal educational experiences to permit them to maintain responsible citizenship, and to prepare them for career changes, retirement, and life at different age stages. Adult education can also be useful in compensating for the deficits that often do occur with aging, as we explain in the following sections.

MEMORY TRAINING STUDIES

Although the research we have reviewed in this chapter suggests that older adults may have more difficulties than young adults in the acquisition or encoding of information and in retrieving stored information, these age differences are surprisingly slight. The clear conclusion is that adults of all ages, barring illness, should have no difficulty in benefiting from formal training and educational opportunities. One area of growing interest is memory training research with the elderly (Poon, Rubin, and Wilson, 1986).

Most research on memory training has focused on the encoding of information into long-term store. This research, which often focuses on training older adults in the encoding strategies described earlier in this chapter, has shown that many older adults do not spontaneously employ encoding strategies, although they can do so when they are instructed in their use (Poon, Walsh-Sweeney, and Fozard, 1980). Thus training in strategy use could be useful to many people.

One of the most common memory problems is face–name recall, remembering people's names when you meet them. In a series of studies examining the effectiveness of mediational procedures involving imagery, Yesavage taught subjects to form associations using visual imagery (Yesavage, 1983; Yesavage and Rose, 1984; the earlier article is summarized at the end of this chapter). Those who learned this imagery mnemonic (a mnemonic is a memory device) were found to have significantly improved face–name recall. Learning of the mnemonic was improved when subjects were given pretraining in forming images. A more recent study suggested that pretraining in muscle relaxation techniques reduced performance anxiety, thereby improving learning and the use of the imagery mnemonic (Yesavage and Rose, 1984).

In another series of studies, the relationship between memory training, memory complaints, and depression was examined (Zarit, 1980; Zarit, Cole, and Guider, 1981). You will recall that memory complaints have been found to be associated with depression, but that there is no relationship between memory complaints and actual memory performance. In these studies, older adults were randomly assigned to one of two groups, a memory training group that focused on encoding strategies and a current events discussion group. The current events group was included to provide group interaction and to allow for the possibility that people's abilities would improve even without actual instruction in procedures likely to enhance memory. Four ninety-minute sessions were held with each group. There were several important findings. First, after training, the group that received memory training did better on several memory tasks. No similar improvement was found for the current events group. Second, the level of subjective complaints about memory, which was the same in both groups prior to training, declined for those who received memory training and for those who discussed current events. Third, since memory complaints decreased in both groups, it could be concluded that the reductions in memory complaints were not related to actual improvements in memory resulting from training.

The study involving imagery mnemonics and the one described in the preceding paragraph both used as subjects elderly people living in the community. Can similar procedures in memory training be used to improve the functioning of those who suffer from dementia? The evidence so far is not very encouraging. In a study of the effectiveness of visual imagery training among those with senile dementia, it was found that subjects improved somewhat in tests given immediately after the training, but that the improvements were not maintained in later tests (Zarit, Zarit, and Reever, 1982). However, some success with very intensive memory training has been reported for amnesiacs and head injury patients (Wilson and Moffat, 1984).

In summary, the memory performance of healthy elderly people can be improved through memory training. Whether this improvement is maintained over time remains to be seen. Neither do we know whether the elderly spontaneously use the training strategies they learn in everyday situations. It appears that participation in a group can lead to a decrease in memory complaints whether or not actual memory performance has improved. Finally, memory training for people with clinical problems shows relatively less promise.

It should be kept in mind that virtually all training research on memory has focused on the use of internal memory aids (encoding strategies). Since we know that old and young people alike often use external aids, such as making lists, it is important that future memory research examine training in this area as well.

THE OLDER ADULT LEARNER

An ultimate goal of most psychological research is to help people function better in their everyday lives. Much of the memory research we have been discussing has practical implications for adults learning and functioning in their daily life. We summarize some of these implications in this section.

As you will recall, research shows that the elderly often do not spontaneously use encoding strategies but that they can use them when instructed or reminded to do so. Whether older adults never acquired these strategies in their youth because of historical changes in educational procedures, or whether their use of these strategies declined with age is still being debated, but it is clear that they benefit greatly when these strategies are used. Thus it may be beneficial for educational programs for the elderly to take into account their need for "instruction in learning" as well as instruction in the substantive material of the course itself.

Use of encoding strategies can be fostered in a number of different ways. The instructor can provide mnemonics to aid the adult in remembering steps in a procedure or in recalling technical terms. Some research indicates that it is particularly effective for students to generate their own mnemonics or imagery mediators, rather than relying on instructor-generated mnemonics. It is also useful to discuss with students which types of memory strategies are appropriate for various memory tasks. For example, rehearsal may be an effective strategy when the goal is to keep information in short-term memory. Thus repeating a phone number several times will help someone remember it until it can be written down. Rehearsal is probably not the most effective strategy, however, for storing information in long-term memory. For encoding information into long-term memory (for example, remembering someone's name or a grocery list), organizational strategies, mnemonics, and imagery mediators are more useful. Likewise, in prospective memory tasks, use of time monitoring strategies (for example, checking one's schedule) or timing devices (kitchen timer) have been shown to be particularly effective.

Older people remember best when appropriate encoding strategies are used *and* when a supportive retrieval context is provided. Thus concern for retrieval cues, as well as encoding strategies, is needed. The elderly, you will recall, do just as well as younger people on recognition tasks but have more trouble when it comes to verbatim recall. Older adults are also more adept at retaining the gist of a text but have trouble remembering details. These findings have implications for the selection of procedures for assessing the learning of older adult students. Multiple-choice and true–false items may be more effective procedures, since both involve recognition memory. Adults might also do well on essay questions that require discussion of the main points or gist of a topic. Short answer or fill-in-the-blank questions, on the other hand, would be difficult because they require recall of specific information. In addition, providing sufficient time for recall is important. Research suggests that older adults particularly benefit from additional time during the retrieval phase.

It is especially important that reading materials for older adults be well organized. Research on prose learning and text recall discussed earlier in this chapter showed that older adults can remember the gist of a well-organized text as well as younger people, but that age differences increase when the key points in text material were difficult to identify (Hultsch and Dixon, 1984). The use of meaningful examples in instructional materials is also helpful. A common rationale given is that adults are more motivated to learn information that is meaningful. In addition, the meaningfulness of the material facilitates deep processing, thereby increasing retention in long-term memory.

Older learners may be anxious about undertaking new learning, in part because stereotypes suggest that the elderly have poor memories and are poor learners. Yesavage and Rose (1984), you will remember, found that pretraining in anxiety reduction accelerated learning of memory mnemonics. Thus it is especially important that the educator and the learning environment be supportive when disseminating information to the elderly.

Finally, older learners may have some loss of vision or hearing, and compensation for this loss can facilitate their processing of information. Use of reading materials with larger print is a well-recognized aid. Another approach is to avoid speaking quickly, not only to make things easier for those who have hearing problems but to allow for slightly slower rates of information processing. Normal speech presents little problem in most cases (see Chapter 11). Seating the hearing-impaired near the speaker where they can see lip movements is helpful too. Repeating the main points several times during a presentation may also be useful. Some research suggests that capacity to pay attention may decline with age (Craik and Byrd, 1982) and repetition ensures that the student may grasp a point even if he or she was inattentive when it was first presented.

ADULT EDUCATION

A surprisingly large number of adults are involved in formal educational pursuits. Some take classes for credit, but most take noncredit classes given by continuing education or extension programs, industry, community agencies, and other organizations. It is variously estimated that between 12 and 30 percent of the adult population takes part in some form of adult education (Cross, 1981).

Those involved in adult education are more likely to be in young or middle adulthood and to be above average in education level and family income (Cross, 1981). Those who work outside the home or who are looking for work outside the home are more likely to be involved than those who do not work. College graduates are more than twice as likely to be involved as high school graduates, and high school graduates are more than twice as likely to be involved as high school dropouts (Carp, Peterson, and Roelfs, 1974). Among adults over age fifty-four, approximately 5 percent participate, compared with 12 percent or more of all adults.

The best single predictor of whether an adult is involved in adult education is his or her level of education, so the lower levels of participation among current cohorts of elderly may be partially a function of these cohorts' lower level of education. High school graduation appears to be a significant benchmark in determining who participates in adult education, and while the median level of education for the adult population as a whole is twelve years, roughly the equivalent of a high school education, the median level for current elderly cohorts

Like these computer programmers, workers in many occupations must return to school now and then to update their knowledge.

is nine to ten years, the equivalent of one or two years of high school. Among adults as a whole, the participation rate in adult education for those with ten years of education is about 4.1 percent, which is comparable to the participation rate among today's elderly. Thus the low participation rate of the elderly may be in part a cohort effect. As the education level of future elder cohorts rises, their participation in adult education may also increase.

Adult education typically involves goals which are different from those of early education (Birren and Woodruff, 1973; McCluskey, 1982; Willis, 1985). These goals are often closely related to the types of transitions experienced in young and middle adulthood (Stagner, 1985). Two broad categories account for over half the formal educational coursework undertaken by adults. These are career-related education and courses related to personal development, hobbies, and recreation. Vocational courses account for the largest proportion of formal educational coursework undertaken by professionals (Houle, 1981). Interestingly, business and industry, rather than universities, are the single largest providers of adult education. Career-related education can take numerous forms. The adult may return to school to upgrade his or her occupation status (for example, promotion to a managerial position). Alternatively, much of career-related adult education involves updating of job-relevant skills to combat the threat of obsolescence. A number of professions (medicine, teaching, accounting) now require continuing education for continued certification in the profession. One study (*The New York Times,* August 22, 1982) identified sixteen different professions requiring continuing education credits for continued credentialing. A growing number of middle-aged women are returning to school. Women now account for two-thirds of all adult students. In the early 1970s women cited personal growth as the major reason for returning to school. Today, they are returning to upgrade their skills in anticipation of returning to the workplace (Adelstein, Sedlacek, and Martinez, 1983). Finally, the middle-aged adults may find themselves in obsolete occupations, and therefore seek further education in making a career transition.

A second major reason for engaging in formal continuing education involves personal development, hobbies, and recreation. Except for professionals, these topics are of greatest interest to the adult learner involved in continuing education (Houle, 1981). The professional's major objective for engaging in adult education is job advancement. For the rest of the adult learner population the primary reason for engaging in adult education is to become better informed and for personal enjoyment and enrichment. This broad category can represent a variety of concerns adults may have. Due to rapid technological change, adults may feel the need to update themselves and to understand the nature of this rapid societal change. For example, computer literacy is a current popular topic. Likewise, adults may seek further information about facilitation of their own development (for example, nutrition, exercise) or may seek further understanding of the aging process being experienced by their elderly parents.

The United States considers itself to be a literate society, and so it comes as a shock to many that there is a need for adult education on basic skills such as reading, spelling, and basic math. Kozol (1985) suggests that perhaps 35 percent of our adult population suffers from inadequate levels of these basic skills. Of the 158 members of the United Nations, the United States ranks 49th in literacy (Kozol, 1985). Kozol argues that the problem of illiteracy is increasing, since a greater degree of literacy is required to cope effectively in today's high-tech job market. While illiteracy is more prevalent among the poor, it is not limited to minorities or immigrants. Many functional illiterates have completed high school. In 1985 our government will have spent $100 million annually on literacy programs.

Unfortunately, very few people participate in programs of retirement preparation (Atchley, 1984). Again, level of education is an important predictor of the need for preparation for retirement. The less education a person has, the more likely he or she is to need retirement preparation. Level of education and occupation go hand in hand, however, and those who have good jobs offering pension plans may be in relatively good shape for retirement. Those who most need preparation for retirement, on the other hand, are at income and occupational levels at which they are least likely to get it. Probably the most important part of any retirement preparation program deals with financial planning, which suggests that the most beneficial programs should begin long before retirement, during middle age.

The theme of the 1971 White House Conference on Aging was "Toward a National Policy on Aging." Over fifteen years later, many of the policy objectives identified at the conference are still relevant and still unmet. One objective focused on education and included these goals:

1. Adult education should be expanded to include more of the specific concerns of the elderly.
2. Federal funds should be earmarked specifically for library services for older people.
3. Material relevant to aging should be included in education curricula from preschool through higher education.
4. Preretirement education should be available to everyone, and well in advance of retirement.

One of the most notable and well-received educational programs for the elderly has been Elderhostel (McCluskey, 1982). The term elderhostel was borrowed from the term youth hostel. In elderhostel, the college campus is the hostel and the elders are the hostelers. Elderhostel involves a U.S.-based national network of colleges and universities engaged in providing short-term, on-campus, college-level courses to the elderly at very low cost. The elderly hostelers live in college dormitories vacant during the summer and take from one- to three-week college courses taught by regular faculty members. There is no homework, examinations, grades, or award of credits. The growth of the Elderhostel movement has been spectacular. Begun in 1975 by a small number of colleges in New Hampshire, the program now has extended to all fifty states and is estimated to serve more than 60,000 participants.

Summary

1.   Human memory is commonly viewed as a three-stage process, involving the *acquisition, storage,* and *retrieval* of information. Human learning, though it has been traditionally viewed in S–R terms as "behavior modification," can be considered as the acquisition or encoding phase of memory. Research suggests that very few significant age changes in learning occur until after the age of sixty-five. The changes after sixty-five may be due to distracting or debilitating disease, changes in motivation, or other factors; that is, these changes may not reflect "normal" deterioration in the nervous system's capability for processing information.

2.   One variable known to affect old learners more than young learners is the *pace of learning*. Old learners prefer a slower pace, especially in the time to make a response. These data suggest retrieval difficulties with older subjects. Motivational factors such as anxiety/arousal (more disruptive in older subjects), cautiousness (leading to more "omission" errors in older subjects), and lack of interest (older subjects are less interested in the silly lists psychologists present for memorization) have all been suggested as causes of the age differences in learning performance.

3.   Problem-solving is a relatively complex mental process. Four stages in problem-solving have been identified: understanding the problem, devising a plan, carrying out the plan, and reviewing what one has done. Concept attainment, twenty-questions, and Piagetian tasks indicate that the elderly are poorer problem-solvers than younger people.

4.   Current research suggests that the memory difficulties of older adults are the result of encoding *and* retrieval problems. There is much evidence that many older subjects do not spontaneously organize information for later recall, nor do they make effective use of mediational strategies as often as younger subjects. With training, however, the performance of older people improves significantly. Older adults also tend to process information at shallower depths; again, training leads to improvements.

5.   New incoming information is initially registered in sensory store for a very brief period. Older people may have minor deficits in sensory store, but they probably don't contribute significantly to loss of long-term memory. Short-term store, which holds information for a period of ten or twenty seconds, does not appear to change much with age. Age differences in long-term store, on the other hand, may be fairly large.

6.   Older people can recognize words that they cannot recall. The widespread belief that the elderly can recall events in the distant past but not in the recent past is apparently without foundation. They are probably comparing important distant events with insignificant recent events.

7.   Critics have claimed that laboratory studies of memory yield results that have little relevance to how people actually use their memories in their everyday lives.

The contextual approach suggests that the influence of a variety of factors should be considered in assessing memory. Prose research indicates that the elderly do better in recalling text passages than they do in list recall. Such age differences as occur are a function of mediating factors. Older adults recall the gist of a well-organized passage as well as young adults.

8. On self-reports of memory, older adults report more memory problems. Contrary to popular belief, memories encoded into long-term store are susceptible to distortion by information received later. Memory complaints do not correlate with scores on objective tests of memory performance, but they do correlate with depression. Drugs can have an adverse effect on memory. There may be some potential that drugs will be developed to improve memory and other aspects of cognitive functioning.

9. The memory performance of healthy older people can be improved through memory training, but training of people suffering from senile dementia shows little sustained benefit. This finding and others have important implications for education programs for the healthy elderly. Many steps can be taken to compensate for problems the elderly may face in education programs. Participation in adult education programs is strongly correlated with level of education; since the elderly have less education, their lower participation rates may be a cohort effect. Much participation in adult education is motivated by the need to remain current in one's occupation. Few people are involved in programs of preparation for retirement.

SUGGESTED READINGS

Craik, F. I. M., and Byrd, M. (1982). Problem solving and complex decision making. In F. I. M. Craik and S. Trehub (Eds.), *Aging and cognitive processes.* New York: Plenum. Review chapter on selected aspects of memory research from an information processing approach

Cross, K. P. (1981). *Adults as learners.* San Francisco, CA: Jossey-Bass. A book focusing on four questions related to adult learners: Who participates in adult learning? Why do they participate? What and how do they learn?

Poon, L. (1985). Differences in human memory with aging: Nature, causes, and clinical implications. In J. E. Birren and K. W. Schaie (Eds.), *Handbook of the psychology of aging* (2nd ed.). New York: Van Nostrand Reinhold. Comprehensive review chapter on age changes and age differences in memory.

Reese, H. W., and Rodeheaver, D. (1985). Problem solving and complex decision making. In J. E. Birren and K. W. Schaie (Eds.), *Handbook of the psychology of aging* (2nd ed.). New York: Van Nostrand Reinhold. Chapter reviews prior research on cognitive problem solving in adulthood

Wilson, B. A., and Moffat, N. (Eds.). (1984). *Clinical management of memory problems.* Rockville, MD: Aspen. The aims of this book are to give persons working with the memory impaired a better understanding of the difficulties faced by the memory impaired and to offer suggestions as to how to handle, bypass, or reduce their memory problems.

Imagery Pretraining and Maintenance and Intellectual Abilities

Elderly adults often complain of memory problems and typically perform more poorly than young adults on tests of long-term memory. Recalling people's names is especially problematic for the aged. In one large survey, it was found that forgetting names was the most frequent memory complaint of the elderly (Zelinski, Gilewski, and Thompson, 1980). This study examined training procedures to aid elderly adults in recalling names.

A mnemonic device based on visual imagery associations has been found to substantially improve name recall in young adults. This mnemonic employs a series of steps for reconstructing a person's name when one sees the face of that person. First, a prominent facial feature is identified (for example, a large mouth). Second, a vivid concrete image is derived from the person's name (for example, Whalen becomes "A whale"). Third, a visual image associating the prominent facial feature with the name transformation is formed. For example, an image of a whale with a big mouth is formed. In recalling a person's name, one uses this mnemonic by first identifying the prominent facial feature (that is, large mouth) and then using the feature to recall the visual image (that is, whale). The person's name is then reconstructed from the visual image (that is, Whalen from whale).

Yesavage suggests that such a mnemonic might be used with older adults to aid name recall. However, prior research suggests that older adults have difficulty developing and remembering visual images, a necessary aspect of this mnemonic. The purpose of this study was to examine whether giving older adults pretraining in use of visual imagery would facilitate their ability to use such a mnemonic.

METHOD

Subjects

Subjects were recruited from local senior citizen centers. The potential subjects were carefully screened for depression and organic brain disease; those who showed symptoms of either ailment were not included in the study. A total of fifty subjects were involved in the study. The mean age of these subjects was seventy-eight with a range of sixty-four to ninety-two years. Eighty percent were female. Subjects were randomly assigned to one of two groups. The groups did not differ on pretest memory measures or on demographic measures such as age, sex, education, or health status.

The subjects participated in six 1.5-hour sessions, two sessions per week for three weeks. In the first session, subjects were given an orientation to the study and a pretest of name recall. In the second and third sessions, one group, hereafter called the imagery group, was taught a series of techniques to improve their ability to form and use visual images. These included (1) procedures to imagine various vivid scenes from poems or literature; (2) procedures to study and review from memory detailed pictures of paintings or line drawings; (3) exercises in the mental "rotation" of three-dimensional objects; (4) exercises based on "find the mistake" problems, in which subjects were asked to find the mistakes in pictures that were slightly different from the stimulus picture. During the second and third sessions, the control group, on the other hand, learned techniques to improve attitudes toward aging and to combat negative stereotypes of the elderly. At the end of the third session, a test of name recall (Test 1) was performed. Both groups spent the fourth and fifth sessions learning the visual imagery mnemonic device for name recall described in the introduction. The sixth session was devoted to posttesting (Test 2) and debriefing.

Testing

For assessing name recall at pretest, Test 1 and Test 2, sets of slides of six males and six females were used. Each slide was paired with a fictitious name written on a piece of paper and presented with the name for a study period of one minute. At the first two testings (pretest, Test 1), subjects were told to study and learn the names as best they could. At the third testing (Test 2), subjects were told to use the mnemonic they had learned to remember the face–name pair. Immediately after the study period, the name recall of subjects was tested by showing them the slides for one minute each and asking them to recall the name.

RESULTS

As you can see in Figure I, both groups improved but the imagery group improved significantly more than the control group. This suggests that techniques that improve visual imagery ability may improve the elderly person's ability to use a visual-image-based mnemonic device. Although recall of the imagery group improved with imagery training alone, the improvement did not become significantly better than that of the control group until after mnemonic training. Thus the visual image mnemonic was greatly enhanced by the effectiveness of pretraining on forming visual images.

FIGURE I.

Proportion of names recalled at three points in the study. Pretest occurred in first session. Test 2 is after imagery training in the imagery group and after attitude training in the control group. Test 3 is after both groups have received training in the face–name mnemonic.

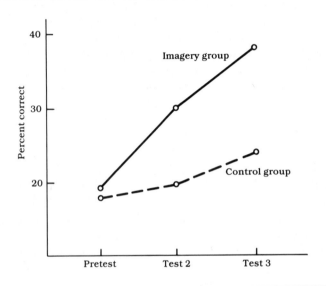

Yesavage, Jerome A. (1983). Imagery pretraining and memory training in the elderly. *Journal of Gerontology, 29,* 271–275.

Chapter Eleven

BIOLOGICAL DEVELOPMENT

The Aging Body

Writers and researchers striving to convey the nature of biological development over the life span have often used the image of the "one-hoss shay," as described in a poem by Oliver Wendell Holmes (1858). The shay was a magnificent piece of work — "the Deacon's masterpiece" — a perfectly constructed horse-drawn carriage that lasted exactly 100 years. Then all its parts collapsed at once: "all at once, and nothing first, — Just as bubbles do when they burst." This is indeed the image we want, the dream that scientific research in biological development holds out to us. We cannot live forever; death awaits us all. But perhaps we can reduce the period of dependency at the end of life and function effectively, almost to the moment of our inevitable demise — just like the one-hoss shay.

In this chapter, we explore the scientific research supporting the image of the human as at least a potential one-hoss shay. But first, for those of you who have not yet had the pleasure of the encounter, we present Holmes' original poem:

THE DEACON'S MASTERPIECE:

or, The Wonderful "One-hoss-shay"

A LOGICAL STORY
by Oliver Wendell Holmes

Have you heard of the wonderful one-hoss-shay,
That was built in such a logical way
It ran a hundred years to a day,
And then, of a sudden, it — ah, but stay,
I'll tell you what happened without delay,
Scaring the parson into fits,
Frightening people out of their wits, —
Have you heard of that, I say?

Seventeen hundred and fifty-five,
Georgius Secundus was then alive, —

Snuffy old drone from the German hive;
That was the year when Lisbon-town
Saw the earth open and gulp her down,
And Braddock's army was done so brown,
Left without a scalp to its crown.
It was on the terrible earthquake-day
That the Deacon finished the one-hoss-shay.

Now in building of chaises, I tell you what,
There is always *somewhere* a weakest spot, —
In hub, tire, felloe, in spring or thill,
In panel, or crossbar, or floor, or sill,
In screw, bolt, thoroughbrace, — lurking still,
Find it somewhere you must and will, —
Above or below, or within or without, —
And that's the reason, beyond a doubt,
A chaise *breaks down* but doesn't *wear out*.

But the Deacon swore (as Deacons, do,
With an "I dew vum," or an "I tell *yeou*,")
He should build one shay to beat the taown
'n' the keounty 'n' all the kentry raoun';
It should be so built that it *couldn't* break daown,
 — "Fur," said the Deacon, " 't's mighty plain
Thut the weakes' place mus' stan' the strain;
'n' the way t' fix it, uz I maintain,
       Is only jest
T' make that place uz strong uz the rest."

So the Deacon inquired of the village folk
Where he could find the strongest oak,
That couldn't be split nor bent nor broke, —
That was for spokes and floor and sills;
He sent for lancewood to make the thills;
The crossbars were ash, from the straightest trees,
The panels of white-wood, that cuts like cheese,
But lasts like iron for things like these;
The hubs of logs from the "Settler's ellum," —
Last of its timber, — they couldn't sell 'em,
Never an axe had seen their chips,
And the wedges flew from between their lips,
Their blunt ends frizzled like celery-tips;

Step and prop-iron, bolt and screw,
Spring, tire, axle, and linchpin too,
Steel of the finest, bright and blue;
Thoroughbrace bison-skin, thick and wide;
Boot, top, dasher, from tough old hide
Found in the pit when the tanner died.
That was the way he "put her through." —
"There!" said the Deacon, "naow she'll dew."

Do! I tell you, I rather guess
She was a wonder, and nothing less!
Colts grew horses, beards turned gray,
Deacon and deaconess dropped away,
Children and grand-children — where were they?
But there stood the stout old one-hoss-shay
As fresh as on Lisbon-earthquake-day!

EIGHTEEN HUNDRED; — it came and found
The Deacon's Masterpiece strong and sound.
Eighteen hundred increased by ten; —
"Hahnsum kerridge" they called it then.
Eighteen hundred and twenty came; —
Running as usual; much the same.
Thirty and forty at last arrive,
And then come fifty, and FIFTY-FIVE.

Little of all we value here
Wakes on the morn of its hundredth year
Without both feeling and looking queer.
In fact, there's nothing that keeps its youth,
So far as I know, but a tree and truth.
(This is a moral that runs at large;
Take it. — You're welcome. — No extra charge.)

FIRST OF NOVEMBER, — the Earthquake-day. —
There are traces of age in the one-hoss-shay,
A general flavor of mild decay,
But nothing local, as one may say.
There couldn't be, — for the Deacon's art
Had made it so like in every part
That there wasn't a chance for one to start.
For the wheels were just as strong as the thills,
And the floor was just as strong as the sills,
And the panels just as strong as the floor,
And the whippletree neither less nor more,
And the back-crossbar as strong as the fore,
And spring and axle and hub *encore.*
And yet, *as a whole,* it is past a doubt
In another hour it will be *worn out!*

First of November, 'Fifty-five!
This morning the parson takes a drive.
Now, small boys, get out of the way!
Here comes the wonderful one-hoss-shay,
Drawn by a rat-tailed, ewe-necked bay.
"Huddup!" said the parson. — Off went they.

The parson was working his Sunday's text, —
Had got to *fifthly,* and stopped perplexed
At what the — Moses — was coming next.

All at once the horse stood still,
Close by the meet'n'-house on the hill.
— First a shiver, and then a thrill,
Then something decidedly like a spill, —
And the parson was sitting upon a rock,
At half-past nine by the meet'n'-house clock, —
Just the hour of the Earthquake shock!
— What do you think the parson found,
When he got up and stared around?

The poor old chaise in a heap or mound,
As if it had been to the mill and ground.
You see, of course, if you're not a dunce.
How it went to pieces all at once, —
All at once, and nothing first, —
Just as bubbles do when they burst.

End of the wonderful one-hoss-shay.
Logic is logic. That's all I say.

Biological Development

Biological aging is usually represented in peoples' minds as biological decline: sagging skin, muscles not so supple, failing eyesight. Considered across the life span, however, the early years are years of biological growth and development. Muscles become stronger and coordination improves; the information from eyes is better integrated with information from other senses and from the brain's repository of previous experience. Most bodily functions reach maximum capacity and efficiency early in life, in late childhood or in young adulthood, but decline is typically slow through the adult years. In many instances, an increase in experience (wisdom) more than compensates for the slight decrease in biological functions, so that even in athletically demanding tasks, a middle-aged adult may be the finest flower. A slight decline in finger dexterity in a concert pianist, for example, is more than balanced by a growing intellectual ability to grasp the poetic insights in a musical composition. Then too decline in some functions is not necessarily something that we should value negatively. Decreasing hormone levels, for example, can be seen as a blessing in some respects: they may result in lessened hostility and anxiety; they probably reduce the chances of a heart attack in males; and, in women, they eliminate the production of ova and thus the fear of pregnancy after menopause.

The data that form the basis of our understanding of biological aging have been derived in large part from cross-sectional studies. But, as with intellectual abilities, younger cohorts seem to compare favorably to older ones in terms of biological factors. Better health care and nutrition have rendered the younger groups more physically fit. Thus cross-sectional data on *today's* elderly may present an unduly pessimistic picture of the early declines associated with increasing age that can be expected by *tomorrow's* elderly. In fact, longitudinal data indicates that physiological deficits are minor until the sixties and that individual patterns of physiological change over the adult life span vary greatly (Shock, 1985).

In this chapter we first discuss general theories of biological aging: What, exactly, *is* biological aging? What causes it? Then we consider the effect of age on sensory capacities, most notably vision and hearing. Age changes that occur inside the body (in the brain, in hormone levels) are reviewed next. Finally, we turn to the relationship between age and disease, a complex and tangled web of theory and research that is basic not only to our understanding of "normal" aging but also to our appreciation of our own individual lives.

Biological Aging

We know them well, the signs of encroaching age. The hair is thinning and gray in color, if it remains at all. Skin is less elastic, and where it is exposed to the sun — on the face and hands — it is wrinkled, leathery, and sprinkled with dark spots. The body moves more slowly and with less agility, the result of muscle atrophy, bone degeneration, and possibly arthritis; posture may be stooped. Teeth may be missing, a few or even all of them, sometimes replaced by dentures. The voice is slightly higher in pitch, and weaker, softer.

Eventually the person dies. The death may have an ostensible cause — heart disease perhaps, or cancer — but if the person is very old, the disease seems less relevant than the general inability of the aging body to fend off environmental insults. Why do people grow old? Why do they die? Literally life-and-death questions, these have earned the attention of scientists for centuries. The answers do not come easily, however. In the words of one noted biologist, "The fundamental causes of biological aging are almost as much a mystery today as they have always been" (Hayflick, 1975, p. 36).

LIFE EXPECTANCIES

Before we discuss the data on human longevity, it is necessary to distinguish between two related concepts: life expectancy and potential life span. *Life expectancy*, as used in vital statistics, refers to the age at which half the population cohort born in the year that statistic is published will have died. For example, the life expectancy at birth of a child born in 1983 was just under seventy-five years (also see Figure 11–1). This means that half the children born in that year could expect to reach or exceed their seventy-fifth birthday. As we shall see life expectancy has been going up rapidly because of medical and technological advances that have kept more and more people from dying before their time. By contrast, *potential life span* refers to the maximum age that could be attained if an

FIGURE 11–1.

Two portraits of life expectancy. The top graph gives average length of life for various times and places. The bottom graph gives the number of people, of each 100,000 born, still living at each age. Note that as conditions become more conducive to survival, the lines become more nearly rectangular, but the maximum span of life does not increase much.

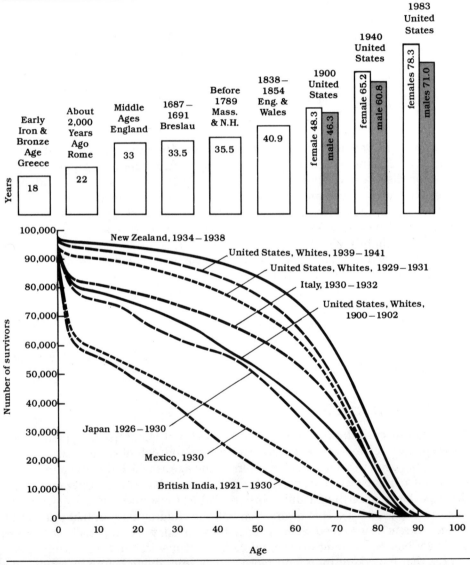

Source: Top graph from National Center for Health Statistics, 1979, and U.S. Bureau of the Census, 1984a. Bottom graph from *Aging: The biology of senescence* by Alex Comfort. Copyright © 1964, 1965 by Alex Comfort. Reprinted by permission of A. M. Heath & Company Ltd.

individual were able to avoid or be successfully treated for all illnesses and accidents. Potential life span, then, represents the absolute limits of human life, that may be genetically determined in part, but may also be set by the limits of our knowledge in compensating for the detrimental effects of aging. The average female infant can look forward to between seven and eight years more in life than her male counterpart. This sex difference has been attributed to a variety of sources, including the "easy life" of the typical female and the "sinful life" of the typical male (smoking and drinking being the obvious life-threatening vices). Nicotine and alcohol probably do play a role, but the "easy life" of the female is an implausible hypothesis, for a number of reasons. Sex differences in life expectancy are found in almost all cultures around the world, including those in which the typical woman works as hard as or harder than the typical man, and receives less than her share of food protein besides. Also, the old saying, "Hard work never killed anybody," is approximately true: the wear-and-tear theory of aging is one of the least tenable, as we shall see, and the worry and anxiety of work, which is its chief life-shortening ingredient, does not seem to have been allotted in disproportionate shares to one sex or the other.

Furthermore, one would expect the increasing number of women in the work force in industrialized countries to have shorter life spans. If anything, however, gender differences in life span have increased over the last three decades, even as more women have taken jobs outside the home (Myers and Manton, 1984). Finally, female advantage in life span is characteristic also of a number of animal species, including rats, mice, flies, and dogs (Shock, 1977). This finding suggests a genetic basis for the sex difference, probably in the second X chromosome that females have but males don't; this same chromosome protects the female against a large number of genetic diseases, including hemophilia (uncontrollable bleeding) and color blindness.

Life expectancies for both sexes have been increasing in the United States at a fairly rapid rate. A child born in 1900, for example, could expect to live only forty-seven years, compared to well over seventy years today. During the 1970s, the life expectancy of a forty-five-year-old increased by 6.6 percent, whereas the life expectancy of a newborn increased by 4 percent (McGinnis, 1982). Among those aged sixty-five to seventy-four, mortality declined 18 percent between 1968 and 1977 (Siegel, 1980). Improved safety, nutrition, hygiene, and medical discoveries account for most of these increases, primarily by reducing the likelihood of illnesses and injuries that bring a person to an "untimely" end. There is no persuasive evidence, however, that the potential life span of humans has increased by much (Hayflick, 1975). For example, medical discoveries typically affect events (such as illnesses) that interrupt the normal life span, reducing death rates among young adults, but they leave death rates among the elderly essentially unchanged.

Cardiovascular disease is the leading cause of death in the United States. If all mortality due to cardiovascular disease were eliminated, the gain in life expectancy would be 11 years at age sixty-five and 12 years at birth. The gain among the elderly is so great because this is a disease that most often strikes the elderly. Even so, mortality from this cause has decreased by more than 30 percent in the past 30 years, with much of the gain occurring between 1970 and 1980 (Levy and Moskowitz, 1982). If all deaths from cancer were eliminated, on the other hand, the gain in life expectancy would be 1½ years at age sixty-five and 2½ years at birth. The gain at age sixty-five would be much smaller for cancer than for cardiovascular disease because cancer has a lower incidence than cardiovascular disease and because half of all cancers occur before age sixty-five. However, over the past 15 years, cancer mortality among those under age forty-five has decreased between 20 and 43 percent. Mortality from cancer has increased in those over forty-five, however, primarily as a result of cancers related to smoking (Frei, 1982). Thus if medical science were able to eliminate heart disease and cancer, the major causes of death in old people, it would simply "reduce the possible ways in which the inevitability of our death will occur, and will allow accidents then to become the leading killer" (Hayflick, 1975, pp. 36–37).

Probably some sort of genetic program sets an upper limit to life span in humans (Shock, 1977). Humans whose parents lived long lives themselves have a greater life expectancy than those with parents who died at a relatively early age. It seems likely, however, that long life is due to the combined effect of many different genes, not just one or a few. Animal experiments designed to "evolve" long-lived specimens by selective inbreeding almost always fail; in fact, the inbred strains almost always have shorter-than-average life spans (Maynard-Smith, 1966). The inbreeding reduces the variety of genes in the offspring, suggesting that variety is the spice of a *long* life.

LONGEVITY

Inbreeding of long-lived humans is not likely to produce offspring who live longer, if the animal studies are any guide. Nevertheless, it has been claimed that certain small groups of people display extraordinary longevity, commonly living to over 100 years of age. Inbreeding, an exceptionally healthy diet, hard work, and a vigorous sex life are among the reasons offered to explain these remarkably old people, who are found in Ecuador, Pakistan, and the Georgian Republic of the USSR. Unfortunately, it now appears that no explanations are necessary. The original reports were simply in error; these people live no longer than anyone else. The Hunzukuts in Pakistan, for example, have no written language and thus, of course, no birth records (Hayflick, 1975).

The people of Vilcabamba in southern Ecuador are similarly difficult to investigate, in this case because of a fire in the church that destroyed many baptismal records. An intensive and extensive study of many kinds of evidence, including census data, survey research, marriage records, and more recent birth records, showed clearly that none of the twenty-three people who claimed to be over 100 years old were in fact centenarians; their true ages ranged from seventy-five to ninety-six (Mazess and Forman, 1979). The Vilcabambans, for some reason, began to exaggerate their ages at about seventy years, to the extent that for anyone who claimed to be 100, the best statistical prediction was eighty-four. Such exaggeration is not uncommon; it can be documented even in the United States (Rosenwaike, 1968).

Lack of reliable birth records and the human propensity to exaggerate very old age probably account for the reports of extraordinary longevity in Soviet Georgia too (Medvedev, 1974). The Russian pseudocentenarians add a further wrinkle: draft dodging. Apparently hundreds of thousands of deserters and draft dodgers of World War I and the Russian Revolutionary War used their fathers' records to falsify their ages, to avoid military service by reason of old age. When large numbers of 100-year-old men (and it is indeed suggestive that men outnumber women in the over-100 age group!) began turning up in Georgia, the aging draft dodgers suddenly found themselves heroes of the Soviet Union, examples of the life-prolonging effects of Communism. That tourism to these parts of Georgia also increased provided even more incentive to continue their masquerade. Despite the misleading information about potential life span provided by some of the accounts of long-lived isolated groups, it should be stressed that cross-cultural studies can be quite useful in informing us on differential rates of biological change and its interaction with different sociocultural influences.

The maximum potential life span of a member of the human species varies between 70 and 110, with 90 or so probably average (Hayflick, 1975). Factors such as one's sex and the longevity of one's ancestors affect maximum span, as we have mentioned. Environmental factors also predict individual differences in life span. Heavy cigarette smoking lowers life expectancy by about twelve years, on the average, and obesity lowers it by about a year and a half for every 10 percent overweight. Pollution of our air and our water, dangerous food additives, overuse of pesticides and weed killers, and other side effects of an industrial economy have negative effects on longevity (U.S. Department of Health, Education, and Welfare, 1974). On the other hand, a good marriage can add five years to life. A study of 1,200 people who had lived to be 100 years old concluded that "usefulness and work remained the most consistently accurate" of all factors that predicted living to a very old age (Segerberg, 1982, p. 190).

People who live to be very old have certain characteristic personality traits (Palmore and Jeffers, 1971). Although individual differences among people aged 90 to 100 are almost as great as in younger groups, one trait they seem to have in common is a moderate and flexible attitude toward life. Very old people are rarely extreme in their habits. They are neither health-food fanatics nor junk-food gluttons; they are likely to enjoy drinking in moderation, and they exercise a bit each day. Their lives are quite varied — some relatively placid, others full of storm and stress. It is not so much the presence or absence of pressure in their lives that marks these unusually old people, but their adaptability, their ability to handle whatever comes their way (Lehr, 1982).

THEORIES OF AGING

It seems clear that some sort of genetic program allows us a certain maximum span of life, but no more. As we grow older, biological changes occur that affect our ability to survive, that is, to avoid accidents, to fight off disease. In very old persons, death is a result not so much of the particular disease or accident that happens to do them in, but of age-related biological decrements that made the disease or accidents more likely. For this reason, aging is often defined as "a decline in physiologic competence" (Timiras, 1972).

But what exactly is the nature of this decline? There is a vast number of theories of biological aging, most of them at least plausible (Shock, 1977). In science, one often finds a large number of theories in an early stage of scientific development; eventually all but one or two are eliminated after relevant scientific research has been conducted. That the field of aging still offers several is thus a sign of scientific infancy. Many of the theories are stated too speculatively and permit no experimental tests. Others could be tested in principle, but the techniques to do so are not yet available. Some theories, for example, specify certain functions of human DNA, the large protein molecule that contains each individual's genetic information. We have just recently discovered the structure of DNA, and we now have some knowledge of how it works in simple organisms, such as bacteria. But the human DNA is incredibly complex — a molecular strand, six feet long and a 250-millionth of an inch wide, repeated in every body cell (Bodmer and Cavalli-Sforza, 1976; Rhodes, 1979). We are many years from understanding its function, and thus we are many years from a test of theories of biological aging that speculate on this function.

Cellular theories   In many theories of aging, genetic mechanisms are presumed to operate at the cellular level to bring about the symptoms of aging. One theory proposes "aging genes" that program biological changes such as menopause, gray hair, and, at a more basic level, partial or complete loss of function of body cells (Hayflick, 1980). Another theory suggests that our genetic mechanisms are designed to promote growth and, eventually, reproduction. Once duty is done for the preservation of the species, the organism has no more useful genetic information and "runs down," like a clock that one no longer winds. Advocates of this theory point out that "old age" is an "unnatural" phenomenon, rarely found among animals in the wild. Wild animals have roughly half the average life span of zoo animals; they are killed off by disease or predators as loss of their speed and strength makes them vulnerable. No genetic code for "later life" is needed, because for most animals there is no such thing.

Probably the most widely accepted theory of aging maintains that the genetic mechanisms begin to use inaccurate, distorted information (Shock, 1977). The genes or the DNA molecules may be damaged by radiation (including heat) or chemicals (such as alcohol), or inevitable mutations may occur in the process of repairing DNA or producing other molecules. "Self-poisons" manufactured (deliberately or by accident) in other parts of the body are another possibility (Strehler, 1973). In any case, damage to DNA or other molecules in the genetic system would result in less efficient replacement and repair of body cells, or abnormal (cancerous) cells might be manufactured instead.

Another theory, the cross-linking theory of aging, begins with the observation that many tissues in the body become less elastic with age. Skin is the most directly observable of these tissues, taking on a leathery look as the individual grows old. The reason for this change is known: proteins called collagen and elastin, which compose the connective tissue in skin and also in various other parts of the body such as the muscles of the heart and lungs and the blood vessels throughout the body, form bonds or *cross-linkages* either within the protein molecule or between molecules. Cross-linking itself has many deleterious effects, decreasing the efficiency of heart and lungs and raising blood pressure (Kohn, 1971). In addition, it has been proposed that the same sort of cross-linking occurs within the body's cells, in the intracellular proteins such as the enzymes and DNA itself (Bjorksten, 1974). If this were true, the efficiency of the intracellular proteins would be significantly reduced, with the same unfortunate results that we described for damaged DNA.

Cross-linking occurs much more rapidly in the presence of a class of chemicals called aldehydes. (Aldehydes, in fact, are used to "tan" leather, a process of cross-linking among the molecules of the leather.) Aldehydes are produced in abundance in the body as a by-product of cell metabolism, a fact that makes the cross-linking theory of aging at least plausible. Aldehyde production also varies as a function of diet, which may offer some hope to those who wish to avoid the ravages of time; low-fat and low-calorie diets with plenty of vitamins are best, and vitamin E may help too.

Perhaps the oldest theory of aging, one that still has a few attractive aspects, is the wear-and-tear theory. In the view of the wear-and-tear theory, people are like machines: the longer in use, the more worn the parts. Unfortunately for the theory, however, people are not very much like machines. Unlike machines, worn out parts of the body usually are replaced or repaired. Also, there is no relationship between hard work and early death. In fact, vigorous exercise in the form of hard work is a factor predicting longer life, not shorter life. Nevertheless, some aspects of the wear-and-tear theory must be considered in a general theory of aging (Finch, 1976). For example, years and years of exposure to sunlight damages the skin, and weaknesses or ruptures in blood vessels are most likely in areas of turbulent blood flow (e.g., near branchings). Agents such as radiation and alcohol destroy irreplaceable cells, including neurons. But wear and tear cannot explain much of the aging process.

Physiological theories In contrast to the cellular theories, which depict age changes in DNA and other intracellular molecules, physiological theories see the primary cause of aging in something outside the individual cell. The thymus gland, for example, controls many important immune reactions; if it functions poorly, the body may lose its ability to fight off disease or to destroy cancerous cells. Or, for some reason, the immune system may lose its selectivity and begin to attack normal body cells as if they were foreign intruders (Adler, 1974; Blumenthal, 1983).

The most widely accepted theory of aging at the physiological level is based on assumptions of a general decline in the adult years of the body's endocrine system, which controls many bodily activities through hormones (Shock, 1977; Minaker, Meneneilly, and Rowe, 1985). Decline in the function of the ovaries in adult women is a prime example; menopause around the age of fifty is the most obvious result. Menopause is clearly not a disease; it is a normal facet of the aging process in women.

Other important glands in the endocrine system include the thymus gland, which controls immune reactions, and the thyroid gland, which controls metabolism. In general, the endocrine system controls many vital balances in the body, such as the level of sugar in the blood, acting to increase it when it is low and to lower it when it is elevated. Other "homeostatic" (balancing) mechanisms keep the body temperature from becoming too high or too low and keep water, salt, and acid levels in the normal range. To the extent that the efficiency of these mechanisms is impaired by age, the body loses its ability to react to stress. In many old people, death is due to a relatively mild stress (for example, a change in the fluid balance caused by diarrhea) to which the aging body can no longer adapt.

Physiological theories of aging, of course, are not incompatible with cellular theories. Indeed, if a theorist views aging primarily as a function of declining endocrine activity, he or she must still answer the cellular question: What is it about the cells of the endocrine system that accounts for the decline? Aging genes? Damaged cells? In the long run, an adequate theory of aging will have to specify the age changes at both the cellular and the physiological level. The interactions between levels are intricate, since damaged cells can cause a decline in physiological function, which in turn can damage more cells. The other major control system of the body — the nervous system — is also involved. One feeds off the others, so that any decline starts a sort of vicious cycle, causing decline elsewhere, and eventually the cell mechanism or physiological system that began the cycle is itself affected; the cycle begins anew. For most of the adult years, the decline in physiological functioning is slight, but it accelerates with age. At the end of life there is a neuroendocrine cascade (Finch, 1976), a catastrophe of errors and malfunctions that results inevitably in death. It is the ultimate collapse of the one-hoss-shay.

The imagery of the one-hoss shay has resurfaced at the proper moment, for it allows us to repeat the significance of these theories for the quality of human life. Although there may be future advances in basic biology that could lead to substantial extensions of the potential life span (cf. Strehler, 1977), it seems unlikely at present that we will be able to extend life much beyond the years allotted by the aging mechanisms. Perhaps our goal instead should be to understand the mechanisms and to deal with them so that life in the later years is satisfying and as free as possible from debilitating disease and unnecessary biological decline. The goal is to have a life like the one-hoss-shay — serviceable 'til the very end.

Sensory Capacities

Now that we've considered the general process of aging, we can consider some of the effects of age on psychologically important components of the whole biological system we call our body. As psychologists we are particularly interested in the

The goal in later years is to enjoy a life as satisfying and as free from disease and unnecessary decline as possible.

biological equipment used for processing information from the environment. In the following section we consider the central nervous system: the brain and the spinal cord. Here we begin our discussion where information processing begins: at the periphery, with the sense organs.

VISION

Several biological changes occur in the visual system during the adult years, especially toward the end of life. These changes affect a person's vision in different ways, sometimes creating problems in coping with life, but usually we can compensate for significant losses of visual ability through external devices such as eyeglasses. Two major classes of biological events occur at somewhat different times in life. The first includes changes in some of the external parts of the eye (most notably the cornea and lens), affecting the transmission of light waves; these changes begin to assume importance between the ages of thirty-five and forty-five (Kline and Schieber, 1985). The second class of changes concerns the retina and the nervous system; these changes, which affect the sensitivity of the retina, begin to become noticeable between fifty-five and sixty-five years of age.

As the average individual ages, the lens of the eye becomes harder and less flexible. The reason for this is that the lens is made up of epithelial tissue, like the skin, hair, and nails. Like all other body parts of this sort, the lens continues to grow throughout life. Unlike the skin, hair, and nails, however, the lens cannot shed excess cells; instead it becomes more compact and hence less flexible (if it did not become more compact, it would grow too large for the eyeball). The result of this loss of lens flexibility is a decrease in the ability to accommodate the shape of the lens for viewing objects that are close to the eye (Spector, 1982). Thus many adults around the age of forty or forty-five begin experiencing difficulty in reading and doing "close work"; however, bifocal lenses can compensate for most of this difficulty.

The lens also becomes yellower with age, although the cause of this change is a mystery. The result is a reduction in the amount of light that reaches the retina and also a change in the quality of light, since yellow absorbs wavelengths from the blue-green end of the spectrum. Older people thus require more illumination than young adults to read, and some mornings they might show up with one blue sock and one purple sock.

Increasingly with age, especially in one's seventies and beyond, the lens may become so clouded as to block or scatter most of the entering light; vision is of course severely impaired. Cataracts (extreme conditions of lens opacity) are found in 20 to 25 percent of seventy-year-olds (Corso, 1981). The appearance of a cataract in one eye is often followed by the appearance of a cataract in the other eye, albeit several years later (Corso, 1981). Data from the Framingham longitudinal study (Kahn et al., 1977) suggest that cataracts might be related to elevated blood sugar level, which would explain the increased incidence of cataracts in old people with diabetes (Chylack, 1979). Excessive exposure to ultraviolet light is another possible cause. A study of Australian aborigines found that those who lived in areas with higher levels of radiation were more likely to develop cataracts at earlier ages and become visually disabled than those who lived in areas of lesser radiation (Hallow and Moran, 1981). Cataracts are fairly easy to cure. A relatively simple operation can remove the faulty lens and with eyeglasses, a contact lens, or a plastic replacement lens nearly normal vision can be restored.

One often overlooked problem with an increasingly opaque lens is glare caused by the scattering of light waves as they enter the eye. Glare puts older adults in a bit of a bind, since they need greater illumination to see well, but more light also makes for more glare. Night driving might be particularly difficult, since most of the viewing must be done in dim light and shadows and, in addition, the lights of oncoming automobiles are exceptionally effective in producing glare, even in younger people (Carter, 1982).

In addition to the lens, the pupil also changes with age (Kline and Schieber, 1985). Older pupils are smaller than young pupils in the same light, and the response to changes in illumination is slower. These changes affect the eye's ability to adapt to changing light conditions, making night driving difficult for still another reason. Also some eye muscles become so much less effective with age that, to cite one example, adults at the age of forty have significantly more difficulty looking up without raising their heads. It's a minor difficulty, perhaps, but it could be a problem when trying to read overhead street signs or see overhead traffic-control signals.

It should be kept in mind again that there are vast individual differences in rate of change also in visual functions. These findings, therefore, suggest that some older persons should avoid driving at night. But for most of us, as we get older, they simply mean that greater care and attention are required to compensate for the slight psysiological changes. Moreover, persons with only minor visual changes find that corrective glasses are particularly helpful in night driving, even though they might be safely dispensed with during the day.

Combined effects   Changes in the lens, the pupil, eye muscles, and other parts of the eye account for a good part of the age differences usually found in common visual abilities such as visual acuity and depth perception. Visual acuity is the ability to see clearly in the sense of being able to read an eye chart in a doctor's office. The decrease in the illumination that reaches the retina through a yellowing lens and a pupil gradually decreasing in size affects acuity. Glare, which is the visual equivalent of static on a radio, also cuts down on the ability to see clearly. The result is a decline in visual acuity that begins around the age of forty or fifty. By the age of seventy-five or so, poor vision is common, although most problems can be corrected with eyeglasses (Anderson and Palmore, 1974; Pitts, 1982).

Depth perception is the ability to estimate the distance objects are from you in three-dimensional space. The perception of depth depends on several cues, many of which are affected by the biological changes we have been discussing. For example, texture is a cue to depth, since the "grain" of something is clearer and less dense up close. Decreases in visual acuity and increases in glare would make it more difficult to discriminate small details in the distance, reducing the texture gradient. Similarly, less flexibility in the lens makes accommodation less effective as a cue to estimates of distance. The result is a general decrease in the accuracy of depth perception after the age of fifty or so (Bell, Wolf, and Bernholz, 1972). In most real-life situations, however, the many redundant cues to distance make it unlikely that this deficit will cause any major problems, at least not until late in life. In other words, if one cue to distance becomes unreliable, the person can turn to other cues (for example, is one object in front of another?) without much loss in the accuracy of depth estimates.

The field of vision is the total area one can see adequately when one is looking straight ahead at a fixed point. The extent of the field of vision has important consequences in daily life. A person with a broad visual field is aware of cars pulling out of side streets when he or she is driving; a person with a narrow field of vision sees only the road he or she is driving down.

Field of vision is generally measured with a technique called "kinetic" perimetry, in which an object is slowly moved from a position outside the person's field of vision to a position where the person can detect it. The latter position is one limit of the person's field of vision. Investigations using kinetic perimetry show that the visual field constricts with advancing age. In a study of the peripheral vision of 17,000 persons between the ages of sixteen and ninety-two, Burg (1968) found that the total horizontal (left and right) visual field remained constant up to age thirty-five, declined slightly between the ages of forty and fifty, and declined more quickly thereafter. A study utilizing a different technique found that the visual field remained stable through age fifty-five and then began to shrink. The total size of the field of vision was found to diminish most markedly in those over seventy-five (Wolf, 1967).

Retinal loss In addition to the effects of changes in the eye as a whole, a second major class of age changes involves the basic receptor cells for light in the retina. These changes result in the destruction or malfunction of retinal cells, mostly because of decreased blood circulation and the resulting starvation of the receptor cells. The changes may be the result of disease; that is, they may not represent "normal" aging, although they are normal in the statistical sense: retinal cell damage can be detected in most people by the age of fifty-five to sixty-five (Fozard et al., 1977; Marmor, 1982).

One retinal ailment that afflicts the elderly is senile macular degeneration (SMD). In this disease, the macula, the area of the retina where vision is most acute, begins to deteriorate. The ailment begins slowly, typically progressing until the visual acuity declines to between 20/50 and 20/100. Within this range, the eyes are damaged such that reading becomes extremely difficult, although it remains possible with a strong, handheld magnifying glass. A television screen is visible only as a blur. Peripheral vision is usually not seriously affected, so the person can still function in familiar environments (Marmor, 1982). The disease usually affects both eyes, and it is untreatable (Lewis, 1979). A devastating variant of SMD, disciform macular degeneration, is accompanied by leakage of blood vessels, which will destroy the nervous tissue of the macula (and central visual acuity) if not halted by laser photocoagulation. About 60 percent of the people who get this disease are legally blind within five years of the first occurrence of visual loss (Lewis, 1979).

Damage to the retina in old age can also be caused by glaucoma. In this group of disorders, increasing intraocular pressure is accompanied by atrophy of the optic nerve and abnormalities in the visual field. It appears that the primary cause of the increasing pressure is resistance to the outflow of liquid in the front of the eye. The increase in pressure leads to subsequent changes in the optic disc (the blind spot at the end of the optic nerve) and the retina. Longitudinal and cross-sectional studies show marked increases in glaucoma among older people in the age range from sixty to eighty-five (Anderson and Palmore, 1974; Kahn et al., 1977). Age-related changes in the prevalence of glaucoma may be related to normative changes in the volume of the lens and the rigidity of the iris and surrounding tissue (Kornzweig, 1972). It has also been demonstrated that intraocular pressure is correlated with systolic blood pressure (the higher number in the blood pressure reading). Recent studies suggest that administering drugs called beta blockers that control blood pressure will also control intraocular pressure (Gillies and West, 1981; Strempel, 1981).

An important aspect of open-angle glaucoma, the most prevalent type among the elderly, is that no symptoms become apparent in many cases until the retina has been irreparably damaged. Advanced cases reveal themselves by a characteristic cupping of the optic disc as seen through the ophthalmoscope. However, the pressure increases that cause glaucoma can now be detected well before significant damage has occurred through the use of tonometry, a method of estimating the pressure in the eye by measuring the force needed to depress the surface of the eye. Since early detection is crucial, people over age fifty should have regular glaucoma screenings.

FIGURE 11–2.

Percentage of persons requiring corrections for visual defects

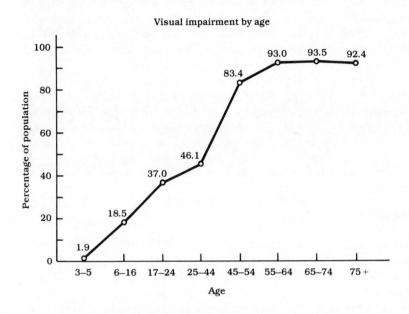

Source: National Center for Health Statistics, 1983b.

Any retinal loss, of course, affects vision directly. Visual acuity is reduced and sensitivity to low levels of illumination decreases, making night driving even more hazardous than before. Color vision is also affected, so much so that in one study, subjects near the age of ninety failed to identify the color of over 50 percent of the objects presented (Dalderup and Fredericks, 1969). Most people do not experience serious problems with vision until the age of eighty or later, but in a few cases, the retinal damage is so severe as to leave the individual legally blind (Padula, 1982). According to a survey by the National Society for the Prevention of Blindness, the incidence of blindness increases from a rate of 2.5 per thousand individuals between the ages of forty and sixty-four to 5.0 per thousand between sixty-five and sixty-nine and to 14.5 per thousand over seventy (Kirchener and Peterson, 1979).

HEARING

Hearing difficulties show approximately the same progression with age that problems with vision do (see Figure 11–2). With both senses, the number of people with impairments begins to increase around the age of forty and shows sharp increases after sixty. In the forty-five to fifty-four age group, about 19 percent experience some difficulties with hearing; between seventy-five and

Most people can compensate for slight loss in sensory capacities with devices such as glasses and hearing aids.

seventy-nine, the percentage is 75 (Harris, 1978). About 15 percent of the people over sixty-five are legally deaf (Corso, 1977).

Although some hearing impairment can be attributed to external factors (excessive accumulations of ear wax, for example, or arthritis in the bones of the middle ear), most of the loss is due to degenerative changes in the cochlea, the primary neural receptor for hearing. The cochlea is to hearing what the retina is to vision. Cochlear problems generally involve the loss of hair cells (the end organs transmitting sound to the brain) or disturbances of the inner-ear metabolism (Corso, 1981). The reduced flexibility of inner-ear membranes and restrictive adhesions may also be implicated. Although particular patterns of hearing loss are associated with the degeneration of specific structures in the ear, a person often suffers from several types of structural degeneration at the same time (Olson, Hawkins, and Lenhardt, 1985).

Hearing loss is generally greater for sounds of high frequency (Corso, 1977). In other words, the average old person will have more difficulty hearing sopranos than basses, more difficulty hearing women than men, more difficulty with tweeters than woofers. Men, who at all ages hear less of high-pitched sounds than women, also show more loss with age, so that by the later years of life, the difference in the abilities of a husband and wife to hear high-frequency sounds can be considerable. Older persons generally have the most trouble hearing under what are called "masking conditions." Masking occurs when a sound is obscured or rendered inaudible by other sounds. In general, a sound must be about 10 decibels louder than background noise to be heard. As the level of masking sounds increases, high-frequency sounds are more likely to be affected than low-frequency sounds. As a result, masking presents problems, especially when one is trying to understand relatively high-frequency speech sounds against a noisy background (Smith and Prather, 1971; Bonding, 1979).

Hearing loss, then, is one of the prime sources of the difficulty old people sometimes have understanding speech. By a standard test of speech understanding, there is not much change between the ages of twenty and fifty, but by eighty, the average loss is about 25 percent (Plomp and Mimpen, 1979; Bond and Garnes, 1980). Speaking more loudly, of course, helps, as does a hearing aid. Rapid speech is particularly hard for old people with hearing loss (see Figure 11–3).

Reductions in the amount one can hear with clarity and comprehension have effects beyond the purely sensory loss. There is often a sense of increasing social isolation, as the familiar sounds of life become dimmer and dimmer; depression and other emotional disorders are a common result. People with a hearing deficit who also have paranoid tendencies will often misinterpret poorly heard conversation as hostile toward them (Corso, 1977). Mental competence may decline also, if the individual begins to avoid interpersonal interactions (Schaie, Baltes, and Strother, 1964).

Fortunately, we can compensate for much hearing loss by modifying the acoustic signal that arrives at the ear by redesigning the acoustic environment. One of the common devices used by people with hearing loss is the hearing aid. The ordinary hearing aid increases the intensity of sounds at the eardrums, but by blocking the ear canal it also reduces the transmission of low frequencies, thereby limiting the hearing of some sounds even as it improves the hearing of others. Furthermore, conventional hearing aids amplify background noise just as much as the desired signal. Binaural hearing aids (for both ears) present problems because transmitted sounds may not stimulate both ears at the proper time, which may introduce distortions. Some of these difficulties can be resolved by ensuring that prescriptions for hearing aids are based on the results of an examination by a competent audiologist; hearing aids should not be purchased directly from hearing aid salespeople without examination by a qualified audiologist. But even when the hearing aid is chosen with the assistance of professionals, it tends to be less useful as people age. One study of a sample of older hearing aid users found that at age sixty, 90 percent found the appliance useful; by age seventy, the figure had dropped to 70 percent, and by age eighty, to less than 40 percent (Davis and Silverman, 1975).

A much-neglected technique that holds particular promise for those who are not helped much by hearing aids involves the modification of the older person's acoustic environment. Modifications of this kind often cost little or nothing. A number of changes can be made. Furniture can be arranged to provide better face-to-face contact, and obstructions can be removed. Noisy appliances can be located where they won't interfere with the intelligibility of speech. Mechanical devices such as telephone amplifiers may be helpful. In some cases, modest structural alterations might be considered. Designers and builders of housing for the elderly might take specific design features into account. Studies show, for example, that the increased reverberation that occurs in narrow rooms helps the hearing-impaired and that the suitable placement of soft and rough surfaces can improve speech discrimination (Schroeder, 1981).

None of those approaches is of much value to the totally deaf, but there are

FIGURE 11–3.

A cross-sectional study of speech intelligibility, shown as percentage decrement from the scores of subjects aged twenty to twenty-nine. Conditions: (1) normal speech; (2) speeded speech, 2½ times the normal rate; (3) selective listening, that is, tracking one speaker among many, as at a cocktail party; (4) reverberated or echoed speech, as in a hall with unfavorable acoustics; (5) interrupted speech, as on a poor telephone connection.

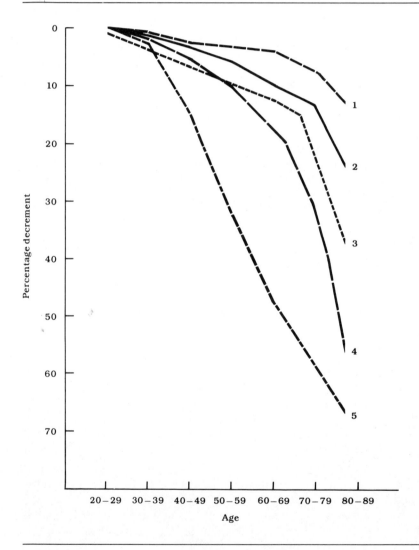

Source: Bergman et al. (1976). Age related decrement in hearing for speech: Sampling and longitudinal studies, *Journal of Gerontology*, 31, 533–538. Reproduced by permission.

some promising advances here also. The FDA has recently approved electronic cochlear implants that allow deaf people to hear such sounds as automobile horns and doorbells and to detect rises and falls in inflection, which is helpful in lipreading.

OTHER SENSES

Sensitivity to tastes and smells appears to decrease slightly with age (Murphy, 1983). With healthy subjects, however, the decrease may be slight indeed; several studies have shown no loss with age in the sense of smell (Engen, 1982). Anecdotal evidence and a few research studies suggest that sensitivity to bitter tastes (unfortunately) lasts longer than to sweet or salty tastes; sour tastes too may be more easily detected by the elderly. Elderly subjects are best at discriminating the smell of fruits from other foods (butter, beans, corn, beef, and so on); they also like the smell of fruits best (Schiffman and Pasternak, 1979).

To the extent that the senses of taste and smell do become less sensitive, old people are robbed of many of life's pleasures: the smell of flowers, the taste of a good meal (which is partly smell as well). People who can no longer appreciate subtle flavors may also be less inclined to meet friends for meals, so they may be deprived of an important social outlet. Fortunately, one can compensate somewhat for the loss of sensitivity to taste through the use of various flavor enhancers. In fact, increasing older adults' enjoyment of food by using healthy food additives may be an effective way to ensure that they eat the correct amount and variety of food (Schiffman, Orlandi, and Erickson, 1979).

Just as important as the loss of pleasure in eating is the fact that the elderly lose some of their ability to avoid poisons, which we often identify by taste. They might be less likely to notice that a potato salad "doesn't taste right" — a clue that deadly bacteria are forming. And they lose some of their ability to detect life-threatening events such as leaking gas or fires, which we often identify by the smell of smoke. An electronic smoke detector is probably a good idea for people of all ages, but for an elderly person living alone, it is a particularly wise augmentation of human sensory capacity.

If there is justice in this world, we will find age-related decreases in sensitivity to pain to compensate the elderly for decreases in the other, more pleasant senses. Although the research evidence is not consistent, the bulk of it suggests that old people do indeed suffer less pain with the same obnoxious stimulus than young people (Harkins and Chapman, 1976; Kenshalo, 1977). Since old people experience more obnoxious stimuli (injuries, diseases, surgery), this is a blessing of sorts. On the other hand, decreasing sensitivity to pain can be dangerous if reduced to the point that injuries, burns, and the like are ignored.

One of the major problems in research on pain is that pain tolerance is only *partly* a function of the painful stimulus; it also depends on the individual's attitude (a young male may submit to considerable pain to validate his macho self-concept), the situation (whether the pain is expected or perceived as part of a healing process), and the culture (British patients have a bit more of the "stiff upper lip" and are willing to accept more pain than Americans).

Sensitivity to temperature also declines in old age. This is a particular problem because temperature regulation also becomes less efficient in the elderly (Fox et al., 1983). From the mid-sixties to the mid-eighties, differences between the temperature of the skin and the body core decline. This probably means that temperatures in the body core cannot be maintained adequately when the outside temperature (and hence the skin temperature) is low (Collins et al., 1977). The combination of lowered awareness and poor temperature regulation means that older people face a greater risk of frostbite and even death from exposure to cold. As would be expected, social isolation increases the risk of sudden temperature drop (hypothermia) (Rango, 1985).

Degeneration of the structures related to balance lead to instabilities of posture and gait among the elderly, and in the very old there is an increased chance of falls (Ochs et al., 1985). Surveys of older persons have shown that about 30 percent of those over sixty-five had fallen at least once during the preceding year (Campbell et al., 1981). In 1980, 69 percent of the deaths from falls occurred in people over sixty-five years old (National Safety Council, 1981). Among those who have poor balance, fear of falling can lead to restrictions in physical activities and social contacts (Bhala, O'Donnell, and Thoppil, 1982). Those who do fall and injure themselves may not be able to care for themselves. They may have to depend on family members for assistance, and some eventually have to be institutionalized.

The Brain and the Nervous System

The brain, which together with the spinal cord constitutes the central nervous system (CNS), is the primary biological basis for intelligence and personality. We are thus very concerned with what happens to the brain (and the CNS) with age. Unfortunately, research on the human brain is very difficult and fraught with the possibility of serious error. For example, much of the research has been done on old people who, for one reason or another, require an autopsy after death; a high percentage of these subjects may have suffered from diseases affecting the brain (Bondareff, 1981; Buell and Coleman, 1981). Thus the fact that these subjects' brains weigh less, on the average, than those of people who died young may not be very meaningful. Caution is further indicated by the fact that brain atrophy with age is not generally found in studies of animals (Finch, 1982).

Nevertheless, our best guess at present is that even healthy people experience some loss of brain neurons over the years. It has been suggested that the neurons that remain lose some of their branches (dendrites) (Scheibel, 1982). A variety of explanations of neuron loss have been offered. Possible causes include accumulation of the pigment lipofuscin, which may impair the neuron's protein metabolism (Ordy, 1981); reduction of the rate of blood circulation through the brain (Frackowiak et al., 1980); a progressive increase in errors in protein synthesis of the nuclei of the neurons (Lynch and Gerling, 1981); and degeneration of the dendrites due to insufficient environmental stimulation (Greenough and Green, 1981).

The efficiency of the aging brain may also be affected by the availability of appropriate amounts of neurotransmitters, which are the chemicals that mediate synaptic communication between neurons. Neurotransmitters control the flow of information in the brain by regulating inhibitory and excitatory patterns. If the supply of neurotransmitters is inadequate, nerve impulses are conducted more slowly. Levels of a neurotransmitter known to effect memory, acetylcholine, have been shown to decrease with age (Drachman et al., 1980; Sims, Bowen, and Davison, 1982). Another neurotransmitter, dopamine, also declines with age; extreme declines result in Parkinson's disease (Carlson et al., 1980).

Much less is known about brain changes that take place at the subcortical level. Age does not seem to affect the neurons in the basal ganglia that are responsible for gross motor movement (Bugiani et al., 1978). The cerebellar cells, on the other hand, appear to decline more rapidly after the age of sixty. This change may result in impaired balance, loss of muscle tone that results in premature muscle fatigue, and increased difficulty in coordinating fine motor movement (Schmidt, 1978).

Estimates of neuron loss in the cortex range from zero to almost 50 percent, another indication of the difficulty of research in this area (Bondareff, 1977; Henderson, Tomlinson, and Benson, 1980). Perhaps 5 to 10 percent is a reasonable figure for people at the age of seventy-five (Leaf, 1973b), with loss at an accelerating rate after that. But other investigators have questioned findings concerning the loss of neurons, regarding them as artifacts of staining and sampling techniques (Buell, 1982). Several researchers have recently proposed that any loss of neurons may be made up by the plasticity of the remaining neurons, which may develop new synaptic connections by elaborating their dendritic branches (Curcio, Buell, and Coleman, 1982). This sort of proliferation of branches may occur in response to environmental stimulation (Greenough and Green, 1981); it has even been suggested that it may result in a net gain in the density of synapses with increasing age (Brody, 1982). All in all, however, it appears that the physical loss in the CNS is remarkably low, considering losses in other systems; kidney filtration, for example, may decline by 50 percent. Since nerve fibers are not replaced in the body (once they die, they're gone forever), the maintenance of neurons is testimony to the protection and repair mechanisms of the brain.

Nevertheless, some theorists have suggested that many of the effects of aging can be attributed to damage to the brain and CNS (Reed and Reitan, 1963). Research on this hypothesis has compared the performance of normal subjects, young and old, with that of people with known brain damage — from alcoholism, for example, or cerebral anoxia (in which the brain is temporarily starved of oxygen). The hypothesis would be supported if it could be shown that old "normal" people perform like brain-damaged subjects or, in a stronger form of the hypothesis, if the old normals look like young brain-damaged. Most of the

Athletic people who remain active as they age may have faster reaction times than young nonathletic people.

research has not been kind to this hypothesis (Goldstein and Shelly, 1975). If the deficits that many old people show in learning and memory are due to brain damage, it is not the same sort of brain damage one incurs by flooding one's brain with dangerous chemicals.

REACTION TIME

One of the most consistent findings in the study of aging is a decline in reaction time as one grows older (Birren, 1965). Typical reaction-time tasks range from the simple (How long does it take to press a button after a light goes on?) to the more complex (How fast can one write or type?). The decrease in speed with which older adults perform such tasks is sizable; the decrease is around 20 percent for simple tasks and can be 50 percent or more for complex tasks (Welford, 1984). In the view of some psychologists, this increasing slowness in response with age "reflects a basic change in the speed with which the central nervous system processes information" (Birren, 1974, p. 808).

Reaction time consists of three major components: sensory transmission time, motor execution time, and a central component that involves interpretation, decision, and association. Through various means, it has been possible to show that sensory input and motor output are usually small components compared to the central processing component (Botwinick, 1978). For example, the time between the onset of a stimulus, like a light, and the arrival of an impulse in the brain, which can be measured electronically, is short. And the first signal to the muscle (of the forearm that controls the finger that is to be lifted, for example) can be detected, so we know how much is "motor time" and how much is "premotor" (Salthouse, 1980). Unless the stimulus or response is unusually complex, the central processing time accounts for up to 80 percent of the total reaction time (Botwinick and Thompson, 1966).

It is an appealing hypothesis, this notion that the central nervous system gets sluggish with age, slowing down reaction time. If it were valid, the decreasing speed of processing information could account for many of the observed age differences in learning, memory, perception, and intelligence (Birren, 1974; Birren, Woods, and Williams, 1980; Salthouse and Kail, 1983). The advantage to older subjects of a slower pace of learning, for example, would be explained directly. Unfortunately, the hypothesis is very difficult to test experimentally, especially since we don't really know what "central processing" means in terms of brain function. In addition, reaction time does not generally correlate very highly with measures of intellectual ability. The correlations are higher for old people than for young; but this can be interpreted in several ways. It may be that, for older adults, speed of response is a more important component of intellectual performance. Or it may be that intelligence tests, for older adults, often measure reaction time instead of intellectual ability.

Recent research has been concerned with the nature of the "neural sluggishness" underlying decreasing reaction times with age. Several possibilities have been suggested — irreversible neural deterioration, decreasing blood flow to the brain (which may be reversible), faltering arousal processes — and, indeed, there are probably several factors at work (Birren, Woods, and Williams, 1980). One relevant consideration is that reaction times can be significantly improved by physical exercise (Botwinick, 1978). Among active old people, such as those who run or play racquetball, average reaction times are faster than among nonathletic young people; in one study, these differences were sizable, even though the oldsters were sixty to seventy years old and were being compared to young men in their twenties (Spirduso and Clifford, 1978). Since exercise increases blood flow to the brain, increases the amount of oxygen in the blood, and may even affect the character of neural tissue, these factors are thereby implicated in the more typical age differences in reaction time (Birren, Woods, and Williams, 1980).

Another possibility is that inefficient coordination of the body's arousal processes with the brain's activity patterns is at fault (Marsh and Thompson, 1977). Reaction-time tasks, especially the more complex tasks, require alertness and penalize both underarousal and overarousal. If the average old person is less easily aroused and, once aroused, is more easily rattled — as we concluded in Chapter 7 on motivation — then we would expect reaction-time performance to suffer.

Still another consideration is evidence from some studies that reaction times in very simple tasks do *not* differ with age (Gottsdanker, 1982). These studies suggest that age differences in more complex tasks result from differences in attention and concentration or, in general, in the way subjects get themselves ready for an impending stimulus. For example, younger subjects typically use warning signals before the stimulus to greater advantage than older subjects

(Gottsdanker, 1980). This "preparation" hypothesis pictures the older subject as something like a sprinter whose speed on the track is equal to that of his or her competitors but whose technique in the starting blocks is inferior. In other words, old people do not typically suffer from irreversible neural deterioration; their reaction times are as quick as those of young adults when the task is so simple that preparation and readiness are not important. Tasks that provide no clues to the imminent appearance of the stimulus (when the stimulus appears at random times, for example) also show no age differences (Gottsdanker, 1982).

The preparation hypothesis may stand in opposition to notions of irreversible neural decline, but it is compatible with theories of increasingly poor alignment of bodily arousal with brain activity. In fact, difficulties in achieving and maintaining the proper degree of alertness may be directly responsible for the problems old people have in reaction-time tasks that require efficient preparation (Loveless and Sanford, 1974). Unlike nerves that have deteriorated, however, inefficient arousal processes can apparently be improved by practice or experience with reaction-time tasks, which significantly enhances performance (Botwinick, 1978; Gottsdanker, 1980; Salthouse, 1985).

BRAIN WAVES

Age changes in the brain's function might be detected through age changes in brain waves, those mysterious electronic broadcasts from the brain we record with electroencephalograms (EEGs). The precise nature of brain waves is unknown, although the frequency and amplitude of the waves appear to be correlated with arousal. In particular, an alert adult who is attending to some task will usually show fast, low-amplitude waves; relaxed, doing nothing in particular, the same individual will show *alpha waves,* higher. in amplitude and slower in frequency; a subject who goes to sleep, will show even slower, more powerful waves (unless he or she is dreaming, when the waves look paradoxically like those of an alert, attentive person). Most of the interest in the relationship between brain waves and aging has centered on alpha waves.

Age differences in EEG are not readily detectable until the late fifties or early sixties (Woodruff, 1978; Obrist, 1980). The most reliable finding is a slowing of the alpha rhythm. In young adults, alpha is found at an average of ten or eleven cycles per second; by the sixties, the average is around nine cycles per second; for people over eighty, alpha cycles around eight times per second.

The EEG can also be used to measure the brain's electrical response when a person's attention is called to a particular visual, auditory, or tactile stimulus. In one task, the subjects were asked to count the number of occurrences of an infrequent tone. In a group ranging in age from fifteen to seventy-one, it was found that the time between the tone and the EEG response to the tone increased linearly with age (Goodin et al., 1978). Thus, like slower reaction times, EEG data seem to suggest an increasing sluggishness of the brain and central nervous system in old age. What this means in terms of intellectual performance is not clear, for EEGs, like reaction times, do not correlate highly with intellectual measures. It may be simply that arousal levels are somewhat lower in old people than in young adults, a hypothesis we have just reviewed in the previous section on reaction time.

SLEEP DISTURBANCES

EEG and other studies have also revealed age-related changes in sleep patterns. Although the total time of actual sleep remains fairly constant throughout adulthood, after age sixty people spend an increasing amount of time awake in bed, trying to fall asleep initially, during wakeful periods throughout the night, and lying awake before rising in the morning. Periods of wakefulness during the night begin in the thirties and increase thereafter; for people over age fifty, an unbroken night's sleep is extremely rare. When it does occur, the sleep of older persons is less restful, with less time spent in deep, dreamless (REM) sleep. Older persons also awaken more readily than do young people. The major causes of sleep disturbances in old age are sleep apnea (a halting of respiration in sleep), periodic leg movements, and heartburn (Williams, Karacen, and Hursch, 1974; Coleman et al., 1981; Dement, Miles, and Bilwise, 1982).

There are two possible reasons that older people spend more time in bed even though they sleep no more than other adults. It may be simply that it takes longer for older people to accumulate a sufficient amount of deep sleep to meet their physiological needs. On the other hand, older people may spend more time in bed because they have more time to spend there; often as many as ten or twelve hours (Williams, Karacen, and Hursch, 1974; Carskadon, 1982). Of course, here too, there are vast individual differences that may be affected by the social context the older person is in as well as by the perpetuation of previously preferred lifestyles.

Although many old persons complain primarily about sleeping less soundly, it has been found that the most damaging aspect of sleep disturbances is the frequent interruption of sleep. This sleep fragmentation has been related to sleepiness and reduced daytime well-being in the aged. Inadequate nighttime sleep is frequently compensated for by daytime naps, and the elderly often make extensive use of drugs to promote sleep. However, the most commonly prescribed sleep medications may actually increase the incidence of apnea and cardiac arrhythmia. Most recent evidence from sleep deprivation studies suggests that sleep loss may actually improve the quality of sleep (that is, increasing the proportion of time in deep sleep) the following night. Consequently, it appears that older persons could improve the quality of their sleep if they avoided sleeping pills and stayed in bed for shorter rather than longer intervals (Woodruff, 1985).

Aging and Disease

It has been remarkably difficult to document significant age changes in the functioning of the central nervous system in the disease-free old person. Several diseases affect the CNS, producing a range of mental disorders that, in old people, are lumped under the catch-all term, senility. These diseases are examined in more detail in the following chapter on mental illness. Here we consider disease in general and its relationship to aging. It is a thorny issue, as we have already indicated more than once.

The probability of disease increases dramatically after the age of sixty-five. People over sixty-five, who constitute about 12 percent of the population, account for 30 percent of the nation's health expenditures (Butler, 1975; Harris, 1978). They consume 25 percent of all drugs; they fill a third of the nation's hospital beds; they account for 40 percent of physicians' office visits. They are the major users of facilities for long-term care and home-care facilities.

The medical picture of the elderly, though hardly a bright one, is often painted in colors too gray for the facts (Harris, 1978). Only about 5 percent of the population over sixty-five are found in nursing homes and other long-term facilities; these are predominantly white (94 percent), widowed (64 percent) females (70 percent) over the age of seventy-five (74 percent). In a given year, around 83 percent of the elderly do *not* require short-term hospital care, only slightly less than the 89 percent of those under the age of sixty-five. Nevertheless, 86 percent of the elderly have some sort of chronic condition — arthritis being the most common (38 percent), with vision and hearing impairments next frequent. Illness incidence also varies by ethnic groups. Higher rates of reported illness among the black indicate that as many as 52.8 percent suffer from arthritis, 54.8 percent report hypertension, and 17.3 percent have diabetes (Chatters and Jackson, 1982).

EFFECTS OF DISEASE

As psychologists, we are interested in the effects of disease on the individual's life and mood, as well as in his or her ability to adjust to the illness. Disease has many effects. There is often pain, for example, with arthritis, chronic pain that steals pleasure from each day and distracts the sufferer from more satisfying pursuits; it may affect motivation, learning, and memory. The financial effects of disease, in spite of Medicare and other government programs, are still significant; elderly citizens still must pay over a fourth of their personal medical costs (Harris, 1978). The fear of becoming financially dependent on others because of lingering illness remains one of the chief concerns of the elderly.

The threat of financial dependence is added to the possibility of physical dependence, if the disease is chronic and handicaps the individual in some degree. Some 11 million persons, almost 40 percent of people over sixty-five, experience some limitation in carrying out major activities, such as work or housekeeping (U.S. Bureau of the Census, 1984a). The diseases most often resulting in such limitations are heart conditions, diabetes, asthma, and arthritis. Arthritis and heart conditions are also among the prime villains in limiting mobility, keeping 5 percent of the noninstitutionalized elderly confined to their homes and another 12 percent from getting around by themselves. These enforced dependencies may lower the self-esteem of the older person; it certainly makes "old age with integrity" more difficult. When a national sample of people of all ages were asked for their opinion of the "worst things a[...] sixty-five years of age," 62 percent cited poor health or poor phys[...] (Harris and associates, 1975).

HEART DISEASE

Heart disease is an illuminating topic to review, as it affects people of differe[...] ages. The heart is probably the most important muscle in the body; when it is [...] diseased, severe limitations on activity and mobility are likely. Among people over sixty-five, heart disease accounts for over 40 percent of deaths, so it also affords a look at the relationship between disease and aging.

The normal age-related changes in the cardiovascular system are difficult to distinguish from pathological changes such as those resulting from high blood pressure and hardening of the arteries. The problem is complicated by the fact that one cannot, of course, perform longitudinal autopsy studies. In addition, it is difficult to relate the structural changes that are discovered to alterations in cardiovascular functioning. There are wide individual variations, which reflect such factors as the rate of physiological aging, the amount of environmental stress, diet, smoking patterns, and amount of exercise. Nevertheless, several types of changes appear to be age-related. First, the heart muscle needs more time to relax between contractions. Second, blood ejected from the left ventricle (heart chamber) into the aorta (the main artery leading from the heart) during contraction meets more resistance from the less flexible wall of the aorta (Weisfeldt, 1981; Gerstenbleth, 1982). Third, the heart muscle is less responsive to the stimulation of the pacemaker cells (Weisfeldt, 1980). Finally, the amounts of elastin, collagen, and fat in the walls of the heart increase, while the amount of muscle decreases. The heart valves show abnormal thickenings and ridges as well as deposits of fatty substances (Pomerance, 1976).

Heart disease is by no means restricted to the elderly, of course. The dreaded phrase, "heart attack," is most often heard in conjunction with middle-aged men, among whom it is actually more common than among older men, or women in general. About 80 percent of the heart-attack victims are male; about one in five men will experience a heart attack before the age of sixty (Taylor, 1976). Although the reasons why middle-aged men are particularly prone to heart attacks are not clear, the best guess is that some combination of stress, bad habits (such as smoking), and the male hormone testosterone is involved; when the level of testosterone drops in later life, so does the probability of a heart attack.

In some respects, a heart attack is to middle-aged men what menopause is to middle-aged women: it is often perceived as a definitive sign of "old age," an end to the "good life," full of activity and fun. Thus it is not surprising to find that reactions to heart attacks vary with the man's age (Rosen and Bibring, 1968). Men under the age of forty seem to need to demonstrate that their virility and vigor are intact. Nurses describe them as cheerful, jovial, even manic, and also flirtatious. They tend to pooh-pooh the dangers of heart disease and, more than older patients, deliberately disobey doctors' orders. The elderly heart-attack victims,

nt

ful but unlike the youngest patients, they are very
ions to the letter. They seem to accept the heart
nate, of course, but as an event that "old men" like
listinct possibility.

eir fifties is not cheerful at all; they are depressed,
for the most part, still see themselves as capable
ife, felled by misfortune. At the same time, they
continue "the struggle" (usually, achievement
), but they were beginning to wonder about their
heart attack. And now. . . . Researchers have
ntuates the normal concerns and worries of a
...g man particularly vulnerable to its psychological effect: ". . .
the immediate demands for passivity and dependence concretely represent the
position toward which advancing age has begun to propel him, but which he is
not yet prepared to accept" (Rosen and Bibring, 1968, pp. 207–208).

CANCER

Cancer is another disease that increases markedly with age. Over half of all
cancers occur in people over sixty-five (Butler and Gastel, 1979). Figure 11–4 gives
age-specific data on the incidence of cancer for a sample representative of the
population of the United States. The solid line indicates what proportion of the
total incidence of cancer occurs in each age group. As you can see, the incidence
peaks in early old age. But this statistic reflects the numbers of older people
remaining in the population: there are relatively few people alive after age eighty-
five, so the number who can get cancer will of course be rather small. Across age
groups, we find that the incidence and the mortality of cancer rise as people grow
older, reaching the highest rates in the eighties. Thus cancer is the second leading
cause of death (after heart disease) among those over sixty-five (Libow and
Sherman, 1981). This is not to say that everyone will get cancer as he or she ages,
of course, but that cancer is much more common in older groups than in younger
ones (Crawford and Cohen, 1984).

Like many other diseases among the elderly, cancer often escapes early
detection because of the prevailing assumption that "feeling bad" is a normal part
of aging and does not necessarily warrant medical attention. On the other hand,
elderly people who do see their doctors often may undergo lab tests that reveal
spurious abnormalities, which can lead to fruitless but expensive and hazardous
exploratory surgery.

There is some controversy as to whether cancer is more virulent or more
benign in old age. Tumor growth is less aggressive in the elderly for breast cancer
(Lemon, 1982) and lung cancer (Ershler, Socinski, and Greene, 1983). Nevertheless, cancer survival rates do decline with age, even when they are adjusted for
age-specific normal life expectancy (Ries, Pollack, and Young, 1983). The adaptive
abilities of the older cancer patient are often exhausted by other diseases occurring
at the same time, lack of a social and financial support system, and the threat of

FIGURE 11–4.

Comparison by age of the proportion of total cancer incidence in the population with age-specific cancer incidence and mortality.

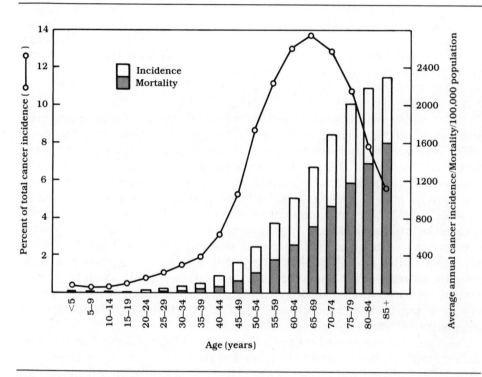

Source: From Crawford, J., and Cohen, H. J. (1984). Aging and neoplasia. *Annual Review of Gerontology and Geriatrics*, 4, 5. Copyright © Springer Publishing Company, Inc. Reprinted by permission.

diagnostic studies and cancer therapy. In the absence of intense family support, it is extremely difficult for the elderly person to cope.

STRESS AND ILLNESS

One of the better predictors of whether or not a man will have a heart attack is his "lifestyle." In particular, medical researchers have identified a behavior pattern called "Type A," which is characterized by competitive achievement strivings, a constant feeling that time is too short, and general hostility, born of the inevitable frustrations an extremely competitive and impatient person will experience (Friedman and Rosenman, 1974). Type A men have more than twice the number of heart attacks of Type B men, who are relatively easygoing and patient. Why this is so is not entirely clear, but several aspects of the different lifestyles probably play a role. Type A men are more likely to smoke cigarettes in large quantities, for example. But, in addition, stress itself results in increases in blood cholesterol, and cholesterol, in turn, has been associated with heart disease. As the researchers state:

> In the absence of Type A Behavior Pattern, coronary heart disease almost never occurs before seventy years of age, regardless of the fatty foods eaten, the cigarettes smoked, or the lack of exercise. But when this behavior pattern is present, coronary heart disease can easily erupt in one's thirties or forties. (Friedman and Rosenman, 1974, p. ix)

Although it may be said that Type A individuals create stress for themselves, stress may also be induced by a stressful environment (Henry and Stephens, 1977). Thus another approach to the study of the relationship between stress and illness begins with an attempt to estimate the degree of stress associated with various life events. Such an attempt is the Social Readjustment Rating Scale, shown in Table 11–1, which assigns a "stress value" to each event listed (Holmes and Rahe, 1967). The most stressful event is the death of a spouse (a common occurrence in old age). Divorce, landing in jail, and getting fired all rank high, but even minor changes, such as a change in sleeping habits, can have their effect, according to this scale. Change, even if it is pleasurable, is presumed to be stressful: marriage, for instance, ranks seventh on the scale. The scale is typically used by tabulating all the events an individual has experienced in a certain period of time (within the last six months or so) and then predicting near-future illness in the people with the higher scores (Rahe, 1972).

An unusual number of life changes, as measured by the Social Readjustment Rating Scale, has been found to be related to an unusual number of illnesses of various kinds (Rahe and Arthur, 1978). The scale also predicts which men are likely to become heart-attack victims (Theorell and Rahe, 1974). The role of stress in these correlations is indicated by studies showing that even among high scorers who do not become ill, there is evidence of increased endocrine-system activity (Rubin, 1974). In short, it appears that significant changes in one's life lead to bodily stress. The body sends out hormones to prepare itself for the "struggle" of dealing with the stress, and this "alarm reaction" eventually results in increased susceptibility to illness. People can and do "worry themselves sick" (Lazarus, 1981).

It should be kept in mind that environmental and psychosocial stresses may have a different effect on the elderly than they would have on younger people. The biological evidence suggests that the elderly have less resilient reactions to stress; they may be more vulnerable because their "reserve" capacities are lower. On the other hand, some stresses, such as loss of a spouse, may have less of an effect on the elderly because they are expected (Kasl and Berkman, 1981). Stress management in the elderly as it affects health might be greatly improved by training in self-regulation skills, since it has been shown that some of the biological factors involved in stress are related to the person's feelings of loss of control (Rodin, 1983). We discuss this topic further in Chapter 12 in relation to the phenomenon of "learned helplessness."

TABLE 11–1.

The social readjustment rating scale.

Life event	Mean value
1. Death of spouse	100
2. Divorce	73
3. Marital separation	65
4. Jail term	63
5. Death of close family member	63
6. Personal injury or illness	53
7. Marriage	50
8. Fired at work	47
9. Marital reconciliation	45
10. Retirement	45
11. Change in health of family member	44
12. Pregnancy	40
13. Sexual difficulties	39
14. Gain of new family member	39
15. Business readjustment	39
16. Change in financial state	38
17. Death of close friend	37
18. Change to different line of work	36
19. Change in number of arguments with spouse	35
20. Mortgage over $10,000	31
21. Foreclosure of mortgage or loan	30
22. Change in responsibilities at work	29
23. Son or daughter leaving home	29
24. Trouble with in-laws	29
25. Outstanding personal achievement	28
26. Wife begins or stops work	26
27. Begin or end school	26
28. Change in living conditions	25
29. Revision of personal habits	24
30. Trouble with boss	23
31. Change in work hours or conditions	20
32. Change in residence	20
33. Change in schools	20
34. Change in recreation	19
35. Change in church activities	19
36. Change in social activities	18
37. Mortgage or loan less than $10,000	17
38. Change in sleeping habits	16
39. Change in number of family get-togethers	15
40. Change in eating habits	13
41. Vacation	13
42. Christmas	12
43. Minor violations of the law	11

Source: From Rahe, R. H. (1972). Subjects' recent life changes and their near-future illness susceptibility. *Advances in Psychosomatic Medicine, 8,* p. 7.

The Type A person is competitive, impatient, and hostile — and likely to have an early heart attack.

PERCEPTIONS OF HEALTH

People's subjective appraisal of their health influences how they react to their symptoms, how vulnerable they consider themselves, and when they decide to obtain treatment. Often a person's self-appraisal of his or her health is a good predictor of physicians' evaluation of health, but such assessments may also differ in many ways. In old age, perceptions of one's health may be determined in large part by one's level of psychological well-being and by whether or not one continues in rewarding roles and activities (Siegler and Costa, 1985).

One interesting study showed that even when age, sex, and health status (as evaluated by physicians) were controlled for, perceived health and mortality from heart disease were strongly related (Kaplan, 1982). Those who rated their health as poor were about 2½ times as likely to die as those who rated their health as excellent. A Canadian longitudinal study of persons over sixty-five produced similar results (Mossey and Shapiro, 1982). Over three years, the mortality of those who described their health as poor at the beginning of the study was about three times the mortality of those who initially described their health as good. Yet despite this apparent awareness among older people of their actual state of health, the elderly are known to fail to report serious symptoms and illnesses and to wait longer than younger persons to seek medical help. It appears that, contrary to the popular view that older people are somewhat hypochondriacal, the elderly generally deserve serious attention when they bring complaints of ill health to a physician.

DISEASE-FREE AGING

What is the effect of age on the heart and circulatory system, free from disease? This is an important question, but one not easily answered. Some loss of elasticity in the major arteries is probably normal, for example, since the cross-linking of molecules is a general phenomenon of aging, as we have mentioned. This slight "hardening of the arteries" is probably a major cause of increasing blood pressure with age in otherwise healthy individuals. But disease can amplify these processes, laying down deposits of fatty tissue in the arteries, producing a further increase in blood pressure. The heart may have to work too hard. Or blood flow may be restricted (blocked), starving body tissue of necessary oxygen, killing cells, damaging organs. The heart, itself a muscle fed by blood, may be damaged too. A vicious cycle ensues, in which a weakened heart provides less oxygen and nutrients to itself, which leads to further weakening, and so on to catastrophe — heart attack. Or an artery in the brain is blocked — stroke, with death of brain tissue. The normal processes, slightly exaggerated, are deadly disease.

More generally, one major fact of aging is that the probability of disease increases with age. The greater the age, the less likely it is that you will be able to find an individual free from disease. Beyond the age of eighty, a disease-free person is very unusual — one could say "abnormal." So what does it mean to ask: What is aging, free from disease? Whatever it is, there's precious little of it.

As in the case of the heart, the biological changes that are generally considered "normal" aging themselves are associated with disease. In most cases, these changes at least make disease and/or injury more likely. A slowing of nerve impulses in the central nervous system; increasing rigidity of body tissue and a lengthened time for damaged tissue to regenerate or repair tissue itself; brittleness of bones: all these "normal" changes reduce the body's capacity to fend off disease, to avoid accidents, and to recover from them.

On the other hand, disease and the normal processes of aging are not the same thing. Changes due to disease are often reversible or at least can be arrested, a fact too often overlooked in the case of an old person who is faltering, either physically or mentally. "They are just getting old," we hear it said. "They will die soon anyway." Or a treatment — surgery in particular — is seen as too dangerous for someone eighty or ninety years old. The truth is that old people respond very well to surgery. At Henry Ford Hospital in Detroit, of 200 hernia operations on patients over seventy years old, 98 percent were successful (Galston, 1975). In a Louisiana community, 98 percent of the gallbladder operations in elderly patients led to marked improvement or complete recovery.

It is true, however, that the nature of the diseases people suffer from changes with age. Among younger people, the most common diseases are acute; that is, they reach a crisis quickly. Among the elderly, chronic diseases are more prevalent. In fact, most premature deaths today are a result of chronic diseases; 80 percent of the years of life lost to acute diseases have been eliminated (Fries, 1980).

Most chronic disorders begin to develop long before their presence is diagnosed by a physician. The longer one lives, the more likely it is that such a disease will develop. It is possible that some chronic diseases are preventable and that the most effective approach is to postpone them rather than attempt to cure them. If a disease can be postponed throughout the person's natural life span, the disease will have been eliminated for all practical purposes (Fries, 1980; Weg, 1983). It may be possible to postpone diseases through changes in lifestyle in such areas as nutrition, exercise, stress management, social support systems, and providing meaningful activities (Richmond, 1979; Fries, 1980). Table 11–2 lists some of the many relationships between disease conditions and lifestyle that have been reliably demonstrated.

A program of moderate exercise, a sensible diet, and the elimination of bad habits like smoking can produce, in the health of even a very old person, a turn for the better.

The concern among young people today about diet and exercise, a relatively new phenomenon, promises to produce generations of old people who will be quite different from those of today. They will probably be healthier both physically and mentally and may even show us that some of the biological changes we consider normal aging are not inevitable at all (Pelletier, 1979; Weg, 1983).

Exercise of one's physical and mental capacities not only makes disease less likely, it also prevents the ravages of *disuse*. "Use it or lose it" is one of the primary messages we can derive from the study of biological aging, and we have to be careful to distinguish the effects of disease from disease-induced (or socially induced) disuse of some function. Even a young adult, immobilized by an accident, will notice a decline in certain physical functions. Even a young adult, socially isolated, may find his or her memory failing. Old people suffer more from lack of physical and mental exercise because of society's expectations; it is "customary" for the elderly to be less active, it is "normal" for the elderly to disengage themselves from social intercourse.

In earlier chapters we discussed the relationship between lifestyle and the maintenance of mental abilities (Schaie, 1984b) as well as the possibility that certain mental functions can be improved by training. In the same way, it is possible to prevent the loss of physical vigor and help prevent disease by physical conditioning. Both middle-aged and older healthy people can participate in physical conditioning programs; their improvement will be proportionally as great as that of young people, although they may start from a lower level. Exercise programs for middle-aged and old persons have been related to important health benefits such as lowered body fat and blood pressure and improved ability to achieve neuromuscular relaxation. Such programs should emphasize the rhythmic activity of large muscle groups. Natural activities such as walking, jogging, running, and swimming seem best suited for this purpose (DeVries, 1983; Buskirk, 1985).

We are not yet able to extend the normal life span by any significant amount. But what we can do is try to maintain a fully functioning system as long as possible, to decrease the period of dependency at the end of life. By keeping oneself physically and mentally active, and also by compensating for minor deficits in eyesight and hearing with eyeglasses, hearing aids, and the like, it is

TABLE 11–2.

Disease conditions and lifestyles.

Disorders/disease	Lifestyle factors
Arteriosclerosis, atherosclerosis, coronary disease, and hypertension	High fat, highly refined carbohydrate diet, high salt; obesity; sedentary lifestyle; cigarette smoking; heavy drinking, alcoholism; unresolved, continual stress; personality type
Cerebrovascular accidents	Sedentary lifestyle; low fiber, high fat or high salt diet; heavy drinking, alcoholism (which contribute to atherosclerosis, arteriosclerosis and hypertension, risk factors for cerebrovascular accidents)
Osteoporosis and periodonitis	Malnutrition — inadequate calcium, protein, vitamin K, fluoride, magnesium and vitamin D metabolite; lack of exercise; immobility; for women, sex steroid starvation
Chronic pulmonary disease	Cigarette smoking; air pollution; stress; sedentary habits
Obesity	Low caloric output (sedentary), high caloric intake; high stress levels; heavy drinking, alcoholism; low self-esteem
Cancer	Possible correlation with personality type; stress; exposure to environmental carcinogens over a long period of time; nutritional deficiencies and excesses; radiation; sex steroid hormones; food additives; cigarette smoking; occupational carcinogens (for example, asbestos); occult viruses; diminution of immune response (immune surveillance)
Dementia and pseudo-dementia	Malnutrition; long illness and bed rest; drug abuse (polypharmacy, iatrogenesis); anemia; other organ system disease; bereavement; social isolation
Sexual dysfunction	Ignorance (the older individual and society at large); societal stereotypic attitudes; early socialization; inappropriate or no partner; drug effects (for example, antihypertensive drugs); psychogenic origin; long periods of abstinence; serious systemic disease

Source: From Weg, R. Changing physiology of aging. In D. W. Woodruff and J. E. Birren (Eds.), *Aging: Scientific perspectives and social issues*, 1983, p. 274. Monterey, CA: Brooks/Cole. Reproduced by permission.

very nearly possible to achieve this ideal. We ride through life in our one-hoss shays; it behooves us to build and to maintain them properly, so they wear out, not break down. "All at once, and nothing first, — Just as bubbles do when they burst. . . . Logic is logic. That's all I say."

Summary

1. Life expectancies have increased dramatically in the United States, from forty-seven in 1900 to nearly seventy-five today. Women live an average of seven to eight years longer than men, probably because they have a second X chromosome or some other source of biological superiority. The increase in life expectancy is due to improved nutrition, sanitation, and medical cures for diseases that formerly interrupted the life span; there is no evidence of an increase in the maximum potential span of life. A longer-than-average life is predicted for people whose ancestors were long-lived, who avoid cigarettes, who keep their weight under control, or who face life with a moderate and flexible attitude. Reports of exceptionally long-lived peoples in Russia, Pakistan, and South America, however-er, are generally believed to be without substance.

2. Theories about the genetic causes of biological aging include the notions of "aging genes"; the absence of genetic control in an organism that is "winding down"; and more or less inevitable damage to genetic molecules, possibly caused by *cross-linking*, which impairs the body's ability to replace and repair body cells. Physiological theories of aging implicate the body's endocrine system and, specifically, the thymus gland, which controls immune reactions; if these reactions are deficient or abnormal, cancerous growths and other diseases are more likely. "Wear and tear" does not appear to be a major factor in aging.

3. The lens of the eye becomes less flexible and yellower with age, the response of the pupil becomes slower, and some retinal receptor cells are lost. As a result, visual acuity declines, as does the ability to perceive depth; bifocal lenses might be needed for close work. Night driving typically becomes more difficult because the old driver needs more light than a young driver, suffers more from the glare of oncoming headlights, and adjusts less rapidly to changes in illumination. The retina may be damaged by senile macular degeneration (SMD) or by glaucoma. The visual field diminishes with age as well. Hearing loss also becomes more probable in late life, especially in the higher frequencies and under "masking" conditions. Wearing a hearing aid prescribed by an audiologist and making changes in the acoustic environment can help many older people compensate for their hearing losses. Sensitivity to taste and smells also appears to decrease with age. A reduction in sensitivity to pain is not always unwelcome, but it can be dangerous if injuries are ignored. Many old people find that loss of sensory abilities increases their sense of social isolation, which may lead to emotional problems or intellectual decline. Declining sensitivity to temperature and degeneration of the structures related to balance may cause additional problems among the elderly.

4. A reasonable estimate is that on the average people lose only 5 to 10 percent of their cortical neurons by the age of seventy-five, providing they remain free of diseases that can destroy brain tissue in larger quantities (for example, cardiovascular diseases, alcoholism). Neuron loss or impairment may result from a variety of factors. Some researchers believe that indications of neuron loss are a research artifact. Some psychologists have used reaction-time tasks to study what they consider to be age-related increases in the "sluggishness" of the *central nervous system* (brain plus spinal cord). Reaction times typically increase with age, especially in complex tasks that require "preparation" for the impending stimulus. Hypotheses that posit irreversible neural deterioration are troubled by studies showing (1) no age differences in simple reaction-time tasks; (2) improved reactions after practice or experience with the task; (3) shortened reaction times in subjects, young and old, who exercise. Reversible deficiencies in blood-oxygen supplies to the brain and in the ability to prepare for an impending stimulus (possibly because of faulty arousal processes) are alternative hypotheses to explain the general slowing of reactions with age. Alpha brain waves, as measured by EEGs, also slow with age; since EEGs, like reaction times, do not correlate highly with measures of intellectual abilities in normal, healthy subjects, these data remain difficult to interpret. EEGs and other studies show that older people sleep less soundly but spend more time in bed than younger people.

5.   The probability of disease increases dramatically after the age of sixty-five, to the point that researchers often find it hard to separate the effects of aging from those of illness. Only 5 percent of those over sixty-five are institutionalized, however, and only 9 percent rate their personal health as poor. Disease has many effects on the elderly; straining their financial resources, limiting their activity and mobility, and in general threatening to place them in the much-feared position of being dependent on others.

6.   Heart disease accounts for 40 percent of the deaths of people over sixty-five, but it is a problem for younger adults too. It is difficult to distinguish normal age-related changes in the cardiovascular system from those resulting from pathology. Men around fifty face a unique threat of heart attack, which many victims interpret as the end of their productive lives. Cancer is the second leading cause of death among those over sixty-five. Stress is a factor in many ailments, especially among the competitive, impatient, and frustrated man known as "Type A." A stressful environment makes illness of various kinds more likely; that is, people can and do "worry themselves sick." The elderly may have less resilient reactions to stress than younger people. Studies show that, contrary to popular belief, the elderly are good judges of their own health and generally deserve serious attention when they bring a problem to a physician.

7.   What is disease-free aging? This is a major question, one not easily answered. It appears that even "normal" aging produces changes in the body that make disease more likely, so that a disease-free person of eighty or ninety is a rare individual. However, disease is at least an exaggeration of normal aging. The elderly are much more likely than younger people to suffer from chronic diseases. Such diseases can sometimes be prevented (through exercise, for example) or reversed (through medical treatment).

SUGGESTED READINGS

Busse, E. W., and Blazer, D. G. (1980). Disorders related to biological functioning. In E. W. Busse and D. G. Blazer (Eds.), *Handbook of geriatric psychiatry* (pp. 390–414). New York: Van Nostrand Reinhold. Describes conditions and treatment of disturbances in physiological functioning affecting behavior, such as sleep disturbances, psychosexual disturbances, psychosomatic reactions, and effects of drug use.

Kline, D. W., and Schieber, F. (1985). Vision and aging. In J. E. Birren and K. W. Schaie (Eds.), *Handbook of the psychology of aging* (2nd ed.) (pp. 296–331). New York: Van Nostrand Reinhold. Comprehensive review of structural changes in the eye, basic visual functioning, visual information processing, and the practical implications of age changes in these processes.

Rossman, I. (1980). Bodily changes with aging. In E. W. Busse and D. G. Blazer (Eds.), *Handbook of geriatric psychiatry* (pp. 125–146). New York: Van Nostrand Reinhold. Describes age changes in stature and posture, muscles, bones, and joints, and declines in organ functions and regulatory systems.

Siegler, I. C., and Costa, P. T., Jr. (1985). Health behavior relationships. In J. E. Birren and K. W. Schaie (Eds.), *Handbook of the psychology of aging* (2nd ed.) (pp. 144–166). New York: Van Nostrand Reinhold. Discusses the reciprocal relationship of the effects of health upon behavior and of behavior upon health.

The Cell Biology of Human Aging

Although more people are living longer today than ever before, the human life span appears to be fixed at about 90 to 100 years. Death can usually be attributed to a specific cause such as heart disease or cancer, but these conditions arise from the gradual degeneration of body functions that begins at about age thirty. Degeneration, in turn, is caused by the body's inability to repair itself effectively. For a person's body does not remain the same from year to year; cells are continually dying and being replaced by their descendents. These new cells do not make the body younger. Aging is expressed in cell *lineages* rather than individual cells. Degeneration may result when cells have trouble reproducing themselves. Leonard Hayflick has shown that normal human fibroblasts, the structural cells of the body's soft tissues, will divide many times over a period of months but that they gradually stop dividing and eventually die. The important implication of this finding is that aging may be an innate property of cells.

Hayflick's research involved a fairly simple technique. After a certain treatment, human cells can be grown on culture mediums. A cell placed on a culture will reproduce for about a week, by which time it will cover the entire surface of the culture in a layer one cell thick. Once the entire surface is covered, reproduction stops due to a phenomenon known as contact inhibition. To continue reproduction, cells can be taken from the mother culture, placed on a fresh medium, and left for another week, at which time reproduction will again cease due to contact inhibition. Continuing the process, Hayflick found that in later "generations" reproduction took place more slowly. By the time of the fiftieth population doubling, they stop reproducing altogether. This suggests that normal cell lineages have a finite lifetime.

This phenomenon appears to be an important cause of human aging and the limitations on the human life span. Cultured tissue samples taken from older people reproduce fewer times than those taken from younger people. Furthermore, evidence suggests not only that the same process occurs in other species, but that there is a direct relationship between the life span of a species and the capacity of its cells to divide in culture. In humans as in other animals, the body begins to deteriorate when cells stop reproducing themselves.

What part of the cell controls the capacity of normal cells to replicate? After a series of experiments that involved joining old nuclei to young cytoplasts (unnucleated cells) and old cytoplasts to young nuclei, the authors came to the preliminary conclusion that the "clock" that controls the cell's ability to continue reproducing is in the nucleus.

Not all human cells divide as rapidly as the fibroblasts. Specialized cells such as nerve cells, muscle cells, and sensory cells divide rarely or not at all after maturity, and gerontologists agree that it is in these slow- or nondividing cells that most important changes occur. It seems likely that most organisms age and die before the fibroblasts have ceased reproduction. However, the mechanisms that limit the division of fibroblasts are probably the same ones that limit the division of specialized cells.

What is the underlying mechanism that causes age changes in most cells? Most gerontologists believe the answer lies in the genes. Three general hypotheses based on the properties of the information-bearing molecules in the cells, RNA and DNA, are now thought to be the most plausible explanation for aging.

The first explanation proposes that, over time, the translation of the genetic message in DNA into RNA, enzymes, and other protein molecules might be increasingly subject to error. This would lead to a decline in the functional abilities of the cell. The situation is analogous to an error in the instructions of a machine that makes parts for other machines: it will turn out faulty parts that, when assembled into the final product, would reduce its efficiency or keep it from working altogether. This hypothesis has been tested, but the results do not yield good evidence in support of it.

The second hypothesis about the genetic basis of aging concerns the fact that many of the genes along the DNA molecule are repeated in identical sequences, making the genetic message highly redundant. These repeated sequences are normally repressed, but if an active gene is extensively damaged, it may be replaced by one of the identical reserve genes. Ultimately, all the repeated genes would be used up, errors would accumulate, and the degeneration associated with age would begin.

The third hypothesis proposes that age changes are simply the continuation of normal genetic signals that regulate the development of animals from the moment of conception until sexual maturation. There may even be "aging genes" that slow or shut down certain biochemical pathways, leading to age changes such as gray hair, menopause, and reduced athletic ability. These genetically programmed events may occur at different times in different types of cells. Thus the root of aging might be deficiencies in a few key cell types that age the fastest and have the greatest effects. These hypothetical aging cells might function in a fashion analogous to that which leads to normal decline and death of cells that occurs on a massive scale during the development of the embryo. In vertebrate animals, for example, development of a limb involves not only the marshalling of millions of cells but also the death and resorption of millions of others. The fate of these latter cells is determined by "death clocks" that operate on a precise schedule. It is conceivable that the same processes continue throughout life, operating at different rates in different tissues and ultimately leading to the normal age changes that increase susceptibility to disease.

The importance of Hayflick's work lies in its demonstration that the mechanisms involved in human cell growth impose finite limits on the human life span. The limits of that span could most likely be broken only by drastic genetic changes or mutations that might markedly alter major species characteristics with unknown and possibly adverse side effects. This conclusion results from the finding that the only cellular structures that seem to escape the limitations of a finite "biological clock" are either life-threatening cancerous growths, or those cells involved in the reproduction of the species, rather than the survival of the individual. A major conclusion to be derived from this fundamental biological research then is that those who wish to improve the condition of our species ought to redirect their efforts from extending the absolute length of life toward increasing the level of functioning and quality of life until as late as possible within the now attainable maximum life span.

Hayflick, L. (1980). The cell biology of human aging. *Scientific American, 242*, 58–65.

Chapter Twelve

MENTAL DISORDERS

Failing to Cope

What is it like to be mentally ill? We who are reasonably rational perhaps can never know the sadness and the frustration of a disordered mind. We can only hope to understand the observable manifestations of the various mental disorders. Consider, for example, the case of E. J.*

E. J. was fifty-five years old when his family began to notice that he was changing (Gardner, 1974). Up until that time, E. J. had been a model citizen: a valued accountant for his employer, a beloved father for his family, and a respected violinist for the local symphony orchestra. One day, while on an outing with his family, E. J. got them lost and could not read the road map. Gradually thereafter, his astonished family watched with distress as he withdrew from social interactions and deteriorated intellectually. He quit the orchestra, frustrated by the numerous mistakes he was making on the violin. His memory began to fail him. He began making computational errors, which created serious problems for him in his job as a professional accountant; finally, at the urging of his employer, he accepted an early retirement.

E. J.'s family thought at first that he was merely depressed, that he would one day "snap out of it" and become his old self. They ignored the signs of intellectual decline until the deterioration was unmistakable — until, for example, E. J. could not recall, for the life of him, the name of the President of the United States. The worried family rushed E. J. to a physician, who diagnosed his illness as Alzheimer's disease, an as-yet-incurable degenerative disease of the brain.

E. J.'s condition continued to worsen. He would forget about things he had put on the stove to heat up. He began to burn himself and the furniture with cigarettes he couldn't seem to hold on to. His speech was affected, and he lost the ability to express himself clearly. His ability to understand events began to fail. For example, once in the shower he found himself unable to open the door; he panicked, and only the timely arrival of his daughter averted a potential disaster. Finally E. J. had to be hospitalized for his own safety.

*Case study of E. J. from *The shattered mind* by Howard Gardner. Copyright © 1974 by Howard Gardner. Reprinted by permission of Alfred A. Knopf, Inc.

Dr. Howard Gardner, a developmental psychologist, interviewed E. J. in the hospital and filed this report:

> I asked him to spell his first name, Elmer. "El . . . uh, M-E-R . . . no, that's not, E-L-R-E, . . . oh, never mind," he replied over a two-minute period in which we both grew extremely uncomfortable. I didn't ask him to spell his last name but instead requested his age.
>
> "I really don't under . . .," he replied.
>
> "Where do you live?"
>
> "In El . . . mer," he said, rather relieved to have gotten something out at least.
>
> "No, where is your home?" I corrected. "Is it in Boston?"
>
> "No."
>
> "Dorchester?"
>
> "No."
>
> "Cambridge?"
>
> "No."
>
> "Belmont?"
>
> "Yes," he responded immediately, evincing marked satisfaction at a successful communication. I asked him to name some objects about the room. Of all those to which I pointed, he only named "glasses" correctly on his own. When he was supplied with terms to choose among, his performance improved, but he still gave the incorrect answer, or no answer at all, on half of the items selected.
>
> We tried some simple calculation problems. Again, he was unable to provide a single answer on his own. After I had repeated the sum $5 + 5$ many times, he did succeed in raising both hands, displaying ten fingers. But the question 2×2 elicited only a sheepish, "Oh, boy, oh, boy," repeated over and over again. When I posed a third problem, he protested: "I just don't . . . you have people who make . . . and so forth . . . and so forth . . . and it becomes . . . I just don't like it" — each phrase accompanied by a helpless wave of the hand. As before, he failed on the name of the President, but when I supplied it, he retorted, "That's it, a real bastard."
>
> "Why?" I asked.
>
> "Because, I don't like him. He's a cookie, what you call it." E. J. also selected the Vice-president's name from among multiple choices, adding the comment, "That's one of them." However, he was unable to pick out the names of the mayor of Boston or the governor of Massachusetts from such lists.
>
> Examination of his language skills revealed that E. J. was better at repeating sentences than at any other task; he was completely unable to write, and could only read single-digit numbers and a few familiar words. He echoed a number of sentences correctly but then began to perseverate on earlier items and I had to discontinue the testing. . . . Rarely could he express an idea verbally, but sometimes one was able to decipher the intended meaning from his tone of voice and accompanying gestures.
>
> Tests of his ability to carry out simple actions produced very pitiful performances. He could neither draw any objects nor copy any figures, not even when I sought to guide his hands. He was unable to light his own cigarette or to comb his hair until I placed his hand in the right position. Given an envelope and a letter and told to place the letter in the envelope, he did not grasp the intent of the command despite numerous explanations and supporting gestures on my part. He did "salute" when I issued the command, but was unable to show me how he waved goodbye, or coughed. Given the appropriate props, he was able to brush his teeth but, when

through, he didn't know where to put the brush. And he retained the paste in his mouth, unable to swallow it or to spit it out. He was somewhat better at imitating gestures that I made with my body but, as with the sentence-repetition task, he quickly reverted to a reenactment of prior sequences and was unable to break out of this "set."

I was unprepared for E. J.'s excellent performance in one area — that of duplicating various rhythmic patterns. Once he had grasped the basic idea, he succeeded in reproducing rhythms of some complexity, and his performance was qualitatively different than it had been at other tasks: he responded immediately and energetically and displayed remarkably few perseverations. His success in the musical sphere stood in stark contrast to the depressed level of his other functions. Although he could neither name melodies he heard nor produce melodies whose names were given, he was able to continue almost any motif which I began, never with the words, but consistently with appropriate rhythm, pitch, and phrasing. Here was a severely demented patient with relative sparing of at least one higher cortical function, possibly due to the great prominence this function had assumed in his earlier life, or to his unusually potent motivation in that domain. (Gardner, 1978, pp. 249–252)

Adult Development and Mental Illness

Mental illness is usually diagnosed from abnormal behavior. A woman is asked the time of day, and she begins to rub her arms and recite the Apostles' Creed. A man is so convinced that someone is "out to get him" that he refuses to leave his apartment. Unusual behaviors like these are taken as evidence that the mental apparatus is not working quite right, and mental illness is proclaimed.

There are many problems with the diagnosis of mental illness (Geiwitz, 1980). The abnormal behaviors are not often as clearly defined as those in the case of E. J. What is considered abnormal by a young white male psychiatrist might be ordinary behavior to an old black woman. For example, she might be seen as abnormally aggressive by a man who believes that women are (or should be) passive and accepting. She might be seen as paranoid by a white person who is insensitive to the years she has spent fighting racial discrimination and protecting herself from ghetto violence. She might be seen as psychotic because she talks to herself; the young psychiatrist does not realize that her friends have died, that her arthritis keeps her from getting around, that she has no one to talk to but herself. She might be a member of a cult or a radical political group, whose attitudes and behaviors would appear like symptoms of mental disorder to the conservative young white male psychiatrist.

The term "mental illness" is itself a matter of some controversy. Before the nineteenth century, people who exhibited bizarre behaviors were considered to be "morally inferior," if their actions were only slightly neurotic, or "possessed by a demon," if their behaviors were extreme. In the early 1800s, a French physician named Philippe Pinel proposed a different view, suggesting that people who behaved in strange ways were "sick people whose miserable state deserves all the consideration that is due suffering humanity" (Zilboorg and Henry, 1941, pp.

323–324). The labeling of mentally disordered people as "ill," rather than as "inferior" or "lazy" or "possessed," had a profound effect on their treatment by society. They were put in "hospitals," and they were called "patients." Compared to the beatings and inhumane confinements previously administered, "medical care" was a distinct improvement.

But problems arose with the label "mentally ill." People began to think of people who behaved in unusual ways in the same ways they thought of people with a broken arm or a touch of pneumonia: "Stick them in a hospital until they recover." Unusual behaviors, such as bedwetting, were seen as "symptoms" of underlying "disease," and "patients" were asked why they wanted to soil the bedsheets of their parents — instead of being given training in bladder control, which for many of them was all the treatment necessary. People with minor "problems in living" were hesitant to see a clinical psychologist (or, worse yet, a psychiatrist with an M.D. degree) because they did not want to label themselves as "sick" (Szasz, 1960). Thus, although the relabeling of people as "mentally ill" resulted in more humane treatment, it sometimes hampers attempts to deliver more effective treatment (Bandura, 1969).

Similarly, mental hospitals were once safe havens ("asylums") for people who were badly abused outside. But, unlike hospitals for the physically ill, mental hospitals do not always promote recovery. People who have problems coping with the world are not likely to solve those problems in an institution. The hospital environment is often radically different from the community environment. Even with the best of intentions, overworked hospital staff often find themselves rewarding passivity and punishing "patients" who make demands on their time. For these and other reasons, many people who would have been in hospitals are now treated in the community; they are trying to adjust.

In this chapter, we consider "mental health" to be adequate adjustment and adaptation to the "real" world. "Mental illness" (or mental disorder) is considered maladaptive. The emphasis is on people's ability to cope with their environment, to handle the developmental tasks placed before them at their stage of life. To be sure, biological factors much like disease are sometimes involved: there may be metabolic deficiencies or brain damage, as there is in the case of E. J. In other cases, however, social stress will be paramount — social isolation, economic hardship, a life crisis of some sort, perhaps the loss of a spouse. Very often, especially in the case of older people, biological and social causes combine in intricate patterns. A hearing loss, for example, might make the comprehension of speech more difficult; individuals might respond to this sensory loss with a paranoid belief that people are deliberately mumbling or speaking about them behind their backs. Simply growing old is a terrible blow to the self-concept of some people, who have a great need to think of themselves as always young and vital.

Many of the criteria for mental health for young adults also apply to the aged. These include freedom from symptoms of psychological pathology, life satisfaction, self-acceptance, mastery of the environment, as well as the ability to work, love, and play. What changes with age, however, are the content areas and

Growing old can be a blow to the self-concept of some people, who like to think of themselves as independent.

operations by which these criteria are met. But the current youth-oriented approach to mental health needs to be balanced by additional criteria that emerge in middle adulthood and become more important as people get older. Birren and Renner (1981) suggest that these include the increasing importance of self-evaluation, life review, and reconciliation. These criteria are deemed important for older individuals because meeting them reflects whether they have exerted good stewardship of their lives and in their responsibilities to younger genera-tions. In response to this position, it has been argued that the very vagueness of such mental health criteria is likely to encourage stereotypes of normal aging that set arbitrary standards. Such standards are said to disregard group norms, cultur-al factors, personal histories, and situational pressures. Instead of dogmatic assumptions about mental health, it might therefore be preferable for pro-fessionals to limit themselves to diagnose psychopathology and leave aside ex-istential issues (Rosow, 1981).

We begin this chapter with a look at the various mental disorders that show relationships with age. Some disorders are more common in late life, including those arbitrarily grouped together under the label "senility." Others are more common among young adults. Following this geographical tour of the territory, we consider (once again) the notion of "life crisis," this time as it applies to stress and mental breakdown.

Depression is a major mental-health problem of elderly people, although it is also common in younger adults. It is a perhaps understandable reaction to frustration and failure (inability to cope), and it is also influenced by body chemistry and drugs. We discuss depression in a life-span perspective and also suicide, to which extreme depression sometimes leads. In addition, we use the case of depression to discuss in some detail both drug therapies and psychotherapies that have been found effective against mental disorders.

The mental disorders known to be associated with brain malfunction or brain damage are reviewed next. Often an overdose of drugs produces a state of confusion that is misdiagnosed as reflecting brain damage; in a section on drug use among the elderly, we look at some of the benefits and dangers derived from these chemical comforts. Finally, we return to psychotherapy, discussing the general issues of goals — how they differ at different life stages — and obstacles to treatment, including the negative attitudes many psychotherapists have toward treating elderly clients.

Psychopathology and Age

Like physical illnesses, mental disorders are often found in different proportions in different age groups. Schizophrenia, a mental disorder marked by loss of contact with reality, is most likely to appear in young adulthood, before the age of thirty (Bernheim and Lewine, 1979). Schizophrenia, in fact, was once called "dementia praecox," which means disturbed thought processes (dementia) that show up early in life (praecox, a word related to "precocious"). Elderly schizophrenics are not uncommon, however, since many forms of schizophrenia resist cure. There are substantial numbers of aged schizophrenics in mental institutions and nursing homes, many of whom were diagnosed early in life and have lived their entire lives in institutions of one sort or another (Redick, Kramer, and Taube, 1973). Others were stabilized and returned to the community, but may in old age be again at risk, since they have typically lived a rather marginal existence (Clausen, 1984).

One of the problems of determining the true relationship of mental disorders to age is that general beliefs about this relationship affect diagnosis. Thus an old person with no history of schizophrenia who exhibits mental confusion, disorientation, and childish emotions is likely to be diagnosed as suffering from senile dementia; the same symptoms in a younger person would almost certainly be called schizophrenia. The primary distinction between senile dementia and schizophrenia, besides age of onset, is evidence of brain cell deterioration in senile dementia. However, such brain damage is quite hard to diagnose, at least until the patient dies and an autopsy is performed. There is an unofficial diagnostic category called "late-life schizophrenia," but some psychiatrists refuse to use it, claiming no such disease exists (Butler and Lewis, 1977).

A similar problem exists with a mental disorder that used to be called "involutional melancholia." "Involutional" refers to body changes that occur later in life and was originally used to describe changes after menopause in women; involutional "melancholia" was diagnosed in cases of severe depression following menopause. So here was a diagnostic category with a built-in age bias (it was never used for young people) and sex bias (it was usually used only for women). The sex bias is gradually waning, as "involutional" is taken more and more to mean "late life" in either sex, but obviously the age bias remains. We can say without fear of contradiction that involutional melancholia occurs more often after the age of fifty than before!

In general, mental disorders in which anxiety is a chief component — the neuroses in particular — appear to be more common in young adults than in middle-aged or elderly people (Public Health Service, 1972). But there may be substantial group differences as is indicated by a national survey of black elderly in which 51 percent of the sample reported that they had a serious personal problem and 26 percent reported that they were near the breakdown level (Chatters and Jackson, 1982; Jackson, Chatters, and Neighbors, 1982).

Mental retardation, like schizophrenia, is usually diagnosed early in life, and like schizophrenia it may continue throughout life. Mania also begins early (Post, 1980), as do histrionic, antisocial, and borderline disorders; all are uncommon among the elderly (Straker, 1982). It has been reported that the incidence of personality disorders decreases in old age (Vaillant and Perry, 1980), but this finding may reflect patterns of service utilization rather than rates of disorder per se.

Middle age, despite the many midlife crises, is not a period characterized by peaks in many disorders, although acute alcoholism is one disorder that peaks in early midlife. During this period of life, rates of mental disorders generally decrease. But, as you can see in Figure 12–1 (first admissions to state and county mental hospitals by age), rates for brain syndromes begin to increase slightly in the midfifties and increase dramatically at about age seventy. Although alcoholism and schizophrenia are the most common disorders among the young and middle-aged, they are so uncommon by age seventy-five that, combined with all mental disorders other than syndromes, they account for only 15 percent of first admissions. Other sources indicate that paranoid, compulsive, narcissistic, and dependent personalities may be more adversely affected by aging and therefore may be more common in older age groups (Straker, 1982). Dependency is particularly painful for many older people. On the one hand, becoming dependent appears to be a prominent fear in old age; on the other hand, learning to do without the help to which one has become accustomed can also present problems.

FIGURE 12-1.

Incidence of organic and psychiatric disorders by first admission rates.

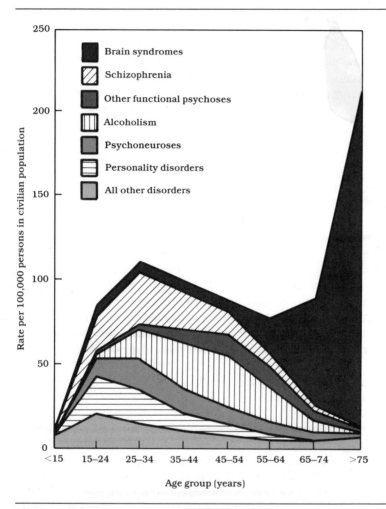

Source: From Kramer, M., (1969). *Application of mental health statistics.* Geneva: World Health Organization. Reprinted by permission.

Many of the serious disorders that lead to the hospital admissions noted in Figure 12–1 involve not only brain disease or alcoholism but may also occur because of severe depression (Cole and Zarit, 1984). The type of depression experienced by old mental patients is different from the depression of young patients: the young patients often experience mood swings, with depression giving way to extreme elation (mania); this disorder is called manic–depressive psychosis or bipolar depression. The old patients more commonly experience only depression — unipolar depression (Butler and Lewis, 1982).

Two points should be made concerning statistics on mental illness among the elderly. First, older people perform differently than young or middle-aged adults on virtually all psychodiagnostic instruments, including personality and mood scales as well as tests of cognitive function (Schaie and Stone, 1982; Zarit, Eiler, and Hassinger, 1985). For example, older persons will typically get a higher (more pathological) score on the depression and hypochondriasis scales of the Minnesota Multiphasic Personality Inventory (MMPI) because it would be normal for them to affirm the presence of minor physical complaints and feelings of loss in interpersonal relationships (see also discussion of personality assessment in Chapter 4). As a result, certain disorders may be over- or underdiagnosed in the aged. The possibility that the assessment instruments used to diagnose the elderly are inaccurate has led to a wave of studies that attempt to "recalibrate" existing instruments for use with older people; how can we estimate the frequency of a disorder if we are not sure how to diagnose it? The issue of age norms is probably most significant for diagnosing mild disorders. It may account, at least in part, for our current inability to distinguish between early forms of dementia and the mental changes normally expected in old age. Thus assessment problems clearly contribute to the current confusion about the presence or absence of age differences in mental disorders.

The second point concerns age differences in the risk factors associated with mental illness. Sensory deficits, physical illness, poverty, bereavement, and social or geographic isolation are all more common among the old than the young. The prevalence of certain conditions such as adjustment disorders and mild depression may be inflated among the elderly because of high rates of physical or psychosocial disability. How these risk factors contribute to more serious disorders such as major depression and various forms of dementia is not clear. Some researchers claim that there is a particularly close association between physical and psychiatric disorders among the aged (Post, 1980; Jarvik and Perl, 1981; Verwoerdt, 1981), but the nature of this interaction and how it differs from that observed in younger groups has not been adequately researched. At this point, all we can say is that risk factors appear to vary with age, but we don't know how these factors affect the development of mental disorders in older people or whether they affect the old differently than the young.

Psychopathology and Sex

In addition to age differences in psychopathology, there are also sex differences. Women are substantially more likely to be diagnosed as mentally disordered than men (Chesler, 1972). There are more women than men in almost all the diagnostic categories, including schizophrenia, depression (both bipolar and unipolar), and the neuroses. Men are more common in categories based on alcoholism, drug addiction, and violent criminal behavior. In some cases, diagnostic categories are *defined* with women in mind; we just mentioned involutional melancholia, which until recently was used exclusively for postmenopausal women. Similarly, women who suffer an emotional letdown after giving birth to a child are said to be in the throes of "postpartum depression"; men have no access to this ailment. Hysteria, a form of neurosis designed to ward off extreme anxiety, was named by the great Greek physician, Hippocrates, who thought the disorder was due to a malfunctioning or "wandering" womb; "hysteria" has the same root as the word "hysterectomy." For 2,000 years after Hippocrates (400 B.C.), the label was used only for women. Even today the tendency toward hysterical behavior is believed by many to be a trait found only in women.

MARITAL STATUS

The higher rate of mental disorders among women is contributed almost entirely by married women (Gove, 1972). Married women have a much greater incidence of mental disorder than married men, but in other categories of marital status — single, divorced, widowed — men have a higher rate than women. Considering this and other evidence, one is led to the conclusion that something about the institution of marriage makes mental disorder more likely for women who enter it and less likely for men (Bernard, 1973; Tavris and Offir, 1977).

The findings that married women are the ones particularly at risk in regard to mental disorder argues against biological interpretations of sex differences. If women in general were biologically more susceptible to mental disorder, one would expect them to exceed men in illness rates in all categories of marital status, not just in the "married" category. Most current interpretations of the sex difference, therefore, place the blame on the social role of "housewife" (Gove, 1972; Unger, 1979). "Housewife" is a position of low prestige, one that does not require a great deal of skill (or so most people believe). Modern society has isolated the nuclear family to some extent, leaving many housewives who have young children with television as their chief source of entertainment; they are often bored and lonely. Even working wives tend to have low-paying, low-status, low-interest jobs. And the job may lead to conflict between family and career goals.

SEX DIFFERENCES IN LATE LIFE

As people grow older, the sex difference in rates of mental disorder decreases and may even reverse; after the age of sixty-five, men may be more likely than women to suffer serious mental disability (Boyd and Weissman, 1982). Retirement, which "lowers" the position of many men to that of "househusband," is considered by some theorists to be a major factor (Gove, 1972). Another factor is cumulative brain damage caused by excessive alcohol consumption, industrial pollution, and the like, which can be expected to be more frequent among men than women. A third possibility is the genetically based difference in life span between men and women: a man at age sixty-five is closer to the end of life than a woman is at the same age. Probably some combination of these factors is necessary to account for the sharper rises in late-life disorders among men than among women.

Psychopathology, Stress, and Helplessness

Although many mental disorders can be traced to genetic bases or physical illnesses, environmental stress is the primary agent in others. The relatively powerless position of women in our society is one such source of stress. The lack of power of people in the lower social classes is another and may help to explain why the rate of mental disorders is ten times as high in the lower classes as it is in the upper classes (Goldstein, Baker, and Jamison, 1980). Some of this difference can be accounted for by the "social drift hypothesis," which proposes that mentally disordered people are found in the lower classes because they cannot hold a job that would give them the status and income necessary to enter the upper classes; "they're poor because they're disordered," not "they're disordered because they're poor." But the constant stress of poverty, poor housing, and deteriorating neighborhoods plays a role too (Kohn, 1973).

In addition to groups that are defined by their lack of power in a society dominated by white, upper-class males, groups defined by the common experience of a particularly stressful life event are also prone to mental disorders. Divorced people form one such group, widowed people another; in both, rates of mental disorder tend to rise, especially in the year or so following the event that defines the group. Retirement or being fired from a job can also trigger mental disorder. People sometimes speak of the stress in a high-powered job with great responsibilities, but the stress of having no job at all appears to be greater, on the average.

HELPLESSNESS

Stress in today's world often means problems with no obvious solutions — helplessness. In Chapter 7, we discussed research on learned helplessness, which is broadly defined as the perception, born of a series of failures, that nothing works. In laboratory experiments, humans or other animals exposed to an aversive event (loud noise, electric shock) over which they had no control eventually gave up trying to do something about it. Even when an effective response was later made available, the subjects who had learned to be helpless did not avail themselves of it; they simply sat and whined or moped.

The feeling that one is helpless to do anything about one's problems is related to several negative emotions, such as anxiety and depression, which in extreme form constitute mental disorder. Psychoanalysts sometimes refer to anxiety as "psychic helplessness," which reflects the fact that nothing is quite so terrifying as the feeling that one is threatened by something and there is no way to combat the threat. Anxiety is probably more common as a response to perceived helplessness among young adults, who are in a life stage in which much is expected of them. They must build a career and choose a mate, both complicated tasks fraught with the dangers of failure and rejection. Not all the determinants of success are controlled by the individual; bosses and prospective mates make many of the important decisions. Thus many times the situation seems helpless and, yet, something should be done. Anxiety is the rather ineffective but common response (Seligman, 1981).

Depression is another response to perceived helplessness. Although young adults are also subject to the debilitating effects of deep depressions, depression is a particularly common problem among older people (Pfeiffer, 1977). Anxiety is an emotion one feels when things look *almost* hopeless, when there is still a chance things might work out. Depression abandons hope; it gives up striving. Older adults might lose their jobs; they have little chance of getting others. When a spouse dies, there is no hope left; it's not like losing a dating partner in one's youth.

A revision of helplessness theory takes into account how people's causal explanations of events may influence their feelings of helplessness (Abramson, Seligman, and Teasdale, 1978). When people face uncontrollable bad events, they ask why; their answers influence how they react.

The researchers contend that three attributes of explanations are influential. First, does the person attribute the events to something in him- or herself (internal explanation) or to something outside (external explanation)? Those who believe the cause of the event is internal are more likely to suffer loss of self-esteem than those who believe the cause is external (and hence beyond their control). Second, does the person believe the cause is a factor that persists across time (stable explanation) or a factor that can change (unstable explanation)? Those who believe the cause to be a stable factor are more prone to chronic helplessness and depression than those who believe in unstable explanations. Third, does the person think the cause is the result of a factor that affects a variety of outcomes (global explanation) or just a few (specific explanation)? Those who choose global causes tend to have pervasive deficits; they may feel helplessness in many areas of their lives. Those who accept more specific explanations may only feel helpless in the areas that the explanation affects.

The relationship among the variables in this theory is diagrammed in Figure 12–2. On the extreme right are the effects, the symptoms of helplessness, such as increased rates of disease, lowered appetite, and so on. These symptoms are the result, helplessness theory says, of the expectation that no action that one takes can control outcomes in the future. The question becomes, then, how do processes and events bring about this expectation? As Figure 12–2 indicates, the expectation is usually triggered when bad events are perceived as uncontrollable. This perception, in turn, is strongly influenced by the causal explanations to which a person is prone. People have a tendency to choose certain kinds of explanations for events; that is, they have different explanatory styles. One person may attribute poor marks in school to biased teachers and meaningless work and his or her resulting lack of interest. Another person may feel that he or she just isn't smart enough and can't manage to do well despite intense efforts. What is most important, however, is that the person attributes the bad events to causes beyond his or her control. Those who tend to give stable, global explanations for bad events are most likely to experience helplessness. A person's ex-

FIGURE 12–2.

The process of learned helplessness.

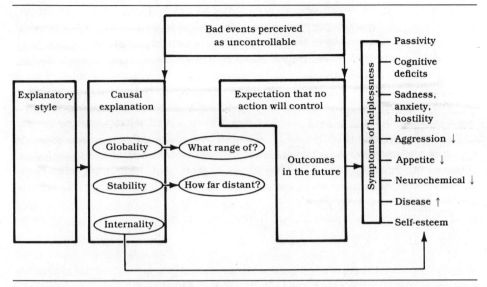

Source: From Peterson, C., and Seligman, M. E. P., (1984). Causal explanations as a risk factor for depression: Theory and evidence. *Psychological Review, 91,* 347–374. Copyright 1984 by the American Psychological Association. Reprinted by permission of the publisher and author.

planatory style and the particular explanation that he or she gives for an event are not sufficient to cause symptoms of helplessness, however. These variables influence expectations, and it is expectations that are a sufficient cause.

What people are likely to perceive themselves as helpless and to believe that control over significant events lies in the hands of fate or other people? Women, relative to men. People in the lower social classes, relative to those in the upper classes. Minority groups, relative to members of the establishment. Old people, over the age of sixty or so, relative to young people. These are the comparatively powerless groups in our society, whose perceptions of helplessness are often realistic. Realistic or not, however, these perceptions can lead to emotional disorders that compound the trials and tribulations of the members of these groups.

Depression and Suicide

It is difficult to imagine someone who has not experienced depression to some degree, so we need not dwell at length on the symptoms of depression. Briefly, however, we can note a few of depression's more prominent characteristics (Pfeiffer, 1977): a painful sadness; a generalized lack of interest in life, combined with general inactivity; a pervasive pessimism that manifests itself as low self-esteem and a gloomy evaluation of one's present and future situation; difficulty in making decisions, even minor ones; dreams of being lost and lonely in isolated, frightening, desolate places, dreams of crying out for help with no one responding. According to the diagnostic manual of the American Psychiatric Association, these symptoms must last at least two weeks to help distinguish clinical depression from an ordinary case of the "blues." Depression has physical symptoms as well: loss of appetite, severe fatigue, sleep disturbances, changes in bowel habits (constipation or diarrhea).

Depression often masks itself in physical symptoms for which there is no discernible cause. Such symptoms may be a mental disorder in and of itself called hypochondriasis, but more often than not, hypochondriasis tends to be closely related to depression (Pfeiffer, 1977). The individual (usually elderly) complains of severe and constant pain, most commonly a headache or backache; a medical examination, however, discovers no physical problem. The person often manifests some of the symptoms of depression — a face full of frowns, low activity level — but denies feeling sad.

Estimates of the incidence of hypochondriasis among the elderly vary.

Although few elderly people are seriously depressed, many aging individuals experience some level of depression as a normal reaction to loss and change.

Among those living in the community, it has been said to be between 10 and 20 percent (Busse and Blazer, 1980). Another researcher found that 31 percent of the aged subjects in his study had negative perceptions of their health even though examinations did not reveal significant medical problems (Maddox, 1964). A study of elderly people hospitalized with depression found that 64 percent claimed to have physical problems for which no physical basis could be found. In nearly half these cases, the depression started with the appearance of hypochondriacal symptoms; other depressive symptoms appeared later. The most common complaints concerned constipation and other digestive system problems, headaches, burning sensations, and tightness and pressure in the head. The reports of relatives and friends indicated that some patients had been preoccupied with health throughout their lives, but in 80 percent of the cases, the physical complaints were considered a new or unusual problem. A most striking finding was that 25 percent of the patients with hypochondriacal complaints had attempted suicide; among the other depressed patients, the rate was only 7 percent (de Alarcon, 1971).

New cases of hypochondriasis peak between the ages of sixty and sixty-five. More women are affected then men. One researcher (Busse, 1976) believes the disorder is a response to accumulated stress. It is especially likely to occur when a person suffers prolonged criticism in a social situation, is isolated as a result of economic restrictions, or has reduced marital satisfaction because a spouse is disabled. The hypochondriacal behavior may indicate (1) withdrawal of psychic interest from other people and events, with interest centering on the self; (2) a shift of anxiety from psychic topics to less-threatening concerns about physical disease; and (3) the use of physical symptoms as a means of self-punishment for unacceptable hostile feelings toward others. Other researchers emphasize the social aspects of hypochondriasis, the central feature of the ailment being that the person cannot convey feelings to others directly and honestly (Goldstein and Birnbom, 1976).

Investigators differ on the probable outcome of hypochondriasis. Busse (1976) maintains that such reactions are often transient and end without intervention, but he provides no supporting data. Verwoerdt (1981) recommends (1) accepting the person's need for a hypochondriacal defense, (2) providing treatment for the symptoms, and (3) ensuring that a physician or therapist remains available for followup appointments. Goldstein and Birnbom (1976) reported that hypochondriacal symptoms in eight elderly depressed patients improved with family therapy; for eight others, family therapy either proved to be impractical or was refused. The latter group were considered failures at a six-month followup. Kline (1974) reports that treatment with drugs or psychotherapy designed to combat depression usually relieves the physical pain, allowing the person to continue normal life.

When a physician or therapist first sees an older patient who has a number of physical complaints, it is often difficult to determine whether they are symptoms of the onset of depression or of a physical disorder independent of depression. For example, since depressed elderly people are quite willing to sit around, doing nothing ("vegetating"), they are often misdiagnosed as having irreversible brain damage (senility). In such cases, treatment for depression can have surprising effects. Therapist Nathan Kline describes one patient:

> a major philanthropist who headed an important foundation. At seventy-eight he resigned his position, retired to Florida, and there sank into what seemed like hopeless senility. He was dependent on hovering attendants for his every need. . . . [Treatment for depression] produced a remarkable reversal not only of mood but also of supposed mental decline. At eighty-three this patient is back in action, serving usefully on diverse boards and committees, and putting in four- to five-hour workdays. (Kline, 1974, pp. 183–184).

In the cases where the diagnosis is uncertain, it is best to refer the patient to a physician with the skill and patience to pursue the complaints. If the evaluation for physical ailments reveals nothing, treating the patient for depression should be considered.

WHAT CAUSES DEPRESSION?

A number of different theories concerning the causes of depression among the elderly have been proposed. Some emphasize purely physiological factors associated with the aging processes. Others place more importance on the social circumstances that may attend aging. It is likely that factors of both types are influential, at least in some cases.

Several theories propose that depressive symptoms result from insufficient supplies of specific neurotransmitter substances or from more general neurotransmitter imbalances in the brain (Maas, 1978). It appears that age does influence a number of neurotransmitter systems (Lipton and Nemeroff, 1978). The fact that depressive symptoms in the elderly often respond to drug treatment also suggests that the problem may be biochemical (Gerner et al., 1980; Gerner and Jarvick, 1984). As yet, however, response to drug therapies has not been directly linked to the functioning of neurotransmitters. Other models emphasize the role of the nondominant hemisphere of the brain in depression (Weingartner and Silberman, 1982). Neuropsychological tests of the right-hemisphere functions of depressives reveal impairments (Flor-Henry, 1979). Electroencephalograms also reveal abnormalities (Davidson et al., 1979). The combined effects of depression and aging on the functioning of the two hemispheres may be a worthwhile area of study.

Depression among the elderly is also strongly correlated with physical illness (Jarvik and Perl, 1981). In a study of 900 people aged sixty-five and older, it was found that 44 percent of the subjects who were depressed were also physically ill. Studies of life satisfaction also show that being healthy is important for a sense of well-being (Morgan, 1976). Physical illness and depression may occur together for several reasons (see Jarvik and Perl, 1981; Ouslander, 1982). Feelings of sadness, anxiety, or fatigue are to be expected when someone is ill, in reaction either to pain or disability itself or to the awareness of the illness. In some cases, these feelings are severe and protracted enough to constitute a depression. Symptoms of depression may also be either a direct consequence of illness or a side effect of medication. Longitudinal and retrospective studies indicate that people who are depressed may be predisposed to develop physical illnesses, so a cycle of physical and emotional illnesses may become established. With our current state of knowledge in this area, it is difficult to disentangle cause and effect when a person has both a psychiatric and physical illness.

Like physical illness, bereavement is disproportionately common among the elderly; 51 percent of the women and 13.6 percent of the men over sixty-five have been widowed at least once (U.S. Bureau of the Census, 1981b). In a group of elderly patients hospitalized for depression, bereavement was reported to be a common precipitating factor (Turner and Sternberg, 1978), but longitudinal studies show relatively low rates of depression among widows and widowers (33 percent one month after the death of the spouse; 13 percent after one year). Studies show that bereaved people who do have symptoms of depression have fewer and less severe symptoms (Gallagher et al., 1982). Thus it appears that relatively few older people develop protracted, disabling depressive illnesses after the loss of loved ones. By paying careful attention to the severity and pattern of depressive symptoms, it should be possible to distinguish major depression from bereavement reactions in most cases.

Depressed people often complain of loneliness and social or emotional isolation, and it may be that having strong social supports decreases the chances that one will have a depressive reaction following a loss (Warheit, 1979). Nevertheless, isolation is not strongly associated with severe depression among the elderly. It may be a more important factor in milder depressions; a number of studies have noted correlations between frequency of social interactions and levels of morale or life satisfaction (Lemon, Bengtson, and Peterson, 1972). In most cases, it seems to be close personal relationships that are important rather than social contact per se. Although low morale or low levels of life satisfaction cannot be equated with depression, research suggests that they are related (Gileard, Willmott, and Vaddadi, 1981). It seems reasonable to assume that isolation may contribute to the high rates of mild depression observed among older people.

Contrary to popular belief, retirement does not generally precipitate serious problems. Men of retirement age do not exhibit increased rates of depression or suicide (Atchley, 1980), and most retired people adjust to retirement with little trauma (George, 1980). It is also widely assumed that relocating to a new residential setting contributes to depression among the elderly. Several studies of involuntary relocation have in fact found that life satisfaction decreases after the move. The relationship between moving and levels of adjustment is complex, however. A number of variables are influential, including the desirability of the move, the nature and quality of the new home, how much the move disrupts the person's social network, and other factors. In addition, factors such as declining physical health may have precipitated the move in the first place (Kasl and Rosenfield, 1980). Thus findings concerning the effects of life satisfactions among the elderly must be interpreted with caution.

In sum, it appears that depression may develop among the elderly in reaction to age-related stresses and losses. One report concluded that "Much of what is called 'depression' in the elderly may actually represent decreased life satisfaction and periodic episodes of grief secondary to the physical, social, and economic difficulties encountered by aging individuals" (Blazer and Williams, 1980, p. 442). Lehmann (1982, p. 29) makes the same observation in stronger terms: "Aging may be regarded as an ongoing process of increasing entropy or a continuous chain of losses. Since depression is the normal reaction to any significant loss, the aging individual seems to be prone, in a tragic existential scenario, to become easy prey to depression." Nevertheless, few elderly people are seriously depressed and most adapt successfully to developments such as bereavement and retirement.

Further research is needed to resolve several unanswered questions related to depression. For example, it is not clear whether mild and severe depression are actually variants of the same illness; they may have different causes and respond to different treatments. Similarly, people who become depressed for the first time in old age may differ in important ways from those who have recurrent depressive illnesses. Until questions such as these have been answered, we cannot assume that we have arrived at a definitive understanding of depression.

TREATMENT OF DEPRESSION

As you have seen, depression is an ailment that comes in all shapes and sizes. We all feel depressed at times, and sometimes our depressions are deep. Psychologists generally distinguish three levels of depression, with one level being "normal" depression, the kind that represents a fairly realistic response to life. The death of a close friend, a child, a parent, or other loved one will trigger in most people a depressive reaction that may last for a long time, perhaps even a year or so. The minor insults of life, such as a poor grade on an examination in which one expected to do well, can also elicit depression, in lesser degree for a shorter time. Neurotic and psychotic depressions are usually more severe and invariably less realistic; psychotic depressions usually involve a serious loss of contact with reality.

All forms of depression, including the normal depressions, can benefit from therapy (Thompson and Gallagher, 1985). Slight depressions that occur in realistic reaction to unfortunate events in life can often be lifted, or at least kept from becoming deeper and more debilitating, with a little insightful advice from an experienced psychotherapist, counselor, or friend. This kind of therapy is called "supportive"; its purpose is something like a cast put on a broken bone, keeping it from more serious injury during a healing process that requires a certain amount of time. For the more severe cases of depression, something stronger than supportive therapy is used. Various drugs have been found useful in combating depression, and several forms of psychotherapy have been found effective; in particularly stubborn cases, electroconvulsive therapy (ECT) may be used.

Drug therapy   The drugs most often used to control severe depression are called the tricyclic antidepressants. ("Tricyclic" refers to the fact that all these drugs have three benzene rings in their molecular structure.) These drugs have been shown to be effective in most cases, and side effects are generally mild; dryness of the mouth is the most common complaint (Morris and Beck, 1974). How they relieve depression is not well known, but apparently they increase the ease with which electrochemical signals are passed along the central nervous system (Baldessarini, 1978).

Another group of drugs used for depression — MAO inhibitors — apparently have a similar effect in the nervous system (they presumably inhibit MAO, a substance that makes signal transmission more difficult). MAO inhibitors are generally less effective than the tricyclic antidepressants and may have severe side effects, including death (Cole and Davis, 1975). In particular, MAO inhibitors react with certain foods — notably cheddar cheese, but also wine, chicken livers, and pickled herring — to create dangerously high blood pressure. MAO inhibitors probably wouldn't be used at all if not for the fact that they work for some patients who are unresponsive to the tricyclics. Obviously a doctor has to monitor the patient closely. (And, as one therapist claims, life without cheese, wine, chicken livers, and pickled herring is so depressing in and of itself, it may overcome the beneficial effects of the drug!)

The danger of side effects is also prominent with lithium salts, which are most commonly used for the treatment of manic states or manic–depressive illness (bipolar depression). Although they are quite effective when used properly, there is a very fine line between a therapeutic dose and a toxic dose, so that lithium levels in the bloodstream must be constantly monitored (Mahoney, 1980). And since lithium salts, like all other salts, raise blood pressure, they are dangerous for people with heart or kidney disease. Moreover, they seem to work in smaller doses in elderly people, which is good, but many doctors do not know this, which leads to overdoses in such patients (Maletta, 1984). Elderly patients are also more likely to require low-salt diets, in which case lithium salts should not be prescribed.

Lithium therapy has also encountered unexpected problems of another sort. In up to 50 percent of the cases in which it is prescribed, the patients stop taking it (Jamison, Gerner, and Goodwin, 1979). Since manics and manic–depressives typically must keep taking lithium to prevent recurrence of symptoms, this usually results in another bout of the mental disorder. Research has shown that two reasons lie behind the frequent noncompliance with lithium prescriptions: First, the patients disliked the whole idea of a chronic mood disorder that had to be controlled by medication; it implied weakness. Second, the lithium kept them on an even keel. They rarely experienced lows or highs, and they missed the highs, even if the highs were manic, unrealistic, and dangerous to their mental health.

Electroconvulsive therapy   Electroconvulsive therapy (ECT) involves passing an electric current of 70 to 130 volts from one of the patient's temples to the other for a period of slightly less than one second (Mahoney, 1980). This results in a seizure not unlike that experienced in severe forms of epilepsy, and in early treatments, broken bones were not uncommon. Today, patients are given a muscle relaxant to prevent this.

Of all therapies for mental disorders, ECT is probably the most frightening to the general public. Books and movies such as *One Flew over the Cuckoo's Nest* portray the procedure in its most frightening aspect, that is, when it is used as a punishment. In addition, it is a seemingly radical therapy that some people think is used only on the most deranged patients; hence the discovery that Senator Thomas Eagleton had received ECT for his depression forced the Democratic Party to drop him as a candidate for vice president in 1972. In fact, however, ECT appears to be an effective treatment for depression that has certain advantages over drugs: usually only a few administrations are necessary (two to ten), compared to long-term maintenance schedules for drugs. And ECT works immediately, unlike drugs whose effects are often not apparent for days — a valuable feature with patients who are dangerously suicidal.

Nevertheless, ECT should not be taken lightly. Why it alleviates depression is almost a complete mystery. It appears to be painless, although we cannot be sure because its most notable side effect is that it destroys memory for itself; in other words, patients cannot remember whether it was painful or not. Memory for other events is also disturbed, but in a week or two, most patients are remembering more than before the treatment (Goldstein, Baker, and Jamison, 1980). In about one of 200 patients, memory problems or other mental complications persist, although whether this is due to ECT or to the mental disorder being treated is not clear.

Psychotherapy Psychotherapy is an approach to treatment that involves discussion and education but not drugs or ECT, although often various combinations are used. All the major types of psychotherapy have been applied to depression. These include psychoanalysis (Freudian therapy), humanistic therapies (Rogers, Maslow, Gestalt), and behavioral therapies (Skinner, Bandura); altogether, more than 130 distinguishable approaches are offered (Weissman, 1978).

Two of the most effective therapies are behavior modification and cognitive therapy. The major assumption of behavioristic therapy is that the depressed person is not receiving enough reinforcements in life (Ferster, 1973). In this view, all animals (not just humans) react with "behavior patterns characteristic of depression" when their responses do not earn the rewards they seek. These "behavior patterns characteristic of depression" include a generally low level of activity combined with behavioral indications that the animal considers this state unpleasant — moping, whining, irritability.

It is worth pointing out that such behaviors are similar to those which define learned helplessness. Learned helplessness is usually defined in the context of responses that do not *eliminate* an *aversive* stimulus, or punishment; the behavioral analysis of depression focuses on responses that do not *produce* a *desired* state of affairs, or reward.

Learning a new and interesting hobby such as photography is a good way to increase the frequency of reinforcements in one's life.

Behavior therapy for depressed humans seeks to increase the number and availability of reinforcements in the individual's environment (Lewinsohn, 1975). One way to do this is simply to increase the individual's level of activity, especially in pleasant activities. A problem arises, however, in that people who are easily depressed are less likely than nondepressed people to *enjoy* any given activity. Talking with friends, catching a big fish, seeing a good movie — all these activities are less rewarding, on the average, to depression-prone individuals. Thus part of the therapy for most patients includes programs designed to teach them how to get pleasure from reinforcements — how to enjoy life! There are a number of ways to do this, and treatment programs are always individualized, since each person's problems are unique. Some programs are similar to art appreciation courses, which are in effect programs designed to enable the student to enjoy art; in therapy, there may be training in "fishing appreciation" or "how to enjoy a talk with a friend." There may be "assertiveness training" so that depressed persons can assert themselves, engaging more fully in the activity they are trying to enjoy. There may be training in how to get along with a spouse, since a good marriage makes depression less likely.

In addition to "accentuating the positive," parts of the therapy work to "eliminate the negative." Depressed people's tendency to think gloomy thoughts, to deprecate themselves, to feel guilty, and to focus on real or imagined physical ailments is handled by nonreinforcement: instead of offering sympathy for such "woe-is-me" behaviors, family and friends are instructed to ignore them. Usually the behaviors decrease in frequency quickly. Positive behaviors, such as smiling and statements of self-praise are quickly rewarded with attention, approval, and sometimes even money or other objects of value. Patients who suffer from anxiety as well as depression are taught how to relax (densensitization therapy). In sum, behavior therapy for depression is a multifaceted attack on the many problems of the depressed patient, each problem carefully specified in behavioral terms. (Gallagher and Thompson, 1981; Gallagher and Thompson, 1982).

Cognitive therapy for depression is based on the assumption that depression results from maladaptive cognitions (thoughts, beliefs, attitudes, expectations). In particular, the individual considers him- or her*self* as inadequate and unworthy, the *world* as insensitive and ungratifying, and the *future* as bleak and unpromising (Beck, 1976). The depressed patient is taught to identify these thought patterns, which in many cases have become so automatic that the patient is unaware of other possibilities. Then the patient is taught how to evaluate self, the world, and the future more realistically. There may be homework assignments, such as charting the relationship among various activities, thoughts, and moods, or trying to experience the power of positive thinking.

Both behavioral and cognitive therapy have been shown to be quite effective with depression, with a combined behavioral/cognitive approach even better than either alone (Taylor and Marshall, 1977). In a study following depressed patients over one year after treatment, it was further found that a combination of cognitive and behavior therapy showed better results than the use of insight therapy (Gallagher and Thompson, 1983). In one study, cognitive theory was compared to drug therapy (Rush et al., 1977). Severely depressed patients receiving cognitive therapy showed marked improvement in 70 percent of the cases, whereas patients on tricyclic antidepressants showed such improvement in only 23 percent of the cases, a difference that was still apparent six months later. Thus, although severe depression may be a genetically induced biochemical disturbance, as many biological psychologists believe, therapy in adapting to the environment (psychotherapy) is still important and may be the crucial element in a life worth living.

Most severely depressed patients today are treated with a combination of all the therapies we have discussed. The drugs have their strongest effect on mood (they keep the individual from feeling so *bad*), whereas psychotherapy permits adjustments in the individual's environment that allow him or her to live a more satisfying life (Goldstein, Baker, and Jamison, 1980; Rosenfeld, 1985).

SUICIDE

Although one need not be depressed to take one's own life, depression is by far the most common cause of suicide (Kleinmuntz, 1980). Suicide for the depressed person is the ultimate reaction to hopelessness, an acting out of the sincere belief that the future holds no promise, that things are not going to get any better. In a given year, United States government statistics will report the successful suicides of about twelve or thirteen people out of every 100,000 — a total of about 25,000 people. Most researchers believe this official figure to be an extreme understatement, mostly because suicide is not given as an official cause of death unless the evidence is overwhelming. If an overdose of sleeping pills can reasonably be ruled an accident, for example, most officials will so rule; the family thus avoids the stigma of family members who "must have been out of their minds" and, in many cases, receives life insurance payments that are not allowed for self-induced deaths. Many single-car accidents are believed to be suicides as well, though proof must usually be indirect. For those reasons, the number of *true* suicides each year is estimated to be at least 50,000 (Schuyler, 1974) and possibly as many as 100,000 (Kline, 1974; Stenback, 1980).

Suicide is related to age, sex, race, and a number of other demographic variables in some informative ways (National Center for Health Statistics, 1978). White males have the highest rate, and both white and nonwhite men are more likely to commit suicide than women (see Figure 12–3). For white males, the first few years of adulthood (ages twenty to twenty-four) show a fairly high rate, perhaps reflecting the pressure of making decisions about career and family. The rate then drops slightly until the age of forty-five, when it begins a rise that continues through the rest of life. The suicide rate of white males over eighty-five was 53.1 per 100,000 of population in 1978, compared to an overall average of 12.5. Nonwhite males also show an early peak, but for them there is no rise after midlife. Theorists commonly attribute this difference to social power: white males have more of it than nonwhite males, which makes them more frustrated and depressed in late life when they are losing it through retirement or illness.

Suicide rates for men in general are three times those for women, although this statistic may reflect no more than the fact that the men are generally more successful in their suicide attempts (Williams, 1977). Women outnumber men in

FIGURE 12–3.
Suicide rate per 100,000 (1978).

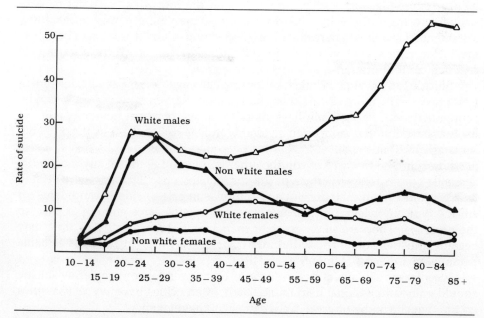

Source: National Center for Health Statistics, U.S. Department of Health and Human Services, 1983a.

unsuccessful attempts by about three or four to one. Some theorists believe women are less sincere, putting out dramatic "cries for help" in the form of apparent suicide attempts. Another possible explanation is that men use more lethal methods (guns, jumping from high places) that women find repulsive, even at death's door; women prefer sleeping pills and poisons, which are clearly less efficient and effective.

Nonwhite women, who have the lowest rate of any group defined jointly by sex and race, show an age pattern similar to that of nonwhite men: an early peak followed by stability or gradual decline. White females, on the other hand, are different from all other groups. They show no peak in young adulthood, but their rate shows a sharp rise in middle age, between forty-five and fifty-nine. Thereafter they show a declining rate through the rest of their lives. No one has a generally accepted explanation of the midlife suicide crisis among white women. Some theorists blame menopause, which seems unlikely since nonwhite women show no suicide peak at this time. The symbolism of this time, however, may play a role; grown children are moving out, biology is closing the gates to more, husband is showing too much interest in younger, prettier women. If the woman's marriage suddenly ends in divorce, and she faces the necessity of finding a job although she has few marketable skills, the future may look bleak indeed.

Considering age by itself, we find that more young adults attempt suicide than actually succeed (Stenback, 1980). The ratio of attempts to deaths is around seven to one. Around the age of fifty, the ratio swings in favor of actual suicides, so that older adults usually manage to take their own lives when they set out to do so. Theorists believe that suicide attempts among young people are often cries for help or expressions of hostility, even though the individual may not be consciously aware of these motives. In this view, the young person is making a statement: "Hey, look! I'm really hurting! It's serious!" Or "If you won't be nice to me, I'll kill myself! Then you'll feel guilty!" Parents and lovers are the usual targets for such communications.

Suicide threats must be taken seriously at any age. The older suicidal person is not necessarily more sincere than the younger. Rather, younger persons who contemplate suicide typically have more extensive personal networks and are likely to be monitored more often by friends and family. That is why the probability is greater that the suicide attempts by young persons will be foiled. Older persons living by themselves, on the other hand, may not have anyone readily available who is likely to interrupt the suicidal act, once it commences. Feeling helpless and viewing the present and future as hopeless, elderly candidates for suicide typically telegraph their intentions, if anyone cares enough to pick up their signals. They are likely to state their intentions explicitly, or they may become unusually quiet and withdrawn. One clue is the giving away of valuable personal possessions (Minkoff et al., 1973).

Needless to say, anyone who suspects that a friend is contemplating suicide should enlist professional help immediately. Many cities have *suicide prevention centers*, which can be of great service in such an emergency.

Brain Disorders

Together with the various mental disorders involving severe depression, organic brain disorders constitute the majority of the mental health problems that develop late in life. The adjective "organic" is used in psychology and psychiatry to identify those mental disorders which are known to be at least partly caused by a malfunction of, or damage to, the brain.

ACUTE BRAIN DISORDERS

Certain mental disorders resulting from brain malfunctions can often be treated successfully, restoring normal mental processes. These are called "acute brain disorders." "Acute" is to be contrasted with "chronic." The acute disorders are usually reversible and, in fact, are often called "reversible brain disorders"; the chronic disorders continue for a long time and are usually irreversible.

Acute brain disorders are characterized by a sudden onset. Their causes are many and varied. A stroke, which cuts off the blood supply to parts of the brain, is one common cause. A heart attack is another, since heart damage affects the ability of the heart to pump blood to the brain; indeed, 13 percent of heart attacks come to the attention of doctors primarily because the individual suddenly begins to "act crazy" (Butler and Lewis, 1982). Malnutrition is another surprisingly frequent cause of acute disorders, especially among the elderly, who may suffer from low income, decreased mobility, illness, loss of appetite, or loss of teeth. Vitamin deficiencies can result in severe depression, irritability, confusion, and memory deficits — the kinds of symptoms that many doctors diagnose as senility (Whanger, 1980). Head injuries, brain tumors, infections, diabetes, thyroid malfunctions, and liver disease are common causes of acute disorders. Drug overdoses, from alcohol abuse and also from improper prescription of dangerous psychoactive drugs by doctors, are often mistaken for irreversible brain damage. All in all, there are nearly 100 reversible conditions that can mimic the symptoms of the few irreversible disorders (Levy et al., 1980).

Acute brain disorders can usually be treated; the patient can usually be returned to a state of physical and mental health. Unfortunately, through misdiagnosis and inadequate medical care for the elderly, many cases go untreated. In the words of the former director of the National Institute on Aging, Robert Butler, "The failure to diagnose and treat reversible brain syndromes is so unnecessary and yet so widespread that I would caution families of older persons to question doctors involved in care about this" (Butler, 1975, pp. 175–176).

CHRONIC BRAIN DISORDERS

Chronic brain disorders more closely correspond to what laypeople call senility. Typically (but not always) these disorders develop gradually, beginning with mild symptoms of depression or anxiety with occasional confusion, becoming progressively more severe with a general loss of intellectual abilities (dementia). Persons suffering from these disorders have trouble recalling common facts that most of us can remember with ease. As a result, simple mental status questions such as those in Table 12–1 may be useful in identifying those who may have these disorders. Neuropsychological testing may also be helpful in differentiating dementia from depression (LaRue, 1984). Emotions are also disturbed so that unexpected outbursts of anger or laughter may become frequent. In advanced cases, motor control is impaired and patients cannot feed themselves or get to the toilet in time. The last stage is one in which patients no longer respond to their own names; coma and death follow. Thus the course of chronic brain disorders is typically degenerative; that is, things get progressively worse and are rarely reversible.

Among elderly patients, there are two major forms of chronic brain disorder: senile dementia (officially, "primary degenerative dementia") and multi-infarct dementia. The average age of onset is seventy-five, and more women are affected than men but this fact may simply reflect the greater average life span of women (Butler and Lewis, 1982). Autopsies show considerable brain damage, as well as two characteristic changes in brain structure called senile plaques and neurofibrillary tangles. In more homely terms, the brains of people who exhibited senile dementia while alive are shrunken, covered with patches (plaques) that look something like rust or mildew, and filled with tiny twisted tubes (Terry and Wisniewski, 1975).

Until 1980, *multi-infarct dementia* was called "cerebral arteriosclerosis" because the mental disorder is an indirect result of a hardening or a narrowing of the arteries supplying blood to the brain. In what is essentially a series of small strokes, several small areas of the brain are destroyed, or "infarcted." These "multiple infarcts" (many small areas of tissue death) are the direct cause of the dementia, hence the name change (American Psychiatric Association, 1980).

TABLE 12-1.
Mental status questions for brain disorders.

---

1. Where are we now?
2. Where is this place (located)?
3. What is today's date — day of month?
4. What month is it?
5. What year is it?
6. How old are you?
7. What is your birthday?
8. What year were you born?
9. Who is President of the United States?
10. Who was President before him?

Source: From A. I. Goldfarb, 1964. The evaluation of geriatric patients following treatment. In P. H. Hoch and J. Zubin (Eds.). *Evaluation of psychiatric treatment*. New York: Grune Stratton. Reprinted by permission.

Symptoms are generally similar to those of senile dementia, although patients with multi-infarct dementia are more variable, with "spotty" rather than complete losses of intellectual abilities (Raskind and Storrie, 1980). Another diagnostic criterion is localized disturbance of cerebral blood flow (Hachinski et al., 1975; Rosen et al., 1980). Often, however, it is nearly impossible to tell if a patient has multi-infarct or senile dementia until an autopsy after death.

Multi-infarct dementia, like all heart and arterial diseases, has been attributed to various factors, including poor diet (too much fat), lack of exercise, smoking, and genetic predisposition. Like most heart ailments, men are more likely to suffer from it than women, with sixty-six the average age of onset (Glatt and Katzman, 1984). Multi-infarct dementia is much less common than senile dementia, accounting for only 12 to 20 percent of the cases of dementia in the elderly (Terry and Wisniewski, 1975).

Physicians have tried to alleviate the effects of cerebral arteriosclerosis by means that share the intention of delivering more oxygen to the oxygen-starved brain. One approach has been to have patients breathe air with a higher-than-normal oxygen content; this approach has been shown to be ineffective (Goldfarb et al., 1972). Another approach is to administer drugs called cerebral vasodilators, which presumably dilate or enlarge the arteries feeding the brain. The effect of these drugs has been questioned, however. The arteries that need to be dilated are usually damaged or diseased and do not respond to vasodilators as normal arteries do; in fact, the drugs may act to dilate other arteries, drawing blood *away* from the areas that need it most (Sathananthan and Gershon, 1975). A third promising approach, although relatively new and untested, is surgery to bypass the damaged arteries.

A number of behavioral symptoms are associated with the development of senile dementia. Most noticeable is progressive intellectual impairment. At first such impairment is noted in the inability to acquire new information. Memory impairment is then noted of the sort where the person with dementia can repeat simple strings of numbers or words, but is not able to repeat more complex material that has to be processed beyond the primary store (see Chapter 10 on memory). Other symptoms include suspicious thoughts, irritability, and depression. Emotional volatility and socially inappropriate behaviors may also occur.

Alzheimer's disease   The symptoms of dementia — intellectual deterioration, emotional and behavioral abnormalities — are also observed among middle-aged adults. Several types of early-onset dementia have been identified. The most common is Alzheimer's disease, the illness suffered by E. J., whose case history opened the chapter, affecting more than 100,000 persons a year. Alzheimer's disease appears to be an early-onset form of senile dementia; brain atrophy, plaques, and neurofibrillary tangles are found on autopsy. It attacks people as early as their forties and fifties with a deadly virulence. Unlike older persons who have Alzheimer-type senile dementia, who generally survive only a few years (Butler and Lewis, 1982), younger victims of the disease may follow a downhill course for ten or twenty years. Alzheimer patients tend to be prone to accidents, strokes, and certain cancers. About one-fifth also suffer from infarcts. Recent studies with positron emission tomography (PET scans) show that different parts of the brain may be affected at different rates (Foster, Chase, and Fedio, 1982). This may account for the fact that behavior changes vary so markedly among Alzheimer victims; the parts of the brain in which metabolic activity is lowered the most will exercise their functions least efficiently.

Several possible causes of Alzheimer's disease are currently being investigated. In fact six alternative, albeit not unrelated, models are being given serious consideration. These models involve genetic defects, abnormal protein mechanisms, infectious agents, toxic substances, abnormal blood flow, and an impaired acetylcholine supply (Wurtman, 1985).

The *genetic* model is based on the observation that there are families in which the incidence of Alzheimer's disease is unusually high, raising the suspicion that there might be one or more faulty genes that render persons vulnerable to some environmental factor that triggers the disease. It is argued that aging might further impair an inborn abnormality in the genetic (DNA) material that leads to the failure to manufacture essential enzymes needed for proper brain function. In spite of the epidemiological evidence on the familiar nature of the disease in some persons, particularly those falling prey to it in middle age, what argues against the genetic theory is the fact that no one has as yet identified an abnormal chromosome in Alzheimer's disease.

More firmly based is the *abnormal protein* model. Recently, attention has been devoted to the finding that the activity of the enzyme choline acetyltransferase (ChAT) progressively decreases in the brain tissue of Alzheimer's disease patients. The decrease appears to be caused by the loss of certain nerve cells in the part of the brain that controls this enzyme (Coyle, Price, and Delong, 1983). Such cell loss is not a normal result of the aging process; recently, it has been suggested that it may be associated with hormonal effects triggered by stress (Henry, 1985). Abnormal biochemical processes may also be implicated in the process that leads to the formation of the plaques and tangles in the cortex that are so typical of Alzheimer's disease (Selkoe, Ihara, and Salazar, 1982). Studies of some rare neurological diseases that can be transmitted under unusual circumstances have led some investigators to consider an *infectious disease* model for Alzheimer's disease also. This idea has been reinforced by the finding that a protein particle called a prion that occurs in these diseases has structural qualities similar to those found in the brains of Alzheimer patients. Experimental attempts to transmit Alzheimer's disease in animals have been unsuccessful thus far. The possibility still exists that, if there is an infectious agent, it may require some prior genetic predisposition, a concurrently occurring immune disease, or exposure to some toxic substance in the environments, before an infection can occur (Wurtman, 1985).

The *toxic substance* model is based on still controversial evidence that aluminum and other trace metals may be present in the brains of Alzheimer patients, accumulating in neurons that have neurofibrillary tangles (Perl, Gajducek, and Garruto, 1982). It is not clear, however, whether the aluminum is absorbed from environmental sources and causes the tangles. What is more likely is that once neurofibrillary tangles appear from other causes of the disease these tangles attract the aluminum. In other words, the accumulation does not arise from the use of aluminum foil or cookware, but rather from disturbances in the brain's metabolic processes once abnormal changes in the brain occur from the disease.

Although Alzheimer's disease is not caused by what used to be called "hardening of the arteries," there appears to be a substantial reduction in *blood flow* to the brain in Alzheimer patients. Recent studies suggest that in this disease blood flow and oxygen consumption in the brain decline some 30 percent of that observed in normal elderly persons. Reduction in blood supply is particularly severe with the frontal and parietal lobe of the cortex, the same areas that show severe pathological changes in brain tissue. The reduction in blood flow is thought to have come about through the loss of neurons that release transmitters that activate regional blood flow in the brain.

Ideally, treatments for a disease result from an understanding of cause. In some cases, however, helpful treatments may be discovered before a disease is fully understood. Quinine was used to treat malaria before the parasite that causes it was discovered, and Parkinson's disease can be treated with the drug L-dopa, which helps relieve deficits in an important neurotransmitter, dopamine. Some proposed treatments for Alzheimer's disease and other dementias are based on the hope that other such compounds may be discovered.

Several of the proposed theories on the causes of Alzheimer's disease have resulted in suggestions for treatment. The finding that the activity of a certain enzyme, *acetylcholine*, decreases in Alzheimer patients, for example, has prompted diet therapy in which the patient is given foods rich in the raw materials that make up the enzyme. The results have been inconclusive. Another approach involves the drug physostigmine, which prevents the rapid breakdown of the enzyme after it is released from nerve cells. There is some evidence that the drug helps Alzheimer's disease patients, but the side effects may be severe.

Investigators pursuing the lead about aluminum are experimentally treating patients with drugs that bind aluminum. Binding this metal is the first step in eliminating it from the body.

Another approach to Alzheimer's disease and other dementias is the use of chemicals to improve memory. Thus far success has been quite limited. One such chemical, however, the hormone vasopressin, has been shown in studies with rats to improve the process by which memories are stored in the brain. It also improves recall. Since the rats were normal, scientists believe the drug may act as a general memory tonic: it might improve memory in normal adults as well as enhance the remaining capacity of patients with brain disease. Memory enhancers have been used in humans in conjunction with behavioral treatment such as supportive counseling and congnitive training. There is some as yet inconclusive evidence that cognitive training in combination with drug treatments may be a useful approach (Yesavage, Westphal, and Rush, 1981).

In general, other drug treatments have also been quite disappointing (Crook and Gershon, 1981). The most promising approaches in recent years have been those involving cholinomimetic agents, either alone or in combination with other drugs. Although drugs such as physostigmine may produce mild improvements in learning and memory performance for short periods, particularly in normal or mildly impaired individuals, longer-term treatments based on the acetylcholine precursors choline and lechithin have usually failed to yield positive outcomes (Barbeau, Growdon and Wurtman, 1979; Bartus et al., 1982). We must conclude that there simply is no known cure for Alzheimer's disease at this time.

Alzheimer's disease is a leading cause of dementia, but it is not the only one. Although the other disorders that lead to dementia are less common and each affects a relatively small group of people, together they account for over a million people with progressive and dementing brain disease in America today.

One of the better known neurological disorders is *multiple sclerosis,* which is characterized by the destruction of the insulating material that covers nerve fibers. The disease usually progresses through a series of acute episodes followed by partial recoveries. In time, both physical and mental deterioration can occur. *Huntington's chorea* is another type of presenile dementia. The disease is sometimes called Woody Guthrie's disease, after the American folksinger who died from it. The ailment is caused by a dominant gene; children of victims (Woody Guthrie's son, Arlo, for example) have a 50-50 chance of inheriting it. The symptoms usually appear in early middle age. They can include personality change, mental decline, psychotic symptoms, and movement disturbance. Restlessness and facial tics may progress to severe uncontrollable flailing of head, limbs, and trunk. At the same time, mental capacity can deteriorate to dementia.

Dementia also develops sometimes (but by no means invariably) in disorders of the central nervous system defined by physical symptoms such as paralysis or "the shakes." *Parkinson's disease,* a disorder that strikes older adults, is one such ailment. The symptoms of Parkinson's disease are tremors and difficulty in originating voluntary movements. Drugs can relieve symptoms but do not halt the progression of the disease. Symptoms of dementia may appear in severe or advanced cases.

Other quite rare conditions include *Creutzfeldt–Jakob disease* and *Pick's disease,* with an onset usually between fifty-five and seventy-five years of age. Creutzfeldt–Jakob disease is caused by an unusual virus that may lie dormant in the body for years (hence it is called a *slow* virus). This disease is contagious. When the virus is activated, it produces a rapidly progressing dementia along with muscle spasms and changes in gait. However, only one new case per million persons is discovered each year (Wurtman, 1985). Pick's disease has symptoms very similar to those of Alzheimer's, but the disease is associated with somewhat different changes in brain tissue.

So there are many different forms of dementia, and many different causes. For most of the dementias, however, the causes and cures remain much of a mystery. The mystery is particularly frustrating in cases of presenile or senile dementia of the Alzheimer type, which afflict the greatest number of adults in the latter half of life.

Drugs, Alcoholism, and Mental Health

As we've indicated in the discussion of treatments for depression, drug therapy is common for mental disorders. Drugs are also prescribed for physical illnesses, of course. In addition, nonprescription drugs such as aspirin are consumed by the cartload, and "recreational" drugs such as alcohol and marijuana are used by millions to relax or get high. Ours is a drug culture in which only a few are not involved, to one degree or another. From our drugs, we derive many benefits: the cures of many diseases and relief from pain, anxiety, depression. But drugs invariably involve risks as well, short-term and long-term "side effects" that range from an upset stomach to death.

Drugs that affect the brain — psychoactive drugs — are particularly dangerous, because their side effects can also affect the brain in less beneficial ways. Each year close to 300 million prescriptions for psychoactive drugs are written in the United States (Prien, 1975). Over 90 percent of the patients of mental hospitals who are under the age of sixty-five receive psychoactive medication of some sort, and over 55 percent of patients over sixty-five; the lower figure among the elderly reflects the greater incidence of chronic brain disorder, for which fewer drugs are effective. Most of the psychoactive drugs can be classified as antipsychotic (used most commonly for schizophrenia), antidepressant, or antianxiety. Most of these drugs are prescribed over a relatively long period of time, making them especially dangerous.

ALCOHOLISM

Harmful effects may also result from the use over a long period of a different type of drug: alcohol. Alcohol abuse and dependence are usually reported to be less common among the elderly than among younger people (Simon, 1980). The proportion of heavy drinkers in both sexes decreases after age fifty and drops still further at about age sixty-five. Of those aged sixty-six or older, about 5 percent of the men and 1 percent of the women are heavy drinkers. On the other hand, 60 percent of the women and 35 to 40 percent of the men in this age group did not drink at all. Some of these age differences are a result of the fact that problem drinkers are less likely to survive to old age, but it has been reported that half the elderly nondrinkers were former drinkers and that most older people who do continue to drink drink less than they did formerly (Cahalan, Cisin, and Crossley, 1969). It is important to recognize, however, that the apparent age decline in alcoholism may actually reflect cohort differences (Glantz, 1981). Today's young and middle-aged adults are less likely to have grown up in environments where drinking was discouraged; as these people age, rates of late-life alcoholism may increase.

Of the elderly people who have drinking problems, at least two-thirds have had the problem for many years. There is some evidence that many late-onset problem drinkers are women; among younger age groups, male alcoholics are more common. A number of studies indicate that the cognitive deficits associated with alcohol abuse are more severe in elderly alcoholics than in younger people with similar drinking histories (Ryan and Butters, 1980; Brandt et al., 1983). It appears that alcoholism accelerates the normal deterioration of central nervous system functioning that occurs with age. Even recovered alcoholics who have not had a drink for years perform more poorly on tests of perceptual-motor speed, tactual-motor ability, abstraction, and other abilities than do nonalcoholics of the same age (Parson and Leber, 1981; Brandt et al., 1983).

It is clear, then, that heavy drinking over a long period can impair an older person's functioning. But the pros and cons of moderate social drinking are still open to debate. On the positive side, older people who drink moderately tend to be more active and sociable and perceive themselves as being in better health than elderly persons who abstain completely. Providing opportunities for limited social drinking in nursing homes has been reported to have beneficial effects on mood and social interaction (Chien, Stotsky, and Cole, 1973). On the negative side, small but statistically significant deficits in the cognitive performance of social drinkers compared to abstainers have been observed (Parker and Noble, 1977). Furthermore, programs providing for the "medicinal" use of alcohol are regarded by some as a sign of excessive reliance on pharmacological approaches to managing problems of the aged (Glantz, 1981).

DRUG EFFECTS

For most old people, iatrogenic illnesses (illnesses caused by doctors or the medication they prescribe) are a much more serious problem than alcoholism. The elderly have a higher overall rate of drug intake than any other age group (Warheit, Arey, and Swanson, 1976). They also have higher usage rates for a number of different prescription medications, including psychoactive drugs such as tranquilizers, sedatives, and hypnotics (Warheit, Arey, and Swanson, 1976). A survey of a group of community residents over age sixty showed that 33 percent were using cardiovascular drugs, 67 percent had taken analgesics, 31 percent took laxatives, 29 percent took vitamins, 26 percent took antacids, 22 percent took antianxiety medications, and 16 percent took diuretics. Only 8 percent were taking no drugs; 83 percent were taking two or more (Chien, Townsend, and Townsend, 1978).

Particularly dangerous are combinations of drugs that have anticholinergic properties. Such drugs include several commonly prescribed tranquilizers, anti-depressants, anti-Parkinsonian drugs, sedatives, and antihistamines. In a survey of 5,902 nursing home residents over sixty-five and a comparable sample of persons living at home, it was found that 60 percent of the nursing home residents and 23 percent of those living at home received prescriptions of drugs with such anticholinergic properties. Based on the recommended dosages it was concluded that 10 percent of the nursing home patients and 7 percent of those living at home received a combination of three or more prescriptions that might result in toxic side effects (Blazer et al., 1983). Often physicians have little or no information on potential drug interactions, which may produce severe reactions, including death. Prescription drugs may also interact with nonprescription drugs as well; patients on tranquilizers, for example, are generally warned to avoid the consumption of alcohol.

There are few adequate investigations of the extent of drug misuse among older adults, but some interesting preliminary statistics are available. First, it appears that misuse of medications in the aged generally occurs in the context of medical treatment. Only 2 to 6 percent of the patients seen in acute-care medical settings for drug-related emergencies are elderly (Petersen and Thomas, 1975); overdoses are most common with psychotropic drugs such as Valium, Tuinal, Luminal, and Darvon. Among younger patients, drug-related emergencies usually involve illicit drugs such as heroin and cocaine. Data suggest that emergency-room statistics severely underestimate the extent of total drug misuse among the elderly, however.

Studies indicate that the elderly are more likely than other age groups to fail to comply with doctors' orders in taking medications (Brand, Smith, and Brand, 1977). For example, people in their seventies are twice as likely as people in their forties to fail to follow doctors' instructions about medication. Of the medication mistakes made by the elderly, 47 percent involve omitting the medication, 20 percent involve inaccurate information, 17 percent involve self-medication, 10 percent involve incorrect dosage, and 4 percent involve incorrect sequence or timing of the dose. Several factors contribute to such mistakes, including incomplete communication between physician and patient, decreased mental competence on the part of the patient, and inadequate supervision of the drug regimen by either professionals or family members. The most frequently cited reason for noncompliance was economic; more than a third of the older patients in the Brand study said they couldn't afford to take their medications in the manner prescribed.

Even when patients adhere strictly to doctors' orders, they may encounter problems with drug side effects. These side effects include general signs of toxic dosages (diarrhea, vomiting, tremor, drowsiness, slurred speech, confusion) as well as specific dangers in specific drugs. Even in the correct dosage, medications taken by the elderly may have such side effects as lethargy, fatigue, depression, and anxiety. One danger of the major antipsychotic drugs is *tardive dyskinesia*, which occurs in 10 to 20 percent of the cases in general and in up to 40 percent of the cases involving elderly patients (Butler and Lewis, 1977). The ailment is characterized by slow, rhythmic, involuntary movements of the face and extremities; the "fly-catcher" tongue is a common symptom, and so are a number of other spastic motions. It is a rather sad state of affairs that the psychotic patient must often choose between dementia that makes adaptation to the real world impossible and potential dyskinesia, which means living a life without complete motor control.

Potential benefits of drug therapy must always be weighed in regard to the risks. When the decision is that the benefit-to-risk ratio is high enough, a program of medication is usually advised. Obviously, however, a certain number of these patients will find such programs to their disadvantage; they will experience more of the risks than the benefits. In addition, many doctors prescribe the wrong drug, or too much of a drug, and thereby induce mental disorders considered iatrogenic. One is reminded of the comment of the eighteenth-century French writer, Voltaire, who said, "Doctors pour drugs of which they know little, to cure diseases of which they know less, into human beings of whom they know nothing" (Butler, 1975, p. 200). Doctor-induced disorders may account for a significant proportion of the mental disorders in the elderly. Perhaps 10 percent are unnecessarily induced (that is, the mental disorder results from medication that was incorrectly prescribed), and perhaps another 10 percent result from medication that was prudently advised but that had unavoidable side effects. Tardive dyskinesia is an example of the latter.

Twelve of the twenty drugs most commonly prescribed for people over sixty-five have a sedating effect (Butler, 1975). Older people who are already experiencing some slowness in response and a decrease in coordination will find these trends exaggerated by sedative drugs. In addition to the problems slower reactions might cause, many elderly patients become frightened or depressed, feeling that their slow behaviors are signs of failing health and approaching death. In high dosages, these drugs can produce severe depression or mental confusion that is sometimes misdiagnosed as chronic brain disorder. These side effects are more likely in elderly patients than in young adults, because drug metabolism is generally less efficient in the elderly. A given dosage has a more pronounced effect in an older patient, on the average, and the drug stays in the body for a longer time before the liver can break it down or the kidneys excrete it (Levy et al., 1980). Furthermore, it is quite possible for an elderly person to develop a drug dependency, particularly if he or she is anxious, depressed, or hypochondriacal. Still, medications remain the preferred treatment for many of the illnesses that affect older people, and the global recommendation that aged people take fewer drugs appears to be an oversimplified answer to a difficult problem (Lamy, 1980). Guidelines for managing medications in the aged are gradually becoming available (Levenson, 1979), and these may help reduce the risk of medication-related problems.

Psychotherapy Across the Life Span

Too often drugs are the only form of treatment of mental disorders, especially among elderly patients. Although we should not discount the significant benefits possible with psychoactive drugs, drug therapy alone is rarely the most effective treatment. Psychotherapy attempts to deal with the environmental pressures and problems the individual faces in relationships with family, friends, business associates, social acquaintances, and the like. The cognitive and behavioral therapies we discussed in the case of depression are examples of psychotherapies that can help the mentally disordered patient cope with difficulties in life. In general, psychotherapy can help even those patients suffering from irreversible, progressive brain disease. An informed, supportive therapeutic program can encourage them to be "the best they can be" within the context of their physical limitations; in fact, much of the current emphasis on self-actualization is based on the observed self-actualization of severely brain-damaged soldiers, as we mentioned in Chapter 7.

GOALS OF PSYCHOTHERAPY

The developmental tasks that one faces in youth — choosing a career, choosing a mate — are different from the tasks one faces in middle age — adjusting career aspirations, adjusting to growing children and aging parents. In old age, the tasks are still different, requiring adaptation to retirement, losses of loved ones, and declining physical abilities. Since the tasks of adaptation to life change with age, the goals of psychotherapy change too.

Young adults, more than middle-aged and elderly adults, are in a position to develop their character or to reconstruct their personality. They are in the final stages of Erikson's "identity crisis" and, at the age of twenty-five or thirty, they may be still uncertain about their most basic attitudes and values. They are still learning social skills, including the interpersonal techniques necessary for a long and satisfying marital relationship. In contrast, middle-aged adults are more likely to be suffering from the failure (or perceived failure) of the adaptations made in young adulthood. Their careers may not be going the way they think they should; their marriages may be disintegrating. Psychotherapy for middle-aged adults, therefore, may focus on transitions, providing emotional support during a change in job or spouse and information about how the transition can be made efficiently and with a minimum of stress.

Psychotherapy for the elderly, on the other hand, presents a number of special problems. Indeed, some have argued that growth-oriented therapies are really not appropriate for the aged. Freud himself offered three reasons why older persons may not benefit from psychotherapy: they have decreased mental "elasticity" and presumably less ability to change; they have accumulated a vast amount of experience, which the therapist might find difficult to work with; and they attach less importance to mental health than younger persons do. The validity of these assumptions might be questioned by many modern therapists. But even today, some researchers assume that older persons would derive few benefits from therapy. Cross, Sheehan, and Kahn (1982) excluded those over age fifty-five from a followup study of patients who had received insight-oriented therapy because they thought such subjects would be influenced more by affective complaints or situational factors, which would make them less amenable to therapy than younger persons. Other researchers have used age cut-offs in their studies because of the increased chances that older subjects would have complications such as organic brain disease and physical illness, would be taking prescription medications, or would present logistical problems such as lack of transportation.

Nevertheless, therapy is undertaken with elderly people, and certain assumptions about how such therapy should proceed have evolved. It is argued that treatment programs should reflect the goals of both client and therapist (Zarit, 1980) and that such goals should be both explicit and realistic (Gallagher and Thompson, 1981). Of course, one's opinion about whether a specific therapy is "realistic" will be influenced by one's views about the aging and about the probable outcome of various disorders. There also seems to be some agreement that the goal of therapy should be equilibration — that is, restoring adequate daily functioning — rather than exploring symptoms as a means of attaining personal growth or development, as might be attempted with younger clients (Mahoney, 1982).

But this view is potentially restrictive. If more limited goals are accepted, psychoanalytic therapy should not attempt to change character; rather than eliminating maladaptive defense mechanisms, the therapist would attempt to restore adaptive defenses (Verwoerdt, 1976). In some cases, such modest goals would be appropriate, but in others they would fall far short of what is actually needed.

Another problem therapists working with the elderly must face is that compensation for the psychological losses the older person faces are relatively difficult. The death of one's spouse, for example, is often extremely trying psychologically, and there is no way that therapy can compensate for such a loss. Given that the client may only live for a few more years anyway, the therapist may be tempted to use therapeutic sessions to discuss such issues as time and death (the latter theme is discussed in the next chapter). But therapy ought not to be devoted to such issues exclusively — the whole purpose is to help people *live* better. Since the older adult expects losses, therapy should take a developmental or existential perspective (Guttman, Griffith, and Grunes, 1982).

Therapy for the elderly may also serve educational functions. As discussed earlier (see Chapters 9 and 10), explicit cognitive training approaches can remediate the moderate deficits that may occur in the early phases of dementia. More traditional therapies may also be offered in the form of psychoeducational programs, if only to avoid clients' fears of seeing a mental health professional (Blum and Tross, 1980; Thompson and Gallagher, 1985). Educational approaches of this sort tend to focus on discussions of the normal aging process, physiological changes, and cultural stereotypes of the aged.

Regardless of the nature of the therapy, many authorities believe that the treatment should be of short duration (Ronch and Maizler, 1977; Brink, 1979; Gallagher and Thompson, 1981, 1982). An average treatment may involve as few as six sessions or take as long as a year. The usual recommendation is to begin with more frequent sessions — perhaps as often as two or more times a week — and then gradually taper off toward the end of the program. The client should be permitted to return as needed for a "booster shot" after the therapy has ended. Clients who have transportation or physical mobility problems may benefit from having telephone "sessions" in between actual face-to-face appointments. Midweek calls to encourage clients to complete self-monitoring "homework" assignments may also be helpful (Gallagher and Thompson, 1981).

Two factors suggest that some exceptions to the policy of brief periods of therapy be made. First, it is widely recognized that change may take longer in older patients. Second, long-term supportive therapy may be a good way to keep older persons out of the hospital (Safirstein, 1972). This type of therapy would require that the therapist take a more active, directive role, emphasizing the client's current circumstances and level of functioning (Zarit, 1980) and expressing greater empathy with the older person's difficulties.

In many people, the prospect of the end of life triggers a kind of retrospective of life, a *life review* (Butler, 1975). In therapy, life reviews can be used in many ways (Lewis and Butler, 1974). Generally, the therapist asks clients to construct their own autobiographies. They might use family albums, old letters, and even interviews with other family members to gain information about their behavior and emotions at crucial points in their lives. By elaborating and formalizing the life-review process, the therapist can explore suppressed guilts, long-standing fears, and unspoken ambitions still unfilled. In some cases, simply having someone who is willing to listen to one's life story can allow the elderly client to integrate the disparate features of his or her life. In other cases, by allowing unresolved conflicts to surface, client and therapist can deal with them more directly. Life review, however, can raise anxiety and feelings of depression over what may be perceived as a wasted life. Such responses can best be handled by a trained professional. That is why, like any other method of psychotherapy, use of life review by nonprofessionals may be fraught with potential danger.

OBSTACLES TO TREATMENT OF ELDERLY CLIENTS

Older people have as much need for psychotherapy as younger adults, perhaps more. Yet they receive less. In mental hospitals, the elderly patients are too often given only custodial care; if there is therapy, most likely it is drug therapy and nothing else. In outpatient mental health clinics, community mental health centers, and the offices of psychotherapists in private practice, elderly clients are seen in far fewer numbers than we would expect on the basis of the proportion of old people in the general population (VandenBos, Stapp, and Kilburg, 1981). Old people who need psychotherapy are not getting it; the question is, why not?

There are a number of reasons. The sheer expense of psychotherapy plays an important role in an age group hampered by dwindling income and rampant inflation. Another reason is that "people will tolerate behavior in an older person that would send them rushing to the authorities if the same behavior occurred in a younger person" (Kalish, 1975, p. 68).

In addition, the generation that is elderly today belongs to a cohort that is not as psychologically minded (Kulka, Veroff, and Douvan, 1979). They were born and raised in an era that stigmatized mental illness as an inherited condition that could not be cured. They may believe that people don't see mental health professionals unless they are really crazy, that those who do have problems are likely to be institutionalized, or that seeing a psychiatrist means lying on a couch and revealing all of your emotional and sexual secrets, which will not help and is immoral to boot. It has been suggested that older people may also have a different understanding of just what constitutes a mental illness, but little research on this matter has been conducted. It may be that older adults tend to deny the existence of problems, stating that they don't want to bother a professional unless the problem is really serious, but actually fearing that they will be institutionalized. People may also be afraid that they will learn that they have a terminal illness or be told that they should no longer live alone (Kovar, 1980). In the future, older adults will have grown up with psychotherapy as a routine part of daily life and will perhaps be more inclined to take advantage of professional mental health services.

Another factor in the underuse of therapy by older persons is simply the desire to be independent. In the United States, older adults emphasize the importance of remaining self-sufficient (Shanas and Maddox, 1976); seeking help may be seen as an admission of failure. Use of mental health services may imply to the older persons that a serious problem exists. One study asked Chicago residents about their knowledge and use of a variety of senior citizen services (not including mental health). It was found that the only service used by more than one-fifth of the respondents was reduced transit fares. The interpretation of the researchers was that a greater stigma was attached to services that implied more infirmity (Bild and Havighurst, 1976). If this interpretation is correct, one would expect mental health services to be used only as a last resort.

It may be that skepticism about the benefits of psychotherapy keeps people from using it (Kovar, 1980; Shanas and Maddox, 1976). Although research on this matter has yielded conflicting results (Harris, 1975; Haug, 1981), older people may tend to assume that their problems are an inevitable result of aging, even though some may be remediable. They may also believe their mental problems have a physical basis and require physical remedies. Even when they do seek medical help, national survey data indicate that the aged have less confidence in the medical profession than other groups do (Kleinman and Clemente, 1976). Many older people assume that physicians are not trained for or interested in working with older adults. They expect physicians to regard their problems as trivial. Indeed, they not only expect to receive no help, they sometimes expect medical intervention to have harmful effects. As we shall see, some of these fears and complaints have some basis in fact.

It has been suggested that older clients may also believe that young therapists have little to offer them. The research findings on this point are inconclusive. Although the influence on therapy effectiveness of degree of demographic "match" between therapist and client has been studied, little research has focused on the age variable (Parloff, Waskow, and Wolfe, 1978). Data do suggest that older therapists are more likely to see older clients (Dorken and Webb, 1979). On variables other than age, it appears that experience with a population is more important than demographic similarity. A young therapist may have different values and a different historical perspective than an older client, but the life experiences of therapist and client are rarely identical. It may be safe to assume that differences in age, although perhaps not an asset, do not preclude a constructive relationship between therapist and client. As far as personal preferences are concerned, one study indicated that people generally do prefer helpers of about the same age as themselves (Furchtgott and Busemeyer, 1981). The study found two exceptions to this trend: age preference for clergy was unrelated to the age of the respondent, and, among more highly educated respondents, older people preferred a slightly younger physician. Interpretations of studies dealing with age preferences should be made with caution, however. Subjects might prefer physicians of a certain age (and presumably therapists as well) for reasons other than their age per se. An older therapist might be preceived as having more experience, for example, or a younger therapist as being more familiar with the most recent developments (Mintz, Steuer, and Jarvik, 1981).

Probably (and unfortunately) the most common reason for the lack of elderly clients in psychotherapy is the lack of interest among therapists. Psychiatrists, clinical psychologists, and psychoanalysts are generally more interested in treating what one reviewer calls the YAVIS — the young, attractive, verbal, intelligent, and successful clients (Schofield, 1974). They often justify such discrimination by suggesting that older clients are usually senile and do not benefit from psychotherapy (Stenmark and Dunn, 1982). One study found that for young and old patients *matched* for symptoms, the elder patients were uniformly rated as "more severely pathological"; probable "usefulness of intervention" (psychotherapy) was rated significantly less in the cases of the older patients (Settin, 1979).

The truth is that almost all elderly patients with mental problems, even people with chronic brain disorders, can benefit from psychotherapy. The negative attitudes of psychotherapists toward treating the elderly have been attributed to prejudice and psychological conflicts in the psychotherapist. A group of psychiatrists listed the following as some of the reasons for the negativism (Committee on Aging, 1971):

1. Old people trigger fears in the therapists about growing old themselves.
2. Old people arouse conflicts the therapists have about their own aging parents.
3. The therapists fear that elderly patients won't respond to treatment, which the therapists interpret as failure.
4. Even if the condition of the old clients improves, the therapists feel it has been a waste of time, since the clients are so near death.
5. The elderly patient might die during treatment, which could challenge the therapist's sense of importance.
6. Colleagues may criticize the therapists' "preoccupation with morbid topics, such as aging and death."

In short, the negative attitude expressed by people in general toward old age is perhaps not surprisingly held by many psychotherapists as well. Therapists feel that treatment of elderly patients is "depressing" and, if they have a choice, they will generally choose to stick with the YAVIS. In one study in England, many psychiatrists in training said they would leave the country if the National Health Service required them to practice geriatric psychiatry (Brooke, 1973).

We can only hope that these negative attitudes will change in the future. There is, however, some basis for hope. Since many of the attitudes are founded in incorrect beliefs (the elderly cannot benefit from therapy, for example), perhaps the attitudes will change as truth spreads. In addition, the coming generations of old people will have different views of therapy; they will not consider it embarrassing, for example, at least not to the degree old people do today (Gatz, Smyer, and Lawton, 1980). The elderly population in the future will be better educated than it is today and probably in better physical condition, making elderly clients more palatable to psychotherapists. Finally, we will know more about chronic brain disorders, which will lessen the psychotherapists' fear of treatment failure (Kahn, 1975).

Summary

1. Schizophrenia and anxiety disorders such as neurosis are more likely to be diagnosed among young adults than among older people. Alcoholism is a problem in disproportionate numbers in early middle age, and depression and organic brain disorders are common among elderly mental patients. Age and sex biases exist in certain diagnostic categories such as "involutional melancholia," which until recently was used only for postmenopausal women. Women, especially housewives, are more likely than men to be diagnosed as mentally disordered; after the age of sixty-five, however, the ratio reverses in disfavor of men. Statistics on mental illness among the elderly must be interpreted with caution, however.
2. Groups of people with less power in society have higher rates of mental disorder: women, lower social classes, minority groups, old people. Feelings of helplessness and an external locus of control, often somewhat realistic in these powerless groups, appear to be related to anxiety and depression. A recent revision of helplessness theory relates helplessness to factors associated with a person's explanatory style.
3. Depression is sometimes masked by physical complaints and sometimes mistaken for irreversible brain disorder, especially among elderly patients. The incidence of new cases of hypochondriasis — physical symptoms for which there is no discernible physiological cause — peaks between the ages of sixty and sixty-five. Although hypochondriasis may mask depression, many depressed elderly people are actually physically ill. Other age-related stresses and losses may also contribute to depression among the aged. To illustrate the kinds of therapies available for mental disorders in general, we discussed those commonly used for severe depression: drugs, electroconvulsive therapy (ECT), and psychotherapy. Behavior modification tries to increase reinforcements in the patient's environment, and cognitive therapy focuses on the patient's maladap-

tive cognitions (self as inadequate, world as ungratifying, future as unpromising); both of these psychotherapies have been shown to be effective.

4. Suicide, which often results from severe depression, may claim as many as 50,000 or 100,000 victims a year. The ratio of unsuccessful to successful suicide attempts is higher among women than men, and higher among young adults than old people, which may reflect a greater tendency of women and young adults to use suicide attempts as a "cry for help." White males have the highest suicide rate, especially in late life; white females peak in midlife, whereas blacks (male and female) peak in young adulthood.

5. Acute brain disorders, which are often reversible, may result from strokes, heart attacks, malnutrition, vitamin deficiencies, head injuries, tumors, infections, diabetes, liver disease, drug overdoses, and many other causes. The two major forms of chronic brain disorder are *senile dementia* (by far the most common) and *multi-infarct dementia*. The latter is due to multiple little strokes, which in turn are related to cerebral arteriosclerosis (hardening or narrowing of the blood arteries feeding the brain). Early-onset dementias (affecting younger adults) include Alzheimer's disease. The causes and possible cures of Alzheimer's disease are currently being investigated. Other types of dementia include multiple sclerosis, Huntington's chorea, Parkinson's disease, Creutzfeldt–Jakob disease, and Pick's disease.

6. Psychoactive drugs (those which affect the brain) have many uses in the control of psychotic symptoms, anxiety, and depression, but they often have dangerous side effects, such as *tardive dyskinesia* (involuntary body movements). Alcoholism and heavy drinking generally decline in old age. Drug misuse among the aged is often the result of mistakes, even though it usually occurs in the context of medical treatment. Drugs are too often overprescribed, with little or no knowledge of drug interactions, or incorrectly prescribed, sometimes producing an "iatrogenic," or doctor-induced, disorder. Sedatives, for example, can produce depression and mental confusion.

7. The goals of psychotherapy shift with the age of the client or patient. Young adults have identity and intimacy crises and middle-aged clients have midlife crises. The elderly present certain special problems for therapists. Older people do not always get the psychotherapy they need because of expense, beliefs that psychotherapy marks an individual as "mentally ill," and the unwillingness of many therapists to treat elderly clients. Times are changing, however, and the future relationships between the providers of mental health care and their elderly clients promise to be more rewarding for everyone concerned.

SUGGESTED READINGS

Blazer, D. G. (1980). The epidemiology of mental illness in late life. In E. W. Busse and D. G. Blazer (Eds.), *Handbook of geriatric psychiatry* (pp. 249–271). New York: Van Nostrand Reinhold. Discusses the distribution of mental illness among the elderly, historical trends, the impact of the social system, and implications for intervention and planning of new mental health services.

Gatz, M., VandenBos, G., Pino, C., and Popkin, S. (1985). Psychological interventions with older adults. In J. E. Birren and K. W. Schaie (Eds.), *Handbook of the psychology of aging* (2nd ed.) (pp. 755–785). New York: Van Nostrand Reinhold. Mental health professionals in the past have been reluctant to conduct psychotherapy or other interventions with the elderly. This review covers the growing experience with such intervention efforts that have characterized the past decade.

La Rue, A., Dessonville, C., and Jarvik, L. F. (1985). Aging and mental disorders. In J. E. Birren and K. W. Schaie (Eds.), *Handbook of the psychology of aging* (2nd ed.) (pp. 664–702). New York: Van Nostrand Reinhold. A thorough review of the incidence and causes of psychopathology in the elderly closely linked to the classifications commonly used in psychiatric diagnosis.

Sloane, R. B. (1980). Organic brain syndrome. In J. E. Birren and R. B. Sloane (Eds.), *Handbook of mental health and aging* (pp. 554–590). Englewood Cliffs, NJ: Prentice-Hall. A discussion of the problems of organic brain disease, their classification, and assessment.

Age and Sex Difference in Somatic Complaints Associated with Depression

Most social research involves making measurements, and investigations of the elderly are no exception. Instruments and tests have been devised to measure a broad spectrum of characteristics, ranging from the most concrete, such as heart rate and blood pressure, to relatively vague concepts, such as intelligence and creativity. As you have undoubtedly gathered by now, the more abstract characteristics are the ones that present most of the measurement difficulties. Depression is an example of such a characteristic. It is often diagnosed correctly, of course, but the use of different assessment techniques may yield different estimates of the general incidence of depression and how the incidences change in different age groups.

On the basis of clinical interviews, for example, Gurland (1976) found that rates of depression were greatest in groups aged twenty-five to sixty-five. But studies relying on instruments that assess depression in terms of symptom counts show that the highest rates are found among those aged sixty-five and over. Why do the different methods of assessment yield different findings? Blumenthal (1975) has suggested an explanation. The diagnosis of depression is based on two types of characteristics — psychological symptoms and somatic (physical) complaints such as lack of energy, poor appetite, and sleep disturbance. In their interviews, the clinicians may have been told about physical complaints by both elderly and younger subjects. In the elderly, however, such symptoms may be dismissed as the ordinary concomitants of aging; among younger subjects, they may be considered to be indicative of depression. Thus the clinicians might be inclined to discover more depression among their younger subjects. In symptom counts, on the other hand, physical symptoms are included for everyone. Since older people may have more physical complaints, one would expect them to have higher scores on such instruments. But higher scores may reflect the physical problems that occur with age rather than depression per se. This type of instrument, then, may be biased toward finding more depression among the aged. To find out if symptom count checklists are actually overrepresenting depression among the elderly, Zemore and Eames (1979) removed the somatic elements from the Beck Depression Inventory (1967). When clients were tested on the remaining psychological elements alone, it was found that the age differences in scores disappeared.

In a study by Berry, Storandt, and Coyne (1984), these findings were tested with a different population and a different symptom checklist, the Zung Self-Rating Depression Scale (SDS). The new population was thought to be healthier than the one used in the Zemore–Eames study. Would they still report more somatic symptoms than younger subjects, as they had in the earlier study? These researchers also assessed the influence of gender on reports of the two types of symptoms. Previous findings indicated that women generally report more depressive symptoms, but that this trend may reverse in later life.

The participants in the study included 179 college students ranging in age from seventeen to twenty-four and 462 older adults between sixty and seventy-nine years old. All were given the Zung Self-Rating Depression Scale, which consists of twenty items ten worded positively and ten negatively. On each item, the subject chooses an answer on a four-point scale. For example, the responses to the statement "I feel downhearted and blue" were (a) none or little of the time, (b) some of the time, (c) a good part of the time, (d) most or all of the time. For the purposes of data analysis, the twenty items were divided into two categories, those that assessed somatic symptoms and those that assessed psychological symptoms. All subjects completed all twenty of the questions on the questionnaire.

The results tended to support Blumenthal's suggestion that such depression checklists may overestimate the number of depressives in the older population. On the basis of the psychological dimension of the test, younger and older adults have comparable rates of the symptomatology of depression. On the somatic questions, college-aged men and women were very similar, but in all older age groups (except those aged seventy to seventy-four), the women had higher scores than the men. Men had stable rates of somatic complaints at all ages, whereas older women had higher scores than younger women. Specifically, older women had more trouble sleeping at night, less interest in sex, loss of appetite, and increased constipation. These somatic changes are similar to the somatic problems that often accompany aging, however. Thus the clinician would do well to explore age-related somatic problems before attributing them to a depressive disorder, especially in older women. This study, then, suggests not only that rates of depression may not be higher among the elderly, but that studies which show higher rates among the aged may in fact be reflecting a problem with the instruments used to measure depression. Since studies of this sort may be used in determining who needs services and how they should be delivered, such conclusions can have important consequences.

Berry, J. M., Storandt, M., and Coyne, A. (1984). Age and sex differences in somatic complaints associated with depression. *Journal of Gerontology, 39*, 465–467.

Chapter Thirteen

LATE LIFE

Reintegration or Despair

"So you want my opinions now, do you?" asked Leonard Leslie, age sixty-nine, father of Larry and grandfather of Linda. "Must be coming to the end of the book!"

"There's still your mother, Lavinia," we pointed out graciously.

"Oh, that will be interesting, for sure. She's even more opinionated than I am."

"It strikes us that you're in a position similar to the one Linda is in. You're thinking of getting a job, and you're thinking about getting married. Just like a young person."

"Well, it's interesting that you put it that way. I've been feeling lately that I have more in common with Linda than with anyone else in this family. I like to see her succeed as she's doing. Things are opening up for women, and I like to see her taking advantage of these new opportunities. And things are opening up for old geezers like me, too. You can do some interesting things now, even if you're over sixty-five. Women and old people are like minority groups: got discriminated against a lot, and now things are opening up."

"Tell us about your jobs — your job before you retired, and the one you're thinking about now."

"Well, I had a bunch of jobs when I was young, but for the last twenty-seven years I was a plumber for the city. Worked for City Power and Water. It wasn't a bad job, I guess. The last few years, it was mostly supervision of young plumbers. Retired at sixty-five, with a small pension. Add to that social security and a little savings. I'm all right financially, though I'm certainly not rich. In fact, I could use a little more money. My car is getting pretty old, keeps needing repairs. Need a new one, but I can't afford it. So I'm thinking about working for Sam Wheatley; he's a local plumber. Maybe part-time, but maybe full-time. We'll see."

"Aren't you working already, at the suicide prevention center?"

"Well, yes, I am. But that's volunteer work. Doesn't pay in money, just in personal satisfaction. I hope I can keep that up, even if I take this job at Wheatley's. This suicide work is really interesting. Mostly, I answer phone calls on the 'hot line.' Talk people out of killing themselves. I like to talk to the old people who call in. They're usually average citizens who feel they're not useful anymore, so why not end it? A lot of them are sick, and depressed about that too. I ask them if they consider it useful to save a person's life. I tell them we need people on the phones, and even if they can't get out of their homes, there's things to do to help. I tell them that if they can play Canasta, they can be on my shift. If they don't play Canasta, I sign them up for Canasta classes — every Tuesday and Thursday. We've got a pretty big group now. Leonard's Legions, they call us. I'd hate to give that up."

"Are you embarrassed by the need to work after sixty-five?"

"Goodness, no! Maybe the politicians should be embarrassed, for inflation and stuff like that. Why should I be embarrassed? Actually, I'm looking forward to working again. I was feeling a little bored, a little useless — in spite of saving all those lives! Sam Wheatley's a good man to work for, too. I'll tell you the truth, though. At first, I had my doubts. Doubts about me. Things have changed, even in the four years I've been retired. I haven't kept up. Lot of plastic pipe now. New techniques. New government regulations. I told Sam I didn't think I'd be of much help — he came to me, you know. Said he'd like me to work at least part-time."

"Sam convinced you that you could do it?" -

"He said he needed me. Said he had too many young pups working for him and he needed somebody he could trust to supervise them — get them out on schedule, handle some of the paper work, handle emergencies. Well, that's what I did the last ten years or so with the city. I never thought of this kind of supervision as a talent, but Sam convinced me it was. I took a look at the mess he's in now and I said to myself, 'Gee, I can improve on this.' "

We changed the subject to biology: "How's your health? Are you in pretty good shape for a person of age sixty-nine? Any definitive signs of age?"

"I'm all right, I guess. A little arthritis in both knees, that keeps me from playing basketball! Doc Winslow says my blood pressure is too high. I told him it was just excitement, thinking about my wedding night, only a month away! Also, it seems to me that my memory is not quite what it used to be."

"Could you give us some examples of that?"

"Examples of what?! Oh, yes, memory. Well, it's a tricky thing. Like Linda's memory isn't so hot, and she's only twenty-two, so a bad memory doesn't mean old age. It's just that I think I forget things now that I used to have no trouble remembering. Plumbing terms, for example. People's names! I'm gonna have to start calling everybody 'Bud' and 'Sweetheart.' But then sometimes I think it's just that remembering is not as important to me as it once was. I forget some names now because the people aren't important in my life. If somebody's not important to my job or to my family, why should I remember his name? Leonard's Legions, however: I can give you the name and description of every single one, and the address and phone number of at least half of them."

"How do you feel about the coming years? Are you apprehensive, are you content, or what?"

"I'm not afraid of death, if that's what you're getting at. I look at it this way: I have ten, maybe twenty years left to live. That's really quite a long time, when you

"Old age" covers thirty to forty years of the lifespan; the differences between the "young-old" and the "old-old" can be considerable.

think about it. I don't want to be a burden to anyone, financially or physically or mentally. I need something to do, which I'm handling with work — real work and volunteer work. I don't want to be alone, so I'm getting married. I know my son Larry doesn't think much of my marriage ideas, but I've got to look out for myself in this matter. I've never been a loner, and I need someone around. But all in all, the future looks pretty good to me. The fears I have are mostly about illness, if I get really sick and start a real money drain on my family. Or senility. That's the deepest fear there is! There ain't nobody over sixty-five who doesn't fear senility, let me tell you! But I don't think about it every moment. Mostly I'm pretty content."

"You should be."

"I know it."

The Young Old, the Old Old, and the Very Old

Old age is often viewed as a single stage of life, and all persons defined as "old" are viewed with the same mixture of awe and pity. In any stage of life, of course, people differ, often radically. Nowhere else in the life span, however, does a single stage so inadequately fit all those in it as in the case of old age. "People over sixty-five" can be divided into at least three stages, the young old (sixty-five to seventy-five or eighty), the old old (seventy-five or eighty to about ninety), and the very old (those in their nineties and older). To compare someone who is ninety-five years old to someone who is sixty-five is not unlike comparing people thirty years different in age at other points in the life span: a five-year-old to a thirty-five-year-old, or thirty-five-year-old to a sixty-five-year-old. Indeed, the physical and mental changes in thirty years toward the end of life are, in most respects, greater than the changes in the same time span at other ages. The probability of physical disease, for example, is much greater for someone over eighty than for someone between sixty-five and eighty. On many variables of mental and physical performance, the young-old people resemble middle-aged adults more than they do old-old people.

Erik Erikson (1979, 1982) defined old age generally as a stage of life in which the individual must try to balance the search for *integrity* with a sense of *despair*. Out of this conflict may emerge *wisdom*, the human virtue most commonly associated with old age. Erikson chose to emphasize those tasks of old age which involve a review of one's life, making sense of it, tying together all the loose ends (integrating it). Despair is a necessary component in this process, for a life's review is bound to turn up ample evidence of human failings; someone who could not remember a single failing would not be called wise but neurotic. The negative emotions associated with this stage, which is the last of Erikson's life crises, are in part a result of the limitations of a person's physical and psychological energy (Gadow, 1983; Skinner, 1983). In addition to being disappointed with one's own failures and those of others, one must also deal with the loneliness that results from the death of people to whom one felt close. But even the despair can be accepted, in an active balance with integrity, which is Erikson's definition of wisdom (Erikson, 1979).

Robert Havighurst (1972) has listed six major developmental tasks that must be faced, one way or the other, in late life. These tasks are listed in Table 13–1. One major theme running through the list is disengagement, the voluntary or involuntary lessening of active participation in society. Retirement is part of disengagement, and decreasing strength and health make activities more difficult; the death of a spouse takes one's companion in previous activities and drains

TABLE 13–1.
Havighurst's developmental tasks of late life.

1. Adjusting to decreasing physical strength and health.
2. Adjusting to retirement and reduced income.
3. Adjusting to death of spouse.
4. Establishing an explicit association with one's age group.
5. Adopting and adapting social roles in a flexible way.
6. Establishing satisfactory physical living arrangements.

emotional resources. To some extent disengagement from the social roles of middle age — the role of worker, for example — is compensated for by the "adopting" of new activities and the "adapting" of old ones. Retired people may take up a new hobby or, as part of their "explicit association" with their new age group, join a political action group or a social-recreational group. They may expand their home-and-family role (taking the grandchildren on excursions, planting a garden) or develop their role in community organizations (in church, a club, the neighborhood). Finally, old people must find a place to live that satisfies their needs — easy access to shopping and other activities, something that isn't a burden to their adult children.

These general notions of issues faced by people over the age of sixty-five do not distinguish between the young old, the old old, and the very old. And clearly there are differences, even in the degree to which the tasks in Table 13–1 are relevant. After the age of eighty, physical decline is usually more evident and may be progressing rapidly, whereas most people between sixty-five and seventy-five are in quite good health. Adjusting to retirement-level income is a "sudden" task, precipitated by the event of retirement; by old-old age, financial adjustments have typically been made, although of course financial difficulties may remain. After young-old age, people typically have to rely more and more on support from children and institutions. Among the very old, financial problems may once again become quite acute because the financial resources planned for in retirement have been "outlived." If the very old person has a fixed income, inflation may well have eroded what may once have been a more-than-adequate income base (Schultz, 1985). People in their nineties may even lose the support of their children because they have died or become too frail themselves to support their parents. Thus the problem of dependency becomes more serious as one grows older. Conspicuous in its absence from Havighurst's list is the task of facing one's own death, which becomes a more preeminent concern the longer one lives.

In this, our concluding chapter, we explore in some detail the concept of *dependency* — the fear of it and the reality of it. Many old people are afraid, to some extent realistically, that they will become dependent on their adult children for money — financial dependency. They also fear becoming physically dependent, needing help getting around, for example, because of severe arthritis or a broken hip. They fear becoming senile due to brain disease, which might make them dependent on others in all facets of their lives, might even make them dependent in such embarrassing matters as bowel control. Then we explore a brighter prospect, the creative accomplishments of older adults, many of which may lean heavily on the wisdom born of years of experience.

Facing death, your own and that of spouse and good friends, is a major task of old people. We explore the sources of anxiety about death and the stages of the dying process. We also consider the survivors — the bereaved — to examine how they deal with grief and loss. Finally we meet Lavinia Leslie, age eighty-seven, the matriarch of the Leslie family, the Leslie in the final stage of the life cycle.

Dependency

In Chapter 2, on the family, we introduced the notion of the family as a set of interdependent relationships. In any family, there is a reciprocal attitude that permits, even encourages, family members to *depend* on kin for financial, physical, and emotional support. Thus old age brings not something new in the form of dependencies that did not exist before, but a change in the nature of the dependencies. Something upsets the curious but fragile balance between dependence and independence that exists for most of an adult's life.

An individual beginning life is almost totally dependent on others for survival. We do not begrudge such people their incapacities; we view child care as a responsibility of the parents. As children grow, the contribution they can make — at least to their own welfare — increases. In adolescence, the balance of dependency and independence becomes a major source of conflict between parent and child. Then comes marriage, and the independence of the two spouses might remain controversial; how much time to do individual things, for example, may be an issue. Another issue in adult life is the relative degree of dependence on, and independence from, one's employer (consider the "company town," for example, in which employees had to depend not only on their employer for wages but also for supplies on which to spend their money). The obligations to one's government and the freedom one should have from its dictates are traditional topics in history and political science.

In old age, people typically retire and face the increasing possibility of disease. To some extent, they must rely on their adult children to provide financial help and physical aid, a reversal in the trend toward increasing independence they have experienced since birth. It is as if they were becoming children again. The dependencies they see developing are not "adult dependencies" — those that grow from, say, a mutual recognition of the benefits of a division of labor, or a mature recognition of everyone's need for emotional support. Instead, they are "childish dependencies," those that go against their values of self-reliance and personal autonomy. These childish dependencies threaten their self-esteem; old people fear them, as Leonard Leslie points out, and they struggle against them.

FINANCIAL DEPENDENCIES

The greatest fears of many old people are of events that actually have very low probability of ever occurring to them. These fears, nevertheless, cannot be called unrealistic, because the effects of such events, if they should indeed occur, could be quite devastating.

Old people, in a sense, are like people who live next to a nuclear plant: chances are nothing will happen, but if something goes wrong, it's a disaster. Thus old people fear crime (and they are indeed prone to certain "highly visible" crimes such as purse snatching), but across the board of criminal activities, they are, relatively speaking, the least victimized of any age group. They fear senility, although brain disease is not very common. And they are afraid that something will happen to wipe out their savings although the majority of old people are financially secure. This was not always the case. Before Medicare, a disastrous illness could lead to large medical bills. Today, the economic impact of disease on the elderly has been mitigated. The rising cost of health care, however, has led to recent political decisions that may require the elderly once again either to contribute a greater share of the cost of their health care or to forego quality care. Probably the most frightening specter, however, is the loss of purchasing power due to inflation that is not properly compensated for by increases in retirement income.

Financial problems are cited as the "worst thing about being over sixty-five years of age" by only 17 percent of the elderly respondents in one national survey (Harris and associates, 1975). (Poor health — physical dependency — was the worst thing, cited by 70 percent, and loneliness was second, with 20 percent.) A more recent study yielded similar results: only 10 percent of the men and 20 percent of the women in a community-based sample thought that their incomes were inadequate (Atchley, 1985, p. 153). This optimistic assessment must be interpreted with caution, however, because it has been found that a person's satisfaction with his or her income is only indirectly related to the actual income. What seems to be most important is whether people feel they are well off relative to the people they compare themselves to and relative to their own past experience (Liang, Kahana, and Doherty, 1980).

Nevertheless, economic statistics do provide some support for the favorable self-appraisal. At the same time, however, these statistics reveal that the elderly are less affluent than the average of the population as a whole. In 1979, the median income of families headed by people sixty-five or older was $8,957; for all families, the median was close to $16,000. The median for people living alone was $4,399 (U.S. Bureau of the Census, 1981a).

It should be recognized that expenditure patterns shift after retirement, so the elderly's income may be more adequate than it would seem. For example, there is a decline in expenses related to employment, such as transportation and meals away from home. In addition, the children have left home, so the average household consists of two or three people rather than the average of four persons for the population as a whole. On the other hand, the physical limitations of many older people may force them to pay for services they could have performed themselves when they were younger. Few old-old or very old people can wash windows, do yard work, or paint their own houses.

Table 13–2 shows three typical budgets developed by the U.S. Bureau of Labor Statistics for an urban retired couple. The low budget is above the poverty line, but it would provide only for the most basic necessities. The moderate and higher budgets would be typical of lower-middle and middle-middle class couples, respectively. The 1980 census showed that about 60 percent of all elderly *couples* had incomes in the middle range or above, but only about 25 percent of all unmarried elderly people had such high incomes. Twenty-one percent of the older couples and 55 percent of the older singles had to function at the bare

TABLE 13–2.

Annual budget for a retired couple, for three levels of living: Urban United States, 1980.

Budget category	Low budget	Moderate budget	Higher budget
Food	$2,082	$2,772	$3,482
Housing	2,169	3,106	4,860
Transportation	487	950	1,748
Clothing	236	396	609
Personal care	184	269	394
Medical care	944	950	956
Other	541	992	1,874
Total	$6,644	$9,434	$13,923

Source: U.S. Bureau of Labor Statistics, 1981.

survival level. Sixteen percent of the elderly had incomes below the official poverty line established by the federal government. In the population as a whole, only 12 percent fall below the poverty line.

About 90 percent of all elderly Americans receive income in the form of a Social Security pension. In 1981, on average, Social Security replaced 66 percent of the earnings in the last year of employment for couples, compared to only 44 percent of the earnings of unmarried persons. (This is because Social Security taxes also provides benefits for spouses.) In the past twenty years, these rates have gone up about 60 percent. The ever-increasing Social Security taxes, however, have gone mostly to reduce poverty; they have not provided lavish pensions (Atchley, 1982b). In fact, the reason that some retired people do reasonably well is not because of Social Security, but because of the gradual development of private pension systems. Such pensions provide additional income to 31 percent of all married elderly couples and 13 percent of all single elderly people. In addition, more than a third of all retired persons receive some income from personal investments (Social Security Administration, 1984).

The data suggest that although most older couples have incomes large enough to support themselves comfortably, most unmarried older people have financial troubles. In general, financial problems in old age tend to occur most often in certain subgroups, particularly minorities and women. In 1980, for example, 16 percent of the elderly population fell below the poverty line, but the figure for whites was only 14 percent, while it was 32 percent for blacks. Only 9 percent of the families headed by white males were below the poverty line, compared with as many as 43 percent of the families headed by black females (U.S. Bureau of the Census, 1981a). Thus the people who suffer discrimination during the adult years before age sixty-five are also most likely to suffer from the income deficits common in the later years of life.

We may conclude that although most old people are not exactly affluent, most of them are not living in poverty, and a substantial proportion experience an acceptable level of comfort. What most old people need, then, is not so much everyday financial support but rather protection from the devastating effects of huge medical bills, galloping inflation, and similar catastrophes.

PHYSICAL AND EMOTIONAL DEPENDENCY

As with financial dependency, physical dependency is a fear not often realized to any significant degree. Only 5.2 percent of the people over sixty-five are in institutions because of incapacitating physical or mental illness. Figures on institutionalization differ markedly, however, between early and late old age. As is to be expected, less than 2 percent of the young old are institutionalized, a proportion not very different from that holding for the younger population. But of the old old, those between seventy-five and eighty-four, about 7 percent are in institutions, and this proportion grows to 22 percent for the very old, those over eighty-five years of age (U.S. Bureau of the Census, 1983a). Only 9 percent of the elderly consider their health to be poor (Harris, 1978). However, almost 18 percent report that they have some difficulty getting around, and nearly 50 percent say they have an infirmity (arthritis, heart condition, and sensory loss being the most common) that keeps them from performing certain activities.

Statistics such as these translate into lives in which physical dependency is severe only in a few cases. Most elderly people must depend on others only slightly more than they did when they were younger. They might need a ride at night, help moving furniture, or confirmation of their reading of a blurry street sign. When help is needed, family members are the most likely source. At present, social agencies provide only a very small percentage of all in-home care for the elderly (Shanas, 1979). Many infirmities that might make one more dependent can be handled with compensatory devices (such as eyeglasses) or compensatory techniques (such as paying professional furniture movers).

Although people need to feel self-reliant both financially and physically, they do not like to be alone. They are increasingly likely to be, however. This is reflected in the changes in housing arrangements that occur in old age (see Figure 13–1). Between the ages of fifty-five and sixty-four, over 80 percent of the men and 65 percent of the women live with their spouses. During the young-old stage, the figure for men doesn't change very much, but the proportion of women living with their spouses drops to 50 percent. Beyond age seventy-five, about 67 percent of the men still have spouses living, compared to only 20 percent of the women (U.S. Senate Special Committee on Aging, 1981).

Old people, of course, need love, affection, and social interaction just as others do. If a spouse has died, however, these needs may be increasingly difficult to meet. People are typically retired from work, and for one reason or another they often reduce their involvement in community organizations. Their parents are dead, and often brothers, sisters, and friends may be dead or ailing too. The emotional response to this growing isolation is loneliness, and next to

FIGURE 13–1.
Living arrangements of noninstitutionalized persons by age and sex: United States, 1980.

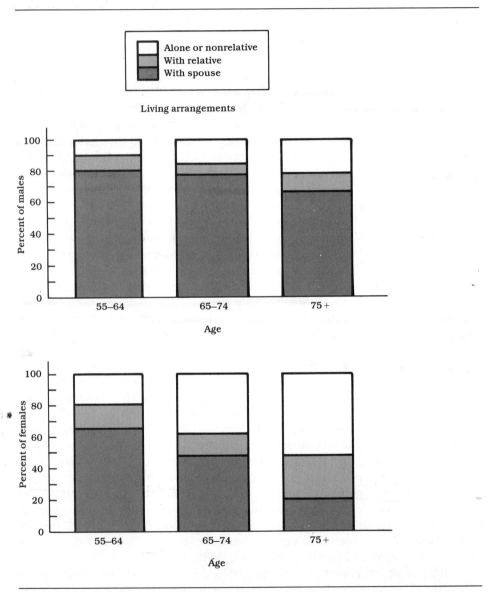

Source: From U.S. Senate Special Committee on Aging, 1981, pp. 15–16.

physical dependency it is one of the greatest fears people associate with old age (Harris and Associates, 1975). Although loneliness is greatest following the death of a spouse, it may also be a result of contextual factors such as the general loneliness of urban existence. It is not surprising that a survey of small-town widows found that only 25 percent considered themselves lonely a lot (Kunkel, 1979).

Loneliness is a dependency issue because, with increasing age, the people one depends on for emotional sustenance are increasingly the members of one's family. Old people like to talk, to discuss current politics, to apply experience to current problems. To whom can they talk? As they grow older, the answer becomes increasingly limited to their adult children. From the old person's point of view, this is just one more "burden" their existence puts on their beloved offspring. In their efforts to avoid being a nuisance, they may choose loneliness.

Because women live longer than men and because husbands tend to be older than their wives, elderly men may often become dependent on their wives, turning them into part-time (or full-time) nurses (Troll, Miller, and Atchley, 1979). This greatly reduces the freedom of many older women to continue participating in activities in the community. Not surprisingly, the life satisfaction expressed by older couples is strongly correlated with health. Interestingly, men seem to be affected more adversely by their wives' poor health than wives are by their husbands' (Atchley and Miller, 1983). This may be because women expect their husbands to become more dependent on them in old age, while men expect just the opposite.

The physical and emotional dependencies of late life have been alleviated for many elderly citizens by the Older Americans Act of 1965 (Atchley, 1984). The Older Americans Act, among its other features, supports "senior centers," which provide information, counseling, meals, and "plain old getting together" for talk and perhaps a game of cards. "Nutrition sites" provide good food in a group setting (as well as the transportation to and from); for those confined to home, there are "Meals on Wheels." Other services (which may be funded by other local, state, and federal agencies, as well as the Older Americans Act) include "visiting nurses," general transportation (for shopping, for example), legal assistance, day-care facilities for seniors, and a number of telephone or mail "reassurance" programs, which make sure the individual living alone is all right (by a daily phone call, for example) and send someone to check if there is any indication of trouble (Monk, 1985).

Some enterprising oldsters have formed *communes* for the elderly, helping each other with financial, physical, and loneliness problems (Butler, 1975). Less radical and more common are social clubs of various types. These clubs may be purely social, serving only as a vehicle for getting together, or they may have an additional purpose, such as travel, old movies, charitable activities, or finance. For some older people, however, dependency needs become great enough that more radical solutions are necessary. For some, this involves moving in with children. When this is not possible or desirable, the older person often ends up

Being able to get around by oneself is a key ingredient for self-reliance at any age.

moving to some kind of sheltered care setting. Such settings, in which the elderly reside with nonrelatives, can be classified along a dimension from facilities providing minimum to those providing maximum services. At one end of the continuum is housing in retirement communities that may provide no more than weekly housecleaning and/or meal programs. At the other end are long-term care settings that include skilled nursing facilities and hospitals for the chronically ill (Moos and Lemke, 1985).

Retirement communities   Some older people deal with their loneliness and the fear that they will become dependent on their children by moving into retirement housing. (Not all people who move to such housing do so for these reasons, of course; some simply want to leave the community to which they were tied by their jobs and to move someplace they like better for their remaining years.) Most of the residents of retirement communities are reasonably affluent people who consciously decide to live in a community of people of the same age. This homogeneity facilitates social interactions and the development of new friendships (Keith, 1982). Full-service retirement communities provide a continuum of services, ranging from arrangements for independent living to semi-independent living to nursing homes that provide full-time care. They typically also offer an extensive array of services in such areas as preventive health care, recreation, transportation, and education. Because most planned retirement communities are relatively expensive, some working-class elderly cannot afford them, moving instead to less expensive mobile home parks for older adults that offer similar services.

In an interesting study, Longino (1981) compared the residents of three types of retirement communities: full-service communities, public housing for the elderly, and unplanned retirement communities that have arisen in certain areas as a result of the migration of retired people to small communities. In the planned full-service communities, the residents tended to be older (average age seventy-six), more affluent, and interested in obtaining such services as meals, housekeeping, and nursing. In public housing, the residents were predominantly elderly women (average age seventy-eight) who had previously lived in the same geographical area but who sought the greater security and lower expense of subsidized housing. In the unplanned retirement communities that arose spontaneously, the residents were typically younger people (average age sixty-eight) who sought independence and enjoyment of the natural environment. These findings support the notion that older people seek housing that satisfies some of their dependency needs. These needs may be met most effectively by the planned retirement community, which often provides a suitable program for the remainder of the residents' lives. Unplanned retirement communities, on the other hand, may be only an intermediate solution because the services they offer may be insufficient when dependency needs increase.

Nursing homes About half of the elderly people who receive care in institutions are in nursing homes. In the United States, there are almost a million people over sixty-five in more than 11,000 such homes. By the year 2003, this number is expected to double given constant mortality figures and to triple if mortality declines at the same rate as has been the case in recent decades. Nursing homes tend to serve most heavily the old old and very old. Currently, three-fourths of their residents are over seventy-five years of age, and 35 percent are eighty-five years of age or older. If mortality declines, forecasts for the year 2003 further suggest that at that time almost 87 percent of nursing home residents would be over seventy-five years old, and as many as 52 percent would be eighty-five or older (National Center for Health Statistics, 1983a).

Keeping fit and having fun at a day camp for the elderly.

In most cases, people move to nursing homes because they or their families recognize a need for a more supportive setting. If the elderly person has a severe illness and is bedridden or requires frequent medications, the move is likely to be voluntary. But emotional problems and mental decline are often denied by older people and their families alike, so in some cases people are placed in nursing homes only when professional intervention establishes that a person has become a safety hazard to him- or herself or others (Bernstein, 1982).

The admission of a person to a nursing home does not mean that interactions with friends, children, and other relatives come to an end. On the contrary, a regular pattern of visits, letters, and phone calls is often established (Miller and Beer, 1977; Smith and Bengtson, 1979). Strong ties between relatives usually persist. Although contacts with friends and former neighbors are less frequent than contacts with relatives, they are often continued as well.

The extent to which contacts are maintained with people outside the institution may be influenced by whether or not the old person is seen as likely to be discharged. If the stay in the institution is likely to be short, concerted efforts may be made to stay in frequent contact. This continuation of relationships offers several advantages, decreasing the adaptation necessary for both the old person and friends and relatives once the return is made to the community. Long-term residents, on the other hand, may be more inclined to get involved in the life of the institution to fill voids in social areas (Aizenberg and Treas, 1985).

The structural arrangement and management of the nursing home have a powerful influence on the residents' social lives. There is some evidence, for example, that as the size of the institution increases, the communication, satisfaction, and activity of the residents decline. Friendships are more likely to develop among people in facilities that have fewer than 50 residents (Curry and Ratliff, 1973). It has also been found that residents of facilities for fewer than 100 people are more likely to form "companion" relationships with nurses' aides than are residents of larger institutions. It appears that smaller facilities more closely resemble the home environment and are better able to meet residents' social needs (Henley and Davis, 1967; Handschu, 1973).

Today, long-term care has become a major health care industry as well as a form of humanitarian service. A great deal of thought has been given in recent years to the planning of facilities that provide economical care while offering optimal services to residents (Breger and Pomeranz, 1985). Very few people who enter nursing homes are completely incapable of self-care, but interactions between staff members and patients often encourage dependency and discourage independence. In some cases, this tendency results from the best of intentions, but more often the nursing staff does tasks for the residents because it is more efficient and cost-effective than allowing residents to struggle along on their own. Staff may also have negative attitudes toward the elderly, to the extent that they may use "baby talk" in speaking to them and otherwise treat them like children (Caporael, 1981; Caporael, Lukaszewski, and Culbertson, 1983). Studies of the social ecology of nursing homes have shown that reinforcing independence reduces dependence, which in turn reduces incidences of disease and death (Baltes, 1982). Changes in nursing home policies are needed to reward staff in terms of the residents' outcomes and to prevent burnout of staff members (Timko and Rodin, in press). If it is assumed that the well-being of nursing home residents can be improved by allowing them more personal control of their lives, it would follow that they should be allowed to determine their daily routines (policy choice) as well as to participate in decisions that determine some aspects of the home's programs and policies (resident controls) (Moos and Lemke, 1985). In a study of ninety-three residential facilities, it was found that higher levels of policy choice and resident control were indeed associated with more cohesive, independence-oriented social environments and with resident activity levels. Women in particular reacted more favorably to the provision of choice over their daily activity as did the more functionally able residents (Moos, 1981).

Accomplishments in Late Life

In some Eskimo societies, people live difficult lives in environments that barely provide sustenance for the small, isolated families (Lidz, 1976). When people in these societies reach an age where they feel that they can no longer contribute to the family's welfare, they go off by themselves to freeze to death on the ice. In one family, the grandmother went to sit on the ice when a grandchild was born; she reasoned that the family would survive if *her* mouth-to-feed was subtracted as the new mouth-to-feed was added (Ruesch, 1959). The parents, however, had never before seen an infant, as can happen in such an isolated existence. They came to believe their toothless, complaining newborn was defective, incapable of survival. They rushed to the grandmother, urging her to take the infant with her to the ice. The grandmother realized she was not yet dispensable. She told the naive parents that she could grow teeth in the infant; she could teach it to survive. Thus the old woman returned to her family for a few more years of life and duty.

In other societies, it is not until quite late in life that positions of power and authority are attained. A social system that is ruled by the old is called a gerontocracy. Such systems were found in ancient as well as modern times; they occur in different environments and in societies of different degrees of complexity that subscribe to different political philosophies. The current leaders of two of the most powerful nations, the United States and China, are all in their seventies.

Gerontocrats acquire power in a variety of ways. In agricultural and pastoral societies, ownership and control of property are acquired through inheritance from senior members, so older people are more powerful in family and village affairs than their juniors. In primitive societies, knowledge of technology and ceremonies and the formation of long-standing social bonds enhances the power of the old (Missinne, 1980; Werner, 1981).

Although the industrialized United States is far more complex than pastoral or primitive societies, elite families apparently control power in ways that resemble those used in clans in tribal societies (Fry, 1985). Senior family members typically control decisions about economic resources, determining which of the younger family members or others they wish to yield power to. Many members of Congress live to an advanced age, and perhaps it's not surprising that Congress also has a seniority system that increases the power of older members. This system is not unlike the power systems found in primitive societies (Weatherford, 1981).

It should be noted, however, that the existence of a gerontocracy does not necessarily ensure the well-being of older people in general. Government by the old is not necessarily government for the old. In general, success and accomplishment in old age seem to be determined by four factors: the degree of respect attained during earlier adulthood, knowledge, the desire to participate, and control of property (Nason, 1981; Fry, 1985).

RESEARCH ON CREATIVITY

For various reasons, the years of young adulthood and middle age are frequently those of the greatest creativity and productivity. Many people in centuries past never reached the age of sixty or seventy, so of course their greatest works were accomplished at an earlier age. Nowadays, people often retire at sixty-five and put a deliberate end to striving for creative or productive goals. Illness, correlated with aging but different from it, can slow and inhibit creative urges. Nevertheless, old age can be a time of significant accomplishments. Many people over sixty or seventy — even over eighty — have made important contributions to art, science, education, and politics. What we would like to explore here is the nature of these accomplishments in late life. Are they age-related? Do they in some sense depend on the fact that the individual involved is old and wise? Or are they better viewed as accomplishments of creative people who have produced something of value *in spite of* their advancing years?

To explore the relationship between age and creativity, psychologists have examined the creative products of scientists, philosophers, artists, businesspeople, politicians, chess players, and other people whose achievements can be said to be important and notable. Major creative works — the one or two accomplishments for which the person is best known — tend to occur relatively early in life (Lehman, 1953). There are, of course, impressive individual exceptions (Goethe completed *Faust* after the age of eighty) and major achievements in certain fields, such as philosophy, seem to occur later than in other fields. But, as shown in Figure 13–2, most artists, scholars, and scientists produce their most remarkable works in their thirties and early forties. When one considers the years of training often necessary before a major contribution is possible, these figures suggest that most major creative works come early indeed.

FIGURE 13–2.

The age of 67 major artists when they painted their best work. The number of "best paintings" for each age period was divided by the number of the artists living at that age, which adjusts to some extent for the lesser number of artists at the older ages. The highest number so obtained was arbitrarily assigned the value of 100, and other periods were assigned a value based on their percentage of the peak.

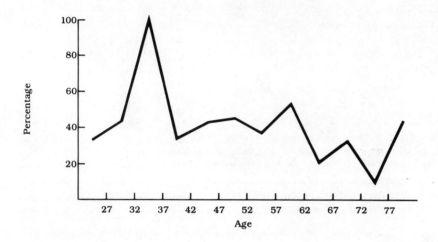

Source: From Lehman, H. C., (1953). *Age and achievement.* Copyright by the American Philosophical Society. Graph, p. 78. Reprinted by permission of Princeton University Press.

The great creative works of young adults are often different in type from those of older people. Elderly adults are known for "wise and mature" works that integrate disparate themes and also for works that depict or elucidate the particular conflicts and problems of old age. Young adults, in contrast, produce works that critics are likely to laud in such terms as "innovative, refreshing, a new look." Young adults tend to play with ideas and come up with new approaches. David Hume contrived some highly original views in *A Treatise of Human Nature*, for example, published before he was twenty-five. Mary Shelley took an even more original look at human nature in her classic novel of horror, *Frankenstein*, written when she was twenty-one. Louis Braille, blind since the age of three, took a more practical view of human nature and the needs of visually handicapped persons to create an alphabet of raised dots — at age twenty.

"Freshness" is a term critics used to describe the works of young people such as Georges Bizet, whose Symphony in C Major was written at the age of seventeen. "It is a work that abounds in youthful vitality," one reviewer said (Lehman,

Maggie Kuhn, founding mother of the Gray Panthers, a radical group of elderly people who fight for the rights of senior citizens.

1953, p. 201). A fresh look at some ancient literature resulted in John Keats's *On First Looking into Chapman's Homer*, considered one of the best sonnets ever written — especially by a twenty-year-old. A new look at the time dimension produced *The Time Machine*, by a twenty-nine-year-old author, H. G. Wells.

Willingness to experiment is another characteristic of young adults. Thus, at twenty-eight, Sigmund Freud tried a strange new drug called cocaine and was, in fact, largely responsible for its introduction to European society. Sir Humphrey Davy was only twenty when the "intoxicating effects of nitrous oxide when respired were discovered by him on April 9, 1799" (Lehman, 1953, p. 204). These drugs, now predominantly used for thrill-seeking purposes, had at the time important anesthetic uses for surgery and other medical procedures.

Decisions about careers and families are the most prominent developmental tasks faced by young adults, but we find very few important works on these topics by young adults. Great discourses, scientific discoveries, and works of art on work and family life seem rather to be the province of older adults, who perhaps have the advantage of having lived through the various stages of processes that only begin, but are by no means completed, in young adulthood. What we do find in young adulthood is a lot of work on love and intimacy. Jane Austen's *Pride and Prejudice*, written when the author was twenty-one, is a remarkably insightful portrayal of manners and traditions that stand in the way of love. Emily Brontë's *Wuthering Heights*, written at twenty-nine, is a brilliant forerunner of the decidedly inferior "gothic romances" that line the bookshelves of our supermarkets today, depicting both the romance (intimacy) and the danger (uncertainty, dependence) that love holds for any young adult.

CREATIVITY IN LATER LIFE

Although the major works of creative people tend to occur early in life, their total output is spread more evenly across the span of life. In a study of 738 persons who lived to age seventy-nine or beyond, the sixties were the most productive years for four groups: historians, philosophers, botanists, and inventors (Dennis, 1966). In terms of more general categories, scholars (history, philosophy, literature) were more productive in their later years — including their seventies. Scientists were most productive in their forties, fifties, and sixties. Artists were most productive slightly earlier, in their thirties and forties.

In a highly sophisticated mathematical analysis of the lives of ten of the most famous composers, creative productivity was found to peak between the ages of forty-five and forty-nine (Simonton, 1977). Productivity was related to age in what was termed an "inverted-backward-J" curve (ʃ) instead of the "inverted-U" curve (∩) the researcher hypothesized. This means that productivity rose to a peak and then fell, but the decline was considerably less than the initial ascent. This relationship held even when the variable of physical illness was controlled for. That is, illness, which becomes more frequent in the later years of life, does *not* explain the decrease in creative productivity in the later years of life.

Another hypothesis to be considered is that major creative works appear to belong to young adulthood simply because the longer one lives, the more competition one has. The number of creative people in any discipline (art, literature, science) has been increasing at a fantastic rate (Dennis, 1958; Simonton, 1977). Consider a hypothetical author — Anthony Owen Colby, we'll call him — whose work at age twenty is considered the best the world of literature has ever experienced. By the time Colby is thirty, two new twenty-year-old geniuses have appeared on the scene; the three of them compete for the plaudits of critics. When Colby reaches forty, his "old" (thirty-year-old) competitors are still around, joined by four new twenty-year-olds. At fifty, we add eight new twenty-year-olds to Colby's previous list of six. At sixty, with sixteen new twenty-year-olds, Colby is only one of thirty-one "great writers." He might be writing as well as before, but the competition is now fierce. Centuries later, looking back, we might decide his creativity failed in his later years because he wasn't discussed as much.

Increasing competition among older creators may explain some of the apparent advantage of young adults (Dennis, 1958). Although competition is not a factor in studies that count *all* works of an artist, scholar, or scientist, it does affect measures of creativity based on mention in historical accounts (Simonton, 1977). In other words, the probability of Anthony Owen Colby's works being cited in a book on the literature of his century depends on his age. His work at age twenty, with no competition, is sure to be mentioned, but his work at age sixty, perhaps equally meritorious, will have about one chance in thirty-one of being listed as the best of that decade.

The productivity of creative old people is indeed amazing. In the retrospective studies of Wayne Dennis (1968), the subjects were eminent scholars, scientists, and artists who had lived at least eighty years. Their creative output was categorized into six decades of adult life, ranging from the twenties to the seventies. We are here concerned with the accomplishments of late life, when the subjects were sixty to eighty years old. If 100 percent of a person's works were evenly divided by decade, we would expect 16.7 percent per decade or a little over 33 percent for the two late-life decades combined. By actual count, we find 41 percent for the scholars (historians, philosophers, scholars of literature), 21 percent in their sixties and 20 percent in their seventies. The sixties was their *most* productive decade! Among scientists, 35 percent of their work was done in late life, 20 percent in their sixties and 15 percent in their seventies. Famous inventors did well over *half* their work after sixty (53 percent). Among artists, 20 percent of their work was done in late life, 14 percent in their sixties and only 6 percent in their seventies. The poorest late-life performance was by dramatists, architects, and opera composers (10 to 15 percent after sixty).

The first thing to note about these data is the remarkable number of significant achievements after the age of sixty. Scholars and scientists seem scarcely to slow down, and even artists are productive, though at a lesser rate. Some of the greatest works of art were done by people in the last years of their lives. Michelangelo, for example, finished painting *The Last Judgment,* one of the most famous pictures in the world, at age sixty-six. At seventy, he completed the dome of St. Peter's in Rome. Goethe was eighty-two when he finished *Faust.* Wagner finished *Götterdämmerung* at sixty-three. Verdi produced *Otello* at seventy-four and *Falstaff* at eighty. Cervantes wrote *Don Quixote* at sixty-eight (Nelson, 1928).

Are the creative productions of old people in some respects dependent on their age? Certainly there are instances in which the impediments of old age add little. One thinks of a deaf Beethoven composing symphonies, a blind Galileo at seventy-four working out the application of pendulum movement to the regulation of clockwork. But there are few works of late life that did not benefit in some way from the accumulated knowledge and wisdom of the creator. Late-life works typically have a maturity, a complexity, and an insight into the interrelationships of things that the work of a younger person lacks. It is difficult to define terms such as wisdom and maturity, although it is not difficult to recognize these traits in finished work. In comparing two works of the French dramatists Molière, one reviewer notes:

> Nothing is more instructive than to compare *Les Precieuses Ridicules,* which is almost his first play, with *Les Femmes Savantes,* which is almost his last. They are so closely connected in subject that the later play has sometimes been called an expanded recast of the earlier. But the improvement in treatment is immense. Amusing as *Les Precieuses Ridicules* is, it is not much more than farce of the very best sort. *Les Femmes Savantes* is comedy of the highest kind, the result of exact observation of life informed by intimate knowledge of character, and clothed with the most accomplished phrase. (Saintsbury, 1896, p. 439)

Many scholarly and scientific works in late life represent an integration of the observations of a lifetime. Personal memoirs are the most individualistic of these integrations, although memoirs are often personalized histories of a field — medicine, law, government. Historians in general produce a high percentage of their best works after the age of sixty (44 percent in Dennis's study), and many people in other disciplines produce insightful histories of their fields (education, mathematics, psychology).

In similar fashion, many of the great works of late life represent the individual's final attempt to make sense of the often conflicting "facts" in his or her field. The work may be a "magnum opus," such as the ten-volume treatise on social psychology that Wilhelm Wundt (the father of modern psychology) finished at the age of eighty-eight. (Wundt followed this work with his memoirs, which he also completed at eighty-eight, shortly before he died, in 1920.) The work may be an important textbook, such as those of John Henry Comstock, who wrote *An Introduction to Entomology* at seventy-one, and Asa Gray, who wrote *Elements of Botany* at seventy-seven; these books advanced and defined their fields and remain classics, important to the history of the field even today (Lehman, 1953). Integrative works such as these require wisdom and maturity; it is difficult to imagine them being done by young adults.

Many great works of late life have to do with old age. With intimate knowledge and a vested interest, old scholars and scientists often turn their creative energies to this topic. G. Stanley Hall, twice president of the American Psychological Association in the early 1900s, was one of the first psychologists to examine aging in his book, *Senescence: The Last Half of Life* (Hall, 1923). Hall was seventy-five years old at the time. In medicine, the first book specifically on diseases of old age was written by a physician at age seventy-five, and the first book on senility as a disease was written by a physician at age seventy-one (Lehman, 1953). Numerous elderly inventors have turned their talents to the problems of old age. The most famous is perhaps Benjamin Franklin, who at age seventy-eight invented bifocal lenses for eyeglasses because he himself could not see both near and far with lenses of a single focus.

The list goes on and on, and we have not even mentioned leadership positions, which old people could be fairly said to dominate. Among leadership positions that have been filled more than half the time by people over the age of sixty are popes of the Roman Catholic Church; justices of the United States Supreme Court; speakers of the United States House of Representatives; presidents of France; British prime ministers; presidents of major United States corporations; top-ranking United States Army and Navy commanders (Lehman, 1953). The world as we know it today has been shaped by such leaders as Charles de Gaulle of France, Winston Churchill of Great Britain, and Mao-Tse-tung of China, all of whom held the reins of government when they were in their seventies. George Meany was head of the powerful AFL–CIO labor organization into his eighties. There are many reasons why older people are generally found in positions of power in a society; among the better reasons is that they commonly display wisdom and maturity; they are not "rash" as younger people tend to be; and they know how to orchestrate the activities of large organizations.

We spoke earlier of eminent scholars, scientists, artists, and leaders, but only to illustrate by their extreme creativity the kinds of things that are possible in the later years of life — indeed, are *made* possible by the experiences of many years of life. Mature wisdom, an ability to integrate information, an interest in the aging process, and a talent for leadership are often found in old people eminent only in a small circle of family and friends (Giesen and Datan, 1979). Fine, handcrafted furniture that distills the accumulated knowledge of an elderly carpenter; a family genealogy written by a retired schoolteacher; a demonstration for government policies aiding old people, organized by an old woman like Maggie Kuhn, head of the Gray Panthers — these too are fruits of old age. Some old people set out in totally new directions, learning a new language or, like Grandma Moses, taking up painting for the first time (Borenstein, 1983).

A significant accomplishment of old age, one that may well be related to the resolution of the conflict between integrity and despair, is the increase in altruism and humanitarian concerns during the last part of life. This may to some degree be a compensatory development. Social exchange theory suggests that people in social interactions attempt to increase rewards and minimize costs, thereby obtaining the most profitable outcomes possible (McDonald, 1981). It may be that the majority of older people hold so little power and are sufficiently aware of the limits of their existence that such motives are less influential. Indeed, a study of old people's motives in relocating found that they often felt a sense of relief and freedom once they escaped from the exchange-oriented worklife (Kahana and Kahana, 1982). At the same time, however, people still have a strong need to leave a psychological legacy (Butler, 1975), and in many cases they channel their energies into contributing to the welfare of others for intrinsic reasons alone. Empirical data do show that humanitarian attitudes among the elderly increase (Schaie and Parham, 1976). By participating in volunteer and community efforts, the older person may also avoid the emotional problems that result from dependency and helplessness. Helping others may provide a sense that one's life is meaningful, leading to a sense of competence and increased self-esteem.

Old age, properly considered, is a time of great potential. It is, in the words of Goethe, a time when "knowledge of the world is much clearer. For I am as one who had in youth many small pieces of copper and silver money, who constantly exchanging them for better, beholds now the property of his youth in pieces of pure gold" (Nelson, 1928, p. 310).

Pick up here.

Death and Bereavement *What does it mean*

Death is the natural, biological end to life, but it is much more than that. It is a social event, affecting family and friends, and usually other people as well. If the person was a figure of importance — a leader, for example, like Charles de

Gaulle — the death may mark the end of an era; on the other hand, the death of Jesus marked the beginning of an era. Death is also a psychological event, one each individual must face and come to grips with.

FACING DEATH

Most people have some conscious or unconscious anxiety about death (Lester, 1967). They don't like the thought of it, either of their own death or of someone else's. Exactly what they fear, however, varies from person to person. Many people fear death because it is an unknown and unknowable experience: Is it painful? Is there "life" after death? Anxiety about death may reflect existential concerns, a philosophical wonderment about the nature of the human soul. It may reflect childhood conflicts that, deep in the psyche, remain unresolved — a fear of separation from the protection of loved ones, for example, or feelings of guilt for having failed to discharge one's responsibilities to one's self, family, and community.

Children go through distinct stages in their beliefs about death (Blueband-Langner, 1977; Gardner, 1978). Preschoolers fail to appreciate the irreversibility of death; they tend to think of death as "going away," a reversible separation. Between the ages of six and eleven or twelve, death tends to be personified; the "death man" comes to take away those of whom it is later said, they died. After the age of twelve, death is perceived more or less accurately, as the end of life.

Lanetto (1980) has speculated that anxiety about death reaches its peak during adolescence. He points out that most people in our society reach adolescence with little help from society in conceptualizing and coping with death. This situation may be changing now with the advent of "death education" in schools and colleges. Instructors have found that many students were keeping emotion-laden concerns about death to themselves for lack of opportunity to discuss them (McLendon, 1979). Often these concerns focused on specific people and events in their lives, not on the abstract idea of death. In fact, the experience of death educators suggests that the freedom to deal with mortality on a conceptual level is often hindered by unresolved personal problems, such as guilt feelings about relationships with persons thought to be close to death. There is some evidence that the supportive classroom environment and material presented in classes do help adolescents develop more flexible and comfortable orientations toward death (Wittmaier, 1979; McDonald, 1981).

Though colored with mystical and religious beliefs, death for most people is frightening primarily because it involves *loss* (Kalish, 1976). Death means at least potentially the end of personal identity — the loss of self. No more will the individual smell jasmine or taste honey, solve a problem or have an orgasm; no joy, no hope, not even sweet sorrow. The dead can no longer love or hate, be loved or be hated — at least if the atheists are correct, and one never knows for sure. Death marks the end of relationships — " 'til death do us part." The prospect of never again seeing a spouse, a friend, or even a beloved pet is saddening, a decidedly unpleasant prospect. Many people think about what their death will mean to others, the loss the living will experience. Young adults tend to think most about the grief of friends, whereas middle-aged adults think more about the hardships their death will impose on their families (Diggory and Rothman, 1961).

Anxiety about death is related in complex ways to factors such as age, religious beliefs, and the degree to which the individual has lived a full and satisfying life. Some people are concerned about death from an early age; others, of a less reflective nature, may move into advanced old age continuing their habitual one-day-at-a-time approach to life. Compared to young adults, old people generally think about death more often but fear it less (Kalish, 1976). Probably the fear is less because old people are "socialized" (taught, or led to believe, by society) to expect death and to prepare for it, emotionally as well as financially; death, even the thought of it, is shocking to many young people. Perceptions of social desirability are also influential. Many older adults think they are expected to say wise and gracious things about life and death and consequently do so. Others may feel a need to review their attitudes toward death and revise and transform the relevant beliefs and attitudes. A full and satisfying life appears to further reduce anxiety about death in old people, but among the young and middle-aged it probably increases one's fears. Death at the end of a life well lived is acceptable, but death in the midst of such a life is viewed as something like a tasteless joke played by inscrutable fate.

Kastenbaum (1985) has suggested that useful clues to adults' orientation toward death can be derived by studying people's practical decisions as well as their expressed attitudes. A number of questions can be asked. Has a person made a will and revised it to keep up with changing circumstances? Has a person changed exercise, dietary, or drinking habits out of concern over his or her longevity? Does a person visit or avoid seriously ill friends and relatives? Does a person turn first to the obituary pages of the newspaper or does he or she purposely skip over them? Faced with the probable death of her husband, does a wife take practical steps to adjust?

Nevertheless, it remains difficult to predict the causes and discover the correlates of anxiety about death. A survey of a random sample of American elderly people has, however, shown us some of the factors to which it is not related. These include the respondent's activity level, purpose in life, and tendency toward repression. Surprisingly, anxiety about death does not seem to be related to chronological age, either (Oleshansky, Gamsky, and Ramsmeyer, in press). It appears that death anxiety may be a function of past experience rather than current life circumstances (Bell and Batterson, 1979).

A few correlates of death anxiety are known. Religious beliefs, as you might expect, are generally associated with less than average anxiety about death. But those subjects who usually show the highest death anxiety are not atheists or agnostics; they are the irregular churchgoers, people who are inconsistent in their beliefs and practices (Kalish, 1976). In another study, Zen meditators and psychedelic drug users showed even less anxiety about death than religion students

(Garfield, 1974). The interpretation? "Perhaps because the altered-state groups have had transcendent experiences and have also encountered the blurring of ego lines, so that the difference between self and nonself is diminished, the prospect of death does not pose a condition that is different from what they have already experienced" (Kalish, 1976, p. 492).

THE PROCESS OF DYING

Know all her stuff.

We have been speaking of the fears of death people in general experience, but what of the people who know they are dying? What do they experience?

Perhaps the best-known research on the process of dying is by Elisabeth Kübler-Ross (1969, 1981), a psychiatrist who has observed and interviewed several hundred dying patients. Kübler-Ross identified five stages of dying, each characterized by a certain attitude. The first stage is *denial*, in which the characteristic attitude is expressed something like, "Oh, no! Not me! It can't be true!" Often obvious symptoms of impending death are ignored or treated as if they were unimportant. Denial is followed by *anger*, in which the approaching death is acknowledged, but with rage: "Why me? Why now?" Hostility toward doctors, nurses, and family is common; it is as if someone must be blamed.

A *bargaining* attitude marks the third stage of the dying process. God or even Satan is inundated with pleas for a pardon from the terrible sentence, or at least a postponement. The patient often becomes very compliant, hoping to win some extra time on earth "for good behavior."

The fourth stage is *depression*, a stage of hopelessness, as death is perceived as unavoidable. This "preparatory" sorrow is perhaps necessary for the fifth and final stage: *acceptance*. Stewart Alsop, a noted journalist, expressed his acceptance of his impending death in these words: "A dying man needs to die as a sleepy man needs to sleep, and there comes a time when it is wrong, as well as useless, to resist" (Alsop, 1973, p. 299). Acceptance is not a happy stage, but neither is it a sad one. "It is almost void of feelings. It is as if the pain had gone, the struggle is over" (Kübler-Ross, 1969, p. 100).

Kübler-Ross' work has awakened interest in the psychological aspects of dying and has undoubtedly been of help to people trying to understand the feelings of a loved one whose death is imminent. As a scientific theory, however, it leaves much to be desired (Shneidman, 1980; Kastenbaum, 1981). Kübler-Ross' interviews were not very systematic; instead of statistical analyses, she offers examples and anecdotes. Other researchers do not find the same five stages (Metzger, 1979). Of the five, only depression is consistently reported (Schulz and Alderman, 1974). Kübler-Ross herself has stated that not everyone expresses each stage, that the stages do not always occur in the same order, and that in fact the patient may exhibit two or even three stages at the same time (Kübler-Ross, 1974). Thus we should not consider Kübler-Ross' ideas as a stage theory of the dying process, as it is so often described, but as an insightful discussion of some of the attitudes that are often displayed by people who are dying.

Denial Of the five attitudes, denial is one of the most frequently discussed (Peterson, 1980). In some people — some of the patients and some of their loved ones — denial takes the extreme form of a defense mechanism. The idea of impending death is denied access to consciousness, and the opposite is asserted, often vehemently: "I am *not* dying!" In some cases, the patient (or loved one) denies even the obvious symptoms: "I am *not* having trouble breathing!" In others, denial breaks the link between symptom and implication: "So I'm having a little trouble breathing. That means *nothing!*" In still other forms, the symptoms and implications are admitted, but the patient blithely maintains that he or she is an exception: "Untreatable lung cancer does *not* always mean death, you know" (Weisman, 1972).

Outright denial is common in some form at some time in the process of dying. More common, however, is the conscious avoidance of talk about death in the presence of the person who is dying. Societal standards of etiquette require that if one person involved in the process — the patient, a loved one, or the doctor or nurse — does not want to talk about it, no one should. Death then becomes a taboo topic, and also no one is permitted to discuss the major symptoms or the future. If someone breaks the code (for instance, if someone starts crying), that person must be ignored; discussions of the weather, the quality of hospital food, and how to sleep in a hospital environment must continue unabated (Glaser and Strauss, 1965, 1977; Shneidman, 1980).

Often those attending a dying person do not desire this conspiracy of silence, but they are in a quandary. In *Anna Karenina,* Leo Tolstoy describes the feelings of Levin as he sits with his dying brother.

> He did not know what to say, how to look, how to walk. To talk of things that did not matter seemed an outrage, something quite impossible to him; to talk of death, of something else that was grim and depressing, was equally impossible. To keep silent was impossible, too. "If I look at him, he'll think I'm watching him, afraid of him; if I don't look at him, he'll imagine that I'm thinking of something else. If I walk on tiptoe, he won't like it; to walk in the ordinary way seems wrong somehow." (Tolstoy, 1961, p. 499)

Although the suppression of discussion of death and dying is typically motivated by humanitarian concerns, it should be realized that sparing someone's feelings has a price tag (Glaser and Strauss, 1965). If the impending death were to be openly discussed, the patient as well as his or her loved ones might benefit from a sharing of sorrow. Typically, problems arise upon the death of a family member; these could be discussed and possible solutions could be formulated. Many times the dying patient has "unfinished business" (a will to be drawn up, a petty argument with a friend that needs to be made up), and a denial that life is ending prohibits him or her from tying up these loose ends.

Anger Anger is a common response to news that one is soon to die. People feel cheated and frustrated, and they "do not go gentle into that good night." They rail against God, Nature, their doctor, and whatever other scapegoat they can imagine. Their loved ones, feeling the same sense of loss, sympathize and may feel anger themselves.

Anger can be a valuable experience, a way of integrating death with the rest of one's life (Peterson, 1980). Two common examples come to mind. One is the death of a young adult — "before his time," as we say. The sense of being cheated out of a full measure of life is particularly strong in such an event, but the search for meaning that results can add immeasurably to life, as many parents of children with cancer can attest. Anger in an older person may represent important values: One young woman spoke of her father, an atheist, who raged against a priest she called in to administer last rites. In his last effort, he rose in bed and said to the priest, "Go to hell!" The woman was embarrassed, of course, and half-afraid that he had alienated God. But she was also half-pleased that he had managed to keep to his own values to the end.

Bargaining   Though the literary view of bargaining at the time of death pictures pacts with God or the devil, probably the most common negotiations involve attempts to live "just a little longer, until. . . ." Usually some important event is anticipated such as the completion of a significant work of some sort, the birth of a grandchild, or the like. There is much anecdotal evidence of dying people "hanging on" until the important event — Thomas Jefferson, for example, who managed to stay alive until July 4, 1826, the "golden anniversary" of the signing of the Declaration of Independence. A considerable amount of research suggests that there is a "death dip" (a lower-than-average death rate) before birthdays, with a corresponding rise in the death rate after the birthdays (Phillips, 1972; Phillips and Feldman, 1973), but recent reanalyses of these data cast suspicion on the conclusion that some people somehow manage to last until their birthday before dying (Schulz and Bazerman, 1980). Nevertheless, the notion that one can put off death for a short time in order to experience a positive event remains an intriguing possibility, though it now has the status of an untested hypothesis (Rowland, 1977).

If the hypothesis should prove to be valid, another question immediately arises:

> How is it that looking forward to something delays death? Does a state of positive anticipation precipitate neurochemical changes that have a positive effect on health . . .? An alternative explanation is that behaviors are changed when important events are anticipated. The vulnerable individual may follow his or her health regimen more closely or may adopt a more pleasant interaction style with others, who then reciprocate and thereby reduce the amount of stress the individual is exposed to. These are important questions that have a bearing not only on these phenomena but on psychosomatic phenomena in general. (Schulz and Bazerman, 1980, p. 260)

Alternative viewpoints   Future research on the process of dying will further clarify the role of attitudes such as denial, anger, and bargaining; their sequence too will be explored in the stage theories of the future. Indeed, stage theories in general will compete with other approaches, as they do in many areas of developmental psychology. For example, stage theories can be contrasted with the views of Edwin Shneidman (1974, 1980), whose research on death and dying is almost as famous as that of Kübler-Ross and considerably more scientific.

Shneidman sees death as imposing burdens of two kinds. First, one must prepare oneself for one's own death. Second, one must deal with the interpersonal aspects of death that will have an effect on one's loved ones. They must prepare themselves to be survivors. The process of confronting these two burdens, he says, involves continual alternation between pervasive emotional states, including grief, anguish, anger, anxiety, and denial. Shneidman describes dying people, for example, who shock a listener one day with their candor in expressing their profound acceptance of imminent death, and then shock the same listener the next day with their unrealistic talk of leaving the hospital and going on a trip. This interplay between acceptance and denial, understanding and disbelieving, reflects a deeper dialogue in which the person's knowing that death is imminent is balanced with the need to "not know" in order to survive the final ordeal.

A third perspective on dying is offered by Pattison (1977). This perspective suggests that death itself is not a problem of life because it is not amenable to treatment or intervention. What is important is the process of dying — especially since advances in medicine have prolonged the period of dying to such an extent that it comprises a new life stage, the living–dying interval. This stage has three phases: the acute crisis phase, the chronic living–dying phase, and the terminal phase.

During the acute crisis phase, Pattison says, we should attempt to prevent the chaotic disintegration of the person's life, integrating the dying process with the person's lifestyle and circumstances. This is the stage when emotional support is most important, especially if anxiety can be reduced by attempts to be realistic.

During the chronic living–dying phase, the dying person must deal with a number of fears, including fears of the unknown, of loneliness, of sorrow, of loss of family and friends, of loss of body, of loss of self-control, of suffering and pain, of loss of identity, and of regression. At the beginning of this phase, the dying person typically has hopeful expectations — for example, that the disease will go into spontaneous remission or that a cure will be discovered.

A change in this attitude signals the onset of the terminal phase. The person may continue to be hopeful — that is, he or she may still wish to keep living — but the expectation that this hope will be realized no longer exists. This change in the quality of hope may be involved in the psychological process of giving up and surrendering to death.

Unanswered questions Research on dying needs to be expanded to investigate a greater variety of influences. For example, the nature of the disease probably affects the way a person dies; dying of cancer, many physicians report, is different from dying of emphysema or heart disease. As one reviewer states, the mere mention of the word "cancer" strikes terror into the hearts of patients (Spikes, 1980). Cancer elicits fantasies of violence and sadism and the idea, sometimes unconscious, that the patient ("victim") is being forced to submit passively to a merciless killer.

The relationship between physical and mental state will certainly be a concern of researchers in the future. As an example of this complex interaction, one study of terminally ill patients who appeared to be in a stage of quiet acceptance (as defined by Kübler-Ross) found that 75 percent were suffering from organic brain disorders, many no doubt induced by the life-threatening illness itself (Spikes, 1980). Also, there might be sex differences, and almost certainly ethnic differences, in the style of dying. A teenager dies differently than someone very old, and dying at home is different from dying in a hospital. Personality is also important: "We approach our death to some extent as the type of person we have always been — reflective or impulsive, warm or aloof, whatever. A view of the dying process that excludes personality as such must also exclude much of reality" (Kastenbaum, 1975, p. 43).

The hospice movement   In the last decade there have been major developments in the effort to improve the humane treatment of the dying. Many of these developments have grown out of the hospice movement, which emphasizes the individuality of patients as well as the needs and right of families and caregivers. Hospices provide an alternative to a final stay in the hospital for terminal patients. At the hospice, the goal is to relieve the pain and preserve the dignity of the dying person, not to use technology in every way possible to prolong a person's life in circumstances that may prove to be destructive to the dying patient and his or her family (Lack, 1978; Hamilton and Reid, 1980). The growth of hospice services has produced a new group of compassionate and skillful caregivers, including many elderly people, whose maturity and coping skills make them valuable volunteers. Hospice research has also added new dimensions to our knowledge of the dying process (Greer, 1983; Kastenbaum, 1985).

One recent focus of attention has been the fact that, in addition to the well-recognized pattern of gradual decline, there may be a more discontinuous pathway to death. For example, sudden falls that are not in themselves serious may signal rapid terminal deterioration (Howell, 1980). A traditional hospital would discharge the patient after he or she recovered from the fall, not recognizing that continuing support is often needed because the fall signals a broader systematic decline. On the other hand, hospices often release patients and provide supportive care when a patient expresses a wish to die at home (Buckingham and Foley, 1978; Buckingham, 1982). Hospices may reverse the trend toward providing less than first-rate care to dying elderly patients (Hamilton and Reid, 1980).

The right to die   A final basic issue that must be addressed is whether people should be allowed to die naturally when keeping them alive through heroic efforts will only bring them unmitigated suffering or permit them a vegetative existence.

Medical advances permit us to keep some people alive who would have died from their ailment a few decades ago. In some cases, however, their level of functioning is minimal and they can no longer experience life in a meaningful way. Others are kept alive to suffer for long periods of time (Butler, 1975).

Most of us would abhor "active" euthanasia, in which those who are presumed to be hopelessly sick or disabled are killed. The issue is far less clear, however, with "passive" euthanasia, in which medical care that might prolong life is withheld. On the one hand, medical technology may be perceived as being cruel when it prolongs the life of a person who would die soon in any event. On the other hand, a similar argument could be used to justify withholding medical care for the elderly because such care is considered wasteful. Furthermore, there is the problem of not knowing the outcome of a procedure in advance. For one terminally ill cancer patient, major surgery may be nothing more than an ordeal; for another, it might have life-enhancing effects, permitting greater mobility, for example (Butler and Lewis, 1982). Another consideration is that prolonging life unnecessarily may have severe psychological and economic consequences for the family of the dying person.

Thus it is difficult to determine when medical efforts should cease. Some patients really are the living dead: they breathe and their hearts beat, but they are incapable of any response that we would characterize as being "human." For this reason, modern definitions are coming to recognize death as the irreversible destruction of the brain, but this too is more difficult to recognize than most people would think. It is also difficult to determine who should decide when life support systems should be turned off and what the rules should be when they are (Baron, 1981).

Matters become even more complicated when we are dealing with a critically ill person who has expressed a wish to die. Should individuals be allowed to make that decision? There has been much discussion of "living wills," formal documents in which physicians and family are directed to refrain from so-called heroic and life-sustaining treatments when all hope of potential recovery is gone. There are problems, however, with such documents, in that their legal status has not yet been clearly established, and that they may be ignored by professional caretakers because of their fear of potential malpractice liability. As it stands now, some suffering persons who are near death may be virtually forced either to commit suicide or to have their loved ones consider killing them (Siegal, 1982). Any alternative that would allow physicians to practice active euthanasia, even at the behest of their patients, could lead to serious abuse, and in any event would be cause for much legitimate public controversy (Levenson and List, 1981; Meiner and Cassell, 1983).

THE SURVIVORS: BEREAVEMENT AND GRIEF

Death ends the suffering of the dying, but the family faces a long period of adjustment. We refer to the family, collectively, as "the bereaved" — that is, those who have lost something dear. We give a name to what they are feeling —

grief. We expect some instability, until they adapt to life without the one who "passed away."

Throughout this book we have described the family as a system of interdependent relationships. The death of a family member disrupts this system; the family is "dismembered" (Peterson, 1980). Adjustment, in family terms, reflects the attempt to restore equilibrium to the system; roles and tasks must be reassigned, and power alignments must be revised. If the deceased was the family leader and primary source of income (the father, for example, of a relatively young family), adjustment obviously must be radical and pervasive, but even the loss of the youngest child may require considerable change. *what pos. in family.*

Rituals Following the death of a family member most families encounter a set of rituals or ceremonies that simultaneously help them handle their grief and express certain societal values and beliefs about death. A funeral service is usually the keystone of this ritualistic structure; the deceased's better qualities are praised, and the beliefs of his or her religion about death and life after death are stated. The family is kept busy with details (making decisions about arrangements, contacting relatives, and so on), while friends and community organizations offer their support (bringing hams and casseroles, for example). Wakes, "sitting shiva," and other rituals complement the funeral service. After burial (or other ceremonies, if the body is cremated or donated to medical research), there is often a ritualistic social gathering, which is not always an unhappy occasion, where the bereaved and their friends can further work out their feelings. In even the simplest of cases, more detail work follows the funeral. If there is a will, it is read and executed. Old clothing must be distributed, old photo albums must be examined, thank-you notes must be written. One need not concern oneself with decisions about dress; in this country, black or dark attire is traditional.

Research evidence on the effect of rituals is lacking, but most psychologists believe the ceremonial behaviors lessen the effect of severe grief. By giving the bereaved some easy work to do, the rituals prevent rumination and wallowing. They also muster community support for people who very much need support at this time. The rituals include formal opportunities for the bereaved to consider their relationships with the deceased and their lives without him or her. And they state facts, values, and beliefs (belief in an afterlife, for example) that promote positive thinking. Even the cemetery plays a role; it is, as one sociologist called it, "the city of the dead," a symbolic replica of the living community (Warner, 1965). The cemetery is an expression of the belief that the "social personality" of the deceased is still with us, though the physical body is without life. One's influence on others remains; it is a sort of eternal life.

Grieving As there are supposedly stages in the acceptance of one's own death, there are probably definable stages also in the acceptance of the death of a loved one. One theorist has proposed three broad stages, which, he claims, are observable not only in humans but in many species of animals as well (Bowlby, 1974). In the first, the bereaved yearn for the deceased; anger born of the inevitable frustration of their craving may also be observed. The second stage is character-ized by apathy and disorganized behavior. Finally, the bereaved get themselves together and reorganize their life. In human terms, these stages might be called (1) denial/anger, (2) depression, and (3) acceptance/readjustment (Spikes, 1980). So put, the stages of grieving are strikingly similar to the stages of dying proposed by Kübler-Ross.

The severity of these reactions and the time span over which they endure vary, depending on factors such as the individual's closeness to the deceased, the social support available, and the degree to which the death was expected (Gal-lagher, Thompson, and Peterson, 1981–82). "Grieving" reactions are even observed in children as young as twelve months of age. When placed with strangers, such children make determined efforts to recover their lost mothers. For days the children cry loudly, throw themselves about, and search eagerly, as if hopefully, for any sight or sound that might prove to be their missing mothers (Bowlby, 1980). For a week or so, hopeful looking about alternates with periods of urgent distress. But eventually despair sets in. The child continues to long for the mother's return, but with less and less hope that she actually will come back. Ultimately, the child's demands cease, and he or she becomes apathetic and withdrawn. At this stage, the child cries intermittently in a state of great misery.

A similar pattern of response is also observed in people who clearly do know that they have suffered bereavement or some other catastrophic loss. Indeed, it is a familiar sight among institutionalized geriatric patients. This behavioral re-sponse, then, is associated with a perception of critical loss (Kastenbaum, 1985).

Of course, all deaths do not have the same meaning or result in the same level of social disruption. It has been suggested that the death of aged people has relatively little influence on society. Several studies have found that the death of an elderly parent was less disruptive, less emotionally debilitating, and generally less significant for adult children than either the death of a spouse or the death of a child (Sanders, 1979; Owens, Fulton, and Markusen, 1983). The survivors of the death of a parent were less likely to have a traditional funeral ritual and less likely to become ill in subsequent months. The impact of the death of an elderly parent may be diminished by its predictability and by the factors that have diminished the influence of the nuclear family. Another factor may be that the adult child repeatedly considers and rehearses the death of a parent; there is certainly less of a taboo associated with anticipating the death of a parent than with anticipating the death of a spouse or a child. By anticipating the death of a parent over many decades, the adult child is prepared for it when it comes (Moss and Moss, 1980). The process may also involve subtle preparation for one's own death.

At the other extreme, some people find the loss of a loved one — spouse, child, or parent — so unbearably painful that the grief can be described as pathological. Such grief may involve feelings of self-hatred and loss of self-esteem; in some cases, mourners may even attempt to take their own lives. Pathological grief has been viewed as an unusually prolonged or intense form of the experience of normal grief. During pathological grief, self-images and modes of interacting with others that were held in check by the existence of the deceased person may reemerge (Horowitz et al., 1980; Kaltreider, Becker, and Horowitz, 1983).

The bereaved have good periods and bad periods; the proportion of bad periods decreases over time. Some social withdrawal by the bereaved is traditional. In one study, widows tended to withdraw from activities for about two months; after that, they reported that they "were themselves" again (Glick, Weiss, and Parkes, 1974). Some disorganization in behavior and emotions typically continues, however, for a year or two (Schulz, 1978).

The newly bereaved person is often treated by society ". . . as a sick person. Employers expect him to miss work, he stays at home, and relatives visit and talk in hushed tones. For a time, others take over responsibility for making decisions and acting on his behalf" (Parkes, 1972, p. 5). Most people believe that it is inappropriate to return to work immediately after the death of someone close, and they also think it improper for someone who has lost a spouse to "go out with" others of the opposite sex for at least six months (Kalish and Reynolds, 1976). There is much variability in such beliefs, however; 20 percent of people over sixty felt that it is unimportant to wait for any length of time before remarrying, whereas 34 percent felt that one should wait at least five years.

Health The health of people who are grieving over the loss of a loved one seems to suffer. Compared to people of the same age, recently widowed people have more physical complaints and visit their doctors more often (Parkes, 1972). The death rate of bereaved persons is generally found to be higher than one would expect, at least for the first six months following the death (Schulz, 1978). Some studies report a rise in death rate only for bereaved people under sixty-five, with no such increase among the elderly (Rees and Lutkins, 1967).

Interpretations of these data include: (1) the stress of bereavement makes illness and death more likely; (2) the stress of bereavement leads to life-threatening behaviors, such as smoking, drinking, a lack of interest in exercise, and poor sleep habits; (3) bereaved people were understandably unwilling to do much about their own medical problems before their loved one died, and thus an increase in doctor's visits represents an averaging-out of medical complaints between the pre- and postdeath periods (untreated problems, of course, can become more serious and even increase the chances of death). Perhaps all these factors are present in some degree or another. Also, some reviewers are sharply critical of the research that underlies these data (Clayton, 1973; Stroebe et al., 1980). Perhaps there is no real increase in illness or death to interpret.

Therapy People who have lost a loved one can usually benefit from supportive psychotherapy or counseling; some are in desperate need of such help (Horowitz et al., 1980). Often another family member provides emotional support, and religion is a source of comfort for many. A good friend serves the need for some (Kalish and Reynolds, 1976). One particularly effective program is the widow-to-widow counseling begun in Boston in the 1960s (Silverman, 1969). This program trains widowed people who have reorganized their lives to help those more recently bereaved.

One of the major problems faced by widows is the inferior status of women in society. The widows cannot (or think that they cannot) function well without their husbands, who provided the bulk of the income and who escorted them to various activities (see also Chapter 6). Thus it should not be surprising to learn that women's consciousness-raising groups are among the most effective forms of therapy for grieving widows (Barrett, 1974). In these groups, the widows consider sex-role stereotypes — the woman as passive, dependent, incompetent — and discuss the ways in which these stereotypes affect their adjustment as widows. They may also be given "assertiveness training" to provide them with the knowledge and the confidence to lead independent lives in a male-oriented, youth-oriented, and couple-oriented society.

The Eldest Leslie

Lavinia Leslie, mother of Leonard, is dying. She is eighty-seven years old. She lives in a nursing home, to which she retired last year after breaking her hip. She has a widespread cancer of the lungs that is developing slowly but threatens to kill her in a year or two; her doctors decided that radiation, chemotherapy, or surgery would be useless, that it would only make her ill. She has no pain, although breathing is sometimes difficult. We asked her how she felt about the nursing home.

"It's all right. It's boring, but then the life of an eighty-seven-year-old woman with a broken hip doesn't promise much in the way of excitement, even in the best of circumstances. I'm glad I'm here, don't get me wrong. What with my hip, my cancer — my age in general — I'd be a problem for Leonard or Larry to handle. This way I feel more independent, even though I depend now on the people here at the home; they get paid for helping me, so they can't complain."

"Leonard says he feels guilty about you being here, and Larry told us he tried to talk you into coming to live with them."

"Oh, no, I couldn't live with them, not with any of them. They're just being dutiful children. I'd guess they're happy I took the decision out of their hands by coming here. I think everyone's better off; everyone's happier this way. Oh, my goodness! The very thought of living with Leonard! He's about to get married again, to some young thing! He's a loving son, don't get me wrong. But he gets a little uneasy around me these days."

"Uneasy? Why?"

"Well, I think he thinks about getting old himself. When we reach Leonard's age, we start peering around the corner, and there's old Mr. Death peering back at us. It's not a pleasant experience, especially when you're about to marry a young woman."

"You seem to be spending a lot of time and energy — and money — to keep from being a burden. Don't you think that you deserve a little tender, loving care? You've worked hard all your life, you've made plenty of sacrifices for your family; there isn't a person in the family that you haven't had to care for at one time or another. Now you're down with a broken hip. Why shouldn't they return a little of the love they're received all these years from you?"

"What you say is true. Our family is very close, and we're all very family-oriented. When one of us needs help, the others are all quick to respond. But we all have our own lives to lead, and I don't see why I should make life difficult for Leonard or Larry when I'm perfectly content here."

"Do you accept any help at all from your family?"

"Oh, goodness, yes! They come to visit, they chauffeur me around when I have to go someplace, Laura helps me buy clothes and things — Linda, too. They bring me home almost every Sunday for dinner. Yes. They do a lot for me."

"Does this much help bother you?"

"No. You know, you're right — about deserving a *little* consideration after all these years. I've earned it! I deserve it! There! Does that make you feel better?"

"Yes."

"I think if you know yourself and your family, it's all right to accept a little help from your family. Let's face it, when you're old, you need more help. You don't want it to be too much, though; keep it in reasonable bounds. And you don't want to use your helplessness as a weapon, as I've seen some of the people here do. They whine and cry and make their children feel just terrible. Guilty. If you make people feel guilty, you've got a lot of power over them."

"Do you think about your own death?"

"Of course! Don't be ridiculous! I'm eighty-seven years old, my good man, and I'm full of cancer. It won't be long now."

"Well, what do you think when you think about it?"

"I don't think about what happens after death, if that's what you mean. There's no way we can know that. My religion has certain beliefs, but I've never taken them literally. It's more like poetry — the poetry of afterlife. What I do think about is that I'll never see my family anymore, I'll never see my friends again. I'll miss my favorite TV shows! Isn't that silly? I think about what I'll lose when I die, and it makes me very sad."

"You mentioned the poetry of afterlife. What do you make of the term, 'eternal life'?"

"I believe in eternal life through your children. I believe that you live forever in the hearts and minds of everyone who knew you. Maybe there's another kind of eternal life, too, more like the kind the preachers are always telling us about; I don't know about that. What's more, I don't care. I don't think that way anymore. I remember reading once that Shakespeare said something about the world being a great stage and all the people were actors. Well, I think he was onto something. You come onto the stage and your purpose is to give the best performance you possibly can — an honest performance, one that moves those who see it. Then you exit, and your part of the play is over. If your performance was well done, you don't have any regrets that the play is over."

"So you wouldn't mind if people applauded at your funeral, instead of crying."

"No, I wouldn't mind that a bit. I'd be very proud."

Summary

1. Old age is often viewed as a single stage of life, but it can be divided into at least three stages: the "young old" (between sixty-five and seventy-five and eighty), the old old (age seventy-five or eighty to about ninety), and the very old (age ninety or above). The three groups differ in significant ways.

2. In Erik Erikson's view, the basic developmental issue of late life is *integrity* versus *despair*. One of the chief impediments to personal integrity is the fear or the reality of financial, physical, or emotional dependency. Most old people, however, are financially secure and in reasonably good health, with friends and family to combat loneliness. Senior centers and other government-sponsored programs have done much to alleviate the problems of dependency in late life. Some older people move to retirement communities or nursing homes. Those who move to retirement communities tend to be relatively affluent; the type of retirement community sought is a reflection of dependency needs. Nursing homes are primarily housing for the old old and very old. Moving to a nursing home does not generally involve severing relationships with family and friends. Studies show that nursing home staff members often encourage dependency among residents.

3. In healthy old people, creativity flourishes in a degree not significantly reduced from the levels exhibited by younger adults. The creative productions of old scholars, scientists, and artists benefit from their experience and wisdom. Often the works represent an intellectual integration of the observations of a lifetime, and many of these works have to do with old age itself. A society ruled by the old is called a gerontocracy. Government by the old is not necessarily government for the old, however. Altruism and humanitarian concerns typically increase in old age.

4. Most people have a certain amount of conscious or unconscious anxiety about death; old people, who expect death soon, are less anxious than young people. Young children often personify death as a being who takes people away, and these personifications continue in adult literature and fantasy, for example, the Grim Reaper. The most fundamental feature of death, to both the dying and the survivors, is *loss* — loss of self, loss of a loved one.

5. Kübler-Ross sees the process of dying in five stages: denial, anger, bargaining, depression, and acceptance. Denial or avoidance of the topic of death in the presence of dying is common and understandable, although it can prevent the

dying person from carrying out important last-minute duties. Anger results from frustration and imminent loss. Bargaining may take the form of changes in behavior that the individual hopes will allow a few more days or weeks of life, perhaps until some important event, like a birthday. Depression, as we might imagine, is the most common emotion among the dying. Although Kübler-Ross has done much to stimulate interest in the emotional life of dying individuals, her stage theory has not received much empirical support. If a stage theory is appropriate at all, it will probably have to be modified to account for age, sex, ethnic, and other differences in the process of dying.

6. Shneidman sees death as imposing two kinds of burdens: one must prepare for one's own death and one must deal with the effects of one's death on one's loved ones. Pattison regards the period of dying as a new life stage, the living–dying interval. This stage has three phases: the acute crisis phase, the chronic living–dying phase, and the terminal phase. The hospice movement provides an alternative to hospital care for terminally ill patients. Hospices emphasize the comfort and dignity of patients rather than the use of elaborate and expensive technology to prolong the lives of suffering patients as much as possible. The question of whether an individual should be able to choose to die is controversial. Most of us would abhor "active" euthanasia, in which the hopelessly sick are killed, but "passive" euthanasia, in which medical care that might prolong life is withheld, is more problematical. The issue is especially complex when the ill patient has expressed a wish to die.

7. "Bereavement" originally meant the state of having been robbed of something and now is used in reference to the family and friends of the person who died. Grief, the extreme sadness most bereaved people feel, is helped by rituals, such as the funeral, which give the bereaved something to do and time to sort out their thoughts and feelings. Stage theories of the grieving process are similar to those of the dying process — from denial/anger to depression to acceptance/ readjustment — which makes sense if loss (anticipated or actual) is the key feature in both processes. Grieving reactions have been noted even in very young children. All deaths do not have the same meaning or result in the same level of social disruption; the deaths of aged people, for example, may have relatively little influence on society. Some people, on the other hand, suffer from a grief so extreme that it can be considered pathological.

SUGGESTED READINGS

Butler, R. N. (1975). *Why survive? Being old in America.* New York: Harper & Row. Pulitzer prize winning exposé on the condition and meaning of life of America's elderly.

Kastenbaum, R. (1985). Dying and death: A life-span approach. In J. E. Birren and K. W. Schaie (Eds.), *Handbook of the psychology of aging* (2nd ed.) (pp. 619–643). New York: Van Nostrand Reinhold. Provides a theoretical basis for analyzing death and dying and discusses the personal and social support for the dying and those left behind during bereavement.

Moos, R. H., and Lemke, S. (1985). Specialized living environments for older people. In J. E. Birren and K. W. Schaie (Eds.), *Handbook of the psychology of aging* (2nd ed.) (pp.

864–889). New York: Van Nostrand Reinhold. A review of specialized housing for the elderly, describing methods for assessing the quality of such settings and discussing the relationship between the characteristics of residents and the facilities that serve them.

Schultz, J. H. (1985). *The economics of aging* (3rd ed.). New York: Van Nostrand Reinhold. Facts and fictions regarding the actual economic status of the elderly, including a review of the adequacy of the money income of the elderly and the status of major pension and welfare programs.

Schulz, R., and Bazerman, M. (1980). Ceremonial occasions and mortality: A second look. *American Psychologist, 35,* 253–261. A critical review of research on the hypothesis that timing of death may be affected by such matters as the impending holiday season, a person's birthday, or other meaningful events.

Intellectual Self-Management in Old Age

Although he is over eighty, B. F. Skinner is continuing his productive work in behavioral psychology. He admits that being older makes it more difficult to do demanding intellectual work, but he also recognizes that it is possible to compensate for many of the deficits of old age. He discussed some of the problems of old age and how he deals with them in an address to the American Psychological Association that was later published in the *American Psychologist*.

Aging, Skinner says, can be seen as a process involving two factors. One is the person, the organism subject to the biological process of growing old. The other is the person's world, the physical and social environment in which he or she lives. Biological aging is an inexorable process, but "environmental aging" is not. As Skinner put it, "If many of the problems of old people are due to shortcomings in their environments, the environments can be improved" (p. 239).

Many remedial steps of this sort are well known. One can wear glasses for vision improvement and hearing aids for hearing improvement. Of particular concern to Skinner, however, are the steps the elderly can take to maintain their creative thinking abilities. He suggests that people can benefit from using a variety of aids — some mental, some material — to compensate for declining abilities.

One common problem is forgetting names. When he has time, Skinner finds, he can almost always remember a name by using prompts such as going through the alphabet and testing for the first letter. When it is impossible to use such a technique and one must admit that one has forgotten a person's name, it is important to keep "name-forgetting" from becoming an anxiety-producing event, which would only complicate the problem. It may help, Skinner says, to accept one's deficiencies calmly and gracefully, perhaps flattering one's listener in the process. If one is skillful at that sort of thing, forgetting may even become a sort of pleasure and so will not exacerbate the problem by causing anxiety.

The problem in old age is not so much how to have ideas but how to have them when one can use them, Skinner says. Thinking of the solution to a problem is of little use if one forgets it before one has taken advantage of it. He suggests keeping a written or recorded record of one's ideas as they occur: "In place of memories, memoranda" (p. 240). Appropriate preparations can be helpful in other contexts too. If one tends to forget the main track of one's thought when one makes a digression, one should resolve not to make digressions. If one tends to lose one's train of thought when saying long sentences, resolve to use short sentences. If one is going to attend a class reunion, check one's alumni register and reacquaint oneself with the names of the people who will be there.

Another common problem for the aged is mental fatigue. It may be necessary, Skinner says, to be content with fewer working hours per day. One should also learn to recognize the symptoms of fatigue. Skinner mentions several, including an unusual use of profanity, bad handwriting, and mistakes in playing the piano. In his writing, he finds that he uses clichés when he is tired. A related concern is the tendency to follow the same well-worn paths in one's thinking. The unique idea is the one most difficult to think of. It helps to do everything one can to make it easy to think novel thoughts, perhaps simply by having pens and pencils conveniently available, by using a good typewriter or word processor, and by having a convenient filing system.

According to Skinner, the lack of motivation often attributed to the elderly might more properly be considered a lack of reinforcement. The activities of the elderly are more likely to be followed by aches and fatigue and less likely to evoke a positive response than the activities of younger people. Our culture does not generously reinforce the behavior of old people. People are often receptive to the personal reminiscences of the elderly, but this can encourage older people to live in the past rather than the present and future. When working on a paper, the older scholar is likely to receive reinforcement less frequently from being able to solve a problem, say precisely what he or she wants in a sentence, or effectively characterize a situation. Whether one will continue to attempt scholarly work, Skinner says, will depend on the schedule on which one was reinforced in the past. Those who are accustomed to sometimes waiting quite a long time before receiving reinforcement will have less trouble remaining active.

A final factor Skinner mentions is the importance of having an audience. Retired persons no longer talk with colleagues in their fields. The solution to this problem is a simple one: organize a discussion group, even if it consists only of two people. Two heads together are better than both apart. At the same time, however, one must avoid those who try too hard to be helpful and who too readily flatter one. Those who help those who can help themselves do people a disservice by making the good things in life no longer properly contingent on behavior. "If you have been very successful," Skinner says, "the most sententious stupidities will be received as pearls of wisdom, and your standards will instantly fall. If you are still struggling to be successful, flattery will more often than not put you on the wrong track by reinforcing useless behavior" (p. 244).

In sum, the secret of doing productive work in old age is to construct a world in which one's behavior is abundantly reinforced and as free as possible from aversive consequences — what Skinner calls a "prosthetic environment." Difficulties are inevitable, but with the correct approach they are not insurmountable. In his address, he concluded by offering himself as an example of what can be accomplished, paraphrasing Dr. Johnson: "Sir, an aged lecturer is like a dog walking on his hinder legs. It is not done well; but you are surprised to find it done at all" (p. 244).

Skinner, B. F. (1983). Intellectual self-management in old age. *American Psychologist, 38,* 77–84.

GENERAL RESOURCES

Handbooks

Binstock, R. H., and Shanas, E. (Eds.) (1985). *Handbook of aging and the social sciences* (2nd ed.). New York: Van Nostrand Reinhold.

Birren, J. E., and Schaie, K. W. (Eds.) (1985). *Handbook of the psychology of aging* (2nd ed.). New York: Van Nostrand Reinhold.

Birren, J. E., and Sloane, R. B. (Eds.) (1980). *Handbook of mental health and aging.* Englewood Cliffs, NJ: Prentice-Hall.

Busse, E. W., and Blazer, D. G. (Eds.) (1980). *Handbook of geriatric psychiatry.* New York: Van Nostrand Reinhold.

Finch, C. E., and Schneider, E. L. (Eds.) (1985). *Handbook of the biology of aging* (2nd ed.). New York: Van Nostrand Reinhold.

International Federation on Ageing (1985). *International glossary of social gerontology.* New York: Van Nostrand Reinhold.

Monk, A. (Ed.) (1985). *Handbook of gerontological services.* New York: Van Nostrand Reinhold.

Wolman, B. B. (Ed.) (1982). *Handbook of developmental psychology.* Englewood Cliffs, NJ: Prentice-Hall.

Serials

Baltes, P. B., and Brim, O. G. (Eds.). *Life-span development and behavior.* New York: Academic Press, 1978, 1979, 1980, 1982, 1983, 1984, 1985. (Volumes 1–7 now available.)

Eisdorfer, C. (Ed.). *Annual Review of Gerontology and Geriatrics.* New York: Springer, 1980, 1981, 1982, 1984, 1985 (Volumes 1–5 now available.)

Volumes with Broad Coverage of Topics

Atchley, R. C. (1985). *The social forces in later life* (4th ed.) Belmont, CA: Wadsworth.

Baltes, P. B., and Schaie, K. W. (Eds.) (1973). *Life-span developmental psychology: Personality and socialization.* New York: Academic Press.

Brim, O. G., Jr., and Kagan, J. (Eds.) (1980). *Constancy and change in human development.* Cambridge, MA: Harvard University Press.

Callahan, E. J., and McKloskey, K. A. (Eds.) (1983). *Life-span developmental psychology: Non-normative life events.* New York: Academic Press.

Datan, N., and Ginsberg, L. H. (Eds.) (1975). *Life-span developmental psychology: Normative life crises.* New York: Academic Press.

Datan, N., and Reese, H. W. (Eds.) (1977). *Life-span developmental psychology: Dialectical perspectives on experimental research.* New York: Academic Press.

Goulet, L. R., and Baltes, P. B. (Eds.) (1970). *Life-span developmental psychology: Research and theory.* New York: Academic Press.

Hendricks, J., and Hendricks, C. D. (1981). *Aging in mass society: Myth and realities* (2nd ed.). Cambridge, MA: Winthrop.

Knox, A. (1977). *Adult development and learning.* San Francisco: Jossey-Bass.

McCluskey, K. A., and Reese, H. W. (Eds.) (1984). *Life-span developmental psychology: Historical and generational effects.* New York: Academic Press.

Nesselroade, J. R., and Baltes, P. B. (Eds.) (1979). *Longitudinal methods in the study of behavior and development.* New York: Academic Press.

Nesselroade, J. R., and Reese, H. W. (Eds.) (1973). *Life-span developmental psychology: Methodological issues.* New York: Academic Press.

Palmore, E., Busse, E. W., Maddox, G. L., Nowlin, J. B., and Siegler, I. C. (Eds.) (1985). *Normal aging III.* Durham, NC: Duke University Press.

Poon, L. W. (Ed.) (1980). *Aging in the 1980s.* Washington, DC: American Psychological Association.

Santos, J., and VanderBos, G. (Ed.) (1982). *Psychology and the older adult: Challenge for training in the 1980s.* Washington, DC: American Psychological Association.

Schaie, K. W. (Ed.) (1983). *Longitudinal studies of adult psychological development.* New York: Guilford.

Schaie, K. W., Campbell, R. C., Meredith, W. A., and Rawlings, S. A. (Eds.) (1986). *Methodological issues in the study of aging.* New York: Springer.

Storandt, M., Siegler, I. E., and Elias, M. P. (Eds.) (1978). *The clinical psychology of aging.* New York: Plenum.

Turner, R. R., and Reese, H. W. (Eds.) (1980). *Life-span developmental psychology: Intervention.* New York: Academic Press.

Woodruff, D. S., and Birren, J. E. (1983). *Aging: Scientific perspectives and social issues.* Monterey, CA: Brooks/Cole.

Journals

Developmental Psychology
Educational Gerontology
Experimental Aging Research
Gerontologist
Human Development
International Journal of Behavioral Development
International Journal of Aging and Human Development
Journal of Gerontology
Journal of Marriage and the Family
OMEGA, The International Journal of Death and Dying
Psychology and Aging

REFERENCES

Aaronson, B. S. (1958). Age and sex influence on MMPI profile peak distribution in an abnormal population. *Journal of Consulting Psychology, 22,* 203–206.

Aaronson, B. S. (1960). A dimension of personality change with aging. *Journal of Clinical Psychology, 16,* 63–65.

Abramson, L. Y., and Alloy, L. B. (1980). Judgment of contingency: Errors and their implications. In A. Baum and J. Singer (Eds.), *Advances in environmental psychology* (Vol. 2). Hillsdale, NJ: Erlbaum.

Abramson, L. Y., Seligman, M. E. P., and Teasdale, J. (1978). Learned helplessness in humans: Critique and reformulation. *Journal of Abnormal Psychology, 87,* 49–74.

Adams, B. N. (1968). *Kinship in an urban setting.* Chicago: Markham Publishing.

Adams, B. N. (1979). Mate selection in the United States: A theoretical summarization. In W. Burr, R. Hill, I. Nye, and R. Reiss (Eds.), *Contemporary theories about the family* (Vol. 1). *Research-based.* New York: Free Press.

Adams, D. (1954). *The anatomy of personality.* New York: Doubleday.

Adelstein, D., Sedlacek, W., and Martinez, A. (1983). Dimensions underlying the characteristics and needs of returning women students. *Journal of the National Association for Women Deans, Administrators, and Counselors, 47,* 32–37.

Adler, W. (1974). An autoimmune theory of aging. In M. Rockstein (Ed.), *Proceedings of a symposium on the theoretical aspects of aging.* New York: Academic Press.

Advisory Panel (1977). *On further examination: Report of the advisory panel on the Scholastic Aptitude Test score decline.* College Entrance Examination Board.

Ahammer, I. M. (1973). Social-learning theory as a framework for the study of adult personality development. In P. B. Baltes and K. W. Schaie (Eds.), *Life-span developmental psychology: Personality and socialization.* New York: Academic Press.

Ainlay, S. C., and Hunter, J. D. (1984). Religious participation among older Mennonites. *Mennonite Quarterly Review, 58,* 70–79.

Ainlay, S. C., and Smith, R. (1984). Aging and religious participation. *Journal of Gerontology, 39,* 357–363.

Aizenberg, R., and Treas, J. (1985). The family in the late life: Psychosocial and demographic considerations. In J. E. Birren and K. W. Schaie (Eds.), *Handbook of the psychology of aging* (2nd ed.). New York: Van Nostrand Reinhold.

Aldous, J. (1978). *Family careers: Developmental change in families.* New York: Wiley.

Alloy, L. B., and Abramson, L. Y. (1979). Judgment of contingency in depressed and nondepressed students: Sadder but wiser. *Journal of Experimental Psychology: General, 108,* 441–485.

Alloy, L. B., and Abramson, L. Y. (1982). Learned helplessness, depression and the illusion of control. *Journal of Personality and Social Psychology, 42,* 1114–1126.

Alloy, L. B., Abramson, L. Y., Viscusi, D. (1981). Induced mood and the illusion of control. *Journal of Personality and Social Psychology, 41,* 1129–1140.

Alloy, L. B., Peterson, C., Abramson, L. Y., and Seligman, M. E. P. (1984). Attributional style and the generality of learned helplessness. *Journal of Personality and Social Psychology, 45,* 681–687.

Allport, G. W. (1937). *Personality.* New York: Holt, Rinehart & Winston.

Alpert, J. L., and Richardson, M. S. (1980). Parenting. In L. W. Poon (Ed.), *Aging in the 1980s.* Washington, DC: American Psychological Association.

Alsop, S. (1973). *Stay of execution.* New York: Lippincott.

American Psychiatric Association. (1980). *Diagnostic and statistical manual of mental disorders* (3rd ed.). Washington, DC: American Psychiatric Association.

American Psychological Association Monitor. (1983, August). *Low-cost, local programs offer support for families,* pp. 1. Washington, DC: American Psychological Association.

491

Ames, L. B. (1965). Changes in the experience balance scores on the Rorschach at different ages in the life span. *Journal of Genetic Psychology, 106,* 279–286.

Anastasi, A. (1976). *Psychological testing* (4th ed.). New York: Macmillan.

Anderson, B., and Palmore, E. (1974). Longitudinal evaluation of ocular function. In E. Palmore (Ed.), *Normal aging II.* Durham, NC: Duke University Press.

Antonovsky, I. (1981). *Health, stress and coping.* San Francisco: Jossey-Bass.

Arenberg, D., and Robertson-Tchabo, E. A. (1977). Learning and aging. In J. E. Birren and K. W. Schaie (Eds.), *Handbook of the psychology of aging.* New York: Van Nostrand Reinhold.

Arlin, P. K. (1983). Adolescent and adult thought: A structural interpretation. In N. Commons and S. Benack (Eds.), *Post-formal operations.* New York: Praeger.

Ash, P. (1966). Pre-retirement counseling. *Gerontologist, 6,* 127–128.

Atchley, R. C. (1975a). Adjustments to loss of job at retirement. *Aging and Human Development, 6,* 17–27.

Atchley, R. C. (1975b). The life course, age grading, and age-linked demands for decision making. In N. Datan and L. H. Ginsberg (Eds.). *Life-span developmental psychology: Normative life crises.* New York: Academic Press.

Atchley, R. C. (1980). Aging and suicide: Reflection of the quality of life. In S. Haynes and M. Feinleib (Eds.), *Proceedings of the Second Conference on the Epidemiology of Aging.* Washington, DC: U.S. Government Printing Office.

Atchley, R. C. (1982a). The aging self. *Psychotherapy: Theory, Research and Practice, 19,* 338–396.

Atchley, R. C. (1982b). Retirement as a social institution. *Annual Review of Sociology, 8,* 263–287.

Atchley, R. C. (1985). *Social forces and aging: An introduction to social gerontology* (4th ed.). Belmont, CA: Wadsworth.

Atchley, R. C., and Miller, S. J. (1980). Older people and their families. *Annual Review of Gerontology and Geriatrics, 1,* 337–369.

Atchley, R. C., and Miller, S. J. (1983). Types of elderly couples. In T. H. Brubaker (Ed.), *Family relationships in later life.* Beverly Hills, CA: Sage.

Atkinson, J. W., and Birch, D. (1978). *Introduction to motivation* (2nd ed.). New York: Van Nostrand.

Atkinson, J. W., and Shiffrin, R. M. (1968). Human memory: A proposed system and its control processes. In K. W. Spence and J. T. Spence (Eds.), *The psychology of learning and motivation* (Vol. 2). New York: Academic Press.

Auster, C. J., and Auster, D. (1981). Factors influencing women's choice of nontraditional careers: The role of family, peers, and counselors. *The Vocational Guidance Quarterly, 29,* 253–263.

Bahr, H. (1970). Aging and religious disaffiliation. *Social Forces, 49,* 59–71.

Baldessarini, R. J. (1978). Chemotherapy. In A. M. Nicholi (Ed.), *The Harvard guide to modern psychiatry.* New York: Belknap.

Baltes, M. M. (1982). Environmental factors in dependency among nursing home residents: A social ecology analysis. In T. A. Wills (Ed.), *Basic processes in helping relationships.* New York: Academic Press.

Baltes, P. B. (1979). Life-span developmental psychology: Some converging observations on history and theory. In P. B. Baltes and O. G. Brim, Jr. (Eds.), *Life-span development and behavior* (Vol. 2). New York: Academic Press.

Baltes, P. B., Cornelius, S. W., and Nesselroade, J. R. (1979). Cohort effects in developmental psychology. In J. R. Nesselroade and P. B. Baltes (Ed.), *Longitudinal research in the study of behavior and development.* New York: Academic Press.

Baltes, P. B., Dittmann-Kohli, F., and Dixon, R. A. (1985). Intellectual development during adulthood: General propositions towards theory and a dual-process conception. In A. B. Sorensen, F. Weinert, and L. Sherrod (Eds.), *Human development: Interdisciplinary perspectives.* Hillsdale, NJ: Erlbaum.

Baltes, P. B., and Labouvie, G. V. (1973). Adult development of intellectual performance: Description, explanation, and modification. In C. Eisdorfer and M. P. Lawton (Eds.), *The psychology of adult development and aging.* Washington, DC: American Psychological Association.

Baltes, P. B., Reese, H. W., and Nesselroade, J. R. (1977). *Life-span developmental psychology: Introduction to research methods.* Monterey, CA: Brooks/Cole.

Baltes, P. B., and Schaie, K. W. (1976). On the plasticity of intelligence in adulthood and old age: Where Horn and Donaldson fail. *American Psychologist, 31,* 720–725.

Baltes, P. B., and Willis, S. L. (1977). Toward psychological theories of aging and development. In J. E. Birren and K. W. Schaie (Eds.), *Handbook of the psychology of aging.* New York: Van Nostrand Reinhold.

Baltes, P. B., and Willis, S. L. (1978). Life-span developmental psychology, cognition and social policy. In M. W. Riley (Ed.), *Aging from birth to death.* Washington, DC: American Association for the Advancement of Science.

Baltes, P. B., and Willis, S. L. (1982). Enhancement (plasticity) of intellectual functioning: Penn State's Adult Development and Enrichment Project (ADEPT). In F. I. M. Craig and S. Trehub (Eds.), *Aging and cognitive processes.* New York: Plenum.

Bandura, A. (1969). *Principles of behavior modification.* New York: Holt, Rinehart & Winston.

Bandura, A. (1977a). Self-efficacy: Toward a unifying theory of behavioral change. *Psychological Review, 84,* 191–215.

Bandura, A. (1977b). *Social learning theory.* Englewood Cliffs, NJ: Prentice-Hall.

Bandura, A. (1981). Self-referent thought: A developmental analysis of self-efficacy. In J. H. Flavell and L. Ross (Eds.), *Social cognitive development: Frontiers and possible futures.* New York: Cambridge University Press.

Barbeau, A., Growdon, J. H., and Wurtman, R. J. (1979). *Choline and lecithin in brain disorders* (Vol. 5). New York: Raven Press.

Barfield, R. E., and Morgan, J. N. (1978). Trends in satisfaction with retirement. *Gerontologist, 8,* 19–23.

Baron, C. H. (1981). Termination of life support systems in the elderly: To die before the Gods please, legal issues surrounding euthanasia and the elderly. *Journal of Geriatric Psychiatry, 14,* 45–70.

Barrett, C. J. (1974). *The development and evaluation of three group-therapeutic interventions for widows.* Unpublished doctoral dissertation, University of Southern California.

Barrett, F. M. (1980). Sexual experience, birth cohort usage, and sex education of unmarried Canadian university students: Changes between 1968 and 1978. *Archives of Sexual Behavior, 9,* 367–390.

Barry, A. J., Steinmetz, J. R., Page, H. F., and Rodahl, K. (1966). The effects of physical conditioning on older individuals: II. Motor performance and cognition function. *Journal of Gerontology, 21,* 182–191.

Bartus, R. T., Dean, R. L., Beer, B., and Lippa, A. S. (1982). The cholinergic hypothesis of geriatric memory dysfunction. *Science, 217,* 408–417.

Basseches, M. (1980). Dialectical schemata: A framework for the empirical study of the development of dialectical thinking. *Human Development, 23,* 400–421.

Bayer, L., Whissell-Buechy, D., and Honzik, M. (1980). Adolescent health and personality: Significance in adult health. *Journal of Adolescent Health Care, 1,* 101–107.

Beck, A. T. (1967). *Depression: Clinical, experimental and theoretical aspects.* New York: Harper & Row.

Beck, A. T. (1976). *Cognitive therapy and the emotional disorders.* New York: International Universities Press.

Beck, S. (1983). Position in the economic structure and unexpected retirement. *Research on Aging, 5,* 197–216.

Bell, A. P., and Weinberg, M. S. (1978). *Homosexualities.* New York: Simon & Schuster.

Bell, B., Wolf, E., and Bernholz, C. D. (1972). Depth perception as a function of age. *Aging and Human Development, 3,* 77–81.

Bell, B. D., and Batterson, C. T. (1979). The death attitudes of older adults: A path-analytic exploration. *Omega, 10,* 59–76.

Bellak, L. (1975). *The Thematic Apperception Test, the Children's Apperception Test and the Senior Apperceptive Technique in clinical use* (3rd ed.). New York: Grune & Stratton.

Bem, S. L. (1978). Beyond androgyny: Some presumptuous prescriptions for a liberated sexual identity. In J. Sherman and F. Denmark (Eds.), *Psychology of women: Future directions of research.* Psychological Dimensions.

Bendig, A. W. (1960). Age differences in the interscale factor structure of the Guilford-Zimmerman Temperament Survey. *Journal of Consulting Psychology, 24,* 134–138.

Bengtson, V. L. (1971). Inter-age differences in perception and the generation gap. *Gerontologist, 11*, Part II, 85–90.

Bengtson, V. L. (1973). *The social psychology of aging.* Chicago: Bobbs-Merrill.

Bengtson, V. L. (1975). Generation and family effects in value socialization. *American Sociological Review, 40*, 358–371.

Bengtson, V. L. (1979). Research perspectives on intergenerational interaction. In P. Ragan (Ed.), *Aging parents.* Los Angeles, CA: University of Southern California Press.

Bengtson, V. L. (1981). Research across the generation gap. In J. Rosenfeld (Ed.), *Relationships: The marriage and family reader.* Glenview, IL: Scott, Foresman.

Bengtson, V. L., and Black, K. D. (1973). Intergenerational relations and continuities in socialization. In P. B. Baltes and K. W. Schaie (Eds.), *Life-span developmental psychology: Personality and socialization.* New York: Academic Press.

Bengtson, V. L., and DeTorre, E. (1980). Aging and family relations. *Marriage and Family Review, 3*, 51–76.

Bengtson, V. L., and Kuypers, J. A. (1971). Generational difference and the developmental stake. *Aging and Human Development, 2*, 249–259.

Bengtson, V. L., Reedy, M. N., and Gordon, C. E. (1985). Aging and self-conceptions: Personality processes and social contexts. In J. E. Birren and K. W. Schaie (Eds.), *Handbook of the psychology of aging* (2nd ed.). New York: Van Nostrand Reinhold.

Benninger, W. B., and Walsh, W. B. (1980). Holland's theory and non-college-degree working men and women. *Journal of Vocational Behavior, 17*, 81–88.

Berger, P. C., and Norsigian, J. (1976). Menopause. In The Boston Women's Health Book Collective (Eds.), *Our bodies, ourselves* (2nd ed.). New York: Simon & Schuster.

Bergman, M., Blumenfeld, V. G., Casardo, D., Dash, B., Levitt, H., and Margulies, M. K. (1976). Age-related decrement in hearing for speech: Sampling and longitudinal studies. *Journal of Gerontology, 31*, 533–538.

Berkerian, D. A., and Bowers, J. M. (1983). Eyewitness testimony: Were we misled? *Journal of Experimental Psychology: Learning, Memory, Cognition, 9*, 139–145.

Bernard, J. (1973). *The future of marriage.* New York: Bantam.

Bernheim, K. F., and Lewine, R. R. (1979). *Schizophrenia.* New York: Norton.

Bernstein, J. (1982). Who leaves — who stays: Residency policy in housing for the elderly. *Gerontologist, 22*, 305–313.

Berry, J. M., Storandt, M., and Coyne, A. (1984). Age and sex differences in somatic complaints associated with depression. *Journal of Gerontology, 39*, 444–465.

Berscheid, E., and Walster, A. (1974). A little bit about love. In T. L. Huston (Ed.), *Foundations of interpersonal attraction.* New York: Academic Press.

Berscheid, E., Walster, E., and Bohrnstedt, G. (1973, November). The happy American body: A survey report. *Psychology Today*, pp. 119–124.

Bhala, R. P., O'Donnell, J., and Thoppil, E. (1982). Ptophobia: Phobic fear of falling and its clinical management. *Physical Therapy, 62*, 187–190.

Bielby, D., and Papalia, D. (1975). Moral development and perceptual role-taking: Their development and interrelationship across the life-span. *International Journal of Aging and Human Development, 6*, 293–308.

Bild, B. R., and Havighurst, R. J. (1976). Knowledge and use of services. *Gerontologist, 16*, 76–79.

Binstock, R. H., and Shanas, E. (Eds.). (1976). *Handbook of aging and the social sciences.* New York: Van Nostrand Reinhold.

Bird, G., Bird, G., and Scruggs, M. (1984). Determinants of family task sharing: A study of husbands and wives. *Journal of Marriage and the Family, 46*, 345–355.

Birkhill, W. R., and Schaie, K. W. (1975). The effect of differential reinforcement of cautiousness in the intellectual performance of the elderly. *Journal of Gerontology, 30*, 578–583.

Birren, J. E. (1961). A brief history of the psychology of aging (Part II). *Gerontologist, 1*, 127–134.

Birren, J. E. (1965). Age changes in speed of behavior: Its central nature and physiological correlates. In A. T. Welford and J. E. Birren (Eds.), *Behavior, aging and the nervous system.* Springfield, IL: Charles C. Thomas.

Birren, J. E. (1970). Toward an experimental psychology of aging. *American Psychologist, 25,* 124–135.

Birren, J. E. (1974). Translations in gerontology — from lab to life. Psychophysiology and speed of response. *American Psychologist, 29,* 808–815.

Birren, J. E., and Cunningham, W. R. (1985). Research on the psychology in aging: Principles and experimentation. In J. E. Birren and K. W. Schaie (Eds.), *Handbook of the psychology of aging* (2nd ed.). New York: Van Nostrand Reinhold.

Birren, J. E., Cunningham, W. R., and Yamamoto, K. (1983). Psychology of adult development and aging. *Annual Review of Psychology, 34,* 543–575.

Birren, J. E., Kinney, D. K., Schaie, K. W., and Woodruff, D. S. (1981). *Developmental psychology: A life-span approach.* Boston: Houghton Mifflin.

Birren, J. E., and Renner, J. V. (1977). Research on the psychology of aging: Principles of experimentation. In J. E. Birren and K. W. Schaie (Eds.), *Handbook of the psychology of aging.* New York: Van Nostrand Reinhold.

Birren, J. E., and Renner, V. J. (1981). Concepts and criteria of mental health and aging. *American Journal of Orthopsychiatry, 51,* 242–254.

Birren, J. E., and Schaie, K. W. (Eds.). (1977). *Handbook of the psychology of aging.* New York: Van Nostrand Reinhold.

Birren, J. E., and Woodruff, D. S. (1973). Human development over the life span through education. In P. B. Baltes and K. W. Schaie (Eds.), *Life-span developmental psychology: Personality and socialization.* New York: Academic Press.

Birren, J. E., Woods, A. M., and Williams, M. V. (1980). Behavioral slowing with age: Causes, organization, and consequences. In L. W. Poon (Ed.), *Aging in the 1980s.* Washington, DC: American Psychological Association.

Bischof, L. J. (1976). *Adult psychology* (2nd ed.). New York: Harper & Row.

Bixby, L. (1976). Retirement patterns in the United States. *Social Security Bulletin, 39,* 3–19.

Bjorksten, J. (1974). Crosslinkage and the aging process. In M. Rockstein (Ed.), *Proceedings of a symposium on the theoretical aspects of aging.* New York: Academic Press.

Blau, P. M., and Duncan, O. D. (1967). *The American occupational structure.* New York: Wiley.

Blau, Z. S. (1961). Structural constraints on friendships in old age. *American Sociological Review, 26,* 429–439.

Blazer, D. G., Federspiel, C. F., Ray, W. R., and Schaffner, W. (1983). The risk of anticholinergic toxicity in the elderly: A study of prescribing practices in two populations. *Journal of Gerontology, 38,* 31–35.

Blazer, D., and Palmore, E. (1976). Religion and aging in a longitudinal panel. *Gerontologist, 16,* 82–85.

Blazer, D., and Williams, C. D. (1980). Epidemiology of dysphoria and depression in the elderly populations. *American Journal of Psychiatry, 137,* 439–444.

Blenkner, M. (1965). Social work and family relationships with some thoughts on filial maturity. In E. Shanas and G. Streib (Eds.), *Social structure and the family: Generational relations.* Englewood Cliffs, NJ: Prentice-Hall.

Blenkner, M. (1969). The normal dependencies of aging. In R. Kalish (Ed.), *The dependencies of old people.* Ann Arbor, MI: University of Michigan Institute of Gerontology.

Blieszner, R., Willis, S. L., and Baltes, P. B. (1981). Training research in aging on the fluid ability of inductive reasoning. *Journal of Applied Developmental Psychology, 2,* 247–265.

Block, J. (1971). *Lives through time.* Berkeley, CA: Bancroft Books.

Block, J. (1981). Some enduring and consequential structures of personality. In A. I. Rabin (Ed.), *Further explorations in personality.* New York: Wiley-Interscience.

Bloom, A. H. (1981). Adult cognitive development. In D. S. Beasley and G. A. Davis (Eds.), *Aging: Communications processes and disorders.* New York: Grune & Stratton.

Bloom, B. L., Asher, S. J., and White, S. W. (1978). Marital disruption as a stressor: A review and analysis. *Psychological Bulletin, 85,* 867–894.

Blueband-Langner, M. (1977). Meaning of death to children. In H. Feifel (Ed.), *New meanings of death.* New York: McGraw-Hill.

Blum, J. E., and Tross, S. (1980). Psychodynamic treatment of the elderly: A review of issues in theory and practice. In C. Eisdorfer (Ed.), *Annual Review of Gerontology and Geriatrics,* (Vol. 1). New York: Springer.

Blumenthal, H. (1983). Diabetes mellitus as a disorder of information flow. In H. Blumenthal (Ed.), *Handbook of the diseases of aging.* New York: Van Nostrand Reinhold.

Blumenthal, M. D. (1975). Measuring depressive symptomatology in a general population. *Archives of General Psychiatry, 32,* 971–978.

Bobele, H. K., and Buchanan, P. J. (1976). Training managers to be better problem-solvers. *Journal of Creative Behavior, 10,* 250–255.

Bodmer, W. F., and Cavalli-Sforza, L. L. (1976). *Genetics, evolution, and men.* New York: Freeman.

Bond, Z. S., and Garnes, S. (1980). Misperceptions of fluent speech. In R. A. Cole (Ed.), *Perception and production of fluent speech.* Hillsdale, NJ: Erlbaum.

Bondareff, W. (1977). The neural basis of aging. In J. E. Birren and K. W. Schaie (Eds.), *Handbook of the psychology of aging.* New York: Van Nostrand Reinhold.

Bondareff, W. (1981). The neurobiological basis of age-related changes. In J. L. McGaugh and S. B. Kiesler (Eds.), *Aging: Biology and behavior.* New York: Academic Press.

Bonding, P. (1979). Critical bandwidth in presbycusis. *Scandinavian Audiology, 8,* 205–225.

Borenstein, A. (1983). *Chimes of change and hours: View of older women in twentieth-century America.* Toronto: Associated University Presses.

Borland, D. C. (1978). Research on middle age: An assessment. *Gerontologist, 18,* 379–386.

Botwinick, J. (1977). Intellectual abilities. In. J. E. Birren and K. W. Schaie (Eds.), *Handbook of the psychology of aging.* New York: Van Nostrand Reinhold.

Botwinick, J. (1978). *Aging and behavior* (2nd ed.). New York: Springer.

Botwinick, J., and Storandt, M. (1974). *Memory, related functions and age.* Springfield, IL: Charles C. Thomas.

Botwinick, J., and Thompson, L. W. (1966). Components of reaction time in relations to age and sex. *Journal of Genetic Psychology, 108,* 175–183.

Bourque, L. B. (1977). Life graphs and life events. *Journal of Gerontology, 32,* 669–674.

Bower, D. W., and Christopherson, V. A. (1977). University student cohabitation: A regional comparison of selected attitudes and behavior. *Journal of Marriage and the Family, 39,* 447–453.

Bowlby, J. (1974). Psychiatric implications in bereavement. In A. H. Kutscher (Ed.), *Death and bereavement.* Springfield, IL: Charles C. Thomas.

Bowlby, J. (1980). *Loss.* New York: Basic Books.

Bowles, N. E., and Poon, L. (1982). An analysis of the effect of aging on memory. *Journal of Gerontology, 37,* 212–219.

Boyd, J. H., and Weissman, M. M. (1982). Epidemiology. In E. S. Paykel (Ed.), *Handbook of affective disorders.* New York: Guilford Press.

Brandt, J., Butters, N., Ryan, C., and Bayog, R. (1983). Cognitive loss and recovery in chronic alcohol abusers. *Archives of General Psychiatry, 40,* 436–442.

Bray, D. W., Campbell, R. J., and Grant, D. L. (1974). *Formative years in business.* New York: Wiley.

Bray, D. W., and Howard, A. (1979, Winter). Keeping in touch with success. *The Wharton Magazine.*

Bray, D. W., and Howard, A. (1980). Career success and life satisfactions of middle-aged managers. In L. A. Bond and J. C. Rosen (Eds.), *Coping and competence during adulthood.* Hanover, NH: University Press of New England.

Bray, D. W., and Howard, A. (1983a). Personality and the assessment center method. In C. D. Spielberger and J. N. Butcher (Eds.), *Advances in personality assessment.* Hillsdale, NJ: Erlbaum.

Bray, D. W., and Howard, A. (1983b). The AT & T longitudinal studies of managers. In K. W. Schaie (Ed.), *Longitudinal studies of adult psychological development.* New York: Guilford Press.

Breger, W., and Pomeranz, W. R. (1985). *Nursing home development: A guide for the planning, financing and construction of long-term care facilities.* New York: Van Nostrand Reinhold.

Breytspraak, L. M. (1984). *The development of self in later life.* Boston: Little, Brown.

Brim, O. G., Jr. (1977). Theories of the male mid-life crisis. In N. K. Schlossberg and A. T. Entine (Eds.), *Counseling adults.* Monterey, CA: Brooks/Cole.

Brink, T. L. (1979). *Geriatric psychotherapy.* New York: Human Sciences Press.

Broderick, C. (1982). Adult sexual development. In B. B. Wolman (Ed.), *Handbook of developmental psychology.* Englewood Cliffs, NJ: Prentice-Hall.

Brody, E. M. (1978). The aging of the family. *The Annals of the American Academy of Political and Social Science, 438,* 13–27.

Brody, E. M. (1979). Aging parents and aging children. In P. K. Ragan (Ed.), *Aging parents*. Los Angeles: University of Southern California Press.

Brody, E. M. (1981). Women in the middle and family help to older people. *Gerontologist, 21,* 471–480.

Brody, E. M. (1985). Parent care as a normative family stress. *Gerontologist, 25,* 19–29.

Brody, E. M., Johnson, P. T., Fulcomer, M. C., and Lang, A. M. (1983). Women's changing roles and help to elderly parents: Attitudes of three generations. *Journal of Gerontology, 38,* 597–607.

Brody, H. (1982). Age changes in the nervous system. In F. I. Caird (Ed.), *Neurological disorders in the elderly*. Bristol: John Wright and Sons.

Brody, H., and Vijayashankar, N. (1977). Anatomical changes in the nervous system. In C. E. Finch and L. Hayflick (Eds.), *Handbook of the biology of aging*. New York: Van Nostrand Reinhold.

Brooke, P. (1973). Psychiatrists in training. *British Journal of Psychiatry,* Special Bulletin No. 7.

Broverman, I. K., Vogel, S. R., Broverman, D. M., Clarkson, F. E., and Rosencrantz, P. S. (1972). Sex role stereotypes: A current appraisal. *Journal of Social Issues, 28,* 59–78.

Brown, J. K. (1982). Cross-cultural perspectives on middle aged women. *Current Anthropology, 23,* 143–156.

Brown, R., and Kulick, J. (1977). Flashbulb memories. *Cognition, 5,* 73–99.

Brownmiller, S. (1975). *Against our will*. New York: Simon & Schuster.

Brozek, J. (1955). Personality changes with age: An item analysis of the MMPI. *Journal of Gerontology, 10,* 194–206.

Buckingham, R. W. (1982). Hospice care in the United States: The process begins. *Omega, 13,* 159–171.

Buckingham, R. W., and Foley, S. H. (1978). A guide to evaluation research in terminal care programs. *Death Education, 2,* 127–144.

Buehler, C. (1968). The general structure of the human life cycle. In C. Buehler and F. Masarik (Eds.), *Human life: A study of goals in human perspective*. New York: Springer.

Buell, S. J. (1982). Golgi-Cox and rapid Golgi methods as applied to autopsied hymna brain tissue: Widely disparate results. *Journal of Neuropathology and Experimental Neurology, 41,* 500–507.

Buell, S. J., and Coleman, P. D. (1981). Individual differences in dendritic growth in human aging and senile dementia. In D. Stein (Ed.), *The psychology of aging: Problems and perspectives*. Amsterdam: Elsevier-North Holland.

Bugiani, C., Salvariania, S., Perdelli, F., Mancardi, G. L., and Leonardi, A. (1978). Nerve cell loss with aging in the putamen. *European Neurology, 17,* 285–291.

Bultena, G. L., and Powers, E. A. (1978). Denial of aging: Age identification and reference group orientations. *Journal of Gerontology, 33,* 748–754.

Bumpass, L. (1981). *Demographic aspects of children's experience in second families*. Paper presented at the annual meeting of the American Sociological Association.

Burg, A. (1968). Lateral visual field as related to age and sex. *Journal of Applied Psychology, 52,* 10–15.

Burgess, E. W., Locke, H. J., and Thomes, M. M. (1963). *The family: From institution to companionship* (3rd ed.). New York: American Book.

Burke, D. M., and Light, L. L. (1981). Memory and aging: The role of retrieval processes. *Psychological Bulletin, 90,* 513–546.

Burlin, F. (1976). The relationship of parental education and maternal work and occupational status to occupational aspiration in adolescent females. *Journal of Vocational Behavior, 9,* 99–104.

Burt, M. R., and Albin, R. S. (1981). Rape myths, rape definitions, and probability of conviction. *Journal of Applied Social Psychology, 11,* 212–230.

Busch, J. W. (1985). Mentoring in graduate schools of education: Mentor's perceptions. *American Educational Research Journal, 22,* 257–265.

Buskirk, E. R. (1985). Health maintenance and longevity: Exercise. In C. E. Finch and E. L. Schneider (Eds.), *Handbook of the biology of aging* (2nd ed.). New York: Van Nostrand Reinhold.

Busse, E. W. (1976). Hypochondriasis in the elderly: A reaction to social stress. *Journal of the American Geriatric Society, 24,* 145–149.

Busse, E. W., and Blazer, D. (1980). Disorders related to biological functioning. In E. W. Busse and D. Blazer (Eds.), *Handbook of geriatric psychiatry*. New York: Van Nostrand Reinhold.

Butler, R. N. (1975). *Why survive?* New York: Harper & Row.

Butler, R. N., and Gastel, B. (1979). Aging and cancer management. Part II: Research perspectives. *Cancer, 29,* 333–342.

Butler, R. N., and Lewis, M. I. (1977). *Aging and mental health* (2nd ed.). St. Louis, MO: Mosby.

Butler, R. N., and Lewis, M. I. (1982). *Aging and mental health* (3rd ed.). St. Louis, MO: Mosby.

Cahalan, D., Cisin, I. H., and Crossley, H. M. (1969). *American drinking practices: A national survey of drinking behavior and attitudes* (Monograph No. 6). New Brunswick, NJ: Rutgers Center of Alcohol Studies.

Calden, G., and Hokanson, J. E. (1959). The influence of age on MMPI responses. *Journal of Clinical Psychology, 15*, 194–195.

Caldwell, B. (1954). The use of the Rorschach in personality research with the aged. *Journal of Gerontology, 9*, 316–323.

Calearo, C., and Lazzaroni, A. (1957). Speech intelligibility in relationship to the speed of the message. *Laryngoscope, 67*, 410–419.

Cameron, P. (1969). Age parameters of young adult, middle-aged, old, and aged. *Journal of Gerontology, 24*, 201–202.

Cameron, P. (1975). Mood as an indicant of happiness: Age, sex, social class, and situational differences. *Journal of Gerontology, 30*, 216–224.

Campbell, A. (1975, May). The American way of mating: Marriage si, children only maybe. *Psychology Today*.

Campbell, A. J., Reinken, J., Allen, B. C., and Martinez, G. S. (1981). Falls in old age: A study of frequency and related clinical factors. *Age and Ageing, 10*, 264–270.

Campbell, D. P. (1974). *Manual for the Strong-Campbell Interest Inventory*. Stanford, CA: Stanford University Press.

Canestrari, R. E. (1968). Age changes in acquisition. In G. A. Talland (Ed.), *Human aging and behavior*. New York: Academic Press.

Canter, A., Day, E. W., Imboden, J. B., and Cluff, J. E. (1962). The influence of age and health status on the MMPI scores of a normal population. *Journal of Clinical Psychology, 18*, 71–73.

Cantor, M. H. (1983). Strain among caregivers: A study of experience in the United States. *Gerontologist, 23*, 597–604.

Caporael, L. R. (1981). The paralanguage of caregiving: Baby talk to the institutionalized aged. *Journal of Personality and Social Psychology, 40*, 867–884.

Caporael, L. R., Lukaszewski, M. P., and Culbertson, G. H. (1983). Secondary baby talk: Judgements by institutionalized elderly and their caregivers. *Journal of Personality and Social Psychology, 44*, 746–754.

Carlson, A., Adolfson, R., Aquilonius, S. M., Gotfries, C. G., Oreland, L., Svennerholm, L., and Winbland, B. (1980). Biogenic amines in human brain in normal aging, senile dementia, and chronic alcoholism. In M. Goldstein, D. B. Caine, A. Lieberman, and M. O. Turner (Eds.), *Ergot compounds and brain function: Neuroendocrine and neuropsychiatric aspects*. New York: Raven Press.

Carlson, R. (1981). Studies in script theory: I. Adult analogs of a childhood nuclear scene. *Journal of Personality and Social Psychology, 40*, 501–510.

Carp, F., Peterson, R., and Roelfs, P. (1974). Adult learning interests and experiences. In K. P. Cross, J. R. Valley and Associates (Eds.), *Planning non-traditional programs: An analysis of the issues for postsecondary education*. San Francisco: Jossey-Bass.

Carskadon, M. A. (1982). Sleep fragmentation, sleep loss, and sleep needs in the elderly. *Gerontologist, 22*, 187.

Carter, H., and Glick, P. C. (1976). *Marriage and divorce* (rev. ed.). Cambridge, MA: Harvard University Press.

Carter, J. H. (1982). The effects of aging upon selected visual functions: Color vision, glare sensitivity, field of vision and accommodation. In R. Sekuler, D. Kline, and K. Dismukes (Eds.), *Aging and human visual function*. New York: Alan R. Liss.

Cattell, R. B. (1971). *Abilities: Their structure, growth and action*. Boston: Houghton Mifflin.

Cavanaugh, J. (1984). Effects of presentation format on adult's retention of television programs. *Experimental Aging Research, 10*, 51–54.

Cavanaugh, J., Grady, J., and Perlmutter, M. (1983). Forgetting and use of memory aids in 20-to-70 year olds' everyday life. *International Journal of Aging and Human Development, 17*, 113–122.

Cerella, J., Poon, L., and Fozard, J. (1982). Age and iconic read-out. *Journal of Gerontology, 37*, 197–202.

Charles, D. C. (1970). Historical antecedents of life-span developmental psychology. In L. R. Goulet and P. B. Baltes (Eds.), *Life-span developmental psychology: Research and theory*. New York: Academic Press.

Chatters, L. M., and Jackson, J. S. (1982). Health and older blacks. *NCBA Quarterly Contact, 5*(1), 1, 7–9

Cherlin, A. (1979). Work life and marital dissolution. In G. Levinger and O. Moles (Eds.), *Divorce and separation: Context, causes and consequences*. New York: Basic Books.

Cherniss, C. (1980). *Staff burnout: Job stress in the human services*. Beverly Hills, CA: Sage.

Chesler, P. (1972). *Women and madness*. New York: Doubleday.

Chien, C. P., Stotsky, B. A., and Cole, J. O. (1973). Psychiatric treatment for nursing home patients: Drug, alcohol and milieu. *American Journal of Psychiatry, 130*, 543–548.

Chien, C. P., Townsend, E. J., and Townsend, A. R. (1978). Substance use and abuse among the community elderly: The medical aspect. *Addictive Diseases, 3*, 357–372.

Chiriboga, D. A. (1982). Adaptations to marital separation in later and earlier life. *Journal of Gerontology, 37*, 109–114.

Chiriboga, D., and Thurnher, M. (1975). Concept of self. In M. F. Lowenthal, M. Thurnher, D. Chiriboga and Associates (Ed.), *Four stages of life*. San Francisco: Jossey-Bass.

Chown, S. M. (1968). Personality and aging. In K. W. Schaie (Ed.), *Theory and methods of research on aging*. Morgantown, WV: West Virginia University.

Christenson, C. V., and Gagnon, J. H. (1965). Sexual behavior in a group of older women. *Journal of Gerontology, 20*, 351–356.

Chylack, L. T., Jr. (1979). Aging and cataracts. In S. S. Han and D. Coons (Eds.), *Special senses in aging*. Ann Arbor, MI: University of Michigan Press.

Clausen, J. (1984). Mental illness and the life course. In P. B. Baltes and O. G. Brim, Jr. (Eds.), *Life-span development and behavior* (Vol. 6). New York: Academic Press.

Clayton, P. J. (1973). The clinical morbidity of the first year of bereavement: A review. *Comprehensive Psychiatry, 14*, 1512–1517.

Clayton, P. J., Halikes, J. A., and Maurice, W. L. (1971). The bereavement of the widowed. *Diseases of the Nervous System, 32*, 597–604.

Cohen, D. (1980, February). Donald Hebb: An inside look at aging. *APA Monitor*.

Cohen, J. (1957). The factorial structure of the WAIS between early adulthood and old age. *Journal of Consulting Psychology, 21*, 283–290.

Cole, J. O., and Davis, J. M. (1975). Antidepressant drugs. In A. M. Freedman, H. I. Kaplan, and B. J. Sadock (Eds.), *Comprehensive textbook of psychiatry — II*. Baltimore: Williams & Wilkins.

Cole, K. D., and Zarit, S. H. (1984). Psychological deficits in depressed mental patients. *Journal of Nervous and Mental Diseases, 172*, 150–155.

Coleman, R. M., Miles L. E., Guilleminault, C. C., Zarcone, V. P., Van den Hoed, J., and Dement, W. C. (1981). *Journal of the American Geriatrics Society, 29*, 289–296.

Collins, K. J., Dore, C., Exton-Smith, A. N., Fox, R. H., MacDonald, I. C., and Woodward, P. M. (1977). Accidental hypothermia and impaired temperature homeostasis in the elderly. *British Medical Journal, 1*, 353–356.

Colwill, N. L., and Holborn, S. W. (1978). Sex and sexuality. In H. M. Lips and N. L. Colwill (Eds.), *The psychology of sex differences*. New York: Spectrum.

Comfort, A. (1980). Sexuality in later life. In J. E. Birren and R. B. Sloane (Eds.), *Handbook of mental health and aging*. Englewood Cliffs, NJ: Prentice-Hall.

Committee on Aging. (1971). *The aged and community mental health*. Washington, DC: Group for the Advancement of Psychiatry.

Commons, M., Richards, F., and Kuhn, D. (1982). Systematic and metasystematic reasoning: A case for levels of reasoning beyond Piaget's stage of formal operations. *Child Development, 53*, 1058–1069.

Conger, J. J. (1977a). A world they never knew: The family and social change. *Daedalus, 100*, 1105–1138.

Conger, J. J. (1977b). *Adolescence and youth* (2nd ed.). New York: Harper & Row.

Connolly, K. J., and Bruner, J. C. (1973). *The growth of competence*. New York: Academic Press.

Constantine, L. L., and Constantine, J. M. (1972). Dissolution of marriage in a nonconventional context. *The Family Coordinator, 21,* 457–462.

Constantinople, A. (1969). An Eriksonian measure of personality development in college students. *Developmental Psychology, 1,* 357–372.

Cool, L. E., Jr. (1981). Role continuity or crisis in later life?: A Corsican case. *International Journal of Social Psychology, 38,* 668–678.

Corso, J. (1977). Auditory perception and communication. In J. E. Birren and K. W. Schaie (Eds.), *Handbook of the psychology of aging.* New York: Van Nostrand Reinhold.

Corso, J. F. (1981). *Aging sensory systems and perceptions.* New York: Praeger.

Costa, P. T., Jr., and McCrae, R. R. (1978). Objective personality assessment. In M. Storandt, I. C. Siegler, and M. P. Elias (Eds.), *The clinical psychology of aging.* New York: Plenum.

Costa, P. T., Jr., and McCrae, R. R. (1980a). Influence of extroversion and neuroticism on subjective well-being: Happy and unhappy people. *Journal of Personality and Social Psychology, 38,* 668–678.

Costa, P. T., Jr., and McCrae, R. R. (1980b). Still stable after all these years: Personality as a key to some issues in adulthood and old age. In P. Baltes and O. G. Brim, Jr. (Eds.), *Life span development and behavior* (Vol. 3). New York: Academic Press.

Costa, P. T., Jr., and McCrae, R. R. (1982). An approach to the attribution of aging, period and cohort effects. *Psychological Bulletin, 92,* 238–250.

Costa, P. T., Jr., and McCrae, R. R. (1985). Personality as a lifelong determinant of well-being. In C. Malatesta and C. Izard (Eds.), *Affective processes in adult development and aging.* New York: Sage.

Costa, P. T., Jr., McCrae, R. R., and Arenberg, D. (1980). Enduring dispositions in adult males. *Journal of Personality and Social Psychology, 38,* 793–800.

Costa, P. T., Jr., McCrae, R. R., and Holland, J. L. (1984). Personality and vocational interests in an adult sample. *Journal of Applied Psychology, 42,* 390–400.

Cottrell, F. (1960). The technological and societal basis of aging. In C. Tibbitt (Ed.), *Handbook of social gerontology: Societal aspects of aging.* Chicago: University of Chicago Press.

Cottrell, L. S., Jr. (1942). The life adjustment of the individual to his age and sex roles. *American Sociological Review, 7,* 617–620.

Cowdry, E. V. (1942). *Problems of aging.* Baltimore: Williams & Wilkins.

Coyle, J. T., Price, D. L., and DeLong, M. R. (1983). Alzheimer's disease: A disorder of cortical cholinergic innervation. *Science, 219,* 1184–1190.

Coyne, J. C., and Gollub, I. H. (1983). The role of cognition in depression: A critical appraisal. *Psychological Bulletin, 94,* 472–505.

Cozby, P. C., and Rosenblatt, P. C. (1971). Privacy, love, and in-law avoidance. *Proceedings of the 79th Annual Convention of the American Psychological Association, 6*(1), 277–278.

Craik, F. I. M. (1977). Age differences in human memory. In J. E. Birren and K. W. Schaie (Eds.), *Handbook of the psychology of aging.* New York: Van Nostrand Reinhold.

Craik, F. I. M., and Byrd, M. (1982). Aging and cognitive deficits: The role of attentional resources. In F. I. M. Craik and S. Trehub (Eds.), *Aging and cognitive processes.* New York: Plenum.

Craik, F. I. M., and Lockhart, R. S. (1972). Levels of processing: A framework for memory research. *Journal of Verbal Learning and Verbal Behavior, 11,* 671–684.

Craik, F. I. M., and Masani, P. A. (1967). Age differences in the temporal integration of language. *British Journal of Psychology, 58,* 291–299.

Craik, F. I. M., and Rabinowitz, J. C. (1984). Age differences in the acquisition and use of verbal information. In J. Long and A. Baddeley (Eds.), *Attention and performance* (Vol. X). Hillsdale, NJ: Erlbaum.

Craik, F. I. M., and Trehub, S. (Eds.). (1982). *Aging and cognitive processes.* New York: Plenum.

Craik, F. I. M., and Tulving, E. (1975). Depth of processing and the retention of words in episodic memory. *Journal of Experimental Psychology: General, 104,* 268–294.

Crawford, J., and Cohen, H. J. (1984). Aging and neoplasia. *Annual Review of Gerontology and Geriatrics, 4,* 3–32.

Crawford, M. P., and Hooper, D. (1973). Menopause, ageing and family. *Social Science and Medicine, 7,* 469–482.

Cronbach, L. J. (1970). *Essentials of psychological testing* (3rd ed.). New York: Harper & Row.

Crook, T., and Gershon, S. (1981). *Strategies for the development of an effective treatment for senile dementia*. New Canaan, CT: Mark Powley Associates.

Cross, D. G., Sheehan, P. W., and Khan, J. A. (1982). Short- and long-term follow-up of clients receiving insight-oriented therapy and behavior therapy. *Journal of Consulting and Clinical Psychology, 50*, 103–112.

Cross, K. P. (1981). *Adults as learners*. San Francisco: Jossey-Bass.

Crouter, A. (1984a). Participative work as an influence on human development. *Journal of Applied Developmental Psychology, 5*, 71–90.

Crouter, A. (1984b). Spillover from family to work: The neglected side of the work-family interface. *Human Relations, 37*, 425–442.

Crovitz, E. (1966). Reversing a learning deficit in the aged. *Journal of Gerontology, 21*, 236–238.

Crowder, R. G. (1980). Echoic memory and the study of aging memory systems. In L. W. Poon, J. L. Fozard, L. S. Cermak, D. Arenberg, and L. W. Thompson (Eds.), *New directions in memory and aging: Proceedings of the George A. Talland memorial conference*. Hillsdale, NJ: Erlbaum.

Cumming, E. (1969). The multigenerational family and the crisis of widowhood. In W. Donahue et al. (Eds.), *Living in the multigenerational family*. Ann Arbor, MI: University of Michigan Institute of Gerontology.

Cumming, E., and Henry, W. (1961). *Growing old: The process of disengagement*. New York: Basic Books.

Cunningham, D. J., and Antill, J. K. (1984). Changes in masculinity and femininity across the family life cycle: A reexamination. *Developmental Psychology, 20*, 1135–1141.

Cunningham, W. R., and Owens, W. A., Jr. (1983). The Iowa State Study of the adult development of intellectual abilities. In K. W. Schaie (Ed.), *Longitudinal studies of adult psychological development*. New York: Guilford Press.

Curcio, C. A., Buell, S. J., and Coleman, B. D. (1982). Morphology of the aging central nervous system: Not all downhill. In J. A. Mortimer, F. J. Pirozzola, and G. L. Maletta (Eds.), *Advances in neurogerontology: The aging motor system*. New York: Praeger.

Curry, T. J., and Ratliff, B. W. (1973). The effects of nursing home size on resident isolation and life satisfaction. *Gerontologist, 13*, 295–298.

Cutler, S., Lentz, S., Muha, M., and Riter, R. (1980). Aging and conservatism: Cohort changes in attitudes about legalized abortion. *Journal of Gerontology, 35*, 115–123.

Dalderup, L. M., and Fredericks, M. L. C. (1969). Colour sensitivity in old age. *Journal of the American Geriatric Society, 17*, 388–390.

Daniels, P., and Weingarten, K. (1982). *Sooner or later: The timing of parenthood in adult lives*. New York: Norton.

Datan, N., and Ginsberg, L. H. (Eds.) (1975). *Life-span developmental psychology: Normative life crises*. New York: Academic Press.

Davidson, R. J., Schwartz, G. E., Saron, C., Bennett, J., and Goleman, D. J. (1979). Frontal vs. parietal EEG asymmetry during positive and negative affect. *Psychophysiology, 16*, 202–203.

Davis, H., and Silverman, S. R. (1975). *Hearing and deafness* (3rd ed.). New York: Holt, Rinehart & Winston.

Davis, K. E. (1985). Near and dear: Friendship and love compared. *Psychology Today, 19*, 22–30.

Davis, R. H. (1981). The middle years. In R. H. Davis (Ed.), *Aging: Prospects and issues* (3rd ed.). Los Angeles: Andrus Gerontology Center.

Davis, W. E., Mozdzierz, G. J., and Macchitelli, F. J. (1973). Loss of discriminative "power" of the MMPI with older psychiatric patients. *Journal of Personality Assessment, 37*, 555–558.

de Alarcon, J. (1971). Social causes and consequences of mental illness in old age. In D. Kay and A. Walk (Eds.), *Recent development in psychogeriatrics*. London: Headley.

deMause, L. (1974). The evolution of childhood. In L. deMause (Ed.), *The history of childhood*. New York: Harper & Row.

Dement, W. C., Miles, L. E., and Bilwise, D. L. (1982). Physiological markers of aging: Human sleep pattern changes. In M. E. Reff and E. L. Schneider (Eds.), *Biological markers of aging*. Washington, DC: U.S. Government Printing Office, NIH Publication No. 82-2221.

Demming, J. A., and Pressey, S. L. (1957). Tests "indigenous" to the adult and older years. *Journal of Counseling Psychology, 2*, 144–148.

Demos, J. (1970). *A little commonwealth.* New York: Oxford University Press.

Denney, N. W. (1974). Classification abilities in the elderly. *Journal of Gerontology, 29,* 309–314.

Denney, N. W. (1979). Problem solving in later adulthood: Intervention research. In P. B. Baltes and O. G. Brim (Eds.), *Life-span development and behavior.* New York: Academic Press.

Denney, N. W. (1980). Task demands and problem-solving startegies in middle-age and older adults. *Journal of Gerontology, 35,* 559–564.

Denney, N. W. (1981). Adult cognitive development. In D. S. Beasley and G. A. Davis (Eds.), *Aging: Communications processes and disorders.* New York: Grune & Stratton.

Dennis, W. (1958). The age decrement in outstanding scientific contributions: Fact or artifact? *American Psychologist, 13,* 457–460.

Dennis, W. (1966). Creative productivity between the ages of 20 and 80 years. *Journal of Gerontology, 21,* 1–8.

Dennis, W. (1968). Creative productivity between the ages of 20 and 80 years. In B. L. Neugarten (Ed.), *Middle age and aging.* Chicago: University of Chicago Press.

Deutsch, H. (1945). *The psychology of women.* New York: Grune & Stratton.

Deutscher, I. (1968). The quality of postparental life. In B. L. Neugarten (Ed.), *Middle age and aging.* Chicago: University of Chicago Press.

DeVries, H. A. (1983). Physiology of exercise and aging. In D. W. Woodruff and J. E. Birren (Eds.), *Aging: Scientific perspectives and social issues.* Monterey, CA: Brooks/Cole.

Diamond, M., and Karlen, A. (1980). *Sexual decisions.* Boston: Little, Brown.

Diggory, J. C., and Rothman, D. Z. (1961). Values destroyed by death. *Journal of Abnormal and Social Psychology, 63,* 205–210.

Doering, M., Rhodes, S. R., and Schuster, M. (1983). *The aging worker: Research and recommendations.* Beverly Hills, CA: Sage.

Doherty, W. J., and Jacobson, N. S. (1982). Marriage and the family. In B. B. Wolman (Ed.), *Handbook of developmental psychology.* Englewood Cliffs, NJ: Prentice-Hall.

Dollard, J., and Miller, N. E. (1950). *Personality and psychotherapy.* New York: McGraw-Hill.

Dorken, H., and Webb, J. T. (1979). Licensed psychologists in health care: A survey of their practices. In C. A. Kiesler, N. A. Cummings, and G. R. VandenBos (Eds.), *Psychology and National Health Insurance.* Washington, DC: American Psychological Association.

Douglas, K., and Arenberg, D. (1978). Age changes, cohort differences, and cultural change on the Guilford-Zimmerman Temperament Survey. *Journal of Gerontology, 33,* 737–747.

Douvan, E. (1979). Differing views on marriage 1957 to 1976. *Newsletter of the Center for Continuing Education of Women* (University of Wisconsin), *12,* 1–2.

Drachman, D. A., Noffsinger, D., Sahakian, B. J., Kurdziel, S., and Fleming, P. (1980). Aging, memory and the cholinergic system: A study of dichotic listening. *Neurobiology of Aging, 1,* 39–43.

Dubin, S. (1972). Obsolescence or lifelong education: A choice for the professional. *American Psychologist, 17,* 486–498.

Durbin, N. E., Gross, E., and Borgatta, E. (1984). The decision to leave work. *Research on Aging, 6,* 572–592.

Edelwich, J., and Brodsky, A. (1980). *Professional burnout in human service organizations.* New York: Praeger.

Educational Testing Service. (1977). *Basic skills test: Reading.* Princeton, NJ: Educational Testing Service.

Eibl-Eibesfeldt, I. (1972). *Love and hate.* New York: Holt, Reinhart & Winston.

Eichorn, D. H., Clausen, J. A., Haan, N., Honzik, M. P. and Mussen, P. H., (Eds.) (1981). *Present and past in middle life.* New York: Academic Press.

Eisdorfer, C. (1960). Rorschach rigidity and sensory decrement in a senescent population. *Journal of Gerontology, 15,* 188–190.

Eisdorfer, C. (1968). Arousal and performance: Experiments in verbal learning and a tentative theory. In G. A. Talland (Ed.), *Human aging and behavior.* New York: Academic Press.

Eisdorfer, C., Nowlin, J., and Wilkie, F. (1970). Improvement of learning in the aged by modification of autonomic nervous system activity. *Science, 170,* 1327–1329.

Eisdorfer, C., and Wilkie, F. (1973). Intellectual changes with advancing age. In L. F. Jarvik, C. Eisdorfer, and J. E. Blum (Eds.), *Intellectual functioning in adults.* New York: Springer.

Ekerdt, D., Bosse, R., and LoCastro, J. (1983). Claims that retirement improves health. *Journal of Gerontology, 38*, 231–236.

Elder, G. H., Jr. (1974). *Children of the great depression.* Chicago: University of Chicago Press.

Elder, G. H. (1979). Historical change in life patterns and personality. In P. B. Baltes and O. G. Brim, Jr. (Eds.), *Life-span development and behavior* (Vol. 2). New York: Academic Press.

Elder, G. H., Jr., Liker, J. K., and Cross, C. E. (1984). Parent-child behavior in the great depression: Life course and intergenerational influences. In P. B. Baltes and O. G. Brim, Jr. (Eds.), *Life-span development and behavior* (Vol. 6). New York: Academic Press.

Elder, G. H., Jr., Liker, J. K., and Jaworski, B. J. (1984). Hardship in lives: Depression influences from the 1930s to old age in postwar America. In K. A. McCluskey and H. W. Reese (Eds.), *Life-span developmental psychology: Historical and generational effects.* New York: Academic Press.

Elias, M. F., and Elias, P. K. (1977). Motivation and activity. In J. E. Birren and K. W. Schaie (Eds.), *Handbook of the psychology of aging.* New York: Van Nostrand Reinhold.

Elwell, F., and Maltbie-Crannell, A. D. (1981). The impact of role loss upon coping resources and life satisfaction of the elderly. *Journal of Gerontology, 36*, 223–232.

Engen, T. (1982). *The perception of odors.* New York: Academic Press.

Erber, J. T. (1981). Remote memory and age: A review. *Experimental Aging Research, 1*, 189–199.

Erber, J. T. (1982). Memory and age. In T. Field, W. Overton, H. Quay, L. Troll, and G. Finley (Eds.), *Review of human development.* New York: Wiley.

Erikson, E. (1963). *Childhood and society* (2nd ed.). New York: Norton.

Erikson, E. (1964). *Insight and responsibility.* New York: Norton.

Erikson, E. (1968). *Identity, youth and crisis.* New York: Norton.

Erikson, E. (1979). Reflections on Dr. Borg's life cycle. In E. H. Erikson (Ed.), *Adulthood.* New York: Norton.

Erikson, E. (1982). *The life cycle completed: A review.* New York: Norton.

Ershler, W. B., Socinski, M. A., and Greene, C. J. (1983). Bronchogenic cancer, metastases and aging. *Journal of the American Geriatric Society, 31*, 673–690.

Eysenck, H. J. (1976). *Sex and personality.* Austin: University of Texas Press.

Farber, B. A. (1983). *Stress and burnout.* New York: Pergamon.

Farrell, M. P., and Rosenberg, S. (1981). *Men at midlife.* Boston: Auburn House.

Favia, S., and Genovese, R. (1983). Family, work, and individual development in dual-career marriages. In H. Lopata and J. H. Pleck (Eds.), *Research in the interweave of social roles: Jobs and families* (Vol. 3). Greenwich, CT: JAI Press.

Featherman, D., Hogan, D., and Sorensen, A. (1984). Entry into adulthood: Profiles of young men in the 1950s. In P. B. Baltes and O. G. Brim, Jr. (Eds.), *Life-span development and behavior* (Vol. 6). New York: Academic Press.

Feldman, H. (1971). The effects of children on the family. In A. Michel (Ed.), *Family issues of employed women in Europe and America.* Leiden: Brill.

Feldman, S. S., Biringen, Z. C., and Nash, S. (1981). Fluctuations of sex-related self-attributions as a function of stage of family life cycle. *Developmental Psychology, 17*, 24–35.

Feldman, S. S., Nash, S. C., and Aschenbrenner, B. G. (1983). Antecedents of fathering. *Child Development, 54*, 1628–1636.

Fengler, A. P. (1976). *Productivity and representation: The elderly legislator in state politics.* Paper presented at the annual meeting of the Gerontological Society, New York.

Ferster, C. B. (1973). A functional analysis of depression. *American Psychologist, 29*, 857–870.

Fiedler, F. (1967). *A theory of leadership effectiveness.* New York: McGraw-Hill.

Fiedler, F. (1978). The contingency model and the dynamics of the leadership process. In L. Berkowitz (Ed.), *Advances in experimental social psychology.* New York: Academic Press.

Finch, C. E. (1976). The regulation of physiological changes during mammalian aging. *The Quarterly Review of Biology, 51*, 49–83.

Finch, C. E. (1982). Rodent models for aging processes in the human brain. In S. Corkin, K. L. Davis, J. H. Growdon, E. Usdin, and R. J. Wurtman (Eds.), *Alzheimer's disease: A report of progress.* New York: Raven Press.

Finch, C. E., and Schneider, E. L. (Eds.). (1985). *Handbook of the biology of aging* (2nd ed.). New York: Van Nostrand Reinhold.

Fiske, M. (1980). Tasks and crises of the second half of life: The interrelationship of commitment, coping, and adaptation. In J. E. Birren and R. B. Sloane (Eds.), *Handbook of mental health and aging.* Englewood Cliffs, NJ: Prentice-Hall.

Fitzgerald, J. M. (1978). Actual and perceived sex and generational differences in interpersonal styles: Structural and quantitative issues. *Journal of Gerontology, 33,* 394–401.

Flavell, J. H. (1963). *The developmental psychology of Jean Piaget.* New York: Van Nostrand.

Flavell, J. H. (1970). Cognitive changes in adulthood. In L. R. Goulet and P. B. Baltes (Eds.), *Life-span developmental psychology: Research and theory.* New York: Academic Press.

Flint, M. (1982). Male and female menopause: A cultural put on. In A. Voda, M. Dinnerstein, and S. O'Donnell (Eds.), *Changing perspective on menopause.* Austin: University of Texas Press.

Flor-Henry, P. (1979). On certain aspects of the localization of the cerebral systems regulating and determining emotion. *Biological Psychiatry, 14,* 677–698.

Ford, C. S., and Beach, F. A. (1951). *Patterns of sexual behavior.* New York: Harper.

Foster, N. L., Chase, T., and Fedio, D. L. (1982). Alzheimer's disease: Focal cortical changes shown by positron emission tomography. *Neurology, 33,* 961–965.

Fox, G. L. (1975). *Before marriage: An assessment of organization and change in the premartial period.* Paper presented at Merrill Palmer Conference on Changing Sex Roles and the Family, Detroit, MI.

Fox, R. H., MacGibbon, R., Davies, L., and Woodward, P. M. (1983). Problem of the old and the cold. *British Medical Journal, 7,* 21–24.

Fozard, J. L. (1980). The time for remembering. In L. W. Poon (Ed.), *Aging in the 1980s.* Washington, DC: American Psychological Association.

Fozard, J. L., and Nuttall, R. L. (1971). Effects of age and socioeconomic status differences in the 16PF questionnaire scores. *Proceedings of the 79th Annual Convention of the American Psychological Association, 6,* 597–598.

Fozard, J. L., Wolf, E., Bell, B., McFarland, R. A., and Podolsky, S. (1977). Visual perception and communication. In J. E. Birren and K. W. Schaie (Eds.), *Handbook of the psychology of aging.* New York: Van Nostrand Reinhold.

Frackowiak, R. S. J., Lenzi, G. L., Jones, T., and Heathe, J. D. (1980). Quantitative measurement of regional cerebral blood flow and oxygen metabolism in man using oxygen-15 and positron emission tomography: Theory, procedure and normal values. *Journal of Computer Assisted Tomography, 4,* 727–736.

Frei, E. (1982). The national cancer chemotherapy program. *Science, 217,* 600–609.

Freilich, M. (1964). The natural trends in kinship and complex systems. *American Sociological Review, 29,* 529–540.

Freud, A. (1946). *The ego and the mechanisms of defense.* New York: International Universities Press.

Freudenberger, H. J. (1974). Staff burn-out. *Journal of Social Issues, 30,* 159–165.

Freudenberger, H. J., and Richelson, G. (1980). *Burn-out: The high cost of high achievement.* Garden City, NY: Anchor Press/Doubleday.

Friedman, M., and Rosenman, R. H. (1974). *Type A behavior and your heart.* New York: Knopf.

Friedrich, M. A. (1982). Aging, menopause, and estrogens: The clinician's dilemma. In A. Voda, M. Dinnerstein, and S. O'Donnell (Eds.), *Changing perspectives on menopause.* Austin: University of Texas Press.

Fries, J. F. (1980). Aging, natural death, and the compression of morbidity. *New England Journal of Medicine, 300,* 130–135.

Fries, J. F. (1985, February 17). Separating death from disease. *New York Times,* p. E5.

Fries, J. F., and Crapo, L. M. (1981). *Vitality and aging.* San Francisco: Freeman.

Frieze, I. H. (1983). Investigating the causes and consequences of marital rape. *Signs: Journal of Culture and Society, 8,* 532–553.

Frodi, A. M., Lamb, M. E., Hawang, C. P, and Frodi, M. (1982). *The Swedish experiment: Paternal involvement in infant care.* Paper presented at the International Conference on Infant Studies, Austin, TX.

Fry, C. L. (1985). Culture, behavior and aging in the comparative perspective. In J. E. Birren and K. W. Schaie (Eds.), *Handbook of the psychology of aging* (2nd ed.). New York: Van Nostrand Reinhold.

Fuller, E. (1970). *2500 anecdotes for all occasions.* New York: Avenel.

Furchtgott, E., and Busemeyer, J. R. (1981). Age preferences for professional helpers. *Journal of Gerontology, 36,* 90–92.

Gadow, S. (1983). Frailty and strength: The dialectic in aging. *Gerontologist, 23,* 144–147.

Gallagher, D., Breckenbridge, J. N., Thompson, L. W., Dessonville, C., and Amaral, P. (1982). Similarities and differences between normal grief and depression in older adults. *Essence, 5,* 127–140.

Gallagher, D. E., and Thompson, L. W. (1981). *Depression in the elderly: A behavioral treatment manual.* Los Angeles, CA: University of Southern California Press.

Gallagher, D. E., and Thompson, L. W. (1982). Treatment of major depressive disorders in older outpatients with brief psychotherapies. *Psychotherapy: Theory, Research and Practice, 19,* 482–490.

Gallagher, D. E., and Thompson, L. W. (1983). Effectiveness of psychotherapy for both endogenous and nonendogenous depression in older adult outpatients. *Journal of Gerontology, 38,* 707–712.

Gallagher, D. E., Thompson, L. W., and Peterson, J. A. (1981–82). Psychosocial factors affecting adaptation to bereavement in the elderly. *International Journal of Aging and Human Development, 14,* 79–82.

Gallup Poll: Public Opinion. (1983, July 31). Wilmington, DE: Scholarly Resources.

Galston, L. (1975, June 29). Don't give up on an aging parent. *Parade Magazine.*

Galton, F. (1883). *Inquiries into human faculty and its development.* New York: Macmillan.

Garber, J., and Seligman, M. E. P. (Eds.). (1980). *Human helplessness: Theory and applications.* New York: Academic Press.

Gardner, H. (1974). *The shattered mind: The person after brain damage.* New York: Knopf.

Gardner, H. (1978). *Developmental psychology.* Boston: Little, Brown.

Garfield, C. A. (1974). *Psychothanatological concomitants of altered state experience.* Unpublished doctoral dissertation, University of California, Berkeley.

Garrett, H. E. (1957). *Great experiments in psychology* (3rd ed.). New York: Appleton-Century-Crofts.

Gatz, M., Smyer, M. A., and Lawton, M. P. (1980). The mental health system and the older adult. In L. W. Poon (Ed.), *Aging in the 1980s.* Washington, DC: American Psychological Association.

Gatz, M., VandenBos, G., Pino, C., and Popkin, S. (1985). Psychological interventions with older adults. In J. E. Birren and K. W. Schaie (Eds.), *Handbook of the psychology of aging* (2nd ed.). New York: Van Nostrand Reinhold.

Geiwitz, J. A. (1979). A book for all seasons. *Contemporary Psychology, 24,* 294–295.

Geiwitz, J. (1980). *Psychology: Looking at ourselves* (2nd ed.). Boston: Little, Brown.

Geiwitz, J., and Moursund, J. (1979). *Approaches to personality.* Monterey, CA: Brooks/Cole.

George, L. K. (1978). The impact of personality and social status factors upon levels of activity and psychological well-being. *Journal of Gerontology, 33,* 840–847.

George, L. K. (1980). *Role transitions in later life.* Belmont, CA: Wadsworth.

George, L., Fillenbaum, G. and Palmore, E. (1984). Sex differences in the antecedents and consequences of retirement. *Journal of Gerontology, 39,* 364–371.

George, L., and Maddox, G. (1977). Subjective adaptation to loss of the work role: A longitudinal study. *Journal of Gerontology, 32,* 456–462.

Gergen, K. J., and Back, K. W. (1966). Communication in the interview and the disengaged respondent. *Public Opinion Quarterly, 30,* 385–398.

Gerner, R., Estabrook, W., Steuer, J., Waltuch, L. Kakkar, P., and Jarvik, L. (1980). A placebo controlled double-blind study of Imipramine and Trazedone in geriatric depression. In J. O. Cole and J. E. Barret (Eds.), *Psychopathology in the aged.* New York: Raven Press.

Gerner, R., and Jarvik, L. F. (1984). Antidepressant drug treatment in the elderly. In E. Friedman, F. Mann, and S. Gerson (Eds.), *Depression and antidepressants: Implications for consideration and treatment.* New York: Raven Press.

Gerstenbleth, G. (1982). Cardiovascular aging. In M. E. Reff and E. L. Schneider (Eds.), *Biological markers of aging.* Washington, DC: U.S. Government Printing Office, NIH Publication No. 82-2221.

Giesen, C. B., and Datan, N. (1979). The competent older woman. In N. Datan and N. Lohmann (Eds.), *Transitions of aging.* New York: Academic Press.

Gilleard, C. J., Wilmott, M., and Vaddadi, K. S. (1981). Self-report measures of mood and morale in elderly depressives. *British Journal of Psychiatry, 138,* 230–235.

Gillies, W. E., and West, R. H. (1981). Timolol maleate and intraocular pressure in low-tension glaucoma. *Transactions of the Ophthalmology Society, 33,* 25–33.

Gilligan, C. (1982). *In a different voice: Psychological theory and women's development.* Cambridge, MA: Harvard University Press.

Giniger, S., Dispenzieri, A., and Eisenberg, J. (1983). Age, experience, and performance on speed and skill jobs in an applied setting. *Journal of Applied Psychology, 68,* 469–475.

Glamser, F. D. (1976). Determinants of a positive attitude toward retirement. *Journal of Gerontology, 31,* 104–107.

Glantz, M. (1981). Predictions of elderly drug abuse. *Journal of Psychoactive Drugs, 13,* 117–126.

Glaser, B. G., and Strauss, A. L. (1965). *Awareness of dying.* Hawthorne, NY: Aldine.

Glaser, B. G., and Strauss, A. L. (1977). *Time for dying.* Hawthorne, NY: Aldine.

Glatt, S., and Katzman, R. (1984). Multi-infarct dementia. *Annual Review of Gerontology and Geriatrics, 4,* 61–86.

Glenn, N. D. (1969). Aging, disengagement, and opinionation. *Public Opinion Quarterly, 33,* 17–33.

Glenn, N. D. (1980). Values, attitudes and beliefs. In O. G. Brim, Jr. and J. Kagan (Eds.), *Constancy and change in human development.* Cambridge, MA: Harvard University Press.

Glick, I. O., Weiss, R. S., and Parkes, C. M. (1974). *The first year of bereavement.* New York: Wiley.

Glick, P. C. (1977). Updating the life cycle of the family. *Journal of Marriage and the Family, 39,* 5–13.

Glick, P. C. (1980). Remarriage: Some recent changes and variations. *Journal of Family Issues, 1,* 455–478.

Glock, C., and Stark, R. (1965). *Religion and society in tension.* Chicago, IL: Rand McNally.

Goldfarb, A. E., Hochstadt, N. J., Jacobson, J. H., and Weinstein, E. A. (1972). Hyperbaric oxygen treatment of organic mental syndrome in aged persons. *Journal of Gerontology, 27,* 212–217.

Goldstein, E. (1979). Effect of same-sex and cross-sex role models on the subsequent academic productivity of scholars. *American Psychologist, 34,* 407–410.

Goldstein, G., and Shelly, C. H. (1975). Similarities and difference between psychological deficit in aging and brain damage. *Journal of Gerontology, 30,* 448–455.

Goldstein, K. (1939). *The organism.* New York: American Book.

Goldstein, M. J., Baker, B. L., and Jamison, K. R. (1980). *Abnormal psychology.* Boston: Little, Brown.

Goldstein, S. E., and Birnbom, F. (1976). Hypochondriasis and the elderly. *Journal of the American Geriatric Society, 24,* 150–154.

Golin, S., Terrell, F., and Johnson, B. (1977). Depression and the illusion of control. *Journal of Abnormal Social Psychology, 86,* 440–442.

Goodin, D., Squires, K., Henderson, B., and Starr, A. (1978). Age-related variation in evoked potentials to auditory stimuli in normal human subjects. *Electroencephalography and Clinical Neurophysiology, 44,* 447–458.

Goodman, M. (1982). A critique of menopause research. In A. Voda, M. Dinnerstein, and S. O'Donnell (Eds.), *Changing perspective on menopause.* Austin: University of Texas Press.

Goodman, M. J., Stewart, C. J., and Gilbert, F. (1977). Patterns of menopause. *Journal of Gerontology, 32,* 291–298.

Gottsdanker, R. (1980). Aging and the use of advance probability information. *Journal of Motor Behavior, 12,* 133–143.

Gottsdanker, R. (1982). Aging and simple reaction time. *Journal of Gerontology, 37,* 342–348.

Gould, R. L. (1978). *Transformations: Growth and change in adult life.* New York: Simon & Schuster.

Gove, W. R. (1972). The relationships between sex roles, marital status and mental illness. *Social Forces, 51,* 34–44.

Grandy, T. C., and Stahmann, R. F. (1974). Family influence on college students' vocational choice: Predicting Holland's personality types. *Journal of College Student Personnel, 15,* 404–409.

Gratton, B., and Haug, M. (1983). Decision and adaptation: Research on female retirement. *Research on Aging, 5,* 59–76.

Green, S. K. (1981). Attitudes and perceptions about the elderly: Current and future perspectives. *Aging and Human Development, 13,* 95–115.

Greenberg, D. (1980, August 19). Till Monday do us part. *New York Times*.

Greenough, W. T., and Green, E. J. (1981). Experience and the changing brain. In J. L. MacGaugh and S. B. Kiesler (Eds.), *Aging: Biology and behavior*. New York: Academic Press.

Greenwald, A. G. (1980). The totalitarian ego: Fabrications and revision of personal history. *American Psychologist, 35*, 603–618.

Greer, D. S. (1983). Hospice: Lessons for geriatrics. *Journal of the American Geriatrics Society, 31*, 67–70.

Gribbin, K., and Schaie, K. W. (1979). Selective attrition in longitudinal studies: A cohort-sequential approach. In H. Orino, K. Shimada, M. Iriki, and D. Maeda (Eds.), *Recent advances in gerontology*. Amsterdam: Excerpta Medica.

Gribbin, K., Schaie, K. W., and Parham, I. A. (1980). Complexities of life style and maintenance of intellectual abilities. *Journal of Social Issues, 36*, 47–61.

Grossman, F. K., Eichler, L. S., and Winickoff, S. A. (1980). *Pregnancy, birth and parenthood*. San Francisco: Jossey-Bass.

Guemple, D. L. (1969). Human resource management: The dilemma of the aging Eskimo. *Sociological Symposium, 2*, 59–74.

Guilford, J. P. (1967). *The nature of human intelligence*. New York: McGraw-Hill.

Guilford, J. P. (1980). Fluid and crystallized intelligence: Two fanciful concepts. *Psychological Bulletin, 88*, 408–412.

Guilford, J. P., and Hoepfner, R. (1971). *The analysis of intelligence*. New York: McGraw-Hill.

Guilford, J. S., Zimmerman, W. S., and Guilford, J. P. (1976). *The Guilford-Zimmerman Temperament Survey handbook*. San Francisco, CA: EdITS Publishers.

Gurland, B. J. (1976). The comparative frequency of depression in various adult age groups. *Journal of Gerontology, 31*, 283–292.

Gurland, B. J., and Cross, P. S. (1982). Epidemiology of psychopathology in old age. In L. F. Jarvik and G. W. Small (Eds.), *Psychiatric clinics of North America*. Philadelphia: Saunders.

Gutmann, D. (1975). Parenthood: Key to the comparative psychology of the life cycle? In N. Datan and L. Ginsberg (Eds.), *Life-span developmental psychology: Normative life crises*. New York: Academic Press.

Gutmann, D. (1977). The cross-cultural perspective: Notes toward a comparative psychology of aging. In J. E. Birren and K. W. Schaie (Eds.), *Handbook of the psychology of aging*. New York: Van Nostrand Reinhold.

Guttmacher Institute. (1976). *11 million teenagers*. New York: Guttmacher Institute.

Guttman, D. (1978). Patterns of legal drug use by older Americans. *Addictive Diseases, 3*, 337–356.

Guttman, D., Griffith, B., and Grunes, J. (1982). Developmental contributions to the late-onset affective disorders. In P. B. Baltes and O. G. Brim, Jr. (Eds.), *Life-span development and behavior* (Vol. 4). New York: Academic Press.

Guzzardi, W. (1966). *The young executives*. New York: New American Library.

Gwenwald, M. (1984). The sage model for serving older lesbians and gay men. *Journal of Social Work and Sexuality, 2*, 53–61.

Gynther, M. D., and Shimkunas, A. M. (1966). Age and MMPI performance. *Journal of Consulting Psychology, 30*, 118–121.

Hachinski, V. C., Iliff, I. D., Zilka, E., Duboulay, G. H., McCallister, V. I., Marshall, J., Russell, R. W. R., and Symon, L. (1975). Cerebral blood flow in dementia. *Archives of Neurology, 32*, 632–637.

Hagestad, G. (1978). *Patterns of communication and influence between grandparents and grandchildren in a changing society*. Paper presented at the World Congress of Sociology, Sweden. Cited in Troll (1980).

Hagestad, G. O. (1981). Problems and promises in the social psychology of intergenerational relations. In R. Fogel, E. Hatfield, S. Kiesler, and J. March (Eds.), *Aging: Stability and change in the family*. New York: Academic Press.

Hagestad, G. O. (1984a). The continuous bond: A dynamic multigenerational perspective on parent-child relations. In M. A. Perlmutter (Ed.), *Minnesota symposium on child psychology* (Vol. 17). Hillsdale, NJ: Erlbaum.

Hagestad, G. O. (1984b, March). *Twentieth century family patterns: A guide for the twenty-first?* Paper presented at the annual meeting of the Eastern Sociological Association, Boston.

Hagestad, G. O., and Neugarten, B. L. (1985). Age and the life course. In R. Binstock and E. Shanas (Eds.), *Handbook of aging and the social sciences* (2nd ed.). New York: Van Nostrand Reinhold.

Hagestad, G. O., Smyer, M., and Stierman, K. (1984). The impact of divorce in middle age. In R. S. Cohen, B. J. Cohler, and S. H. Weissman (Eds.), *Parenthood: A psychodynamic perspective*. New York: Guilford Press.

Hall, G. S. (1923). *Senescence: The last half of life*. New York: Appleton-Century-Crofts.

Hallow, F., and Moran, D. (1981). Cataract — the ultraviolet risk factor. *Lancet, 8258,* 1249–1253.

Hamilton, M., and Reid, H. (Eds.) (1980). *A hospice handbook*. Grand Rapids, MI: Eerdmans.

Handler, P. (1960). Radiation and aging. In N. W. Shock (Ed.), *Aging*. Washington, DC: American Association for the Advancement of Science.

Handschu, S. S. (1973). Profile of the nurse's aide — Expanding her role as the psycho-social companion to the nursing home resident. *Gerontologist, 13,* 315–317.

Hardyck, C. D. (1964). Sex differences in personality changes in age. *Journal of Gerontology, 19,* 78–82.

Harkins, S. W., and Chapman, R. C. (1976). Detection and decision factors in pain perception in young and elderly men. *Pain, 2,* 253–264.

Harlow, H. F. (1975). Lust, latency, and lover: Simian secrets of successful sex. *Journal of Sex Research, 11,* 79–90.

Harragan, B. L. (1977). *Games Mother never taught you*. New York: Warner.

Harris, C. S. (1978). *Fact book on aging*. Washington, DC: National Council on the Aging.

Harris, L., and Associates. (1975). *The myth and reality of aging in America*. Washington, DC: National Council on the Aging.

Harris, R. (1975). Breaking the barriers to better health-care delivery for the aged. *Gerontologist, 15,* 52–56.

Hartley, A. A. (1981). Adult age differences in deductive reasoning processes. *Journal of Gerontology, 36,* 700–706.

Hartley, J. T., Harker, J. O., and Walsh, D. A. (1980). Contemporary issues and new directions in adult development of learning and memory. In L. W. Poon (Ed.), *Aging in the 1980s*. Washington, DC: American Psychological Association.

Haug, M. R. (1981). Age and medical care utilization patterns. *Journal of Gerontology, 36,* 103–111.

Havighurst, R. J. (1972). *Developmental tasks and education* (3rd ed.) New York: McKay.

Havighurst, R. J., and Albrecht, R. (1953). *Older people*. New York: Longmans Green.

Havighurst, R. J., Neugarten, B. L., and Tobin, S. S. (1968). Disengagement and patterns of aging. In B. L. Neugarten (Ed.), *Middle age and aging*. Chicago: University of Chicago Press.

Hayflick, K. (1980). The cell biology of human aging. *Scientific American, 242,* 58–65.

Hayflick, L. (1975). Why grow old? *The Stanford Magazine, 3*(1), 36–43.

Heidbreder, E. (1972). Factors in retirement adjustment: White-collar/blue-collar experience. *Industrial Gerontology, 12,* 69–72.

Heisel, M., and Faulkner, A. (1982). Religiosity in an older black population. *Gerontologist, 22,* 354–358.

Helmreich, R. L., Spence, J. T., Beane, W. E., Lucker, G. W., and Mathews, K. (1980). Making it in academic psychology: Demographic and personality correlates of attainment. *Journal of Personality and Social Psychology, 39,* 896–908.

Henderson, G., Tomlinson, B., and Benson, P. H. (1980). Cell counts in human cerebral cortex in normal adults throughout life using an image analyzing computer. *Journal of the Neurological Sciences, 46,* 113–136.

Hendrick, C., and Hendrick, S. (1983). *Liking, loving, and relating*. Monterey, CA: Brooks/Cole.

Hendricks, J., and Hendricks, C. D. (1977). *Aging in mass society: Myths and realities*. Cambridge, MA: Winthrop.

Henley, B., and Davis, M. S. (1967). Satisfaction and dissatisfaction: A study of the chronically-ill aged patient. *Journal of Health and Social Behavior, 8,* 65–75.

Henry, J. P. (1985). Relation of psychosocial factors to the senile dementias. In J. E. Birren, M. L. Gilhooly, and S. H. Zarit (Eds.), *The dementias: Policy and management*. Englewood Cliffs, NJ: Prentice-Hall.

Henry, J. P., and Stephens, P. N. (1977). *Stress, health and the social environment*. New York: Springer-Verlag.

Hertzog, C., Schaie, K. W., and Gribbin, K. (1978). Cardiovascular disease and changes in intellectual functioning from middle to old age. *Journal of Gerontology, 33,* 872–883.

Hess, A. L., and Bradshaw, H. L. (1970). Positiveness of self-concept and ideal-self as a function of age. *Journal of Genetic Psychology, 117,* 57–67.

Hess, B., and Waring, J. M. (1978). Parent and child in later life: Rethinking the relationship. In R. M. Lerner and G. B. Spanier (Eds.), *Child influences on marital and family interaction.* New York: Academic Press.

Hill, R., Foote, N., Aldonus, J., Carlson, R., and MacDonald, R. (1970). *Family development in three generations.* New York: Schenkman.

Himes, N. E. (1963). *Medical history of contraception.* New York: Gamut.

Hiroto, D. S. (1974). Locus of control and learned helplessness. *Journal of Experimental Psychology, 102,* 187–193.

Hobbs, D. F., and Wimbish, J. M. (1977). Transition to parenthood by black couples. *Journal of Marriage and the Family, 39,* 677–689.

Hockschild, A. R. (1975). *The unexpected community.* Englewood Cliffs, NJ: Prentice-Hall.

Hoffman, L. W. (1983). Increased fathering effects on the mother. In M. Lamb and A. Sagi (Eds.), *Social politics and legal issues pertaining to fatherhood.* Hillsdale, NJ: Erlbaum.

Hoffman, L. W. (1984). Work, family, and the socialization of the child. In R. D. Parke (Ed.), *Review of child development research* (Vol. 7). Chicago: University of Chicago Press.

Hoffman, L. W., and Manis, J. D. (1979). The value of children in the United States: A new approach to the study of fertility. *Journal of Marriage and the Family, 41,* 583–596.

Holahan, C. K. (1984). Marital attitudes over 40 years: A longitudinal and cohort analysis. *Journal of Gerontology, 39,* 49–57.

Holland, J. L. (1966). *The psychology of vocational choice.* Waltham, MA: Blaisdell.

Holland, J. L. (1973). *Making vocational choices: A theory of careers.* Englewood Cliffs, NJ: Prentice-Hall.

Holland, J. L. (1985). *Making vocational choices: A theory of vocational personalities and work environments.* Englewood Cliffs, NJ: Prentice-Hall.

Holmes, O. W. (1858). *The autocrat of the breakfast table.* New York: Heritage Press.

Holmes, T. H., and Rahe, R. H. (1967). The Social Readjustment Rating Scale. *Journal of Psychosomatic Research, 11,* 213–218.

Hooper, F. H., Hooper, J. D., and Colbert, K. K. (1984). *Personality and memory correlates of intellectual functioning: Young adulthood to old age.* New York: Karger.

Hooper, F. Fitzgerald, J., and Papalia, D. (1971). Piagetian theory and the aging process: Extensions and speculations. *Aging and Human Development, 2,* 3–20.

Horn, J. L. (1978). Human ability systems. In P. B. Baltes (Ed.), *Life-span developmental psychology* (Vol. 1). New York: Academic Press.

Horn, J. L. (1982). The theory of fluid and crystallized intelligence in relation to concepts of cognitive psychology and aging in adulthood. In F. J. M. Craik and S. Trehub (Eds.), *Aging and cognitive processes.* New York: Plenum.

Horn, J. L., and Donaldson, G. (1976). On the myth of intellectual decline in adulthood. *American Psychologist, 31,* 701–719.

Hornblum, J. N., and Overton, W. F. (1976). Area and volume conservation among the elderly: Assessment and training. *Developmental Psychology, 12,* 68–74.

Horowitz, M. J., Wilner, N., Marmar, C., Krupnick, J. (1980). Pathological grief and the activation of latent self-images. *American Journal of Psychiatry, 137,* 1157–1162.

Houle, C. O. (1981). *Continuing learning in the professions.* San Francisco: Jossey-Bass.

Howard, A. (1984, August). *Cool at the top: Personality characteristics of successful executives.* Paper presented at the Annual Meeting of the American Psychological Association, Montreal, Canada.

Howard, A., and Bray, D. W. (1980). *Career motivation in mid-life managers.* Paper presented at the Annual Meeting of the American Psychological Association, Montreal, Canada.

Howard, A., and Wilson, J. A. (1982). Leadership in a declining work ethic. *California Management Review, 24,* 33–46.

Howard, J. (1978). *Families.* New York: Simon & Schuster.

Hoyer, W. J., and Plude, D. J. (1980). Attentional and perceptual processes in the study of cognitive aging. In L. Poon (Ed.), *Aging in the 1980s*. Washington, DC: American Psychological Association.

Hultsch, D. (1971). Adult age differences in free classification and free recall. *Developmental Psychology, 4*, 338–342.

Hultsch, D., and Deutsch, F. (1981). *Adult development and aging*. New York: McGraw-Hill.

Hultsch, D., and Dixon, R. (1984). Memory for text materials in adulthood. In P. B. Baltes and O. G. Brim, Jr. (Eds.), *Life-span development and behavior* (Vol. 6). New York: Academic Press.

Hultsch, D. F., and Plemons, J. K. (1979). Life events and life-span development. In P. B. Baltes and O. G. Brim, Jr. (Eds.), *Life span development and behavior* (Vol. 2). New York: Academic Press.

Humphreys, L. G., and Parsons, C. K. (1979). Piagetian tasks measure intelligence and intelligence tests assess cognitive development: A reanalysis. *Intelligence, 3*, 369–382.

Hunt, M. (1974). *Sexual behavior in the 1970s*. New York: Playboy Press.

Hunt, R., and King, M. (1971). The intrinsic-extrinsic concept. *Journal for the Scientific Study of Religion, 10*, 339–356.

Hurlock, E. (1975). *Developmental psychology* (4th ed.). New York: McGraw-Hill.

Huston, P., McHale, S., and Crouter, A. (1984). When the honeymoon's over: Changes in the marriage relationship over the first year. In R. Gilmour and S. Duck (Eds.), *Key issues in personal relations*. Hillsdale, NJ: Erlbaum.

Huston-Stein, A., and Higgins-Trenk, A. (1978). Development of females from childhood through adulthood: Career and feminine role orientations. In P. B. Baltes (Ed.), *Life-span development and behavior* (Vol. 1). New York: Academic Press.

Hyde, J. S., and Phyllis, D. E. (1979). Androgyny across the life span. *Developmental Psychology, 15*, 334–336.

Jackson, J. S., Chatters, L. M., and Neighbors, H. W. (1982, January/February). The mental health status of older black Americans: A national study. *The Black Scholar*, 21–35.

Jackson, J., and Gibson, R. (1984). Work and retirement among the black elderly. In Z. Blau (Ed.), *Current perspectives on aging and the life cycle*. Greenwich, CT: JAI Press.

Jamison, K. R., Gerner, R. H., and Goodwin, F. K. (1979). Patient and physician attitudes toward lithium: Relationships to compliance. *Archives of General Psychiatry, 36*, 866–869.

Jaques, E. (1965). Death and the mid-life crisis. *International Journal of Psychoanalysis, 46*, 502–514.

Jarvik, L. F., and Bank, L. (1983). Aging twins: Longitudinal aging data. In K. W. Schaie (Ed.), *Longitudinal studies of adult psychological development*. New York: Guilford Press.

Jarvik, L. F., and Cohen, D. A. (1973). A biobehavioral approach to intellectual changes with aging. In C. Eisdorfer and M. P. Lawton (Eds.), *The psychology of adult development and aging*. Washington, DC: American Psychological Association.

Jarvik, L. F., and Perl, M. (1981). Overview of physiologic dysfunctions related to psychiatric problems in the elderly. In A. Levenson and R. C. W. Hall (Eds.), *Psychiatric management of physical disease in the elderly*. New York: Raven Press.

Johannson, C. B., and Campbell, D. P. (1971). Stability of the strong vocational interest blank for men. *Journal of Applied Psychology, 55*, 34–36.

Jones, L. Y. (1980). *Great expectations: America and the baby boom generation*. New York: Coward, McCann & Geoghegan.

Jung, C. G. (1960). The stages of life. In *Collected Works* (Vol. 8). Princeton, NJ: Princeton University Press.

Kagan, J. (1980). Perspectives on continuity. In O. G. Brim, Jr. and J. Kagan (Eds.), *Constancy and change in human development*. Cambridge, MA: Harvard University Press.

Kahana, E., and Coe, R. M. (1969). Perceptions of grandparenthood by community and institutionalized age. *Proceedings of the 77th Annual Convention of the American Psychological Association, 4*, 735–736.

Kahana, B., and Kahana, E. (1970). Grandparenthood from the perspective of the developing grandchild. *Developmental Psychology, 3*, 98–105.

Kahana, B., and Kahana, E. (1982). Environmental continuity, discontinuity, futurity and adaptation of the aged. In G. Rowles and R. Ohta (Eds.), *Aging and milieu: Environmental aperspectives on growing old*. New York: Academic Press.

Kahn, H. A., Leibowitz, H. M., Ganley, S. P., Kini, M. M., Colton, J., Nickerson, R. S., and Dawber, T. R. (1977). Framingham eye study: I. Outline and major prevalences and findings. *American Journal of Epidemiology, 106,* 17–32.

Kahn, R. L. (1975). The mental health system and the future aged. *Gerontologist, 15,* 24–31.

Kahn, R., Zarit, S, and Hilbert, N. (1975). Memory complaint and impairment in the aged. *Archives of General Psychiatry, 32,* 1569–1573.

Kalish, R. A. (1975). *Late adulthood.* Monterey, CA: Brooks/Cole.

Kalish, R. A. (1976). Death and dying in a social context. In R. H. Binstock and E. Shanas (Eds.), *Handbook of aging and the social sciences.* New York: Van Nostrand Reinhold.

Kalish, R. A., and Reynolds, D. K. (1976). *Death and ethnicity.* Los Angeles: University of Southern California Press.

Kaltreider, N., Becker, T., and Horowitz, M. J. (1983). Relationship testing after parental bereavement. *American Journal of Psychiatry, 141,* 243–246.

Kanin, E. (1971). Sexually aggressive college males. *Journal of College Student Personnel, 112,* 107–110.

Kaplan, G. A. (1982). *Psychological factors and ischemic heart disease mortality: A focal role for perceived health.* Paper presented at the annual meeting of the American Psychological Association, Washington, DC.

Kaplan, H. S. (1974). *The new sex therapy.* New York: Brunner/Mazel.

Karabel, J., and Astin, A. W. (1975). Social class, academic ability and college quality. *Social Forces, 53,* 381–398.

Kasl, S. V., and Berkman, L. S. (1981). Some psycho-social influences on the health status of the elderly: The perspective of social epidemiology. In J. L. McGaugh and S. B. Kiesler (Eds.), *Aging: Biology and behavior.* New York: Academic Press.

Kasl, S. V., and Rosenfield, S. (1980). The residential environment and its impact on the mental health of the aged. In J. E. Birren and R. B. Sloane (Eds.), *Handbook of mental health and aging.* Englewood Cliffs, NJ: Prentice-Hall.

Kastenbaum, R. (1975). Is death a life crisis? On the confrontation with death in theory and practice. In N. Datan and L. H. Ginsberg (Eds.), *Life-span developmental psychology: Normative life crises.* New York: Academic Press.

Kastenbaum, R. (1981). *Death, society and human experience* (2nd ed.). St. Louis, MO: Mosby.

Kastenbaum, R. (1985). Dying and death: A lifespan approach. In J. E. Birren and K. W. Schaie (Eds.), *Handbook of the psychology of aging* (2nd ed.). New York: Van Nostrand Reinhold.

Kaszniak, A. W., Garron, D. C., Fox, J. H., Bergen, D., and Huckman, M. (1979). Cerebral atrophy, EEG slowing, age, education, and cognitive functioning in suspected dementia. *Neurology, 29,* 1273–1279.

Kausler, D. H. (1982). *Experimental psychology and human aging.* New York: Wiley.

Kausler, D., and Hakami, M. (1983). Memory for activities: Adult age differences and intentionality. *Developmental Psychology, 19,* 889–894.

Kaye, I. (1973). Transportation problems of the older American. In J. G. Cull and R. E. Hardy (Eds.), *The neglected older American: Social and rehabilitation services.* Springfield, IL: Charles C. Thomas.

Kegan, R. (1982). *The evolving self.* Cambridge, MA: Harvard University Press.

Keith, J. (1982). *Old people, new lives: Community creation in a retirement residence* (2nd ed.). Chicago: University of Chicago Press.

Keith, P. N. (1979). Life change perceptions of life and death among older men and women. *Journal of Gerontology, 34,* 870–878.

Keller, W. D., Hilebrandt, K. A., and Richards, M. E. (1981). *Effects of extended father-infant contact during the newborn period.* Paper presented at the meeting of the Society for Research in Child Development, Boston.

Kelly, E. L. (1955). Consistency of the adult personality. *American Psychologist, 10,* 659–681.

Kelly, J. (1977). The aging male homosexual: Myth and reality. *Gerontologist, 17,* 328–332.

Kelly, J. B. (1982). Divorce: The adult perspective. In B. B. Wolman (Ed.), *Handbook of development psychology.* Englewood Cliffs, NJ: Prentice-Hall.

Kenshalo, D. R. (1977). Age changes in touch, vibration, temperature, kinesthesis, and pain sensitivity. In J. E. Birren and K. W. Schaie (Eds.), *Handbook of the psychology of aging.* New York: Van Nostrand Reinhold.

Kerckhoff, A. C., and Davis, K. (1962). Value consensus and complementarity in mate selection. *American Sociological Review, 27,* 295–303.

Kinsey, A. C., Pomeroy, W. B., and Martin, C. E. (1948). *Sexual behavior in the human male.* Philadelphia: Saunders.

Kinsey, A. C., Pomeroy, W. B., Martin, C. E., and Gebhard, P. H. (1953). *Sexual behavior in the human female.* Philadelphia: Saunders.

Kirchener, C., and Peterson, R. (1979). The latest data on visual disability from NCHS. *Journal of Visual Impairment and Blindness, 73,* 151–153.

Kitson, G., Lopata, H., Holmes, W., and Myering, S. (1980). Divorces and widows: Similarities and differences. *American Journal of Orthopsychiatry, 50,* 291–301.

Klaus, M. H., and Kennell, J. H. (1982). *Parent-infant bonding* (2nd ed.). St. Louis, MO: Mosby.

Kleemeier, R. W. (1962). Intellectual change in the senium. *Proceedings of the Social Statistics Section of the American Statistical Association,* 290–295.

Kleinman, M. B., and Clemente, F. (1976). Support for the medical profession among the aged. *International Journal of Health Services, 6,* 295–299.

Kleinmuntz, B. (1980). *Essentials of abnormal psychology* (2nd ed.). New York: Harper & Row.

Kline, D. W., and Schieber, F. (1985). Vision and aging. In J. E. Birren and K. W. Schaie (Eds.), *Handbook of the psychology of aging* (2nd ed.). New York: Van Nostrand Reinhold.

Kline, N. S. (1974). *From sad to glad.* New York: Putnam.

Klineberg, S. L. (1984). Social change, world views, and cohort succession: The United States in the 1980s. In K. A. McCluskey and H. W. Reese (Eds.), *Life-span developmental psychology: Historical and generational effects.* New York: Academic Press.

Klonoff, H., and Kennedy, M. (1966). A comparative study of cognitive functioning in old age. *Journal of Gerontology, 21,* 239–243.

Knaub, P. K., Eversoll, D. A., and Voss, J. H. (1983). Is parenthood a desirable adult role? An assessment of attitudes held by contemporary women. *Sex Roles, 9,* 355–362.

Kohlberg, L. (1973). Continuities in childhood and adult moral development revisited. In P. B. Baltes and K. W. Schaie (Eds.), *Life-span developmental psychology: Personality and socialization.* New York: Academic Press.

Kohlberg, L. (1981). *The philosophy of moral development: Moral stages and the idea of justice* (Vol. 1). San Francisco: Harper & Row.

Kohn, M. L. (1973). Social class and schizophrenia. *Schizophrenia Bulletin, 7,* 60–79.

Kohn, M. L. (1977). *Class and conformity: A study in values.* Chicago: University of Chicago Press.

Kohn, M. L., and Schooler, C. (1983). *Work and personality: An inquiry into the impact of social stratification.* Norwood, NJ: Ablex.

Kohn, R. R. (1971). *Principles of mammalian aging.* Englewood Cliffs, NJ: Prentice-Hall.

Kornzweig, A. L. (1972). The prevention of blindness in the aged. *Journal of the American Geriatric Society, 20,* 383–386.

Koss, M., and Oros, C. (1980). *The unacknowledged rape victims.* Paper presented at the meeting of the American Psychological Association, Montreal, Canada.

Kotelchuck, M. (1976). The infant's relationship to the father: Experimental evidence. In M. E. Lamb (Ed.), *The role of the father in child development.* New York: Wiley.

Kozol, J. (1985) *Illiterate America.* New York: Anchor Press-Doubleday.

Kovar, M. G. (1980). Morbidity and health care utilization. In S. G. Havnes and M. Feinleib (Eds.), *Proceedings of the second conference on the epidemiology of aging.* Washington, DC: U.S. Government Printing Office.

Kramer, M., Taube, C., and Redick, R. (1973). Patterns of use of psychiatric facilities by the aged: Past, present, and future. In C. Eisdorfer and M. P. Lawton (Eds.), *The psychology of adult development and aging.* Washington, DC: American Psychological Association.

Kreps, J. M. (1977). Intergenerational transfers and the bureaucracy. In E. Shanas and M. Sussman (Eds.), *Family, bureaucracy and the elderly.* Durham, NC: Duke University Press.

Kubler-Ross, E. (1969). *On death and dying.* New York: Macmillan.

Kubler-Ross, E. (1974). *Questions and answers on death and dying.* New York: Macmillan.

Kubler-Ross, E. (1981). *Living with death and dying.* New York: Macmillan.

Kuhlen, R. G. (1968). Developmental changes in motivation during the adult years. In B. L. Neugarten (Ed.), *Middle age and aging*. Chicago: University of Chicago Press.

Kuhn, D., Langer, J., Kohlberg, L., and Haan, N. S. (1977). The development of formal operations in logical and moral judgment. *Genetic Psychology Monograph, 95*, 97–188.

Kuhn, D., Pennington, N., and Leadbeater, B. (1983). Adult thinking in developmental perspective. In P. B. Baltes and O. G. Brim, Jr. (Eds.), *Life span development and behavior* (Vol. 5). New York: Academic Press.

Kulka, R. A., Veroff, J., and Douvan, E. (1979). Social class and the use of professional help for personal problems: 1957 and 1976. *Journal of Health and Social Behavior, 20*, 2–17.

Kunkel, S. R. (1979). *Sex differences in adjustment to widowhood*. Unpublished master's thesis, Miami University, Oxford, OH.

Labouvie-Vief, G. (1977). Adult cognitive development: In search of alternative interpretations. *Merrill-Palmer Quarterly, 23*, 227–263.

Labouvie-Vief, G. (1982). Growth and aging in life-span perspective. *Human Development, 25*, 65–79.

Labouvie-Vief, G. (1985). Intelligence and cognition. In J. E. Birren and K. W. Schaie (Eds.), *Handbook of the psychology of aging* (2nd ed.). New York: Van Nostrand Reinhold.

Labouvie-Vief, G., and Blanchard-Fields, F. (1982). Cognitive aging and psychological growth. *Aging and Society, 2*, 183–209.

Labouvie-Vief, G., and Chandler, M. J. (1978). Cognitive development and life-span developmental theory: Idealistic versus contextual perspectives. In P. B. Baltes (Ed.), *Life-span developmental psychology* (Vol. 1). New York: Academic Press.

Labouvie-Vief, G., and Gonda, J. N. (1976). Cognitive strategy training and intellectual performances in the elderly. *Journal of Gerontology, 31*, 327–332.

Labouvie-Vief, G., and Schnell, D. (1982). Learning and memory in later life. In B. B. Wolman (Ed.), *Handbook of developmental psychology*. Englewood Cliffs, NJ: Prentice-Hall.

Lacey, J. I. (1967). Psychophysiological approaches to the evaluation of psychotherapeutic process and outcome. In E. A. Rubenstein and M. B. Parloff (Eds.), *Research in psychotherapy*. Washington, DC: American Psychological Association.

Lack, S. A. (1978). Characteristics of a hospice program of care. *Death Education, 2*, 41–52.

Lamb, M. E., Frodi, A. M., Hwang, C. P., and Frodi, M. (1982). Varying degrees of paternal involvement in infant care: Attitudinal and behavioral correlates. In M. E. Lamb (Ed.), *Nontraditional families*. Hillsdale, NJ: Erlbaum.

Lamy, P. P. (1980). Misuse and abuse of drugs by the elderly. *American Journal of Pharmacology, 20*, 14–17.

Lanetto, R. (1980). *Children's conceptions of death*. New York: Springer.

Langer, E. J. (1975). The illusion of control. *Journal of Personality and Social Psychology, 32*, 311–328.

Langer, E. J. (1977). The psychology of change. *Journal for the Theory of Social Behavior, 7*, 185–207.

Langer, E. J. (1982). Old age: An artifact? In *Biology, behavior and aging*. New York: National Research Council.

Langer, E. J., and Benevento, A. (1978). Self-induced dependence. *Journal of Personality and Social Psychology, 36*, 886–893.

Langer, E. J., and Rodin, J. (1976). The effects of choice and enhanced personal responsibility for the aged: A field experiment in an institutional setting. *Journal of Personality and Social Psychology, 34*, 191–198.

La Rue, A. (1984). Neuropsychological testing. *Psychiatric Annals, 14*, 201–204.

La Rue, A., Dessonville, C., and Jarvik, L. F. (1985). Aging and mental disorders. In J. E. Birren and K. W. Schaie (Eds.), *Handbook of the psychology of aging* (2nd ed.). New York: Van Nostrand Reinhold.

Lasswell, M., and Lobsenz, N. M. (1980). *Styles of loving*. Garden City, NY: Doubleday.

Laurence, M. W. (1967). Memory loss with age: A test of two strategies for its retardation. *Psychonomic Science, 9*, 209–210.

Lawrence, B. (1980). The myth of the midlife crisis. *Sloan Management Review, 21*, 35–49.

Lazarus, R. S. (1981). The stress and coping paradigm. In C. Eisdorfer, D. Cohen, A. Kleiman, and P. Maxim (Eds.), *Theoretical bases in psychopathology*. New York: Spectrum.

Leaf, A. (1973a). Every day is a gift when you are over 100. *National Geographic, 143*, 93.

Leaf, A. (1973b, September). Getting old. *Scientific American*.

Leech, S., and Witte, K. L. (1971). Paired-associate learning in elderly adults as related to pacing and incentive conditions. *Developmental Psychology, 5*, 174–180.

Lehman, H. C. (1953). *Age and achievement*. Princeton, NJ: Princeton University Press.

Lehmann, H. E. (1984). Affective disorders in the aged. In L. F. Jarvik and G. W. Small (Eds.), *The psychiatric clinics of North America*. Philadelphia: Saunders.

Lehr, U. M. (1982). Social-psychological correlates of longevity. *Annual Review of Gerontology and Geriatrics, 3*, 102–147.

LeMasters, E. E. (1957). Parenthood as crisis. *Marriage and Family Living, 19*, 352–355.

Lemon, B. W., Bengtson, V. L., and Peterson, J. A. (1972). An exploration of the activity theory of aging: Activity types and life satisfactions among in-movers to a retirement community. *Journal of Gerontology, 27*, 511–523.

Lemon, H. M. (1982). Estrogens. In J. F. Holland and E. Frei (Eds.), *Cancer medicine*. Philadelphia: Lea and Febiger.

Lerner, R. M., and Spanier, G. (1978). A dynamic interactional view of child and family development. In R. M. Lerner and G. B. Spanier (Eds.), *Child influences on marital and family interaction*. New York: Academic Press.

Levenson, A. J. (1979). *Neuropsychiatric side-effects of drugs in the elderly*. New York: Raven Press.

Levenson, S. A., and List, N. D. (1981). Ethical considerations in critical and terminal illness in the elderly. *Journal of the American Geriatrics Society, 29*, 563–567.

Levin, C., Kohlberg, L., and Hewer, A. (1985). The current formulation of Kohlberg's theory and a response to critics. *Human Development, 28*, 94–100.

Levinger, G. (1979). A social psychological perspective on marital dissolution. In G. Levinger and O. C. Moles (Eds.), *Divorce and separation*. New York: Basic Books.

Levinson, D. J. (1978). *The seasons of a man's life*. New York: Knopf.

Levy, R. I., and Moskowitz, J. (1982). Cardiovascular research: Decades of progress, a decade of promise. *Science, 217*, 121–129.

Levy, S. M., Derogatis, L. R., Gallagher, D., and Gatz, M. (1980). Intervention with older adults and the evaluation of outcome. In L. W. Poon (Ed.), *Aging in the 1980s*. Washington, DC: American Psychological Association.

Lewinsohn, P. M. (1975). The behavioral study and treatment of depression. In M. Hersen, R. M. Eisler, and P. M. Miller (Eds.), *Progress in behavior modification*. New York: Academic Press.

Lewinsohn, P., Mischel, W., Chaplin, W., and Barton, R. (1980). Social competence and depression: The role of illusory self-perceptions. *Journal of Abnormal Psychology, 89*, 203–212.

Lewis, M. I., and Butler, R. N. (1974). Life review therapy. *Geriatrics, 29*, 165–173.

Lewis, M., and Fiering, C. (1981). Direct and indirect interactions in social relationships. In L. P. Lipsitt (Ed.), *Advances in infancy research* (Vol. 1). New York: Ablex.

Lewis, R. A. (1979). Macular degeneration in the aged. In S. S. Han and D. H. Coons (Eds.), *Special senses in the aged*. Ann Arbor, MI: University of Michigan Press.

Liang, J., Kahana, E., and Doherty, E. (1980). Financial well-being among the aged: A further elaboration. *Journal of Gerontology, 35*, 409–420.

Libow, L. S., and Sherman, F. T. (1981). *The core of geriatric medicine*. St. Louis, MO: Mosby.

Lidz, T. (1976). *The person* (rev. ed.). New York: Basic Books.

Linton, R. (1949). The natural history of the family. In R. N. Anshen (Ed.), *The family: Its function and destiny*. New York: Harper.

Lipton, M. A., and Nemeroff, C. B. (1978). The biology of aging and its role in depression. In G. Usdin and C. K. Hofling (Eds.), *Aging: The process and the people*. New York: Brunner/Mazel.

Litwak, E. (1960a). Geographical mobility and extended family cohesion. *American Sociological Review, 25*, 9–21.

Litwak, E. (1960b). Geographical mobility and extended family structure. *American Journal of Sociology, 25*, 385–394.

Litwak, E. (1981). *The modified extended family, social networks, and research continuities in aging*. New York: Center for Sciences at Columbia University.

Livson, F. B. (1976). Patterns of personality development in middle-aged women: A longitudinal study. *International Journal of Aging and Human Development, 7,* 107–115.

Livson, F. B. (1981). Paths to psychological health in the middle years: Sex differences. In D. Eichorn, J. Clausen, N. Haan, M. Honzik, and P. Mussen (Eds.), *Present and past in middle life.* New York: Academic Press.

Loevinger, J. (1966). The meaning and measurement of ego development. *American Psychologist, 21,* 195–206.

Loftus, E. (1983). Misfortunes of memory. *Philosophical Transactions of the Royal Society London, 302,* 413–421.

Loftus, E. F. (1985). To file, perchance to cheat. *Psychology Today, 19,* 35–39.

Loftus, E., Fienberg, S., and Tanur, J. (1985). Cognitive psychology meets the national survey. *American Psychologist, 40,* 175–180.

Loftus, E. F., and Loftus, G. R. (1980). On the permanence of stored information in the human brain. *American Psychologist, 35,* 409–420.

Long, B. H. (1983). Evaluations and intentions concerning marriage among unmarried female undergraduates. *Journal of Social Psychology, 119,* 235–242.

Longino, C. F., Jr. (1981). Retirement communities. In F. J. Berghorn and D. E. Schafer (Eds.), *The dynamics of aging.* Boulder, CO: Westview Press.

Longino, C. F., and Kart, C. S. (1982). Explicating activity theory: Formal replication. *Journal of Gerontology, 37,* 713–722.

Looft, W. R. (1972). Egocentrism and social interaction. *Psychological Bulletin, 78,* 73–92.

Lopata, H. Z. (1973). *Widowhood in an American city.* Cambridge, MA: Schenkman.

Lopata, H. Z. (1975). Widowhood: Societal factors in life-span disruptions and alternatives. In N. Datan and L. H. Ginsberg (Eds.), *Life-span development psychology: Normative life crises.* New York: Academic Press.

Lopata, H. Z. (1980a). The widowed family member. In N. Datan and N. Lohmann (Eds.), *Transitions of aging.* New York: Academic Press.

Lopata, H. (1980b). The Chicago woman: A study of patterns of mobility and transportation. *Journal of Women in Culture and Society, 5,* 161–169.

Lopata, H. (1981). Widowhood and husband sanctification. *Journal of Marriage and the Family,* 349–450.

Lougee, M., and Packard, G. (1981). *Conformity and perceived competence in adulthood.* Paper presented at the bi-annual meeting of the Society for Research in Child Development, Boston, MA.

Loveless, N. E., and Sanford, A. J. (1974). Effects of age on the contingent negative variation and preparatory set in a reaction-time task. *Journal of Gerontology, 29,* 52–63.

Lowenthal, M. F., and Berkman, P. L. (1967). *Aging and mental disorder in San Francisco.* San Francisco: Jossey-Bass.

Lowenthal, M. F., and Chiriboga, D. (1972). Transition to the empty nest: Crisis, change or relief? *Archives of General Psychiatry, 26,* 8–14.

Lowenthal, M. F., Thurnher, M., and Chiriboga, D. (1975). *Four stages of life.* San Francisco: Jossey-Bass.

Lowther, M. A. (1977). Career change in mid-life: Its impact on education. *Innovator, 8(7),* 1, 9–11.

Lynch, G., and Gerling, S. (1981). Aging and brain plasticity. In J. L. McGaugh and S. B. Kiesler (Eds.), *Aging: Biology and behavior.* New York: Academic Press.

Maas, H. S., and Kuypers, J. A. (1974). *From thirty to seventy.* San Francisco: Jossey-Bass.

Maas, J. W. (1978). Clinical and biochemical heterogeneity of depressive disorders. *Annals of Internal Medicine, 88,* 556–563.

Mace, D., and Mace, V. (1960). *Marriage East and West.* New York: Dolphin.

Macklin, E. (1972). Heterosexual cohabitation among unmarried college students. *The Family Coordinator, 12,* 463–471.

Maddison, D., and Viola, A. (1968). The health of widows following bereavement. *Journal of Psychosomatic Research, 12,* 297–306.

Maddox, G. L. (1964). Self assessment of health status: A longitudinal study of selected elderly subjects. *Journal of Chronic Disease, 17,* 449–460.

Maddox, G. L. (1968). Retirement as a social event in the United States. In B. L. Neugarten (Ed.), *Middle age and aging*. Chicago: University of Chicago Press.

Mahoney, M. J. (1980). *Abnormal psychology*. New York: Harper & Row.

Mahoney, M. J. (1982). Psychotherapy and human change processes. In *Master Lecture Series on Psychotherapy Research and Behavior*. Washington, DC: American Psychological Association.

Maletta, G. J. (1984). Use of antipsychotic medication in the elderly. *Annual Review of Gerontology and Geriatrics, 4,* 175–220.

Marcia, J. E. (1967). Ego identity status: Relationships to change in self-esteem, "general adjustment" and authoritarianism. *Journal of Personality, 35,* 118–133.

Maret, E., and Finlay, B. (1984). The distribution of household labor among women in dual-earner families. *Journal of Marriage and the Family,* 357–364.

Markus, H. (1977). Self schemata and processing information about the self. *Journal of Personality and Social Psychology, 35,* 63–78.

Marmor, M. F. (1982). Aging and the retina. In R. Sekuler, D. Kline, and K. Dismukes (Eds.), *Aging and human visual function*. New York: Alan R. Liss.

Marsh, G. R. (1980). Introduction to psychopharmacological issues. In L. W. Poon (Ed.), *Aging in the 1980s*. Washington, DC: American Psychological Association.

Marsh, G. R., and Thompson, L. W. (1977). Psychophysiology of aging. In J. E. Birren and K. W. Schaie (Eds.), *Handbook of the psychology of aging*. New York: Van Nostrand Reinhold.

Martin, C. E. (1981). Factors affecting sexual functioning in 60–79 year old married males. *Archives of Sexual Behavior, 10,* 339–420.

Marwell, G., Rosenfeld, R., and Spilerman, S. (1979). Geographic constraints on women's careers in academia. *Science, 205,* 1225–1231.

Maslow, A. (1953). Deficiency motivation and growth motivation. In M. Jones (Ed.), *Nebraska symposium on motivation* (Vol. 3). Lincoln, NE: University of Nebraska Press.

Maslow, A. H. (1970). *Motivation and personality* (2nd ed.). New York: Harper & Row.

Masnick, G., and Bane, M. J. (1980). *The nation's families: 1960–1990*. Joint Center for Urban Studies of MIT and Harvard.

Masters, W. H., and Johnson, V. E. (1966). *Human sexual response*. Boston: Little, Brown.

Masters, W. H., and Johnson, V. E. (1970). *Human sexual inadequacy*. Boston: Little, Brown.

Masters, W. H., Johnson, V. E., and Kolodny, R. C. (1982). *Human sexuality*. Boston: Little, Brown.

Maynard-Smith, J. (1966). Theories of aging. In P. L. Krohn (Ed.), *Topics in the biology of aging*. New York: Interscience.

Mazess, R. B., and Forman, S. H. (1979). Longevity and age exaggeration in Vilcabamba, Ecuador. *Journal of Gerontology, 34,* 94–98.

McCary, J. L. (1978). *Human Sexuality* (3rd ed.). New York: Van Nostrand.

McClelland, D. C. (1973). Testing for competence rather than for "intelligence." *American Psychologist, 28,* 1–14.

McCluskey, H. (1982). Education for older adults. In C. Eisdorfer (Ed.), *Annual review of gerontology and geriatrics* (Vol. 3). New York: Springer.

McCluskey, N. G., and Borgatta, E. F. (Eds.) (1981). *Aging and retirement: Prospects, planning, and policy*. Beverly Hills, CA: Sage.

McConnel, C., and Deljavan, F. (1983). Consumption patterns of the retired household. *Journal of Gerontology, 38,* 480–490.

McCrae, R. R., and Costa, P. T., Jr. (1982). The self-concept and the stability of personality: Cross-sectional comparisons of self-reports and ratings. *Journal of Personality and Social Psychology, 43,* 1282–1292.

McCrae, R. R., and Costa, P. T., Jr. (1983). Psychological maturity and subjective well-being: Toward a new synthesis. *Developmental Psychology, 19,* 243–248.

McCrae, R. R., and Costa, P. T., Jr. (1984). *Emerging lives, enduring dispositions: Personality in adulthood*. Boston: Little, Brown.

McDonald, G. W. (1981). Structural exchange and marital interaction. *Journal of Marriage and the Family, 43,* 825–839.

McDowell, J. (1982). Obsolescence of knowledge and career publication profiles: Some evidence of differences among fields in costs of interrupted careers. *The American Economic Review, 72,* 752–768.

McGinnis, J. M. (1982). Recent health gains for adults. *New England Journal of Medicine, 306,* 671–673.

McKain, W. C. (1972). A new look at older marriages. *The Family Coordinator, 21,* 61–69.

McKinney, F. (1965). *Understanding personality: Cases in counseling.* Boston: Houghton Mifflin.

McKluskey, K. A., Killarney, J., and Papini, D. R. (1983). Adolescent pregnancy and parenthood: Implications for development. In E. C. Callahan and K. A. McKluskey (Eds.), *Life-span developmental psychology: Non-normative life events.* New York: Academic Press.

McLendon, G. H. (1979). One teacher's experience with death education for adults. *Death Education, 3,* 57–66.

Meacham, J. (1983). Wisdom and the context of knowledge: Knowing that one doesn't know. In D. Kuhn and J. Meacham (Eds.), *On the development of developmental psychology.* Basel: Karger.

Mead, M. (1970). *Culture and commitment.* San Francisco: Natural History Press.

Medvedev, Z. A. (1974). Caucasus and Altay longevity: A biological or social problem? *Gerontologist, 14,* 381–387.

Meiner, D. E., and Cassel, C. K. (1983). Euthanasia in old age: A case study and ethical analysis. *Journal of the American Geriatrics Society, 31,* 294–298.

Metropolitan Life Insurance Co. (1977). Current patterns of dependency. *Statistical Bulletin, 58,* 10–11.

Metzger, A. M. (1979). A Q-methodological study of the Kübler-Ross stage theory. *Omega, 10,* 291–302.

Meyer, B., and Rice, G. (1983). Learning and memory from text across the adult life span. In J. Fine and R. O. Freedle (Eds.), *Developmental studies of discourse.* Norwood, NJ: Ablex.

Meyerowitz, J., and Feldman, H. (1967). Transitions to parenthood. In I. Cohn (Ed.), *Family structure, dynamics and therapy.* New York: American Psychiatric Association.

Myers, G. C., and Manton, K. G. (1984). Recent changes in the U. S. age at death distributions: Further observations. *Gerontologist, 24,* 571–575.

Migdel, S., Abeles, R. P., and Sherrod, L. R. (1981). *An inventory of longitudinal studies of middle and old age.* New York: Social Science Research Council.

Miles, W. R. (1931). Measures of certain human abilities through the life-span. *Proceedings of the National Academy of Sciences, 17,* 627–632.

Miller, B. C. (1976). A multivariate developmental model of marital satisfaction. *Journal of Marriage and the Family, 38,* 643–657.

Miller, K., and Kohn, M. (1983). The reciprocal effects of job conditions and the intellectuality of leisure-time activities. In M. L. Kohn and C. Schooler (Eds.), *Work and personality.* Norwood, NJ: Ablex.

Miller, K., Schooler, C., Kohn, M. L., and Miller, K. (1979). Women and work: The psychological effects of occupational conditions. *American Journal of Sociology, 85,* 66–94.

Miller, M. B., and Beer, S. (1977). Patterns of friendship among patients in a nursing home setting. *Gerontologist, 17,* 269–275.

Minaker, K. L., Meneneilly, G. S., and Rowe, J. W. (1985). Endocrine systems. In C. E. Finch and E. L. Schneider (Eds.), *Handbook of the biology of aging* (2nd ed.). New York: Van Nostrand Reinhold.

Mindel, C. H., and Vaughan, C. E. (1978). A multidimensional approach to religiosity and disengagement. *Journal of Gerontology, 33,* 103–108.

Mineka, S., and Hendersen, R. W. (1985). Controllability and predictability in acquired motivation. *Annual review of psychology, 36,* 495–529.

Minkoff, K., Berman, E., Beck, A. T., and Beck, R. (1973). Hopelessness, depression, and attempted suicide. *American Journal of Psychiatry, 130,* 455–459.

Mintz, J., Steuer, J., and Jarvik, L. (1981). Psychotherapy with depressed elderly patients: Research considerations. *Journal of Consulting and Clinical Psychology, 49,* 542–549.

Mischel, W. (1968). *Personality and assessment.* New York: Wiley.

Missinne, L. E. (1980). Aging in Bakongo culture. *International Journal of Aging and Human Development, 11,* 283–295.

Mitchell, J., Wilson, K., Revicki, D., and Parker, L. (1985). Children's perceptions of aging: A multidimensional approach to differences by age, sex and race. *Gerontologist, 25,* 182–187.

Mitchell, T. (1979). Organizational behavior. *Annual Review of Psychology, 30,* 243–281.

Moberg, D. O. (1968). Religiosity in old age. In B. L. Neugarten (Ed.), *Middle age and aging.* Chicago: University of Chicago Press.

Moles, O. C. (1979). Public welfare payments and marital dissolution: A review of recent studies. In G. Levinger and O. C. Moles (Eds.), *Divorce and separation.* New York: Basic Books.

Monge, R. H. (1975). Structure of the self-concept from adolescence through old age. *Experimental Aging Research, 1,* 281–291.

Monge, R., and Hultsch, D. (1971). Paired-associate learning as a function of adult age and the length of the anticipation and inspection intervals. *Journal of Gerontology, 26,* 157–162.

Monk, A. (Ed.) (1985). *Handbook of gerontological services.* New York: Van Nostrand Reinhold.

Moore, L. M., Neilsen, C. R., and Mistretta, C. M. (1982). Sucrose taste thresholds: Age-related differences. *Journal of Gerontology, 37,* 64–69.

Moos, R. H. (1981). Environmental choice and control in community care settings for older people. *Journal of Applied Social Psychology, 11,* 23–43.

Moos, R. H., and Lemke, S. (1985). Specialized living environments for older people. In J. E. Birren and K. W. Schaie (Eds.), *Handbook of the psychology of aging* (2nd ed.). New York: Van Nostrand Reinhold.

Morgan, L. A. (1976). A re-examination of widowhood and morale. *Journal of Gerontology, 31,* 687–695.

Morgan, L. A. (1981). Aging in a family context. In R. H. Davis (Ed.), *Aging: Prospects and issues* (3rd ed.). Los Angeles: Andrus Gerontology Center.

Morris, J. B., and Beck, A. T. (1974). The efficacy of antidepressant drugs: A review of research (1958–1972). *Archives of General Psychiatry, 30,* 667–674.

Morris, J. N., Sherwood, S., and Mor, V. (1984). An assessment tool for use in identifying functionally vulnerable persons in the community. *Gerontologist, 24,* 373–378.

Morrison, M. H. (1983). The aging of the U.S. population: Human resource implications. *Monthly Labor Review, 106,* 15–19.

Mortimer, J. T. (1974). Patterns of intergenerational occupational movements: A smallest-space analysis. *American Journal of Sociology, 5,* 1278–1295.

Mortimer, J. T. (1976). Social class, work and family: Some implications of the father's occupation for family relationships and son's career decisions. *Journal of Marriage and the Family, 38,* 241–256.

Mortimer, J. T., Finch, M. D., and Kumka, D. (1982). Persistence and change in development: The multidimensional self-concept. In P. B. Baltes and O. G. Brim, Jr. (Eds.), *Life span development and behavior* (Vol. 4). New York: Academic Press.

Mortimer, J. T., and Kumka, D. (1982). A further examination of the occupational linkage hypothesis. *The Sociological Quarterly, 23,* 241–256.

Mortimer, J. T., and Lorence, J. (1979). Occupational experience and the self-concept: A longitudinal study. *Social Psychology Quarterly, 42,* 307–323.

Moss, H. A., and Sussman, E. J. (1980). Longitudinal study of personality development. In O. G. Brim, Jr. and J. Kagan (Eds.), *Constancy and change in human development.* Cambridge, MA: Harvard University Press.

Moss, M. S., and Moss, S. Z. (1980, November). *The impact of parental death on middle-aged children.* Paper presented at the 38th Annual Meeting of the American Society of Marriage and Family Therapy, Toronto, Canada.

Moss, M. S., Moss, S. Z., and Moles, E. L. (1985). The quality of relationships between elderly parents and their out-of-town children. *Gerontologist, 25,* 134–140.

Mossey, J. M., and Shapiro, E. (1982). Self-rated health: A predictor of mortality among the elderly. *American Journal of Public Health, 72,* 800–808.

Murphy, C. (1983). Age-related effects on the threshold psychophysical function, and pleasantness of menethol. *Journal of Gerontology, 38,* 217–222.

Murray, H., and Associates. (1938). *Explorations in personality.* New York: Oxford University Press.

Muhs, P. J., Hooper, F. H., and Papalia-Finlay, D. E. (1980). An initial analysis of cognitive functioning across the life-span. *International Journal of Aging and Human Development, 10,* 311–333.

Mussen, P. H., Conger, J. J., Kagan, J., and Geiwitz, J. (1979). *Psychological development: A life-span approach.* New York: Harper & Row.

Mussen, P., and Haan, N. (1981). A longitudinal study of patterns of personality and political ideologies. In D. Eichorn, J. Clausen, N. Haan, M. Honzik, and P. Mussen (Eds.), *Present and past in middle life.* New York: Academic Press.

Nadelson, T. (1969). A survey of literature on the adjustment of the aged to retirement. *Journal of Geriatric Psychiatry, 3,* 3–20.

Nagy, M. (1948). The child's theories concerning death. *Journal of Genetic Psychology, 73,* 3–27.

Nahemow, N. R. (1984). Grandparenthood in transition. In K. A. McCluskey and H. W. Reese (Eds.), *Life-span developmental psychology: Historical and generational effects.* New York: Academic Press.

Naisbitt, J. (1984). *Megatrends.* New York: Warner Books.

Nason, J. D. (1981). Respected elderly or old person: Aging in a Micronesian community. In P. T. Amoss and S. Harrell (Eds.), *Other ways of growing old.* Stanford, CA: Stanford University Press.

National Center for Health Statistics. (1978). *Vital and health statistics.* Washington, DC: U.S. Government Printing Office.

National Center for Health Statistics. (1980). *Vital statistics of the United States, 1976, Vol. II Mortality, Part A.* Washington, DC: U.S. Government Printing Office.

National Center for Health Statistics. (1983a). Changing mortality patterns, health services utilization and health care expenditures: United States, 1978–2003. *Vital and Health Statistics, Series 3,* No. 23.

National Center for Health Statistics. (1983b). Eye care visits and use of eyeglasses or contact lenses: United States, 1979–80. *Vital and Health Statistics, 10,* No. 145.

National Center for Health Statistics. (1983c, August). Advance report of final marriage statistics, 1980. *Monthly Vital Statistics Report, 32* (Supp. 9).

National Center for Health Statistics. (1984a). Advance report of final divorce statistics, 1981. *Monthly Vital Statistics Report, 32,* 3.

National Center for Health Statistics. (1984b). Health characteristics by geographic region. Large metropolitan areas, and other places of residence, United States, 1980–81. *Vital and Health Statistics, 10,* No. 146.

National Crime Survey (1980). *Criminal victimization in the United States, 1978.* Washington, DC: U.S. Department of Justice, Bureau of Justice Statistics.

National Safety Council. (1981). *Accident facts.* new York: National Safety Council.

Neapolitan, J. (1981). Occupational change in mid-career: An exploratory investigation. In R. E. Hill, E. L. Miller, and M. A. Lowther (Eds.), *Adult career transitions: Current research and perspectives.* Ann Arbor: University of Michigan, Michigan Business Papers, No. 66.

Nehrke, M. F., Hulicka, I. M., and Morganti, J. R. (1980). Age differences in life satisfaction, locus of control, and self-concept. *International Journal of Aging and Human Development, 11,* 25–33.

Nelson, H. (1928). The creative years. *American Journal of Psychology, 40,* 303–311.

Neugarten, B. L. (1968). The awareness of middle age. In B. L. Neugarten (Ed.), *Middle age and aging.* Chicago: University of Chicago Press.

Neugarten, B. L. (1969). Continuities and discontinuities of psychological issues into adult life. *Human Development, 12,* 121–120.

Neugarten, B. L. (1973). Personality change in late life: A developmental perspective. In C. Eisdorfer and M. P. Lawton (Eds.), *The psychology of adult development and aging.* Washington, DC: American Psychological Association.

Neugarten, B. L. (1977). Personality and aging. In. J. E. Birren and K. W. Schaie (Eds.), *Handbook of the psychology of aging.* New York: Academic Press.

Neugarten, B. L. (1979). The middle generations. In P. K. Ragan (Ed.), *Aging parents.* Los Angeles: University of Southern California Press.

Neugarten, B. L., and Associates. (1964) *Personality in middle and late life.* New York: Atherton Press.

Neugarten, B. L., and Gutmann, D. L. (1958). Age-sex roles and personality in middle age: A thematic apperception study. *Psychological Monographs: General and Applied, 17* (Whole No. 470).

Neugarten, B. L., and Gutmann, D. L. (1968). Age-sex roles and personality in middle age. In B. L. Neugarten (Ed.), *Middle age and aging.* Chicago: University of Chicago Press.

Neugarten, B. L., Havighurst, R. J., and Tobin, S. S. (1968). Personality and patterns of aging. In B. L. Neugarten (Ed.), *Middle age and aging*. Chicago: University of Chicago Press.

Neugarten, B. L., and Moore, J. W. (1968). The changing age status system. In B. L. Neugarten (Ed.), *Middle age and aging*. Chicago: University of Chicago Press.

Neugarten, B. L., Moore, J. W., and Lowe, J. C. (1968). Age norms, age constraints, and adult socialization. In B. L. Neugarten (Ed.), *Middle age and aging*. Chicago: University of Chicago Press.

Neugarten, B. L., and Weinstein, K. K. (1964). The changing American grandparent. *Journal of Marriage and the Family, 26*, 299–304.

Neugarten, B. L., Wood, V., Kraines, R. J., and Loomis, B. (1968). Women's attitudes toward the menopause. In B. L. Neugarten (Ed.), *Middle age and aging*. Chicago: University of Chicago Press.

Newman-Hornblum, J., Attig, M., and Kramer, D. A. (1980, August). *The use of sex-relevant Piagetian tasks in assessing cognitive competence among the elderly*. Paper presented at the annual meeting of the American Psychological Association, Toronto, Canada.

Norton, A. J. and Glick, P. C., (1979). Marital instability in America: Past, present, and future. In G. Levinger and O. C. Moles (Eds.), *Divorce and separation*. New York: Basic Books.

Obrist, W. D. (1978). Noninvasive studies of cerebral blood flow in aging and dementia. In R. Katzman, R. D. Terry, and K. L. Bick (Eds.), *Alzheimer's disease: Senile dementia and related disorders*. New York: Raven Press.

Obrist, W. D. (1980). Cerebral blood flow and EEG changes associated with aging and dementia. In E. W. Busse and D. G. Blazer (Eds.), *Handbook of geriatric psychiatry*. New York: Van Nostrand Reinhold.

Ochs, A. L., Newberry, J., Lenhardt, M. L., and Harkins, S. W. (1985). Neural and vestibular aging associated with falls. In J. E. Birren and K. W. Schaie (Eds.), *Handbook of the psychology of aging* (2nd ed.). New York: Van Nostrand Reinhold.

Offenbach, S. I. (1974). A developmental study of hypothesis testing and cue selection strategies. *Developmental Psychology, 10*, 484–490.

Ohrbach, H. (1961). Aging and religion: Church attendance in the Detroit metropolitan area. *Geriatrics, 16*, 530–540.

Okun, M. A., and DiVesta, F. J. (1976). Cautiousness in adulthood as a function of age and instructions. *Journal of Gerontology, 31*, 571–576.

Okun, M. A., and Elias, C. S. (1977). Cautiousness in adulthood as a function of age and instructions. *Journal of Gerontology, 32*, 451–455.

Oiesen, V. (1982). Sociological observations on ethical issues implicated in estrogen replacement therapy at menopause. In A. Voda, M. Dinnerstein, and S. O'Donnell (Eds.), *Changing perspective on menopause*. Austin: University of Texas Press.

Oleshansky, M. E., Gamsky, N. R., and Ramsmeyer, G. C. (In press). Activity level, purpose in life and repression as predictors of death anxiety in the aged. *Omega*.

Oliver, L. W. (1975). The relationship of parental attitudes and parent identification to career and homemaking orientation in college women. *Journal of Vocational Behavior, 7*, 1–12.

Olson, L. W., Harkins, S. W., and Lenhardt, M. (1985). Aging and the auditory system. In J. E. Birren and K. W. Schaie (Eds.), *Handbook of the psychology of aging* (2nd ed.). New York: Van Nostrand Reinhold.

O'Neill, N., and O'Neill, G. (1972). *Open marriage*. New York: Evans.

O'Rand, A., and Henretta, J. (1982). Delayed career entry, industrial pension structure, and early retirement in a cohort of unmarried women. *American Sociological Review, 47*, 365–373.

Ordy, J. M. (1981). Neurochemical aspect of aging in humans. In H. M. Praag, M. H. Lader, O. J. Rafaelson, and E. J. Sacher (Eds.), *Handbook of biological psychiatry*. New York: Dekker.

Orthner, D. (1975). Leisure activity patterns and marital satisfaction over the marital career. *Journal of Marriage and the Family, 37*, 91–102.

Ouslander, J. G. (1982). Illness and psychopathology in the elderly. In L. F. Jarvik and G. W. Small (Eds.), *The psychiatric clinics of North America*. Philadelphia: Saunders.

Owens, G., Fulton, R., and Markusen, E. (1983). Death at a distance: A study of family survivors. *Omega, 13*, 191–226.

Owens, W. A. (1966). Age and mental abilities: A second adult follow-up. *Journal of Educational Psychology, 57*, 311–325.

Padula, M. V. (1982). Low vision related to function and service delivery in the elderly. In R. Sekuler, D. W. Kline, and K. Dismukes (Eds.), *Aging and human visual function*. New York: Alan R. Liss.

Paine, W. S. (Ed.). (1982). *Job stress and burnout: Research, theory, and intervention perspective*. Beverly Hills, CA: Sage.

Palmore, E. (1970). The effects of aging on activities and attitudes. In E. Palmore (Ed.), *Normal aging*. Durham, NC: Duke University Press.

Palmore, E. (Ed.) (In press). *Retirement: Causes and consequences*. New York: Springer.

Palmore, E., Busse, E., Maddox, G. L., Nowlin, J. B., and Siegler, I. C. (Eds.) (1985). *Normal aging III*. Durham, NC: Duke University Press.

Palmore, E., and Jeffers, F. C. (Eds.) (1971). *Prediction of life span*. Lexington, MA: Heath.

Papalia, D., and Bielby, D. (1974). Cognitive functioning in middle and old age adults: A review of research based on Piaget's theory. *Human Development, 17*, 424–443.

Papalia-Finlay, D. E., Blackburn, J., Davis, E., Dellmann, M., and Roberts, P. (1980). Training cognitive functioning in the elderly — inability to replicate previous findings. *International Journal of Aging and Human Development, 12*, 111–117.

Parke, R. D., and Sawin, D. B. (1976). The father's role in infancy: A reevaluation. *The Family Coordinator, 25*, 365–371.

Parke, R. D., and Tinsley, B. R. (1981). The father's role in infancy: Determinants of involvement in caregiving and play. In M. E. Lamb (Ed.), *The role of the father in child development* (2nd ed.). New York: Wiley.

Parke, R. D., and Tinsley, B. R. (1984). Fatherhood: Historical and contemporary perspectives. In K. A. McCluskey and H. W. Reese (Eds.), *Life-span developmental psychology: Historical and generational effects*. New York: Academic Press.

Parker, E. S., and Noble, E. P. (1977). Alcohol consumption and cognitive functioning in social drinkers. *Journal of the Study of Alcoholism, 38*, 1224–1232.

Parkes, C. M. (1972). *Bereavement*. New York: International Universities Press.

Parkes, C. M., Benjamin, R., and Fitzgerald, R. A. (1969). Broken heart: A statistical study of increased mortality among widowers. *British Medical Journal, 1*, 740–743.

Parloff, M. B., Waskow, I. E., and Wolfe, B. E. (1978). Research on therapist variables in relation to process and outcome. In S. L. Garfield and A. E. Bergin (Eds.), *Handbook of psychotherapy and behavior change*. New York: Wiley.

Parnes, H., and King, R. (1977). Middle-aged job losers. *Industrial Gerontology, 4*, 77–96.

Parnes, H. S., and Nastel, G. (1981). The retirement experience. In H. S. Parnes (Ed.), *Work and retirement*. Cambridge, MA: MIT Press.

Parron, E., and Troll, L. (1978). Golden wedding couples: Effects of retirement on intimacy. *Alternate Life Styles, 1*, 447–464.

Parson, D. A., and Leber, W. R. (1981). The relationship between cognitive dysfunction and brain damage in alcoholics: Causal, interactive or epiphenomenal? *Alcoholism: Clinical and Experimental Research, 5*, 326–343.

Parsons, T. (1949). The social structure of the family. In R. N. Anshen (Ed.), *The family: Its function and destiny*. New York: Harper.

Pascual-Leone, J. (1983). Growing into human maturity: Toward a metasubjective theory of adult stages. In P. B. Baltes and O. G. Brim, Jr. (Eds.), *Life-span development and behavior*. New York: Academic Press.

Pattison, E. M. (1977). *The experience of dying*. New York: Prentice-Hall.

Pearlin, L. I. (1982). Discontinuities in the study of aging. In T. K. Hareven and K. J. Adams (Eds.), *Aging and life course transitions: An interdisciplinary perspective*. New York: Guilford Press.

Pellegrino, J. W., and Glaser, R. (1979). Cognitive correlates and components in the analysis of individual differences. In R. J. Sternberg and D. K. Detterman (Eds.), *Human intelligence*. New York: Ablex.

Pelletier, K. R. (1979). *Holistic medicine: From stress to optimum health*. New York: Descorte Press/ Seymour Lawrence.

Perl, D. P., Gajdusek, D. C., and Garruto, R. M. (1982). Intraneuronal aluminum accumulation in amyotrophic lateral sclerosis and parkinsonism-dementia in Guam. *Science, 217*, 1053–1055.

Perlmutter, M. (1978). What is memory aging the aging of ? *Developmental Psychology, 14*, 330–345.

Perry, D. K. (1955). Validities of three interest keys for U. S. Navy Yeomen. *Journal of Applied Psychology, 39*, 134–138.

Perry, W. I. (1968). *Forms of intellectual and ethical development in the college years.* New York: Holt, Rinehart and Winston.

Perun, P., and Bielby, D. (1979). Midlife: A discussion of competing models. *Research on Aging, 1*, 275–300.

Peskin, J. (1982). Measuring household production for the GNP. *Family Economics Review, 3*, 16–25.

Petersen, D. M., and Thomas, C. W. (1975). Acute drug reactions among the elderly. *Journal of Gerontology, 30*, 552–556.

Petersen, D. W., Whittington, F. J., and Beer, E. T. (1979). Drug use and misuse among the elderly. *Journal of Drug Issues, 9*, 5–26.

Peterson, C., and Seligman, M. E. P. (1984). Causal explanations as a risk factor for depression: Theory and evidence. *Psychological Review, 91*, 547–574.

Peterson, G. H., Meehl, L. E., and Leiderman, P. H. (1979). The role of some birth-related variables in father attachment. *American Journal of Orthopsychiatry, 49*, 330–338.

Peterson, J. A. (1980). Social psychological aspects of death and dying and mental health. In J. E. Birren and R. B. Sloane (Eds.), *Handbook of mental health and aging.* Englewood Cliffs, NJ: Prentice-Hall.

Pfeiffer, E. (1977). Psychopathology and social pathology. In J. E. Birren and K. W. Schaie (Eds.), *Handbook of the psychology of aging.* New York: Van Nostrand Reinhold.

Pfeiffer, E., Verwoerdt, A., and Davis, G. C. (1972). Sexual behavior in middle life. *American Journal of Psychiatry, 128*, 1262–1267.

Phillips, D. P. (1972). Deathday and birthday: An unexpected connection. In J. M. Tanner (Ed.), *Statistics: A guide to the unknown.* New York: Holden-Day.

Phillips, D. P., and Feldman, K. A. (1973). A dip in deaths before ceremonial occasions: Some new relationships between social integration and mortality. *American Sociological Review, 38*, 678–696.

Piaget, J. (1967). *Six psychological studies.* New York: Random House.

Piaget, J. (1972). Intellectual evolution from adolescence to adulthood. *Human Development, 15*, 1–12.

Pierce, R. C., and Chiriboga, D. A. (1979). Dimensions of adult self-concept. *Journal of Gerontology, 34*, 83–85.

Pines, A., and Aronson, E. (1981). *Burnout: From tedium to personal growth.* New York: Free Press.

Pitts, D. G. (1982). The effects of aging on selected visual functions: Dark adaptation, visual acuity, stereopsis and brightness contrast. In R. Sekuler, D. W. Kline, and K. Dismukes (Eds.), *Aging and human visual function.* New York: Alan R. Liss.

Pleck, J. H. (1983). Husbands' paid work and family roles: Current research issues. In H. Z. Lopata and J. H. Pleck (Eds.), *Research on the interweave of social roles. Vol. 3: Families and jobs.* Greenwich, CT: JAI Press.

Pleck, J. H., and Staines, G. L. (1982). Work schedules and work-family conflict in two earner couples. In J. Aldous (Ed.), *Two paychecks: Life in dual-earner families.* Beverly Hills, CA: Sage.

Plemons, J. K., Willis, S. L., and Baltes, P. B. (1978). Modifiability of fluid intelligence in aging: A short-term longitudinal training approach. *Journal of Gerontology, 33*, 224–231.

Plomp, R., and Mimpen, A. M. (1979). Speech-reception threshold for sentences as a function of age and noise level. *Journal of the Acoustical Society of America, 66*, 1333–1342.

Plutchik, R., Weiner, M. B., and Conte, H. (1971). Studies of body image: I. Body worries and body discomforts. *Journal of Gerontology, 35*, 49–55.

Pocs, O., Godrow, A., Tolone, W. L., and Walsh, R. H. (1977, June). Is there sex after 40? *Psychology Today.*

Polya, G. (1971). *How to solve it: A new aspect of mathematical method* (2nd ed.). Princeton: Princeton University Press.

Pomerance, A. (1976). Pathology of myocardium and valves. In F. T. Caird, J. L. C. Doll, and R. D. Kennedy (Eds.), *Cardiology in old age.* New York: Plenum.

Poon, L. (1985). Differences in human memory with aging: Nature, causes, and clinical implications. In J. E. Birren and K. W. Schaie (Eds.), *Handbook of the psychology of aging* (2nd ed.). New York: Van Nostrand Reinhold.

Poon, L., and Fozard, J. (1980). Speed of retrieval from long-term memory in relation to age, familiarity and datedness of information. *Journal of Gerontology, 5*, 711–717.

Poon, L., Fozard, J., Paulshock, D., and Thomas, J. (1979). A questionnaire assessment of age differences in retention of recent and remote events. *Experimental Aging Research, 5,* 401–411.

Poon, L., Rubin, D., and Wilson, B. (1986). *Everyday cognition and memory.* Hillsdale, NJ: Erlbaum.

Poon, L., and Schaffer, G. (1982, August). *Prospective memory in young and elderly adults.* Paper presented at the meeting of the American Psychological Association, Washington, DC.

Poon, L., Walsh-Sweeney, L., and Fozard, J. (1980). Memory skill training for the elderly: Salient issues on the use of imagery mnemonics. In L. Poon et al. (Eds.), *New directions in memory and aging: Proceedings of the George A. Talland Memorial Conference.* Hillsdale, NJ: Erlbaum.

Poon, L. W., and Welford, A. T. (1980). Prologue: A historical perspective. In L. W. Poon (Ed.), *Aging in the 1980s.* Washington, DC: American Psychological Association.

Post, F. (1980). Paranoid, schizophrenia-like, and schizophrenic states in the aged. In J. E. Birren and R. B. Sloane (Eds.), *Handbook of mental health and aging.* Englewood Cliffs, NJ: Prentice-Hall.

Powell, R. R. (1974). Psychological effects of exercise therapy upon institutionalized geriatric mental patients. *Journal of Gerontology, 29,* 157–161.

Power, T. G., and Parke, R. D. (1982). Play as a context for early learning: Lab and home analyses. In I. E. Siegel and L. M. Laosa (Eds.), *The family as a learning environment.* New York: Plenum.

Pratt, M. W., Golding, G., and Hoyer, W. J. (1983). Aging as ripening: Character and consistency of moral judgements in young, mature, and older adults. *Human Development, 26,* 277–288.

Prien, R. F. (1975). A survey of psychoactive drug use in the aged at Veterans Administration Hospitals. In S. Gershon and A. Raskin (Eds.), *Aging* (Vol. 2). New York: Raven Press.

Public Health Service. (1972). *Age, sex and diagnostic composition of resident patients in state and county mental hospitals — United States, 1961–1970.* Washington, DC: U.S. Government Printing Office.

Quirk, D., and Skinner, J. (1973). Physical capacity, age, and employment. *Industrial Gerontology, 19,* 49–62.

Rabinowitz, J. C., Craik, F. I. M., and Ackerman, B. P. (1982). A processing resource account of age differences in recall. *Canadian Journal of Psychology, 36,* 325–344.

Rahe, R. H. (1972). Subjects' recent life changes and their near-future illness susceptibility. *Advances in Psychosomatic Medicine, 8,* 2–19.

Rahe, R. H., and Arthur, R. T. (1978). Life changes and illness studies. *Journal of Human Stress, 4*(11), 3–15.

Ramey, J. W. (1972). Communes, group marriage, and the upper-middle class. *Journal of Marriage and the Family, 34,* 647–655.

Rango, N. (1985). The social epidemiology of accidental hypothermia among the aged. *Gerontologist, 25,* 424–430.

Rapoport, Rh., and Rapoport, Ro. (1971). *Dual-career families.* New York: Pelican.

Rapoport, R., and Rapoport, R. N. (1980). Three generations of dual-career family research. In F. Pepitone-Rockwell (Ed.), *Dual career couples.* Beverly Hills, CA: Sage.

Raskind, M. A., and Storrie, M. C. (1980). The organic mental disorders. In E. W. Busse and D. G. Blazer (Eds.), *Handbook of geriatric psychiatry.* New York: Van Nostrand Reinhold.

Raynor, J. O., and Entin, E. E. (Eds.). (1982). *Motivation, career striving, and aging.* Washington, DC: Hemisphere.

Redick, R. W., Kramer, M., and Taube, C. A. (1973). Epidemiology of mental illness and utilization of psychiatric facilities among older persons. In E. W. Busse and E. Pfeiffer (Eds.), *Mental illness in later life.* Washington, DC: American Psychiatric Association.

Reed, H. B. C., and Reitan, R. M. A. (1963). A comparison of the effects of the normal aging process with the effects of organic brain-damage on adaptive abilities. *Journal of Gerontology, 18,* 177–179.

Reedy, M. N., Birren, J. E., and Schaie, K. W. (1981). Age and sex differences in satisfying love relationships across the adult life span. *Human Development, 24,* 52–66.

Rees, J., and Botwinick, J. (1971). Detection and decision factors in auditory behavior of the elderly. *Journal of Gerontology, 26,* 133–136.

Rees, W. D., and Lutkins, S. G. (1967). Mortality of bereavement. *British Medical Journal, 4,* 13–16.

Reese, H. W., and Rodeheaver, D. (1985). Problem solving and complex decision making. In J. E. Birren and K. W. Schaie (Eds.), *Handbook of the psychology of aging* (2nd ed.). New York: Van Nostrand Reinhold.

Reid, B. (1984). An anthropological reinterpretation of Kohlberg's stages of moral development. *Human Development, 27,* 57–64.

Reinert, G. (1970). Comparative factor-analytic studies of intelligence throughout the human life-span. In L. R. Goulet and P. B. Baltes (Eds.), *Life-span development psychology: Research and theory.* New York: Academic Press.

Rhodes, R. (1979, June). Intimations of immortality. *Playboy Magazine.*

Rhodes, S. (1983). Age-related differences in work attitudes and behavior: A review and conceptual analysis. *Psychological Bulletin, 93,* 328–367.

Ribot, T. (1882). *Diseases of memory.* New York: Appleton.

Richmond, J. B. (1979). *Healthy people: The Surgeon General's report on health promotion and disease prevention.* Washington, DC: U.S. Government Printing Office, DHEW Publication No. 79-55071.

Ridgeway, C. (1978). Parental identification and patterns of career orientation in college women. *Journal of Vocational Behavior, 12,* 1–11.

Riegel, K. F. (1975). Adult life crises: A dialectical interpretation of development. In N. Datan and L. H. Ginsberg (Eds.), *Life-span developmental psychology: Normative life crises.* New York: Academic Press.

Riegel, K. F. (1976a). The dialectics of human development. *American Psychologist, 31,* 689–700.

Riegel, K. F. (1976b). From traits and equilibrium toward developmental dialectics. In W. Arnold (Ed.), *Nebraska Symposium on Motivation* (Vol. 24). Omaha, NE: University of Nebraska Press.

Riegel, K. F. (1977). The dialectics of time. In N. Datan and H. W. Reese (Eds.), *Life-span developmental psychology: Dialectical perspective on experimental research.* New York: Academic Press.

Riegel, K. R., and Riegel, R. M. (1972). Development, drop, and death. *Developmental Psychology, 6,* 306–319.

Ries, L. G., Pollack, E. S., and Young, J. L. (1983). Cancer patient survival: Surveillance, epidemiology, and end results program, 1973–1979. *Journal of the National Cancer Institute, 70,* 693–712.

Riley, M. W. (1985). Age strata in social systems. In R. H. Binstock and E. Shanas (Eds.), *Handbook of aging and the social sciences.* New York: Van Nostrand Reinhold.

Riley, M. W., and Foner, A. (1968). *Aging and society: An inventory of research findings.* New York: Russell Sage Foundation.

Roberts, M. A., and Caird, F. L. (1976). Computerized tomography and intellectual impairment in the elderly. *Journal of Neurology, Neurosurgery and Psychiatry, 39,* 986–989.

Robertson, J. F. (1975). Interaction in three-generation families; parents as mediators: Toward a theoretical perspective. *International Journal of Aging and Human Development, 6,* 103–110.

Robertson, J. F. (1976). Significance of grandparents: Perceptions of young adult grandchildren. *Gerontologist, 16,* 137–140.

Robertson, J. F. (1977). Grandmotherhood: A study of role concepts. *Journal of Marriage and the Family, 39,* 165–174.

Robertson-Tchabo, E. A., Hausman, C. P., and Arenberg, D. A. (1976). A classic mnemonic for old learners: A trip that works. *Educational Gerontology, 1,* 215–226.

Robinson, I. E., and Jedlicka, D. (1982). Change in sexual attitudes and behavior of college students from 1965 to 1980: A research note. *Journal of Marriage and the Family, 44,* 237–240.

Rodgers, W. L., and Thornton, A. (1984). *Changing patterns of first marriages in the United States.* Ann Arbor, MI: University of Michigan Survey Research Center.

Rodin, J. (1981). Current status of the internal-external hypothesis for obesity. *American Psychologist, 36,* 361–372.

Rodin, J. (1983). Behavioral medicine: Beneficial effects of self-control training in the aged. *International Review of Applied Psychology, 32,* 153–181.

Rodin, J., and Langer, E. J. (1977). Long-term effects of a control-relevant intervention with the institutionalized aged. *Journal of Personality and Social Psychology, 35,* 897–902.

Rodin, J., and Langer E. (1980). Aging labels: The decline of control and the fall of self-esteem. *Journal of Social Issues, 36,* 12–29.

Rogers, C. (1972). *Becoming partners: Marriages and its alternatives.* New York: Dell.

Rollins, B. C., and Feldman, H. (1970). Marital satisfaction over the life cycle. *Journal of Marriage and the Family, 32,* 20–28.

Ronch, J. L., and Maizler, J. S. (1977). Individual psychotherapy with the institutionalized aged. *American Journal of Orthopsychiatry, 47,* 257–283.

Rosen, J. L., and Bibring, G. L. (1968). Psychological reactions of hospitalized male patients to a heart attack: Age and social-class differences. In B. L. Neugarten (Ed.), *Middle age and aging.* Chicago: University of Chicago Press.

Rosen, J. L., and Neugarten, B. (1960). Ego functions in the middle and later years: A thematic apperception study of normal adults. *Journal of Gerontology, 15,* 62–67.

Rosen, W. G., Terry, R. D., Fuld, P. A., Katzman, R., and Peck, A. (1980). Pathologic verification of the ischemic score in differentiation of dementias. *Annals of Neurology, 7,* 53–59.

Rosenfeld, A. H. (1985, June). Depression: Dispelling despair. *Psychology Today,* 28–34.

Rosenwaike, I. (1968). On measuring the extreme aged in the population. *Journal of the American Statistical Association, 63,* 29–40.

Rosin, A. J., and Glatt, M. M. (1971). Alcohol excess in the elderly. *Quarterly Journal of Studies on Alcoholism, 32,* 53–59.

Rosow, I. (1974). *Socialization in old age.* Berkeley, CA: University of California Press.

Rosow, I. (1981). Docs: Ortho and para. *American Journal of Orthopsychiatry, 512,* 255–259.

Rossi, A. (1980). Aging and parenthood in the middle years. In P. B. Baltes and O. G. Brim, Jr. (Eds.), *Life-span development and behavior* (Vol. 3). New York: Academic Press.

Rossman, I. (1980). Bodily changes with aging. In E. W. Busse and D. G. Blazer (Eds.), *Handbook of geriatric psychiatry.* New York: Van Nostrand Reinhold.

Rotter, J. (1966). Generalized expectancies for internal versus external control of reinforcement. *Psychological Monograph,* No. 609.

Rougemont, D. (1956). *Love in the western world.* New York: Pantheon.

Rowland, K. F. (1977). Environmental events predicting death for the elderly. *Psychological Bulletin, 84,* 349–372.

Rubin, I. (1973). The "sexless older years" — a socially harmful stereotype. In A. M. Juhasz (Ed.), *Sexual development and behavior.* New York: Dorsey.

Rubin, K. H. (1973). Decentration skills in institutionalized and noninstitutionalized elderly. *Proceedings of 81st Annual Convention, American Psychological Association, 8* (Part 2), 759–760.

Rubin, L. B. (1980). The empty nest: Beginning or ending? In L. A. Bond and J. C. Rosen (Eds.), *Competence and coping in adulthood.* Hanover, NH: University Press of New England.

Rubin, R. T. (1974). Biochemical and neuroendocrine responses to severe psychological stress. In E. K. E. Gunderson and R. H. Rahe (Eds.), *Life stress and illness.* Springfield, IL: Charles C. Thomas.

Ruesch, H. (1959). *The top of the world.* New York: Pocket Books.

Ruggles, N., and Ruggles, R. (1974). The anatomy of earnings behavior. In National Bureau of Economic Research, *The economics of well-being.* Conference on Research in Income and Wealth.

Rush, A. J., Beck, A. T., Kovacs, M., and Hollon, S. (1977). Comparative efficacy of cognitive therapy and pharmacotherapy in the treatment of depressed out-patients. *Cognitive Therapy and Research, 1,* 17–37.

Russell, C. (1974). Transition to parenthood: Problems and gratification. *Journal of Marriage and the Family, 36,* 244–303.

Russell, D. E. (1975). *The politics of rape.* New York: Stein & Day.

Russell, G. (1982). Share-caregiving families: An Australian study. In M. E. Lamb (Ed.), *Nontraditional families.* Hillsdale, NJ: Erlbaum.

Russo, V. (1981). *The celluloid closet: The treatment of homosexuality in American film.* New York: Harper & Row.

Ryan, C., and Butters, N. (1980). Further evidence for a continuum of impairment encompassing male alcoholic Korsakoff patients and chronic alcoholic men. *Alcoholism: Clinical and Experimental Research, 4,* 190–198.

Rybash, J. M., Roodin, P. A., and Hoyer, W. J. (1983). Expressions of moral thought in later adulthood. *Gerontologist, 23,* 254–260.

Rychlak, J. R. (1968). *A philosophy of science for personality theory.* Boston: Houghton Mifflin.

Ryff, C. (1984). Personality development from the inside: The subjective experience of change in adulthood and aging. In P. B. Baltes and O. G. Brim, Jr. (Eds.), *Life-span development and behavior* (Vol. 6). New York: Academic Press.

Ryff, C., and Baltes, P. B. (1976). Value transition and adult development in women: The instrumentality-terminality hypothesis. *Development Psychology, 12,* 567–568.

Ryff, C., and Migdal, S. (1984). Intimacy and generativity: Self-perceived transitions. *Signs: Journal of Women in Culture and Society, 9,* 470–481.

Sabatini, P., and Labouvie-Vief, G. (1979). *Age and professional specialization in formal reasoning.* Paper presented at the annual meeting of the American Psychological Association, Washington, DC.

Safirstein, S. L. (1972). Psychotherapy for geriatric patients. *New York State Journal of Medicine, 72,* 2743–2748.

Sagi, A. (1982). Antecedents and consequences of various degrees of paternal involvements in child rearing: The Israeli project. In M. E. Lamb (Ed.), *Nontraditional families.* Hillsdale, NJ: Erlbaum.

Saintsbury, G. (1896). Molière. *Chambers Encyclopedia.*

Salthouse, T. A. (1979). Adult age and the speed-accuracy tradeoff. *Ergonomics, 22,* 811–821.

Salthouse, T. A. (1980). Age and memory: Strategies for localizing the loss. In L. W. Poon, J. L. Fozard, L. S. Cermak, D. Arenberg and L. W. Thompson (Eds.), *New directions in memory and aging.* Hillsdale, NJ: Erlbaum.

Salthouse, T. A. (1982). *Adult cognition: An experimental psychology on human aging.* New York: Springer-Verlag.

Salthouse, T. A. (1984). Effects of age and skill in typing. *Journal of Experimental Psychology: General, 113,* 345–371.

Salthouse, T. A. (1985). Motor performance and speed of behavior. In J. E. Birren and K. W. Schaie (Eds.), *Handbook of the psychology of aging* (2nd ed.). New York: Van Nostrand Reinhold.

Salthouse, T. A., and Kail, R. (1983). Memory development throughout the life span: The role of processing rate. In P. B. Baltes and O. G. Brim, Jr. (Eds.), *Life-span development and behavior* (Vol. 5). New York: Academic Press.

Sanders, C. M. (1979). A comparison of adult bereavement in the death of a spouse, child and parent. *Omega, 10,* 303–322.

Sanders, J. A. C., Sterns, H. L., Smith, M., and Sanders, R. E. (1975). Modification of concept identification performance in older adults. *Developmental Psychology, 11,* 824–829.

Sanders, R. E., and Sanders, J. C. (1978). Long-term durability and transfer of enhanced conceptual performance in the elderly. *Journal of Gerontology, 33,* 408–412.

Sanders, R. E., Sanders, J. A. C., Mayes, G. J., and Sielski, K. A. (1976). Enhancement of conjunctive concept attainment in older adults. *Developmental Psychology, 12,* 485–486.

Santos, J. F., and VandenBos, G. R. (1982). *Psychology and the older adult: Challenges for training in the 1980s.* Washington, DC: American Psychological Association.

Sarason, S. B. (1977). *Work, aging, and social change.* New York: Free Press.

Sathananthan, G. L., and Gershon, S. (1975). Cerebral vasodilators: A review. In S. Gershon and A. Raskin (Eds.), *Aging* (Vol. 2). New York: Raven Press.

Savage, R. D., Gaber, L. B., Britton, P. G., Bolton, N., and Cooper, A. (1977). *Personality and adjustment in the aged.* New York: Academic Press.

Schaie, K. W. (1965). A general model for the study of developmental change. *Psychological Bulletin, 64,* 92–107.

Schaie, K. W. (1973). Methodological problems in descriptive developmental research on adulthood and aging. In J. R. Nesselroade and H. W. Reese (Eds.), *Life-span developmental psychology: Developmental issues.* New York: Academic Press.

Schaie, K. W. (1977). Quasi-experimental research designs in the psychology of aging. In J. E. Birren and K. W. Schaie (Eds.), *Handbook of the psychology of aging.* New York: Van Nostrand Reinhold.

Schaie, K. W. (1977/78). Toward a stage theory of adult cognitive development. *Aging and Human Development, 8,* 129–138.

Schaie, K. W. (1978). External validity in the assessment of intellectual development in adulthood. *Journal of Gerontology, 33,* 695–701.

Schaie, K. W. (1979a). Age changes in intelligence. In R. L. Sprott (Ed.), *Aging and intelligence.* New York: Van Nostrand Reinhold.

Schaie, K. W. (1979b). The primary mental abilities in adulthood: An exploration in the development of psychometric intelligence. In P. B. Baltes and O. G. Brim, Jr. (Eds.), *Life-span development and behavior* (Vol. 2). New York: Academic Press.

Schaie, K. W. (1980). Cognitive development in aging. In L. K. Obler and M. Alpert (Eds.), *Language and communication in the elderly*. Lexington, MA: Heath.

Schaie, K. W. (1982a). Longitudinal data sets: Evidence for ontogenetic development or chronicles of cultural change? *Journal of Social Issues, 38*, 65–72.

Schaie, K. W. (1982b). The aging in the coming decade. In K. W. Schaie and J. Geiwitz (Eds.), *Readings in adult development*. Boston: Little, Brown.

Schaie, K. W. (Ed.) (1983a). *Longitudinal studies of adult psychological development*. New York: Guilford Press.

Schaie, K. W. (1983b). Consistency and changes in cognitive functioning of the young-old and old-old. In M. Bergener, U. Lehr, E. Lang, and R. Schmitz-Scherzer (Eds.), *Aging in the eighties and beyond*. New York: Springer.

Schaie, K. W. (1983c). The Seattle Longitudinal Study: A twenty-one year exploration of psychometric intelligence in adulthood. In K. W. Schaie (Ed.), *Longitudinal studies of adult psychological development*. New York: Guilford Press.

Schaie, K. W. (1984a). Historical time and cohort effects. In K. A. McCluskey and H. W. Reese (Eds.), *Life-span developmental psychology: Historical and generational effects*. New York: Academic Press.

Schaie, K. W. (1984b). Midlife influences upon intellectual functioning in old age. *International Journal of Behavioral Development, 7*, 463–478.

Schaie, K. W. (1985). *Manual for the Schaie-Thurstone Adult Mental Abilities Test (STAMAT)*. Palo Alto, CA: Consulting Psychologists Press.

Schaie, K. W., and Baltes, P. B. (1975). On sequential strategies and developmental research. *Human Development, 18*, 384–390.

Schaie, K. W., Baltes, P., and Strother, C. R. (1964). A study of auditory sensitivity in advanced age. *Journal of Gerontology, 19*, 453–457.

Schaie, K. W., Gonda, J. N., and Quayhagen, M. (1981). The relationship between intellectual performance and perception of everyday competence in middle-aged, young-old, and old-old adults. *Proceedings of the XXIInd International Congress of Psychology*. Leipzig: International Union of Psychological Sciences.

Schaie, K. W., and Hertzog, C. (1982). Longitudinal methods. In B. B. Wolman (Ed.), *Handbook of developmental psychology*. Englewood Cliffs, NJ: Prentice-Hall.

Schaie, K. W., and Hertzog, C. (1983). Fourteen-year cohort-sequential studies of adult intelligence. *Developmental Psychology, 19*, 531–543.

Schaie, K. W., and Hertzog, C. (1985a). Measurement in the psychology of aging. In J. E. Birren and K. W. Schaie (Eds.), *Handbook of the psychology of aging*. New York: Van Nostrand Reinhold.

Schaie, K. W., and Hertzog, C. (1985b). Toward a comprehensive model of adult intellectual development: Contributions of the Seattle Longitudinal Study. In R. J. Sternberg (Ed.), *Advances in human intelligence* (Vol. 3). New York: Academic Press.

Schaie, K. W., and Labouvie-Vief, G. (1974). Generational versus ontogenetic components of change in adult cognitive behavior: A fourteen-year cross-sequential study. *Developmental Psychology, 10*, 305–320.

Schaie, K. W., Labouvie, G. V., and Barrett, T. J. (1973). Selective attrition effects in a fourteen-year study of adult intelligence. *Journal of Gerontology, 28*, 328–334.

Schaie, K. W., and Marquette, B. (1972). Personality in maturity and old age. In R. M. Dreger (Ed.), *Multivariate personality research*. New York: Claitor's.

Schaie, K. W., and Parham, I. A. (1974). Social responsibility in adulthood: Ontogenetic and sociocultural changes. *Journal of Personality and Social Psychology, 30*, 483–492.

Schaie, K. W., and Parham, I. A. (1976). Stability of adult personality traits: Fact or fable? *Journal of Personality and Social Psychology, 34*, 146–158.

Schaie, K. W., and Stone, V. (1982). Psychological assessment. *Annual Review of Gerontology and Geriatrics, 3*, 329–360.

Schaie, K. W., and Strother, C. R. (1968). A cross-sequential study of age changes in cognitive behavior. *Psychological Bulletin, 70*, 671–680.

Schaie, K. W., and Willis, S. L. (In press). Can decline in adult cognitive functioning be reversed? *Developmental Psychology*.

Scheibel, A. B. (1982). Age-related changes in the human forebrain. *Neurosciences Research Progress Bulletin, 20,* 577–583.

Scheidt, R. J., and Schaie, K. W. (1978). A situational taxonomy for the elderly: Generating situational criteria. *Journal of Gerontology, 33,* 848–857.

Schiffman, S., Orlandi, M., and Erickson, R. P. (1979). Changes in taste and smell with age: Biological aspects. In J. M. Ordy and K. Brizzes (Eds.), *Sensory systems and communication in the elderly.* New York: Raven Press.

Schiffman, S., and Pasternak, M. (1979). Decreased discrimination of food odors in the elderly. *Journal of Gerontology, 34,* 73–79.

Schmidt, F. (Ed.) (1978). *Fundamentals of neurophysiology* (2nd ed.). New York: Springer-Verlag.

Schmitt, F. A., Murphy, M. D., and Sanders, R. E. (1981). Training older adult free recall rehearsal strategies. *Journal of Gerontology, 36,* 329–337.

Schmitz-Scherzer, R., and Thomae, H. (1983). Constancy and change of behavior in old age: Findings from the Bonn Longitudinal Study of Aging. In K. W. Schaie (Ed.), *Longitudinal studies of adult psychological development.* New York: Guilford Press.

Schneider, B. (1985). Organizational behavior. *Annual Review of Psychology, 36,* 573–613.

Schofield, W. (1974). *Psychotherapy: Purchase of friendship.* Englewood Cliffs, NJ: Prentice-Hall.

Schonfield, D., and Robertson, E. A. (1966). Memory storage and aging. *Canadian Journal of Psychology, 20,* 228–236.

Schooler, C. (1984). Psychological effects of complex environments during the life span: A review and theory. *Intelligence, 8,* 259–281.

Schroeder, M. R. (1981). Acoustics in human communications: Room acoustics, music and speech. *Journal of the Acoustical Society of America, 68,* 22–28.

Schuckit, M., and Pastor, P. (1978). The elderly as a unique population: Alcoholism. *Alcoholism: Clinical and Experimental Research, 2,* 31–38.

Schulenberg, J. E., Vondracek, F. W., and Crouter, A. C. (1984). The influence of the family on vocational development. *Journal of Marriage and the Family, 46,* 129–143.

Schultz, J. H. (1976). Income distribution and the aging. In R. H. Binstock and E. Shanas (Eds.), *Handbook of aging and the social sciences.* New York: Van Nostrand Reinhold.

Schultz, J. H. (1985). *The economics of aging* (3rd ed.). New York: Van Nostrand Reinhold.

Schultz, N. R., and Hoyer, W. J. (1976). Feedback effects on spatial egocentrism in old age. *Journal of Gerontology, 31,* 72–75.

Schulz, R. (1978). *The psychology of death, dying, and bereavement.* Reading, MA: Addison-Wesley.

Schulz, R. (1980). Aging and control. In J. Garber and M. E. P. Seligman (Eds.), *Human helplessness: Theory and applications.* New York: Academic Press.

Schulz, R., and Alderman, D. (1974). Clinical research and the "stages of dying." *Omega, 5,* 137–144.

Schulz, R., and Bazerman, M. (1980). Ceremonial occasions and mortality: A second look. *American Psychologist, 35,* 253–261.

Schulz, R., and Hanusa, B. H. (1978). Long-term effects of control and predictability-enhancing interventions: Findings and ethical issues. *Journal of Personality and Social Psychology, 36,* 1194–1201.

Schuyler, D. (1974). *The depressive spectrum.* New York: Jason Aronson.

Schwartz, A. N. (1979). Psychological dependency: An emphasis on the later years. In P. K. Ragan (Ed.), *Aging parents.* Los Angeles: University of Southern California Press.

Schwartz, P., and Blumstein, P. (1983). *American couples: Money, work, and sex.* New York: William Morrow.

Sealy, A. P. E., and Cattell, R. B. (1965). *Standard trends in personality development in men and women of 16 to 70 years, determined by 16 PF measurements.* Paper presented at the British Psychology Society Conference.

Seligman, M. E. P. (1972). For helplessness: Can we immunize the weak? In *Readings in Psychology Today* (2nd ed.). Monterey, CA: CRM.

Seligman, M. E. P. (1975). *Helplessness: On depression, development and death.* San Francisco: Freeman.

Seligman, M. E. P. (1981). A learned helplessness point of view. In L. P. Rehm (Ed.), *Behavior therapy for depression: Present status and future directions.* New York: Academic Press.

Selko, D. J., Ihara, Y., and Salazar, F. J. (1982). Alzheimer's disease: Insolubility of partially purified paired helical filaments in sodium dodecyl sulfate and urea. *Science, 215,* 143–1245.

Serrin, W. (1984, November 25). Experts say job bias against women persists. *New York Times,* p. 32.

Settin, J. (1979). *Client age, gender and class as determinants of clinicians' perceptions.* Unpublished paper cited in Levy et al. (1980).

Severne, L. (1982). Psychosocial aspects of the menopause. In A. M. Voda, M. Dinnerstein, and S. O'Donnell (Eds.), *Changing perspectives on menopause.* Austin: University of Texas Press.

Seward, R. R. (1973). The colonial family in America: Toward a sociohistorical restoration of its structure. *Journal of Marriage and the Family, 35,* 58–70.

Shanan, J., and Jacobowitz, J. (1982). Personality and aging. *Annual Review of Gerontology and Geriatrics, 3,* 148–178.

Shanas, E. (1972). Adjustment to retirement. In F. M. Carp (Ed.), *Retirement.* Berkeley, CA: Behavioral Publications.

Shanas, E. (1979). The family as a social support system in old age. *Gerontologist, 19,* 169–174.

Shanas, E. (1980). Older people and their families: The new pioneers. *Journal of Marriage and the Family, 42,* 9–18.

Shanas, E., and Maddox, G. L. (1976). Aging, health, and the organization of health resources. In R. H. Binstock and E. Shanas (Eds.), *Handbook of aging and the social sciences.* New York: Van Nostrand Reinhold.

Shanas, E., and Sussman, M. B. (1981). The family in later life: Social structure and social policy. In R. W. Fogel, E. Hatfield, S. B. Kiesler, and J. March (Eds.), *Aging: Stability and change in the family.* New York: Academic Press.

Shanas, E., Townsend, P., Wedderburn, D., Friis, H., Milhoj, P., and Stehouwer, P. (Eds.) (1968). *Old people in three industrial societies.* London: Routledge & Kegan Paul.

Sheehy, G. (1976). *Passages.* New York: Dutton.

Shiffrin, R. M., and Schneider, W. (1977). Controlled and automatic human information processing: II. Perceptual learning, automatic attending and a general theory. *Psychological Review, 84,* 127–190.

Shneidman, E. S. (1974). *Deaths of man.* New York: Penguin.

Shneidman, E. S. (1980). *Voices of death.* New York: Harper & Row.

Shock, N. W. (1977). Biological theories of aging. In J. E. Birren and K. W. Schaie (Eds.), *Handbook of the psychology of aging.* New York: Van Nostrand Reinhold.

Shock, N. W. (1985). Longitudinal studies of aging in humans. In C. E. Finch and E. L. Schneider (Eds.), *Handbook of the biology of aging.* New York: Van Nostrand Reinhold.

Shock, N. W., Greulick, R. C., Andres, R., Arenberg, D., Costa, P. T., Lakatta, E. G., and Tobin, J. D. (1984). *Normal human aging: The Baltimore Longitudinal Study of Aging.* Washington, DC: U.S. Government Printing Office, NIH Publication No. 84-2450.

Shotland, R. L. (1985). When bystanders just stand by. *Psychology Today, 19,* 50–55.

Shotland, R. L., and Goodstein, L. (1983). Just because she doesn't want to doesn't mean it's rape: An experimentally based causal model of the perception of rape in a dating situation. *Social Psychology Quarterly, 46,* 220–232.

Siegel, J. S. (1980). Recent and prospective demographic trends for the elderly population and some implications for health care. In S. G. Haynes and M. Feinleib (Eds.), *Epidemiology of aging.* Washington, DC: U.S. Government Printing Office, NIH Publication No. 80–969.

Siegel, K. (1982). Rational suicide: Considerations for the clinician. *Psychiatric Quarterly, 54,* 77–84.

Siegler, I. C. (1983). Psychological aspects of the Duke longitudinal studies. In K. W. Schaie (Ed.), *Longitudinal studies of adult psychological development.* New York: Guilford Press.

Siegler, I. C., and Botwinick, J. (1979). A long-term longitudinal study of intellectual ability of older adults: The matter of selective attrition. *Journal of Gerontology, 34,* 242–245.

Siegler, I. C., and Costa, P. T., Jr. (1985). Health behavior relationships. In J. E. Birren and K. W. Schaie (Eds.), *Handbook of the psychology of aging* (2nd ed.). New York: Van Nostrand Reinhold.

Siegler, I. C., George, L. K., and Okun, M. A. (1979). Cross-sequential analysis of adult personality. *Developmental Psychology, 15,* 350–351.

Siegler, I. C., McCarthy, S. M., and Logue, P. E. (1982). Wechsler Memory Scale scores, selective attrition and distance from death. *Journal of Gerontology, 37,* 176–181.

Silverman, P. R. (1969). The widow-to-widow program: An experiment in preventive intervention. *Mental Hygiene, 53,* 333–337.

Silverstone, B., and Hyman, H. K. (1976). *You and your aging parents.* New York: Pantheon.

Simon, A. (1980). The neuroses, personality disorders, alcoholism, drug use and misuse, and crime in the aged. In J. E. Birren and R. B. Sloane (Eds.), *Handbook of mental health and aging.* Englewood Cliffs, NJ: Prentice-Hall.

Simonton, D. K. (1977). Creative productivity, age, and stress: A biographical time series analysis of 10 classical composers. *Journal of Personality and Social Psychology, 35,* 791–804.

Sims, N. R., Bowen, D. M., and Davison, A. N. (1982). Acetylcholine synthesis and glucose metabolism in aging and dementia. In E. Giacobini, G. Filogano, and A. Vernadakis (Eds.), *The aging brain: Cellular and molecular mechanisms of aging in the nervous system.* New York: Raven Press.

Skinner, B. F. (1983). Intellectual self-management in old age. *American Psychologist, 38,* 239–244.

Skolnick, A. (1978). *The intimate environment* (2nd ed.). Boston: Little, Brown.

Skolnick, A. (1981). Married lives: Longitudinal perspectives on marriage. In D. H. Eichorn, J. A. Clausen, N. Haan, M. J. Honzik, and P. H. Mussen (Eds.), *Present and past in middle life.* New York: Academic Press.

Smith, A. (1980). Age differences in encoding, storage, and retrieval. In L. W. Poon et al. (Eds.), *New directions in memory and aging: Proceedings of the George A. Talland Memorial Conference.* Hillsdale, NJ: Erlbaum.

Smith, D. S. (1981). Historical change in the household structure of the elderly in economically developed societies. In R. W. Fogel, E. Hatfield, S. B. Kiesler, and J. March (Eds.), *Aging: Stability and change in the family.* New York: Academic Press.

Smith, K. R., and Bengtson, V. L. (1979). Positive consequences of institutionalization: Solidarity between elderly parents and their middle-aged children. *Gerontologist, 19,* 438–447.

Smith, R., and Prather, W. F. (1971). Phoneme discrimination in older persons under varying signal-to-noise conditions. *Journal of Speech and Hearing Research, 14,* 630–635.

Snow, R., and Crapo, L. (1982). Emotional bondedness, subjective well-being, and health in elderly medical patients. *Journal of Gerontology, 37,* 609–615.

Social Security Administration. (1984). Current operating statistics. *Social Security Bulletin, 41*(12), 31–98.

Spanier, G. (1983). Married and unmarried cohabitation in the United States: 1980. *Journal of Marriage and the Family,* 277–288.

Spanier, G., and Furstenberg, F. (1982). Remarriage after divorce: A longitudinal analysis of well being. *Journal of Marriage and the Family,* 709–720.

Spanier, G., and Glick, P. (1981). Marital instability in the United States: Some correlates and recent changes. *Family Relations, 31,* 329–338.

Spark, R. F., White, R. A., and Connolly, P. B. (1980). Impotence is not always psychogenic: Newer insights into hypothalamic-pituitary-gonadal dysfunction. *Journal of the American Medical Association, 243,* 750–755.

Spector, A. (1982). Aging of the lens and cataract formation. In R. Sekular, D. W. Kline, and K. Dismukes (Eds.), *Aging and human visual function.* New York: Alan R. Liss.

Spence, K. W. (1958). A theory of emotionally based drive (D) and its relation to performance in simple learning situations. *American Psychologist, 13,* 131.

Spikes, J. (1980). Grief, death, and dying. In E. W. Busse and G. D. Blazer (Eds.), *Handbook of geriatric psychiatry.* New York: Van Nostrand Reinhold.

Spirduso, W. W., and Clifford, P. (1978). Replication of age and physical activity effects on reaction and movement time. *Journal of Gerontology, 33,* 26–30.

Stagner, R. (1985). Aging in industry. In J. E. Birren and K. W. Schaie (Eds.), *Handbook of the psychology of aging* (2nd ed.). New York: Van Nostrand Reinhold.

Staples, R. (1976). The black American family. In C. H. Mindel and R. W. Habenstein (Eds.), *Ethnic families in America.* New York: Elsevier.

Starr, B, and Weiner, M. (1981). *The Starr-Weiner report on sex and sexuality in the mature years.* New York: McGraw-Hill.

Stegner, W. (1971). *Angle of repose.* New York: Doubleday.

Steinitz, L. (1981). The local church as support for the elderly. *Journal of Gerontological Social Work, 4,* 43–53.

Stenback, A. (1980). Depression and suicidal behavior in old age. In J. E. Birren and R. B. Sloane (Eds.), *Handbook of mental health and aging.* Englewood Cliffs, NJ: Prentice-Hall.

Stenmark, D. E., and Dunn, V. K. (1982). Issues related to the training of geropsychologists. In J. F. Santos and G. R. VandenBos (Eds.), *Psychology and the older adult.* Washington, DC: American Psychological Association.

Sternberg, R. J. (1980). Sketch of a componential subtheory of human intelligence. *The Behavioral and Brain Sciences, 3,* 573–584.

Sternberg, R. J. (1982). A componential approach to human intelligence. In R. J. Sternberg (Ed.), *Advances in the psychology of human intelligence* (Vol. 1). Hillsdale, NJ: Erlbaum.

Sternberg, R. J. (1984). Toward a triarchic theory of human intelligence. *Behavioral and Brain Sciences, 7,* 269–315.

Sternberg, R., and Grajek, S. (1984). The nature of love. *Journal of Personality and Social Psychology, 47,* 312–329.

Stewart, P. L., and Cantor, M. G. (Eds.) (1982). *Varieties of work.* Beverly Hills, CA: Sage.

Stimpson, C. R. (1982). The fallacy of bodily reductionism. In A. Voda, M. Dinnerstein, and S. O'Donnell (Eds.), *Changing perspective on menopause.* Austin: University of Texas Press.

Stinnett, N., and Walters, J. (1977). *Relationships in marriage and family.* New York: Macmillan.

Stoll, C. S. (1974). *Female and male.* New York: Brown.

Storandt, M. (1983). Psychology's response to the graying of America. *American Psychologist, 38,* 323–326.

Straker, M. (1982). Adjustment disorders and personality disorders in the aged. In L. F. Jarvik and G. W. Small (Eds.), *The psychiatric clinics of North America.* Philadelphia: Saunders.

Strehler, B. L. (1973, February). A new age for aging. *Natural History.*

Strehler, B. L. (1977). *Time, cells, and aging* (2nd ed.). New York: Academic Press.

Streib, G. F., and Schneider, C. J. (1971). *Retirement in American society.* Ithaca: Cornell University Press.

Strempel, E. (1981). Long-term results in the treatment of glaucoma with beta-adreanergic blocking agents. *Transactions of the Ophthalmology Society, 33,* 21–23.

Stroebe, M. S., Stroebe, W., Gergen, K. J., and Gergen, M. (1980). *The broken heart: Reality or myth.* Unpublished manuscript, cited in Schulz and Bazerman, 1980.

Strong, E. K., Jr. (1955). *Vocational interests 18 years after college.* Minneapolis: University of Minnesota Press.

Sundberg, N. D. (1977). *Assessment of persons.* Englewood Cliffs, NJ: Prentice-Hall.

Sussman, M. B. (1977). Family, bureaucracy and the elderly individual: An organizational/linkage perspective. In E. Shanas and M. B. Sussman (Eds.), *Family, bureaucracy and the elderly.* Durham, NC: Duke University Press.

Sussman, M. B., and Burchinal, L. (1962). Parental aid to married children: Implications for family functioning. *Marriage and Family Living, 24,* 320–332.

Swenson, C. F. (1983). A respectable old age. *American Psychologist, 38,* 327–333.

Swenson, M. W., Pearson, J. S., and Osborne, D. (1973). *An MMPI source book.* Minneapolis: University of Minnesota Press.

Szasz, T. (1960). The myth of mental illness. *American Psychologist, 15,* 113–118.

Tapp, J. L., and Levine, F. J. (1972). Compliance from kindergarten to college: A speculative research note. *Journal of Youth and Adolescence, 1,* 233–249.

Taub, H. A. (1967). Paired associates learning as a function of age, rate and instructions. *Journal of Genetic Psychology, 111,* 41–46.

Tavris, C., and Offir, C. (1977). *The longest war: Sex differences in perspective.* New York: Harcourt Brace Jovanovich.

Taylor, F. G., and Marshall, W. L. (1977). Experimental analysis of a cognitive-behavioral therapy for depression. *Cognitive Therapy and Research, 1,* 59–72.

Taylor, R. (1976). *Welcome to the middle years.* New York: Acropolis Books.

Taylor, R. J., and Chatters, L. M. (1984). *Church-based informal support among elderly blacks.* Paper presented at the American Sociological Association meeting, San Antonio, TX.

Terkel, S. (1974). *Working.* New York: Pantheon.

Terry, R. D., and Wisniewski, H. M. (1975). Structural and chemical changes of the aged human brain. In S. Gershon and A. Raskind (Eds.), *Aging* (Vol. 2). New York: Raven Press.

Terry, R. D. (1978). Aging, senile dementia, and Alzheimer's disease. In R. Katzman, R. D. Terry, and K. L. Bick (Eds.), *Alzheimer's disease: Senile dementia and related disorders.* New York: Raven Press.

Theorell, T., and Rahe, R. H. (1974). Psychosocial characteristics of subjects with myocardial infarction in Stockholm. In E. K. E. Gunderson and R. H. Rahe (Eds.), *Life stress and illness.* Springfield, IL: Charles C. Thomas.

Thomae, H. (1980). Personality and adjustment to aging. In J. E. Birren and R. B. Sloane (Eds.), *Handbook of mental health and aging.* Englewood Cliffs, NJ: Prentice-Hall.

Thompson, L. (1980). Testing and mnemonic strategies. In L. Poon et al. (Eds.), *New directions in memory and aging: Proceedings of the George A. Talland Memorial Conference.* Hillsdale, NJ: Erlbaum.

Thompson, L. W., and Gallagher, D. E. (1985). Treatment of depression in elderly outpatients. In G. Maletta (Ed.), *Advances in neurogerontology, Vol. 5: Treatment of the elderly neuropsychiatric patient.* New York: Praeger.

Thompson, L., and Spanier, G. (1983). The end of marriage and acceptance of marital termination. *Journal of Marriage and the Family,* 103–114.

Thornton, A., Chang, M. C., and Sun, T. H. (1984). Social and economic change, intergenerational relationships, and family formation in Taiwan. *Demography, 21,* 475–499.

Thurstone, L. L., and Thurstone, T. G. (1941). Factorial studies of intelligence. *Psychometric Monographs,* No. 2.

Thurstone, L. L., and Thurstone, T. G. (1949). *Examiner manual for the SRA Primary Abilities Test.* Chicago: Science Research Associates.

Time. (1982, January 25). Marital tale of two cities (pp. 83–85).

Timiras, P. S. (1972). *Developmental physiology and aging.* New York: Macmillan.

Timko, C., and Rodin, J. (In press). Staff-patient relationships in nursing homes: Sources of conflict and rehabilitation potential. *Journal of Rehabilitation Psychology.*

Titus, H. E., and Goss, R. G. (1969). Psychometric comparison of old and young supervisors. *Psychological Reports, 24,* 727–733.

Tobin, S., and Neugarten, B. (1961). Life satisfaction and social interaction in aging. *Journal of Gerontology, 16,* 344–346.

Toffler, A. (1970). *Future shock.* New York: Random House.

Tolstoy, L. (1961). *Anna Karenina.* New York: New American Library.

Tomlinson, B. E., Blessed, G., and Roth, M. (1968). Observations on the brains of nondemented old people. *Journal of Neurological Sciences, 7,* 331–356.

Treas, J. (1977). Family support systems for the aged: Some social and demographic considerations. *Gerontologist, 17,* 486–491.

Treas, J., and Bengtson, V. L. (1982). The demography of middle and late-life transitions. *Annals of the American Academy of Political and Social Science, 464,* 11–21.

Treat, N., and Reese, H. (1976). Age, imagery, and pacing in paired associate learning. *Developmental Psychology, 12,* 119–124.

Treloar, A. (1982). Predicting the close of menstrual life. In A. Vonda, M. Dinnerstein, and S. O'Donnell (Eds.), *Changing perspective on menopause.* Austin: University of Texas Press.

Troll, L. E. (1971). The family of later life: A decade review. *Journal of Marriage and the Family, 33,* 263–290.

Troll, L. E. (1980). Grandparenting. In L. W. Poon (Ed.), *Aging in the 1980s.* Washington, DC: American Psychological Association.

Troll, L. E., Miller, S. J., and Atchley, R. C. (1979). *Families in later life.* Belmont, CA: Wadsworth.

Tsitouras, P. D., Martin, C. E., and Harman, S. M. (1982). Relationship of serum testosterone to sexual activity in healthy elderly. *Journal of Gerontology, 37,* 288–293.

Tulving, E. (1972). Episodic and semantic memory. In E. Tulving and W. Donaldson (Eds.), *Organization of memory.* New York: Academic Press.

Turkel, S. (1984). *The second shift: Computers and the human spirit.* New York: Simon & Schuster.

Turner, R. K., and Sternberg, M. P. (1978). Psychosocial factors in elderly patients admitted to a psychiatric hospital. *Age and Ageing, 7,* 171–177.

Udry, J. R. (1971). *The social context of marriage* (2nd ed.). New York: Lippincott.

Udry, J. R. (1974). *The social context of marriage* (3rd ed.). New York: Lippincott.

Uhlenberg, P., & Myers, M. (1981). Divorce and the elderly. *Gerontologist, 21,* 276–282.

Unger, R. K. (1979). *Female and male.* New York: Harper & Row.

U.S. Bureau of the Census. (1973). Employment status and work experience. *Census of Population: 1970, Subject Report PC* (2)-6A. Washington, DC: U.S. Government Printing Office.

U.S. Bureau of the Census. (1976a). Number, timing, and duration of marriages and divorces in the United States. *Current Population Reports,* Series P-20, No. 297. Washington, DC: U.S. Government Printing Office.

U.S. Bureau of the Census. (1976b). *Statistical abstract of the United States: 1976* (97th ed.). Washington, DC: U.S. Government Printing Office.

U.S. Bureau of the Census. (1981a). Money income of individuals: 1980. *Current Population Reports,* Series P-60, No. 127. Washington, DC: U.S. Government Printing Office.

U.S. Bureau of the Census. (1981b). *Statistical abstract of the United States* (102nd ed.). Washington, DC: U.S. Government Printing Office.

U.S. Bureau of the Census. (1982a). Marital status and living arrangements: March, 1981. *Current Population Reports,* Series P-20, No. 372. Washington, DC: U.S. Government Printing Office.

U.S. Bureau of the Census. (1982b). Projections of the population of the United States. *Current Population Reports,* Series P-25, No. 922. Washington, DC: U.S. Government Printing Office.

U.S. Bureau of the Census. (1983a). Persons in institutions and other group quarters. *1980 Census of Population: Subject reports* (Vol. 2). Washington, DC: U.S. Government Printing Office.

U.S. Bureau of the Census. (1983b). *U.S. census of population and housing, 1980: Summary* (Vol. 2). Washington, DC: U.S. Government Printing Office.

U.S. Bureau of the Census. (1984a). *National data book and guide to sources: Statistical abstract of the United States, 1985* (105th ed.). Washington, DC: U.S. Government Printing Office.

U.S. Bureau of the Census. (1984b). Household and family characteristics, March 1983. *Current Population Reports,* Series P-20, No. 388. Washington, DC: U.S. Government Printing Office.

U.S. Bureau of Labor Statistics. (1981). Three budgets for a retired couple. *News, U.S. Department of Labor, 81,* 384.

U.S. Department of Health, Education and Welfare. (1974). *Working with older people (Vol. II). Biological, psychological and sociological aspects of aging.* Washington, DC: U.S. Government Printing Office.

U.S. Department of Labor. (1974). *Job satisfaction: Is there a trend?* Manpower Research Monograph No. 30. Washington, DC: U.S. Government Printing Office.

U.S. Department of Labor. (1982, January). *Employment and earnings.* Washington, DC: U.S. Government Printing Office

U.S. Department of Labor. (1983). *Manpower report to the President, 1983.* Washington, DC: U.S. Government Printing Office.

U.S. Senate Special Committee on Aging. (1981). *Developments in aging: 1981.* Washington, DC: U.S. Government Printing Office.

Vaillant, G. E. (1977). *Adaptation to life.* Boston: Little, Brown.

Vaillant, G. E., and Perry, J. C. (1980). Personality disorders. In H. Kaplan, A. Freedman, and B. Sadock (Eds.), *Comprehensive text on psychiatry* (3rd ed.). Baltimore: Williams & Wilkins.

Valenstein, E. (1981). Age-related changes in the human central nervous system. In D. S. Beasley and G. A. Davis (Eds.), *Aging: Communication processes and disorders.* New York: Grune & Stratton.

VandenBos, G. R., Stapp, J., and Kilburg, R. R. (1981). Health service providers in psychology: Results of the 1978 APA Human Resources Survey. *American Psychologist, 36,* 1395–1418.

Van Dusen, R. A., and Sheldon, E. B. (1976). The changing status of American women. *American Psychologist, 31,* 106–116.

Van Maanen, J., and Schein, E. H. (1977). Career development. In J. R. Hackman and J. L. Suttle (Eds.), *Improving life at work.* New York: Goodyear.

Veroff, J., Atkinson, J. W., Feld, S., and Gurin, G. (1960). The use of thematic apperception to assess motivation in a nationwide interview survey. *Psychological Monographs, 74,* Whole No. 499.

Veroff, J., Douvan, E., and Kulka, R. (1981). *The inner American: A self-portrait from 1957 to 1976.* New York: Basic Books.

Veroff, J., and Feld, S. (1970). *Marriage and work in America.* New York: Van Nostrand Reinhold.

Verwoerdt, A. (1976). *Clinical geropsychiatry.* Baltimore, MD: Williams & Wilkins.

Verwoerdt, A. (1981). *Clinical geropsychiatry* (2nd ed.). Baltimore: Williams & Wilkins.

Vietze, P. M., MacTurk, R. H., McCarthy, M. E., Klein, R. P., and Yarrow, L. J. (1980). *Impact of mode of delivery on father- and mother-infant interaction at 6 and 12 months.* Paper presented at the International Conference on Infant Studies, New Haven, CT.

Voda, A., Dinnerstein, M., and O'Donnell, S. (Eds.) (1982). *Changing perspective on menopause.* Austin: University of Texas Press.

Wagner, E. E. (1960). Differences between old and young executives on objective psychological test variables. *Journal of Gerontology, 15,* 296–299.

Waldman, D., and Avolio, B. (1984). *A meta-analysis of age difference in job performance: An addendum to Rhodes.* Unpublished manuscript, State University of New York at Binghamton, School of Management.

Walker, K., and Woods, M. (1976). *Time use: A measure of household production of family goods and services.* Washington: American Home Economics Association.

Walker, L. (1984). Sex differences in the development of moral reasoning: A critical review. *Child Development, 55,* 677–691.

Walsh, D., Till, R. E., and Williams, M. V. (1978). Age differences in peripheral perceptual processing: A monoptic backward masking investigation. *Journal of Experimental Psychology: Human Perception and Performance, 4,* 232–243.

Walsh, W. B., Horton, J. A., and Gaffey, R. L. (1977). Holland's theory and college degreed working men and women. *Journal of Vocational Behavior, 10,* 180–186.

Wang, H. S., and Busse, E. W. (1975). Correlates of regional cerebral blood flow in elderly community residents. In A. M. Harper, W. B. Jennett, J. D. Miller, and J. O. Rowan (Eds.), *Blood flow and metabolism in the brain.* London: Churchill Livingstone.

Wang, H. S., Obrist, W. D., and Busse, E. W. (1970). Neurophysiological correlates of the intellectual function of elderly persons living in the community. *American Journal of Psychiatry, 126,* 1205–1212.

Warheit, G. J. (1979). Life events, coping, stress and depressive symptomatology. *American Journal of Psychiatry, 136,* 502–507.

Warheit, G. J., Arey, S. A., and Swanson, E. (1976). Patterns of drug use: An epidemiological overview. *Journal of Drug Issues, 6,* 223–237.

Warner, W. L. (1965). The city of the dead. In W. L. Warner (Ed.), *The living and the dead.* New Haven, CT: Yale University Press.

Weatherford, M. J. (1981). *Tribes on the hill.* New York: Rawson, Wade.

Wechsler, D. (1972). "Hold" and "Don't Hold" tests. In S. M. Chown (Ed.), *Human aging.* New York: Penguin.

Weg, R. B. (1983). Changing physiology of aging: Normal and pathological. In D. W. Woodruff and J. E. Birren (Eds.), *Aging: Scientific perspectives and social issues* (2nd ed.). Monterey, CA: Brooks/Cole.

Weingartner, H., and Silberman, E. (1982). Models of cognitive impairment: Cognitive changes in depression. *Psychopharmacological Bulletin, 18,* 27–42.

Weisfeldt, M. L. (1981). Left ventricular function. In M. L. Weisfeldt (ed.), *The aging heart: Its function and response to stress.* New York: Raven Press.

Weisman, A. D. (1972). *On dying and denying.* New York: Behavior Publications.

Weiss, R. S. (1973). *Loneliness: The experience of emotional and social isolation.* Cambridge, MA: MIT Press.

Weiss, R. S. (1979). The emotional impact and marital separation. In G. Levinger and O. C. Moles (Eds.), *Divorce and separation.* New York: Basic Books.

Weissman, M. (1979). Environmental factors in affective disorders. *Hospital Practice, 14,* 103–109.

Weisz, J. R. (1983). Can I control it? The pursuit of verdical answers across the life span. In P. B. Bales and O. G. Brim, Jr., (Eds.), *Life-span development and behavior* (Vol. 5). New York: Academic Press.

Weisz, J. R., and Stipek, D. J. (1982). Competence, contingency, and the development of perceived control. *Human Development, 25,* 250–281.

Weitz, S. (1977). *Sex roles.* New York: Oxford University Press.

Welford, A. (1984). Psychomotor performance. *Annual Review of Gerontology and Geriatrics, 4,* 237–274.

Werner, D. (1981). Gerontocracy among the Mekranoti of Central Brazil. *Anthropological Quarterly, 54,* 15–27.

West, R. L. (In press). Practical memory mnemonics for the aged: Preliminary thoughts. In L. Poon, D. Rubin, and B. Wilson (Eds.), *Everyday cognition and memory.* Hillsdale, NJ: Erlbaum.

Whalen, R. E., and Simon, N. G. (1984). Biological motivation. *Annual review of psychology,* 257–276.

Whanger, A. D. (1980). Nutrition, diet and exercise. In E. W. Busse and D. G. Blazer (Eds.), *Handbook of geriatric psychiatry.* New York: Van Nostrand Reinhold.

Whitbourne, S. K. (1985). The psychological construction of the life span. In J. E. Birren and K. W. Schaie (Eds.), *Handbook of the psychology of aging* (2nd ed.). New York: Van Nostrand Reinhold.

Whitbourne, S. K., and Waterman, A. S. (1979). Psychosocial development during the adult years: Age and cohort comparisons. *Developmental Psychology, 15,* 373–378.

Whitbourne, S. K., and Weinstock, C. S. (1979). *Adult development: The differentiation of experience.* New York: Holt, Rinehart & Winston.

Wigdor, B. (1980). Drives and motivation with aging. In J. E. Birren and R. B. Sloane (Eds.), *Handbook of mental health and aging.* Englewood Cliffs, NJ: Prentice-Hall.

Wilkening, E. A., Guerrero, S., and Ginsberg, S. (1972). Distance and intergenerational ties of farm families. *Sociological Quarterly, 13,* 383–386.

Williams, J. H. (1977). *Psychology of women.* New York: Norton.

Williams, R. L., Karacan, I., and Hursch, C. (1974). *Electroencephalography (EEG) of human sleep: Clinical applications.* New York: Wiley.

Willis, S. L. (1985). Towards an educational psychology of the older adult learner: Intellectual and cognitive bases. In J. E. Birren and K. W. Schaie (Eds.), *Handbook of the psychology of aging* (2nd ed.). New York: Van Nostrand Reinhold.

Willis, S. L., Blieszner, R., and Baltes, P. B. (1981). Intellectual training research in aging: Modification of performance on the fluid ability of figural relations. *Journal of Educational Psychology, 73,* 41–50.

Willis, S. L., and Schaie, K. W. (1981). Maintenance and decline of adult mental abilities: II. Susceptibility to intervention. In F. W. Grote and J. Feringer (Eds.), *Adult learning and development.* Bellingham, WA: Western Washington University.

Willis, S. L., and Schaie, K. W. (1985a). *Ability correlates of real life tasks in the elderly.* Unpublished manuscript, The Pennsylvania State University, University Park, PA.

Willis, S. L., and Schaie, K. W. (1985b). Practical intelligence in later adulthood. In R. J. Sternberg and R. K. Wagner (Eds.), *Intelligence in the everyday world.* New York: Cambridge University Press.

Wilson, B., and Moffat, N. (Eds.) (1984). *Clinical management of memory problems.* Rockville, MD: Aspen.

Winch, R. F. (1974). Complementary needs and related notions about voluntary mate selection. In R. F. Winch and G. B. Spainer (Eds.), *Selected studies in marriage and the family.* New York: Holt, Rinehart & Winston.

Winsborough, H. H. (1980). A demographic approach to the life cycle. In K. W. Back (Ed.), *Life course: Integrative theories and exemplary populations.* Boulder, CO: Westview Press.

Wissler, C. (1901). *The correlation of mental and physical tests.* New York: Columbia University Press.

Wittels, I. (1972). Age and stimulus meaningfulness in paired-associate learning. *Journal of Gerontology, 27,* 372–375.

Wittmaier, B. C. (1979). Some unexpected attitudinal consequences of a short course on death. *Omega, 10,* 271–275.

Wohlwill, J. F. (1973). *The study of behavioral development.* New York: Academic Press.

Wolf, E. (1967). Studies on the shrinkage of the visual field with age. *Highway Research Record, 167,* 1–7.

Wolk, R. L., and Wolk, R. B. (1971). *The Gerontological Apperception Test.* New York: Behavioral Publications.

Wood, V., and Robertson, J. F. (1978). Friendship and kinship interaction: Differential effect on the morale of the elderly. *Journal of Marriage and the Family, 40,* 367–375.

Woodruff, D. S. (1978). Brain electrical activity and behavior relationships over the life span. In P. B. Baltes (Ed.), *Life-span development and behavior* (Vol. 1). New York: Academic Press.

Woodruff, D. S. (1983a). Physiology and behavior relationships in aging. In D. S. Woodruff and J. E. Birren (Eds.), *Aging: Scientific perspectives and social issues* (2nd ed.). Monterey, CA: Brooks/Cole.

Woodruff, D. S. (1983b). The role of memory in personality continuity: A 25 year follow-up. *Experimental Aging Research, 9,* 31–34.

Woodruff, D. S. (1985). Arousal, sleep, and aging. In J. E. Birren and K. W. Schaie (Eds.), *Handbook of the psychology of aging* (2nd ed.). New York: Van Nostrand Reinhold.

Woodruff, D. S., and Birren, J. E. (1972). Age changes and cohort differences in personality. *Developmental Psychology, 6,* 252–259.

Woodworth, R. S. (1920). *The personal data sheet.* New York: Stoelting.

Wurtman, R. J. (1985, January). Alzheimer's disease. *Scientific American,* 62–74.

Yankelovich, D. (1974). *The new morality.* New York: McGraw-Hill.

Yankelovich, D. (1981). *New rules: Searching for self-fulfillment in a world turned upside down.* New York: Random House.

Yerkes, R. M. (Ed.). (1921). Psychological examining in the United States Army. *Memoirs of the National Academy of Sciences, 15,* 1–890.

Yesavage, J. A. (1983). Imagery pretraining and memory training in the elderly. *Gerontology, 29,* 271–275.

Yesavage, J. A., and Rose, T. (1984). The effects of a face-name mnemonic in young, middle aged, and elderly adults. *Experimental Aging Research, 10,* 55–57.

Yesavage, J. A., Westphal, J., and Rush, L. (1981). Senile dementia: Combined pharmacologic and psychologic treatment. *Journal of the American Geriatrics Society, 29,* 164–171.

Yogman, M. W. (1983). Development of the father-infant relationship. In H. Fitzgerald, B. Lester, and M. W. Yogman (Eds.), *Theory and research in behavioral pediatrics* (Vol. I). New York: Plenum.

Zander, A. (1979). The psychology of group processes. *Annual Review of Psychology, 30,* 417–451.

Zarit, S. H. (1980). *Aging and mental disorders.* New York: Free Press.

Zarit, S. H., Cole, K., and Guider, R. (1981). Memory training strategies and subjective complaints of memory in the aged. *Gerontologist, 21,* 158–164.

Zarit, S. H., Eiler, J., and Hassinger, M. (1985). Clinical assessment. In J. E. Birren and K. W. Schaie (Eds.), *Handbook of the psychology of aging* (2nd ed.). New York: Van Nostrand Reinhold.

Zarit, S., Zarit, J., and Reever, K. (1982). Memory training or severe memory loss: Effects of senile dementia. *Gerontologist, 22,* 373–377.

Zeits, C., and Prince, R. (1982). Child effects on parents. In B. B. Wolman (Ed.), *Handbook of development psychology.* Englewood Cliffs, NJ: Prentice-Hall.

Zelinski, E., Gilewski, M., and Thompson, L. (1980). Do laboratory tests relate to self assessment of memory ability in the young and old? In L. Poon et al. (Eds.), *New directions in memory and aging: Proceedings of the George A. Talland Memorial Conference.* Hillsdale, NJ: Erlbaum.

Zelinski, E. M., Schaie, K. W., and Gribbin, K. (1977). *Omission and commission errors: Task-specific adult life-span differences.* Paper presented at the 85th annual convention of the American Psychological Association, San Francisco.

Zemore, R., and Eames, N. (1979). Psychic and somatic symptoms of depression among adults, institutionalized aged and noninstitutionalized aged. *Journal of Gerontology, 34,* 716–722.

Zilboorg, G., and Henry, G. W. (1941) *A history of medical psychology.* New York: Norton.

Zimberg, S. (1974). The elderly alcoholic. *Gerontologist, 14,* 221–224.

Zimberg, S. (1978). Diagnosis and treatment of the elderly alcoholic. *Alcoholism: Clinical and Experimental Research, 2,* 27–29.

Zuboff, S. (1982). New worlds of computer mediated work. *Harvard Business Review, 60,* 1142–1152.

Index

Author Index